Principles of Macroeconomics
Fifth Edition

PRINCIPLES OF MACROECONOMICS
FIFTH EDITION

RYAN C. AMACHER
Professor of Economics and
Dean, College of Commerce and Industry
Clemson University

HOLLEY H. ULBRICH
Alumni Professor of Economics
Clemson University

COLLEGE DIVISION South-Western Publishing Co.
Cincinnati Ohio

Sponsoring Editor: James M. Keefe
Developmental Editor: Alice Denny
Production Editor: Sue Ellen Brown
Production House: Lifland et al., Bookmakers
Cover and Interior Designer: Craig LaGesse Ramsdell
Photo Editor: Diana Robbins Carter
Marketing Manager: Scott D. Person
Cover and Interior Illustrator: Jean Tuttle ©1992

HB67EA1
Copyright ©1992
by South-Western Publishing Co.
Cincinnati, Ohio

ALL RIGHTS RESERVED
The text of this publication, or any part thereof, may not be reproduced or transmitted in any form or by any means, electronic or mechanical, including photocopying, recording, storage in an information retrieval system, or otherwise, without the prior written permission of the publisher.

Library of Congress Cataloging-in-Publication Data

Amacher, Ryan C.
    Principles of macroeconomics / Ryan C. Amacher, Holley H. Ulbrich.
  — 5th ed.
      p.   cm.
    Includes bibliographical references and index.
    ISBN 0-538-81306-7
    1. Macroeconomics.   I. Ulbrich, Holley H.   II. Title.
HB172.5.A4 1991
339—dc20   91-20450
                                                                                                       CIP

Printed in the United States of America

1 2 3 4 5 6 7 RN 6 5 4 3 2 1

Photo Credits: p. 18: (*top*) Hoover Institution, Stanford University; (*bottom*) Massachusetts Institute of Technology; p. 63: The Bettmann Archive; p. 172: Historical Pictures Service, Inc., Chicago; p. 202: The Bettmann Archive

PREFACE

Each revision of a textbook presents a major challenge. This fifth edition was no exception. We had to decide what to keep, what to change, and what additions or modifications were needed to make the textbook up to date and responsive to changing ideas, methods, and interests. In putting together a fifth edition, we have benefited from comments and suggestions from users of earlier editions, colleagues at Clemson University, and some careful and thoughtful reviewers.

We reiterate our goal that guided the earlier editions. We do not want to make professional economists out of students. A common complaint is that instructors and textbook authors treat the principles of economics course as the first step in work toward a Ph.D. This text is intended not to train professional economists but rather to describe the analytical tools that economic theory offers the policy analyst or adviser to governments and business firms. This book teaches enough theory to enable students to understand policy and presents enough policy situations to give them an understanding of how to apply the theory. In addition, where relevant, we present the historical context of the theory.

CHANGES IN THE FIFTH EDITION

The multi-color format allows us to be more creative with the graphs and to make the book more attractive. The figures have been prepared so that all demand-related curves are blue and all supply-related curves are red. Historical and other nonspecific information is shown in gold. Throughout the text, special features, including the International Perspectives, Economic Profiles, Economic Insights, and summary boxes, are presented in a consistent color and format.

We have expanded the integration of the international sector in this edition. The gold-colored International Perspective pages in each chapter extend the scope of the material from the purely domestic scene to the worldwide implications and focus on related real-world international issues. Some of the perspectives show what happens to the model or theory when it is placed in the context of an open economy. Thus, we add exports and imports to aggregate supply and demand in macroeconomics. We look at the link between the budget deficit and the trade deficit. Other perspectives consider how particular problems are addressed or how particular institutions work in other countries. For example, the chapter on financial markets looks at how financial markets work in Japan.

We recognize that students appreciate having important material summarized frequently, so we continue to include concise summaries of main points in order to make the book as user friendly as possible. Other features that are especially helpful to students have been retained, including key terms and their definitions in the margins and the numbered chapter summaries. Chapter learning objectives have been reintroduced at the request of users. The number of end-of-chapter questions has been expanded, including more problem-solving and brainstorming questions along with those that review chapter material.

On the basis of reviewer recommendations, a major effort was made in this edition to reorganize and streamline the material in the introductory chapters. The number of introductory chapters has been reduced from four to three. Each chapter emphasizes a single model and uses that model to develop basic methodological concepts. Thus, Chapter 1, "Economics, Economic Issues, and Economic Methods," now introduces the production possibilities curve. Chapter 2, "Markets, Governments, and Nations: The Organization of Economic Activity" describes the circular flow model, building on the introductory material on scarcity and choice in Chapter 1 while creating a broad overview of both microeconomics and macroeconomics. This chapter blends some materials from Chapter 2 of the previous editions with a discussion of the role of governments and the international economy, in order to set the stage for the remaining chapters. Some methodological material, which appeared in the opening chapter in earlier editions, is best understood in the context of the circular flow model. Thus, Chapter 3, "Supply and Demand," now incorporates the topics of comparative statics and equilibrium and disequilibrium. The materials that were presented in Chapter 4 in previous editions have been assigned to various chapters as appropriate, but the basic material on the role of government has been incorporated into the new Chapter 2.

The significant changes in macroeconomics begin with Chapter 9, "Fiscal Policy." Materials on the size and composition of the federal budget are now found in Chapter 9 in connection with discussion of the budget as a policy tool. Because the broad and complex issue of the national debt and deficits dominates any discussion of fiscal policy, we have split this critical current policy debate off into a separate chapter (Chapter 10), drawing materials from several earlier chapters and incorporating new data and arguments.

In the area of money and interest rates, we felt that it was necessary to include some discussion of financial markets, as banks are increasingly becoming merely one among a host of financial intermediaries. After the discussion of money demand in Chapter 11 and banks and the Federal Reserve in Chapter 12, a new chapter has been added. Chapter 13, "Financial Markets and Interest Rates," includes materials on the interest rate, investment, and the loanable funds market, as well as a new discussion of the economic role of financial intermediaries such as the stock and bond markets. We have reorganized the final chapters of the macro part of the text so that the discussion of demand issues ends in Chapter 15 with another look at inflation and employment, as well as a brief summary of various schools of thought. Chapter 16, "Aggregate Supply and Economic Growth," includes an expanded treatment of the productivity issue and industrial policy. We have moved "Economic Development and the Third World" from the end of the textbook to Chapter 17 in the macroeconomics section, since it is logically linked to the growth chapter.

The international section comprises three chapters. Chapter 18, "International Trade," now includes an introduction to two additional arguments for tariffs: the optimum tariff argument and the theory of the second best. To show the role of services in the balance of payments, Chapter 19 contains an International Perspective that discusses how the United States has become a net exporter of tourism. Chapter 20, which deals with comparative systems, was revised at the last minute to incorporate the rapid changes in Eastern Europe.

IMPORTANT FEATURES OF THE FIFTH EDITION

The previous editions of *Principles of Macroeconomics* have been used by thousands of students at hundreds of institutions. The following features have made this text a useful and well-regarded teaching and learning tool.

ORGANIZATION

The length and content of the fifth edition represent a very careful weighing of thoroughness against brevity. Although we did not go quite so far as to apply "zero-based editing" by requiring each item to justify its inclusion, we did carefully rethink what to include and we did some pruning to make room for new material and ideas.

SPECIAL PAGES

Each chapter includes special pages. At least one special page, color-keyed gold, is an International Perspective, extending the scope of the material in the chapter to a global view. Other special pages may be Economic Profiles of important economists or Economic Insights into important institutions, relevant historical events, or pressing current issues. The special pages are placed close to the relevant chapter material and highlight the development of the theory or its application to current domestic or global problems.

PEDAGOGICAL FEATURES

Each chapter begins with learning objectives, to introduce the students to the materials that will be covered. Key terms and their definitions are highlighted in the margin of the text. A feature introduced in the fourth edition and continued in the fifth edition is the capsule summaries of the preceding section or sections, placed at strategic points in each chapter. We have again expanded the selection of end-of-chapter questions, which can be used for review, homework, or class discussion. Suggested answers are provided in the *Instructor's Manual*. The carefully annotated Suggestions for Further Reading in each chapter have been updated and expanded to include current material. All terms that appear in boldface type and in the margins of the book are defined in the Glossary.

SUPPLEMENTARY MATERIALS

In addition to the pedagogical features in the textbook—the learning objectives, key terms, questions, and summaries—there is also a *Study Guide*, an *Instructor's Manual*, and a *Test Bank*. The *Study Guide* was prepared by Patricia Pando of Houston Baptist University. The revised *Test Bank* for the fifth edition was developed by Ryan Amacher, Holley Ulbrich, and Dennis Placone of Clemson University and has again been expanded to accommodate instructors' needs. The *Instructor's Manual* was prepared by the authors of the textbook.

THE STUDY GUIDE

The *Study Guide* will be a real asset for your students. Each chapter corresponds to a chapter in the textbook. It includes a chapter overview; matching exercises based on the important terms in the chapter; a three-part self-test consisting of true/false questions, problems requiring numerical and/or graphical solutions (where appropriate), and multiple choice questions; a review of the learning objectives for the chapter; complete answers to all questions in the self-test; and chapter exercises. The chapter exercises can be used for homework or for quizzes. (Answers are provided in the *Instructor's Manual*.)

THE INSTRUCTOR'S MANUAL

The *Instructor's Manual* also contains a chapter corresponding to each chapter in the text. Each chapter of the *Manual* includes a short discussion of the purposes of the chapter; the chapter outline, learning objectives, and summary; key terms from the chapter with their definitions; suggestions for lectures, extensions, and applications; suggested answers to all end-of-chapter questions; and answers to the chapter exercises in the *Study Guide*. Transparency masters are also included in the *Instructor's Manual*.

THE TEST BANK

An extensive *Test Bank* is available to adopters. It consists of multiple choice and true/false questions, including those in the *Study Guide* (marked with an asterisk). The *Test Bank* is also available on disk for use with MicroSWAT III test generation software. This easy-to-use, menu-driven software allows instructors to quickly and efficiently produce high-quality tests. Instructors can enter and edit questions, scramble questions and choices, and print graphs as part of a test. Included in the software is a grade book.

TRANSPARENCIES

Important illustrations from *Principles of Macroeconomics* have been reproduced on a set of color acetate transparencies available to adopters to enhance classroom presentations. The most critical illustrations appear on overlay transparencies, an innovative teaching tool.

THE MICROCOMPUTER TUTORIALS

Tutorial software, available for IBM® or IBM-compatible machines, contains four modules designed for either individual or group use in reviewing basic concepts.[1] The tutorials have been thoroughly revised in response to suggestions from users and are available to adopters. Copies may be made for student use.

ACKNOWLEDGMENTS

We are grateful to the many colleagues who made specific comments concerning the fourth edition or reviewed drafts of this fifth edition:

Jack E. Adams
University of Arkansas

Andy Barnett
Auburn University

Dan Barszcz
College of DuPage

Greg Brown
Lincoln Memorial University

Heinrich H. Bruschke
St. Louis University

Gary W. Burbridge
Grand Rapids Junior College

Camille P. Castorina
Florida Institute of Technology

Rick L. Chaney
St. Louis University

Abdur Chowdhury
Marquette University

Dave Clark
Marquette University

David L. Cleeton
Oberlin College

Donald A. Coffin
Indiana University Northwest

Dean S. Dutton
Brigham Young University

Bernard Feigenbaum
California State University–Northridge

David W. Findley
Colby College

Vivek Ghosal
University of Florida

Patricia E. Graham
University of Northern Colorado

Ralph Gunderson
University of Wisconsin–Oshkosh

R. W. Hafer
Southern Illinois University

David L. Hames
University of Hawaii, Hilo

Raza Hamzaee
Missouri Western College

---

1. IBM® is a registered trademark of International Business Machines Corporation. Any reference to IBM refers to this registered trademark.

Stephen Happel
Arizona State University

Dannie E. Harrison
Murray State University

Thomas R. Ireland
University of Missouri–St. Louis

David Jobson
Keystone Junior College

Andrew Larkin
St. Cloud State University

Anton D. Lowenberg
California State University–Northridge

Robert McAuliffe
Babson College

Rob Roy McGregor
University of South Carolina

Patrick McMurry
Missouri Western State College

Robert Main
Butler University

John E. Marthisen
Babson College

Richard F. Measell
St. Mary's College

Hamid Milani
University of Wisconsin–Marathon County

Clark Nardinelli
Clemson University

Michael V. Olds
Orange Coast College

Eugene Ottle
McKendree College

John Pisciotta
Baylor University

Dennis Placone
Clemson University

Gary Quinlivin
St. Vincent College

Richard Robertson
Hinds Community College

Barbara Sherman Rolleston
Baldwin Wallace College

Malcolm Russell
Andrews University

Jody L. Sindelar
Yale University

Lawrence G. Smith
Grossmont College

Fred A. Tarpley, Jr.
Georgia Institute of Technology

Percy O. Vera
Sinclair Community College

Doug Wakeman
Meredith College

John Warner
Clemson University

Mellie Warner
Clemson University

Dale Warnke
College of Lake Country

William F. Watson, Jr.
Brunswick Junior College

Donald A. Wells
University of Arizona

Arthur L. Welsh
Pennsylvania University

Bernard J. Widera
University of Wisconsin, Madison

Jehad Yasin
Fort Valley State College

In addition, we owe a significant debt of gratitude to users and reviewers of the earlier editions of the textbook for numerous suggestions and comments. Our team at South-Western Publishing Co. has been a significant part of our textbook life. Our developmental editors—Dennis Hanseman and, for the last two editions, Alice Denny—have greatly improved our work. Sponsoring Editor Jim Keefe and Marketing Manager Scott Person have developed a classy final product. Over the years we have learned a great deal about the market from the College Division publisher's representatives, and we have enjoyed our interactions with them. We also want to thank our spouses, Susan and Carl, who continue to provide encouragement and inspiration through many editions of this textbook.

Finally, we would like to dedicate the fifth edition to the memory of Professor Jack Livingston of Ripon College and Professor Dorothy Goodwin of the University of Connecticut. Their skill and enthusiasm for teaching attracted us to economics as a profession. If they were alive to read this textbook, they would find their inspired teaching living on in its pages.

Ryan C. Amacher
Holley H. Ulbrich

CONTENTS

PART 1
INTRODUCTION TO ECONOMICS 1

CHAPTER 1 ECONOMICS, ECONOMIC ISSUES, AND ECONOMIC METHODS 2
Introduction 2
What Is Economics? 2
Economics in Relation to Other Fields 3
Why Study Economics? 3
Scarcity: Limited Resources, Insatiable Wants 4
International Perspective: The Nobel Prize for Economics 7
Society's Choices: The Production Possibilities Curve 8
Theories, Hypotheses, and Models 13
Basic Elements of the Economic Approach 17
Economic Profile: Milton Friedman (1912–) and Paul A. Samuelson (1915–) 18
Three Common Fallacies 20
International Perspective: The United States and the Rest of the World 22
Making Policy Choices 23
Summary 25
New Terms 25
Questions for Discussion 26
Suggestions for Further Reading 27
Appendix: Economic Relationships and Graphs 29

CHAPTER 2 MARKETS, GOVERNMENTS, AND NATIONS:
   THE ORGANIZATION OF ECONOMIC ACTIVITY 41
Introduction 41
Limited Resources: The Factors of Production 41
The Basic Economic Questions 43
The Circular Flow of Economic Activity 48
The Economic Role of Government 52

INTRODUCTION TO ECONOMICS

1

AFTER STUDYING THIS CHAPTER, YOU SHOULD BE ABLE TO:

1. Define economics and distinguish between microeconomics and macroeconomics.
2. Explain why you should study economics.
3. Discuss how economics is related to other social sciences.
4. Explain the relationship between scarcity and choice.
5. Define and give examples of opportunity cost.
6. Use a production possibilities curve to show:
   a. opportunity cost,
   b. increasing opportunity cost,
   c. economic growth,
   d. unemployment of the factors of production.
7. Identify the basic elements of an economic model and explain how it can be tested.
8. Interpret the self-interest assumption and explain why it is important in economics.
9. Explain and give examples of:
   a. the association-causation fallacy,
   b. the fallacy of composition,
   c. the *ceteris paribus* fallacy.
10. List the steps followed in policy analysis.

CHAPTER 1

ECONOMICS, ECONOMIC ISSUES, AND ECONOMIC METHODS

INTRODUCTION

In this chapter, we explore what economics is, stressing the basic economic problem of scarcity and choice. In order to do that, we introduce you to your first economic model—the production possibilities curve. We then generalize from this model to some properties of models in general. Finally, we explain how economists use models to think about economic problems and develop policies to address those problems. By the end of this chapter, you will have begun to think like an economist.

WHAT IS ECONOMICS?

economics
The study of how people and institutions make decisions about production and consumption and how they face the problem of scarcity.

microeconomics
The study of individual market interactions, focusing on production and consumption by the individual consumer, firm, or industry.

Economics is the study of how people, individually and through institutions, make decisions about producing and consuming goods and services and how they face the problem of scarcity. The word *economics* comes from the Greek *oikonomos*, which means household management. The study of economics is divided into microeconomics and macroeconomics.

Micro, or *mikros*, is a Greek prefix meaning small. **Microeconomics** describes the interactions of producers and consumers in individual markets, such as the market for cars. It also examines interactions between such markets, for example, the impact of changes in the demand for steel on the price of aluminum.

The Greek prefix *macro*, or *makros*, means long or large. So, as you might expect, the study of the economy as a whole is called **macroeconomics**. Macroeconomics is concerned with **aggregates**, or quantities whose values are determined by adding across many markets. Macroeconomics studies the behavior of variables that describe the whole economy, such as the value of the total output that the economy produces in a given time period. Macroeconomics also examines the behavior of such aggregates as the price level and total employment or unemployment. Values of these aggregates are derived from many individual markets taken together.

In both microeconomics and macroeconomics, the most important tools are demand and supply, which are developed in Chapter 3. Demand and supply help to explain prices and outputs in individual markets. These tools also explain the relation between prices and outputs in different markets. In microeconomics, you may look at the demand for the output of a single industry, such as bicycle manufacturing. In macroeconomics, you look at the level of prices and output for the economy as a whole, using aggregate demand and aggregate supply as the main tools. Even though microeconomics and macroeconomics are often studied separately, they are closely related.

macroeconomics
The study of the economy as a whole or of economic aggregates, such as the level of employment and the growth of total output.

aggregates
Quantities whose values are determined by adding across many markets.

ECONOMICS IN RELATION TO OTHER FIELDS

Economics is usually classed as a **social science**. This label makes economics an academic relative of political science, sociology, psychology, and anthropology. All of these fields look at the behavior of human beings, individually and in groups. They study different subsets of the actions and interactions of human beings. (For this reason, they are also sometimes termed *behavioral sciences.*)

Economics focuses on the consumption, production, and use of scarce resources by individuals and groups. Economics is also concerned with the processes by which households and firms make decisions about the use of scarce resources. This definition of the "territory" of economics leads to some overlap with the other social sciences. Psychologists and economists share an interest in what causes people to take certain actions. However, economists are primarily interested in actions that are reflected in market activity or in economic decisions made through government. Sociologists are interested in all facets of organized human activity. Economists, however, are interested mainly in organized activities that relate to the production and consumption of goods and services.

In general, economists assume that individuals pursue their own self-interest and respond to various signals or incentives in light of that self-interest. Although that assumption may seem obvious, it is a somewhat different view of human behavior from that of psychologists and sociologists. It often leads economists to draw different conclusions. As you learn more about economics, you will better understand how it overlaps with—and differs from—other social sciences.

social science
An academic field that studies the behavior of human beings, individually and in groups, and examines their interactions.

WHY STUDY ECONOMICS?

Economics is a required course for many different majors. You may be wondering why this is so. One reason is that economics interacts with almost all other academic subjects. It affects and is affected by current events. Also, it has a major effect on politics, both domestic and international.

A second reason for studying economics is the impact that economic ideas and theories have on world leaders. Much of what political decision makers do is based on economic theory. As John Maynard Keynes, an economist who has had great influence on macroeconomic policy in this century, wrote:

The ideas of economists and political philosophers, both when they are right and when they are wrong, are more powerful than is commonly understood. Indeed, the world is ruled by little else. Practical men, who believe themselves to be quite exempt from any intellectual influences, are usually the slaves of some defunct economist. Madmen in authority, who hear voices in the air, are distilling their frenzy from some academic scribbler of a few years back.[1]

Keynes was saying that if you want to understand what politicians, great or mad, are trying to do, you must understand the economic theories on which they are acting.

A third reason for studying economics is that it provides a better understanding of how society functions. Economic theory is very useful in understanding behavior because it allows the development of models with predictive power. As Alfred Marshall, another noted economist, wrote, "Economics is the study of mankind in the ordinary business of life."[2]

Finally, economics is fun, and people who are trained in economics find rewarding jobs and careers. If you like to think in a logical fashion, you will enjoy studying economics.

SCARCITY: LIMITED RESOURCES, INSATIABLE WANTS

scarcity
The central economic problem that there are not enough resources to produce everything that individuals want.

Whether you are just taking one course or planning a career in economics, the most important single problem you will address is that of **scarcity.** That is, there are not enough resources to produce all the goods and services people would like to consume. The first tool we will develop is an economic model that is used to explain how any economic system deals with the basic problem of scarcity. Human wants and desires are vast, relative to the resources available to satisfy them. Thus, in every economic system, there has to be some method for making choices among different desirable ends.

We live in a world of limited resources. Resources are whatever can be used to produce goods and services for human consumption. Some resources, such as oil and coal, are converted to energy and used up in the course of production or consumption. Others are not used up in that sense but are virtually fixed in quantity. Examples are land, diamonds, and copper. At any given time, even the quantity of resources created by people—roads, factories, machines, and skilled labor—cannot be changed quickly or cheaply.

insatiable wants
The needs and desires of human beings, which can never be completely satisfied.

Limited resources conflict with **insatiable wants**. Human wants are said to be insatiable (unable to be satisfied) because no matter how much peo-

---
1. J. M. Keynes, *The General Theory of Employment, Interest, and Money* (London: Macmillan, 1936), 383.
2. Alfred Marshall, *Principles of Economics*, 8th ed. (Don Mills, Ontario: Macmillan of Canada, 1920), 323.

ple have, they always want more of something. You may know people who seem perfectly content with what they have. If you questioned them carefully, however, you would probably find that they would like cleaner air, more time to play tennis or golf, or more shelters for the homeless. Since not all wants can be satisfied, individuals have to choose which ones to satisfy with limited available resources. In fact, every society is faced with the problem of scarcity and choice. Without scarcity, there would be no need to make choices about what desires or needs to satisfy—and thus no need to study economics.

OPPORTUNITY COSTS

Every decision to produce or consume something means sacrificing the production or consumption of something else. For instance, the cost of going to a football game includes the value of what is given up in order to attend. Economists use the term **opportunity cost** to denote the full value of the best alternative that is given up, or forgone. Part of the cost of attending a football game is the price of the ticket. This price represents the other goods and services you could have purchased with that money instead. However, there is another important part of the cost. This second part is the most valuable alternative use of those three hours, such as studying for a test. The opportunity cost of attending the game consists of both the price of the ticket and the difference in your test grade that three more hours of study would have produced. Even if the ticket had no monetary price, going to the game would still have an opportunity cost.

Many people have problems grasping the concept of opportunity cost because they are used to thinking of cost as price, or the amount of money spent on an item or an activity. In economics, however, the concept of cost is much broader. It includes not only the dollar outlay (the other goods you could have purchased) but also the time cost (the earnings or satisfaction you could have produced for yourself in some other activity) and other sacrifices you might have made. Sometimes it is difficult to place a dollar value on these other costs, but they still play an important role in economic decisions.

opportunity cost
The value of the other alternatives given up in order to enjoy a particular good or service.

SOME APPLICATIONS OF OPPORTUNITY COST

Your everyday life provides many illustrations of the concept of opportunity cost. For example, what is the opportunity cost of attending college? It is not simply the dollar figure given in your college's catalog. Money spent on books and tuition is certainly part of the opportunity cost. However, the expense of your room, meals, and clothing is not, because you would have incurred those costs even if you weren't in college. The catalog may list them as costs, but economists don't count them because they are not opportunity costs.

One important opportunity cost not listed in any college catalog is the income you could have been earning during the years you are spending in classes. For most students, that lost income will eventually be made up in higher future earnings. However, right now it is an opportunity cost that should be included. Even if you can earn only $5 an hour, if you have to cut your working hours by 30 hours a week during the 32 weeks a year you are in school, the lost earnings represent a cost of $4,800 a year.

For some students, the opportunity cost of going to college is even higher. Suppose you are a talented athlete who could play professionally right after high school, as many baseball and tennis players do. Your college education may cost as much as $100,000 a year in lost earnings. After several years of college, many football and basketball players face this dilemma. Even if they are straight-A students, the opportunity cost of completing a degree in terms of lost income is very high. It is not surprising that many of them choose to "turn pro" and postpone or abandon getting a degree.

Another illustration of opportunity cost is provided by the proposal of some politicians that there should be two years of national service for all young adults. This service would be in the military or some other part of the public sector and would pay very low wages. For some, the opportunity cost would be very low because they have few good employment opportunities. But for someone with an engineering or accounting degree, athletic skills, or other potential for good earnings, the opportunity cost would be very high. Universal national service is a tax on being young. Such a tax would be very different for different individuals.

OPPORTUNITY COST AND THE CHOICE CURVE

We can illustrate the concept of opportunity cost and its relationship to choice using a very simple example. Assume that you have $40 to spend and you have two choices: pizza and cola. Pizzas cost $8 each, and colas cost $2 for a six-pack. To keep things simple, we assume that you wish to spend the whole $40. Figure 1 shows the various combinations of pizza and cola that you can buy with $40. If you spend the entire $40 on pizza, you can purchase 5 pizzas (the *y*-intercept in Figure 1). On the other hand, you can

FIGURE 1
CHOICE AMONG ALTERNATIVES
If six-packs of cola cost $2 and pizzas cost $8, a person with $40 to spend has many attainable combinations of cola and pizza. The line *PR* represents the boundary between attainable and unattainable combinations. Along line *PR*, the opportunity cost of 1 pizza is 4 six-packs of cola.

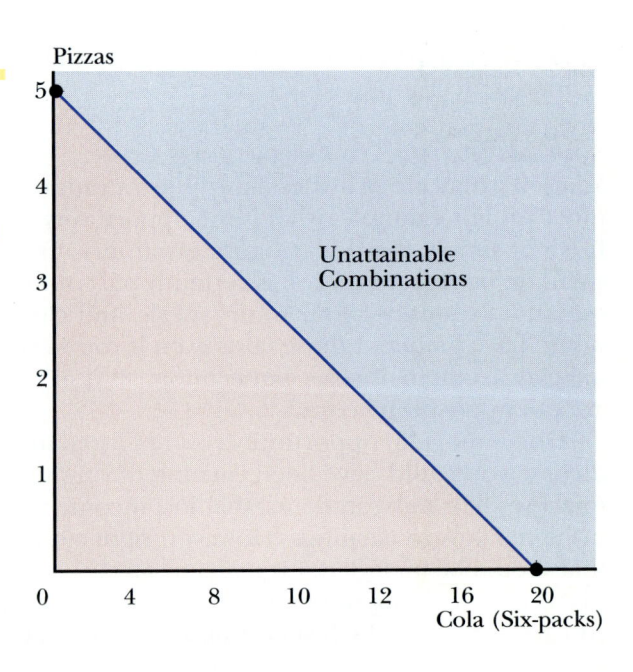

International Perspective

The Nobel Prize for Economics

The Nobel Committee, established by the Swedish Royal Academy of Sciences, awarded the first Nobel Prize in 1901. These prizes include awards for peace, as well as physics, chemistry, literature, and medicine. They were originally funded by a bequest from the inventor of dynamite, Alfred Nobel. It wasn't until 1969, however, that the first Nobel Prize for Economics was awarded. The Bank of Sweden funded this prize to celebrate its 300th anniversary.

The addition of an economics prize puts economics in a distinguished family of academic disciplines. It is the only social science to be so honored. Receipt of a Nobel Prize is a high honor for an economist and financially rewarding.

The Nobel Prize winners in economics have made profound and very diverse contributions to this field. Many of the European winners are noted for their work in international or development economics. These include Myrdal, Meade, Ohlin, and Lewis. More than half the winners have been Americans. The following are the winners of the prize since 1969:

1969 Ragnar Frisch, Norway
     Jan Tinbergen, Netherlands
1970 Paul A. Samuelson, United States
1971 Simon Kuznets, United States
1972 Kenneth J. Arrow, United States
     Sir John R. Hicks, Great Britain
1973 Wassily Leontief, United States
1974 Gunnar Myrdal, Sweden
     Friedrich A. von Hayek, Great Britain
1975 Leonid V. Kantorovich, Soviet Union
     Tjalling C. Koopmans, Netherlands/United States
1976 Milton Friedman, United States
1977 James E. Meade, Great Britain
     Bertil Ohlin, Sweden
1978 Herbert A. Simon, United States
1979 Sir Arthur Lewis, Great Britain
     Theodore Schultz, United States
1980 Lawrence R. Klein, United States
1981 James Tobin, United States
1982 George Stigler, United States
1983 Gerard Debreu, France/United States
1984 Sir Richard Stone, Great Britain
1985 Franco Modigliani, United States
1986 James M. Buchanan, United States
1987 Robert Solow, United States
1988 Maurice Altais, France
1989 Trigve Haavelmo, Norway
1990 Harry M. Markowitz, United States
     Merton H. Miller, United States
     William F. Sharpe, United States

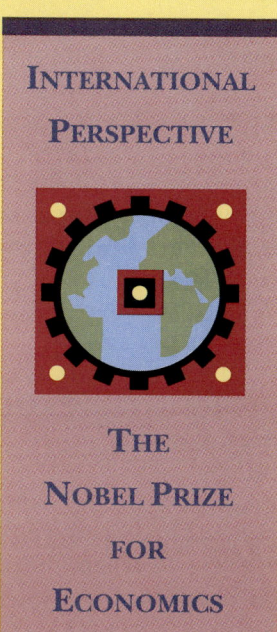

buy 20 six-packs of cola with $40 (as shown by the *x*-intercept in Figure 1). Other possibilities lie along the line that connects these two intercepts. The line represents all possible combinations of pizza and cola that total $40.[3] Of course, all combinations in the shaded area of Figure 1 are also attainable. However, these combinations wouldn't exhaust your entire $40.[4] Combinations above and to the right of the line are not attainable because they cost more than $40.

Figure 1 illustrates the array of choices and the concept of opportunity cost. The price of 1 pizza is the same as the price of 4 six-packs of cola. The decision to purchase a pizza means the sacrifice of those six-packs that could have been purchased instead. Opportunity cost is measured by the slope of the choice line.[5]

SOCIETY'S CHOICES: THE PRODUCTION POSSIBILITIES CURVE

From the perspective of the economy as a whole, the choice is not how to spend income between alternative purchases but how to allocate available productive resources between alternative goods that could be produced. This problem is illustrated by a close relative of the choice curve of Figure 1. Society's choice curve is called a **production possibilities curve**. This curve shows the various output combinations of two goods or groups of goods that can be produced in an economy with the available resources. This simple economic model is based on a few assumptions:

production possibilities curve
A graph that depicts the various combinations of two goods that can be produced in an economy with the available resources.

1. All of the economy's productive resources are fully employed. This means that everyone who wants a job has one. Also, factories, land, and other resources are being used to full capacity. (These resources will be discussed in greater detail in the next chapter.)
2. There are only two goods (or types of goods) in the economy.
3. The resources used in production are interchangeable. One worker is the same as another, one machine can be substituted for another, and all land is equally useful for producing the two goods.
4. We are looking at the economy at a specific period of time (the short run). During this time period, both the quantity and quality of resources are fixed, and the technology does not change.

Given these four assumptions, we can look at a simple example of a

---

3. The line *PR* is a continuous line. It is easy to see that points *A* and *B* represent attainable combinations because both contain whole numbers of colas and pizzas. Connecting these points implies that you can purchase fractional units of cola and pizza, for example, half of a six-pack of cola. Since we usually purchase goods in whole units, it might seem strange to show fractional units as attainable combinations. This is merely a convenient assumption. If the numbers on the axes are large enough, for example, hundreds of pizzas and thousands of colas, then there is less problem in visualizing the array of choices as a continuous line.
4. We have ruled out the possibility of saving part of the $40 because we are assuming only two alternative uses of funds: pizza and cola. If saving were an option, there would really be three goods: pizza, cola, and savings. Faced with only two alternatives, we can only choose how to divide the money between them.
5. If you have forgotten how to measure the slope of a line, you should refer to the appendix on graphs to refresh your memory.

Chapter 1 Economics, Economic Issues, and Economic Methods

**TABLE 1
PRODUCTION POSSIBILITIES SCHEDULE**

SOYBEANS (TONS)	MISSILES
20	0
16	1
12	2
8	3
4	4
0	5

production possibilities curve. Table 1 shows combinations of missiles and soybeans that an economy can produce. Figure 2 plots the numbers of Table 1 on a graph. Line *PR* in Figure 2 is a production possibilities curve. It represents all the combinations of missiles and soybeans that can be produced in this economy when the available resources are fully employed.

In Figure 2, points *A* and *B* represent two different combinations of missiles and soybeans that both lie on the production possibilities curve. Points *A* and *B* are both output combinations that can be attained in this economy with the available resources. Point *C* is also attainable. Since it lies inside of line *PR*, however, it represents unemployed resources. There are points on *PR* that have to be better than *C* because they represent more missiles, more soybeans, or more of both. The economy can do better, that is, can produce more. Therefore, *C* is inferior to points on the production possibilities curve.

The line *PR* in Figure 2 can also be used to measure opportunity cost for the economy. Line *PR* is a straight line. This fact implies that the opportunity cost of one product in terms of the other is constant. That is, the number of missiles given up to get another ton of soybeans doesn't

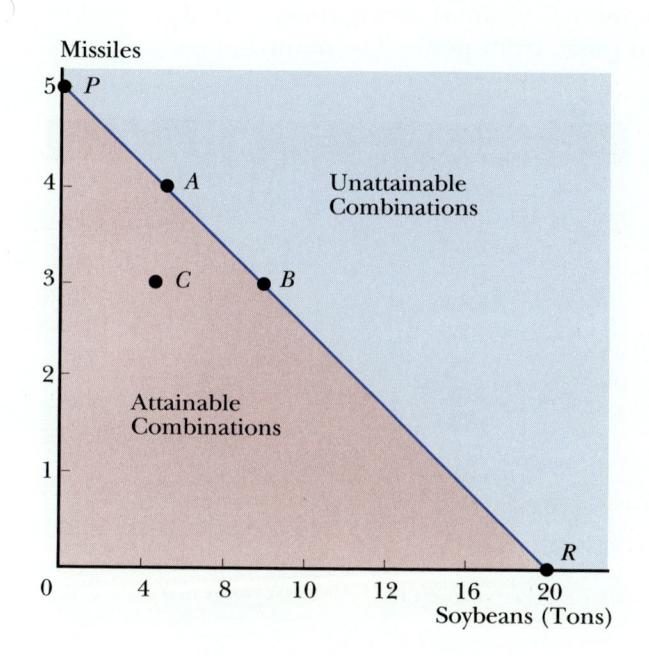

**FIGURE 2
PRODUCTION POSSIBILITIES CURVE**
A production possibilities curve shows combinations of two goods that can be produced in an economy, with fixed resources and technology. Points on the curve represent the full employment of resources.

change along line *PR*. Each time the production of soybeans is increased by 1 ton, one-quarter of a missile is sacrificed. The opportunity cost of 1 more ton of soybeans is one-quarter of a missile. Conversely, the opportunity cost of 1 more missile is 4 tons of soybeans.

Opportunity cost of one good in terms of another is constant along line *PR* in Figure 2 because we assumed that all resources are alike for production purposes. That is, any unit of resources is just as good as any other unit in producing either soybeans or missiles. This assumption produces a straight-line production possibilities curve.

INCREASING OPPORTUNITY COSTS

After an economist has constructed a model, the next step is to go back and vary the assumptions to see what difference they make. Consider what happens when we drop the third assumption stated above—that productive resources are interchangeable. That is, we no longer assume that one unit of labor or land is just as productive as another for producing either good. Table 2 shows a different set of combinations of missiles and soybeans that can be produced in this economy. These combinations are plotted on the graph in Figure 3. At point *A* in Figure 3, output is 10 missiles and 200 tons of soybeans. At point *B*, output consists of more missiles, 100, but fewer soybeans, only 100 tons.

The production possibilities curve in Figure 3 is bowed, or curved, instead of being a straight line. This new shape reflects the change in the assumption that resources are alike. Here we are being more realistic and assuming that some resources are better suited to the production of missiles and others to the production of soybeans. This change in assumptions produces a model that differs from the first one in what it implies about opportunity cost.

If the economy is at point *A* in Figure 3, we can get another 10 missiles by shifting resources from soybean production to missile production. In moving from point *A* to point *C*, we must give up only a small amount of soybeans, 5 units. But to move from point *B* to point *D*, producing an-

TABLE 2
PRODUCTION POSSIBILITIES SCHEDULE

SOYBEANS	MISSILES
205	0
(A) 200 ⎱ −5	10 ⎱ +10
(C) 195 ⎰	20 ⎰
187	30
179	40
169	50
158	60
146	70
133	80
117	90
(B) 100 ⎱ −23	100 ⎱ +10
(D) 77 ⎰	110 ⎰
50	120
0	130
0	130

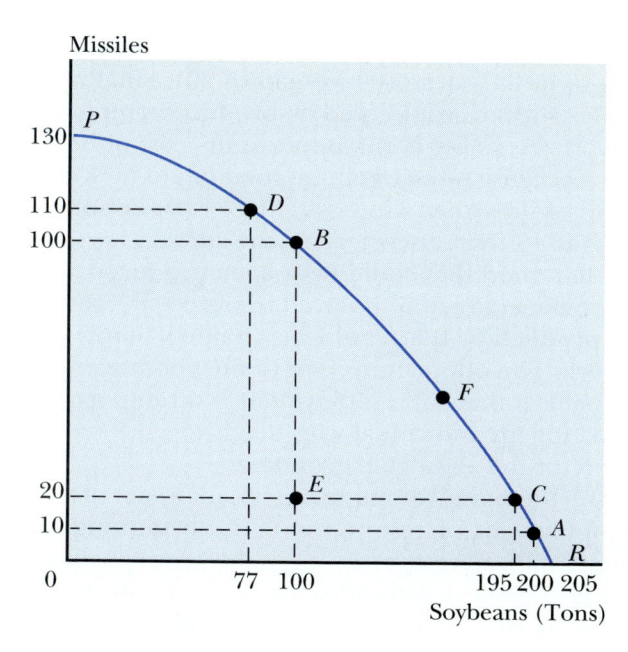

Chapter 1 Economics, Economic Issues, and Economic Methods   11

**FIGURE 3
PRODUCTION POSSIBILITIES AND INCREASING OPPORTUNITY COSTS**
On this production possibilities curve, the opportunity cost of additional units of soybeans increases as the economy becomes more specialized in soybeans: producing each additional unit of soybeans requires a larger sacrifice of missiles than before (increasing opportunity cost). If the economy is inside the production possibilities curve at some point such as E, more of both goods could be produced.

other 10 missiles requires a larger sacrifice of soybeans, 23 units instead of 5. This curved production possibilities curve illustrates the very important principle of **increasing opportunity cost**. That is, the more missiles that are already being produced, the larger the sacrifice of soybeans required to get additional missiles. Table 2 shows that between points A and C, ten more missiles cost 5 units of soybeans. Between points B and D, however, ten more missiles cost 23 units of soybeans.

Increasing opportunity costs are obvious in wartime. As more war goods are demanded, civilian sacrifices increase. Initially, as military production expands, additional labor and other resources are used that are relatively more productive for making missiles and relatively less productive for growing soybeans. As the switch to missiles continues, however, military production takes resources that are relatively less productive for making missiles, although they were highly productive for growing soybeans. Soybean production falls by larger and larger amounts, therefore, because more resources are stripped away from soybeans for every extra missile produced. These resources are increasingly those best suited to producing soybeans and least adaptable to missile production.

increasing opportunity cost
The principle that as production of one good rises, larger and larger sacrifices of another are required.

UNEMPLOYMENT
For the straight-line version of the production possibilities curve, another important assumption was that all resources are fully employed. If we drop that assumption, the production possibilities curve can also illustrate unemployment and the effect of reducing it. Suppose the economy is at point E in Figure 3. This point is inside the production possibilities curve because some workers, factories, land, and machines are unemployed. If the economy could move from point E to point C, it would be possible to have more soybeans (195 tons instead of 100) with no sacrifice of missiles.

Moving from point E to point B would mean producing the same amount of soybeans (100 tons) but more missiles (100 instead of 20). Finally, at point F, more of both missiles and soybeans could be produced simply by putting idle resources to work. At point E, the opportunity cost of both soybeans and missiles is zero because none of either good has to be sacrificed to increase production of the other. However, there is an opportunity cost to being at point E rather than elsewhere on the curve. This cost is equal to the output of either good that could have been produced.

From a macroeconomic perspective, unemployed resources are wasteful. They represent extra production that could be attained simply by putting idle resources to work. The opportunity cost of the goods gained is zero. Thus, economists believe that full employment is an important goal. It is important not just for the individual who needs to work in order to earn income, but also for the aggregate economy.

Both World War II and the Vietnam War made Americans aware of the importance of the full employment of resources. At the beginning of World War II, there were unemployed resources. It was therefore possible to produce more war goods (missiles) without a sacrifice of consumer goods (soybeans). Eventually, all the idle resources were employed. Then further expansion of the production of war goods required the sacrifice of consumer goods. No cars were produced for several years during World War II as auto factories switched to making military tanks and trucks. Other consumer goods were also in short supply. The Vietnam War occurred at a time of relatively low unemployment in the late 1960s. Thus, expanding production of military hardware and diverting labor from civilian activities to soldiering led immediately to reduced production of consumer goods. The economy was already on the production possibilities curve when the United States was drawn into the Vietnam War.

One of the main concerns of macroeconomics is explaining how an economy can find itself inside the production possibilities curve at a point such as E in Figure 3. How can an economic system avoid the idleness and waste of unemployed resources? If an economy finds itself at a point such as E, what can be done to get back on the production possibilities curve? These are important questions in the study of macroeconomics. The production possibilities curve is a useful technique for identifying these questions.

ECONOMIC GROWTH

Another macroeconomic issue that can be illustrated by the production possibilities model is economic growth. If technology can improve and the quantity of resources can increase, then output can grow beyond the limits of the production possibilities curve. Better technology or more resources means a change in the fourth assumption stated earlier—that both resources and technology are fixed. As labor becomes more skilled and productive, and as producers acquire new machines and plants embodying the latest technology, the production possibilities curve shifts outward.

An outward shift of a production possibilities curve is shown in Figure 4. If the economy is at point A on PR, production consists of D_1 units of soybeans and C_1 units of missiles. With the shift of the curve to P_1R_1, it is

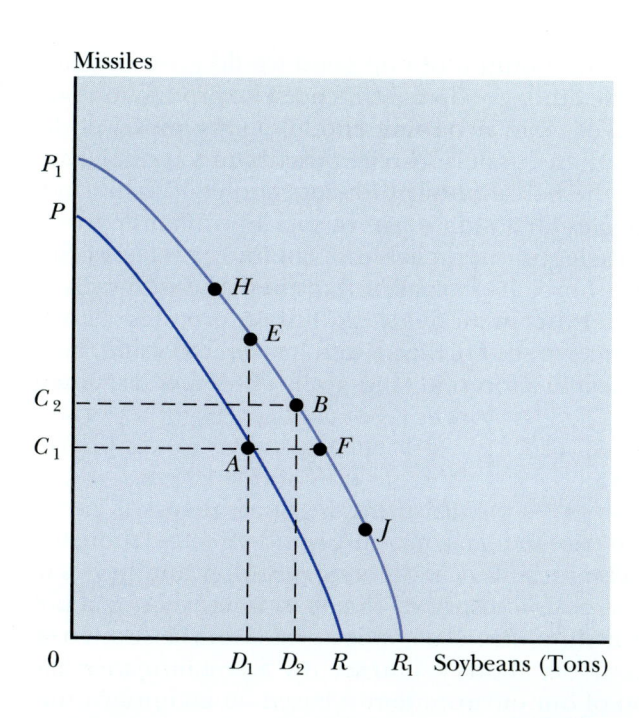

FIGURE 4
SHIFT OF THE PRODUCTION POSSIBILITIES CURVE
An outward shift of the production possibilities curve from PR to P_1R_1 means that the economy can produce more of both goods (economic growth).

possible to reach some point, such as point B, that includes more of both soybeans (D_2 units) and missiles (C_2 units). Other possible combinations on the new production possibilities curve include the same amount of one good and more of the other (such as point E or F) or less of one good and more of the other (such as point H or J). No matter which combination is produced, the important thing about an outward shift of a production possibilities curve is that it increases the economy's capacity to respond to human wants.

Added resources, usually labor or capital, are sources of economic growth. New technology can also shift a production possibilities curve outward and account for economic growth. Invention, innovation, discovery of resources, and improvements in productivity all contribute to economic growth.

THE PRODUCTION POSSIBILITIES CURVE SHOWS:	
• Attainable combinations	Points on the curve
• Opportunity cost	The slope of the curve
• Unemployment of resources	Points below or inside the curve
• Economic growth	A shift of the curve to the right

THEORIES, HYPOTHESES, AND MODELS

The production possibilities curve is a theoretical model. Based on certain assumptions (two products, a brief time period, fixed resources, given technology), we theorized that output of one good would grow in a predictable way if output of the other good was reduced. The production possibilities curve is just one of many economic models. This book will develop and use a variety of these models. You can use them to understand the workings of markets, the behavior of producers and consumers, and the effects of various policies on a wide range of social problems.

A model represents a scientific approach to examining problems. Scientists of all kinds differ from nonscientists in that they deal with facts in a systematic way. Early scientists in all fields did little more than classify the facts they or others uncovered. This approach has limited value, however. It is very easy to get lost in a forest of facts, even when they are neatly filed and classified.

THEORIES AND HYPOTHESES

theory
A set of principles that can be used to make inferences about the world.

Theories play an important role in everything we do. A **theory** is an abstraction from reality that tries to focus on a cause-and-effect relationship between two variables. The variables can be money supply and prices in macroeconomics or labor costs and prices of cars in microeconomics. A theory is useful in that it simplifies observations by clearing away irrelevant details. In a way, a theory allows you to see the forest instead of the trees. Any interpretation of our environment is based on an implicit theory about cause-and-effect relationships. Our senses receive information, and we interpret that information on the basis of some theory about the world we have developed over time. These theories are constantly being revised and improved to better explain the facts. A good theory will develop **testable hypotheses**, which are mini-theories that can be verified or disproved by checking them against facts or experiences. Even small children, for example, quickly develop testable hypotheses based on experience: "My finger will hurt if I touch the hot stove," or "The cat will scratch me if I pull its tail."

testable hypothesis
An inference from a theory that can be subjected to real-world testing.

MODELS

Economic theorists, like other scientists, develop theories that will yield testable hypotheses.[6] Then they test these hypotheses by comparing them with the facts and seeing if they are consistent.

model
A set of assumptions and hypotheses that is a simplified description of reality.

A **model** is a formal statement of a theory, usually in the form of graphs or equations. In the simpler model of the production possibilities curve as a straight line, we assumed that all productive resources were alike. As a result, the relationship between outputs of the two goods was a constant one. In the more complex model, we introduced an alternative assumption—that all resources were not alike. The model then predicted that increased production of one good would require increasing sacrifices of the other.

An economic model will generate one or more "if-then" hypotheses about what will happen in the real world. These hypotheses are then

---

6. Not everyone agrees that economics, or any of the other social sciences, is scientific in the same sense as the natural sciences. This debate has been going on for a century. It started with an essay by Thorstein Veblen in the *Quarterly Journal of Economics* in 1889. For a more recent discussion of this issue, see Alfred Eichner, "Can Economics Become a Science?" *Challenge* (November-December 1986): 4–12.

tested in real situations or experiments. The production possibilities model offers several such testable hypotheses. For example, according to this model, if a larger share of resources is devoted to production of military goods (missiles), then less will be available for consumer goods (soybeans). During the Vietnam War, President Lyndon Johnson was convinced that there were enough idle resources in the U.S. economy to expand both military and civilian output at the same time. As the economy quickly reached full employment, it became apparent that continuing to produce military goods and to divert some productive resources (young men) into fighting could be done only at the expense of producing less housing, education, and other goods and services for consumers.

At the beginning of the 1990s policy makers were anticipating another test of the above hypothesis—in the opposite direction. If reforms in the Soviet Union and Eastern Europe did indeed lead to reduced spending on defense in the United States, most economists expected that the resources released from military use would lead to a large increase in output of civilian goods. Politicians named those released resources the "peace dividend." They were making plans to divert them to such civilian uses as education, housing, anti-drug programs, and bailing out the savings and loan industry, when war broke out in the Persian Gulf. A peace dividend may still occur, but not as soon as many people had hoped.

ASSUMPTIONS

Unlike physical scientists, economists rarely have the chance to conduct controlled experiments to validate their models. Instead, economists most often test hypotheses by looking at actual experiences in markets. Such experiments are often referred to by economists as *ceteris paribus* experiments. *Ceteris paribus* is a Latin phrase that means "all else being equal." An economist changes one variable in a theoretical model (for example, the technology for producing missiles in the production possibilities model). The economist then predicts what would happen *ceteris paribus*, or if everything else remained constant. The **ceteris paribus assumption**, or holding everything else constant, is the most common and most important assumption in economic models. If the technology of missile production improved but there was no change in the technology of producing soybeans, the production possibilities curve would shift out as in Figure 5, from *PR* to *PR*₁. The economist would predict an increase in output of both commodities, but a relatively larger increase in the output of missiles. The economist must then untangle the effects of the change in missile technology on the mix of output (missiles and soybeans) from anything else that changed in the real world in the time period when this model is being tested.

In addition to the *ceteris paribus* assumption, one other assumption is a basic part of most economic models. This assumption is that most people behave in a self-interested way. In general, **self-interested behavior** consists of trying to get the most of something they want (to maximize some goal) out of available resources. For consumers, self-interested behavior means maximizing their satisfaction. For owners of productive resources, self-interest is expressed by seeking to maximize income or wealth. For busi-

ceteris paribus assumption The assumption that everything else will remain constant, used for most economic models. (*Ceteris paribus* is Latin for "all else being equal.")

self-interested behavior A basic assumption of economic theory that individual decision makers do what is best for themselves.

**FIGURE 5
TECHNOLOGICAL CHANGE AND THE PRODUCTION POSSIBILITIES CURVE**
A change in the technology of producing soybeans shifts the production possibilities curve from PR to PR_1. This shows that if all resources were devoted to soybeans, more could be produced. If all resources were devoted to missiles, however, no increase in output could occur. Increases in both are also possible.

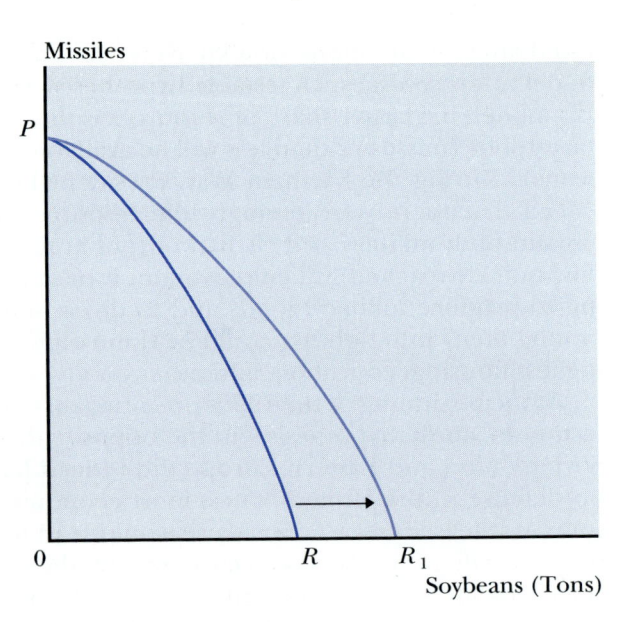

ness firms, self-interest means maximizing profits.[7] In the production possibilities model, self-interested behavior will direct the decision as to which combination to produce out of all possible combinations. That combination is the one that maximizes the welfare or satisfaction of consumers.

The self-interest assumption has given economics, and economists, a good deal of undeserved bad press. This has occurred because self-interest is confused with selfishness. Critics of market economies argue that encouraging and rewarding self-interested behavior is a basic flaw in such systems. The ideas of social reformers such as Karl Marx and Mao Zedung have led to many experiments in socialism, such as the Fourier settlements in the United States and the Cultural Revolution in China. These experiments have been attempts to devise alternative ways of organizing economic activity. All of these experiments have tried to rebuild societies in such a way that individuals would act on nobler or higher motives than self-interest.

In fact, concern for others and for the community as a whole is not incompatible with self-interest because individuals define their own self-interest in terms of what is satisfying to them. Some individuals derive their greatest satisfaction from material possessions, others from leisure or enjoyment of the arts, and still others from helping others and building better communities. Some persons may derive satisfaction from all of these! So self-interested behavior is not inconsistent with volunteer work or charitable contributions. Such unselfish activities are not, by our definition, un-self-interested. This definition of self-interest is broad enough to cover the actions of Albert Schweitzer and Mother Teresa as well as those of the most unlovable of "greedy capitalist pigs."

When economists use the self-interest assumption in developing theory, they are simply saying that they expect individual behavior to be

---

7. Maximization of various kinds is a central concern of microeconomics. You can refer to the appendix on graphs to review the geometry of maximization.

influenced by costs and benefits. If the cost of a course of action declines or the benefits rise, relative to alternatives, more people will choose that course of action. For example, if the price of soybeans rises relative to that of missiles, some firms will switch production from missiles to soybeans, attracted by the higher price. If salaries for public school teachers rise relative to those of accountants, more people are likely to prepare for a teaching career and fewer to study accounting. If the penalty for speeding falls, *ceteris paribus*, more people are likely to drive faster than the posted speed limit. If the cost of giving to charity rises because it is no longer tax-deductible, less will be given to charity.

Furthermore, economists do not use the concept of self-interest to predict any one person's or firm's behavior but rather to predict average or group behavior. Such predictions are similar to the use of attributes of certain groups by insurance companies to predict how often certain events will occur. Insurance companies develop norms for various groups—life expectancies, accident rates, or numbers of house fires—and use them to set prices for policies. These norms say nothing about how likely any particular member of a group is to live past the age of 80, run a car off the road, or have a house burn to the ground.

Even economists do not always agree about the best way to develop theories and construct models. Specifically, the role of assumptions has been fiercely debated by two American Nobel Prize winners in economics, Paul Samuelson and Milton Friedman. The traditional view, taken by Samuelson, is that once a theory is demonstrated to be logically correct, its usefulness depends on whether its assumptions are realistic. This view is consistent with the role of theory in the natural sciences. Friedman disagrees, arguing that the true test of the usefulness of a theory is whether it works. That is, does it accurately predict what happens in the real world? In this book, we will be looking for logically correct theories and models that pass both kinds of tests: realistic assumptions, and accurate predictions.

BASIC ELEMENTS OF THE ECONOMIC APPROACH

This discussion of theories and models suggests that economics is much like other sciences in its methods. What is unique or different about the economic approach? There are a few emphases and ideas that help set economics apart.

1. *Like the natural sciences, economic theory is positive, or nonnormative.* **Positive statements** are if-then propositions about *what is*. In contrast, **normative statements** describe *what ought to be*. In other words, economic theory strives to be scientific. However, when economists try to apply economic theory to policy questions, they often find it difficult to keep their work positive. Economic theory is value-free. However, appliers of the theory are often tempted to mix in their values in order to favor a preferred outcome or policy. It is a positive statement to say that production of more missiles will require increasing sacrifices of soybeans. It is a normative statement to say that more missiles and fewer soybeans should be produced.

positive statements
A set of propositions about what is, rather than what ought to be.

normative statements
A set of propositions about what ought to be (also called value judgements).

Milton Friedman and Paul A. Samuelson are two of the best-known contemporary American economists. Both are winners of the Nobel Prize in economics. The two men represent polar extremes with respect to economic policy. Samuelson sees an important role for government in modern industrial society. Friedman advocates a *laissez-faire* economic policy. He argues that the market economy operates very well and that the interventions Samuelson supports do more harm than good. Samuelson is a leader of the Eastern liberal school of economics. Friedman represents the conservative Chicago School.

Samuelson, a professor at the Massachusetts Institute of Technology (MIT), has an A.B. degree from the University of Chicago and A.M. and Ph.D. degrees in economics from Harvard University. His Ph.D. dissertation, *Foundations of Economic Analysis,* written when he was only 23 years old, was published as a book. It still ranks as a monumental work in the application of mathematics to economics. Graduate students still study it. Many of today's economists were introduced to economics with Samuelson's textbook, *Economics.* Samuelson is largely responsible for making MIT's economics department one of the best in the country.

Friedman is retired from the University of Chicago, where he taught for 30 years. He is presently a senior research fellow at the Hoover Institution at Stanford University. Friedman received an A.B. degree from Rutgers, an A.M. degree from the University of Chicago, and a Ph.D. degree from Columbia University. He has made notable contributions to economic theory. His policy ideas are readily available in three popular books: *Essays in Positive Economics* (1953), *Capitalism and Freedom* (1962), and *Free to Choose* (1980). Recently, Friedman has angered some of the conservatives who usually agree with him by arguing that illegal drugs should be legalized. He argues that legalizing such drugs will reduce both the profits in selling them and the crime and violence among sellers and users.

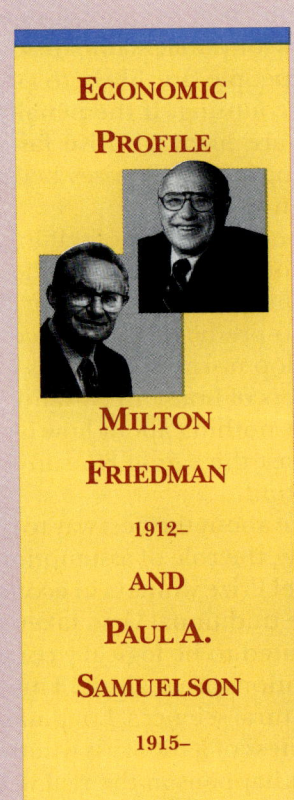

ECONOMIC PROFILE

MILTON FRIEDMAN
1912–
AND
PAUL A. SAMUELSON
1915–

2. *Economic theory cannot predict the future.* It can only explain the effects of certain events. Economic theory consists of statements of the if-*A*-then-*B* type. The prediction that *B* will occur depends on whether or not *A* happens. (Note that theory does not predict the occurrence of *A*. Economists do not have a crystal ball.) In the production possibilities model, an increase in resources will result in economic growth, *ceteris paribus*. In this case, part of the *ceteris paribus* assumption is that the increased resources will be put to work and not left unemployed. There is, however, some difference between what economics *is* and what many economists actually *do*. Many economists, especially macroeconomists, spend a great deal of time forecasting future conditions. To do this, they make use of economic theory. In forecasting, an economist guesses the likelihood that *A* will occur and then uses economic theory to predict the occurrence of *B*. Sometimes, however, forecasts are wrong. This doesn't necessarily mean that the theory is incorrect. The forecaster may have been wrong in expecting *A* to occur.
3. *Most economists look first to market processes for solutions to social problems.* This market bias reflects a preference for the freedom and efficiency arising from decentralized processes. However, most economic theory is applicable to nonmarket systems as well, even though the legal and political institutions differ. Economists can apply tools developed for analyzing market economies to the workings of socialist economies and to a wide variety of nonmarket behavior.
4. *Economists pay a great deal of attention to cost.* The emphasis on opportunity cost, scarcity, and choice is fundamental to economics. Nobel Prize winner Milton Friedman underscored the importance of opportunity cost in this famous remark: "There is no such thing as a free lunch. This is the sum of my economic theory. The rest is elaboration." Harping on the subject of cost often puts economists in conflict with policy makers. Environmentalists don't like to hear economists talk about the opportunity cost of environmental purity in terms of forgone output. College admissions or recruitment officers seeking students don't like economists reminding students that the opportunity cost of a college education includes income not earned while in college.
5. *Economists are very interested in chances to substitute among alternatives.* Substitution and cost are closely related because the decision to substitute is based on the costs of the various alternatives. Sometimes substitutes are obvious, such as plastic for aluminum or electric heat for gas. Other substitutes are less apparent. A tree, for example, can substitute for gas or oil as heat or for aluminum siding on houses. Trees can also substitute for air conditioning or awnings by providing shade. An important task of economic analysis is identifying alternatives that can serve as substitutes and evaluating the costs of substituting one for another.
6. *Economists think in terms of incremental, or marginal, analysis.*[8] The marginal approach means looking at the effects on other variables of small increases or decreases in one important variable. Should we produce another (marginal) missile? If we do, what will be the (marginal) cost in terms of soybeans not produced? Most decisions in economics are

---

8. Remember that *marginal* means extra, or incremental, rather than inferior.

not all-or-nothing choices but are made at the margin. Decisions about how to spend the next hour, whether to eat another slice of pizza, and whether to hire an extra worker are all marginal decisions.

7. *Economists take the individual, rather than the group, the industry, or the community, as the basic decision-making unit.* They regard the behavior of individuals as an important influence on public policy and on decisions made in the private sector. The emphasis on individuals rather than groups reflects the importance of incentives in economics. Changes in prices, costs, profits, wages, substitutes, and opportunities are the driving forces behind individual economic decisions. It is the individual, not the group or community, that responds to incentives.

THREE COMMON FALLACIES

There are three dangerous fallacies, or errors in logical thinking, that can lead to false conclusions in economics. The following three statements could appear in the news and would seem logical to most readers. Each, however, contains a fallacy.

1. "The stock market closed up today in active trading. Analysts attributed the gain to optimism generated by the recent U.S.-Soviet summit on arms control."
2. "Layoffs in the auto industry were attributed to rising imports of cars, especially from Japan. Union leaders called for renewed emphasis on buying American goods, predicting severe unemployment in all manufacturing industries if the tide of imports continues to rise."
3. "The long expected decline in college enrollment, caused by fewer high school graduates since the mid-1980s and sharply rising tuitions, has not taken place. College enrollments appear to be stable or rising, in contradiction to forecasts."

THE ASSOCIATION-CAUSATION FALLACY

The Latin phrase *post hoc, ergo propter hoc* translates as "after this, therefore, because of this." This kind of reasoning is called the **association-causation fallacy**. The fact that *A* changes and then *B* changes does not mean that the change in *A* caused the change in *B*. Suppose an increase in the number of students taking driver education programs is followed by an increase in accidents involving teenaged drivers. We could not conclude that driver education causes accidents. A statistical or observed association does not imply a causal relationship.

The stock market news item presented above is a familiar example. Newscasters know that the market has either risen or fallen, and they want a cause to offer as an explanation to report to their audiences. They can always find such a reason by identifying another important news event of the same day as *the* cause. The best way to avoid this fallacy is to search for a theoretical explanation for the suggested cause-and-effect relationship. Why, in terms of models and theories, should we expect a change in *A* to cause *B* to change in a certain way? There are sound theoretical reasons why an increase in profits or a decline in interest rates might lead to a

association-causation fallacy
The false notion that association implies causality.

Chapter 1 Economics, Economic Issues, and Economic Methods

> **THINKING LIKE AN ECONOMIST**
>
> As you start to think about problems and policies from an economic perspective, here are some guidelines to help you.
>
> | | |
> |---|---|
> | • Positive, not normative | Try not to confuse what theory tells you will happen with what you *want* to happen |
> | • Can the market solve it? | Economists tend to prefer market solutions because they are more efficient. |
> | • Costs | I know there is no free lunch, but have I really counted all the costs? |
> | • Substitutes | What are the substitutes? Where are they? What are their costs? |
> | • Individuals and incentives | What incentives (positive and negative) does this policy create for individual buyers, sellers, and workers? |
> | • Fallacies | Have I carefully reviewed my analysis to avoid the three common fallacies? |

stock market boom. Is there any reason for an arms agreement to affect the stock market? Avoiding the association-causation fallacy is a good reason for studying and using economic theory.

THE FALLACY OF COMPOSITION

The second news item given above illustrates the **fallacy of composition**. This is the erroneous view that what holds for the parts holds for the whole as well. It is true that rising auto imports hurt auto producers and auto workers as a group. Even if most of the auto industry suffers, that is not true of all manufacturing industries. If Americans import more, some American manufacturers will manage to sell more to foreigners who earn those dollars. Thus, there will be gainers as well as losers. What is true for auto workers and auto producers is not true for the economy as a whole. In fact, the U.S. economy did quite well during some of the worst years for the auto industry in the 1980s.

fallacy of composition The false notion that what holds for the parts holds for the whole.

THE *CETERIS PARIBUS* FALLACY

The third news item offers an example of the *ceteris paribus* fallacy. The ***ceteris paribus* fallacy** occurs when a variable does not change as predicted because the analyst has overlooked the fact that other variables have also changed. When economists make statements or predictions, they qualify them with the phrase *ceteris paribus*, meaning other things being unchanged. What happens to college enrollment when tuition rises, *ceteris paribus*? Economic theory tells us that enrollment should fall. Instead, enrollment in the 1980s held steady and even rose slightly.

The rise in tuition and decline in high school graduates, taken together, should have caused a decline in college enrollment. However, at the same time, incomes rose. Even though there were fewer students, they came from smaller families that could more easily afford to educate all their children. Also, a growing population of retired people provided a

ceteris paribus **fallacy** The false notion that arises because an observer fails to recognize that variables other than the one in question have changed.

INTERNATIONAL PERSPECTIVE

THE UNITED STATES AND THE REST OF THE WORLD

From the end of World War II until the mid-1970s, American students learned economics almost as though the United States were on a different planet from the rest of the world. A few textbooks had a chapter or two on international economics at the end. This material was rarely covered in class, however. This approach to economics reflected two common attitudes. The first was that the U.S. economy was so large and the share of foreign trade in U.S. economic activity was so small that the rest of the world could safely be ignored. The second was that it was important for students to learn how the U.S. economy worked, but not necessarily how institutions, policies, and solutions to common problems worked in other countries.

In the 1980s, Americans learned the economic importance of the rest of the world. The rest of the world has had a significant effect on the U.S. economy. The price of the dollar has seen some dramatic ups and downs in the last fifteen years. These fluctuations have affected imports, exports, employment, and price levels in the United States. Clearly, U.S. economists can no longer ignore the macroeconomic effects of the rest of the world.

At the microeconomic level, individual American firms, workers, and consumers have also become increasingly aware of the rest of the world. Americans who eat bananas from Central America on their cereal and drink coffee from Colombia, tea from India, or hot chocolate from Ghana for breakfast start their days in an international market. They may ride to work or school on a Japanese bicycle or in a Japanese car—although the car may have been built in the United States! When students graduate, many take jobs with multinational firms, American or foreign, in the United States or abroad. Their parents may have suffered spells of unemployment related to imports competing with domestic production of steel, autos, shoes, or textiles.

As Americans have become more aware of the impact of the rest of the world on their own economy at both the micro and macro levels, they have also become increasingly interested in learning from others. Europe has taught Americans the benefits of economic integration, which is being applied in the newly created U.S.–Canada free trade area. Americans have looked to Europe and Canada to study experiments in social policy, such as national health insurance and children's allowances. Japan has much to show U.S. firms about management and innovation. Japanese educators have been studying U.S. higher education while Americans are interested in their system of year-round education in the lower grades.

Recognizing the growing importance of the international economy as both an influence on the U.S. economy and a source of ideas, we have chosen not to relegate the rest of the world to the back of the book. Each chapter offers one or more international perspectives. Some of these extend the material in that chapter to the open, or international, economy. This allows you to see the impact of the rest of the world on economic decisions and events at home. Others look at how a model, analysis, or solution to an economic problem might be different in another environment. You will see how tax systems work in Europe, why antitrust policy in the United States is stricter than in other nations, or why unemployment is always so high in the United Kingdom. Theories and models will explore the similarities between economic systems and the impact of one nation on another. Specific institutions and solutions will highlight the variety of possible approaches to solving the common problem of scarcity and choice.

When you finish this course, you should understand not only how the U.S. economic system operates but also how it appears in perspective with many others. We hope you will use the international perspectives to broaden your horizons and your understanding of the U.S. economy as one among many.

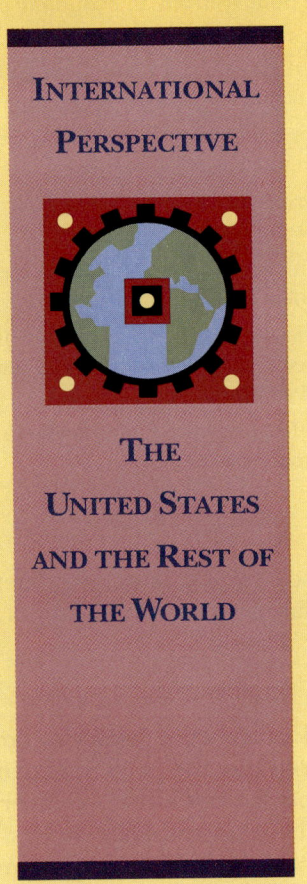

new pool of students. Income, family size, and number of retirees were all assumed to be *ceteris paribus* conditions. However, they did not remain constant but changed. These changes offset the effects of higher tuition and fewer high school graduates. Thus, college enrollments continued to increase. The statement predicting falling enrollment is wrong because the observer failed to examine fully the *ceteris paribus* conditions. In this case, as with the other two, a careful application of economic theory will help avoid the fallacy.

MAKING POLICY CHOICES

When economic models are applied to public policy issues, it is difficult to decide when the economist's task ends and the policy maker takes over. When economic methods are used for policy analysis, there is a five-step process.

1. *State the problem.* The choice of what problem to consider and how to state it is the task of the policy maker. How a problem is stated often determines what tools the economist applies and what solutions are considered. For example, suppose the problem is illegal parking on campus, especially parking by students in faculty spaces. Let's follow that problem through the next four steps.
2. *Apply the relevant economic model.* The economist turns to the toolkit to select the most useful theoretical model. In this case, there is a fairly simple technique called cost-benefit analysis that is not a formal model. This technique simply assumes that people are self-interested, that they are aware of the opportunity costs and benefits of their actions, and that they will choose the course of action that maximizes the excess of benefits over opportunity costs. This simple model predicts that an increase in the opportunity cost of illegal student parking or a reduction in benefits will reduce the amount of such illegal parking.
3. *Identify solutions.* The most common error at this stage is to leave out some solutions. Cost-based solutions to illegal parking might include higher fines. Do you think a student would be less likely to park in a faculty space if the fine were $100 instead of $10? More police officers would raise the cost by increasing the probability of being caught. The university could reduce the benefits of illegal parking by providing more bicycle racks or free bus transportation around campus and to and from commuter parking lots. Campus officials could even sell reserved parking spaces, and let students and faculty bid for parking rights.
4. *Evaluate solutions.* This is the stage where economists are most useful, pointing to costs, substitutes, and incentives. A good economic model predicts how various solutions will affect the amount of illegal parking, who will gain and who will lose, and which solution costs least to implement. For example, more police officers would be more expensive than higher fines. On the other hand, higher fines are a burden on students, many of whom have limited incomes. Bicycle racks are cheaper than shuttle buses. However, racks are not as helpful as buses would be to commuting students, unless they live very close to campus.
5. *Choose and implement one or more solutions.* This step is *not* the task of the

economist, although it is hard to stop after carrying the process this far. The policy maker (who may have been trained as an economist) takes the economist's list of possible solutions and the evaluation and makes a policy choice.

Most arguments among economists occur when they overstep the boundaries of scientific analysis and advocate a particular solution to an economic problem. Newspapers and TV news programs often quote economists who disagree. However, economists agree far more often than they disagree. Disagreements make headlines; agreement isn't news. Throughout this book, we will point out where most economists agree and also where and why they disagree. The models we describe represent a broad range of agreement among most economists on how markets work and how individuals respond to incentives.

Economics is an exciting social science. The individual who understands the economic way of thinking will gain insight into an endless array of interesting policy questions. We wish you well. Let's get on with it!

Summary

1. Economics is the study of how decisions about producing and consuming goods and services are made and how individuals and groups face the problem of scarcity.
2. Microeconomics looks at the interactions of producers and consumers in individual markets. Macroeconomics is the study of the economy as a whole and is concerned with aggregates, numbers that are determined by adding across many markets.
3. Economics is one of the social sciences, along with psychology, sociology, and political science. These fields focus on the behavior of individuals in their interactions with one another.
4. Economic theory is an abstract way of thinking that allows the development of principles, or tools, that can be used to study social issues.
5. Resources are finite, but human wants are insatiable. This conflict is the basic economic problem of scarcity. People cannot have everything they want and must make choices.
6. The production possibilities curve illustrates the problem of scarcity. In order to have more of one good, people must settle for less of another. The cost of extra units of one good is the number of units of the other sacrificed, or the opportunity cost.
7. The principle of increasing opportunity cost says that the more of one good people have, the greater the amount of other goods they must sacrifice to obtain one more unit of that good.
8. The production possibilities curve can be used to describe unemployment of resources (points inside the curve) and economic growth (a shift of the curve to the right).
9. Self-interested behavior is a basic assumption of economic theory. Although economists recognize that economic behavior is a complex process, they assume that human beings pursue their own self-interest.
10. Economic theory is positive, or nonnormative. It can't tell us what we should do, but it can make statements of an if-A-then-B type.
11. Economists tend to rely on the market to solve social problems. In analyzing problems, economists stress identifying options and looking at costs and benefits, particularly at the margin.
12. The association-causation fallacy is the false notion that association implies causality.
13. The fallacy of composition is the false idea that what holds for the parts holds for the whole.
14. The *ceteris paribus* fallacy occurs when changes in one variable fail to have the predicted effect on another variable because the observer has ignored changes in other important variables.
15. A policy decision is analyzed in five steps: state the problem, apply the relevant economic model, identify solutions, evaluate solutions, and choose and implement solutions.
16. Although economists agree on many things, their disagreements are often highlighted. Most of their disagreements are over policy choices rather than economic theory.

New Terms

economics
microeconomics
macroeconomics
aggregates
social science
scarcity
insatiable wants
opportunity cost
production possibilities curve
increasing opportunity cost
theory
testable hypothesis
model
ceteris paribus assumption
self-interested behavior
positive statements
normative statements
association-causation fallacy
fallacy of composition
ceteris paribus fallacy

QUESTIONS FOR DISCUSSION

1. Do you think people exhibit behavior patterns that confirm the self-interest assumption? Does your own behavior confirm this assumption? Is a contribution to charity or volunteer work a contradiction of the self-interest assumption?

2. Why do economists theorize rather than attempt to describe reality exactly?

3. Do assumptions have to be realistic in order for a theory to work?

4. What is the difference between using theory to predict and forecasting?

5. Consider the following simple predictive model: if the speed limit is reduced, fewer highway deaths will occur. What assumptions are being made? What *ceteris paribus* conditions could change and make this prediction invalid?

6. Identify and explain the fallacy in each of the following statements.
   a. "There was a transit strike in April, and unemployment in the city rose in May. Clearly the transit strike created unemployment."
   b. "The new subway system is finally working, but downtown parking spaces are harder to find than before. The subway system hasn't relieved congestion."
   c. "Our state competed heavily to attract industry, and it worked. Unemployment is down. If all states did the same, national unemployment would fall."

7. Which of the following quantities are microeconomic, and which are macroeconomic? Which might fall between the two?
   a. price of shoes
   b. number of men aged 18 to 24 in the U.S. labor force
   c. level of interest rates
   d. unemployment in Tulsa
   e. production of agricultural products
   f. average level of prices
   g. production of butter
   h. average price of imported goods
   i. unemployment in the United States
   j. total output
   k. unemployment of carpenters
   l. number of nurses in the U.S. labor force
   m. unemployment in the northeastern states

8. What is the opportunity cost of working 10 hours a week flipping burgers while in college? If you worked more hours per week, would you experience increasing or constant opportunity cost? That is, would the extra hours require giving up alternative uses of your time that have the same value or an increasing value?

9. a. Given the following data, plot a production possibilities curve and calculate the opportunity cost of bicycles in terms of skateboards.

BICYCLES	SKATEBOARDS
10	0
8	10
6	20
4	30
2	40
0	50

   b. Assume that new technology increases the possible output of both skateboards and bicycles by 50 percent. Draw the new production possibilities curve. Calculate the new opportunity cost of bicycles in terms of skateboards.
   c. Now assume that new technology increases the amount of bicycles that can be produced by 6 units if all resources are devoted to bicycles, but does not change the amount of skateboards that can be produced. Draw a new curve, and calculate a new opportunity cost.

10. You know that the opportunity cost of books in terms of cassettes not produced is 1 book for 2 cassettes and that available resources can produce a maximum of 100 books. Can you draw the production possibilities curve for these two goods? If so, what is the maximum possible output of cassettes? If you choose to produce 40 books, how many cassettes can be produced?

11. Using the following economic data, plot a production possibilities curve for tomatoes and tomahawks:

TOMATOES	TOMAHAWKS
100	0
80	15
60	30
40	45
20	60
0	75

What is the opportunity cost of a tomato? A tomahawk? If 50 tomatoes are produced, how many tomahawks can be produced?

12. Using the data in question 11, suppose a change in technology makes it possible to increase tomato production to a maximum of 150 units. There is no change in the technology of producing tomahawks. Draw the new production possibilities curve. Now what is the opportunity cost of each good? If this economy chooses to produce 60 tomatoes, how many tomahawks can it produce?

13. Try developing a simple economic model to predict how students will respond to an increase in dormitory rents. What are your assumptions? What will happen to the number of dormitory spaces rented? What will happen to the number of off-campus apartments rented and their prices?

14. Which of the following statements are normative, and which are positive? Rewrite the normative statements to make them positive and the positive ones to make them normative.

   a. "Women earn less than men."
   b. "Defense spending has grown too rapidly in the last decade."
   c. "Because their child-care duties interfere with their work, women with children should earn less than men."
   d. "Twenty-three percent of the federal budget is spent on defense."
   e. "An estimated 14 percent of the U.S. population lives in poverty, according to government standards defining poverty."
   f. "The government is not doing enough to reduce poverty."

15. The economy of Southland can only produce two goods: food and clothing. Both are subject to constant costs. Draw a production possibilities curve for Southland that shows the maximum output of food as 50 cartons and the maximum output of clothing as 100 suits. Now locate each of the following on your diagram.

   a. Output of 25 cartons of food and 25 suits of clothing. Label this point *U*. Does it lie on the curve? What does this point represent? What is the opportunity cost of another suit of clothing at this point?
   b. Output of 50 cartons of food and 100 suits of clothing. Label this point *G*. Does this point lie on the curve? Is it attainable? If not, what must happen for *G* to be a possible output combination?
   c. Output of 25 cartons of food and 50 suits of clothing. Label this point *A*. Does it lie on the curve? What is the opportunity cost of another carton of food at this point?

16. a. Suppose the two goods in question 15 are subject to increasing costs, but the end points remain the same. Draw a new production possibilities curve for food and clothing in Southland.
   b. Suppose the economy of Southland has a technological change that increases the capacity to produce food but not clothing. How will the production possibilities curve shift? Is it possible to produce more of both food and clothing after this shift?
   c. Suppose the economy of Southland has an increase in resources that affects both food and clothing production equally. How will the production possibilities curve shift?

Suggestions for Further Reading

Boulding, Kenneth. *Human Betterment.* Beverly Hills, CA: Sage, 1985. This recent book by one of America's best known economic philosophers makes a case for normative analysis when the values behind the analysis are clearly spelled out.

Huff, Darrell, and Irving Geis. *How to Lie with Statistics.* New York: W. W. Norton, 1954 (copyright renewed 1982). This classic guide to interpreting and misinterpreting graphs and statistics is must reading for any serious student of the social sciences.

Rhoads, Stephen E. *The Economist's View of the World: Government, Markets, and Public Policy.* New York: Cambridge University Press, 1985. Written by a political scientist, this book looks at both the useful contributions of economics to other social sciences and the limitations of economics.

Stigler, George. *Memoirs of an Unregulated Economist.* New York: Basic Books, 1988. A Nobel Prize–winning economist looks at the training of economists and the uses of economics in an account of his own experiences in the field.

Chapter 1 Economics, Economic Issues, and Economic Methods

APPENDIX:
ECONOMIC RELATIONSHIPS AND GRAPHS

Economic theories and models are often expressed in the form of mathematical relationships among variables. These relationships can be described by algebraic equations. Economists more often express them visually in the form of graphs. Graphs make it possible to illustrate economic theories and models in ways that make them easier to remember and to apply to the real world. Remember that everything that can be said in graphs can also be said in words. Graphs are only an aid to understanding the theory. Mastering and applying the theory is what you should be trying to achieve. If you can learn to feel comfortable with graphs as visual presentations of economic ideas, reading this textbook and understanding your professor's lectures will be much easier.

RELATIONSHIP BETWEEN TWO VARIABLES

A relationship between two variables, variable x and variable y, can be expressed in a number of ways. One is a table of values of x and y. For example, Table 1A shows the various amounts of fertilizer applied per acre and the corresponding yields of corn per acre. What does this table mean? It means that different amounts of fertilizer were applied to different plots of land and that those plots of land yielded varying amounts of corn.

This relationship could also be expressed in the form of a graph.[a] A

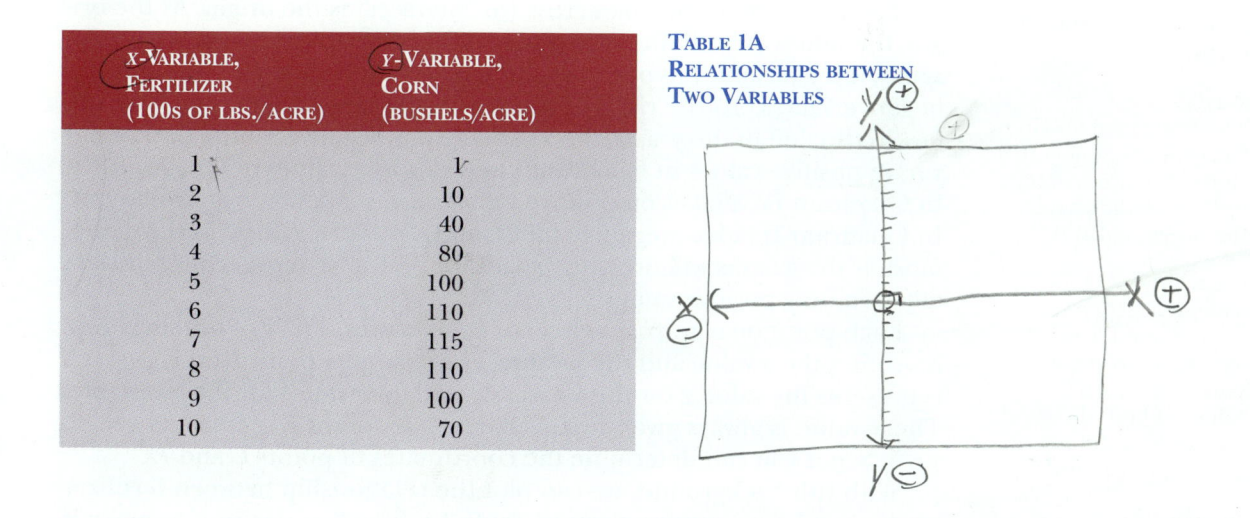

TABLE 1A RELATIONSHIPS BETWEEN TWO VARIABLES

X-VARIABLE, FERTILIZER (100s OF LBS./ACRE)	Y-VARIABLE, CORN (BUSHELS/ACRE)
1	1
2	10
3	40
4	80
5	100
6	110
7	115
8	110
9	100
10	70

a. A third way to represent such a relationship is with an equation, $y = f(x)$. We will be using some equations in this book but will rely more heavily on graphs to display relationships between variables.

FIGURE 1A
QUADRANT SYSTEM
A four-quadrant system makes it possible to represent combinations of positive and negative values in two dimensions. Point C represents an x-value of 0 and a y-value of –6. The quadrants are labeled I to IV in the counterclockwise direction.

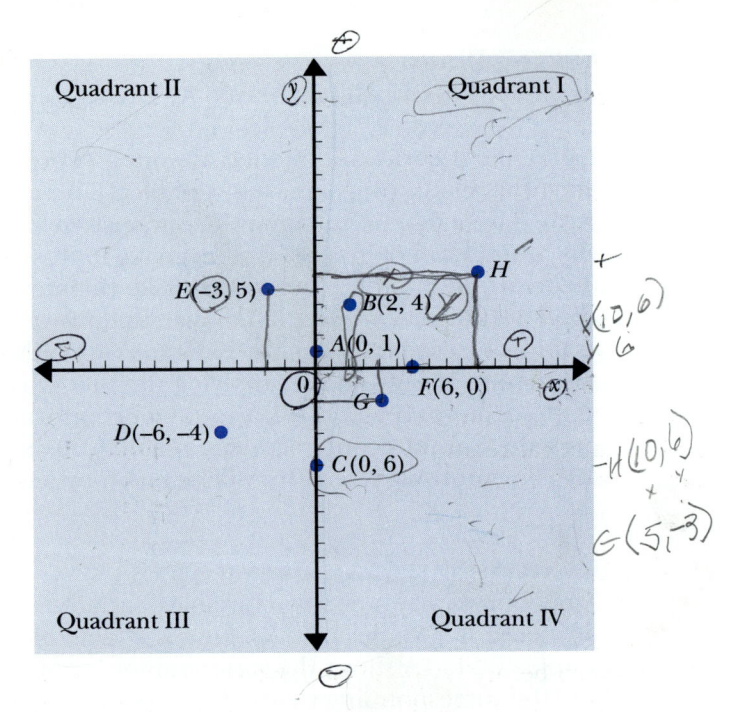

y-axis
The upright line in a coordinate system that shows the values of the dependent variable; the vertical axis.

x-axis
The horizontal line in a coordinate system that shows the values of the independent variable; the horizontal axis.

origin
The intersection of the vertical and horizontal axes of a coordinate system, at which the values of both the x-variable and the y-variable are zero.

coordinates
The values of x and y that define the location of a point in a coordinate system.

graph shows how the quantity of one variable changes when another variable changes. Figure 1A shows the system most commonly used for graphing. The vertical line is referred to as the **y-axis** (or vertical axis). The horizontal line is referred to as the **x-axis** (or horizontal axis). The x-axis and y-axis divide the graph into four quadrants.

The point where the axes cross (or intersect) is the **origin**. At the origin, the values of both the x-variable and the y-variable are zero. Above the x-axis, the y-variable has positive values. Below the x-axis, the y-variable has negative values. To the right of the y-axis, the x-variable has positive values. To the left of the y-axis, the x-variable has negative values. Both x and y have positive values in Quadrant I and negative values in Quadrant III. In Quadrant IV, x takes on positive values, and y takes on negative values. In Quadrant II, x has negative values, and y positive values. In this book, most of the graphs will use only Quadrant I because most economic data takes on only positive values.

Each point on a graph has a set of **coordinates**, a pair of numbers representing the x-value and the y-value. For example, point B on Figure 1A represents the value 2 for the x-variable and the value 4 for the y-variable. The x-value is always given first. For example, point E represents $x = -3$, $y = 5$. See if you can determine the coordinates of points G and H.

With this background, we can plot the relationship between fertilizer applied and corn output given in Table 1A. The first decision to make is which variable goes on which axis. If there is a cause-and-effect relationship, we usually put the "causing" variable on the horizontal axis and the variable being affected on the vertical axis. In mathematics, the causing variable is the **independent variable**, and the affected variable is the **dependent variable**. Since we think that fertilizer causes increased corn yields, we plot it on the horizontal axis (*x*-axis). Corn yield is plotted on the vertical axis (*y*-axis).

The next decision concerns establishing a scale for each axis. The scales can be whatever is convenient and do not need to be the same. In this case, the fertilizer units are hundreds of pounds per acre, and the corn units are bushels per acre. Once a scale is established and the axes are labeled, we can plot the coordinates of the points in Table 1A. Then we connect the plotted points with a smooth curve to produce a graph, shown in Figure 2A.

The value of a graph is that it gives you a visual picture of the mathematical relationship between the variables. In Figure 2A, you can easily see that as fertilizer is increased up to 700 pounds per acre, corn output increases. After that level, more fertilizer causes a decrease in output. The corn plants grow too rapidly and don't produce many ears, or the roots suffer fertilizer burn.

Not all relationships produce as tidy a graph as the one for fertilizer and corn yield. Sometimes researchers plot data to see if there is any visual pattern before trying to understand what, if any, is the relationship between the two variables. Such a plot of actual data is called a **scatter diagram**. Scatter diagrams are useful in searching for possible mathematical relationships between two variables.

Figure 3A plots actual data on the rate of inflation (vertical axis) and the rate of unemployment (horizontal axis) for the United States from 1975 to 1989. In this diagram, there doesn't seem to be a consistent rela-

---

independent variable
The variable, usually plotted on the horizontal axis, that affects or influences the other variable.

dependent variable
The variable, usually plotted on the vertical axis, that is affected or influenced by the other variable.

scatter diagram
A graph that plots actual pairs of values of two variables to determine whether there appears to be any consistent relationship between them.

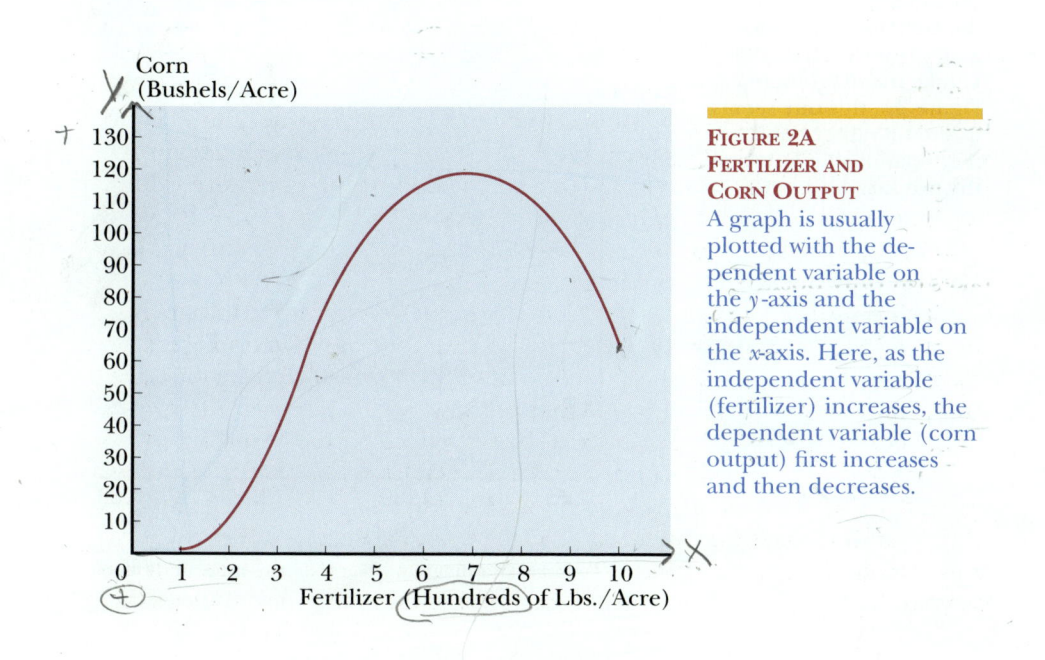

FIGURE 2A
FERTILIZER AND CORN OUTPUT
A graph is usually plotted with the dependent variable on the *y*-axis and the independent variable on the *x*-axis. Here, as the independent variable (fertilizer) increases, the dependent variable (corn output) first increases and then decreases.

FIGURE 3A
INFLATION AND UNEMPLOYMENT
A scatter diagram plots the coordinates for the values of two variables that may or may not have a consistent relationship. This diagram plots the unemployment rate and the inflation rate for the United States from 1976 to 1989. It shows no consistent relationship between these two variables.

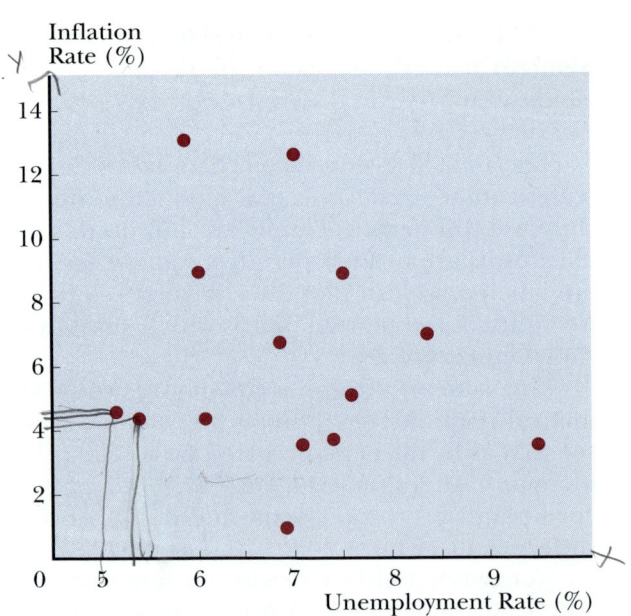

Source: Council of Economic Advisers, *Economic Report of the President* (Washington, DC: U.S. Government Printing Office, 1990).

FIGURE 4A
GNP AND MONEY SUPPLY (BILLIONS OF DOLLARS)
This scatter diagram plots the money supply and the GNP for the United States from 1976 to 1989. Unlike the diagram in Figure 3A, this one seems to show a rather consistent relationship between the two variables.

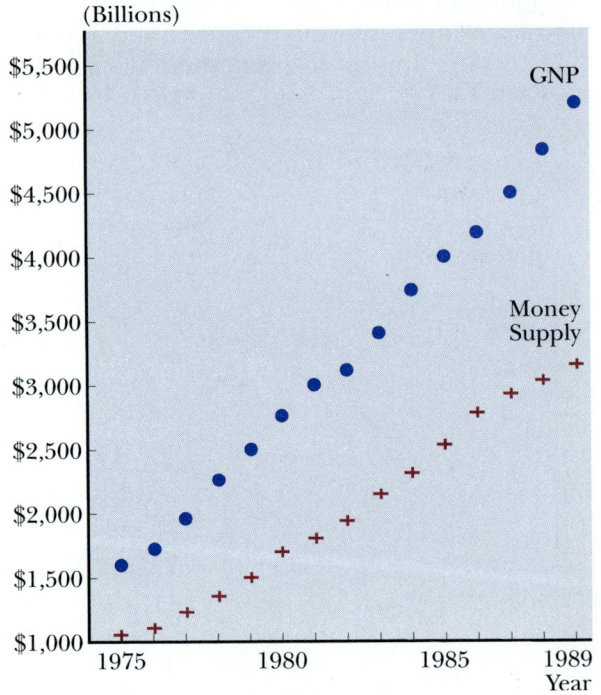

Source: Council of Economic Advisers, *Economic Report of the President* (Washington, DC: U.S. Government Printing Office, 1990).

tionship of any kind between the rate of inflation and the rate of unemployment, at least for the years plotted. Figure 4A plots the relationship between the money supply and total output, or GNP, for the United States from 1975 to 1989. As you can see, there appears to be a more consistent relationship between these two variables.

POSITIVE AND NEGATIVE RELATIONSHIPS AND SLOPES

A graph shows how two variables are related. This relationship may be positive or negative. A **positive relationship** means that an increase in the value of the *x*-variable is associated with an increase in the value of the *y*-variable, as in Figure 4A. A **negative relationship** means that an increase in the value of the *x*-variable is associated with a decrease in the value of the *y*-variable. Some relationships in economics, such as the one between fertilizer and corn output plotted in Figure 2A, are positive for some values of the *x*-variable and negative for others.

Most of the economic relationships you will encounter in this book are represented by straight lines. A straight line can have a positive slope, as in Figure 5A, or a negative slope, as in Figure 6A. The **slope** is a measure of the steepness of the line. It is the ratio of the change in the dependent variable (*y*) to the change in the independent variable (*x*). If the slope is designated by the letter *m*, then the equation of a straight line can be written as

$$y = mx + b,$$

where *b* is the value of *y* when *x* = 0. (The value *b* is also known as the *y*-intercept, because at this value the line crosses the *y*-axis.)

Even though both lines in Figure 5A are positively sloped, the rela-

positive relationship
A relationship between two variables in which an increase in one is associated with an increase in the other and a decrease in one is associated with a decrease in the other.

negative relationship
A relationship between two variables in which an increase in the value of one is associated with a decrease in the value of the other.

slope
The ratio of the change in the dependent variable (*y*) to the change in the independent variable (*x*).

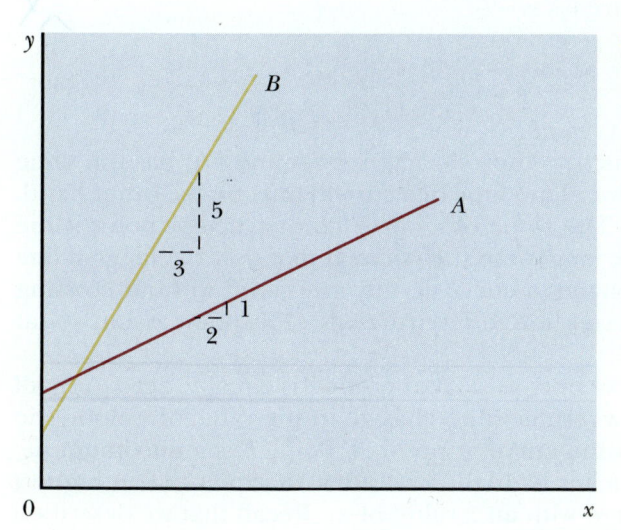

FIGURE 5A
POSITIVELY SLOPED LINES
The slope of a line is the ratio of the change in the *y*-value to the change in the *x*-value. A line sloping upward to the right has a positive slope, indicating a positive relationship between the two variables.

FIGURE 6A
NEGATIVELY SLOPED LINE
A negative slope represents a relationship between the variables in which an increase in the value of the independent variable is associated with a decrease in the value of the dependent variable.

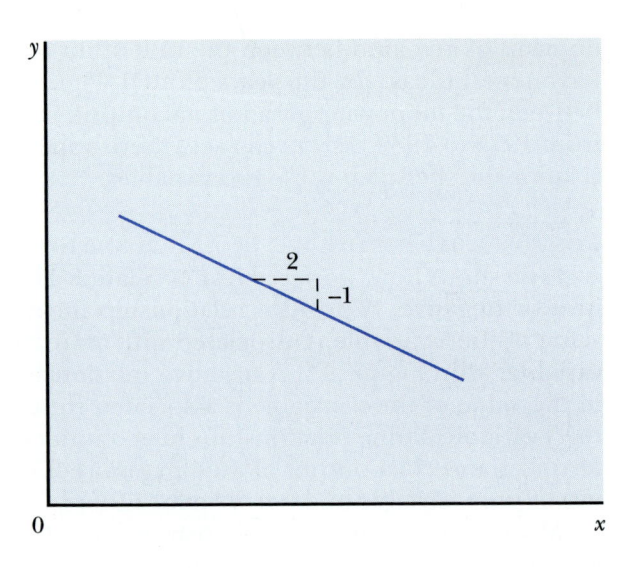

tionship between the x-variable and the y-variable represented by line A is very different from that represented by line B. The same amount of change in x leads to a larger change in y along line B than it does along line A. In Figure 5A, the slope of line A is equal to $+\frac{1}{2}$ because the y-value changes by one unit for each two-unit change in the x-value. The slope of line B is $+\frac{5}{3}$, or $+1.67$. The steeper slope of line B indicates that a larger change in the value of y will result from a given change in the value of x than along line A. The sign of the slope is also very important. It indicates whether the relationship between the two variables is positive or negative. A slope with a positive sign designates a positive relationship. A slope with a negative sign, as in Figure 6A, indicates a negative relationship. The slope of the line in Figure 6A is $-\frac{1}{2}$.

NONLINEAR GRAPHS AND MAXIMA AND MINIMA

tangent line
A straight line just touching a curve (nonlinear graphic relationship) at a single point. The slope of the tangent line is equal to the slope of the curve at that point.

maximum
The point on a graph at which the y-variable, or dependent variable, reaches its highest value.

A straight-line graph, such as those in Figures 5A and 6A, has the same slope along the entire line. The slope of a curved line, on the other hand, varies along the curve. The slope of a curve at a particular point is the slope of the straight line tangent to the curve at that point. A **tangent line** is a straight line that touches a curve at only one point without crossing it. The slope of the curved line in Figure 7A is $+1$ at point A and $-\frac{3}{2}$ at point C.

The slope of the curve in Figure 7A at point B is equal to zero. A small change in the value of x results in no change in the value of y along the straight line tangent to the curve at point B. Point B is a **maximum** because the y-variable reaches its highest value at that point. The highest value of y, y_1, is associated with an x value of x_1. Recall that we described

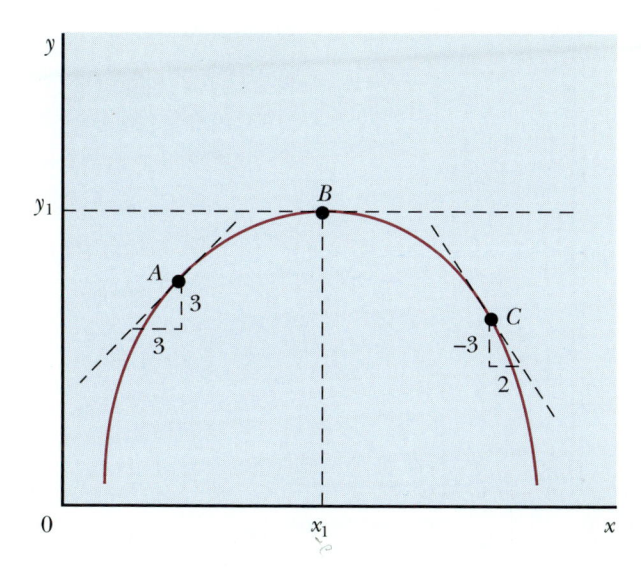

FIGURE 7A
NONLINEAR GRAPHS: SLOPE AND MAXIMUM
On a nonlinear graph, the slope changes along the curve. The slope of the curve at any point is the slope of a straight line tangent to the curved line at that point. When the slope is zero, the value of the y-variable is either at a maximum or at a minimum. At point B, y is at its maximum value, y_1, when x has the value x_1.

self-interested behavior as consumers maximizing satisfaction, resource owners maximizing income, and firms maximizing profit. Being able to find the maximum is very important in economics.

Sometimes a slope of zero is associated with a **minimum** rather than a maximum, as in Figure 8A. The y-variable assumes its lowest value, Y_1, at point B in Figure 8A. This y-value is associated with an x-value of X_1. A firm that is trying to minimize costs, or losses, may be interested in finding a minimum point. It is also important for many kinds of economic questions to determine whether a point of zero slope is a maximum or a minimum.

minimum
The point on the graph at which the y-variable, or dependent variable, reaches its lowest value.

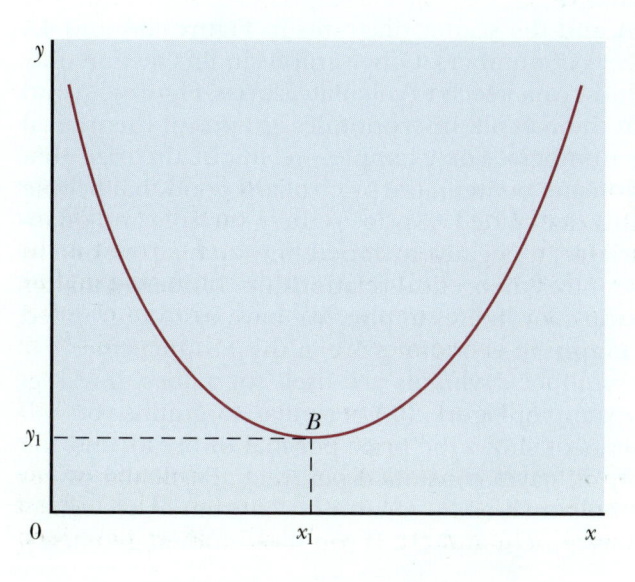

FIGURE 8A
NONLINEAR GRAPHS: MINIMUM
This nonlinear graph also has a slope of zero at point B. In this case, point B represents the minimum value of y, y_1, which is associated with an x-value of x_1.

FIGURE 9A
THE 45° LINE
A 45° line drawn in the first quadrant has a slope of +1. If both axes are measured in the same units, the 45° line shows all points where the *x*-value and the *y*-value are equal.

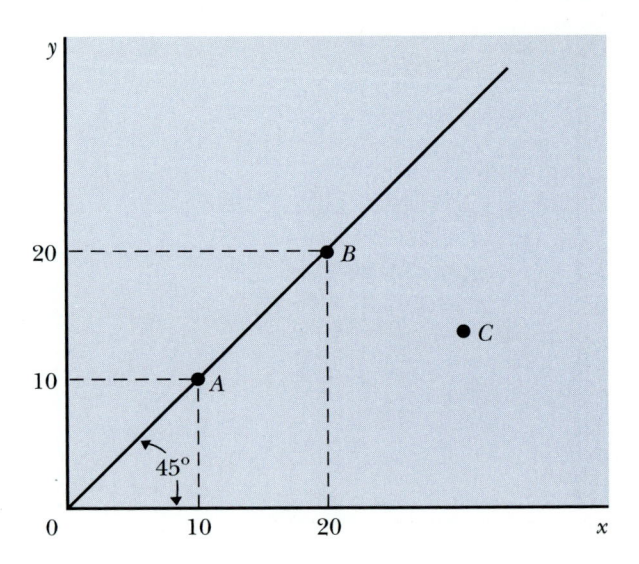

45° line
A line in the first quadrant, passing through the origin, with a slope of +1, which divides the quadrant in half. If the scales on the axes are the same, the value of the *x*-variable is equal to the value of the *y*-variable along the 45° line.

THE 45° LINE

A geometric construction that proves very useful in economic analysis is a **45° line**. This is a straight line through the origin that divides Quadrant I into two equal sections. If both axes are measured in the same units, the values of the *x*-variable and the *y*-variable will be equal at any point on the line, and the slope will be +1. A 45° line is shown in Figure 9A. Suppose, for example, you want to know whether the value of *x* is less than, equal to, or greater than the value of *y* at point *C*. A 45° line gives you a quick answer to that question. The value of *x* is greater than the value of *y* at point *C* because point *C* lies below the 45° line.

GRAPHS WITHOUT NUMBERS

The graph in Figure 2A and the scatter diagrams in Figures 3A and 4A were constructed from sets of numbers. Other graphs in this section only give a few numerical values from which to calculate slopes. Figures 7A and 8A have no numbers on them at all. In economics, graphs of theoretical concepts often use no numbers. For example, we might theorize that there is a negative relationship between the price of any good that people consume and the quantity demanded. If price is the *y*-variable and quantity demanded the *x*-variable, a negatively sloped line such as the one in Figure 5A could represent this theoretical relationship. It doesn't matter that we don't have specific coordinates to plot. We have instead graphed an abstract idea. Many graphs in economics are of this abstract type.

On graphs without numbers, symbols are used for values, line segments, and areas. For example, Figure 10A is similar to graphs you will study in Chapter 3. The *y*-axis shows the price per loaf of bread, and the *x*-axis shows the quantity of loaves consumed per week. Particular prices are represented by symbols such as P_1. Quantities consumed are represented by symbols such as Q_1, Q_2, and Q_3. If you have studied geometry,

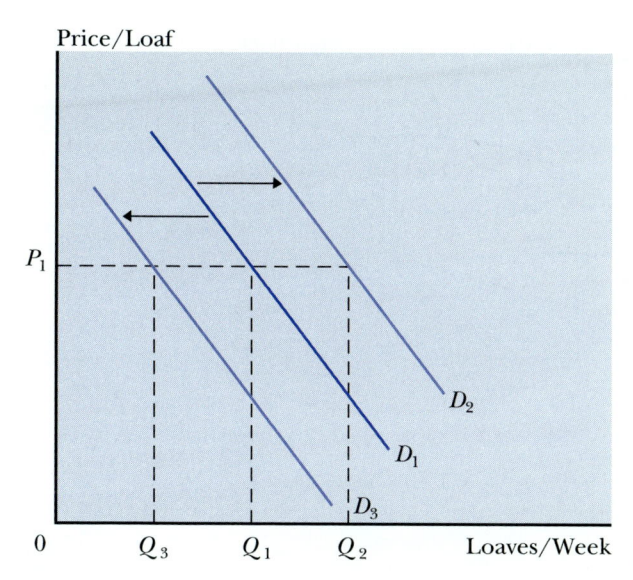

Chapter 1 Economics, Economic Issues, and Economic Methods

FIGURE 10A
EFFECTS OF CHANGES IN TASTES ON THE DEMAND FOR BREAD
Many graphs in economics use symbols rather than numbers on the axes. The symbol P_1 represents a hypothetical price, and Q_1, Q_2, and Q_3 represent hypothetical quantities.

you will note that it would be technically correct to refer to quantity Q_1 as quantity $\overline{0Q_1}$. We will, however, use the shorthand Q_1 to minimize clutter.

In addition to using symbols to represent quantities, we will also make frequent use of the symbol delta, Δ, to represent changes in a variable. For example, the symbol ΔQ is a shorthand expression for the change from Q_1 to Q_2 in Figure 10A.

PIE CHARTS AND BAR CHARTS

All of the graphs considered so far, except for the scatter diagrams, represent theoretical relationships of one kind or another. Economists also use graphs to describe the real world. Such graphs display descriptive statistics. These include the allocation of government funds between types of programs, the growth of output or the money supply over time, and the different growth rates of imports and exports.

Two common types of descriptive graphs encountered in economics are pie charts and bar charts. **Pie charts** are used to show the division of some whole into parts, usually designated by percentages. Figure 11A is a pie chart depicting the sources of household income in 1989. Pie charts have become very popular because they are easy to create on a personal computer. This visual representation often conveys a clearer sense of the relative sizes of various components than you could obtain from reading a table of numbers.

Another popular type of descriptive graph is a **bar chart**, such as Figure 12A. This diagram describes the behavior of two variables, federal government revenue and expenditures, in a series of "snapshots" from 1970 to 1989. This graph gives a much more vivid impression of how much expenditures have grown relative to revenues than you could derive from a set of numbers.

pie chart
A graphic representation in the shape of a pie that expresses actual economic data as parts of a whole. The sizes of the slices of the pie correspond to the percentage shares of the components.

bar chart
A graphic representation that expresses data using columns of different heights.

FIGURE 11A
PIE CHART OF HOUSEHOLD INCOME FOR THE UNITED STATES, 1989
A pie chart depicts the division of a whole into parts (percentages). This pie chart shows that the largest component of household income is wages and salaries. Transfer payments and interest are much smaller components.

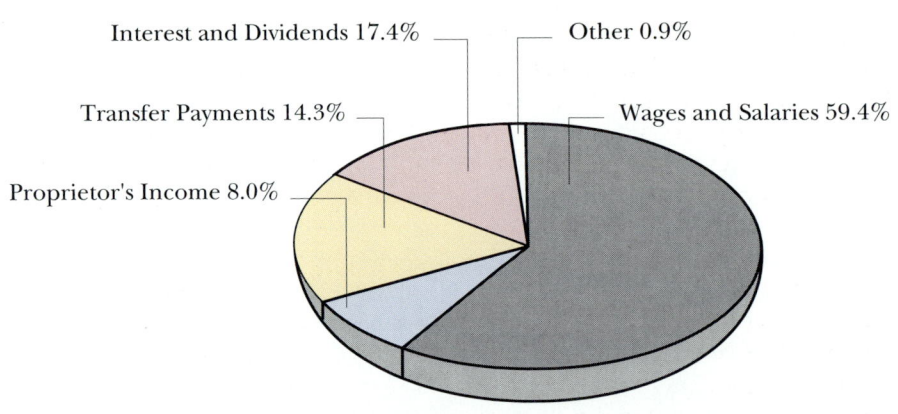

Interest and Dividends 17.4%
Other 0.9%
Transfer Payments 14.3%
Wages and Salaries 59.4%
Proprietor's Income 8.0%

Source: Council of Economic Advisers, *Economic Report of the President* (Washington, DC: U.S. Government Printing Office, 1990).

FIGURE 12A
BAR CHART OF FEDERAL REVENUES AND EXPENDITURES, 1980–1989
A bar chart can be used in a variety of ways to present economic data in a visual fashion. This bar chart compares federal revenues and expenditures for various years.

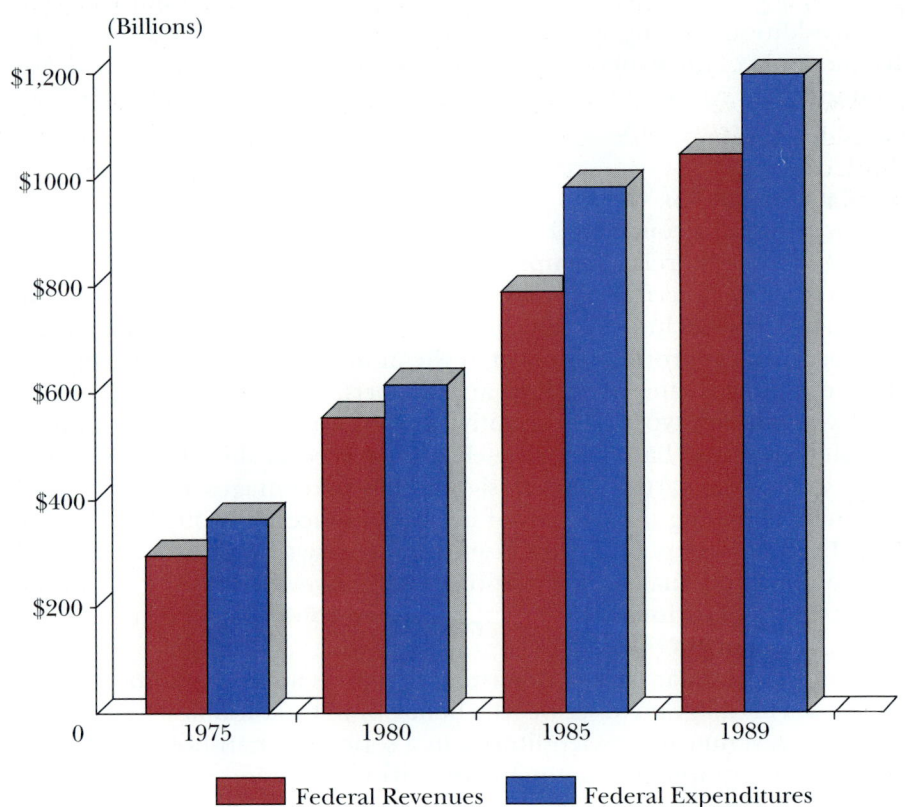

Source: Council of Economic Advisers, *Economic Report of the President* (Washington, DC: U.S. Government Printing Office, 1990).

Theoretical graphs, such as those in Figures 5A through 10A, and descriptive graphs, such as Figures 11A and 12A, are spread throughout this book. Both types are also common in textbooks in social sciences and business and in popular magazines such as *Newsweek*, *Time*, and *Business Week*. Economics is a very visual subject. Be sure that you feel secure with reading and interpreting graphs before proceeding further.

Caution: Graphs and Numbers Can Mislead as Well as Inform!

Graphs and statistics can be very informative. They put some concrete, real-world content into abstract models and economic relationships. However, it is very easy to present data in a misleading way. The choice of a scale along an axis can make changes look bigger than they really are. The use of averages conceals a great deal of information about variation. For example, three families with incomes of $24,000, $25,000, and $26,000 have an average income of $25,000. The same average could be the result of three incomes of $5,000, $5,000, and $65,000. The same average income describes two very different distributions of income.

A classic guide to the use and abuse of numbers and graphs is *How to Lie with Statistics*, by Darrell Huff and Irving Geis. This book has been through numerous paperback editions since it was first published in 1954. It should be required reading for anyone taking courses in the social sciences. It is a useful guide through the pitfalls of the means, medians, averages, bar charts, surveys, samples, and growth rates that are the daily news of the economic and political worlds.

Always be very cautious in accepting someone's graphs or numbers. Consider carefully what that person may be trying to persuade you to think or do and how the statistics could be manipulated to put that position in a more favorable light.

AFTER STUDYING THIS CHAPTER, YOU SHOULD BE ABLE TO:

1. Identify the factors of production.
2. List the three basic economic questions that must be addressed by every economic system.
3. Use a circular flow model to show the relationships between firms and households in product markets and in factor markets in a market economy.
4. Describe how traditional, command, and market economies answer the three basic economic questions.
5. Explain and give examples of the basic economic functions of government.
6. Describe and calculate the benefits of specialization and exchange based on comparative advantage.

CHAPTER 2
MARKETS, GOVERNMENTS, AND NATIONS: THE ORGANIZATION OF ECONOMIC ACTIVITY

INTRODUCTION

Chapter 1 introduced the basic economic problem of scarcity and choice that every economy must address, regardless of its level of development or form of government. In this chapter, we explore some of the common problems and choices faced by people in all societies in using their scarce resources to satisfy their wants. We will also examine the different ways in which choices are made in different kinds of societies. Throughout this book, a series of international perspectives will remind you that the way economic problems are addressed in American society is not necessarily the way they are addressed in other countries.

In the last two decades, economists have become more aware of the importance of interactions between national economies. These interactions include trade in goods and services and movements of labor and capital. They affect the growth rate, production, employment, price level, and other important macroeconomic variables in both countries. Competition from foreign producers, foreign markets for products, and the use of foreign inputs also have important effects on prices and quantities in individual markets. Thus, another issue we introduce in this chapter is the difference between an isolated, or closed, economy and an open economy. An open economy is one that trades goods, services, and productive resources with other nations.

LIMITED RESOURCES: THE FACTORS OF PRODUCTION

To examine the process of choice, we can begin by identifying the scarce resources that exist. Scarce resources used to produce goods and services are called **factors of production**. The factors of production are divided into four broad categories: labor, land, capital, and enterprise. All resources used to produce goods and services fit into one of these four categories.

LABOR

Labor is the factor of production with which you are probably most familiar. **Labor** is the physical and mental exertion of human beings. The

factors of production
The inputs of land, labor, capital, and enterprise that a firm uses to produce outputs.

labor
The physical and mental exertion that human beings put into production activities.

efforts of a factory worker, a professional basketball player, a university professor, and a carpenter are all labor.

Wages are the payments labor receives for its productive services. Some labor is valued (and paid) more than other labor. Why? One reason is that some labor is more productive. Workers are born with different talents and abilities. Some are more intelligent. Others are physically stronger or better coordinated. Still others have artistic or musical ability. It is also possible to make labor more productive by devoting money and time to improving skills. Individuals invest in their labor skills by going to college, serving as apprentices, or practicing. Economists refer to this development of labor skills as an investment in human capital. **Human capital** consists of labor-enhancing abilities that increase labor's productivity. A large part of wage differences can be explained by differences in human capital.

LAND

The second factor of production is land. **Land**, to an economist, is not just rocks and soil, but all natural resources that can be used as inputs to production. By this definition, land includes minerals, water, air, forests, oil, and even rainfall, temperature, and soil quality. The income payment to this factor of production is called **rent**.

A key distinction between land and other productive resources is that land consists of natural resources or conditions, unimproved by any human activity. For example, acreage in Arizona that has been irrigated represents more than land. It also represents capital, the third factor of production. Thus, part of the payment that is called rent is a return to land, but part of it may be a return to capital.

CAPITAL

The third factor of production, **capital**, is defined as all aids to production that are human creations rather than resources found in nature. Capital includes tools, factories, warehouses, and inventories. You have also seen that capital can become attached to land or to labor (human capital) when investment is made in improvements or in skills and training. In common usage, real capital is often confused with financial capital. Financial capital is money lent to purchase real, physical capital. Economists reserve the term *capital* for real inputs to production, not for financial assets.

Capital, like land, receives a flow of income. The payments to capital are called **interest**. Interest is a reward for giving up present consumption in order to make resources available for the creation of more capital for future production. **Investment** is the act of adding to capital. Although the term *investment* is used by noneconomists for such activities as buying stocks and bonds, to an economist the term means the creation of real, tangible assets, such as machines, factories, or inventories that can be used to produce other goods and services.

ENTERPRISE

The last factor of production is **enterprise**, which consists of the activities of combining the factors of production to produce goods and services, taking risks, and introducing new methods and new products (innovation). Entrepreneurs combine other factors of production by buying or

---

wages
The return to labor, one of the factors of production.

human capital
The investment made to improve the quality of people's labor skills through education, training, health care, and so on.

land
Natural resources that can be used as inputs to production.

rent
The return to land, one of the factors of production.

capital
The durable inputs into the production process created by people. Machines, tools, and buildings are examples of capital.

interest
The return to capital, one of the factors of production.

investment
Purchases of real, tangible assets, such as machines, factories, or inventories, that are used to produce goods and services.

enterprise
The input to the production process that involves organizing, innovation, and risk taking.

Chapter 2   Markets, Governments, and Nations   43

renting them to produce a saleable product. The reward for innovation, risk taking, and organization is **profit**.

Profit is the most difficult of the four factor returns to measure in practice because it is whatever is left over after paying for land, capital, and labor. Noneconomists frequently count profit as what is left after the bills are paid. However, this measure is likely to overlook such opportunity costs as the value of the owner's labor (wages) or the return to the owner's capital (interest).

profit
The return to enterprise, one of the factors of production. Profit is whatever remains after all other factors have been paid.

THE BASIC ECONOMIC QUESTIONS

The process of choosing how to allocate scarce resources can be broken down into three broad economic questions.

- *What* goods and services will be produced and in what quantities?
- *How* will they be produced? (That is, what methods of production and combinations of inputs will be used?)
- *For whom* will they be produced? (That is, who gets what share of the goods and services produced?)

Different kinds of economic systems answer these three questions in different ways. However, people in all economic systems are faced with the problem of how to allocate scarce resources among an unlimited number of wants.

The market provides at least a partial answer to these three questions in many societies. A **market** is any setting in which buyers and sellers meet to exchange goods, services, or productive resources. A market system is an economic system that relies primarily on market transactions to answer the three basic economic questions.

market
A place where buyers and sellers meet to exchange goods, services, and productive resources.

The production possibilities curve introduced in Chapter 1 showed attainable levels and combinations of outputs, or the choices available. The production possibilities curve, however, does not explain how to choose among these combinations. What determines if an economy is at one particular point on the production possibilities curve instead of another, and who makes that choice?

WHAT, HOW, AND FOR WHOM

The *what* question asks exactly what mix of goods and services is to be produced—how many tons of wheat, thousands of textbooks, yards of fabric, pairs of jeans, and gallons of milk will make up the total national output. It is a difficult enough question in the simple two-product world of the production possibilities curve. With thousands and thousands of possible combinations of outputs, the *what* question is extremely complex. In a market system, the answer to the *what* question is determined by consumers, who "vote" in the marketplace by using their dollars to obtain particular goods and services. In other economic systems, other methods are used to determine what kinds of goods and services are produced and in what amounts.

A market economy may result in choices about the output mix that some economists or policy makers find peculiar or distasteful. Many policy makers may not share the public's taste for rock videos, gambling palaces, country music, or skateboards. However, unless people's consumption of these items can be shown to be harmful to others, a market society does not pass normative judgment on tastes. Markets produce what people want to buy.

The *how* question asks what input combination will be used to produce the chosen goods and services. Should missiles be produced by combining many workers with a few units of capital or by a more capital-intensive method? Is it better to produce soybeans using lots of tractors and machinery intensely cultivating a few acres of land or using more land and workers and relatively little capital? Should college students be taught in large classes by professors (highly skilled labor) or in small sections by teaching assistants (substituting less skilled labor)? Such questions must be answered in a systematic way. In a market system, prices guide suppliers and buyers of inputs to decisions that maximize profits or minimize costs.

The *for whom* question asks who will get the goods and services produced and how much each person will receive. This is a way of asking which of many possible distributions of income will be chosen. Should the distribution be equal or unequal? Should an individual's share be based on contributions to production, on need, or on some combination of the two? A pure market system answers this question directly: a person's rewards depend on contributions to production. Other systems, including a mixed market system, use a mixture of guidelines to determine the distribution of income.

The answers to the three questions are not independent of one another. The distribution of income will determine whether there is more demand for bread and milk or luxury yachts. The production process chosen may determine the amount of each kind of output that can be produced.

Tradition, Command, and the Market

Every society has to find a way to answer the three basic economic questions. The study of the different ways of organizing economic activity, or answering these questions, is called comparative economic systems. There are many ways of classifying economic systems, such as by who owns the productive resources or by the form of government. One useful way of classifying economic systems is by the method used to answer the three basic economic questions. This classification identifies three broad types of economies: the traditional economy, the command (planned) economy, and the market economy. Of course, no economy fits neatly into any one of these categories. All economies are mixed in that they contain elements of traditional, command, and market processes.

traditional economy
An economy in which the three basic questions are answered by custom, or how things have been done in the past.

The Traditional Economy. The **traditional economy** answers the basic economic questions by appeals to tradition, or custom. That is, the answers are determined by how the questions have been answered in the past. What is produced is whatever parents have taught their children to produce on the basis of customs developed in the past. A heavily traditional society is usually not highly sophisticated. Most of people's efforts are devoted to simple production of food, clothing, and shelter. Tradition determines what kinds of food are grown, what kinds of clothing are made, and what kinds of houses are built. It also determines what combination of these three is produced in any given period.

In a traditional economy, the techniques of production (how to produce) are also passed on, with little change, from one generation to the next. In many parts of Asia and Africa, the methods of building houses and of farming have been the same for many generations. These methods use simple materials, much labor, and very little capital equipment.

Traditional societies also have established answers to the distribution question (for whom). If you have studied cultural anthropology, you know that traditional societies often have rules on how to divide the spoils of the hunt or the fruits of the harvest. Medieval Europe was a highly traditional society, with shares of crops assigned to various claimants. There were also customary duties of military service or payments to the lord of the manor. In such a traditional society, a person's claim on society's resources is determined primarily by status in the hierarchy from peasant to king.

You may recognize elements of tradition that persist even in modern industrial societies. For example, there are still many small, rural communities almost untouched by modern farming techniques. Some ethnic groups have strong traditions of sons following their fathers' occupations. Women's roles and responsibilities continue to follow tradition in many respects. For the most part, however, tradition plays a limited role in the decision-making process in modern industrial economies.

THE COMMAND ECONOMY. The **command economy**, or planned economy, answers the basic economic questions through central command and control. A central planning authority makes all decisions regarding what and how to produce. Individual production units receive detailed plans and orders that carry the weight of law. The question concerning income distribution is answered in the process of determining what and how to produce. The central planners also set wage rates and levels of production. This planning process was the primary method of organization in the Soviet Union and other countries in Eastern Europe, before the recent rapid movement toward market economies. The major goal of perestroika was to decentralize decision making and reduce the amount of central control in the Soviet Union. The nations of Eastern Europe have made an even more rapid journey toward decentralization and the use of markets.

In any economy, people plan. That is, they think about the future and prepare for it. In a traditional society, people plan for a future that will be much like the past. In a command economy, the government plays the primary role in planning how to answer the production and consumption questions for society. This kind of planning is very different from the individual planning that goes on in a market economy. Decision making is highly decentralized in a market system.

THE MARKET ECONOMY. The third type of economic system is the market economy. The **market economy** relies on incentives and the self-interested behavior of individuals to direct production and consumption through

command economy
An economy in which the three basic questions are answered through central planning and control (also called a planned economy).

market economy
An economy in which the three basic questions are answered through the market, by relying on self-interested behavior and incentives.

market exchanges. Consumers, "voting" with their dollars, determine what is produced. The result of this market process determines what goods and services are available.

Suppliers determine how to produce. Since suppliers are self-interested and seek to maximize their profits, they tend to combine inputs so as to produce a good or service at the lowest possible cost. The answer to the *how* question depends on the prices of productive resources. Suppliers will use more of abundant resources because they are relatively cheap.

The goods and services are distributed to consumers who have the purchasing power to buy them. Households that have more purchasing power (because they own more valuable productive resources) receive more goods and services. The quantity and quality of the labor skills the individual sells are the most important determinants of individual income. About 75 percent of the income in the United States is wages and salaries. Those with high-quality, scarce skills that are in great demand receive high salaries and have more influence on the output mix. People with higher earnings have more "votes" in the form of dollars spent in the marketplace.

One essential condition for undirected markets to answer the basic economic questions is the institution of **property rights**. In a command economy, most property belongs to the state. There is very limited private ownership. In fact, the process of restoring private ownership and private property rights has been slow in Eastern Europe, requiring changes in the constitutions in many cases. In a market economy, however, private property and property rights play an essential role. Markets will function only if individual buyers and sellers possess the property rights to the goods and services they want to exchange.

property rights
The legal rights to a specific piece of property, including the rights to own, buy, sell, or use in specific ways. Markets can exist and exchanges can occur only if individuals have property rights to goods, services, and productive resources.

In a market economy, productive resources are owned by individuals. Owners of capital will not invest unless they are certain that they can claim the ownership of that capital and the products that it produces. They also need to be assured that their capital and its interest will not be taken away by the state or by force or violence. Workers will not offer their labor for hire if their rights to be paid cannot be enforced or if they know their earnings are likely to be stolen. Agreements to use productive resources and to make payments for them have to be protected from violence or breach of contract. What a market system needs, then, is a legal system that defines property rights and enforces them against any violations. Defining and enforcing property rights is an important function of government even in a pure market economy.

Beyond enforcing property rights, governments undertake some amount of central planning in all economies, including that of the United States. Federal and state governments play a substantial role in determining what is produced and how it is produced. Government policy makers make decisions about highways, schools, public parks, national defense, and other goods and services produced in the public sector. Their actions also change the distribution of income through taxes and social welfare programs. However, politicians and public policy makers are not the primary decision makers in the U.S. economy or in most other modern industrial economies, such as those of Japan, Canada, Australia, and the nations of the European Community. In these countries, most decisions are made by individuals through markets.

RESPONDING TO CHANGE. One way to compare the workings of these three types of economic systems is to consider how each responds to change. Suppose an earthquake closes some copper mines, and the supply of copper is suddenly cut in half. A traditional economy would probably have rules to ensure a fair distribution of the reduced supply. It would not, however, be very flexible in adjusting production processes or the output mix. In a command economy, government officials would determine the possible effects of the copper shortage and estimate how long it was likely to last. They would then decide which uses of copper had the highest priority and make sure that the available copper was distributed so that those uses could occur. For example, orders might be sent to firms producing electric generators to substitute some other metal for copper, in order to conserve it for uses such as house wiring.

Contrast these processes with what occurs in a market economy. When the mines close and less copper is available, copper prices rise. Consumers of copper know immediately that the price has gone up. The high price leads consumers to search for cheaper substitutes. It also attracts a sudden flow of imported copper or scrap copper to the market. The allocation of copper might not meet the traditional economy's criterion of fairness or the command economy's priorities. However, the market response is much faster. Substitution and increased supplies occur very quickly with no need for the government to process and send information. Acquiring relevant information for decisions requires the use of scarce resources. The market system economizes on the amount of costly information needed to make production and consumption decisions.

Clearly, a market system has advantages over command and traditional economies in flexibility and capacity for dealing with change. However, the market system also has some drawbacks. Many observers criticize the distribution of income that results from the workings of the market, which can create extremes of wealth and poverty. Market systems have also been criticized for encouraging self-centered behavior at the expense of community interests.

MIXED ECONOMIES

Because of the advantages of the market system, even primarily traditional or command economies incorporate some elements of markets. Conversely, the pure market system is often modified to soften some of the harshness of pure capitalism.

The blend of tradition, command, and market-decision methods varies, but most modern industrial countries such as Canada, Japan, the United States, Australia, and some of the nations of Western Europe have mixed economies. In a **mixed economy**, the basic decision method is the market, but some economic choices are made by government. These choices are designed to modify the answers to the basic economic questions reached in the course of unregulated market activity while keeping most of the benefits of markets intact. The goal is to leave economic decisions to the market when it works well, but to intervene in the economy when the market outcome is not acceptable. On a macroeconomic level, a high rate of unemployment is an example of an unacceptable market outcome. On a microeconomic level, air pollution caused by coal-fired power plants is an example of an undesirable market outcome. In both

mixed economy
An economy in which the three basic questions are answered partly by market forces and partly through government.

instances, some people argue that the government should step in to correct the performance of the market and alter its results.

All noncommunist industrial nations are properly classed as mixed economies. Increasingly, the formerly communist nations of Eastern Europe are moving in that direction as well. The mix varies significantly from country to country. Governments are much more heavily involved in the economy in Poland, Sweden, and France than in the United States and Germany. The differences in the degree of governmental involvement in economic decisions reflect variety in political systems, national values, and historical experiences. Even within economies, the division of labor between the market and the public sector changes from time to time. The movement to privatize certain activities (to shift them from the public sector to the private sector) was very strong in the 1980s in several industrial countries, including the United States and Britain. That movement has taken hold in the formerly communist nations of Eastern Europe as their governments sell off state-owned land and enterprises to private individuals.

Most of this book presents economic theory in the context of a mixed, but primarily market, economy. When we want to cite examples of how things work in reality, we will draw mostly on the experiences of the U.S. economy. The international perspectives will offer some illustrations of how things work in other countries. Despite the emphasis on the mixed economy as the model and the United States as the chief example, the economic theory we will develop is universally applicable. What differs is how often and for what purpose different governments choose to intervene in the market.

THE CIRCULAR FLOW OF ECONOMIC ACTIVITY

circular flow model
A visual representation of the relationships between the factor market (in which income is obtained) and the product market (in which income is used to purchase goods and services).

factor market
Set of markets in which owners of the factors of production sell these to producers.

product market
Set of markets in which goods and services produced by firms are sold.

Chapter 1 discussed the use of models by economists in developing simple descriptions from which wider conclusions and inferences can be made. One model that is often used to describe a mixed economy in which the market is the primary source of decisions is the **circular flow model**. This model provides an overview of the central concerns of both macroeconomics and microeconomics. The circular flow model is a visual picture of the relationships between the **factor market**, in which income is earned, and the **product market**, in which income is used to purchase goods and services.

The first economist to describe a circular flow model was François Quesnay (1694–1774), the leader of a group of French economists known as the Physiocrats. The name *Physiocrats* comes from a French word that means "rule of nature." Physiocrats believed that the economy was a part of the natural order and that there were natural laws governing the causes of wealth. Quesnay, who was also a physician, was inspired by William Harvey's discovery that blood circulated in the human body. This led him to develop the circular flow model of the macro economy. His model was based on the view that the circulation of resources and products in the economy was similar to the circulation of blood in the human body. And, like a loss of blood, any reduction in this flow was a cause for concern.

THE TWO-SECTOR CIRCULAR FLOW MODEL

In a pure market economy, there are only two kinds of actors: households and business firms.[1] Firms and households interact in two types of markets: the factor and product markets. As shown in Figure 1, households purchase goods and services produced by firms, creating a flow of dollars to firms in payment for these goods and services. The individual markets in which these exchanges take place, shown in the upper part of Figure 1, make up the product market. Firms buy factors of production (inputs or resources) from households (who own all the productive resources) in order to produce the goods and services they sell to the households. The total of the individual markets in which these transactions take place, shown

**FIGURE 1
CIRCULAR FLOW OF INCOME**
Households purchase goods and services in the product market and supply land, labor, capital, and enterprise in the factor market. Firms buy the services of these inputs in the factor market and supply goods and services in the product market.

---

1. Sometimes firms and households are one and the same. A family-owned grocery store, a home-based accounting service, or a day-care facility may operate from within a household. For simplicity, we treat them as though they can be separated. That is, we assume that households own all factors of production and firms produce all goods and services.

in the lower part of Figure 1, is the factor market. The flow of productive resources to firms generates a reverse flow of dollar payments (wages, rent, interest, and profits). Quesnay saw such a system as a closed one, in which the flow would be continuous, like the flow of blood in the human body.

As you saw in Chapter 1, models are an important part of economic analysis because they permit more orderly thinking about the world. The circular flow in Figure 1 is a very simple model of the way a market economy operates. This model is a broad overview of the economy that you need to keep in mind as we proceed to look at its various specific components. We will add a few simple refinements to the model in this chapter.

Most of macroeconomics is concerned with measuring and changing the sizes of the flows of output and income, represented by the sizes of the shaded arrows. Most of microeconomics is devoted to a closer look at the operation of the individual markets that make up the circular flow and at the behavior of individual actors (households, firms, and governments).

THE CIRCULAR FLOW MODEL WITH SAVING, GOVERNMENT, AND INTERNATIONAL TRADE

We can make the simple circular flow model more realistic in several important ways. To keep things as simple as possible, however, we will limit the model to just one flow in each market instead of two. The diagrams will show the flow of income payments through the factor market to households and the flow of purchases through the product market to the business sector.

The first adjustment to the model is to relax the assumption that the flow of income from firms to households (the lower half of Figure 1) and the flow of payments from households to firms (the upper half of Figure 1) are equal. If firms pay out all of their revenues to households and households spend every dollar they receive on purchases of goods and services, then the flows will be equal. But if households save part of their incomes, there is a leakage out of the circular flow. If firms invest (buy new capital equipment), there is an injection into the circular flow. Either an injection or a leakage can change the size of the flow. Figure 2 shows a flow of savings out of the income stream and an injection of investment spending into the income stream.

A second adjustment of the simple model is to add a government sector. You know that local, state, and federal governments produce, or cause the production of, goods ranging from schools and libraries to missiles and post offices. Governments take part of household incomes in taxes—a leakage out of the spending stream. They also purchase productive inputs from households—an injection, just like investment. Government plays an important microeconomic role because its actions affect the mix of goods and services produced and the distribution of output. At the macroeconomic level, government actions affect the amount of total production, as well as unemployment and economic growth. Figure 3 on page 52 shows a circular flow diagram with a government that collects taxes from households and purchases goods and services from business firms.

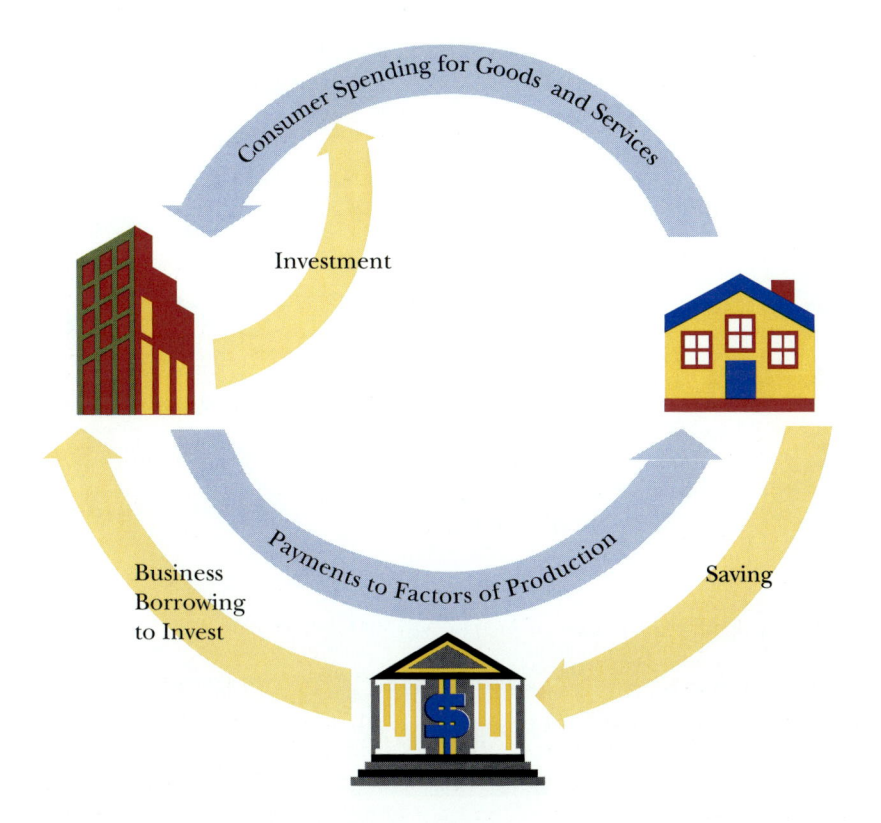

FIGURE 2
CIRCULAR FLOW WITH SAVING AND INVESTMENT
If households do not spend all their income, some of it will leak out of the circular flow in the form of savings. If business firms borrow in order to invest, their investment will be an injection into the circular flow.

Even this model ignores some important government transactions such as taxes on business, transfer payments to households, purchases of labor from households, and borrowing.

Finally, the simple circular flow model describes a closed economy (one that has no interaction with the rest of the world). Except for Albania, which has chosen to minimize its interactions with the rest of the world, most nations are affected by transactions with other countries. Figure 4 on page 53, therefore, adds one final change. Households purchase imports from the foreign sector (other nations). Business firms sell exports to that sector. Imports are a leakage out of the spending stream. Income earned is not directly spent on purchases of consumer goods from the domestic business sectors. Exports represent an injection of spending into the flow. Exports often represent a large part of sales and income, especially in small countries. Imports may provide a large share of total consumption. In the United States, the ratio of exports to total output is only 12 percent. In some smaller countries, this ratio is much higher. Mexico, for example, exports about 16 percent of its output, and the Netherlands exports 49 percent of what it produces.

The government sector and the foreign sector are two very important additions to the circular flow model. The government is what makes the economy a mixed economy, one in which some decisions are made outside the market. The foreign sector makes the economy an open rather

**FIGURE 3
CIRCULAR FLOW WITH GOVERNMENT**
Government is a third actor in the circular flow model. It interacts with households and firms in collecting taxes from households and purchasing goods and services from firms. Here households have two leakages not spent on consumption. Business firms have three customers for output: households (consumption), other business firms (investment), and government.

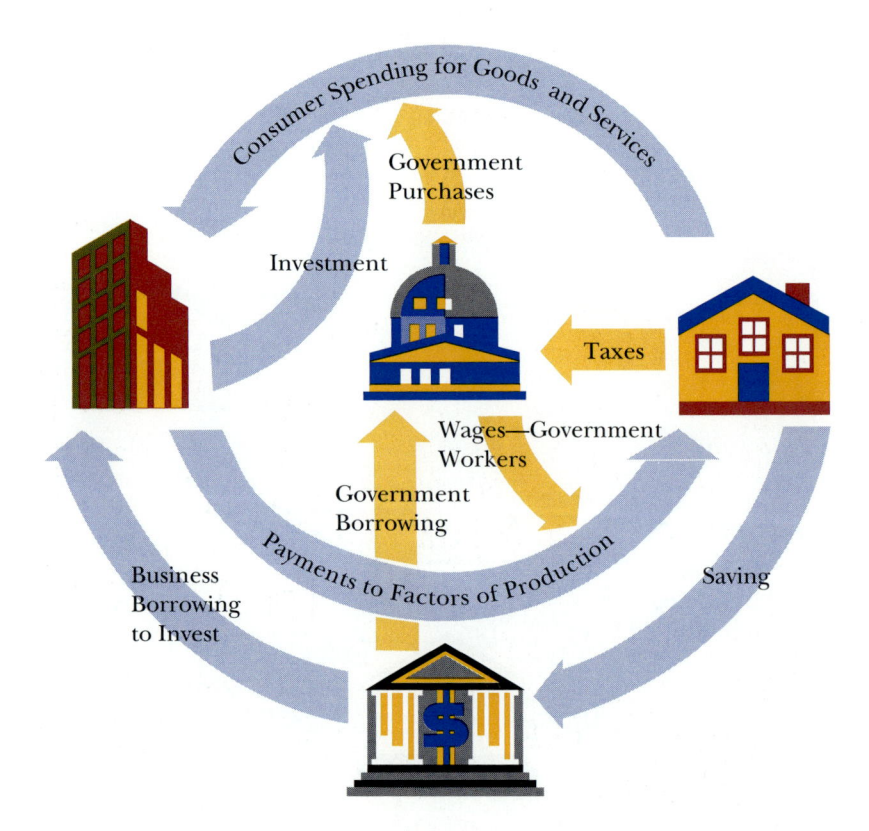

than a closed one. Actions by the three "inside" actors (households, businesses, and government) will have very different effects from what would occur in a closed economy. We will consider each of these sectors in turn.

THE ECONOMIC ROLE OF GOVERNMENT

The next chapter will introduce you to the workings of a market. All markets work in basically the same way in any economy. Supply and demand determine prices and quantities. In some economies or for some kinds of exchanges, however, the market may not be allowed to perform this function. Then some other decision-making process must be used to answer the three basic economic questions.

The most common method other than the market is to allow choices concerning the use of resources to be made by politicians or other agents of government. The kinds of decisions made through governments and the kinds made through the private sector vary among nations. In the United States, health care is private. In Canada, it is publicly financed but privately provided. In most European countries, health care is both paid

Chapter 2 Markets, Governments, and Nations

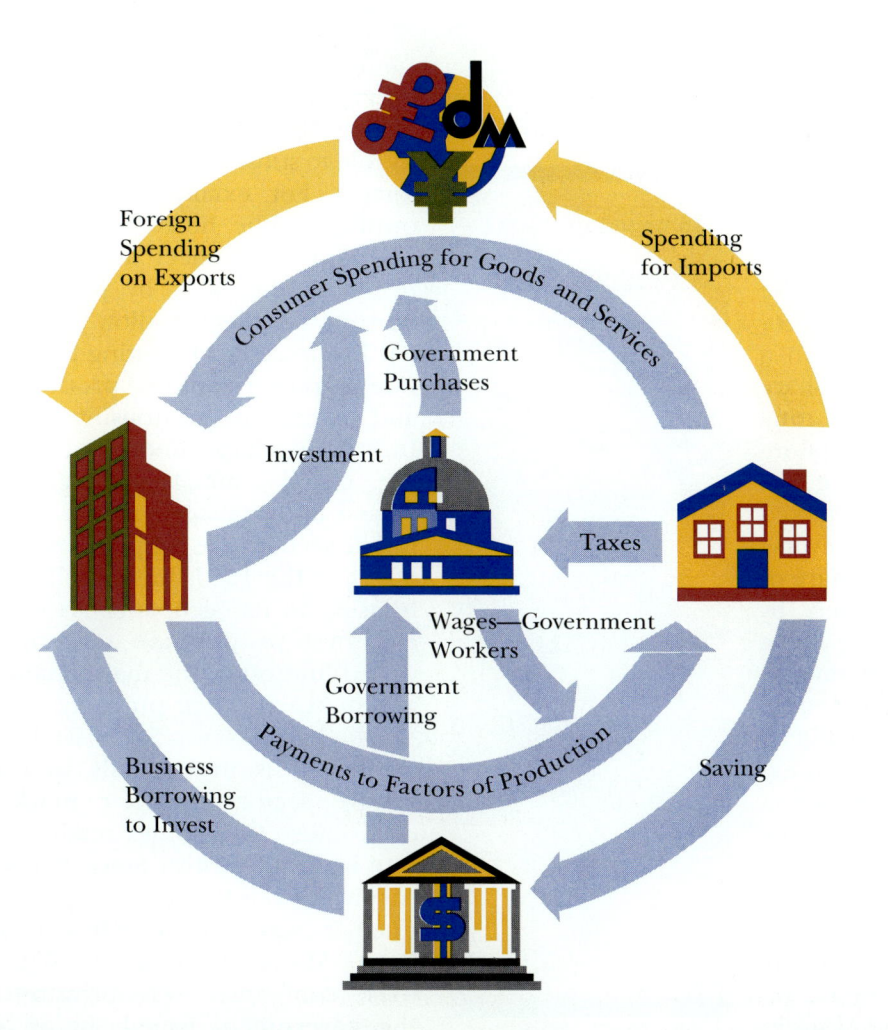

FIGURE 4
CIRCULAR FLOW WITH A FOREIGN SECTOR
Still another source of production and buyer of output is the rest of the world, or the foreign sector. Sales to foreign buyers are exports, and purchases from foreign suppliers are imports.

for and provided by government. Some governments (such as Sweden's) use taxes and social welfare programs to greatly modify the market distribution of income. Others (such as Japan's) do very little to change the distribution of income that results from market decisions.

In the United States, the preference is to make most decisions through the market. However, there are some things that the market cannot do or cannot do well. Many economists argue that the market does not do a very good job of addressing such problems as poverty, pollution, inflation, unemployment, and the market power of large firms. It is also difficult for private markets to provide enough of such collective goods and services as defense, education, and sewer systems.

Recall that a market system requires clearly defined property rights. That is, someone has to decide who owns what goods and services and to define their rights to use and trade those goods and services. The market cannot define and enforce property rights very well, so this role is usually assigned to governments. Citizens in most modern mixed economies cannot legally drive a car without a license, park in a handicapped space without a sticker,

International Perspective: Privatization in Britain

The division of economic activity between public and private spheres in a mixed economy is not fixed. In wartime, the share of economic activity commanded by government increases. When there are changes in citizens' preferences or political philosophy, government's share of total dollars spent may rise or fall in response. For most Western economies, there has been a gradual upward trend in the share of government spending to total GNP and the share of personal income paid in taxes. In the last decade, however, several mixed economies have tried to reverse that trend and reduce the share of economic activity controlled by government. In particular, there has been a move to spin off some allocation activities of government to the private sector. This change is called privatization. In Eastern Europe, a large part of the transition away from communism has consisted of shifting activities from government to the private sector.

Privatization has been strongly advocated in a number of countries. Nowhere was it pushed as far as in Britain under Prime Minister Margaret Thatcher. There the public sector was cut 40 percent in the 1980s. This privatization effort in Britain was stronger than in the United States in part because there had been more public sector involvement in economic activity in Britain.

Privatization can mean a variety of things. It may mean that the government continues to provide a service—for example, garbage collection—but is no longer the producer of that service. Instead, the government collects taxes to pay for the service but contracts with a private firm to actually perform it. Alternatively, the government may get out of the business of providing a service. It will either leave provision completely to the private market or limit its role to subsidizing buyers or producers. For example, instead of owning public housing, the government could meet the housing needs of the poor by providing housing vouchers to allow them to pay for housing and letting the private market respond by producing and managing the housing units. In Britain, a large amount of housing, called council housing, was owned and managed by the local public sector. One big privatization effort in the 1980s was to sell that housing to its occupants. As owners, these people have a stronger vested interest in the maintenance and upkeep of their property.

Much of what was first privatized in Britain is traditionally in the private sector in other market economies. Companies made private included British Steel, British Airways, Rolls-Royce, and Jaguar. (Jaguar was later purchased by Ford Motor Company.) When these companies were privatized, the government issued shares of stock sold to the public, creating private ownership while raising revenue for the public treasury. It was hoped that private, profit-minded managers would be more efficient, lowering costs and prices and increasing output and exports. In the last few years, however, the British government met resistance in trying to privatize such traditionally public services as water, electricity, and roads. The privatization movement has been an important episode in the continuing search for balance between the public and private sectors.

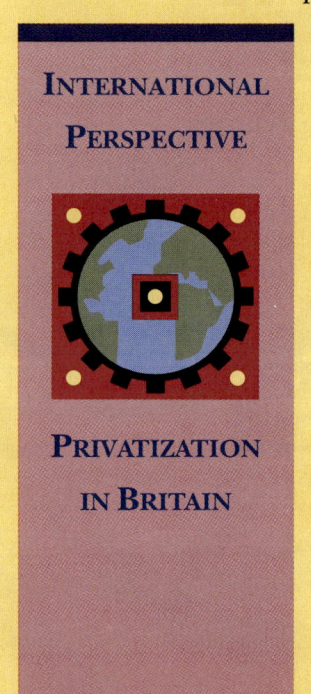

or build a fast-food restaurant in a neighborhood zoned residential. These rules represent restrictions on property rights. An unrestricted market would allow people to do all of these things, whether or not they were considered desirable by the majority. Even in a pure market economy, government is needed to establish and protect property rights.

The activities of government are grouped into three categories: allocation, redistribution, and stabilization. Stabilization and redistribution are conducted primarily through governments in all economic systems. Allocation is a microeconomic activity that is shared by the government and the market to different extents in different systems. Much of the dispute over what government should or should not do relates to its allocation activities. Also, much of the difference between market and command economies involves how allocation is divided between the market and the agencies of government.

THE ALLOCATION FUNCTION

Allocation refers to any activity of government that affects the quantity and quality of goods and services produced (that is, anything that affects the answer to the *what* question). Allocation activities in a market-based mixed economy may include producing public education, subsidizing higher education, taxing cigarettes, regulating factory and automobile emissions, setting safety standards for cars, placing quotas on steel imports, building highways, and setting prices for electric power produced by private firms.[2] In a command economy, the array of government allocation activities is much broader. Some, maybe even most, allocation activities also affect the answer to the *for whom* question because they increase the incomes of some firms and individuals at the expense of others.

allocation
Any activities by government or its agents that affect the distribution of resources and the combination of goods and services produced.

PUBLIC GOODS AND POSITIVE EXTERNALITIES. In mixed economies, allocation activities are usually assigned to the public sector only when the good or service is considered a public good or when its production or consumption creates substantial external effects. We will explore each of these criteria in turn.

Economists define **public goods** as those goods that are nonrival in consumption and not subject to exclusion. What do these technical phrases mean? Sunsets and lighthouses are both nonrival in consumption. *Nonrival* means that a good or service is not used up in consumption. The fact that you are watching a sunset leaves no less sunset for someone else to enjoy. Sunsets and lighthouses are also hard to subject to exclusion. *Exclusion* means that nonpayers, or free riders, can be kept from consuming the good. **Free riders** are people or business firms who consume collective goods without contributing to the cost of their production. In addition to sunsets and lighthouses, national defense and mosquito spraying are examples of services for which it is very difficult, or at least expensive, to exclude nonpayers. Because nonpayers cannot easily be excluded, there is not much incentive for a self-interested private firm to produce such goods.

public goods
Goods that are nonrival in consumption and not subject to exclusion.

free riders
People or business firms who consume collective goods without contributing to the cost of their production.

---

2. Some government allocation activities (for example, setting prices for electric power) relate to the regulation of monopoly.

positive externalities
Spillover benefits to third parties (free riders) that result from production or consumption of certain goods.

Some economists extend the term *public good* to include goods with weak rivalry or high costs of exclusion. Examples of such nearly public goods include fire fighting, education, and highways. In all these cases, benefits spill over to nonpayers. These spillover benefits to third parties are called **positive externalities**. Where there are such positive effects, the private market may not produce enough of the good or service because some who benefit can free-ride. Note that this broader group of nearly public goods can imply an expanded role for government. In fact, all of the services mentioned have at some point been produced in the private sector. Volunteer fire departments in some rural areas still will not put out fires in nonsubscribers' homes. Education through the twelfth grade is produced in both the public and the private sector. Private toll roads were the earliest form of highways in New England.

negative externalities
Harmful spillovers to third parties that result from production or consumption of certain goods.

public bads
Negative external effects of production or consumption that impact a large number of individuals—for example, acid rain.

NEGATIVE EXTERNALITIES. When people or firms consume certain goods or engage in certain activities, they pass some of the costs of production or consumption along to others. These are **negative externalities**. Those who create noise, litter, hazards, and pollution do not bear the full cost. If the negative externalities are strong enough and widespread enough, they may constitute **public bads**. These are negative effects that impact on everyone to some degree. Public bads are the polar opposite of public goods and include such broad negative effects as global warming, depleting of the ozone layer, and extinction of endangered species. Too many negative externalities and public bads are produced if all decisions are left to private markets and individuals. Many of the regulatory activities first undertaken in the 1960s and 1970s in the United States were intended to reduce such effects.

THE SCOPE OF ALLOCATION BY GOVERNMENT. Most economists agree that the government does have some responsibility to produce public goods, to encourage the production of goods with positive externalities, and to discourage the production of negative externalities and public bads. But the lines are drawn differently by different individuals within any nation. They are certainly drawn very differently in different countries. How big do spillovers have to be before government gets involved? Does the government itself have to produce public goods, or can their production be contracted out to the private sector or encouraged through subsidies? Do negative externalities have to be addressed by prohibitions or standards, or can taxes and fines do the job? An individual's, or a nation's, answers to these questions will reflect certain underlying values, ideas about the relative importance of efficiency, equity, and freedom.

Figure 5 shows a spectrum from public bads through goods with negative externalities to private goods and then to goods with positive externalities, ending with public goods. In almost all economies, it is agreed that the two ends of the spectrum call for government intervention to promote public goods and deter public bads. It is also fairly generally agreed that the market works best in the middle of the spectrum, producing and distributing private goods and nearly private goods. Nations disagree on

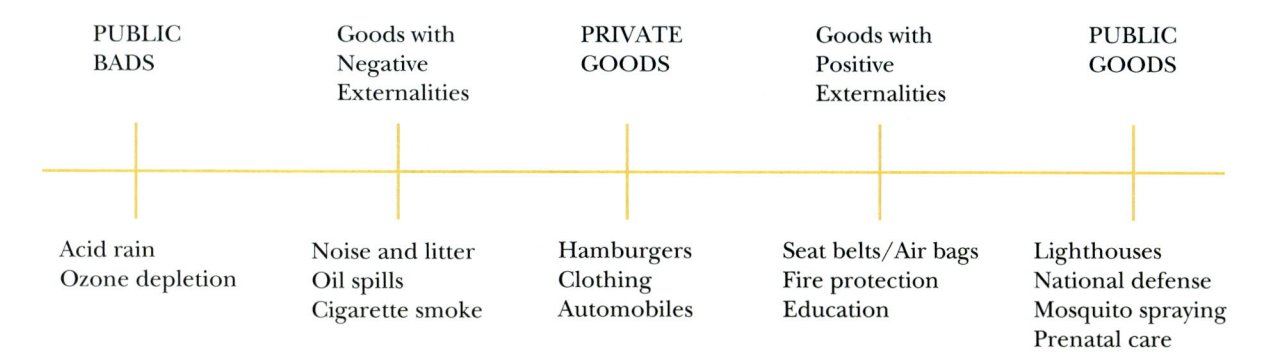

PUBLIC BADS	Goods with Negative Externalities	PRIVATE GOODS	Goods with Positive Externalities	PUBLIC GOODS
Acid rain Ozone depletion	Noise and litter Oil spills Cigarette smoke	Hamburgers Clothing Automobiles	Seat belts/Air bags Fire protection Education	Lighthouses National defense Mosquito spraying Prenatal care

FIGURE 5
PUBLIC GOODS, PRIVATE GOODS, AND PUBLIC BADS
Goods and services fit on a spectrum from pure public goods such as defense through weak public goods, to private goods, and then to goods that cause negative external effects to some parties. At the far end of the spectrum are activities that cause widespread harm, public bads.

where to draw the lines on either side of the middle, dividing the private from the public sphere.

In the United States, there is another division of responsibility, because the United States has a federal system of government. A federal system has another layer of government (besides the national level) with independent responsibility. In the United States, a large part of allocation by government occurs at the state and local levels. Some public goods are provided on a national scale—defense, for example. But many are provided at the community level. Different cities and towns choose different combinations of public services. One city may choose more street lights and snow removal. Another may vote for public parks and better roads. Allowing this kind of variety in local choices makes governments more responsive to the values and desires of the people who are paying the bills. This diversity is an attractive feature of fiscal federalism, a system in which the economic responsibilities of government are not concentrated at a single level but dispersed among several levels. The United States, Canada, Germany, and Australia are examples of countries in which governments at the state or province level have notable power and responsibility. Economists find a federal system attractive because the autonomous lower levels of governments are in competition for residents and business firms. This competition creates diversity and choice, and perhaps greater efficiency.

THE REDISTRIBUTION FUNCTION

The distribution of income in a market economy is based on each person's contributions to production. There is no denying that the distribution of income determined by the market is quite unequal. Some people are very wealthy, and others are very poor. One way in which economies differ greatly is the extent to which the political process is involved in redistribution. **Redistribution** means taking income from one group and giving it to another through taxes and transfer payments.

In any economy, when the government taxes individuals with high incomes, they have less incentive to work, save, and invest to increase output in future years. On the other hand, some individuals cannot earn an income through the market. They may be too old, too young, too sick, or too handicapped. Others work as hard as they can with the skills and resources at their disposal but still cannot earn enough to get by. There is some private redistribution, but private charity is subject to a free rider problem. (Many people will not participate because they know others

redistribution
Actions by government that transfer income from one group to another.

will.) Such free-riding behavior makes income redistribution more or less a public good that falls within the domain of government.

How much income should be redistributed? To whom should it go? How can redistribution be managed to minimize the negative effects on work incentives? These are difficult questions to answer. As a result, the answers are very different in different countries. In general, there is more redistribution and greater equality of income in countries at the middle of the mixed economy spectrum than in countries at either the command or the market extreme.

An obvious way to redistribute income is to use taxes and transfer payments. In the United States, transfer payments take the form of Social Security benefits, food stamps, and welfare payments. Taxes that collect relatively more from the rich than the poor, such as the U.S. federal income tax, mean that the rich pay more than the poor do for the same level of public services. This difference is a form of redistribution. In the United States, transfer payments are primarily financed by the federal government rather than state governments. The states do administer the programs and pay part of the cost. Redistributing income at the federal level makes it possible to reduce inequality between rich and poor states, as well as between rich and poor individuals within states.

Transfer payments are the most visible form of income redistribution. However, there is a redistributive side to almost everything the government does. If increased funds are spent on public education, families with school-aged children benefit more than childless households. Increased spending on health care benefits those who are sick. Quotas on steel imports benefit steelworkers but not steel users. Expanded student loan programs help college-aged people who qualify at the expense of all other taxpayers and would-be borrowers. Since it is virtually impossible for the government to spend money on anything without redistributing income, it is difficult to measure how much redistribution takes place.

Indirect kinds of income redistribution often benefit those who are not poor, that is, the middle class or the rich. Income redistribution through taxes and transfer payments is often criticized because of its effect on incentives. However, other government programs are equally vulnerable to criticism as "welfare for the rich." Examples are subsidies for large farms, tax loopholes for real estate owners and developers and oil and gas producers, bailouts for savings and loan institutions, and cost overruns by large defense contractors. This kind of redistribution is a consequence of democracy, where the rich and the middle class have more political clout than the poor. In any economy, however, how much redistribution is enough, from whom it should come, and to whom it should go are very difficult questions.

THE STABILIZATION FUNCTION

The last and most recently developed task of government is stabilization. **Stabilization** refers to government actions to reduce changes in output, employment, and prices. Until recently, many people believed that stabilization problems were unique to market economies, which tended to go through severe ups and downs in output, employment, and prices. It is now clear, however, that unemployment and inflation were problems for the command economies of Eastern Europe as well.

stabilization
Actions by government to reduce changes in output, employment, and prices.

Stabilization is mainly a macroeconomic function. However, the ways in which stabilization policies are carried out also affect the mix of goods produced (allocation) and the distribution of costs and benefits (redistribution). Government attempts to stabilize the economy consist of increasing spending or cutting taxes to increase output and employment or cutting spending and increasing taxes to control inflation. In addition, changes in the money supply are used to expand or contract economic activity.

Economists disagree about how stable a market economy would be if it were left alone. Historically, in the U.S. economy (and most market economies), there have been periods of high unemployment combined with low inflation, or occasionally even deflation (falling prices). These downturns have alternated with periods of more rapid inflation (increasing prices) and lower unemployment in a cyclical pattern. Even though such cycles have been less severe since World War II, it cannot be concluded that the U.S. economy has been more stable with government intervention than it was when the government played a much smaller role.

When spending and taxes are used to try to stabilize the economy, budget deficits or surpluses are likely to result. The rationale for deficits is that price stability and full employment should dictate whether or not the budget is balanced. However, the U.S. government has run deficits that cannot be justified on the basis of stabilization activity. The central governments of both the United States and the Soviet Union had substantial budget deficits throughout the 1980s. Since 1958, the U.S. federal budget has been in deficit in all but two years.

ECONOMIC ROLES OF GOVERNMENT

FUNCTION	EXAMPLE
• Allocation	
Public goods	Defense, courts
Goods with positive external effects	Education, seat belts
Negative external effects	Pollution controls
• Redistribution	Social Security
• Stabilization	Cutting taxes to end recession

THE ROLE OF THE FOREIGN SECTOR

The last of the four sectors is the foreign sector. All nations engage in trade with other nations to some extent, because there are goods and services they cannot produce for themselves or can produce only at a very high cost. In most nations, there is also some inflow and outflow of the factors of production—labor, capital, land, and enterprise. Some nations, including the United States, allow goods and factors to flow relatively freely. Others, especially China, Japan, and the Soviet Union, restrict the movement of one or both with tariffs, quotas, immigration restrictions, capital controls, and exchange controls.

International Perspective

The Size of the Foreign Sector

In the circular flow diagram, the sizes of the arrows labeled "imports" and "exports" indicate the size of the foreign sector, or the importance of markets and suppliers in other countries. If the foreign sector is small, the economy is more like a closed economy. In a closed economy, activities of governments or private individuals have all or most of their impact within the economy and do not spill over to the rest of the world. Also, actions in the rest of the world have little or no impact on this kind of economy. With a large foreign sector, however, an economy is more likely to affect and be affected by the rest of the world. It is more vulnerable to the effects of inflation or recession in other countries. When its export sales fall, since exports are a large share of total output, the impact is felt throughout the economy.

The larger its land area, population, and total output or income, the less dependent an economy is likely to be on trade. Trade averages 20 to 40 percent of GNP across the broad range of all countries, but there is tremendous variety within this range. The ratio of exports to total output, or GNP, in 1986 was relatively low for such large countries as India (9 percent) and China (11 percent). Countries that are geographically isolated, such as Australia (17 percent), also tend to have a lower ratio of trade to GNP because the cost of shipping is so high. At the other extreme, small countries that produce primary products (agricultural or mineral) often have very high ratios of trade to GNP. The small oil-producing nation of Bahrein exports 92 percent of its total output.

The tiny duchy of Luxembourg exports 72 percent of what it produces. The Caribbean nation of Jamaica, whose revenues derive from tourism, exports 62 percent of its GNP.

The importance of trade can be measured by comparing either exports or imports to GNP. For many nations, the two measures will be about the same, but some countries are very unbalanced. Japan, for example, exports 12 percent of what it produces but imports less than 8 percent of what it consumes. Imports greatly exceeded exports for the United States for most of the 1980s. By 1990, however, the two were close to equal, with exports being about 11 percent of GNP and imports about 12 percent. One of the largest gaps between exports and imports occurs in the small, developing nation of Guinea-Bissau. Its ratio of trade to GNP is only 10 percent for exports but 53 percent for imports.

By either measure, the share of trade in the GNP is a good indicator of how dependent on other nations a nation is. The higher the trade ratio, the more sensitive a country is to events in foreign markets and the more dependent it is on foreign sources of supply. The benefits of trade are substantial, but one of the prices nations pay for those benefits is less control over their own economic destiny.

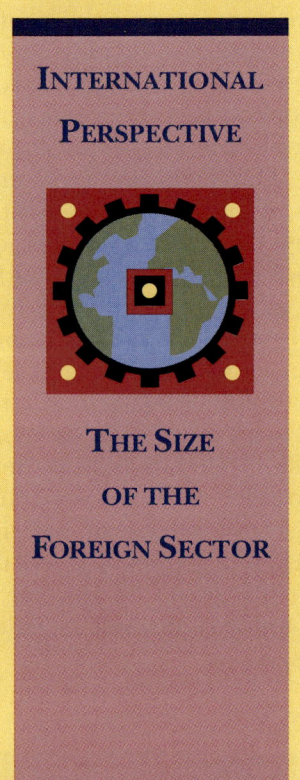

Chapter 2 Markets, Governments, and Nations

BENEFITS AND COSTS OF INTERNATIONAL TRADE

In general, a nation benefits from trade in both goods and factors. Trade enables households to consume goods that are not produced at home or would be much more costly to produce there. Trade enables firms to produce for larger markets, often lowering their costs of production. Trade also forces firms to respond to competitors in other countries that are producing products that are cheaper, more appealing, or safer. A flow of labor or capital may help a country overcome its shortages in certain factors of production.

Those who work for or own firms whose products compete with imports as well as workers who compete directly with immigrant workers may not have a positive attitude toward such trade. These groups are likely to lobby for tariffs and other forms of protection in order to shield themselves from the effects of foreign competition. In addition, an economy that depends on international trade to market its products or supply needed goods and services will be affected by the actions of other countries. Interdependence with other countries reduces the amount of control that the government can exert over domestic economic activities.

For a nation as a whole, however, there are substantial gains from trade with other nations. Let's explore one of the main benefits of such trade, the gains that result from specializing on the basis of comparative advantage.

SPECIALIZATION AND COMPARATIVE ADVANTAGE

A major benefit of international trade is that it permits a nation to go beyond its production possibilities curve without acquiring more resources or improving technology. A nation can attain better combinations of output through specialization and exchange. **Specialization**, or the division of labor, means that individuals will produce more than they intend to consume of one or only a few items and will trade the excess for other things they want.

specialization Limiting production activities to one or a few goods and services that one produces best in order to exchange for other goods.

Specialization allows individuals to take the fullest advantage of their unique talents and skills. Some people who are strong and agile can become professional athletes. Some people who are intelligent and gifted talkers can become lawyers. Specialization allows individuals to concentrate on what they do best and to produce more than they could if they tried to engage in a variety of production activities. For people with very valuable specialized skills, such as basketball stars or brain surgeons, the opportunity cost of using their time for other purposes is very high. Think about the value of the time an NBA star spends in cooking his own dinner or mowing his lawn!

Nations, states, and regions also specialize. The phrase *banana republic* used to refer to small Latin American countries that were heavily specialized in producing bananas for export. These countries used the earnings from bananas to import and consume a wide variety of products that they did not produce. Other small countries are highly specialized in oil, coffee, cocoa, sugar, and other agricultural products and raw materials. Within the United States, pineapples come from Hawaii, oranges from Florida and California, wheat from the midwest and plains states, and peaches from Georgia and South Carolina. Nations, states, and regions also specialize in certain types of goods and services. Japan is famous for small cars and electronic products, Switzerland for watches and banking, and France and Italy for wines.

By specializing, individuals, regions, and nations can produce more total output with no increase in resources or breakthroughs in technology. Thus, specialization improves a nation's standard of living and lets it move outside the production possibilities curve. Small countries especially can consume more goods and enjoy a wider range of goods and services through specialization and trade than if they were limited to what they produced. This point was strongly emphasized by the founder of modern economics, Adam Smith. In his 1776 classic *The Wealth of Nations*, he saw specialization and trade as the engine of growth.

SPECIALIZATION AND EXCHANGE. The benefits of specializing require that people or nations engage in exchange. If you choose to specialize, you will have to engage in trade because you will give up producing all the other goods and services you need. If you are concentrating on what you do well, you don't have time to spend cutting your own hair, growing your own vegetables, or repairing your own car. You certainly don't have time to build your house or manufacture your car! One thing that distinguishes modern industrial societies from less developed countries is the extent of specialization and exchange. The average American produces very little of what he or she consumes. Instead, individuals specialize in one or two products or services and purchase everything else in the market.

COMPARATIVE ADVANTAGE. How do individuals, regions, or nations decide what products to produce for exchange? How do they answer the question "In what should we specialize?" Sometimes the answer is obvious, determined by climate or other resources. In general, the answer lies in the **principle of comparative advantage**. This principle states that each person, group, or country should specialize in that product or service for which the opportunity cost of production is lowest. If that principle is followed, the total output of a group of people, an entire economy, or, for that matter, the entire world will be maximized. Higher total output will result, with no increase in resources or improvement in technology.

Figure 6 illustrates comparative advantage using two straight-line production possibilities curves. Both George and Karen can produce various combinations of cookies and hamburgers with their available resources, as the curves illustrate. Before specializing, Karen is producing 30 hamburgers and 10 dozen cookies a month for her own consumption (point *A* in Figure 6). George is producing 10 hamburgers a month and 40 dozen cookies for himself (point *R* in Figure 6). Karen, who has had some experience working in a fast-food restaurant, is better at making hamburgers. Each hamburger she makes requires that she give up production of only ½ dozen cookies. George's hamburgers cost him 2 dozen cookies per hamburger produced. Karen has a lower opportunity cost for hamburgers, which means that George must have a lower opportunity cost for cookies. Clearly, they should specialize.

If they decide to specialize, Karen will produce 50 hamburgers (point *B* in Figure 6). George will turn out 60 dozen cookies (point *S*). Total out-

---

principle of comparative advantage The idea that output will be maximized if people specialize in producing those goods or services for which their opportunity costs are lowest and engage in exchange to obtain other things they want.

Adam Smith is regarded as the founder of modern economics. He was born in Kirkcaldy, Scotland. He was educated at the University of Glasgow and at Oxford University in England and eventually became a professor at Glasgow. *The Wealth of Nations*, published in 1776, marked a break with previous economic thought. Smith stressed the role of individual self-interest in promoting overall welfare. In his view, the "invisible hand" of self-interest leads people to act in socially desirable ways. For example, you know when you arrive at a hotel in a strange city in the evening that you can count on being able to buy breakfast in the morning. People who hope to make a profit will have restaurants and coffee shops open for your business.

Before Smith, people who wrote on economic issues emphasized what government could and should do to run the economy in the national interest. Smith, however, argued that the role of government should be minimal. It should provide for national defense, produce and regulate the money supply, and support a system of laws with swift, efficient justice in the courts. Beyond these activities, private individuals pursuing their own self-interest would provide direction for economic activity. There was no need for government to intervene. For more than a century, Adam Smith's ideas led economists to view the best economic role of government as minimal.

Smith was not naive about the risks of relying on self-interest. He argued that whenever producers of the same product get together, their thoughts rapidly turn to conspiring to raise prices and increase profits. He was opposed to this type of monopoly behavior and thought that government should do nothing to encourage such practices. But as long as the government does not promote monopoly, market forces and competition will limit the ability of firms to take advantage of their customers.

Opportunity cost is another useful concept developed from the work of Adam Smith. He used the example of a village where people could hunt deer or beaver. As he pointed out, the opportunity cost of bagging one deer was the number of beaver that could have been trapped with the same time and trouble. Smith recognized that the only true cost in economics is opportunity cost.

ECONOMIC PROFILE

ADAM SMITH
1723–1790

**FIGURE 6
SPECIALIZATION AND
EXCHANGE**
When Karen and George specialize, total output increases from 40 hamburgers (Karen 30, George 10) and 50 dozen cookies (Karen 10, George 40) to 50 hamburgers (Karen) and 60 dozen cookies (George). After exchange, both can consume more than before. Karen is at point *C* instead of *A* and George is at point *T* instead of *R*.

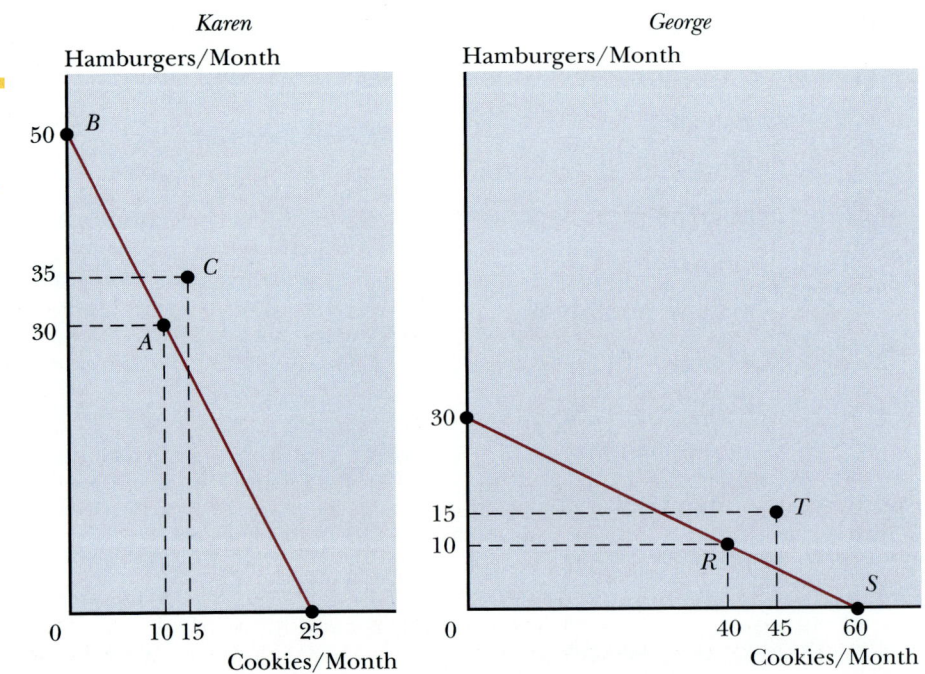

put increases by 10 hamburgers and 10 dozen cookies. All that remains is to divide up the gains. One combination that makes both better off is to split the increase equally. Thus, Karen consumes at point *C* in Figure 6 and enjoys 35 hamburgers and 15 dozen cookies. George consumes at point *T*, with 15 hamburgers and 45 dozen cookies. Both have gained because they are consuming more than before. There is more total output with no new resources and no improvement in technology.

The principle of comparative advantage means that both trading partners gain when individuals and nations specialize in the products for which their opportunity cost is lower and trade for what others produce more efficiently. Comparative advantage is the basis of all trade, not just international trade. We will return to comparative advantage in great detail in the chapter on international trade.

Chapter 2 Markets, Governments, and Nations

Summary

1. The factors of production consist of labor, land, capital, and enterprise. Labor receives wages, land receives rent, capital receives interest, and enterprise receives profit.

2. Every economy must address three basic economic questions: what to produce, how to produce it, and for whom to produce. Processes for answering these questions are tradition, command, and the market.

3. In different degrees, industrial nations have tried to answer the basic economic questions by using a mixed economy, where the market is the primary method, but government officials often intervene in the marketplace in an attempt to improve economic performance.

4. The circular flow model is a useful overview of the relations among sectors in a market economy. The basic model shows the interactions of households and businesses in the factor and product markets. More realistic versions add saving and investment, government, and a foreign sector.

5. There are some necessary functions that the market cannot perform or cannot perform well. These include defining and protecting property rights, providing public goods and correcting for external effects, bringing about a "fair" distribution of income, and stabilization.

6. Allocation by government includes not only the production of public goods and the reduction of public bads, but also any activities that affect private decisions about production and consumption. These activities include taxes, subsidies, and regulation. Different societies make different choices about how much allocation is carried out by government.

7. Redistribution changes the unequal distribution of income that results from the market. Redistribution occurs mainly through taxes and transfer payments, but any action of government will have redistributive effects.

8. Stabilization refers to the activities of government aimed at creating full employment, stable prices, and a satisfactory rate of economic growth. These actions include changes in taxes, transfer payments, and spending as well as changes in the money supply.

9. International trade in goods, services, and factors of production benefits both trading partners. Some workers and firms in a nation experience losses because of foreign competition. The gains usually exceed the losses, but the losers may succeed in persuading the government to restrict trade for their protection.

10. Individuals and nations can gain a higher standard of living with the same resources and technology if they engage in specialization and exchange. Total output will be larger if individuals, regions, and nations produce those goods for which their opportunity costs are lowest and trade for other things. This is the principle of comparative advantage.

New Terms

factors of production
labor
wages
human capital
land
rent
capital
interest

investment
enterprise
profit
market
traditional economy
command economy
market economy
property rights

mixed economy
circular flow model
factor market
product market
allocation
public goods
free riders
positive externalities

negative externalities
public bads
redistribution
stabilization
specialization
principle of comparative advantage

Questions for Discussion

1. Is your college degree an investment in human capital? What is the opportunity cost of your degree?
2. Suppose you own a farm with buildings and machinery, all five members of your family work on the farm, and you take the risks and manage the production. Identify all the factors of production involved and classify them correctly.
3. How are macroeconomic problems handled in a mixed economy?
4. In what ways are factor markets and product markets similar? In what ways are they different?
5. List all the leakages and all the injections you have observed in circular flow diagrams.
6. Which of the following institutions or actions represent tradition, command, or market processes?
    a. the military draft
    b. the volunteer army
    c. encouraging daughters to be teachers and nurses
    d. requiring women to be teachers and nurses
    e. offering financial incentives to anyone who becomes a teacher or nurse
    f. five generations of farmers tilling the same land
    g. prohibiting the sale of marijuana
    h. taxing the sale of alcoholic beverages
7. What should be the role of government in providing education? Should it produce, subsidize, or get out of education altogether? Why do you suppose that education through the twelfth grade is "free" (actually, paid for through taxes) but only subsidized beyond that level? Does it have anything to do with who gets the benefits?
8. Can you find examples of services produced in the public sector in your area that are produced in the private sector elsewhere, or vice versa? Can you explain why the choice might not be the same in different sections of the country or in communities of different sizes?
9. Classify each of the following government actions as primarily allocation, redistribution, or stabilization.
    a. cutting taxes to end a recession
    b. making Social Security payments to the elderly
    c. paying farmers not to produce corn
    d. putting restrictions on the amount of sulphur dioxide factories are allowed to emit into the air
    e. buying paper shredders for government offices
10. Where would you put each of the following items on the spectrum in Figure 5?
    a. hospital wastes that wash up on beaches
    b. noise from a student apartment complex that bothers the neighbors
    c. highways
    d. Christmas decorations that make a house more attractive
    e. flu shots
11. Why is specialization necessary for exchange, and vice versa?
12. Angela and Arthur have been assigned the tasks of filing folders and grading papers. Angela can file 50 folders an hour and grade 20 papers. Arthur can file 25 folders per hour and grade 25 papers. The total output for these two work-study students is to grade 100 papers and file 200 folders. How long will it take if they divide the task equally? How long will it take if they specialize based on the principle of comparative advantage? How much time do they gain?
13. In Question 12, what is Angela's opportunity cost for filing in terms of grading not done? What is Arthur's? How does this information help you to determine comparative advantage?
14. Use the following information on the production of bushels of peaches and tomatoes in two countries, Upland and Downland. Plot a pair of production possibilities curves like those in Figure 6. Before trade, each country is producing 20 bushels of peaches and 30 bushels of tomatoes. Locate their initial production

UPLAND		DOWNLAND	
PEACHES	TOMATOES	PEACHES	TOMATOES
40	0	50	0
30	15	40	10
20	30	30	20
10	45	20	30
0	60	10	40
		0	50

combinations on the graphs. Determine who should specialize in what, locate the production points after specialization, and determine how much the total output will increase.

15. Individuals as well as nations have comparative advantages, which can change. How will going to college and getting a degree change your comparative advantage?

SUGGESTIONS FOR FURTHER READING

Carson, Robert B. *Economic Issues Today: Alternative Approaches,* 5th ed. New York: St. Martin's, 1991. The introduction gives an overview of alternative values and approaches underlying different economic systems.

Hoover, Kenneth, and Raymond Plant . *Conservative Capitalism in Britain and the United States: A Critical Appraisal.* London and New York: Routledge, Chapman and Hall, 1989. Offers a good discussion of the division of responsibilities between the state and the market and the ideological foundations for that choice.

Radford, R. A. "The Economic Organization of a P.O.W. Camp." *Economica* (November 1945): 189–201. This classic article demonstrates how a market economy quickly established itself in a P.O.W. camp during World War II and highlights the gains from exchange.

Wolf, Charles. *Markets or Governments: Choosing Between Imperfect Alternatives.* Cambridge, MA: MIT Press, 1988. Compares market and nonmarket alternatives for various kinds of productive activities.

AFTER STUDYING THIS CHAPTER, YOU SHOULD BE ABLE TO:

1. Define supply and demand and list the factors influencing each.
2. Demonstrate the concepts of supply and demand using:
   a. words,
   b. numbers or functions,
   c. graphs.
3. Identify on a graph the differences between:
   a. changes in demand and changes in the quantity demanded, and
   b. changes in supply and changes in the quantity supplied.
4. Show how changes in the *ceteris paribus* conditions affect demand and supply.
5. Explain how equilibrium is reached, and what disequilibrium and equilibrium mean.
6. Use the supply and demand model to illustrate the concepts of
   a. marginal analysis,
   b. equilibrium,
   c. comparative statics,
   d. endogenous and exogenous variables,
   e. primary and secondary effects.
7. Discuss the functions of prices in a free market.
8. Explain how interference with the market distorts its allocative mechanism.

CHAPTER 3

SUPPLY AND DEMAND: THE BASICS OF ECONOMIC ANALYSIS

INTRODUCTION

Markets are places where buyers and sellers meet to engage in exchange. In the process of exchanging, they determine prices and quantities produced. The supply and demand model explains how buyers and sellers interact to determine prices and quantities. It is the most basic and most widely used model in economics.

Economists view **demand** as the desire and ability to consume certain quantities at various prices over a certain time period. Demand is not seen as needs or wants that can be measured in some social or biological way. The concept of need is reserved for policy makers and political decision making. For needs and wants to be demands, they must be viewed not as wishes or dreams but as what people will actually do when confronted with different sets of prices. Similarly, **supply** refers to what firms are actually willing and able to produce and offer for sale at various prices over a period of time.

demand
The desire and ability to consume certain quantities of a good at various prices over a certain period of time.

supply
The quantity of a good offered for sale at various prices during a certain time period.

DEMAND

Many things affect the demand for a good or service. There is much evidence that price is a very important determinant of demand. Thus, we focus first on what happens when the price of a good or service changes relative to the prices of other goods and services. In looking at the relationship between price and quantity, economists hold constant everything else that affects demand.

69

law of demand
The quantity demanded of a good or service is negatively related to its price, *ceteris paribus*.

The **law of demand** states that the *quantity demanded* of a good or service is negatively related to its price, *ceteris paribus*. In other words, if everything else is held constant, consumers will purchase more of a good or service at a lower price than at a higher price. As price rises, *ceteris paribus*, consumers will purchase less of a good or service, because its opportunity cost in terms of other goods is higher. Note that we are saying quantity demanded—not demand—is a function of price. This distinction is critical. Demand refers to a whole set of price-quantity combinations. Quantity demanded is the amount consumers want to buy at a particular price.

demand schedule
A table that shows quantities demanded at various prices during a specific time period.

A **demand schedule** shows the various quantities demanded at various prices during a specified period of time. How can we generate a demand schedule for an individual? We could develop Mary's demand schedule for potato chips since she knows all of the *ceteris paribus* conditions that apply (tastes, income, prices of substitutes, and so on). We might suggest various prices and ask her how many bags of potato chips she would buy at each price. Actual experiments with a variety of subjects support the validity of the law of demand.

The demand schedule in Table 1 shows Fred's demand for bread. As price falls, Fred chooses to consume larger quantities of bread per week as he substitutes bread for other items he might purchase. Table 1 is consistent with the law of demand because Fred demands larger quantities of bread at lower prices. Note that there is a time dimension—a week. We cannot determine how many loaves Fred will buy without specifying a time frame—per day, per week, per month, per year, or per lifetime.

demand curve
A graph representing a demand schedule and showing the quantity demanded at various prices in a certain time period.

We can represent the demand schedule of Table 1 on a graph called a demand curve, as shown in Figure 1. A **demand curve** is a graph representing a demand schedule. When we draw a demand curve, the vertical axis shows the price per unit and the horizontal axis shows the quantity per time period.[1]

MARKET DEMAND

Table 1 and Figure 1 show a demand schedule and a demand curve for a single consumer. Sellers, however, are more interested in the market demand curve for a brand of bread or even the market demand curve for all

**TABLE 1
FRED'S DEMAND
FOR BREAD**

PRICE PER LOAF (CENTS)	QUANTITY DEMANDED PER WEEK
50	1
40	7
30	13
20	19
10	25
5	28

1. If graphing the schedule is confusing, review the appendix to Chapter 1. We usually draw linear curves for convenience.

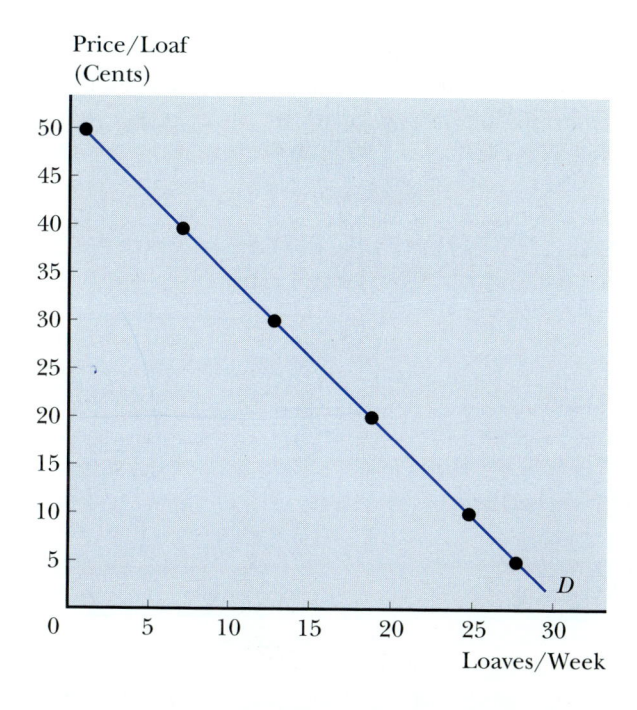

Chapter 3 Supply and Demand: The Basics of Economic Analysis

FIGURE 1
FRED'S DEMAND FOR BREAD
An individual's demand curve shows the quantity that he or she will purchase during a specific period at different prices.

bread. A **market demand curve** shows what quantities will be demanded by all consumers in a certain market at various prices. The market demand curve is the sum of all of the individual demand curves. We add the demand curves for individual consumers horizontally. For example, to determine the market quantity of bread demanded at a price of 40 cents per loaf, we add the 7 loaves demanded by Fred to 2 loaves demanded by Mary, a loaf demanded by Joanna, and so on. We find a total (market) quantity demanded of 10,000 loaves at a price of 40 cents per loaf. These two numbers represent one point on the market demand curve. We then repeat the addition of quantities demanded for every other price. The result is the downward-sloping market demand curve shown in Figure 2, showing a negative relationship between price and quantity. At higher prices, buyers want fewer loaves. At lower prices, they want more.

As price changes in the market, the quantity demanded changes in the opposite direction, just as it did for Fred. Figure 2 shows that 13,000 loaves of bread are purchased at a price of 35 cents per loaf. If the price falls to 20 cents per loaf, the quantity demanded increases to 25,000 loaves. If the price rises to 45 cents per loaf, the quantity demanded decreases to 5,000 loaves.

CETERIS PARIBUS CONDITIONS AND SHIFTS IN DEMAND
Many things can affect the demand for a good or service. Economists generally focus on a few, separated into two important categories: price, and everything else. Because price is so important, economists express demand as a function of price. The price of a good affects the quantity demanded. Everything else affects demand. We held the nonprice determinants of demand constant while we focused on price. Now we want to look at the nonprice determinants and how they affect the demand curve.

market demand curve
The sum of all of the individual demand curves. A market demand curve shows what quantities will be demanded by all consumers in a specific time frame in a certain market at various prices.

**FIGURE 2
MARKET DEMAND FOR
BREAD**
A market demand curve is a graph depicting how much will be purchased in the market at various prices. It is the sum of all of the individual demand curves.

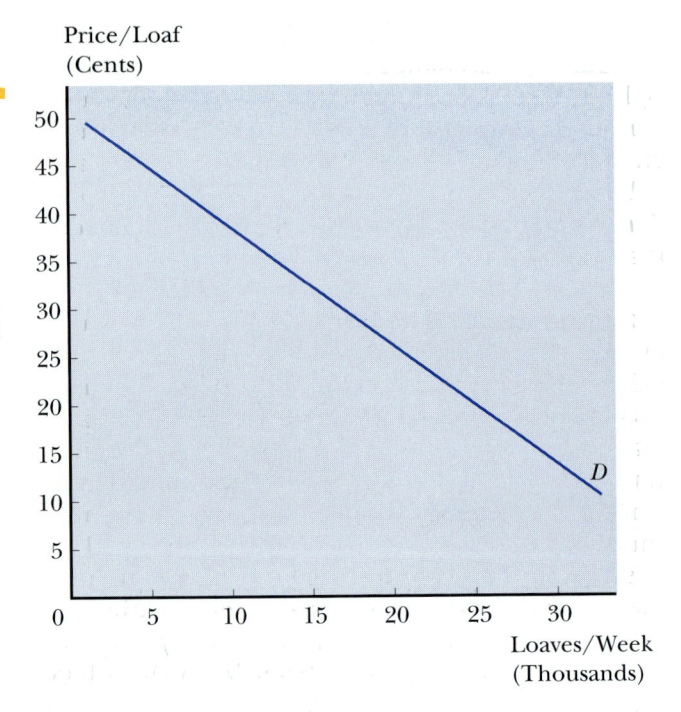

The nonprice determinants of demand are as follows:

1. tastes of the group demanding the good or service,
2. size of the group demanding the good or service,
3. income and wealth of the group demanding the good or service,
4. prices of other goods and services,
5. expectations about future prices or income.

Nearly everything that affects demand does so by working through one of these determinants. Weather, for example, may affect demand for bread by changing tastes. People may eat more cold sandwiches instead of hot meals in warmer weather. Economists study demand by holding all but one of these determinants constant and determining what happens when that one changes. Nonprice determinants of demand are the *ceteris paribus* conditions discussed in Chapter 1.

Changes in the *ceteris paribus* conditions change the demand for the good or service. On the graph, a change in demand is seen as a shift of the curve. Economists are careful to distinguish clearly between movements along a demand curve and changes (or shifts) of the curve itself. Movements along the curve are *changes in quantity demanded*, caused solely by a change in the *price* of the good. When the price of bread goes up, fewer loaves are demanded—a change in quantity demanded. Changes (or shifts) of the curve are *changes in demand* caused by changes in any of the *ceteris paribus* conditions. When the weather gets hot or population increases, more loaves are demanded at every possible price—a change in demand.

TASTES. How do changes in the *ceteris paribus* conditions affect the market demand for a good? Suppose people's tastes change in favor of bread be-

Chapter 3 Supply and Demand: The Basics of Economic Analysis   73

cause the weather is hot or a fad develops for high-fiber diets. As shown in Figure 3, this change in demand shifts the entire demand curve to the right, from D_0 to D_1. An **increase in demand** means that at every price, consumers demand a larger amount than before. The opposite would occur if tastes changed away from bread. Such a change in tastes would cause a decrease in demand, represented by a shift from D_0 to D_2. A **decrease in demand** means that at every price, consumers demand a smaller quantity than before.

SIZE OF THE GROUP. The market demand curve, as you saw earlier, is found by adding the individual demand curves. Thus, if the number of individuals in the group of potential consumers changes, market demand will also change. Suppose demand curve D_0 in Figure 3 represents the demand for automobiles in a state with a minimum driving age of 16 years. If the law is changed to allow 15-year-olds to drive, the group of potential consumers increases. Some of them, or their families, will want an extra car for the extra driver. The demand curve will shift from D_0 to D_1. The size of the group has increased. Therefore, there has been an increase in the demand for the good, or a larger quantity demanded at every price.

On the other hand, if the size of the group decreases, there will be a decrease in demand, a shift from D_0 to D_2 in Figure 3. The big drop in the birth rate in the late 1960s and early 1970s decreased demand first for baby food and diapers and then for public school teachers. In the 1990s, it is affecting demand for automobiles and college teachers.

INCOME AND WEALTH. Income changes can also shift the demand curve. You might expect that demand for all goods would increase as income increases. However, this is not always true. Whether demand increases in this case depends on whether the good is a normal good or an inferior

> **increase in demand**
> A shift in the demand curve indicating that at every price, consumers demand a larger amount than before.
>
> **decrease in demand**
> A shift in the demand curve indicating that at every price, consumers demand a smaller amount than before.

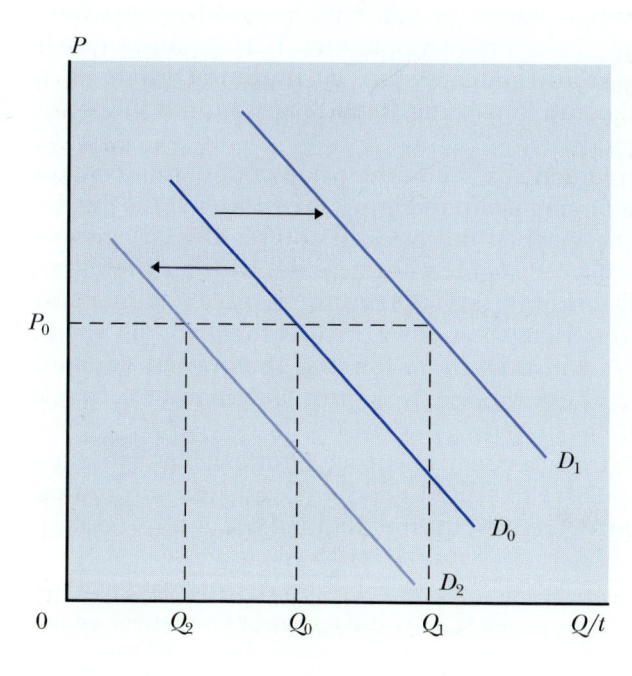

**FIGURE 3
EFFECTS OF CHANGES IN THE CETERIS PARIBUS CONDITIONS ON DEMAND**
If a change causes more of a good to be demanded at every price, the demand curve will shift to the right, as from D_0 to D_1. A change that causes less to be demanded at every price causes a shift to the left, as from D_0 to D_2.

normal good
A good for which demand increases as income increases.

inferior good
A good for which demand decreases as income increases.

good. A **normal good** is a good for which demand increases as income increases, *ceteris paribus*. If demand falls when income rises, the good is an **inferior good**. Most goods are normal goods. However, there are a few inferior goods.

Consider, for example, the difference between steak and hamburger. If, as an individual's income increases, the individual consumes less hamburger and more steak, then hamburger is an inferior good and steak is a normal good. However, meat or beef in general is still considered a normal good.[2] Likewise, a trailer might be considered inferior to a house, but housing in general is a normal good.

For a normal good, an increase in income would cause demand in Figure 3 to shift from D_0 to D_1. For an inferior good, an increase in income would shift demand from D_0 to D_2, as buyers could afford the more expensive substitute. For a normal good, a decrease in income would shift demand from D_0 to D_2 in Figure 3. For an inferior good, a decrease in income would increase demand from D_0 to D_1 as buyers were forced to economize with less appealing goods.

Changes in wealth have the same effect as changes in income. If the value of assets falls, leaving people less wealthy, demand for normal goods will decline. When the stock market crashed in October 1987, many analysts predicted a recession. They expected the decline in wealth to cause consumer spending to decrease. Though there was a decline in wealth, it was not large enough to spark a recession. It did, however, affect the demand for some goods and services.

PRICES OF OTHER GOODS. The fourth nonprice determinant of demand is the prices of other goods and services. There are two classes of other goods: complements and substitutes. **Complementary goods** are goods that are jointly consumed. If consuming two goods together enhances the enjoyment of both, the goods are called complements. Examples are bacon and eggs, lamps and light bulbs, or hamburgers and ketchup. Substitute goods have the opposite relationship. Rather than enhancing each other's consumption, **substitute goods** replace each other. Orange juice and grapefruit juice, Coke and Pepsi, and Reebok and Adidas shoes are examples of substitute goods.

complementary goods
Goods that are jointly consumed. The consumption of one enhances the consumption of the other.

substitute goods
Goods that can be interchanged. The consumption of one replaces the consumption of the other.

If two goods are complements, a rise in the price of one will decrease demand for the other. Referring again to Figure 3, consider D_0 as the demand curve for good x (bagels). If the price of complementary good y (lox) goes up, the demand for bagels will decrease, shifting the curve from D_0 to D_2. Buyers will consume less lox because its price is higher and will thus would demand fewer bagels at every price. If the price of lox fell, consumers would want to consume more lox and thus would demand more bagels to go with it at every price. In Figure 3, demand for bagels would shift from D_0 to D_1.

If two goods are substitutes, a rise in the price of one will increase demand for the other. Good x (Coke) and good y (Pepsi) are substitutes. Suppose curve D_0 in Figure 3 represents the demand for good x (Coke).

---

2. A good example of an inferior good is an outhouse. As a community's income rises, the demand for outhouses decreases. In the United States, outhouses have almost become extinct.

Chapter 3 Supply and Demand: The Basics of Economic Analysis

The price of good y (Pepsi) increases relative to the price of Coke. Since this makes the opportunity cost of Coke lower, consumers will demand more Coke at every price. The demand for Coke shifts from D_0 to D_1 in Figure 3. If the price of Pepsi decreased relative to the price of Coke, the opposite would happen. The opportunity cost of Coke would be higher, and consumers would demand less of it at every price as they shifted consumption to Pepsi. The decrease in demand for Coke is shown by a shift from D_0 to D_2 in Figure 3. The shift to substitutes as price rises means that the quantity demanded of the good falls, exactly as predicted by the law of demand.

In a broad sense, all goods are substitutes for each other because they are all alternatives on which people can spend income. Some goods are closer substitutes than others, however. The more easily that good A can be substituted for good B, the more a change in the price of one will affect the demand curve for the other. A rise in the price of watches, for example, would have much less impact on the demand for hot dogs than on the demand for clocks, bracelets, or other substitutes.

People often make the error of assuming a good has no satisfactory substitutes. How often have you heard someone say, "There is no substitute for victory (or success, steak, a new car...)." In fact, there are substitutes for anything. If the price rises sharply enough, consumers will start searching harder for acceptable substitutes.[3]

REASONS FOR A CHANGE IN THE QUANTITY DEMANDED

- The quantity demanded will *increase* if the price of the good or service *decreases*.
- The quantity will *decrease* if the price of the good or service *increases*.

REASONS FOR A CHANGE IN DEMAND

- The demand for a normal good or service will *increase* if:
  buyers' tastes change to favor that good or service,
  the number of buyers in the market increases,
  the income or wealth of buyers increases,
  the prices of complementary goods fall,
  the prices of substitute goods increase, or
  buyers' expectations for the future cause them to purchase more now.

- The demand for a normal good or service will *decrease* if:
  buyers' tastes change against that good or service,
  the number of buyers in the market decreases,
  the income or wealth of buyers decreases,
  the prices of complementary goods increase,
  the prices of substitute goods decrease, or
  buyers' expectations of the future cause them to delay purchases.

---

3. This point often makes economists seem cynical. Does honesty have a substitute? Yes. If the price becomes too high, many people (but not all) will become dishonest.

expectations
Feelings that individuals have about future conditions.

EXPECTATIONS. The last *ceteris paribus* condition that affects demand is **expectations**. If individuals expect anything important to change in the future, they may take action now that they would otherwise postpone. For example, if you expect that the demand for automobiles will be so high next year that their prices will rise, you may decide to buy a car now to avoid paying a higher price. If you expect your income to be higher in the future, you may demand more goods and borrow to pay for them so that you do not have to delay consumption until your income actually rises.

SUPPLY

supply schedule
A table that shows quantities offered for sale at various prices over a particular time period.

A **supply schedule** shows the quantities offered for sale at various prices during a specific period of time. Price is the primary determinant of quantity supplied.

THE (NOT QUITE) LAW OF SUPPLY

(not quite) law of supply
The quantity supplied of a good or service is usually a positive function of price, *ceteris paribus*.

Assume everything else is held constant but the price of the good or service. We can then state the **(not quite) law of supply** as follows: the *quantity supplied* of a good or service is *usually* a positive function of price, *ceteris paribus*.

With all else held constant, suppliers usually will supply less of a good or service at lower prices. As prices rise, the quantity supplied will increase, because it becomes more profitable to produce and sell the good. It is important to note that quantity supplied is a function of price. Note also the word *usually*. This is not quite a law because of two exceptions to this relationship. The first is when there is no time to produce more units (for example, theater seats at a sold-out performance) or when a unique supplier no longer exists (for example, paintings by Picasso). In these unusual cases, quantity supplied does not respond to price at all. The second exception occurs for certain products for which increased volume allows costs per unit to fall. For example, as a utility company increases its output of electricity, its costs per unit typically fall. These lower costs may be passed on to customers in the form of lower prices.

Table 2 shows a hypothetical supply schedule for an individual supplier—Susan's Lemonade Stand. A supply schedule shows the quantities supplied during a period of time at various prices. Like a demand schedule, a supply schedule includes a time frame—in this case, a day. Table 2 is consistent with the law of supply because Susan supplies larger quanti-

TABLE 2
SUSAN'S SUPPLY OF LEMONADE

PRICE PER GLASS (CENTS)	QUANTITY SUPPLIED PER DAY
5	0
10	5
15	10
20	15
25	20
30	25

ties of lemonade at higher prices. The supply schedule of Table 2 can be drawn on a graph as shown in Figure 4. This **supply curve** is a diagram showing the quantity supplied in a particular time and at various prices. It shows a positive relationship—more will be offered for sale at higher prices. Price per unit is on the y-axis, and quantity per time period is on the x-axis, just as it was for the demand curve. Supply curves usually have a positive y-intercept, indicating that at some low price, suppliers may offer none of the good.

supply curve
A graph representing a supply schedule and showing the quantities supplied at various prices in a certain time period.

MARKET SUPPLY

The **market supply curve** is the sum of all of the individual supply schedules. Figure 5 is a market supply curve for lemonade, showing the total quantity supplied over a period of time at various prices. As price changes in the market, quantity supplied changes in the same direction. Figure 5 shows that 5,000 glasses of lemonade are supplied at a price of 10 cents per glass. If price falls to 5 cents per glass, quantity supplied decreases to zero glasses. If price rises to 20 cents per glass, quantity supplied increases to 15,000 glasses. These changes occur because most producers are willing to sell more units if the price rises enough to cover the added costs of production.

market supply curve
The sum of all of the individual supply curves. A market supply curve shows what quantities will be supplied by all firms at various prices during a specific time period.

CHANGES IN SUPPLY AND THE *CETERIS PARIBUS* CONDITIONS

A supply curve is drawn to show a relationship between price and quantity supplied, with everything else held constant. A change in one of the *ceteris paribus* conditions will cause the entire supply curve to shift. The most important of these are as follows:

1. the state of technology,
2. prices of the factors of production,
3. the number of suppliers,
4. expectations about the future,
5. prices of related goods.

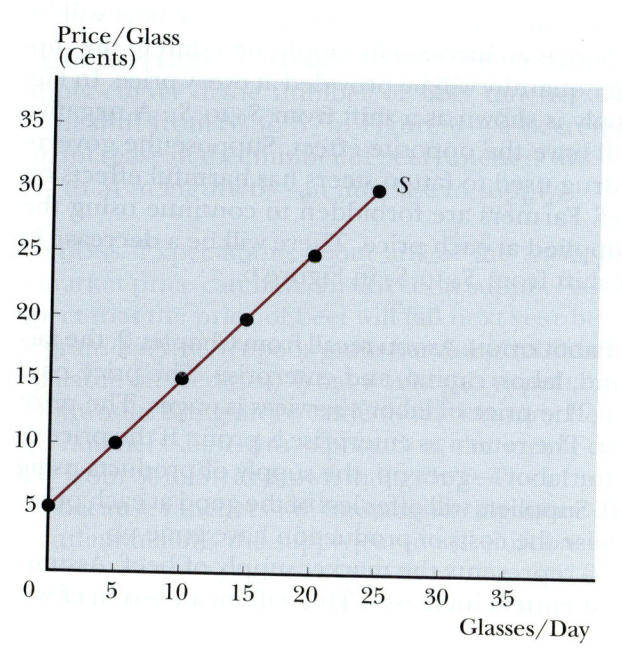

FIGURE 4
SUSAN'S SUPPLY OF LEMONADE
A supply curve for an individual (or firm) shows how much of a good will be offered for sale at various prices.

PRICES OF RELATED GOODS. Changes in the prices of other goods can affect supply. If the price of a good that uses a similar production technique increases, a firm may switch production. A farmer may switch from corn to wheat when the price of corn increases relative to the price of wheat. A sewing factory might switch from men's shirts to babies' nightwear if the price of men's shirts fell and the price of babies' nightwear rose.

> ### REASONS FOR A CHANGE IN THE QUANTITY SUPPLIED
>
> - The quantity supplied will *increase* if the price of the good or service *increases*.
> - The quantity supplied will *decrease* if the price of the good or service *decreases*.
>
> ### REASONS FOR A CHANGE IN SUPPLY
>
> - The supply of a good or service will *increase* if:
>   new technology allows the good or service to be produced at lower cost,
>   the prices of the factors of production decrease,
>   the number of suppliers increases,
>   the prices of other goods or services that can be produced with the same resources decrease, or
>   suppliers' expectations for the future cause them to produce more now.
> - The supply of a good or service will *decrease* if:
>   the prices of the factors of production increase,
>   the number of suppliers decreases,
>   the prices of other goods or services that can be produced with the same resources increase, or
>   suppliers' expectations for the future cause them to produce less now.

MARKET EQUILIBRIUM

market equilibrium
A point at which quantity demanded by consumers is equal to quantity supplied by producers. The price at which this occurs is the equilibrium price, or market-clearing price.

market-clearing price
The equilibrium price, which clears the market because there are no frustrated consumers or suppliers.

disequilibrium
An unstable situation in which variables are moving toward equilibrium but are not yet at equilibrium.

We can combine market supply and market demand schedules to determine the market equilibrium. **Market equilibrium** occurs at that price for which quantity demanded by consumers is equal to quantity supplied by producers. This equilibrium price is also called the **market-clearing price**.

EQUILIBRIUM AND DISEQUILIBRIUM

In Table 3, at a price of $2, suppliers *want* to supply 4 million pounds of coffee, and consumers *want* to purchase 8 million pounds. A price of $2 is not an equilibrium price because quantity demanded exceeds quantity supplied by 4 million pounds at that price. This situation is one of **disequilibrium**, in which variables are moving toward equilibrium but are not yet there. This is an unstable position. Some consumers will not be able to purchase the amount they desire at a price of $2. As they shop for coffee, they will offer a higher price. As the price rises, quantity supplied will rise, and quantity demanded will fall. This process will continue until the price reaches $3. At $3, the amount consumers wish to purchase is exactly equal to the amount suppliers wish to sell. This quantity is the equilibrium quan-

International Perspective

Adding Foreign Demand and Supply

The number of suppliers and the number of buyers can shift the supply and demand curves, respectively. Sometimes the suppliers are offering imported goods, and sometimes the buyers live in foreign countries.

In an open economy, the market demand curve faced by producers is the sum of the domestic demand for the product and the foreign demand for the product. Consider the market demand for American corn. If there were no foreign demand, the market price would settle at P_d, and corn producers would sell Q tons of corn. (See the graph titled "Foreign Demand for Corn.") When foreign demand, D_f, is added, the price rises to P_{d+f}, and the amount sold rises to Q_{d+f}. The price of corn and the amount of corn sold have both increased. Consumers in the domestic market are paying a higher price because they now pay P_{d+f}. Since the domestic demand curve has not shifted and the price has increased, the quantity of corn demanded by domestic consumers will fall. In this example, domestic consumption falls to Q_d.

It appears that domestic corn producers have gained at the expense of domestic corn consumers. After all, consumers now pay a higher price for less corn. This conclusion is correct, but it ignores the other side of the coin. Foreign consumers can only buy the corn if they sell something that earns the currency necessary to pay for the corn. The domestic supply of the product that foreigners sell to pay for the corn will have an effect in other markets.

The graph titled "Foreign Supply of Automobiles" shows the U.S. market for automobiles. Without a foreign supply, the domestic price and quantity would be P_d and Q_d. Adding foreign supply, S_f, changes the equilibrium. There is a decline in price to P_{d+f} and an increase in quantity demanded to Q_{d+f}. In this case, the domestic consumption of automobiles increased by $Q_{d+f} - Q_d$. Domestic consumers can purchase more automobiles at a lower price.

There is an important lesson in this example of supply and demand in an open economy. Relative to a no-trading situation, the opening of foreign trade will result in higher prices and less consumption of exported items and lower prices and more consumption of imported items. So there are winners and losers as a result of international trade. But, as you learned in Chapter 2, the principle of comparative advantage shows that the net effect of trade is an expansion of choices and an increase in total consumption for consumers in the domestic market.

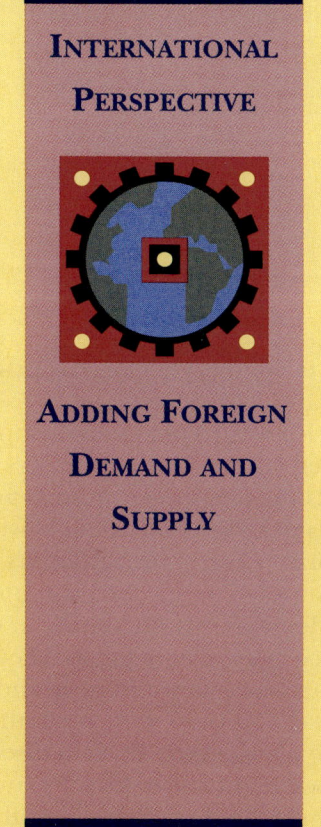

Foreign Demand for Corn

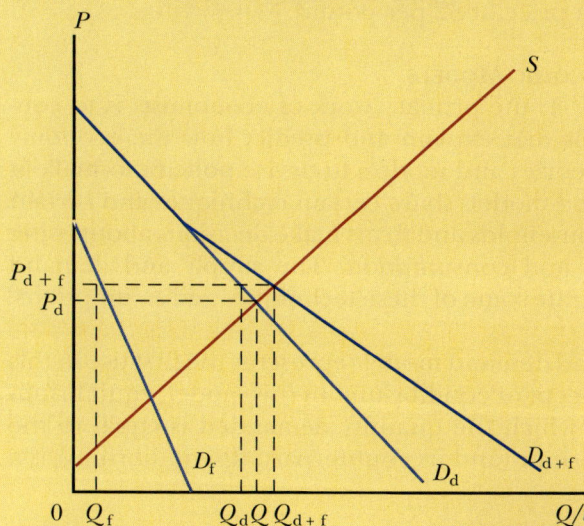

Foreign Supply of Automobiles

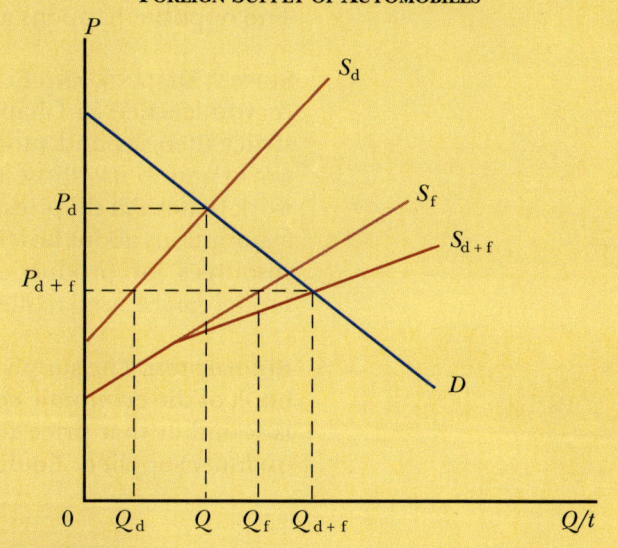

TABLE 3
SUPPLY OF AND DEMAND FOR COFFEE

PRICE PER POUND (DOLLARS)	POUNDS SUPPLIED PER MONTH	POUNDS DEMANDED PER MONTH	DIFFERENCE
1	2 million	10 million	8 million excess quantity demanded
2	4 million	8 million	4 million excess quantity demanded
3	6 million	6 million	equilibrium
4	8 million	4 million	4 million excess quantity supplied
5	10 million	2 million	8 million excess quantity supplied

tity, and $3 is the market-clearing price, because there is no tendency for price or quantity to change.

If the price was $4 per pound, suppliers would offer 8 million pounds of coffee per month, but consumers would only wish to purchase 4 million pounds. At this price, there is an excess quantity supplied of 4 million pounds per month. Suppliers with unsold coffee will accept a lower price. As price falls, some suppliers reduce their output (a movement along the supply curve), and some consumers buy more (a movement along the demand curve) until the equilibrium price of $3 is reached. This $3 price again clears the market.

Note that the equilibrium price and quantity do not simply represent the point where the amount sold equals the amount bought. Quantities bought and sold are *always* equal, even in disequilibrium. Four million pounds per month were bought and sold at $2 and at $4. Equilibrium occurs at a price for which the quantity supplied and the quantity demanded are equal.

Figure 7 shows market supply and market demand curves for coffee, based on the supply and demand schedules in Table 3. The equilibrium price is $3, and 6 million pounds per month are sold at equilibrium. At $4, there is an excess quantity supplied, and price will fall. This causes the quantity demanded to increase and the quantity supplied to decrease. The opposite happens at a price of $2 per pound.

SUPPLY, DEMAND, AND ECONOMIC MODELS

As you learned in Chapter 1, the primary work of economists is to construct theories and models that explain and predict how the economy works and to use those theories and models to devise policies to make it work better. All theories and models share certain techniques and certain assumptions about how households and firms make decisions about using resources for production and consumption. The supply and demand model can be used to illustrate some of these techniques and assumptions.

EQUILIBRIUM. The supply and demand model represents the first use in this book of the economic concept of equilibrium. In this model, equilibrium is found at that price for which the quantity demanded is equal to the quantity supplied. Equilibrium (and its counterpart, disequilibrium) is a

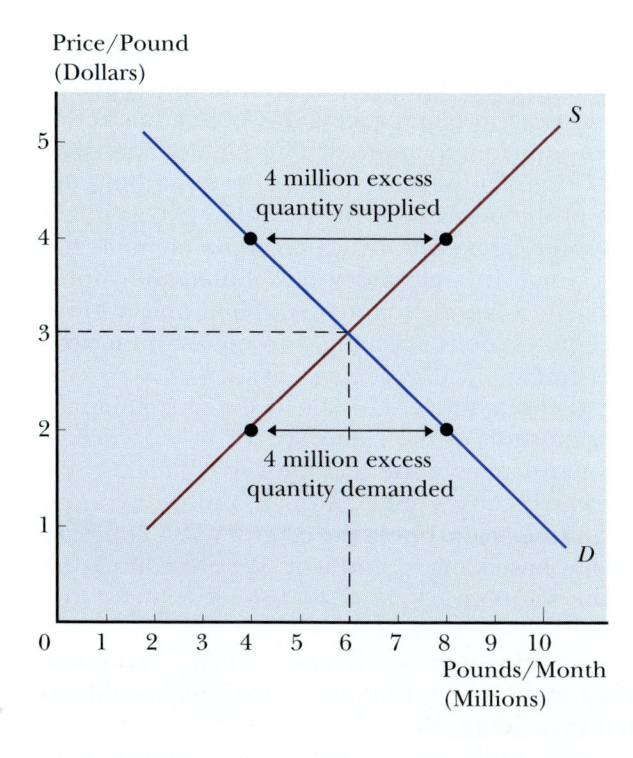

Chapter 3 Supply and Demand: The Basics of Economic Analysis

FIGURE 7
SUPPLY OF AND DEMAND FOR COFFEE
At equilibrium, the amount consumers wish to purchase is equal to the amount suppliers wish to sell. The price established at equilibrium is called the market-clearing price. At prices above the market-clearing price, quantity supplied exceeds quantity demanded. At prices below the market-clearing price, quantity demanded exceeds quantity supplied.

term that you will encounter often. This book will discuss equilibrium prices, equilibrium quantities, equilibrium levels of employment, equilibrium levels of gross national product (GNP), and so forth. Almost every economic model includes a definition of equilibrium. If the model has an equilibrium position, it will have a set of forces that can change that position. In the supply and demand model, these forces are called supply shifters and demand shifters. There are also forces that move an economy toward a new equilibrium position. In the supply and demand model, sellers' and buyers' responses to price changes will move the economy toward a new equilibrium.

Economists' notion of equilibrium is borrowed from the physical sciences. A system is in equilibrium when it is at rest or when it is moving at a constant rate in the same direction. That is, all the forces acting on the system are in balance, and there is no tendency to change. Equilibrium carries no sense of being good or bad, desirable or undesirable. In economics (as in physics or chemistry), if a system is left alone, equilibrium is where it will come to rest. Disequilibrium is a state in which the variables are moving away from old equilibrium values and toward new equilibrium values but have not yet arrived there. If the supply curve has shifted to the right but the demand curve is unchanged, there is a surplus at the old price. This situation is a disequilibrium. A surplus means that the quantity supplied is greater than the quantity demanded at the current price. Market forces are putting downward pressure on the price in order to move to a new equilibrium. If the price was too low for equilibrium to exist, there would be a shortage. Quantity demanded would exceed quantity supplied, and there would be upward pressure on the price.

COMPARATIVE STATICS. When a supply curve or a demand curve shifts, the diagram always identifies the original equilibrium and the new equilibrium. Economists are able to describe the process by which a market or economy moves from one equilibrium to another. This kind of analysis is called **comparative statics**. Comparative statics begins by describing the initial equilibrium position of the market (or the economy). This initial state is then compared to some later state in which some element has changed. For example, a change in technology has shifted the supply curve to the right, resulting in a larger quantity supplied and a lower price. That is, comparative statics looks at changes in equilibrium positions between two different times.

Another way of looking at comparative statics is to see such an analysis as a comparison of two snapshots of the economy (or of a particular market). We take a snapshot and analyze the relationships that exist. We then change one variable, which causes the economy to move to a new equilibrium. Next, we take another snapshot of the economy. We compare the two snapshots to see what has changed and why. We are comparing static (frozen) pictures of the economy.

> **comparative statics**
> A technique of comparing two equilibrium positions to determine the changing relationships between variables.

MARGINAL ANALYSIS. Supply and demand is just one of many economic models that involve **marginal analysis**, a technique for analyzing problems by examining the results of small changes.

Marginal refers to the extra, additional, or next unit of output, consumption, or any other measurable quantity that can be increased or decreased by incremental amounts. The concept of the margin is central to economic analysis, although it is probably new to you. Most economic decisions are made at the margin: Should I consume the extra slice of pizza or work the extra hour? Should we produce the extra unit or take on a new client at our accounting firm? These kinds of daily decisions made by households and firms determine prices, output, and other important economic quantities. In the supply and demand model, the supply curve reflects the decisions of suppliers to offer extra or additional (marginal) units for sale at higher prices. The demand curve reflects the decisions of buyers to purchase extra or additional (marginal) units at lower prices. When the price of a good falls, consumers decide at the margin whether to substitute a little more of that good for other goods whose prices have not changed.

> **marginal analysis**
> A technique for analyzing problems by examining the results of small changes.

ENDOGENOUS AND EXOGENOUS VARIABLES. All economic models contain variables. Variables that a model attempts to explain or determine are called **endogenous variables**. Variables that have an impact on the endogenous variables but are themselves determined outside the model are called **exogenous variables**. In mathematics (and sometimes in economics), these are referred to as dependent and independent variables, respectively.

In the supply and demand model, both price and quantity are endogenous variables that affect one another and are determined by the model. For example, the price of oranges is endogenous to this model. Some of the other variables in a supply and demand model are exogenous. For example, in the market for oranges, the weather in Florida is an exogenous variable. The weather affects the price of oranges, but the price of oranges does not affect the weather.

> **endogenous variables**
> Variables that are explained or determined within a model.
>
> **exogenous variables**
> Variables that are determined outside of a model and affect endogenous variables.

In the supply and demand model, the exogenous variables are the nonprice determinants that cause the position of the supply or demand curve to change. These determinants are technology, tastes, number of suppliers, income, prices of related goods, and so forth. Most economic models concentrate on just one or two endogenous (or dependent) variables and explain them by the behavior of a larger number of exogenous (or independent) variables.

PRIMARY AND SECONDARY EFFECTS. Economists often analyze the effect of a change in one variable on other related variables. The **primary effect** is the dominant effect they seek to analyze. For instance, the demand curve shows how doubling the price of oranges would affect the quantity of oranges consumed. But there are also **secondary effects** in related markets. These effects may not be immediately apparent and may take time to work through the economy. For example, if the price of oranges doubled, the sales of cranberry juice might increase, or the consumption of bacon and eggs might decrease. These are related goods whose demand depends on the price of oranges (or orange juice). Such changes would not be as obvious or as immediately apparent as the primary effect.

primary effect
The dominant or immediate effect of a change in an economic variable.

secondary effects
Effects indirectly related to the immediate effect, often smaller and felt after some time.

A THEORY OF PRICE FORMATION

The law of demand and the (not quite) law of supply support a very powerful theory of how markets work to set and change prices. That theory is based on two propositions. The first is that quantity demanded is negatively related to price. The second is that quantity supplied is positively related to price. When these two propositions are combined, they imply several things:

1. When the quantity demanded exceeds the quantity supplied, ($Q_d > Q_s$), price will rise.
2. When the quantity demanded is less than the quantity supplied, ($Q_d < Q_s$), price will fall.
3. When the quantity demanded equals the quantity supplied, ($Q_d = Q_s$), price is at equilibrium.

This theory, combined with the possible shifts in *ceteris paribus* conditions, produces all of the basic elements of a model of how prices (and quantities) are determined in a market system.

CHANGES IN DEMAND AND SUPPLY

When changes occur in any of the *ceteris paribus* conditions that affect demand, the model can be used to trace the effect on market equilibrium. Assume first that there is an increase in demand, that is, an outward shift of the entire curve. This increase in demand could be a result of a change in any of the *ceteris paribus* conditions. It could result from an increase in income (for a normal good), a change in tastes in favor of the good, an increase in the price of a substitute or a decrease in the price of a complement, an increase in the size of the consuming group, or a change in expectations. The increase in demand is shown as an outward shift in the demand curve from D_0 to D_1 in Figure 8. The equilibrium price rises from

P_e to P_1, and the price increase causes quantity supplied to increase to Q_1. Consumers demand a larger quantity of the good at every price than before the shift of the curve.

Now consider a decrease in demand. A decrease in demand means that consumers will demand less of a good at every price. This decrease could result from a fall in income, a change in tastes away from the good, a decrease in the price of a substitute or an increase in the price of a complement, a decrease in group size, or a change in expectations. The decrease in demand is shown as an inward shift in the demand curve from D_0 to D_2 in Figure 8. The decrease in demand causes equilibrium price to fall from P_0 to P_2, and quantity supplied responds by falling from Q_0 to Q_2.

Changes in any condition that affects supply will shift the supply curve. An increase in supply could result from an advance in technology, a decrease in the price of a factor of production, an increase in the number of suppliers, or a change in expectations. The increase in supply appears on a graph as a rightward shift of the supply curve, from S_0 to S_1 in Figure 9. This increase in supply would cause the equilibrium price to fall from P_0 to P_1, leading to an increase in the quantity demanded from Q_0 to Q_1.

A decrease in supply could result from an increase in the price of a factor of production, a decrease in the number of suppliers, or a change in expectations. A decrease in supply is shown as a leftward shift from S_0 to S_2 in Figure 9. This decrease in supply causes the equilibrium price to rise from P_0 to P_2, causing quantity demanded to decrease from Q_0 to Q_2.

The supply and demand model is very useful in analyzing a variety of economic problems and issues. As you apply this model, keep in mind the difference between changes in demand and supply (that is, shifts in the positions of the curves) and changes in the quantity demanded and quan-

FIGURE 8
CHANGES IN DEMAND
An increase in demand from D_0 to D_1 causes the equilibrium price to rise from P_0 to P_1 and the quantity supplied to increase from Q_0 to Q_1. A decrease in demand from D_0 to D_2 causes the equilibrium price to fall from P_0 to P_2 and the quantity supplied to fall from Q_0 to Q_2.

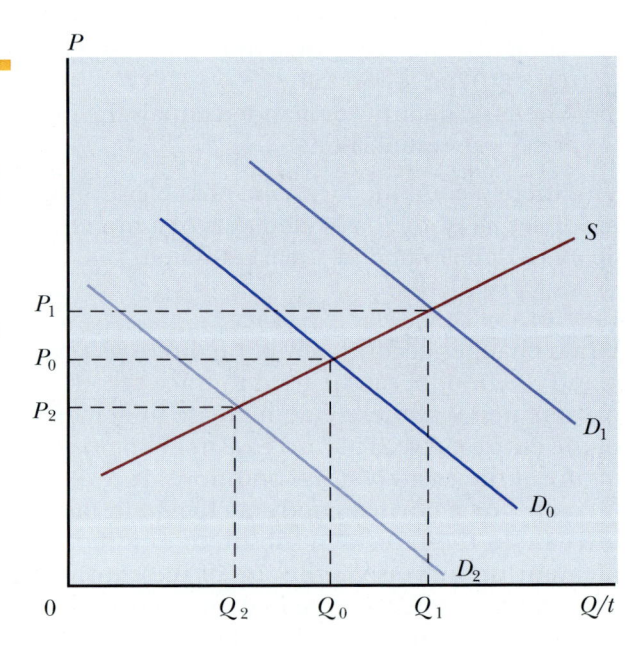

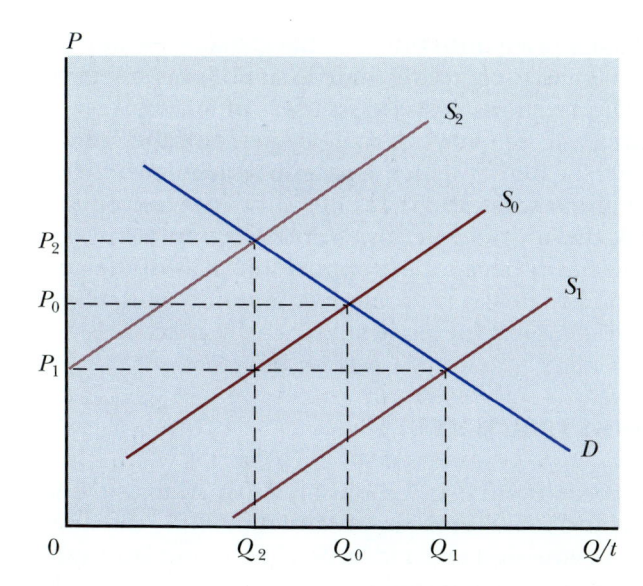

Chapter 3 Supply and Demand: The Basics of Economic Analysis

FIGURE 9
CHANGES IN SUPPLY
An increase in supply from S_0 to S_1 causes the equilibrium price to fall from P_0 to P_1 and the quantity demanded to increase from Q_0 to Q_1. A decrease in supply from S_0 to S_2 causes the equilibrium price to rise from P_0 to P_2 and the quantity demanded to fall from Q_0 to Q_2.

tity supplied (that is, movements along the curves). The importance of this difference will become very clear as you attempt to untangle situations that involve several changes in *ceteris paribus* conditions.[4]

ARE PRICES FAIR?

The analysis of supply and demand presented in this chapter has been positive rather than normative. No mention has been made of what constitutes a fair or just price. Nor has there been any comment as to whether certain minimal levels of consumption of certain goods are necessary for a fair society. Supply and demand theory predicts how an increase in demand for a good will affect price and quantity. A higher price may mean that some people can no longer afford the item, regardless of how "necessary" or "basic" it may appear to be. The supply and demand model offers no moral evaluation of what prices should be.

DIFFERENT PRICES FOR DIFFERENT BUYERS

A second adjustment to the supply and demand model is the observation that, in reality, people often pay different prices for the same good. In the supply and demand model, the equilibrium price is a single, unique price that is paid by all buyers and received by all sellers. There may be different prices for different buyers and sellers because of transactions costs. **Transactions costs** are costs associated with gathering information about markets (prices and quantities supplied) for consuming or producing. Organizing, negotiating, and searching take time and involve opportunity costs. Firms are organized to reduce transactions costs on the producing side. For consumers, the existence of transactions costs means that different people pay different prices for the same good or service.

transactions costs
Costs associated with gathering information about markets (prices and quantities supplied) for consuming or producing.

---

4. To test yourself, work through these shifts. Determine the effect that changes in supply and demand have on price and quantity. For example, ask yourself: What is the effect on equilibrium of an increase in demand coupled with a decrease in supply?

A familiar example of such price differences is that gas stations next to expressways charge higher prices for gasoline than do stations farther away from expressways. Why? Transactions costs. Most users of an expressway are unfamiliar with the area and are in a hurry. They perceive the cost of searching for a lower price to be higher than the potential saving produced by such searching. Think about what gas prices might be in a retirement community. Do you think there would be lower and more uniform gas prices in a retirement community because the opportunity cost of the customers' time is lower? If you live near a retirement community, you might want to check on the prices charged for gasoline in nearby areas.

EVALUATING THE MARKET PROCESS

In Chapter 2, you saw that each and every economy must address three basic questions: what, how and for whom? Supply and demand—the market process—provide important signals to inform, direct, and motivate economic agents in answering these questions.

FUNCTIONS OF PRICES

Prices play a central role in a market system in allocating scarce resources and answering the basic economic questions. The primary functions of prices are to inform, direct, and motivate consumers and business firms.

INFORMING. Market prices condense a great deal of complex information into a simple form. This condensed information is useful to consumers and producers in making decisions. An increase in demand causes a market price to rise. The supplier of a product does not have to know what caused demand to change. All suppliers need to know is that the price has risen. They will respond by increasing the quantity supplied. Likewise, consumers do not need to understand anything about the production process or the associated costs. All they need to know is the market price. If the price rises, consumers decrease the quantity demanded. The market price, then, provides all participants in the market with up-to-the-minute information on the relative scarcity of goods.

DIRECTING. Market participants act on price information. If suppliers are bringing too much of a good to market, its price will fall. The decisions of consumers and producers will move the market to a new equilibrium. Market prices will signal for an increase in the production of those products of which consumers are demanding more. Firms will produce these goods by bringing resources together in a way directed by the market prices of those resources. All of this takes place without any individual or group of individuals telling consumers and entrepreneurs how or why to act. All of the necessary information is found in market prices.

MOTIVATING. The *for whom* question is also a reminder that price is a powerful motivator. Supply and demand establish a reward structure for owners and users of productive resources. Households and firms will seek to produce those goods or develop those skills that are highly desired by oth-

International Perspective

Emerging Markets in Eastern Europe

When the Berlin Wall was opened in the fall of 1989, writer Gloria Steinem observed that it was a very peaceful revolution. There was no violence, and everyone went shopping. In fact, the East Germans were hungry for markets, especially supermarkets and large department stores stocked with many kinds of goods. All of the nations of Eastern Europe are scrambling to relearn how markets work as they attempt to decentralize their economies, restore incentives, and obtain a greater variety of consumer goods for their citizens.

Some of the first foreign entrepreneurs attempting to become a part of the emerging markets in Eastern Europe have found the going rough. They were accustomed to working in a network of suppliers rather than interacting with government factories and collective farms to obtain their materials. McDonald's opened its first restaurant in Moscow after hurdling numerous obstacles in obtaining ingredients for its food products and materials for constructing the building. Finding workers, however, was not difficult. With meat always in short supply, prospective workers were attracted as much by the free meals as by the wages.

In spite of years of central planning, however, the market has shown a remarkable resiliency in some of the nations of Eastern Europe, where central planning has only dominated economic activity since the end of World War II. A black market—an illegal market, mostly for foreign goods and foreign currencies—has operated in these nations for the entire period. Even in the Soviet Union, some people working on collective farms were allowed to have private plots as well and to sell the output of those plots in a free market. A significant part of Soviet farm output came from those private plots, because the incentives to work hard and produce more were stronger when the workers could capture the benefits.

Private restaurants and retail shops have been quickly revived, along with farmers' markets and even one private, foreign-owned hotel in Moscow. The process of restoring the use of markets in production of manufactured goods will be slower, but the nations of Eastern Europe see markets—decentralized, efficient, with strong incentives—as their best hope for a higher standard of living in the future.

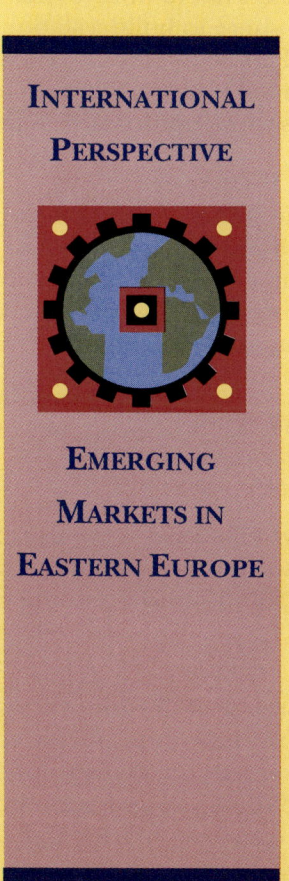

ers, in order to earn rewards in the form of higher incomes. All of this happens without any government agency or central planning bureau telling people what to do. No one has to tell a gas station owner when to be open or where to build a station, or a bright young person to invest in education. People pursue certain activities because they perceive it to be in their own self-interest. This whole process of self-interested response to incentives is what Adam Smith referred to as the **invisible hand**.[5]

invisible hand
The idea advanced by Adam Smith that individuals pursuing their own self-interest direct the market system toward socially desirable outcomes.

ALLOCATIVE EFFICIENCY

According to Adam Smith, the invisible hand informs, directs, and motivates the self-interest of market participants. Suppliers are motivated to guide resources into the production of the goods most wanted by consumers and to produce those goods with the most efficient methods and resource combinations possible. In the words of Nobel Laureate George Stigler,

...an economic actor on average knows better the environment in which he is acting and the probable consequences of his actions than an outsider, no matter how clever the outsider may be.[6]

allocative efficiency
The use of resources to produce the goods most desired by society. Free markets allow allocative efficiency.

Allocative efficiency is the use of resources to produce the goods most desired by society. It is the reason why most economists look to the market first for solutions to economic problems.

FREEDOM

Finally, an important result of a market system is that individuals enjoy a great deal of freedom to pursue their own self-interest. In a market system, the production and distribution of goods and services take place on a basis of voluntary cooperation in the pursuit of individual self-interest. Nobel Laureate Milton Friedman, like Stigler a champion of the market system, describes this advantage in these terms:

So long as effective freedom of exchange is maintained, the central feature of the market organization of economic activity is that it prevents one person from interfering with another in respect to most of his activities. The consumer is protected from coercion by the seller because of the presence of other sellers with whom he can deal. The seller is protected from coercion by the consumer because of other consumers to whom he can sell. The employee is protected from coercion by the employer because of other employers for whom he can work, and so on. And the market does this impersonally and without centralized authority.[7]

NONMARKET ALLOCATION AND THE SHORTCOMINGS OF MARKETS

Although the market is a highly efficient way to allocate resources, it does have some drawbacks, as we observed in Chapter 2. Some of those drawbacks include failure to provide public goods or to correct negative external effects, instability, and inequality in the distribution of income. Markets perform poorly when there is a lack of competition. The above

---

5. See the profile of Adam Smith in Chapter 2.
6. George J. Stigler, "Economists and Public Policy," *Regulation* (May/June 1982): 16.
7. Milton Friedman, *Capitalism and Freedom* (Chicago: University of Chicago Press, 1981): 14–15.

quotation from Friedman does not apply when monopolies interfere with freedom of choice. Often the failings of the market lead to government intervention, resulting in a mixed economy rather than a pure market economy.

Critics of the market system range from those who would replace it with central direction to those with a more middle-of-the-road approach. The latter see a variety of ways of dividing responsibilities between markets and government. If prices are not allowed to direct resources in certain situations, some other mechanism must be developed for their allocation. Government directives, waiting in line, or appeals to "good behavior" are possible allocative mechanisms. The benefits of government intervention must be weighed against the very strong advantages of markets in terms of efficiency and flexibility. The following examples suggest some areas where government intervention has reduced the efficiency of resource allocation.

TAXI FARES. One well-known example of a problem created by intervention in the market is poor taxi service in New York City. The Taxi and Limousine Commission allowed only 11,787 cabs to operate there in 1987. Because the medallions (permits) required to operate a cab were so scarce, owners paid up to $100,000 per medallion. There are a few "gypsy" cabs in New York, but the supply is limited because these drivers face severe penalties if caught operating without the required medallion. Other cities, such as Washington, D.C., allow a large number of cabs to operate and charge a relatively minimal fee for a permit. Both cities regulate the fares that cab drivers can charge, with a fixed price per mile plus a charge for standing time.

At peak traffic hours, it is difficult to get around in New York. Therefore, many cab drivers avoid working during these periods, making it even more difficult to hail a cab. Lines of well-dressed people standing forty-deep outside exclusive hotels attest to this allocation problem. In contrast, you can wave a hand at any street corner in downtown Washington, and three cabs will be immediately at your service.

What are the solutions to New York's problem? The experience in Washington suggests that visitors and residents would be better off if New York City allowed more cabs on the streets. But if you were a driver who paid $100,000 for a medallion, would you be in favor of this solution? Of course not. Another possibility would be to allow the market to set prices for taxi services. *Fortune* magazine suggested that cab drivers be allowed to change rates at peak times with "some sort of electronic display...perched atop the cab that would periodically announce new rates."[8] If cabbies could set rates and vary them by time of day, some riders would be discouraged by higher prices. Also, some cab drivers would be encouraged to put in more hours to earn higher fares. Do you think the lines outside the hotels would decrease?

ORGAN DONATIONS. Another example of markets at work occurs in the relatively new medical field of organ transplanting. Certain organs such as

---

8. "Yellow Power," *Fortune* (15 September 1986): 144.

hearts, lungs, and eyes are donated only at death, usually from accident victims. Other organs, such as kidneys, can be donated by live donors, because humans have two kidneys and can function with just one. There have also been some successful transplants of part of a liver, since this organ can regenerate itself. As organ transplants have become more popular and more successful, a shortage of organs has developed. Newspapers and television frequently carry heartrending appeals. Some hospitals even have donor seekers who contact relatives of accident victims. One explanation for the shortage of organs is that the price is being held at too low a level. In fact, the price is zero.

One writer, Barry Jacobs, proposed establishing a market for kidneys.[9] Since individuals can get along quite well with one kidney, Jacobs's proposal was to let individuals who are cash-poor and kidney-rich sell a kidney to those who are cash-rich and kidney-poor. Also, Congressional hearings were held to consider what could be done about the shortage of kidneys for transplant. Two members of Congress proposed a federal program to fund a computer organ-marketing system and a 24-hour kidney hotline. The program would, however, establish no financial incentives for donors. What do you think might happen if there were a market for kidneys?

Some idea of the possible effect of paying for kidneys comes from an experiment by two British economists, Michael Cooper and Anthony Culver. They tried to determine the supply of blood that would be offered at various prices.[10] They found that there was a moderate supply at a price of zero. At this price, blood was given by those who were motivated by charity, altruism, or other noneconomic reasons. The supply actually fell at a nominal price of about $1.00 a pint, because the payment did not compensate some potential donors for the loss of the good feeling they obtained from giving blood for free. But as the price rose, more and more donors came forward. For many years, some people in American cities have sold their blood when they needed money. The quantity supplied is positively related to price, just as our models would predict. Do you think that kidneys would be any different?

FACULTY OFFICES. A final example of market versus nonmarket allocation comes, appropriately, from an economics department trying to allocate faculty offices in a new building. The other five departments in the school of business used various methods of allocation: seniority, first come first served, and a roll of the dice. None of these methods reflected the intensity of people's preferences for corner offices, offices with windows, large offices, and so forth. There was great dissatisfaction with the outcomes. Only in the economics department was there an attempt to use the market for allocating office space. Faculty members were invited to submit sealed bids. The highest bidders got to choose first, and the proceeds went to student scholarships. A bid indicated how important the "perks" associated with a particular office were to the bidder. Those who

---

9. "Socialized Kidneys," *Fortune* (19 March 1984): 190.
10. Institute of Economic Affairs, *The Economics of Charity: Essays on the Comparative Economics and Ethics of Giving and Selling, with Applications to Blood* (Surrey, England: Gresham Press, 1973).

worked at home more or were away from campus more would presumably bid less than those who used their offices more regularly and cared more intensely about aspects of their workplace.

The experiment was quite successful. The highest bidder paid $500 for the first choice of office, and bidders down to $75 were able to secure the more desirable offices with windows. Since those who bid too low were free to recontract with others if they changed their minds, there was general satisfaction with the outcome.[11]

SUMMARY

1. Demand depends on the current price of the good or service as well as nonprice determinants. These other influences on supply include the size of the group demanding the good, the tastes of the consuming group, the incomes of that group, the prices of related goods and services, and the expectations concerning the future.

2. The law of demand states that the quantity demanded of a good or service is negatively related to its price, *ceteris paribus*.

3. Changes in the price of a good affect the quantity demanded of that good. That is, a price change leads to a movement along the demand curve.

4. Changes in the *ceteris paribus* conditions that affect demand cause demand to either increase or decrease. That is, there is a shift in the position of the entire demand curve.

5. When income increases, the demand for a normal good will increase, and the demand for an inferior good will decrease.

6. Two goods are complements when a price increase in one will cause a decrease in demand for the other. Two goods are substitutes if an increase in the price of one causes an increase in demand for the other.

7. Supply depends on the price of the good or service as well as on nonprice determinants. These include the prices of the factors of production, the level of technology, the number of suppliers, and expectations.

8. The law of supply states that the quantity supplied of a good or service is usually a positive function of its price, *ceteris paribus*.

9. Changes in a good's price affect the quantity supplied of that good. Changes in factors of production that affect supply cause supply to either increase or decrease. When the prices of factors of production increase, there will be a decrease in supply. An advance in technology will usually cause supply to increase.

10. The market-clearing (equilibrium) price is the price at which the amount consumers wish to purchase is equal to the amount suppliers wish to sell. When supply or demand shifts, the market is in disequilibrium until natural forces determine a new equilibrium price and quantity. The comparison of two equilibrium positions is called comparative statics.

11. The supply and demand model has two endogenous variables that are determined within the model. These variables are price and quantity. The exogenous variables are determined outside the model but influence what goes on in the model by shifting supply and demand. These variables include prices of related goods, tastes, income, expectations, and technology.

12. The supply and demand model, like most economic models, uses marginal analysis. It focuses on decisions about the next unit purchased or sold rather than on aggregate or all-or-nothing decisions.

13. Prices play an important role in informing, directing, and motivating consumers and producers.

14. Markets maximize individual freedom by allowing individuals to pursue their own self-interest.

15. Transactions costs result from the fact that organizing, negotiating, and searching take time and involve costs. The existence of transactions costs means that different people pay different prices for the same good or service.

---

11. William J. Boyes and Stephen K. Happel, "Auctions as an Allocation Mechanism in Academia: The Case of Faculty Offices," *Journal of Economic Perspectives* (Summer 1989): 37–40.

New Terms

demand	normal good	market supply curve	endogenous variables
supply	inferior good	increase in supply	exogenous variables
law of demand	complementary goods	decrease in supply	primary effect
demand schedule	substitute goods	market equilibrium	secondary effects
demand curve	expectations	market-clearing price	transactions costs
market demand curve	supply schedule	disequilibrium	invisible hand
increase in demand	(not quite) law of supply	comparative statics	allocative efficiency
decrease in demand	supply curve	marginal analysis	

Questions for Discussion

1. Develop a simple theory to explain (predict) student grades in this course. Identify at least two exogenous variables and one endogenous variable.

2. How can expectations about economic conditions affect supply?

3. Does the fact that some people appear to buy more of some goods, such as mink coats and diamonds, as their prices go up negate the law of demand?

4. How can belief in a future change in the availability of gasoline affect the demand for automobiles?

5. Pat, a professional student, failed an economics course and decided to sell flowers on a street corner to make ends meet. A second flower seller established a business directly across the street from Pat. Pat, unconcerned, came up with the following hypothesis: "When supply increases, demand will increase. Therefore, I will be just as well off as I was before the second flower seller arrived." Did Pat deserve to fail economics? Why or why not?

6. A market-clearing price is the price at which the amount sold equals the amount purchased. Is this correct?

7. List all of the conditions that can decrease demand or supply.

8. List all of the conditions that can increase demand or supply.

9. Why is it so important to distinguish changes in demand and changes in supply from changes in quantity demanded and changes in quantity supplied?

10. Why do some people shop at convenience stores, knowing they will pay higher prices, even when a supermarket with lower prices is open in the same block?

11. The following table lists market information you gathered about landing slots at the Atlanta airport. Suppose you are asked to make a recommendation to the airport manager about pricing the slots to reduce crowding and delays. What will you recommend?

The Market for Landing Slots from 8:00 a.m. to 9:00 a.m.

Price($)	Quantity Supplied	Quantity Demanded
0	12	50
250	12	40
500	12	20
1,000	12	15
1,500	12	8
2,000	12	2

12. Draw a supply curve for personal computers that slopes upward and a demand curve for personal computers that slopes downward. They intersect at an equilibrium price of $2,000 and an equilibrium quantity of 6,000 units per month. Now experiment with each of the following.

   a. A breakthrough in the technology of making chips substantially lowers the cost of production. Which curve shifts, and which way? (Draw it on your diagram.) Find the new equilibrium price and quantity. Did they increase or decrease?

   b. The baby boom generation has bought large numbers of personal computers, and the market is saturated. The number of potential customers in the following generation is much smaller because the birth rate fell sharply during the late 1960s and early 1970s. Does this affect supply or demand? Which curve shifts, and in which direction? What is the effect on price and quantity?

   c. A foreign firm enters the market, adding a new source of supply. How does this change affect the price, quantity, and market supply curve? What is the impact on domestic firms?

13. Explain whether each of the following will shift the supply curve or the demand curve for milk and in which direction.

   a. The birth rate rises. (There are more babies.)

   b. The price of beef is very high, tempting dairy farmers to slaughter their milk cows.

   c. There is a drought, creating a shortage of feed for dairy herds.

   d. Scientists find that drinking too much milk increases the risk of heart disease.

   e. Scientists find that drinking more milk reduces the chances of developing osteoporosis.

14. If both supply and demand shift to the right, what happens to price and quantity? What happens if both supply and demand shift to the left?

15. In 1989, one of the hot gift items was the Nintendo entertainment system, which was used to play games. Only Nintendo games could be played on this system, and Nintendo games could not be played on other systems. How would a shortage of Nintendo systems affect the demand for Nintendo games?

SUGGESTIONS FOR FURTHER READING

Friedman, Milton. *Capitalism and Freedom.* Chicago: University of Chicago Press, 1981. This book presents the case for free markets by perhaps the most respected and passionate of their advocates.

Hayek, F. A. "The Use of Knowledge in Society." *American Economic Review* (September 1945): 519–528. This classic, very readable article shows the importance of markets as a source of information and coordination.

Miller, Roger LeRoy, Daniel K. Benjamin, and Douglass C. North. *The Economics of Public Issues,* 7th ed. New York: HarperCollins, 1990. An easy-to-read book that uses supply and demand to analyze issues of current interest.

Introduction to Macroeconomics

2

AFTER STUDYING THIS CHAPTER, YOU SHOULD BE ABLE TO:

1. Draw and explain the expanded circular flow model, including all leakages and injections.
2. Identify the major macroeconomic goals and tell how each is measured.
3. Discuss the costs and benefits of economic growth and the costs of unemployment and inflation.
4. Define productivity and explain its importance.
5. Draw a typical business cycle diagram, and explain how output, employment, prices, and productivity change over the course of the cycle.
6. Explain the political and economic importance of the Great Depression.

CHAPTER 4

MACROECONOMIC GOALS AND FLUCTUATIONS

INTRODUCTION

Macroeconomics is concerned with the behavior of economic aggregates, including total output and income, total employment and unemployment, and price levels and inflation. In contrast, microeconomics is focused more narrowly on the quantities and prices of specific goods, such as pizza or textbooks, and the employment of certain factors of production, such as farmland or textbook writers. If a few people are unemployed, this is probably a microeconomic problem of finding the right wage rate or the right information on job openings or of developing the right skills. If 10 million people are unemployed, this is a macroeconomic problem. If the price of eggs rises, it is a microeconomic matter. If the average price of everything rises, it is a macroeconomic problem. When one person's income rises, there is a microeconomic explanation in terms of skills or productivity. When the economy's total income rises, there is a macroeconomic explanation in terms of economic growth.

This chapter is an overview of some major macroeconomic concerns. In this chapter, we will begin to explore the issues of the rate of economic growth, price stability and inflation, and employment and unemployment.

THE CIRCULAR FLOW MODEL REVISITED

In Chapter 2, we introduced the circular flow model as a way to see the interrelationships in a market economy. The individual markets and actors that make up the circular flow constitute microeconomics. The sums of their actions constitute macroeconomics. In this chapter, we want to focus on circular flow from a macroeconomic perspective.

A simple two-sector circular flow model shows the flow of goods and services from business firms to households in the upper flow as well as a return flow of payments from households for their purchases. In the lower flow, business firms purchase the services of productive inputs from households, creating a flow of income back to households. Even in this very simple two-sector world, it is possible to identify some important macroeconomic relationships. The upper part of the diagram, the product market, represents the aggregate of the individual markets in which final goods and services are bought and sold. The lower half, the factor market, is the aggregate of the individual markets in which the services of productive inputs are bought and sold. These markets represent the total of thousands of individual markets for steelworkers, bread, rental housing, cars, machine tools, and other inputs and outputs. That is, the product market and the factor market are both macroeconomic markets.

Another important macroeconomic concept that is suggested by the circular flow diagram is the view of national income or output as a *flow*. The flow of factor income from firms to households becomes a flow back to firms to pay for purchases of goods and services. The upper flow is total output, and the lower flow is total income. The two flows are the same size in the simple circular flow model because all of the income received by households is spent to purchase the output of firms.

SAVING, INVESTMENT, AND THE CREDIT MARKET

Figure 1 adds two flows to the simple circular flow model—saving and investment.[1] These flows were introduced in Chapter 2 and are developed

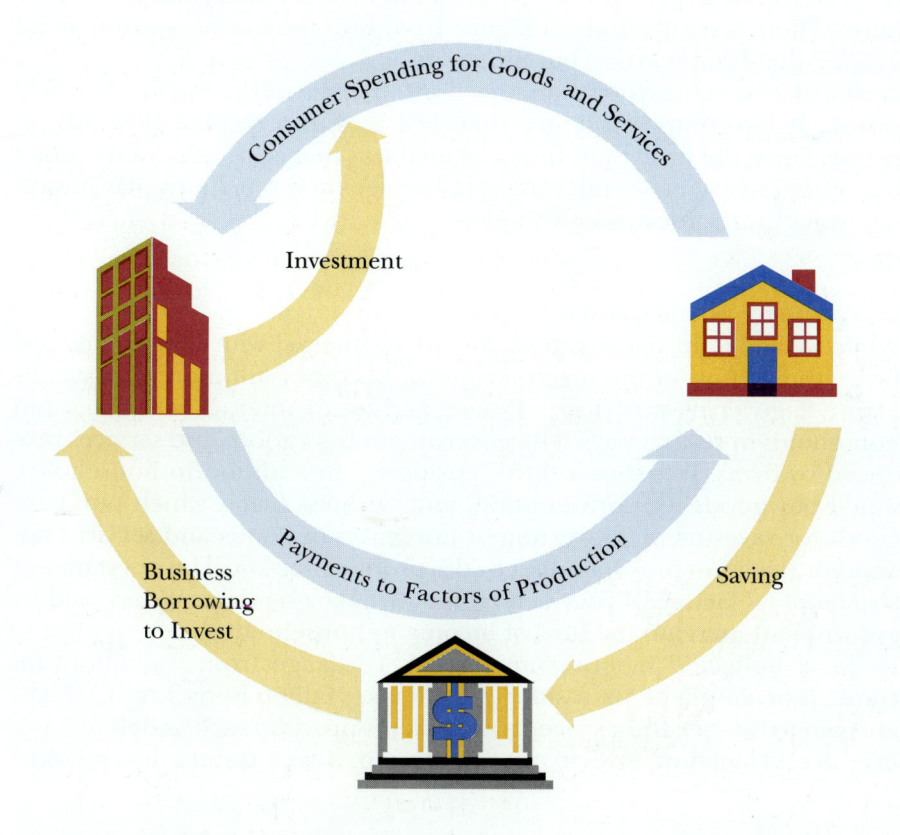

FIGURE 1
THE CIRCULAR FLOW WITH SAVING, INVESTMENT, AND A CREDIT MARKET
When there are leakages, not all household income is spent on consumption. A credit market allows saving (nonconsumption) by households to be converted into investment funds for firms. These investment funds are then spent by firms on capital goods and further production.

---

1. Recall from Chapter 2 that we simplified this diagram before adding other flows. We reduced the original two pairs of flows to just two flows: income payments to productive factors in the lower half and expenditure payments for goods and services in the upper half.

saving
The part of households' income flow not spent on purchases of goods and services.

investment
Purchases by firms of some real, tangible asset, such as a machine, a factory, or a stock of inventory.

credit market
The aggregate market consisting of financial institutions that channel household savings to business firms that want to invest.

leakages
Flows out of the circular pattern that occur when factor income is received but not spent directly on purchases from domestic firms. Savings, taxes, and purchases of imports are leakages.

injections
Spending added to the circular flow that is not paid for out of factor income. Business investment, government expenditures, and sales of exports are injections.

here in more detail. **Saving** is a flow from households that occurs because they refrain from spending part of their income flow on goods and services. These funds flow into the credit market instead of the product market. **Investment** is a flow from firms. Firms borrow from households through the credit market in order to purchase new plants or equipment or to add to their inventories. That is, they use the borrowed funds to purchase new capital goods from other firms or to finance the "purchase" of their own output in the form of increased inventories.[2] The **credit market** consists of financial institutions channeling household savings to business firms that want to invest. The credit market is an important macro market.

Another important pair of macroeconomic concepts is illustrated in Figure 1. These are leakages out of the income stream and injections into the income stream. **Leakages** are flows out of the circular pattern that occur when factor income is received but not spent directly on purchases from domestic firms. Examples of leakages are saving, taxes, and purchases of imports. Income leaks out of the income stream if households do not spend all of their income on consumption of goods produced by business firms. **Injections** are added flows into the circular pattern that represent spending not paid for out of factor income. Examples of injections are business investment, government expenditures, and sales of exports. There are injections in Figure 1 because the business firms spend income that is not earned but borrowed.

If leakages are greater than injections, the size of the income flow will shrink. If injections are larger than leakages, the income flow will increase. Since the level of output and income (that is, the size of the flow) is a central macroeconomic concern, leakages and injections play important roles in macroeconomic models.

GOVERNMENT IN THE CIRCULAR FLOW

When we add a third actor, government, to interact with households and firms, the picture of the macro economy becomes still more realistic. In Figure 2, governments (federal, state, and local) interact with firms and households in several ways. The government buys goods and services produced by firms. It is thus a third "customer" in addition to households, which buy goods for consumption, and business firms, which purchase goods for investment. Government purchases of goods and services are another injection into spending in the product market. The government also employs factors of production, mainly labor services. Wages paid by government increase the flow of income to households.

Taxes collected by governments are a leakage from household income. (For simplicity, we assume that all taxes fall on households.) Taxes are paid to finance the services governments provide, such as defense, police, fire protection, streets, and education. Taxes reduce households'

---

2. Some business firms may actually save and lend to others, and some households may be net borrowers. For simplicity, however, we treat all saving as coming from the household sector and all borrowing as done by the business sector.

FIGURE 2
THE CIRCULAR FLOW WITH A CREDIT MARKET AND GOVERNMENT
Government subtracts from the circular flow by taxing households (leakages). It adds to the upper flow (expenditures) by buying goods and services from firms. It adds to the income flow by purchasing the services of labor from households. Governments, like businesses, also borrow in the credit market.

consumption by lowering their after-tax (disposable) incomes. Therefore, less is available to spend. Taxes may also reduce household saving.

Finally, if the government spends more than it collects in taxes, it must borrow funds in the credit market. There it will compete with business firms for the supply of household savings. A government that spends more than the revenue it takes in is running a **deficit**. A government that collects more in taxes than it spends on wages and purchases is showing a **surplus**.

The government, then, enters the circular flow model at a number of points. It takes funds out of the stream by taxing households and by borrowing in the credit market. It adds to the spending flow by purchasing goods and services from firms. It adds to the income flow by purchasing labor services from households. Taxes are leakages out of the flow. Government purchases of goods and services are injections.

deficit
A situation in which the government spends more than it collects in taxes.

surplus
A situation in which the government collects more in taxes than it spends.

THE FOREIGN SECTOR: EXPORTS AND IMPORTS
Adding the foreign sector completes the picture of the macro economy. As Figure 3 shows, it is not only another "customer" for firms' output but also another supplier of goods and services besides the domestic business sector. Buying from foreign countries and selling to other countries add a new source of leakages and a new source of injections. Purchases from foreign

FIGURE 3
THE CIRCULAR FLOW WITH A CREDIT MARKET, GOVERNMENT, AND FOREIGN SECTOR
Purchases from foreign sellers represent a leakage from the circular flow when households buy imports. Sales of exports to foreign buyers are an injection into the expenditure stream.

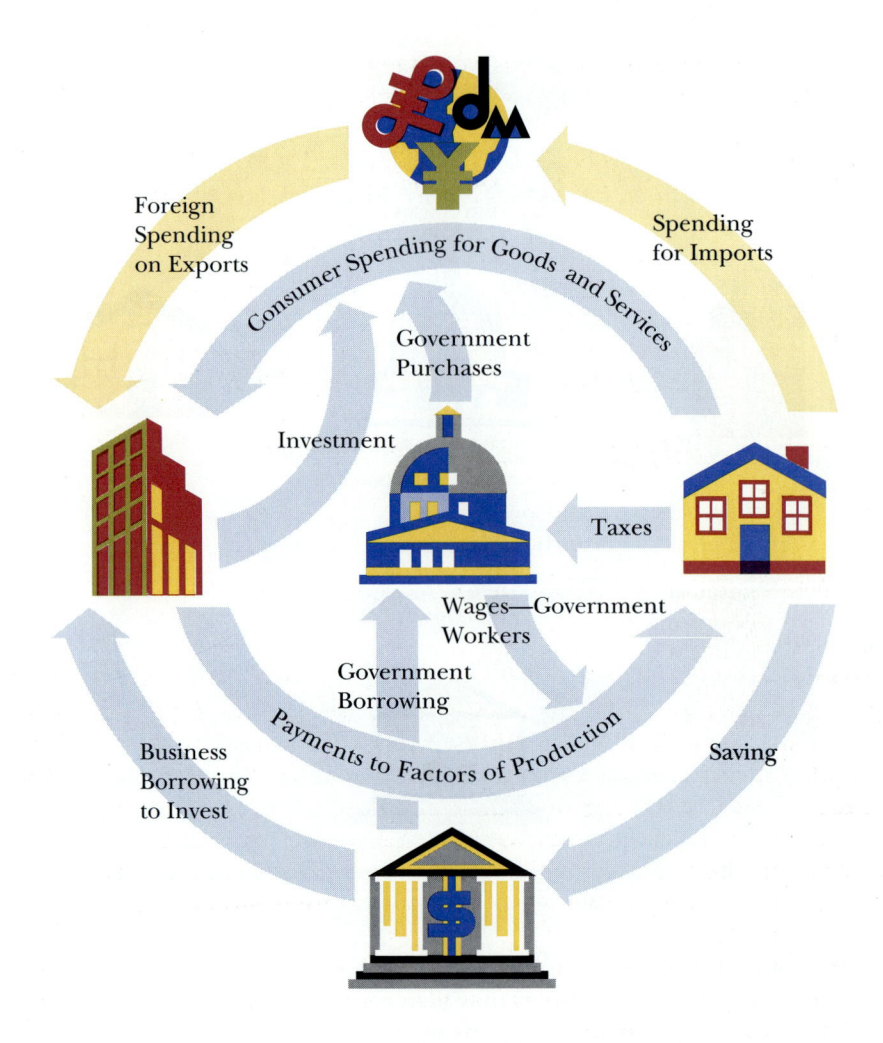

imports
Goods and services purchased from foreign sellers.

exports
Goods and services sold to foreign buyers.

balance on goods and services
The difference between the value of exports and the value of imports for a country in a given year.

firms are **imports**. Goods and services sold to foreign buyers are **exports**. Purchases of imports are flows out of the stream (leakages). Sales of exports are flows into the stream (injections). Thus, if a country increases its purchases from foreigners, *ceteris paribus*, the size of the flow will shrink. If the same country increases its sales to foreigners, *ceteris paribus*, the size of the flow will increase. The difference between exports and imports for a given country for a given year is called the **balance on goods and services**. A surplus in the balance on goods and services means that injections from the foreign market exceed leakages to it. A deficit in the balance on goods and services means that foreign market leakages are greater than injections.

For many years, exports and imports were so small relative to the total flow of income and product in the United States that they were often omitted from the circular flow diagram. In the early 1960s, the ratio of both imports and exports to total domestic output was only about 5 or 6 percent. Since then, not only has the ratio of both imports and exports to total output risen sharply in the United States, but trade has become increasingly unbalanced. By the late 1980s, exports were about 9 percent of total output, and imports accounted for 12 percent of spending. Ignoring exports and imports in the 1990s would lead to serious errors in predicting the size of the income and output flow.

THE COMPONENTS OF THE CIRCULAR FLOW DIAGRAM			
FOUR MARKETS	**FOUR ACTORS**	**THREE LEAKAGES**	**THREE INJECTIONS**
Product	Households	Saving	Investment
Factor	Firms	Taxes	Government purchases
Credit	Government	Imports	Exports
Foreign	Exports and imports		

MACROECONOMIC GOALS

What do people want from the economy as a whole? What are the macroeconomic goals? How can a nation measure whether it is better off or worse off? The circular flow diagram provides a picture of the macro economy. In that visual model we can implicitly identify at least one macroeconomic goal—to encourage the steady growth of the flows of income and output. The levels of income and output and the rate at which they grow are the central focus of macroeconomics. Expressed as a goal, the focus is on economic growth at a steady and sustainable rate. However, there are other important macroeconomic concerns that are not directly observed in the circular flow diagram. Two other major goals are price stability and full employment. There is almost total agreement about the centrality of these three goals, because economists and policy makers are aware of the high costs of lack of growth, price instability, and unemployment. In this chapter, we explore what these goals mean and how performance on each is measured.

ECONOMIC GROWTH

Economic growth is defined as an increase in real output per capita. The word *real* means that the number describing output has been corrected for price changes.[3] For example, if the value of the total output of soup has gone from $1 million to $2 million, you need to know what has happened to the price of a can of soup before you jump to the conclusion that there is twice as much soup. If the price of soup rose 40 percent, the real output of soup has not doubled. In fact, there is really only about 43 percent more soup.

An increase in real output per capita means that the average person has more goods and services and a higher standard of living than before. It is generally believed that a growth rate of 3 to 4 percent per year is the highest that can be sustained for any length of time. Producing more output requires more productive resources and/or improvements in technology. A rate of growth of 3 to 4 percent corresponds to an attainable combined rate of change in these two important sources of economic growth.

economic growth
An increase in the level of real output per capita.

---

3. In contrast, the word *nominal* indicates that a value has *not* been corrected for price changes.

COSTS AND BENEFITS OF ECONOMIC GROWTH. For a long time, economic growth was the most widely accepted of the macroeconomic goals. Economists and others believed that if some production is good, more must be better. A higher standard of living is better than a lower one. As population grows, output has to grow just to keep per capita output and income from falling. Generally, people want economic growth to provide some improvements in the standard of living as well. Additional capacity to produce means that some more of those insatiable wants can be fulfilled. These may be private wants for better housing or collective wants for better roads.

Beginning in the 1960s, however, many people began to question the value and, especially, the costs of economic growth. More industry and a larger population created more air and water pollution, noise, and litter. Questions were raised about the effects of growth on the environment. In addition, as the birth rate dropped in the late 1960s and early 1970s, the need for growth in order to provide for additional population became much less pressing.

Critics of economic growth as a central policy goal raise a number of objections. Some point out that we live on a finite planet, with limited natural resources. Thus, growth cannot be sustained indefinitely. Growth also creates undesirable by-products, such as solid waste, hazardous wastes, and air pollution. Doubts have also been expressed about whether continued economic growth has resulted in improvements in the quality of life. Gains in productivity have seemed to go into producing more output instead of more leisure. In the 1980s, the typical European worker had a four- to six-week annual vacation in contrast to the typical two weeks for an American worker. Some Americans asked whether economic growth was worth the cost in terms of lifestyle. At the same time, younger Japanese workers questioned the benefits of their nation's rapid economic growth. Most of them had to put up with cramped housing, long commutes, and high prices for consumer goods.

Another concern that surfaced in the late 1970s was that the existing infrastructure might not be able to support continued growth. **Infrastructure** is the basic facilities and equipment that provide community services. The support system of roads, water, sewers, electric power, schools, hospitals, and parks is important to residents and businesses. Demand for infrastructure rises with economic growth. The infrastructure not only needs to grow with the population in a community but also requires regular maintenance and repair.

Many of these concerns really point to disagreements about the composition of output rather than about economic growth. If there is an increase in productive capacity, it can be directed toward more output or more leisure, more private goods or more collective goods (including infrastructure). With more resources, a society can devote more effort to improving the environment without sacrificing other goods and services. Many of these apparent objections to economic growth are really objections to how output is measured and how priorities are set for using new resources and technology.

The last two recessions, in 1981–82 and 1990–91, made Americans more aware of the costs of not growing. When economic growth is slow or

infrastructure
The basic facilities and equipment, usually publicly owned, that provide community services.

stops, tax revenues decline or grow slowly. Politicians hate to raise tax rates. Rising unemployment further reduces tax revenues and creates pressures on government to spend in order to relieve unemployment. There are even political battles between generations. Retirees want a greater share of the public budget to support them, and younger people want funding for public schools. Thus, for most Americans, a steady and sustainable rate of economic growth, along with attention to the quality of life and the state of the environment, remains a central economic goal.

MEASURING GROWTH. The most widely used measure of economic growth is the rate of increase in output, which is shown in Figure 4.[4] As this figure suggests, the United States has experienced periods of rapid growth alternating with stretches of slow growth or even decline in output. The 1970s were a period of very slow growth. The rate of growth picked up again by the mid-1980s but slowed at the end of the decade. A recession developed in late 1990. The overall (compounded) rate of growth in Figure 4 has been about 3.6 percent a year, with a wide range from –9 percent a year (briefly) in 1980 to over 12 percent a year in the late 1940s.

PRICE STABILITY

Another important macroeconomic goal is price stability. Prices can either rise or fall. In recent years, however, the United States has experienced a continued rise in the general, or average, level of prices. This is **inflation**. The measure of inflation is the change in the price index. A **price index** measures the price level in any year relative to some base year. The best-known such measure is the **Consumer Price Index (CPI)**, popularly known as the cost-of-living index. The CPI measures the cost of a mar-

inflation
A sustained rise in the general, or average, level of prices.

price index
A measure of the price level in a given year relative to some base year.

consumer price index (CPI)
A well-known measure of inflation based on the cost of a selected market basket of consumer goods (also known as the cost-of-living index).

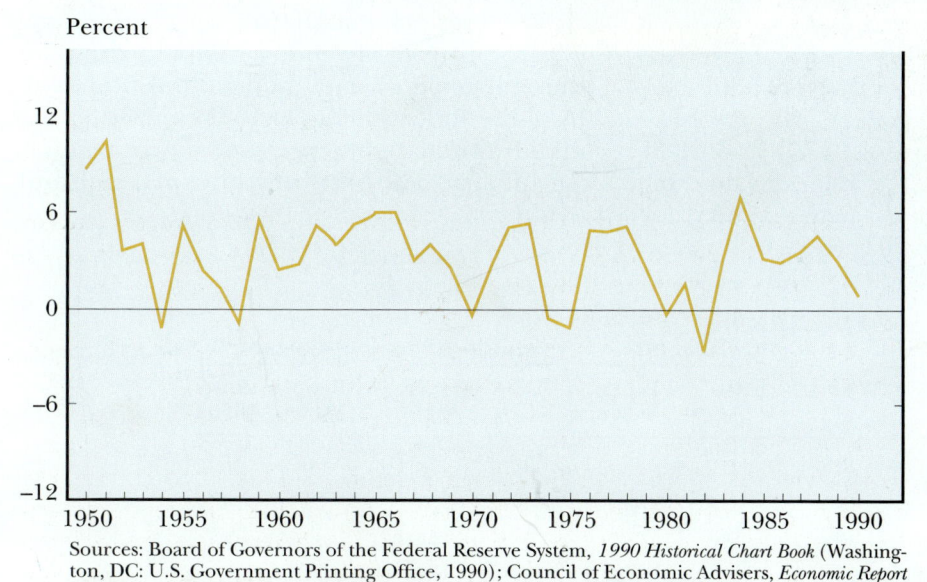

FIGURE 4
ANNUAL GROWTH RATE OF REAL GNP, 1933–1990
Growth rates of output, or real gross national product (output in constant dollars), show much variation over time. It is easy to identify recessions in this diagram as periods when real output fell (growth rates were negative).

Sources: Board of Governors of the Federal Reserve System, *1990 Historical Chart Book* (Washington, DC: U.S. Government Printing Office, 1990); Council of Economic Advisers, *Economic Report of the President* (Washington, DC: U.S. Government Printing Office, 1991).

4. The output growth rates in Figure 4 have been corrected for price changes.

Economic Insight

Constructing an Index

Both prices and productivity are measured in this chapter (Figures 5 and 7) using an index. An index is simply a weighted average, for which the absolute value has relatively little meaning. The important thing about an index is the year-to-year change in its value or the comparison of its values for different individuals, firms, cities, states, or countries.

Suppose you were asked to develop an index of academic quality of colleges. You might set up your index to reflect the number of books in the library, the average SAT scores of entering students, the average starting salary of graduates, and the faculty-to-student ratio. The table presents such data for three colleges. You assign a high weight to SAT scores (40) and equal weights (20 each) to the other three variables (weights must add to 100).

For each item, the index value is calculated by multiplying the weight (which is the same for an item for all three colleges) by the raw value of the item for each college. For example, an SAT score of 10 (1,000 raw score) multiplied by a weight of 40 percent gives a value of 4.0. The weighted index values are added to create an index for each college. The absolute values of the numbers 15.0, 17.7, and 23.8 don't mean very much. The relative values of an index are what matter. These are used to make comparisons over time (how fast prices are rising according to the price index) or space (how the productivity index in the United States compares to that of Japan).

Note that according to this index, college 3 is the "best" primarily because of high SAT scores and secondarily because of graduates' starting salaries. On the other two items, faculty-to-student ratio and number of library books, this college is weaker. If the index gave greater weight to these other items and less weight to entering SAT scores, college 3 might not rank as high. You can see from this example that it is possible to "rig" the weights to make a particular school look good. This is why you need to interpret indices with care. Note also that the indices for a school will record changes in its performance from year to year. Thus, this index can be used for one school over time as well as for comparisons among schools.

Economists use a variety of indices in their work. The price index is the most familiar. Other indices include the productivity index, the stock market index, and the quality-of-life index. Used to compare the well-being of states and nations, the quality-of-life index includes the literacy rate, the infant mortality rate, per capita income, average life span, and other measures of health and wealth.

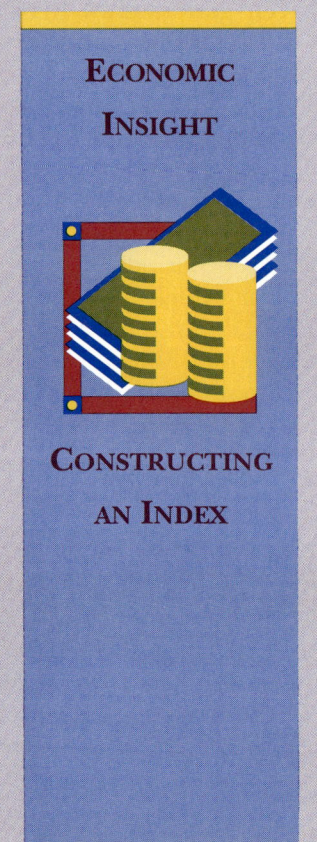

Index of College Quality

Item	Weight	College 1 Raw Value	College 1 Index Value	College 2 Raw Value	College 2 Index Value	College 3 Raw Value	College 3 Index Value
Books	20%	10	2.0	20	4.0	50	10.0
SAT scores	40%	10	4.0	9	3.6	12	4.8
Salaries	20%	25	5.0	20	4.0	30	6.0
F/S ratio	20%	20	4.0	30	6.0	15	3.0
Index			15.0		17.7		23.8

Note: Number of books is in 1,000s, SAT scores in 100s, salaries in $1,000s, and F/S ratio in faculty per 100 students.

ket basket of a selected array of consumer goods each year. The percentage change in the CPI from one year to the next is the inflation rate. The inflation rate from 1933 to 1990 is shown in Figure 5. You can see that, except for World War II, prices were relatively stable until the 1970s. High inflation in the late 1970s and early 1980s increased awareness of the many problems caused by inflation, especially when it is unexpected. Lower inflation rates in the rest of the 1980s helped to calm fears that high rates of inflation would become a permanent feature of the American economy. However, the inflation rate in 1990 was 6 percent—perhaps the start of a new round of higher inflation rates in the 1990s.

GAINERS AND LOSERS FROM INFLATION. One reason why governments try to restrain inflation is that it causes unintended and often undesirable redistribution of income and wealth. Redistribution is more likely to occur when inflation is unexpected. People make contracts and decisions on the assumption of an expected rate of inflation. Suppose, for simplicity, you are expecting zero inflation. You lend someone $100 for a year at an interest rate of 5 percent. This rate is enough to cover your risk of not being repaid and the cost of not using the money for a year, assuming no inflation. Then there is unexpected inflation of 10 percent. At the end of a year, you receive $105, but it will only purchase $95.45 in goods and services ($105/1.10). Who gained? The borrower. If you had anticipated the inflation, you would have charged a higher interest rate to cover the loss

**FIGURE 5
INFLATION RATE,
1933–1990**
The rate of change in the CPI is shown for each year since 1933. Note the negative inflation rates during the Depression of the 1930s, when prices were falling. There was a gradual rise from the 1940s through the 1960s, a sharp increase from 1975 to 1982, and finally a leveling off in the mid-1980s.

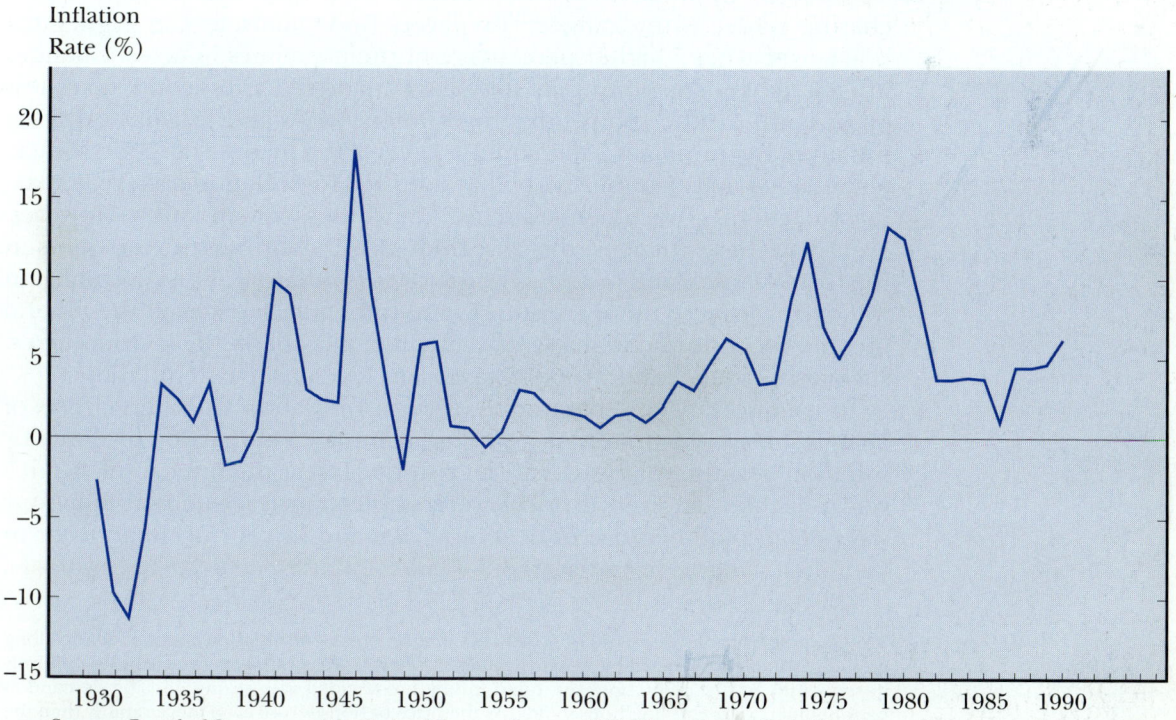

Sources: Board of Governors of the Federal Reserve System, *1990 Historical Chart Book* (Washington, DC: U.S. Government Printing Office, 1990); Council of Economic Advisers, *Economic Report of the President* (Washington DC: U.S. Government Printing Office, 1991).

of purchasing power. Unexpected inflation redistributes income from lenders to borrowers.

Lenders and borrowers are not the only ones who are affected by income redistribution from unexpected inflation. People who hold any kind of fixed-dollar assets, such as life insurance policies, lose purchasing power. People who hold real, physical assets, such as land, houses, or jewelry, often find that the value of those assets rises faster than the rate of inflation. As more people shift to real assets in response to expected inflation, the increase in demand for those assets will drive their prices up even faster than the inflation rate.

Buying as much house as you could possibly afford was a popular inflation hedge in the 1970s and 1980s. Many home buyers were later able to sell their houses for much more than they paid for them as house prices increased rapidly. This pattern ended in the late 1980s. In the 1990s, the smaller number of new home buyers has led real estate experts to predict that house prices will be stable in nominal terms (falling in real terms). Thus, housing does not look like a good inflation hedge in the 1990s. Sometimes common stocks, which represent ownership claims on the real, physical assets of firms, also do better than the inflation rate. However, the future course of the price of any given stock is highly uncertain. Thus, stocks are a risky inflation hedge. Hedging against anticipated inflation is an important way to protect the value of assets, but there is no perfect instrument to use for that purpose.

Governments are often winners during times of inflation because of the progressive nature of state and federal income taxes. As prices rise, households' nominal incomes also rise, even if their real income or purchasing power is unchanged. Taxpayers find themselves in higher tax brackets, paying a higher percentage of their incomes in taxes. Changes in U.S. tax laws beginning in 1987 have made federal income taxes less progressive. In the future, the government will stand to gain less from inflation. Beginning in 1990, some aspects of the income tax code (brackets and personal exemptions) will be adjusted for inflation each year, making the federal government even less of a winner from inflation. However, even with these changes, the government will continue to reap gains in the form of increased revenues when there is inflation. This revenue gain will occur because there are still several rates and brackets in the federal income tax code and in many state income tax codes as well. Other taxes, such as sales taxes and property taxes, are less sensitive to inflation.[5]

It is important to separate the effects of inflation from the effects of changes in *relative* prices. As a worker, you may feel that you are hurt by inflation because your wages aren't rising as fast as the price level. But it's very possible that even if prices were stable your wages might fall. Your wages could fall because of declining demand in your occupation or in your area. Wages of some workers—for example, accountants, engineers,

---

5. Generally, property taxes do not rise with inflation unless the inflation is sustained for a long period of time and reflected in property values. Property is reassessed for tax purposes relatively infrequently. In the 1970s, however, rapid inflation coincided with strong housing demand as baby boomers were forming households. As the price of houses rose even more rapidly than the general price level, property taxes also shot up rapidly, especially in California. The result was the property tax revolt from about 1978 to 1983.

and nurses—have been rising faster than the rate of inflation. Wages of other workers—such as retail clerks—have been rising more slowly. In recent years, wages for fast-food work and other entry-level jobs traditionally held by teenagers and college students have been rising sharply because of the relatively small number of people in that age group. Such relative wage changes have been caused by changes in supply and demand in those markets. As long as the average wage keeps pace with inflation, workers are not hurt by inflation, even though some workers may be suffering from a decline in demand for their particular skills.

The same is true of prices of consumer products. Even when most prices are rising, the prices of some goods are falling or rising much more slowly. If the market basket of goods you purchase is very different from that used to compute the CPI, then you will feel the effects of both inflation and changing relative prices. If your basket is full of items whose prices are rising faster than average, both inflation and changing relative prices will hit your budget. But if you are consuming less popular goods such as bicycle tires, granola, and diapers when most other consumers are driving up the prices of gasoline, oat bran, and college tuition, the cost of your basket may not be rising as fast as the CPI.

Market Signals, Inflation Psychology, and Menu Costs. Our discussion of relative prices versus the price level suggests another problem due to inflation. Inflation confuses the market signals on which individuals rely to make good decisions about earning, spending, saving, and investing. It is difficult to tell what is happening to relative prices when all prices are moving at once. This confusion of signals due to inflation is a major problem in market economies.

Another problem from high rates of inflation is an inflation psychology that leads people to "buy now before the price goes up." This expectation encourages consumption but discourages saving and investment. Saving and investment are important because they increase the nation's stock of capital and result in a higher rate of economic growth. Thus, high rates of inflation can have a negative effect on economic growth.

A third problem is the menu cost of inflation. Have you ever gone into a restaurant and seen prices crossed out and written over? Such price changes happen more often with inflation. Firms have to get new menus, price lists, catalogs, and other price information printed more often. All of these adjustments use real resources that could be used more productively in other ways.

Given all these drawbacks to inflation, why not try to reduce the inflation rate to zero? In fact, a target inflation rate of zero has been proposed by Alan Greenspan, the chairman of the Federal Reserve System (the central bank). One of the problems with this target, however, is that the measurement of inflation is not very precise. Therefore, what appears to be modest inflation of about 2 percent might actually be closer to zero inflation if the index were correctly computed.[6] A stronger argument

---

6. The pros and cons of Greenspan's zero-inflation proposal are discussed by Michelle Garfinkel in "What Is an 'Acceptable' Rate of Inflation?—A Review of the Issues," *Review*, Federal Reserve Bank of St. Louis (July-August 1989): 3–15.

against the goal of zero inflation is that the costs of reducing the inflation rate to zero may be greater than the benefits. Often moderate inflation is associated with rapid economic growth, which is usually considered a desirable goal. Since most of the problems from inflation are related to high rates of inflation, rapid inflation, or unexpected inflation, a low and stable rate of inflation may be desirable.

> **WHAT'S WRONG WITH INFLATION?**
>
> The costs of inflation are:
> - unintended redistribution of income and wealth,
> - transfer of resources to government,
> - confused market signals,
> - lower levels of saving and investment (inflation psychology), and
> - menu costs.

FULL EMPLOYMENT

The third macroeconomic goal is full employment. The precise amounts of employment and unemployment that constitute full employment are difficult to pinpoint. Clearly, full employment does not mean that 100 percent of the population is employed or even that 100 percent of those able are willing to take a job. One way of defining **full employment** is to identify some level of unemployment as "normal," or acceptable, and only count unemployment in excess of that amount. A level of 5 to 6 percent is currently considered normal. Thus, by this definition, an economy is at full employment when 94 to 95 percent of those who want to work are employed.[7]

full employment
The level of employment at which approximately 94 to 95 percent of those who want to work are employed.

FRICTIONAL AND STRUCTURAL UNEMPLOYMENT. It is not possible to have a situation where everyone is always employed. Some unemployment is normal because there are new entrants into the labor force searching for jobs. Finding a job takes time. During that time, a person will be unemployed. Other workers are between jobs. They have quit one job to look for a better one, are recovering from an illness, or have moved with their families to a different part of the country. Such short-term unemployment is called **frictional unemployment**.

frictional unemployment
Unemployment due to workers being temporarily between jobs or new entrants to the work force.

Another normal source of unemployment is a mismatch of workers and jobs. There may be a surplus of teachers and a need for pipefitters. There may be excess labor in Montana and a shortage of workers in Virginia. Whenever the available workers do not match the jobs in terms of skills or location, there is **structural unemployment**. This kind of unemployment tends to last longer than frictional unemployment because it takes longer for workers to retrain or relocate to match available jobs. When plants

structural unemployment
Unemployment due to a mismatch between the skills or locations of unemployed workers and those of available jobs.

---

7. Still another way to define full employment is that the number of job seekers should be about equal to the number of vacancies.

close, either permanently or because the firm is moving production to another place, the result is usually some structural unemployment.[8]

Some economists argue that both frictional and structural unemployment are higher than necessary because government "subsidizes" unemployment. Workers take longer to search for a job when they can collect unemployment compensation and other benefits. That's not necessarily undesirable. They may wind up with more suitable jobs, in which they can earn more and be more productive. It does, however, raise the measured rate of unemployment, and the cost of the search falls on taxpayers.[9]

Frictional unemployment calls for better information and employment services. Structural unemployment may call for retraining and assistance in relocating. Since these policies try to make specific segments of the labor market work more efficiently, they are really closer to being microeconomic than macroeconomic.

CYCLICAL UNEMPLOYMENT. Some unemployment is related to declines in the level of aggregate output. This **cyclical unemployment** is a major policy concern in macroeconomics. Workers are laid off because of a fall in demand generally or specifically for the products they produce. Cyclical unemployment tends to be most severe in heavy industry (manufacturing equipment and some consumer goods such as cars and refrigerators). Macroeconomic policies intended to reduce cyclical employment try to create more jobs by increasing demand for total output.

cyclical unemployment Unemployment caused by a decline in the level of total output.

Unemployment rates since 1929 are shown in Figure 6. Note the extremely low rate of unemployment during World War II and the gradual rise in unemployment during the late 1970s and early 1980s. This period was followed by a gradual decline in unemployment to the end of that decade. Unemployment rates began to rise slowly again in late 1990, as the United States entered a recession.

COSTS OF UNEMPLOYMENT. Why are macroeconomic policy makers concerned about the level of unemployment? First, unemployment is wasteful. If unemployment exists, the economy is not operating on the production possibilities curve. Unemployed labor should be producing goods and services. Although other resources can also be unemployed, policy makers and people in general are usually more concerned about unemployed labor than unemployed capital or land.

The second reason for concern about unemployment is that the system of income distribution in a market economy is very dependent on employment. If people don't have jobs, they earn no income. Employed

---

8. The Bureau of Labor Statistics studied the experiences of workers displaced by plant closings during the recessions in 1980 and 1981–1982. The study found that 60 percent were working again by 1984 although many were receiving lower wages.
9. These same economists would argue that some structural unemployment is caused by the minimum wage, which eliminates entry-level jobs worth less than that wage. Lack of job openings at the entry level keeps unskilled workers from acquiring the skills and experience to move up the employment ladder. In the period 1967–1981, the minimum wage more than tripled in dollar terms (from $1.00 to $3.35). However, the minimum wage was not increased from 1981 until 1990, when it was raised to $3.80, with further increases in 1991 and 1992. During this period, the value of the minimum wage in real terms (adjusted for inflation) fell by about 36 percent. Thus, the minimum wage has probably had little if any impact on employment in the 1980s.

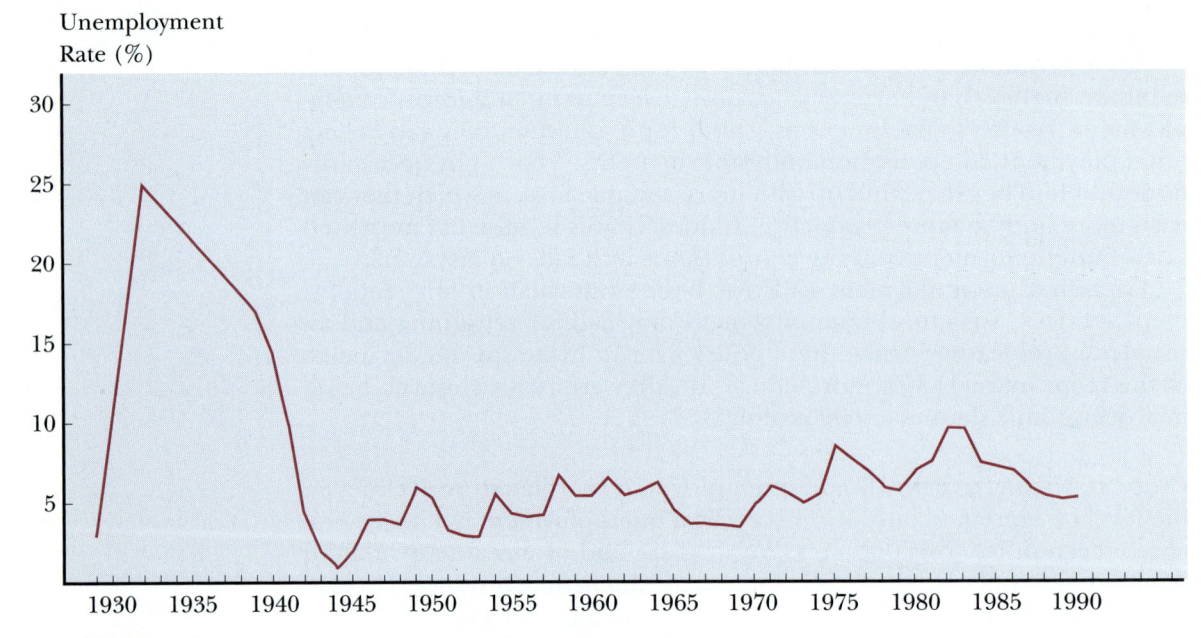

FIGURE 6
U.S. UNEMPLOYMENT RATES AS A PERCENTAGE OF THE CIVILIAN LABOR FORCE, 1929–1990
Unemployment rates soared between 1929 and 1933. Unemployment remained high until World War II, when war production required almost complete employment of the civilian labor force. A gradual upward trend in unemployment rates can be observed, with peaks in the recessions of 1959–1960, 1970, 1975, and 1980–1982.

productivity
A measure of economic performance that shows changes in output per worker hour from one year to the next.

Source: Council of Economic Advisers, *Economic Report of the President* (Washington, DC: U.S. Government Printing Office, various issues).

persons wind up supporting unemployed persons through unemployment benefits, food stamps, and other social welfare programs.

Finally, unemployment is both psychologically demoralizing and harmful to future earnings. Each period of unemployment is a lost opportunity to develop skills and experience that will make a worker more valuable to an employer. That is, unemployment means less investment in human capital.

PRODUCTIVITY AND MACROECONOMIC GOALS

There is one other macroeconomic variable that plays an important role in determining changes in output, employment, and the price level. This variable is productivity. The other three variables are goals, but productivity is a means to a goal. **Productivity** is a measure of economic performance that shows changes in output per worker hour from one year to the next.

The productivity index for the United States is shown in Figure 7. The growth of productivity was very high in the early postwar period. It had slowed considerably by the 1970s and remained low into the early 1980s. When productivity improves rapidly, there tends to be rapid economic growth, high employment, and low inflation. When productivity grows more slowly or not at all, there is usually slow growth, high unemployment, and higher inflation. Thus, productivity plays a key role in achieving the three major economic goals.

Much effort was devoted to trying to explain the slowdown in the growth of productivity in recent decades and to suggest ways to improve productivity. Inexperienced or poorly trained workers, low savings rates,

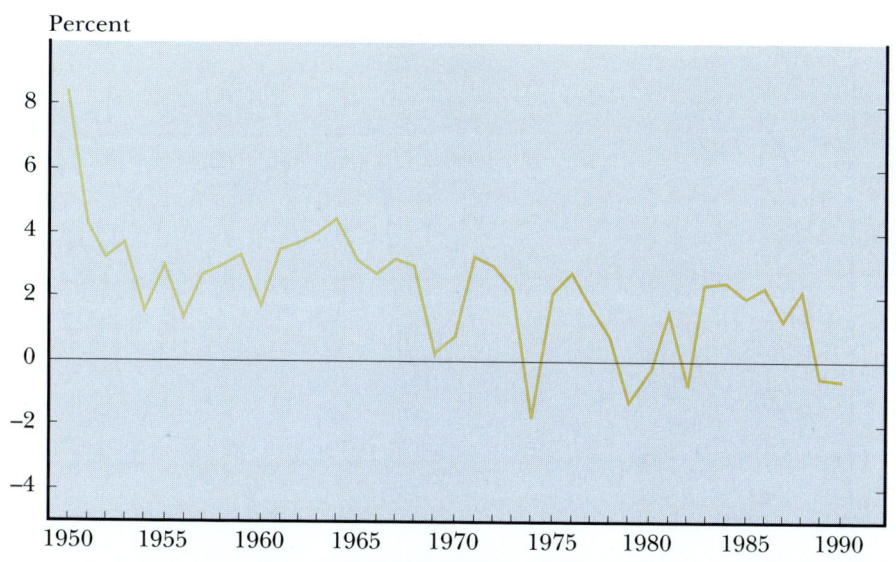

Chapter 4 Macroeconomic Goals and Fluctuations

**FIGURE 7
PRODUCTIVITY INDEX, 1948–1990**
The index of productivity per worker hour in the private sector increased at an average rate of just under 2 percent a year, doubling in the last 40 years. The growth rates were rapid in the 1950s and 1960s, slowed down in the 1970s, and picked up slightly in the 1980s.

Source: U.S. Department of Commerce, *Business Statistics* (Washington, DC: U.S. Government Printing Office, various issues).

and not enough investment in developing new products and technology were all cited as possible causes. Some of the approaches suggested included adopting Japanese management techniques and encouraging more investment in human and physical capital. Certainly, better human capital, more physical capital, and improvements in technology are all key elements in productivity. Other economists, however, have suggested that the high rates of increase in productivity of the early postwar period were not typical and that current rates are more nearly normal.

Productivity is important because it is a major source of growth in per capita income and also a major source of wage increases not due to inflation. In order to earn more, a worker must add more to a firm's revenues. More output per hour is the key to a higher standard of living. In the last fifteen years, most increases in real household income in the United States have come from having more workers per household rather than higher real earnings per worker.

FLUCTUATIONS IN OUTPUT, EMPLOYMENT, AND PRICES

What happens when we put output, employment, and prices together? Figure 8 shows the inflation rate, the unemployment rate, and the growth rate of real output in a single diagram. As you can see, the unemployment rate and growth of output track each other quite closely, though in opposite directions. The inflation rate is less consistently related to the other two. Until the 1970s, inflation rates in the United States tended to be low when growth was slow and unemployment was high. Higher inflation rates went with rapid growth and low unemployment rates. In the 1970s, however, the U.S. economy experienced slow growth, high unemployment, and high inflation all at once. The mid-1980s saw stable growth with both unemployment and inflation rates lower than before.

**FIGURE 8
GROWTH,
UNEMPLOYMENT, AND
INFLATION, 1950–1990**
Combining the three major macroeconomic variables in a single graph shows some pattern of their moving together. Economic growth and unemployment, in particular, move rather consistently in opposite directions. The link between these two variables and inflation is stronger in earlier periods but quite weak in the last two decades.

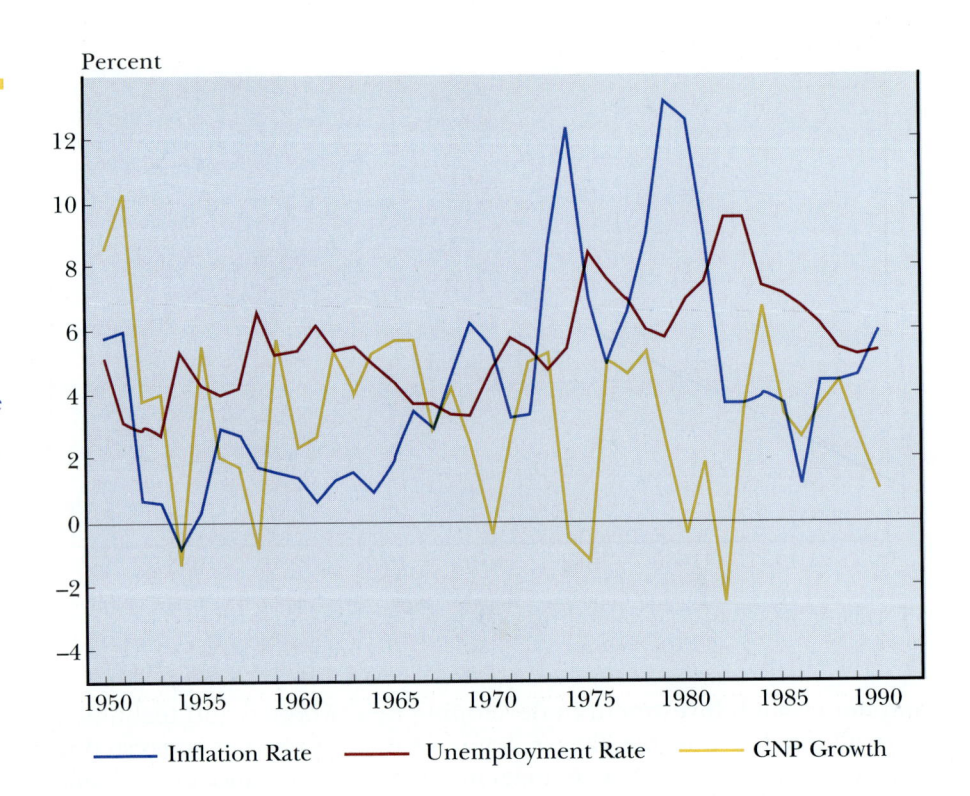

Over the course of a longer period, the major macroeconomic variables tend to move together in a rather predictable fashion, although not always in the "right" direction. When there is slow growth or even falling output, rising unemployment, and/or high inflation rates, the government often intervenes to try to "correct" the course of these variables. **Stabilization policy** consists of those actions of government designed to smooth out ups and downs in output, employment, and prices.

stabilization policy
Government actions designed to smooth out sharp changes in output, employment, and the price level.

business cycle
An observed and repeated pattern of ups and downs in real output, employment, and prices.

peak
A high point in a business cycle, where output turns downward.

recession
A state of an economy marked by a decline in real output for two or more successive quarters.

BUSINESS CYCLES

An observed and repeated pattern of ups and downs in output, employment, and prices was named the **business cycle** in the nineteenth century. A simplified business cycle is shown in Figure 9. In the expansionary phase of the cycle (from upturn through peak), output increases, prices rise rapidly, and unemployment falls. Productivity tends to increase as the economy emerges from the trough of a recession. Firms have kept some workers on during the recession but have not used them fully. As sales increase, firms employ these workers more fully, and productivity rises. As expansion continues, new and less experienced workers are hired. Then the increase in both productivity and output starts to slow, although employment continues to rise.

RECESSIONS, TROUGHS, EXPANSIONS, AND PEAKS. As output reaches a high point, or **peak**, and turns down, prices tend to fall also, or at least to rise at a slower rate. The downturn of output is called a **recession**. The Com-

Level of Economic Activity
(Real GNP)

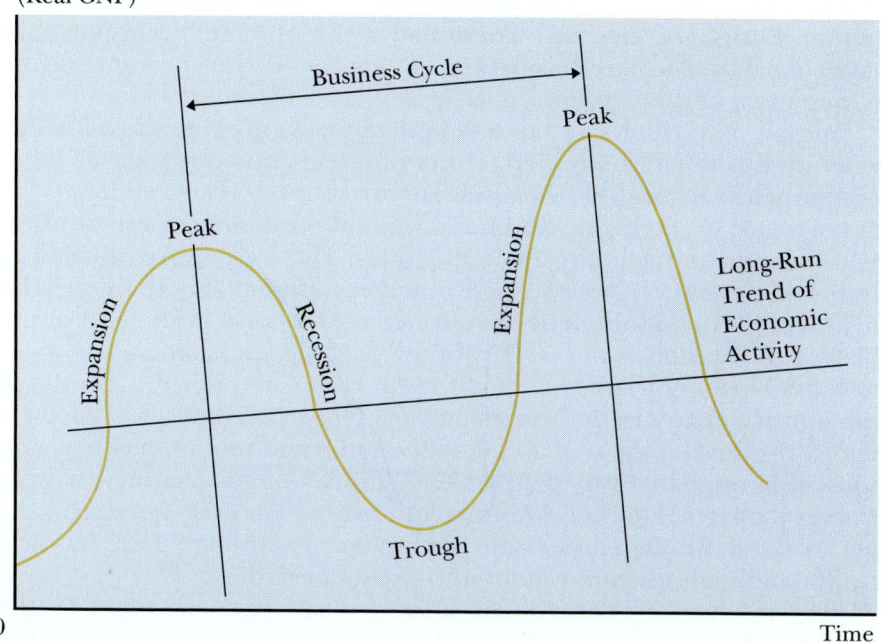

FIGURE 9
THE BUSINESS CYCLE This typical business cycle shows changes in the level of economic activity over time. In this case, the peaks and troughs are equal in magnitude, and the upturn and downturn take the same length of time. Actual cycles may be less symmetric, with upturns greater or smaller than downturns in size or duration. The cycle is measured from peak to peak. The trend line is the underlying growth rate of output.

merce Department's rule is that the economy is in a recession when output (adjusted for price changes) declines for two or more successive quarters. Unemployment increases and income and output fall, until the lower turning point, or **trough**, when output reaches its lowest level. Then the process starts over again. The upturn from trough to peak is an **expansion**. A complete cycle goes from peak to peak.

Each successive peak (and trough) should occur at a higher level of output because the business cycle is a fluctuation around a trend line of growing output over time. For example, a six-year business cycle with a trend growth rate of output of 2 percent a year should see a final peak of output that is 12 to 13 percent above the previous peak.

trough
A low point in a business cycle, where output turns upward.

expansion
A period of economic growth extending from a trough to the next peak in a business cycle.

EARLY BUSINESS CYCLE THEORIES. Much of the early measurement work in macroeconomics was related to the study of business cycles. Researchers identified recurring patterns of upturns and downturns at intervals of eight years (the general business cycle) and twenty years (linked to activity in building construction). In the nineteenth century, macroeconomics meant describing and attempting to explain these business cycles.

These observed ups and downs in economic activity were explained in some rather creative ways. One of these explanations was the sunspot theory, developed by English economist William Stanley Jevons. Unusually severe radioactive storms on the surface of the sun, known as sunspots, seemed to be closely linked to business cycles. This link may sound like a perfect example of the association-causation fallacy discussed in Chapter 1, but there was some plausible reasoning behind it. Sunspots do affect weather patterns on earth, and the agricultural sector (then the largest single sector of the economy) has always been highly dependent on the weather. However, even with the declining relative importance of agriculture, business cycles have continued to be observed. Sunspots may have contributed to early business cycles, but they do not appear to be the driving force in this century.

Another contributor to the mystique of business cycles was a Russian economist, Nikolai Kondratieff. Other observers noted regular cycles of eight to ten years, with shorter cycles of two to three years and longer cycles of about twenty years. Kondratieff found even longer periods of expansion and contraction of about fifty years. These cycles are called Kondratieff cycles, or long waves. Some observers argue that both the regular eight-year cycle and the long-wave cycle turned down at the end of the 1920s, contributing to the severity of the Great Depression.

It has been suggested that the fifty-year cycles are related to the development of entire new industries and complexes of industries—for example, the development of automobiles, radio and motion pictures, and household appliances in the first few decades of this century. If Kondratieff was right, another downturn in the fifty-year cycle was due in the late 1970s. However, a depression did not occur, although there was slow growth and high unemployment during that period.

Most nineteenth-century economists focused their attention on the shorter eight- to ten-year cycle and the twenty-year cycle. They looked to patterns of consumption and investment for their explanations.

U.S. Economic Fluctuations since the Civil War

Some recent business cycles in the United States can be identified in Figure 8. There was a trough in 1953–1954 and another in 1957–1958. There were particularly severe downturns in 1974–1975 and 1980–1982. The data in this figure, however, are too recent to include the most famous downturn of the twentieth century: the Great Depression, which occurred from 1929 to 1937.

The U.S. economy experienced twenty-seven recessions between the end of the Civil War and 1990. On the average, a recession has occurred in the United States every 4½ years. The 1929–1933 recession was so severe it was given a special name: depression. A **depression** is a very severe recession. President Harry Truman once said that when your neighbor is out of work, that's a recession; but when you lose your job, that's a depression. In a depression, people suffer unemployment, inability to get credit, and losses of their homes, farms, savings, and businesses.

There were upturns and downturns in real output and employment in the nineteenth century. However, the variable for which the best data is available for that period is the price level. From the end of the Civil War in 1865 until the early 1900s, wholesale prices in the United States showed a downward trend. You might think that falling prices would have been greeted with enthusiasm. This, however, was not the view of most farmers, who were in debt for equipment, seed, livestock, and land. The payments on these debts were fixed in dollars, but the prices for farm products were falling. Falling prices made it difficult for farmers to meet the payments. This problem explains why people in the western areas of the United States were enthusiastic about **bimetallism** at the end of the nineteenth

depression
A very severe recession.

bimetallism
The use of both gold and silver as parts of the money stock.

International Perspective

The Great Depression in Europe and Canada

The Great Depression of the 1930s was not an American event but a worldwide event. The triggering event for the United States was the stock market crash of Black Friday, October 29, 1929. For Europeans, it was the collapse of the Kredit Anstalt Bank in Austria in 1930, a major bank. Other banks failed in its wake.

Two important conditions in the early 1930s made the Depression spread from country to country. One of these conditions was the remnants of the international gold standard, battered by World War I but still in effect. The gold standard linked the banking systems of many countries and limited the power of national banking systems to expand their money supply unless they had enough gold backing for any added currency. Nations that lost gold to foreigners were forced to contract their money supplies at a time when expansion of the money supply would have been a more suitable policy. As the Depression deepened, one country after another abandoned the gold standard, usually only after the domestic money supply had shrunk to a much smaller size.

The second condition was protectionism. Many countries, including the United States, reacted to falling output and rising unemployment by trying to "keep jobs at home." They tried to substitute domestic production for imported goods by imposing high tariffs and other restrictions—a policy known as "beggar thy neighbor." Some economists even argue that protectionism caused the Great Depression. Most economists would agree that it made the Depression even more severe. The physical volume of trade fell by one-third in the early years of the Depression. Because of falling prices, the value of trade fell by two-thirds.

The Depression's effects in each country can be measured by what happened to output and unemployment during the worst period, 1929–1932. Partly because of their great prosperity in the 1920s, the United States and Canada experienced the largest declines in total output, measured in current dollars. The market value of output fell 25 percent in Canada and 26 percent in the United States in that worst period. Part of the decline was in real output and part was due to falling prices. In Europe, where the 1920s had not been as prosperous, declines in the market value of output were less drastic but still striking: 12 percent in France, 16 percent in Germany, and 10 percent in Sweden. (The United Kingdom, coming off a bad decade in the 1920s, actually saw a slight rise in output of about 2 percent from 1929 to 1932.) The unemployment statistics were even grimmer. The table below shows the unemployment rates for 1929 and 1932.

The political effects of the Great Depression were far-reaching. In the United States, it spawned Social Security, unemployment compensation, welfare programs, bank regulation, and other government programs. The role of government was thus greatly expanded. In Germany and Italy, the frustrations of the Great Depression led to the rise of fascist governments under Hitler and Mussolini. Canada and many Western European nations followed the same path as the United States in building a social safety net for those who lost their source of income. Most Western European governments, however, went much further, creating welfare states that provided health care, public housing, income support programs, and similar services.

Unemployment Rates for 1929 and 1932

Year	Germany	Sweden	United Kingdom	Canada	United States
1929	5.9%	2.4%	5.9%	2.9%	3.1%
1932	17.2%	6.8%	13.1%	17.6%	23.5%

century. This policy would have expanded the U.S. money stock by making silver serve as money along with gold.[10] Farmers hoped that this increase in the money supply would raise prices or at least help curtail falling prices. Bimetallism was not adopted, although it was an important issue in the 1896 presidential campaign. The Democratic candidate for President, William Jennings Bryan, made an electrifying speech against the gold standard and in favor of bimetallism. His theme was "You shall not crucify mankind upon a cross of gold!" and it nearly won him the election.

Price levels rose sharply during World War I, so sharply that efforts were made to measure the effects of inflation on the purchasing power of wages for shipbuilders and other war workers. The outcome of this measurement effort was the first consumer price index. After World War I, prices dropped sharply from the high levels reached in wartime. This fall was accompanied by a sharp contraction in industrial production during the postwar recession of the early 1920s. (Reliable measures of real output and changes in real output began to be available only early in the twentieth century. Growth of real output is the single best measure of the ups and downs in economic activity.)

After a relatively prosperous and mildly inflationary period for the rest of the 1920s, there was a sharp and prolonged fall in prices, output, and employment between 1929 and 1933. This downturn marked the beginning of the Great Depression. It occurred not only in the United States but in many other countries as well. Wholesale prices fell by about one-third between 1929 and 1933. As production in the United States began to recover after 1933, prices also began to rise. Then there was a sharp setback in output, employment, and prices in 1937–1938.

With the outbreak of World War II, prices began a sharp rise, both output and employment rose dramatically, and unemployment almost disappeared. The United States experienced more minor ups and downs in the late 1940s and 1950s, followed by a period of fairly steady growth from 1961 to 1968. The ups and downs resumed with the recession of 1969–1970. There was a severe downturn in 1973–1975 and another in 1980–1982.

In the years since World War II, the most significant change from the prewar period is that declining real output has been much less likely to be accompanied by a fall in prices. When prices have declined, they have not fallen nearly as much as in periods before World War II. A decline in economic activity that is not accompanied by a fall in the price level is referred to as **stagflation**. A combination of the words *stagnation* and *inflation*, this term means that the economy is stagnant (not growing), but there is also inflation at the same time. In the 1974–1975 recession, prices continued to rise sharply. Not until the relatively severe 1980–1982 recession did the rate of inflation fall sharply. Inflation rates remained low through the late 1980s.

stagflation
An economic condition of slow growth, high unemployment, and inflation.

A Case Study in Business Cycles: The Great Depression
The Great Depression brought severe economic hardships to a large portion of the U.S. population. Real output fell by more than one-third. Un-

---

10. The bimetallic standard was used in the United States from the early 1800s until 1878. Then it was abandoned and replaced by the gold standard.

employment rose to almost 25 percent of the work force in the depths of the Depression. People who had jobs were worried they would lose them. Many jobs were converted to a part-time basis in order to spread the work among more people. In addition, banks were failing. Between 1929 and 1933, the number of commercial banks in the United States fell by one-third. More than a fifth of all surviving banks had to suspend operations for some time because of financial problems. Few depositors ever recovered any of the funds they lost.

The effect on people went beyond economic hardships. America seemed to have lost its bright promise. People who had worked hard all their lives, who had saved and planned for the future, and who had believed in the work ethic found themselves wiped out. They lost homes, businesses, and jobs—through no fault of their own. Retired people found their stocks and bonds nearly worthless, and their savings vanished in bank failures. Many people's self-images and status depend on their jobs, on their success in the workday world, and on their ability to provide for their families. The Depression sowed doubt and fear among those who lost their jobs and those in danger of losing theirs. In his first inaugural address, President Franklin D. Roosevelt said, "The only thing we have to fear is fear itself." He was talking about the social, spiritual, and moral crisis in America as well as the economic problems.

The suffering during the Depression was not eased by programs available today, such as unemployment insurance, welfare, Social Security, and food stamps. These programs were in large part inspired by the experiences of the Depression. In 1933, people out of work had to rely mainly on private charity and relief from state and local governments, which were facing hard times themselves. Many city governments were unable to pay their bills because property owners had defaulted on local property taxes. Thus, local governments were in no position to help their residents. In addition, many people were reluctant to accept help either from private charities or from the government.

Economic conditions were no better abroad. The Depression affected every European country. Banks failed, and the European financial system was badly shaken. The United States and European countries raised tariffs and took other antitrade measures in an effort to create jobs by substituting domestic production for imported goods. Trade fell drastically. (The consequences of this policy will be discussed in detail in the chapter on international trade.)

The Roosevelt administration tried to deal with both the immediate emergency and the long-term issues. People had to be put back to work and, in the meantime, had to be given help. To put people back to work, Roosevelt and his advisers experimented with emergency government hiring programs. This policy was one of the early instances of the proposal that government should be the employer of last resort for people who can't find jobs elsewhere.

Beyond the emergency needs, the Roosevelt administration felt that policies had to be adopted to ensure that the Great Depression would never happen again. There should be programs to aid people in hard times as a matter of "right," so they didn't have to feel ashamed. The safety net of social welfare programs, such as Old Age and Survivors Insurance

(Social Security), Aid to Families with Dependent Children, and unemployment compensation, was created during this period. In addition, deposit insurance and other banking regulations were put in place during the Great Depression to safeguard people's savings.

Within the field of economics, the Depression and the resulting policies of the Roosevelt administration set the stage for importing the new ideas of the Keynesian revolution from England. The impact of the Great Depression on policy, programs, and economic thinking far outlasted the soup kitchens and federal relief agencies it spawned.

The misery and fear of the Depression led to political changes in many countries. In January 1933, Adolf Hitler became Chancellor of Germany, a country having severe economic problems. The Depression is also credited with helping Mussolini rise to power in Italy. In the United States, unhappy voters rejected Herbert Hoover in the 1932 election in favor of Franklin Roosevelt. The Socialist candidate, Norman Thomas, received almost 900,000 votes in that election. The Communist candidate received more than 100,000 votes.

Despite his campaign promise to balance the federal budget, Roosevelt was a pragmatic politician, willing to try various tactics to solve the pressing economic problems. One such scheme was to put people back to work by employing them on government projects such as constructing dams and public buildings, sewers and streets. Naturally, the jobless who found work on these projects were pleased. Not only were they making money, but they had also regained the dignity of having worthwhile work and providing for their families. There seemed to be no harm and much good in such projects. Jobless workers were once again providing things people could use. One of the most disturbing aspects of the Depression was the terrible paradox that many people were living in great need of goods and services while many workers couldn't get jobs to produce those things. There were, however, some abuses of these "make work" projects. A standard joke told of the government's hiring some workers to dig ditches and other workers to fill them in again. There were stories of public workers spending their days in parks, leaning on rakes or shovels. On balance, however, the majority of the American public supported such schemes to move the country out of the Depression.

By the presidential election of 1936, the country was hardly back to normal, as the unemployment rates in Figure 6 show. But in a definite sign of approval of Roosevelt's policies, the people re-elected him overwhelmingly. He carried every state except Maine and Vermont.

STABILIZATION POLICY AND THE GREAT DEPRESSION

The Depression influenced the direction of future macroeconomic policy because it was so severe that it brought many new programs and experimental policies into being as part of an effort to "do something." Roosevelt and his advisers developed their plans for government spending and government jobs to reduce unemployment during the Depression on an *ad hoc* basis, with little theory behind them. Economists had already begun to provide theoretical reasons for such approaches. Swedish economists such as Erik Lindahl and Gunnar Myrdal, members of the Stockholm School, had proposed in the late 1920s and early 1930s that governments abandon the goal of balancing the budget annually.[11] Instead, they argued, the budget should be balanced over the course of the business cycle. According to the Stockholm School, when output is falling and unemployment is rising, government should spend more to put people back to work, even if this produces a government deficit. In boom times, the government could run a surplus by cutting back on its projects. This surplus would cool off the boom while paying off the money borrowed during the deficit years. Only over the entire course of a business cycle, then, would the government budget be balanced. This kind of government stabilization policy is called countercyclical policy. **Countercyclical policy** is any set of government actions intended to offset the cyclical ups and downs of the macro economy.

Much more influential than the Stockholm School was a book that came out in 1936, the year of Roosevelt's re-election. That book was *The General Theory of Employment, Interest, and Money*, by British economist John Maynard Keynes. At that time, the Depression in the United States still had five more years to run before it would end as the country entered World War II. Recovery from the Depression was already progressing in Great Britain and in some other countries, including Germany. Keynes, his theories, and his followers did not really have much influence on either the British or the American recovery. However, the Depression convinced many people that Keynesian theory was right and that it provided sound guidelines for economic policy making. Not until the 1970s were there serious challenges to Keynesian ideas about macroeconomic policy.

The Great Depression was a painful and difficult experience for almost all Americans. It forced economists and politicians to think more carefully about macroeconomics and economic policy. The Depression set the stage for Keynes's ideas to challenge the theories and models economists had been working with. In order to test these new ideas, it was necessary to have better measures of output, employment, prices, and other variables than had been developed in the past. Beginning in the 1930s, economists devoted much more attention to measuring economic aggregates in order to have the information needed to carry out a countercyclical policy. The next chapter will address the measurement of these economic aggregates.

countercyclical policy Government actions designed to offset the cyclical ups and downs of the macro economy.

SUMMARY

1. The circular flow model represents the aggregate level of economic activity. Adding a credit market, the government, and a foreign sector provides a more realistic picture of the workings of the macro economy.
2. The major macroeconomic goals are economic growth, price stability, and full employment.
3. Economic growth is measured by changes in real output (or sometimes industrial production). Economic growth of about 4 percent a year is generally regarded as feasible and desirable because it raises the standard of

---

11. Myrdal was awarded the Nobel Prize in economics in 1974. His early work in macroeconomics was noted as well as his later work in sociology and development economics.

living and reduces unemployment. However, economic growth creates some costs in terms of environmental quality and strains on the infrastructure.

4. Price stability is measured by the inflation rate, or changes in the Consumer Price Index (CPI). Unstable prices are usually rising prices. A sustained general rise in the price level is inflation. Inflation causes a redistribution of income and wealth, confuses market signals, discourages saving and investment, and creates menu costs.

5. Full employment is usually reached when about 94 to 95 percent of the labor force is employed. That is, there is an unemployment rate of about 5 to 6 percent. Normal unemployment is partly frictional (due to new entrants in the job market or workers between jobs) and partly structural (due to a mismatch between workers and job openings). Unemployment in excess of a normal level is usually due to declines in real output. This kind of unemployment is called cyclical unemployment and is a macroeconomic policy concern.

6. Productivity is a measure of output per worker and is important for sustained economic growth.

7. Business cycles describe the ups and downs of output, employment, and prices.

8. The most significant macroeconomic event in the twentieth century was the Great Depression. It not only had important economic and political effects but also led to many changes in macroeconomic theory and policy.

NEW TERMS

saving
investment
credit market
leakages
injections
deficit
surplus
imports
exports

balance on goods and services
economic growth
infrastructure
inflation
price index
Consumer Price Index (CPI)
full employment

frictional unemployment
structural unemployment
cyclical unemployment
productivity
stabilization policy
business cycle
peak
recession

trough
expansion
depression
bimetallism
stagflation
countercyclical policy

QUESTIONS FOR DISCUSSION

1. What are the costs and benefits of rapid economic growth?

2. Can you think of any benefits of having high rates of inflation? Of having high rates of unemployment?

3. Using the figures in this chapter, see if you can trace the relationship between changes in output and consumer prices, unemployment, and productivity for each of the following years, all of which showed signs of a recession: 1955, 1958, 1961, 1970, 1974–1975, 1980, 1982.

4. Why is productivity important? How is it likely to be affected by a large increase of new entrants into the labor force? By improvements in technology? By investment in new and better equipment? Why was there a connection among all of these in the 1970s in the United States?

5. How do you think interest rates would be affected if inflation occurred that took everyone by surprise? How would the effect be different if the inflation were expected?

6. What kinds of changes will increase the size of the circular flow? What kinds of changes will decrease the flow?

7. What is a leakage? What is an injection? Identify three kinds of leakages and three kinds of injections.

8. Which of the following are structurally unemployed, frictionally unemployed, or cyclically unemployed?
   a. a new college graduate seeking a first job
   b. a teenager who quit a fast-food job because she didn't like the hours
   c. farmers in Iowa who had to sell their farms because of inadequate demand for farm products and who are looking for a different line of work in a different area
   d. a person with a Ph.D. in classical languages, a field in which there are a hundred applicants for every available teaching position
   e. a person laid off because of a recession

9. How will each of the following affect the flow of real output in the circular flow diagram?
   a. an improvement in technology
   b. a decline in business investment
   c. an increase in taxes, with no increase in government spending as the government attempts to balance its budget
   d. an increase in exports
   e. a rise in the price level

10. Suppose there is a decline in real output. What

would you expect to happen to employment and to the inflation rate? Why?

11. Use the given data to calculate each rate of change.
   a. Year 1, output index = 100; year 2, output index = 110. What is the rate of growth of output from year 1 to year 2?
   b. Year 1, price index = 140; year 2, price index = 155. What is the inflation rate between year 1 and year 2?
   c. Year 1, productivity index = 25; year 2, productivity index = 27. What is the rate of growth of productivity from year 1 to year 2?

12. Suggest three ways in which the Great Depression affected economic policy in the United States.

13. Why is it unlikely that a rate of economic growth in excess of 3 or 4 percent can be sustained for a long period?

14. Why were farmers in favor of expanding the U.S. money supply in the late nineteenth century?

15. How can you tell when an economy is in a recession?

16. Try constructing an index of your own, using the following data. Suppose that 40% of the cost of car repairs is labor, 50% is parts, and 10% is miscellaneous. Suppose that in the first year the cost of labor is $12 an hour, parts cost an average of $15 each, and miscellaneous costs run about $5. In the second year, labor rises to $15, parts average $20, and miscellaneous costs are unchanged. What is your "price index" for car repairs? By how much has the cost risen?

SUGGESTIONS FOR FURTHER READING

Barber, William J. *From New Era to New Deal: Herbert Hoover, the Economists, and American Social Policy.* London: Cambridge University Press, 1985. Examines attempts to stem the flood of decline in the Hoover years before Roosevelt's New Deal.

Bird, Caroline. *The Invisible Scar: The Great Depression and What It Did to American Life, From Then Until Now.* New York: Longman, 1966. A lively account of the aftereffects of the Great Depression.

Galbraith, John K. *The Great Crash of Nineteen Twenty-Nine.* Boston: Houghton Mifflin, 1979. A classic and well-written account of the events leading up to the Great Depression.

Hibbs, Douglas A., Jr. *The American Political Economy: Macroeconomics and Electoral Politics.* Cambridge, MA: Harvard University Press, 1987. Chapters 2 and 3 of this very readable blend of history, economics and politics offer a thorough discussion of the costs of unemployment and inflation.

Hughes, James J., and Richard Perlman. *The Economics of Unemployment: A Comparative Analysis of Britain and the United States.* London: Cambridge University Press, 1984. A nontechnical discussion of how unemployment is measured in both countries, why it is different, which groups are unemployed, and other unemployment issues.

James, Harold. *The German Slump: Politics and Economics 1924–1936.* Cambridge, England: Cambridge University Press, 1987. A look at the experience of the Great Depression from the perspective of the German economy.

AFTER STUDYING THIS CHAPTER, YOU SHOULD BE ABLE TO:

1. Distinguish between stocks and flows and between income statements and balance sheets.
2. Explain the purposes and uses of national income accounting.
3. Describe how gross national product (GNP), net national product (NNP), national income (NI), and personal income (PI) are computed.
4. Explain the relation between the national income accounts and the circular flow model.
5. Explain why actual saving and investment must always be equal in the national income accounts.
6. Describe the drawbacks of the GNP as a measure of economic well-being.
7. Compute a simple price index.
8. Identify the major price indices and explain how each is used.
9. Describe the process by which unemployment figures are calculated.

CHAPTER 5
MEASURING ECONOMIC PERFORMANCE AND NATIONAL INCOME ACCOUNTING

INTRODUCTION

Chapter 4 introduced the basic macroeconomic goals of economic growth, full employment, and price stability. In order to determine how well an economy is doing in terms of those goals, economists have to be able to measure output, employment, and the price level. Measurement of macroeconomic variables is the subject of this chapter. All nations make some effort to track the behavior of output, employment, and prices. In the United States, measurement of output, known as national income accounting, is the responsibility of the Department of Commerce. The Department of Labor collects and reports data on employment and price level.

BASIC ACCOUNTING CONCEPTS

Two basic kinds of accounting statements are used in economics as well as in all business fields. These statements are balance sheets and income statements. In accounting, balance sheets measure stocks of assets and liabilities at a point in time. Income statements record flows of income and expenditure over time. National income accounts take the form of an income statement.

STOCKS AND FLOWS

Economists find it useful to distinguish between stock variables and flow variables. Stock variables appear on balance sheets, and flow variables appear on income statements. A **stock variable** is a variable that is defined at a point in time, such as December 31, 1991. Stocks are existing quantities of goods or assets. An example of a stock variable is the number of apartment units that exist today. Notice the date on this stock—today. A year from today, there will be more or fewer units, depending on how many new apartments are built and how many old ones are torn down.

A **flow variable** is a variable that is defined over a period of time, such as

stock variable
A variable that is defined at a point in time.

flow variable
A variable that is defined over a period of time.

TABLE 3
U.S. GROSS NATIONAL PRODUCT BY PRODUCING SECTOR, 1990 (BILLIONS OF DOLLARS)

Business sector		$4620.3
Government sector		579.4
Federal	$178.5	
State and local	400.9	
Household and nonprofit sector		224.8
Foreign sector (net imports)		38.6
Gross national product		$5,463.0

Source: Council of Economic Advisers, *Economic Report of the President* (Washington, DC: U.S. Government Printing Office, 1991).

final goods
Goods that will not be further processed or resold.

intermediate goods
Goods that will be further processed before final sale.

intermediate goods. **Final goods** are those that will not be further processed or resold. **Intermediate goods** are those that will be further processed into final goods. For example, flour sold to consumers in supermarkets is counted in the GNP but flour sold to bakers is not, because they use the flour to make bread. That sale of flour will be counted in the GNP as part of the value of bread produced.[2]

The output of the business sector reflects sales of final product, measured in dollars. Most U.S. output is produced by the business sector, as you would expect in a market economy. National income accountants get a large share of their data from various financial reports of the business sector, such as sales tax returns, income tax returns, and reports by corporations to their stockholders.

Governments—federal, state, and local—also produce services such as public education, police protection, and national defense. Data for the public sector is easy to find, because all governments must report to their citizens each year how much money was received and how it was spent. Although the data is easy to come by, the market value of government output is difficult to measure because these services are not sold. Since government agencies hire employees to produce these services, national income accounts measure the value of government output by the compensation paid to employees. The services may actually be worth more or less than this amount. In the absence of a market price, however, labor cost is the only available measure of the value of government output.

A relatively small part of the GNP is produced in the household and nonprofit sector and by the foreign sector. The household and nonprofit sector accounts for the value of goods and services produced by nonprofit, nongovernmental agencies, such as private schools, museums, charitable organizations, and social clubs, as well as some small in-home businesses, such as family day care. This data is assembled primarily from income tax returns and other sources.

The foreign sector consists of producers who buy from and sell to

---

2. Another way of computing GNP is the value-added approach. With this method, each product or service is counted when it is sold, regardless of whether the sale is final. However, the cost of goods and services that went into its production is subtracted. For example, if a baker buys flour, the flour is counted when it is sold to the baker. The bread that the baker sells is also counted, but the value of the baker's purchases of flour is subtracted. The difference between the value of goods and services purchased and the value of goods and services sold is the value added. This method should give the same result as adding final goods and services.

other countries. This data is easy to collect because exports and imports pass through a limited number of points of entry and exit, where they are checked by customs officials.

Gross National Product by Buying Sector

The upper half of the circular flow diagram accounts for GNP as spending by buying sectors. A basic assumption behind the national income accounts is that everything that is produced is also sold. If the business sector produces goods that are not sold, these goods must be added to inventories. The changes in these inventories are counted as "sales" of output to the business sector. **Business inventories** are stocks of goods held by firms from which they can make sales to meet demand.

Table 4 shows how U.S. GNP for 1990 was divided among the four groups of buyers to which it could be sold: households, business firms, government, and the foreign sector. These four groups correspond to the four actors in the circular flow model. This second (and more widely used) way of accounting for output also provides a cross check on the data collected for the producing sector.

The Household Sector. Sales to the household sector are called **consumption expenditures**. Since consumer purchases are final sales, they are all counted as part of GNP. Consumption expenditures in turn can be divided into various categories, which are useful because each one responds a little differently to changes in economic conditions. **Consumer durables** are such long-lasting items as refrigerators and washing machines. **Consumer nondurables** are items that have a very short useful life, such as a loaf of bread or a shirt. **Consumer services** are that part of household consumption composed of nontangible activities. Examples of services

business inventories Stocks of goods held by firms from which they can make sales to meet demand.

consumption expenditures Sales to the household sector.

consumer durables Goods that last, on average, a substantial length of time.

consumer nondurables Goods that last, on average, only a short period of time.

consumer services That part of household consumption composed of nontangible activities.

		Percentage of GNP
Gross national product		$5,463.0	100.0
Personal consumption expenditures		$3,658.1	67.0
Consumer durables	$ 481.6		8.8
Consumer nondurables	1,194.2		21.9
Consumer services	1,982.3		36.3
Gross private domestic investment		745.0	13.6
Fixed investment (plant and equipment)	$ 524.3		9.6
Residential construction	222.9		4.1
Change in inventories	−2.2		0.4
Government purchases of goods and services		1,098.0	20.1
Federal government	$ 424.2		7.8
State/local government	673.8		12.3
Net exports of goods and services		−38.0	−0.7
Exports	$ 670.4		12.3
Imports	−708.4		−13.0

Table 4 U.S. Gross National Product by Buying Sector, 1990 (billions of dollars)

Source: Council of Economic Advisers, *Economic Report of the President* (Washington, DC: U.S. Government Printing Office, 1991).

gross private domestic investment
Purchases by the business sector of final output.

fixed investment
The part of business investment that does not add to inventories; consists of new plants and equipment and residential construction.

are haircuts, concerts, being waited on at a restaurant, or having a gardener tend your yard. Services form a large part of total personal consumption, as Table 4 indicates.

THE BUSINESS SECTOR. Purchases by the business sector of final output are called **gross private domestic investment**. Gross investment is measured before subtracting capital goods that have worn out or become so obsolete they aren't worth using. Thus, if the business sector buys 10,000 tractors during one year but has to scrap 1,000 old tractors that year, the net change in the number of tractors is 9,000. Gross investment, however, is still 10,000 tractors. Net investment is 9,000.

What about the words *private* and *domestic*? The word *private* means investment by business firms, rather than by the government. The word *domestic* means that the investment was made in the United States, not in another country. In national income accounting, *investment* means the purchase of some real, tangible asset, such as a machine, a factory, or a stock of inventories. To an economist, buying bonds and making deposits in banks are actually forms of lending. When business firms use borrowed funds to purchase new plants or equipment or expand their inventories, they are investing in the sense meant by economists and national income accountants.

The components of gross private domestic investment are given in Table 4. Most investment consists of **fixed investment**, which is new plants or equipment, such as factories, tractors, drill presses, and computers. A second major component of gross private domestic investment is residential construction. If you think of investment as something that will be used to provide goods and services in the future, the idea that housing should be classed as investment rather than consumption makes a great deal of sense. Houses last a long time and produce "shelter services" to consumers in the future. (Those shelter services are counted under consumption.) Furthermore, many housing units, especially apartments, are owned by firms and rented to households. These housing units are even more like other business investments. Even when individuals purchase houses for their own use, this transaction is more like a business investment than an ordinary consumer purchase of a final good. A housing purchase, like a business investment, is a large expenditure, usually of borrowed money, that will provide a stream of services in the future.

There is no market transaction between the owner and the occupant of an owner-occupied house, because they are the same person. To determine a dollar value for those shelter services that owners "purchase" from themselves, national income accountants have to estimate the equivalent rental value. This value is what the owner-occupied housing would rent for in the market. This estimated value is then counted as a purchase of consumption services by the household sector.

The last component of gross private domestic investment is changes in business inventories. National income accountants treat inventory changes as sales by businesses to other businesses or to themselves. Since these inventories aren't used up in the current year, they are treated as final products, not intermediate goods. Inventories are counted in GNP for the year in which they are produced, not the year sold. Whatever firms produce that is not sold to other sectors becomes part of their investment in inventories. This method of accounting for inventories assures that the national income accounts balance. Every dollar of output produced has a buyer. If no one else wants some output, the accounts show that the firm that produced it has "bought" it to add to its own inventories. Business inventory is an important category to watch in the national income accounts. If firms experience undesired inventory changes, their efforts to restore inventories to desired levels will have a significant impact on output and employment.

THE GOVERNMENT SECTOR. A large part of a nation's income is claimed by government—federal, state and local—and a substantial share of output is produced by or for government. Total government expenditures account for about a third of U.S. national income. The federal government spent $1,273 billion in 1990. State and local governments added another $765 billion. Some of this money was spent to produce or to purchase goods and services, such as defense, health care, highways, police, education, and courts.[3] Other government expenditures were transfer payments, such as veterans' benefits, interest on the national debt, and Social Security benefits, which are not counted in GNP.

Purchase of goods and services by governments at all levels is a major component of GNP. The largest part of government expenditures is for salaries and wages for government employees. Governments produce services such as defense, education, and road repair using the labor of these employees. These services are treated as though the government "sold" them to itself.

Another component of government purchases in the national income accounts is spending for goods and services produced by other sectors, mainly the business sector. State and local governments actually purchase more goods and services than the federal government does. Some government purchases are used up almost immediately, such as food for army mess halls. Other government expenditures, such as those for dams or highways, result in goods that will last for years. These can be regarded as a form of "government investment." The national income accounts, however, do not distinguish between government consumption and government investment, but treat all government expenditures alike.

The value of government purchases in the national income accounts does not correspond to the size of the federal budget for two reasons. First, as we already indicated, national income accounts include state and local as well as federal expenditures. Second, a large part of government expenditures is not in payment for goods or productive services. About two-thirds of total government spending is for goods and services, but the rest is for transfer payments. **Transfer payments** are income payments to individuals who provide no goods or services in exchange. Veterans' benefits, welfare payments, unemployment compensation, and Social Security benefits are all examples of transfer payments. Most transfer payments

transfer payments
Income payments to individuals who provide no goods or services in exchange.

---

3. As you should recall from Chapter 4, total spending by the federal government is higher than that of state and local governments, but a large part of federal spending consists of transfer payments to individuals and grants to state and local governments.

come from the federal level, although many of them are administered by state and local governments.

THE FOREIGN SECTOR. The final group of buyers is the foreign sector. Consumption, investment, and government expenditures all include some imported goods, which must be subtracted from the GNP because they are produced elsewhere. Exports are part of domestic production, so they need to be included in GNP. Thus, exports are added and imports are subtracted to arrive at gross national product, or what was produced by a country's own factors of production. For convenience, national income accounts usually group these exports and imports together and report the difference between them as net exports of goods and services.

Net exports are usually a fairly small part of GNP but receive more attention than any of the other three components. The balance on goods and services (another name for net exports) can be either positive or negative. When it is negative, there is much concern about the effects of the "flood" of imports on competing American firms and of reduced export sales on American exporting industries. The use of net exports makes the foreign sector look less significant than it really is. Exports are now approximately 12 percent of GNP, and imports account for about 13 percent of total spending. The ratios of both exports and imports to GNP have increased in the last twenty years.

TOTAL SPENDING AND GNP. The sum of spending by the four buying sectors is GNP. Adding consumption spending by households (C), investment spending by business (I), purchases of goods and services by government (G), and spending by the foreign sector, or net exports ($EX-IM$), gives this formula for GNP:

$$GNP = C + I + G + (EX - IM).$$

This formula states that everything that is produced in a year must be purchased by one of the four buying sectors.

NATIONAL INCOME

The top half of the circular flow diagram measures the flow of output, or GNP. In the process of producing GNP, income is generated. This income is paid to the factors of production and corresponds to the accounting concept of national income. **National income (NI)** is income earned by the factors of production—land, labor, capital, and enterprise. It consists of wages, rent, interest, profit, and proprietors' net income and is shown on the bottom half of the circular flow.

The key to understanding NI is that all of the income generated in producing GNP must be accounted for in some way. Most of it is paid to the four factors of production. Thus, NI consists of rent, wages and salaries, interest, and profits. In a very simple economy, all of the value of final goods and services produced (GNP) would become payments to factors of production. GNP, which measures the flow in the product market of

national income (NI) Income earned by the four factors of production; consists of wages, rent, interest, profit, and proprietors' net income.

Chapter 5 Measuring Economic Performance

the circular flow diagram, and NI, which measures the flow in the factor market, would be identical. Since the actual economy is not so simple, some adjustments must be made in order to convert GNP to NI.

DEPRECIATION AND NET NATIONAL PRODUCT

The first adjustment to GNP is correcting to account for the fact that part of the capital stock is used up in the production process. Depreciation (called capital consumption allowance in the GNP accounts) is a cost of production that is not received as income by any factor of production.[4] The **capital consumption allowance** is the national income accountants' estimate of the depreciation of the nation's capital stock. In Table 5, GNP minus capital consumption allowance is equal to **net national product (NNP)**. Similarly, **net private domestic investment** is defined as gross private domestic investment minus the capital consumption allowance (depreciation). Net national product is equal to

$$NNP = C + I_n + G + (EX - IM),$$

where I_n represents net, rather than gross, investment. The only difference between GNP and NNP is that GNP includes gross private domestic investment but the investment term in NNP is net private domestic investment.

NNP is a more meaningful measure of production than GNP, because it excludes all intermediate products, including capital used up in the course of the year's production. GNP is more widely used, however, for two reasons. First, GNP figures are more precise than NNP figures because depreciation is difficult to measure or even estimate accurately. Second, GNP is more closely related than NNP to the behavior of employment and prices.

The World Resources Institute, a Washington-based environmental or-

capital consumption allowance
The national income accountants' estimate of the amount of the nation's capital stock used up in production during a year.

net national product (NNP)
Equal to GNP minus the capital consumption allowance (depreciation).

net private domestic investment
Gross private domestic investment minus the capital consumption allowance (depreciation).

GNP		$5,463.0
Less:	Capital consumption allowance	−575.7
Equals:	NNP	4,887.4
Less:	Indirect business taxes and nontax liability and business transfer payments	−475.4
Plus:	Net subsidies less surplus of government enterprises	+2.5
Plus (or minus):	Statistical discrepancy*	−3.1
Equals:	NI	$4,417.5

*The statistical discrepancy reconciles errors that arise from the two different data sources used. GNP is estimated from sales data. NI is estimated from factor income. The discrepancy is the remaining difference in estimates after the "plus" and "less" items have been added to or deducted from GNP.

TABLE 5
RELATION OF GNP, NNP, AND NI FOR 1990 (BILLIONS OF DOLLARS)

Source: Council of Economic Advisers, *Economic Report of the President* (Washington, DC: U.S. Government Printing Office, 1991).

---

4. Firms use the capital consumption allowance more for determining their corporate income tax liability than for providing a good estimate of actual economic depreciation. If tax laws allow businesses to overstate depreciation, firms will take advantage of this opportunity to reduce their taxes. If tax laws don't allow businesses to claim all of their actual depreciation, then the official capital consumption allowance figures will understate depreciation. Federal tax laws have been very generous in allowing depreciation in the past, especially from 1981 to 1986. However, the 1986 tax reform bill greatly reduced this loophole.

ganization, has developed another version of NNP. It is arrived at by subtracting depletion of natural resources as well as depreciation of capital equipment from GNP.[5] This group argues that if capital used up is subtracted, it makes sense to also subtract nonrenewable resources that are used up. The group's first set of estimates of this new concept was made for Indonesia, because so much of that country's output is based on natural resources, mainly oil and natural gas. The correction reduced the estimate of Indonesia's output by 17% and reduced the country's estimated growth rate from 1971 to 1984 from an average of 7 percent to an average of 4 percent. No such estimates have yet been made for the United States.

FROM NET NATIONAL PRODUCT TO NATIONAL INCOME

There are a few more adjustments that must be made to NNP to obtain NI. We must subtract costs of production not paid to factors of production. These costs are indirect business taxes and business transfer payments. We need to add payments to factors of production that are not reflected in market prices. These payments consist of *net* subsidies to farmers and other businesses. Finally, the net surpluses of government enterprises, such as the U.S. Postal Service or a municipal water department, are subtracted. The resulting figure is NI, or that part of NNP that was earned by the factors of production.

Indirect business taxes, such as license fees, excise taxes, and business property taxes, are subtracted from NNP. They are reflected in the prices of final products but are not earned by any factor of production. Business transfer payments, such as private pension payments, bad debts, and prizes in promotional contests, are subtracted for the same reason. Also subtracted is the net surplus (or "profit") of any government enterprise that charges for services. Although this surplus is part of the price paid for services of the government enterprise, it is not earned by any owner of factors of production. Some such enterprises are subsidized, so their market prices reflect less than factor cost. These subsidies are *added* to NNP to determine NI. The sum of these corrections is the *net* amount added to (or subtracted from) NNP to obtain NI.

In Table 6, NI is computed as the sum of factor payments. NI consists of the total of wage and salary income, rental income, corporate profits, net interest earnings, and income of proprietors. (Proprietors are owners of small retail stores, independent farmers, and other businesses that are not corporations.) All of this income is earned by households. However, some of it is not actually paid out—such as the part of corporate profits that firms keep as undistributed profits or pay in corporate income taxes to the government.

Wages, interest, and corporate profits need no explanation, but proprietors' net income is more complicated. Net income for proprietorships consists mostly of wages and profits to the owner-worker. If the proprietor has invested funds in the business, some of this income is interest. Some of the proprietor's income is probably profit to enterprise. It is not possible to separate proprietors' net income into these components. Thus, it is listed as a single item in the national income accounts.

---

5. *Wasting Assets: Natural Resources in the National Income Accounts* (Washington, DC: World Resources Institute, June 1989).

TABLE 6
NATIONAL INCOME BY RECIPIENT, 1990 (BILLIONS OF DOLLARS)

NATIONAL INCOME	$4,417.5
Wages and supplements (including contributions to social insurance)	3,244.2
Proprietors' income	402.4
Rental income of persons*	6.7
Corporate profits	297.1
Net interest	467.1

*Includes the estimated rental value of owner-occupied housing.

Source: Council of Economic Advisers, *Economic Report of the President* (Washington, DC: U.S. Government Printing Office, 1991).

Note that a large part of rental income is *imputed*. National income accountants estimate how much owners would have to pay if they rented their homes instead of owning them. This imputed value of the shelter services of owner-occupied housing is included in NI. Rent paid by one business to another will be netted out, since this is an intermediate rather than a final service. One reason the rental income figure is so small is that it is net of depreciation. Gross rent was $61.4 billion in 1990, but depreciation reduced that amount by $54.8 billion.

Net interest omits all payments of interest from one member of the household sector to another. For example, the interest paid to a relative for a loan to buy a car is not included in national income. Also, interest on government bonds is treated as a transfer payment. It is included in personal income but not in national income because it is not regarded as a cost of production.

NI measures the value of factor services and provides a useful cross check on the accuracy of the GNP and NNP figures. However, from the standpoint of households, the important income flow is not what they *earn* (NI) but what they *receive*. What they receive is personal income.

PERSONAL INCOME AND DISPOSABLE INCOME

Personal income (PI) is the income *received* by households (whether earned or not). National income (NI) is the income *earned* by the household sector. The major differences between NI and PI are corporate income taxes, undistributed corporate profits, and transfer payments. The first two items are subtracted from NI to compute PI because they are earned by households but not actually paid out to them. Net transfer payments are added because they are received but not earned.

Transfer payments are not a part of NI because they represent only a movement of spending power from sector to another. These payments are not related to any current production in the top half of the circular flow model. Transfer payments include a modest amount of business transfer payments and a much larger volume of government transfer payments ($660 billion in 1990).[6] The latter include Social Security, unemployment compensation, Aid to Families with Dependent Children, and veterans'

personal income (PI) The income received by households; computed from NI by subtracting corporate profits taxes and undistributed corporate profits and adding net transfer payments.

---

6. Transfers from households to other households do not change personal income because they remain within the household sector.

TABLE 7
CONVERSION OF NATIONAL INCOME TO PERSONAL INCOME FOR 1990 (BILLIONS OF DOLLARS)

NATIONAL INCOME		$4,417.5
Less:	Undistributed corporate profits,	− 173.3
	corporate profits taxes (includes inventory valuation adjustments), and social insurance contributions	− 506.9
Plus:	Net interest payments	+ 213.8
	Government transfer payments	+ 659.5
	Business transfer payments	+ 35.0
Equals:	Personal Income	$4,699.6

Source: Council of Economic Advisers, *Economic Report of the President* (Washington, DC: U.S. Government Printing Office, 1991).

benefits. *Net* transfer payments are arrived at by subtracting contributions of firms and employees to social insurance from gross transfer payments. Net interest payments are also treated like transfer payments, since such payments are not related to current output. Table 7 shows how 1989 national income is converted to personal income for that year.

The household sector can use its personal income in three ways: (1) to pay personal taxes to various levels of government, (2) to spend on consumption goods, or (3) to save. The income the household sector has left after taxes is called **disposable income**. Disposable income can be spent on consumption or saved. It is very useful for forecasting household consumption, the largest component of GNP.

disposable income
Income received by households and available to spend or save; equals PI less personal taxes.

NATIONAL INCOME ACCOUNTS AND THE CIRCULAR FLOW

The concepts of NI, NNP, and GNP reflect the income and spending flows of the circular flow model discussed in Chapters 2 and 4. Let's begin with the fact that personal income can be used in three ways:

(1) PI = consumption + personal saving + personal taxes.

The relationship between NI and PI is given by

(2) NI = PI + (corporate saving + corporate profits taxes)
− net transfer payments.

Thus, we can substitute for PI from equation (1) into equation (2) to account for all the uses of NI as follows:

(3) NI = consumption + personal saving + personal taxes
+ (corporate saving + corporate profits taxes)
− net transfer payments.

Taxes minus transfer payments are called net tax payments, since they represent income transferred to the government less income transferred back to households. Equation (3) says that NI is spent on consumption *or* used for net tax payments (business taxes and personal taxes less transfers) *or* used for some form of saving, either by households (personal saving) or by business firms (corporate saving). By definition, whatever income is not spent or paid in taxes has to be saved.[7]

If we let T represent net taxes and S the sum of household and business saving, then

$$NI = C + S + T.$$

This equation describes how households use the income received in the lower half of the circular flow model. Ignoring depreciation, the top half of the circular flow model can be represented by

$$GNP = NNP = C + I + G + (EX - IM).$$

If we ignore some of the smaller differences between NNP and NI (indirect business taxes, business transfer payments, and net subsidies to government enterprises), then NNP = NI. That is,

(4) $C + I + G + (EX - IM) = C + S + T.$

Subtracting consumption from each side of equation (4) gives

(5) $I + G + (EX - IM) = S + T.$

If we move imports to the right-hand side of equation (5), we have

$$I + G + EX = S + T + IM.$$

Note that the terms on the left-hand side of the equation correspond to the three kinds of injections into the circular flow discussed in Chapter 4. The terms on the right-hand side of the equation are the leakages out of the circular flow. Thus, when the national income accounts are balanced, the sum of expenditures, $C + I + G + (EX - IM)$, is always equal to the sum of factor earnings, or NI. Also, the leakages out of the circular flow are always equal to the injections. This relationship is a very important one in macroeconomics, as you will see in later chapters.

PRICES AND PRICE INDICES

The values of GNP, NNP, and NI that we have been discussing are all nominal values. In order to use GNP either to measure economic well-being or to forecast output or employment, economists need to know what is happening to real, physical production. A price index makes it possible to correct GNP figures for changes in the price level.

A price index, like any index, is a weighted average. Index values are composites of many numerical values, which are assigned weights based on their relative importance. The absolute value of any index has little meaning. The *relative value*, especially changes in the relative value, of an index is important. The fact that the Dow Jones industrial stock index passed the 2500 mark in 1987, for example, was only meaningful if you knew what its value was in earlier years.

---

7. Remember that consumption is defined as household expenditures on current output of final goods. If you buy an Impressionist painting (or a used bicycle or car), then you have merely passed on some of your income to someone else, who must decide whether to spend it or save it.

How Price Indices Are Constructed: The Consumer Price Index

A price index can be constructed in two different ways. One is to take a current-year market basket of goods and services and ask what it would have cost to buy the same collection last year or several years ago. This kind of index, a current weights index, assigns weights to the various items based on the composition of output or the consumption in the current year. The other way to construct a price index is to start with a market basket or output mix in some benchmark, or base, year. Then the behavior of the cost of that market basket is followed in succeeding years.

The most familiar price index, the Consumer Price Index (CPI), uses base-year weights. The current CPI is based on the mix of goods bought by a typical urban family of four in 1982–1983.[8] Suppose that typical family bought twenty pounds of ground beef, three pairs of jeans, five rolls of paper towels, and eight pounds of apples. Those goods and the amounts of each are used in computing the index. That basket of goods is priced at regular intervals to see what is happening to the CPI, or the "cost of living." Table 8 constructs a price index for those four items after determining their base-year and current-year prices.

Since the items in the market baskets are the same for both years, the increase from $75.00 to $88.90 must be due entirely to price changes. The index is 88.90/75.00 = 1.18, or, as it is usually written, 118. This means that prices rose, on the average, 18 percent. Note, however, that two prices rose more than 18 percent, one price rose less, and one price actually fell.

The actual CPI is based on a market basket of hundreds of items. To find out what is happening to the prices of particular groups of goods or services—such as housing, food, energy, and health care—you can check their price indices each month in the *Monthly Labor Review*. Indices for different regions of the country are also available. Some colleges and universities compute and publish a price index for their immediate areas.

Forbes magazine constructs a price index each year called "The Forbes Four Hundred Cost of Living Extremely Well Index."[9] This index includes such items as a Russian sable coat, tuition at Harvard, season tickets at the Metropolitan Opera, a private plane, an Olympic-size swimming pool, Cuban cigars, and other luxury items. In the late 1980s, this index was rising more rapidly than the CPI. However, little sympathy was generated in political circles for the plight of the extremely well-to-do.

Another tongue-in-cheek index was constructed by James Schick for the cost of the equipment that colonists were required to provide in order to accompany Captain John Smith to the New World in 1624.[10] Schick's list of food, clothing, household equipment, tools, and transportation included such hard-to-find items as powder and shot, swords, and muskets. A careful search for equivalent items led to the conclusion

---

8. The items in the market basket are not changed very often because of the cost and difficulty of carrying out the survey and processing the results. Until 1987, the most recent survey available was that for 1972–1973. Beginning in 1987, the 1982–1983 survey results became available and have since been used in constructing and revising price indices.

9. "Are You Watching, Chairman Greenspan?" *Forbes* (23 October 1989): 388–390. This figure is reported in the magazine each fall.

10. James B. M. Schick, "John Smith's Bill: Then and Now," *American Heritage* (November 1989): 158–165.

TABLE 8
COMPUTING A PRICE INDEX

ITEM	QUANTITY Q	BASE YEAR PRICE VALUE P_1	BASE YEAR TOTAL $(Q \times P_1)$	CURRENT YEAR PRICE VALUE P_2	CURRENT YEAR TOTAL $(Q \times P_2)$
Ground beef	20	$ 1.10	$22.00	$ 1.50	$30.00
Jeans	3	16.00	48.00	18.00	54.00
Paper towels	5	.60	3.00	.50	2.50
Apples	8	.25	2.00	.30	2.40
Value of market basket			$75.00		$88.90

that in 1989 these items would cost $3,190 (plus transatlantic passage for the settler and possessions). John Smith's estimate for the same list of goods was 12 pounds, 6 shillings, and 3 pence, or about $55 at the old dollar/pound exchange rate. Comparing these two figures gives you a very rough estimate of inflation over the last 365 years!

USES FOR THE CONSUMER PRICE INDEX

Price indices are useful for a number of purposes. If you are comparing job offers in different parts of the country, you will want to adjust salary offers to take into account differences in the local cost of living in each area. If you want to see if your real income has improved since last year, you need to adjust this year's nominal income for price changes.[11] Suppose, for example, that between 1988 and 1989 your nominal income rose from $20,000 to $22,000, a 10 percent increase. How much did your real income increase? The value of the CPI was 118.3 at the end of 1988 and 124.0 at the end of 1989 (compared to the base value of 100 for 1982–1984). The 1989 index divided by the 1988 index is 1.048 (a 4.8 percent price increase). In 1989 dollars, your $22,000 income is worth $22,000/1.048, or $20,992. Your real income rose by $992, or 4.96 percent. Note that the 10 percent increase in nominal income is roughly equal to the sum of the real increase of about 5 percent and the price increase of 4.8 percent. This observation offers a shortcut for estimating a change in real income. You can approximate real income changes using

$$\%\Delta Y_r = \%\Delta Y_n - \%\Delta P,$$

where Y_r is the real income, Y_n is the nominal income, and P is the price level. If the change in nominal income (10 percent in this case) and the change in the price level (5 percent) are known, then their difference will be approximately equal to the percentage change in real income.

Changes in the CPI are used to adjust poverty income levels, Social Security benefits, and wages for workers who have contracts providing for cost-of-living adjustments. Even where no contract is involved, the CPI plays a role in many wage negotiations and other business and personal decisions. Housing became an attractive investment in the 1970s, for example, because of figures showing that the value of the average house was

---

11. Nominal income (income not adjusted for changes in the price level) is also often referred to as money income or dollar income.

International Perspective

A Price Index for the Dollar

Until 1973, the price of the dollar in terms of gold and other currencies was established by the U.S. government. From 1935 to 1971, $35 of U.S. currency was the equivalent of one ounce of gold. Prior to 1935, the price of an ounce of gold was $20.67. From December 1971 to February 1973, the price was $38. In 1973, the U.S. government abandoned efforts to control the price of the dollar, and the price was left for the market to determine. In the jargon of central bankers, the United States had "closed the gold window."

Since most other major currencies also had market-determined prices, the problem of measuring the ups and downs of the dollar surfaced immediately. The price of the dollar is important because it is reflected in the prices of exports and imports. Thus, it is important to have some way of measuring changes in its value. But what could be used to measure the value of the dollar? Measuring what was happening to the dollar in terms of Japanese yen would give a different picture from what was happening to it in British pounds or French francs. For example, between 1980 and 1990 the price of the dollar rose from 29.2 to 33.4 in Belgian francs. During the same period, it fell from 227 to 145 in Japanese yen. Any bilateral exchange rate reflects not only what is happening to the market for the U.S. dollar but also anything affecting the value of the second currency in terms of all other currencies.

The solution to this problem was to construct a price index for the dollar, much like the CPI or the GNP deflator. This price index is called the trade-weighted dollar. It is computed as the change in the weighted average of the values of the dollar in terms of fourteen other currencies. Weights are assigned to these values on the basis of the proportion of U.S. trade that each nation represents. The fourteen nations include all of the United States' major trading partners, including Canada, Japan, and the nations of Western Europe.

As you can see from the diagram, this index was set at 100 in 1973 when the U.S. dollar began to float. Between 1980 and 1990, when the dollar rose in terms of Belgian francs but fell in terms of Japanese yen, the index rose from 87.4 to 89.1, an increase of 2 percent. This increase represents the net effect of a large rise in the dollar's price in terms of Belgian francs and British pounds, a more modest increase in Canadian dollars, almost no change in terms of Dutch guilders, and a decline in terms of both Japanese yen and German marks. The index rose sharply from 1980 to 1985 (from 87.4 to 143.2) before falling back at the end of the decade to almost the same value it had in 1973.

TRADE-WEIGHTED VALUE OF THE DOLLAR, 1967–1990*

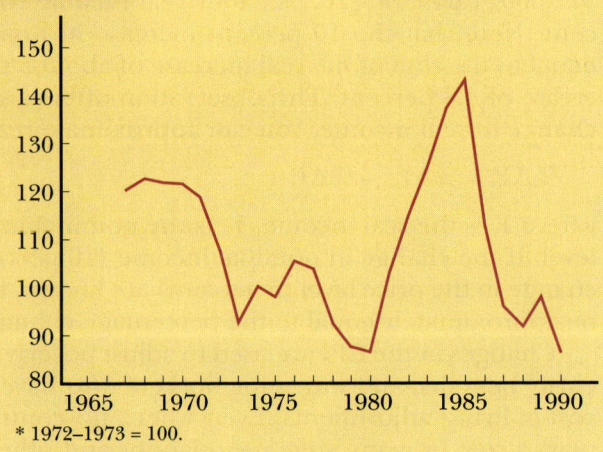

* 1972–1973 = 100.

Source: Council of Economic Advisers, *Economic Report of the President* (Washington, DC: U.S. Government Printing Office, 1991).

How to Construct Your Own Price Index

- Step 1. By survey or some other method, come up with a typical market basket of purchases.
- Step 2. Determine the market price for each item in the base, or beginning, period.
- Step 3. Multiply prices by quantities and add to find the total value of the market basket in the base period.
- Step 4. Find the prices for the same set of items in the next period.
- Step 5. Compute the new value of the market basket as in Step 3.
- Step 6. Divide the value of the current-year market basket in Step 5 by the value of the base-year market basket in Step 3, and multiply the result by 100.

rising faster than the CPI. (It is expected to fall behind the CPI in the 1990s, however.) Probably no other economic data is quoted as often as the CPI.

Problems with the Consumer Price Index

Because the CPI is used so widely, it is important to recognize its drawbacks and limits. One of these is the fact that the market basket is fixed or changed very infrequently on the basis of extensive consumer surveys. The current CPI is based on a survey taken in 1982–83. Since that time, changes in the age distribution of the population, changes in tastes and technology, and development of new products have changed the mix of goods consumers buy. The longer the time that passes since the survey that was used to find the weights, the more inaccurate the CPI becomes.

A second problem has to do with changes in relative prices. The CPI measures changes in the *average* price of a representative market basket of goods and services. If your household consumes those goods and services in about that proportion, then the CPI will reflect changes in your cost of living. If, however, you spend more than average amounts on medical care and housing (whose prices have risen rapidly) and less than average amounts on clothing and furniture (whose prices have risen more slowly), then your personal price index will rise faster than the CPI. Thus, using the CPI to compare incomes over time or to adjust wages or Social Security benefits is likely to lead to overadjusting at some times and undercorrecting for inflation at others.

Other Price Indices

There are two other widely used price indices. One is the **GNP implicit price deflator**. This index is used to correct GNP for price changes to determine what is happening to real output. It has a broader base than the CPI because it reflects all of the goods and services in the GNP, not just consumer goods. Unlike the CPI, the GNP deflator is a current-weights index. The weights for the various components are based on the proportions sold or produced in the current year, not a base year. Once the GNP deflator is computed, it is used to compute real GNP. Each of a series of

GNP implicit price deflator
A current-weights index used to correct the GNP for price changes.

nominal GNP figures is divided by its respective current-year GNP deflator in order to create a series of real, or price-adjusted, GNP figures. These figures allow economists to examine year-to-year growth without being confused by rising prices.

Nominal GNP (uncorrected for inflation) and real GNP can give very different pictures of economic performance. For example, in 1982 (a recession year), nominal GNP rose to $3,069 billion from $2,958 billion in 1981, a modest increase of $111 billion, or 3.6 percent. However, after dividing by the GNP deflator, real GNP actually fell by 2.1 percent between 1981 and 1982. The GNP deflator gives a different measure of inflation than the CPI does. The difference is partly due to the deflator's broader coverage and partly due to the fact that it uses current weights rather than base-year weights. Table 9 compares inflation measured by the CPI and by the GNP deflator for 1975 to 1990.

Another major price index, the **Producer Price Index**, is actually a family of indices. There are three indices: one for raw materials, one for semifinished goods, and one for finished goods. These indices show what is happening to prices paid by producers and wholesalers, which will eventually affect the prices of retail goods and services. The Producer Price Index is useful in forecasting changes in the CPI and the GNP deflator.

Producer Price Index
A group of three indices (for raw materials, semifinished goods, and finished goods) that shows what is happening to prices paid by producers and wholesalers.

PROBLEMS IN USING GNP FIGURES

Adjusting GNP for price changes is a very important correction. Price changes, however, are not the only problem with GNP. Omitted items, both positive and negative, limit the usefulness of GNP.

TABLE 9
COMPARISON OF INFLATION RATES MEASURED BY THE CPI AND THE GNP DEFLATOR, 1975–1990

YEAR	INFLATION RATE MEASURED BY CPI (%)	INFLATION RATE MEASURED BY GNP DEFLATOR (%)
1975	7.0	9.8
1976	4.8	6.4
1977	6.8	6.7
1978	9.0	7.3
1979	13.3	8.9
1980	12.4	9.0
1981	8.9	9.7
1982	3.9	6.4
1983	3.8	3.9
1984	4.0	3.7
1985	3.8	3.0
1986	1.1	2.6
1987	4.4	3.2
1988	4.4	3.3
1989	4.6	4.1
1990	6.1	4.1

Source: Council of Economic Advisers, *Economic Report of the President* (Washington, DC: U.S. Government Printing Office, 1991).

One major use of GNP is to measure economic well-being. Are Americans better off than last year? Are Americans better off than Russians or Japanese? Another use of GNP is as a forecasting tool. Changes in GNP affect employment, prices, interest rates, government tax revenues, and exchange rates. The GNP measure that best reflects economic well-being is not necessarily the one that makes the most reliable forecasting tool. In choosing what to include or exclude, national income accountants usually base their decision on the usefulness of GNP as a forecasting tool rather than as a measure of economic welfare.

This choice leads to some interesting omissions. We have already observed that GNP does not correct for either depreciation of capital equipment or depletion of natural resources. Other omissions are nonmarket production, changes in leisure, illegal activities, and some quality improvements. To convert GNP from a forecasting tool to a welfare measure, a correction would also have to be made for any increase in negative external effects and public bads, such as noise, water pollution, and global warming.

Nonmarket production is not included in GNP. If you repair your own car, only the parts that you purchase are counted. If you take your car to a service station, all of the repairs enter into GNP. Excluding nonmarket transactions understates economic well-being and also distorts the comparative use of GNP figures. This omission of nonmarket production may not make a big difference in year-to-year comparisons within a country or comparisons of similar countries such as the United States and Canada. It does distort comparisons between 1900 and 1990 or between the United States and India. For example, as a country gets wealthier, there are more professional laundries. Less laundry is done at home. This change says nothing about how clean the clothes of the population are. In the last twenty years, as more women have entered the work force in the United States, a larger share of household services (including laundry, meals, and day care) is being purchased in the market. The change in GNP overstates the actual increase in economic well-being.

On the other hand, activities that are paid for "under the table" or by barter are difficult to track, so GNP accountants are not able to include such transactions. This omission understates economic welfare. Some transactions are excluded on purpose. Since the GNP is limited to legal markets, national income accountants exclude illegal activities such as drugs, prostitution, or gambling.[12]

An important aspect of well-being not reflected in GNP is change in leisure time. Since 1900, the average factory work week has dropped from 70 hours to less than 40 hours. That reduction clearly represents an increase in economic well-being, but it is not reflected in GNP. A partial indicator is spending for leisure-type activities (such as travel, theater tickets, and health-club memberships) or equipment (VCRs, tennis racquets, and skis), but these are poor proxies for actual consumption of leisure.

Finally, in many cases what appear to be price increases are actually quality improvements. Products may be safer, more durable, or more use-

---

12. Gambling is counted in states where it is legal (such as Nevada) but not in states where it is illegal.

ful. However, unless a specific feature can be separated out and assigned a price tag, GNP accountants have no good way of correcting for quality improvements.

There are also undesirable activities that increase measured GNP while reducing economic well-being. Suppose there is a rise in the crime rate, resulting in the hiring of more police and the building of more jails. Is the average person better off? Probably not. But the government-spending component of the GNP registers an increase in purchases of police services. In the process of producing more goods and services, the economy may be creating more air and water pollution, more noise, more litter, and more congestion. Not only are these side effects of growth not subtracted, but the costs of combating pollution, noise, and litter are added into GNP as production of additional goods and services. These costs are known as "defensive" expenditures. One estimate places such defensive expenditures (for West Germany before reunification) as high as 10 percent of measured GNP.[13]

Some economists have attempted to develop an alternative to GNP as a measure of changes in the quality of life. William Nordhaus and James Tobin estimated the value of leisure time, household work and other nonmarket production, and quality improvements to add to GNP.[14] They also estimated negative influences on the quality of life (pollution, crime, etc.) and subtracted those from the GNP. The result was their **Measure of Economic Welfare (MEW)**, an alternative to GNP that focuses more closely on changes in economic welfare. Nordhaus and Tobin found that, in general, MEW appears to have grown more slowly than real GNP.

Measure of Economic Welfare (MEW)
An alternative to GNP that tries to provide a better indicator of economic well-being by adding leisure and nonmarket production and subtracting public bads.

MEASURING UNEMPLOYMENT

The last important macroeconomic variable to be measured is the unemployment rate. The number of unemployed as well as the number of employed will grow with the population and with the fraction of the population that is of working age and employable. Thus, it is more helpful to measure unemployment as a percentage of the labor force than to just count the number of unemployed. The **unemployment rate** is defined as the percentage of the labor force that wants to work but does not currently have a job. That is,

unemployment rate
The percentage of the labor force that wants to work but does not currently have a job.

$$(6) \quad \frac{\text{Unemployed workers}}{\text{Labor force}} = \frac{\text{Unemployed workers}}{\text{Employed workers} + \text{Unemployed workers}}$$

The first step in measuring unemployment is to determine the size of the labor force. Until recently, only the civilian labor force was counted.

---

13. Leipert, Christian, "National Income and Economic Growth: The Concept of Defensive Expenditures," *Journal of Economic Issues* (September 1989): 843–855.
14. William Nordhaus and James Tobin, "Is Growth Obsolete?" *Economic Growth, Fiftieth Anniversary Colloquium V* (Cambridge, MA: National Bureau of Economic Research, 1972). A number of other extensions and qualifications to GNP are summarized in Robert Eisner, "Extended Accounts for National Income and Product," *Journal of Economic Literature* (December 1988): 1611–1684.

International Perspective

Comparing GNP, Inflation, and Unemployment

Once statistics are compiled, they are almost always used for comparisons. Is GNP higher than last year? Is U.S. GNP growing faster than GNP in other countries? How does the unemployment rate or inflation rate in the United States compare with that in other developed countries?

There are problems in comparing these figures between nations because GNP, unemployment, and price indices are not computed exactly the same way in all countries. The share of economic activity going through the market is much different in less developed countries. This difference affects all three indicators but especially GNP. Comparisons of the United States, Canada, Japan, Australia, and the countries of Western Europe are a little more reliable because these countries are all at similar levels of economic development. The share of economic activity passing through the market is roughly the same, and the ways statistics are collected and presented are similar, but differences still remain.

With this warning, how does the United States compare with similar countries? As the table shows, it is *not* number one, at least not on many measures, but it doesn't fare too badly. The United States is behind Japan and about even with Canada in industrial production. It ranks in the middle of the seven countries in economic growth and inflation and is only worse than Japan in the unemployment rate.

Country	Industrial Production, 1988*	Real Growth Rate (% change in real GNP) 1976–1983 Average	Real Growth Rate 1990	Unemployment Rate, 1989 (%)	Inflation Rate, 1988 (%)[†]
Canada	136.3	2.7	2.7	7.5	5.7
France	114.0	2.5	2.5	9.6	4.6
Great Britain	118.1	1.7	1.7	7.0	3.6
Italy	126.4	3.3	3.3	7.8	5.9
Japan	159.2	4.4	4.4	2.3	9.3
United States	137.2	2.5	2.5	5.3	5.7
West Germany	117.8	2.4	2.4	5.7	3.6

*For the index of industrial production, the base year in 1977.
[†]Inflation is measured by changes in the CPI.
Source: Council of Economic Advisers, *Economic Report of the President* (Washington, DC: U.S. Government Printing Office, 1990, 1991).

labor force
Those who are working or actively seeking work.

Those who were employed in the military services were excluded. Newer measures include the military in the labor force, which results in lower measured unemployment rates.

The **labor force** consists of those who are working and those who are actively seeking work. A full-time homemaker, a child, a retiree, a full-time student, a prisoner, or anyone else not employed is not counted in either the numerator or the denominator of equation (6). People who had been seeking work but have given up and stopped looking are also excluded from the measured labor force.

The measures of both the labor force and the number of unemployed are obtained from door-to-door surveys and payroll data from business firms.[15] Respondents in door-to-door surveys are only considered unemployed if they have made some effort to find work in the last four weeks.

Like the GNP and the CPI, the unemployment rate is an imperfect indicator. Discouraged workers (those who sought work for a while, became discouraged, and gave up) are not counted as unemployed. This omission makes unemployment appear lower than it really is. Some workers may be underemployed—working below their ability or fewer hours than they would like. These workers, however, are counted as employed. On the other hand, some workers leave jobs, make a modest effort to find work in order to qualify for unemployment benefits, and avoid taking a job until their unemployment benefits run out. These people should probably not be counted as "actively seeking work." Their inclusion overstates unemployment.

The major source of short-term changes in unemployment is changes in total demand for labor that result from changes in total output. Over longer periods, total labor supply also affects the unemployment rate. An indicator that is helpful in sorting out the relative importance of these two sources of changes in unemployment is the labor force participation rate. The **labor force participation rate** measures the fraction of the adult population that is employed or actively seeking work. In 1948, the labor force participation rate was 59 percent. It remained near that level until the 1960s, when it began to rise. By 1990, 66.6 percent of the population over the age of 16 was in the labor force. This increased fraction of the population in the labor force meant that even though the U.S. unemployment rate was reaching new highs, the employment rate (the percentage of the population with jobs) was fairly stable. Part of the increase in unemployment was caused by the larger fraction of the population that was seeking employment.

In the 1990s, the labor force participation rate is expected to level off, primarily because there will be fewer new entrants to the labor force. (A smaller number of people will be in their late teens and early twenties.) Unemployment will remain low as the labor force grows at an average rate of only 1.2 percent a year, compared to 2.3 percent from 1976 to 1990.[16]

The increased labor force participation rate in the last two decades

labor force participation rate
The percentage of the adult population that is employed or actively seeking work.

---

15. There are discrepancies between household and establishment surveys. These differences arise partly from variations in coverage and definitions, partly because some jobs are held by illegal aliens and workers holding more than one job. See Paul O. Flain, "How Many New Jobs since 1982? Two Surveys Differ," *Monthly Labor Review* (August 1989): 10–15.
16. Howard N. Fullerton, Jr., "New Labor Force Projections Spanning 1988 to 2000," *Monthly Labor Review* (November 1989): 3–11.

Chapter 5 Measuring Economic Performance

reflects two factors. One is that the baby-boom generation—due to the jump in the birth rate between 1946 and 1962—grew up and entered the labor force. Thus, a larger proportion of the population was of working age. The other change was in female participation in the labor force, which rose from 38 percent at the beginning of the 1960s to 58 percent in 1990. Some of the high unemployment rates of the 1970s reflect the time required to absorb the large increase in labor force participants. The declining unemployment rates of the late 1980s, which are expected to continue into the 1990s, are as much a result of a slowdown in new entrants to the labor force as any other factor. Female participation is expected to peak, and the baby boom was followed by a "baby bust" (period of low birth rates). The number of new high school and college graduates reached a low in 1990 and is gradually increasing again. Thus, prospects are bright for a low unemployment rate in the next decade simply for demographic reasons.

SUMMARY

1. Stocks are existing quantities. Flows measure quantities over time. An income statement measures flows. A balance sheet measures stocks.
2. Gross National Product (GNP) measures final output produced in a country over a given period of time. It can be measured by producing sector or by buying sector. Its value should be the same whether it measures output produced or income created in the production process.
3. Other measures of output and income are national income (NI), net national product (NNP), personal income (PI), and disposable income. National income corresponds to the flow in the lower half of the circular flow diagram.
4. A price index, which is a weighted average of prices, is used to measure changes in price level. A price index is used to correct for price changes and measure real income or output. The most commonly used price indices are the Consumer Price Index (CPI) and the GNP deflator.
5. GNP is not perfect either as a measure of economic well-being or as a means of making comparisons in time and space. The Measure of Economic Welfare (MEW) is one alternative that tries to compute economic well-being.
6. Problems with the GNP include the omission of nonmarket and illegal transactions and leisure and the failure to correct for economic bads.
7. Unemployment is measured as the percentage of the labor force not working but actively seeking work. Some changes in unemployment arise from changes in the size of the labor force relative to the population rather than from changes in total output or the demand for labor.

NEW TERMS

stock variable
flow variable
depreciation
income statement
balance sheet
net worth
gross national product (GNP)
final goods
intermediate goods
business inventories
consumption expenditures
consumer durables
consumer nondurables
consumer services
gross private domestic investment
fixed investment
transfer payments
national income (NI)
capital consumption allowance
net national product (NNP)
net private domestic investment
personal income (PI)
disposable income
GNP implicit price deflator
Producer Price Index
Measure of Economic Welfare (MEW)
unemployment rate
labor force
labor force participation rate

Questions for Discussion

1. Suppose that during a certain period GNP rises from $3,000 billion to $3,500 billion, while GNP deflator goes from 100 to 125. What has happened to real GNP?

2. Suppose another baby boom occurred and a significant number of parents dropped out of the labor force to stay home and do child care. What would happen to the unemployment rate, the labor force participation rate, and the employment rate?

3. Why is GNP not entirely satisfactory as a measure of economic well-being? Why is it better for comparisons over short time periods or between countries that are similar in economic and social conditions?

4. How would an increase in Social Security taxes affect GNP, NNP, national income, and PI?

5. Draw up a personal income statement. See if it helps you to understand why national income accountants wind up with a statistical discrepancy in matching the income side to the expenditure side.

6. Given the following information, compute the unemployment rate.

Civilian noninstitutional population	186,393,000
Civilian labor force	125,557,000
Total civilian employment	117,342,000

There were an additional 1,688,000 people in the armed forces. What would happen to the unemployment rate if these persons were counted?

7. Use the following data to compute GNP, NNP, and NI. If NI computed at factor cost is $3,387 billion, what is the statistical discrepancy? (All figures are in billions; any omitted items are zero.)

Consumption	$2,762
Government purchases	865
Gross investment	675
Depreciation	455
Indirect business taxes	349
Net exports	−106

8. Use the data in Question 7 to compute the percentage of GNP going to each buying sector. Present the results as a bar chart or pie chart.

9. Use the following data to compute NI, PI, and disposable income for the year. (All figures are in billions; any omitted items are zero.)

Wages and salaries	$2,499
Personal taxes	513
Government transfers	491
Social insurance taxes	376
Corporate profits	300
Net interest	295
Proprietors' income	279
Corporate profits taxes	103
Dividends	88
Undistributed profits	46
Business transfers	23
Rental income	16

10. Given the information in the table, compute a price index for a ten-year-old child. This child receives a weekly allowance and would like to request a raise based on the increase in the cost of the market basket of goods purchased. By how much has this consumer's cost of living risen?

Item	Quantity	Last Year's Price	This Year's Price
Movie admission	1	$3.00	$3.25
Soft drinks	3	.50	.50
Candy bars	4	.30	.35
Pencils	2	.15	.12
Comic books	2	.75	.85

11. Explain this statement: "Everybody's CPI is nobody's CPI."

12. Suppose the government decided not to tax corporate profits, and as a result the extra funds were all paid out as dividends. How would this change affect GNP, NNP, NI, and PI?

13. Suppose a hurricane struck the coast of New England, destroying millions of dollars' worth of housing. What would be the immediate effect on GNP, NNP, NI, and PI?

14. Identify whether each of the following would be an asset or a liability on your personal balance sheet.
   a. government bonds   d. a TV set
   b. car loan   e. a bicycle
   c. bill due for doctor's care   f. a condominium

15. Why is unemployment likely to remain low in the 1990s? If the birth rate rises in the 1990s, when and how will it affect employment and unemployment? Suppose, instead, that the birth rate does not change but immigration increases. What effect would that have on employment and unemployment?

Suggestions for Further Reading

Carlson, Keith M. "Do Price Indices Tell Us about Inflation? A Review of the Issues," *Review*, Federal Reserve Bank of St. Louis (November/December 1989): 12–30. This excellent and not very technical article discusses the historical development of the major price indices and how they are used. Provides details on some of the components for the CPI.

Council of Economic Advisers. *Economic Report of the President.* Washington, DC: U.S. Government Printing Office, annual. Gives a summary of economic developments and a variety of statistics.

Franklin, Norman. *Tracing America's Economy.* Armonk, NY: M.E. Sharpe, 1987. A guide to locating and interpreting economic data.

Sommers, Albert T. *The U.S. Economy Demystified: What the Major Economic Statistics Mean and Their Significance for Business.* Lexington, MA: Lexington Books, 1985. A guide to macroeconomic data, its interpretation, and sources, especially the national income accounts.

U.S. Department of Labor. *Monthly Labor Review.* Washington, DC: U.S. Government Printing Office. Best source of data for the CPI; also reports regularly on changes in the CPI and interpretations of movements in consumer prices.

AFTER STUDYING THIS CHAPTER, YOU SHOULD BE ABLE TO:

1. Describe the uses of the aggregate demand and aggregate supply curves.
2. Explain why the aggregate demand curve has a negative slope.
3. Discuss the different views of the slope and shape of the aggregate supply curve.
4. Identify the basic viewpoint of each of the major schools of macroeconomic thought.
5. Explain how differences in values and goals are related to differences in emphasis and interpretation in macroeconomics.

INTRODUCTION

CHAPTER 6
AGGREGATE DEMAND AND AGGREGATE SUPPLY

Chapters 4 and 5 introduced three important macroeconomic variables that measure aggregate economic performance: total output, price level, and unemployment. The level of each of these variables and how they change are explained by an economic model. For a century, economists have been in agreement on the basic microeconomic model of supply and demand, which determines individual prices and quantities, although they have disagreed about how well the market works in certain industries. There has been little agreement on what kind of model best explains how output, employment, and the price level are determined. This chapter is the first step toward developing a macroeconomic model. Recall from Chapter 1 that any model offers a simplified description of reality that can be used to understand a system and predict the effects of various changes. The aggregate supply and demand model is both simple and predictive. Thus, it is a useful way to organize the study of macroeconomics.

A GENERAL FRAMEWORK FOR MACROECONOMICS

Before looking at the details of macroeconomic theory, we need a general model, or framework. The framework we will use to explain the levels of output, employment, and prices is the aggregate supply and demand model. This framework is general enough to support a number of macroeconomic viewpoints. Once we have established this framework, we will use it to introduce some macroeconomic schools of thought, whose competing ideas will recur in later chapters.

AGGREGATE DEMAND
Think back to the microeconomic supply and demand curves for individual products developed in Chapter 3. Your first thought might be to obtain aggregate supply (*AS*) and aggregate demand (*AD*) curves by adding the supply and demand curves for all the products in the marketplace. Unfortunately, this is not the way to proceed. Why not? First, there are technical problems with adding such unlike goods as cars, toothpaste, and haircuts on the horizontal axis and the prices of each on the vertical axis. What units can you use to combine very different products, and how do you construct an aggregate price index that accurately represents all their prices?

Second, when you add across many markets, many of the effects that can shift the individual supply and demand curves drop out of the picture. For instance, the demand for toothpaste is affected by the prices of mouthwash (a substitute) and toothbrushes (a complement). On the aggregate demand curve, however, it is not possible to distinguish among individual prices. The vertical axis measures only the aggregate, or average, price level. On the horizontal axis, it doesn't matter whether consumers are buying toothpaste or mouthwash, as long as they are buying some item. More toothpaste offsets less mouthwash when both goods are combined into total real output on the horizontal axis. Thus, there is no substitution effect.

A microeconomic market demand curve shows how much of a given product consumers will buy at various prices, *ceteris paribus*. The **aggregate demand curve** shows the amounts of total real output that all buyers in an economy will purchase at various price levels. Figure 1 shows an aggregate demand curve (*AD*). On the vertical axis, *P* represents the price level, measured by a price index. On the horizontal axis, *Y* represents real output, or output adjusted for changes in the price level. Economists generally believe that the aggregate demand curve has a negative slope, as pictured in Figure 1. For convenience, we will usually use a straight-line aggregate demand curve.

aggregate demand curve
A graph showing the amounts of total real ouput that all buyers in an economy wish to purchase at various price levels.

Economists use the symbol *Y* to stand for different concepts of the flow of income or output. However, if we overlook some of the smaller differences between GNP and national income (NI), then *Y* can represent both the flow of output and the flow of income. Nominal GNP or NI is then the product of *P* and *Y* at any point. For example, at point *A* in Figure 1, a price level of $3 and total output of 1,000 units give a GNP of $3,000.

THE AGGREGATE EXPENDITURE APPROACH. One way of looking at aggregate demand is in terms of the components of GNP by purchasing sector. These components are consumption spending by households (*C*), investment spending by business (*I*), government purchases of goods and ser-

FIGURE 1
AGGREGATE DEMAND
An aggregate demand curve shows a negative relationship between the price level and real output.

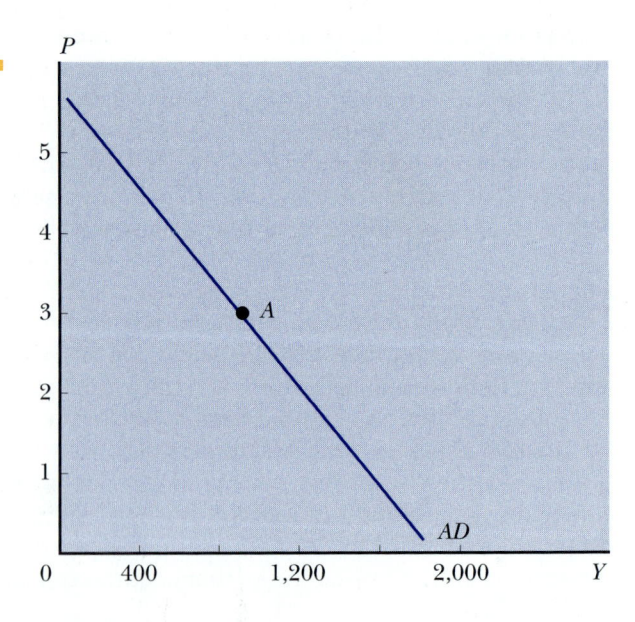

vices (G), and spending by the foreign sector, or net exports (EX – IM). As you learned in Chapter 5, the national income accounts measure actual expenditures in these four categories. However, actual spending and planned spending may be different if the market is not in equilibrium. In order to plot the demand curve, you need to know, not what was actually spent, but the planned or intended level of purchases at each price level.

The only unplanned component of GNP by purchasing sector is unplanned changes in inventories, which is a component of business investment. Everything else is assumed to be planned. Thus, $C + I + G + (EX - IM)$ less unplanned changes in inventory represents a point on a demand curve—one combination of P and Y that buyers choose. However, total GNP by purchasing sector (less unplanned inventory changes) represents "demand" at only one price level, the current one. For this reason, we will refer to the sum of planned purchases, or $C + I + G + (EX - IM)$, as aggregate expenditure, or *AE*. In order to use information on aggregate planned expenditure in plotting an aggregate demand curve, we would have to know what real *C, I, G*, and $(EX - IM)$ would be at various price levels.

Although it is not possible to observe directly what $C + I + G + (EX - IM)$ would be at various price levels, there are some clues to what happens to real demand for output as the price level changes. The slope of the aggregate demand curve implies that higher prices have a negative effect on planned purchases of real output. Dollar spending $(P \times Y)$ may be higher if P is sufficiently higher, but Y will be lower. People tend to be reluctant to buy as much real output at higher price levels as they do at lower ones. This is especially true if prices rise ahead of wages or more rapidly than wages or income. Several explanations based on the theory of self-interested behavior can be offered for the negative slope of the aggregate demand curve.

If the price level rises, even with no change in employment and real output, nominal income $(P \times Y)$ will increase. As you saw in Chapter 4, when nominal income increases and the tax code is progressive, then tax revenues rise more than in proportion to the income increase, even if *real* income (Y) is unchanged. Households' disposable incomes fall relative to total real income and output. Higher taxes, by reducing disposable income, reduce people's ability to buy at higher prices.[1]

When the price level rises, usually exports fall and imports rise. The resulting change in net exports $(EX - IM)$ will change real quantity demanded. Higher domestic prices mean that a country's exports become more expensive to foreigners. Also, imports become more attractive to residents of the country because they are relatively cheaper. Both foreigners and residents will substitute cheaper foreign products for more expensive domestic ones, reducing exports and increasing imports. A fall in net exports means that real quantity demanded is lower at a higher price level.[2] Conversely, a lower price level, *ceteris paribus*, will lead to substitution of home products for foreign products. Then real quantity demanded will be greater at lower price levels.

---

1. The negative impact of collecting higher taxes on total spending will not be as severe if there is an increase in government spending to offset any reduction in consumption.
2. Part, but not all, of the effect of higher prices on exports and imports is likely to be offset by changes in the price of the country's currency. We will explore this topic in more detail in the chapter on international finance.

International Perspective

Foreign Trade and Aggregate Demand

Aggregate supply and demand are concepts developed for a closed economy (one with no foreign sector). But shifts in exports or imports can be quite large and can have a visible effect on output, employment, and prices. Between 1976 and 1990, both imports and exports grew faster in real terms than GNP for the United States. Over this period, exports rose 130 percent, imports rose 134 percent, and real GNP increased by only 47 percent. Clearly, trade is becoming a larger component of economic activity.

Aggregate supply and demand can be adapted to include goods and services that are consumed within a country but produced in foreign countries, or vice versa. To do this, it is necessary to define aggregate supply and aggregate demand a little more precisely. In an economy with a foreign sector, aggregate supply is defined as the supply of goods and services *produced* in the country, not the supply of goods and services available for consumption. Thus, aggregate supply is a production concept, not a consumption concept. In a closed economy, the two supplies would be the same.

Aggregate demand in an open economy consists of demand for goods and services produced in the country, whether the demanders are residents or foreigners. Thus, exports show up in an aggregate supply and demand diagram as an increase in aggregate demand. Imports are shown as a decrease in aggregate demand rather than an addition to aggregate supply. These definitions of aggregate supply and demand in an open economy are used because they reflect the impact of imports and exports (through aggregate supply and demand) on the level of output, employment, and prices.

The total spending by the foreign sector ($EX - IM$) is small relative to the rest of output. Because its two components enter into aggregate demand separately, however, each of them can have a major impact on real output and the price level. An increase in exports is an added source of demand for a nation's output, shifting aggregate demand to the right. Rising exports drive up real output and employment. Exports also tend to put upward pressure on the price level because there are fewer goods left for domestic consumers, who must compete for that limited supply.

Rising imports appear in an aggregate supply and demand diagram as a reduction in demand. Increased imports shift aggregate demand to the left, driving down domestic output and employment but also holding down the price level. From 1981 to 1985, falling exports and rising imports in the United States were blamed for slow growth of output and high unemployment. However, they also deserve some of the credit for a lower rate of inflation.

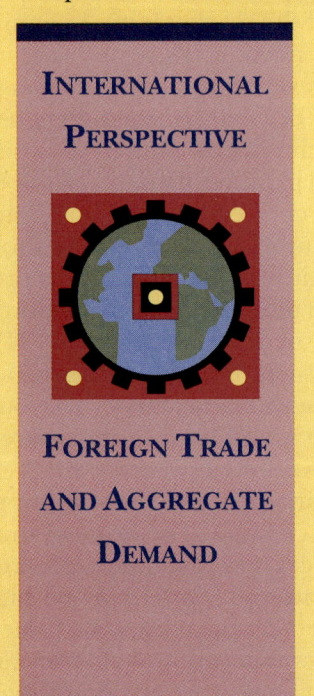

Higher prices also reduce the value of financial assets owned by households. These include savings accounts, bonds, certificates of deposit, pension funds, and insurance policies. As the value of these assets falls, households will cut back on spending in order to rebuild their assets to the desired levels. Changes in aggregate assets or wealth have the same effect on the aggregate demand curve that changes in individual wealth have on the individual demand curve. When the price level falls, the real purchasing power of financial assets rises, making households feel wealthier. Such an increase in wealth means that households are willing and able to purchase more goods and services at every level of real income (Y).

If you are thinking like an economist, it may occur to you that one household's or firm's asset may be another's debt. Your savings deposit (asset) has been loaned by the bank as someone else's mortgage (liability). Your bonds (asset) are the liability of some corporation. When the price level rises, the decreased spending by asset holders may be offset by the increased spending of debtors, who feel less burdened by their debt. This would be true if it were not for the fact that the government is a major net debtor. When the price level rises, there is a fall in the value of government debt held by households. As their wealth decreases, households spend less. However, government officials do not necessarily respond by spending more. Similarly, a fall in the price level would increase the value of government debt held by households, raising their spending. Again, there is no reason to expect that public officials would respond by spending less.

Spending by state and local governments is also sensitive to price level changes. Many of these governments are constrained by their constitutions or in other ways to limit their spending to what they receive in revenues. When the price level rises, two of the three major sources of state and local revenue—property taxes and sales taxes—tend to lag behind. These taxes are not highly sensitive to changes in the price level.[3] Therefore, state and local governments must limit their purchases to what they can buy with revenues that are rising more slowly than the price level.

Finally, higher price levels are associated with higher interest rates, for reasons we will explore in later chapters. Rising interest rates increase the opportunity cost of borrowing by business for investment, by households for purchase of consumer durables, and by state and local governments to finance construction. Lower price levels lead to lower interest rates and more of all three of these kinds of borrowing.

All of the effects described here—taxes, net exports, household wealth, government spending, and interest rates—support the notion of a downward sloping aggregate demand curve. However, none of them are very powerful—certainly not as powerful as the substitution effect in the demand for individual products. Consider, for example, the effect of a change in the value of households' financial assets. Some estimates suggest that a $1 change in a household's wealth only leads to a 6¢ change in its spending. Although all of these effects on price levels are weak, they all work in the same direction—yielding an aggregate demand curve that slopes down-

---

3. The property tax revolt in the late 1970s was a response to rising house prices that led to sharp increases in property taxes as well as income taxes. But, under more normal circumstances, there is a long time lag between rising house prices and rising property tax assessments.

ward from left to right. Because none of these effects are very powerful, the aggregate demand curve is generally believed to be quite steep.

THE MONETARY APPROACH. Another view of the aggregate demand curve is shown in Figure 2. In this figure, the curved line shows the various ways that a given national income can be divided between prices and real output. For example, a national income of $2,000 could consist of a price level of $1 and real output of 2,000 units, a price level of $5 and real output of 400 units, or any of a number of other combinations.

This aggregate demand curve is consistent with a classical explanation of how output and prices are determined. Its origins go back at least to the eighteenth-century British economist and philosopher David Hume. The classical explanation of the price level is based on the equation of exchange and the quantity theory of money. The **quantity theory of money** states that changes in the price level are proportional to changes in the money supply. This theory, like many theories in macroeconomics, developed as a way to explain certain economic events.

Classical economists believed that there was a very simple relationship between the money supply and the price level:

$$M_s \times V = P \times Y.$$

This relationship is called the **equation of exchange**. The idea behind this relationship is that the value of spending must be equal to the value of what was bought. M_s is the money supply, and V is the velocity of money, or the number of times the average dollar is spent per year. Thus, $M_s \times V$ equals total spending. For example, if the money supply is $2,000 and $V = 3$, then total spending will be $6,000. If dollars turn over more often, then the same amount of spending could be supported by a smaller money supply. For example, with $V = 5$, the same $6,000 in spending could be sustained by a money supply of only $1,200. Classical economists generally believed

quantity theory of money
The theory that changes in the price level will be proportional to changes in the money supply.

equation of exchange
An identity based on the quantity theory of money that says that the money supply times the velocity of money equals the price level times real output.

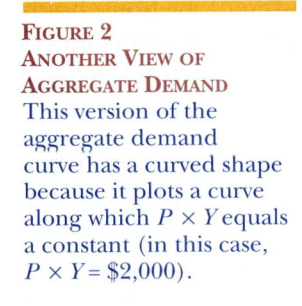

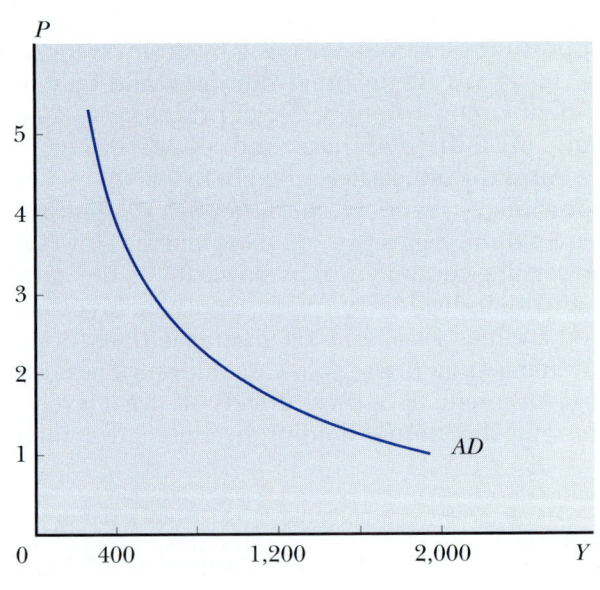

FIGURE 2
ANOTHER VIEW OF AGGREGATE DEMAND
This version of the aggregate demand curve has a curved shape because it plots a curve along which $P \times Y$ equals a constant (in this case, $P \times Y = \$2,000$).

Chapter 6 Aggregate Demand and Aggregate Supply 159

that velocity (V) was quite stable. Therefore, any change in the money supply would result in a proportional change in spending ($P \times Y$).

The variables on the right-hand side of the equation of exchange should look familiar. P is the price level, and Y is real output, so $P \times Y$ is (nominal) national income. If $M_s \times V$ is what was spent, $P \times Y$ is what was bought, and the two have to be equal. In fact, the equation of exchange is an identity. It states that what was spent has to equal the market value of what was bought.

In terms of the aggregate demand curve, the equation of exchange implies that a fixed money supply (M_s) combined with a stable velocity (V) will yield a constant value of nominal GNP, which is equal to $P \times Y$. That is, a fixed amount of money available to spend and a fairly stable frequency of spending for each unit of currency each year will determine nominal GNP. However, for any given nominal GNP, various combinations of P and Y are possible. Those combinations lie along a curve such as the one in Figure 2. You might experiment with drawing such a curve for given values of M_s and V. For example, the combinations of money supply and velocity that resulted in total spending of $6,000 could imply a price level of $1 and real output of 6,000 units or a price level of $4 and real output of 1,500 units, or various other combinations.[4]

We will explore the development of the quantity theory of money in more detail in the next chapter. For now, you can see that any given nominal money supply will determine an aggregate demand curve that slopes downward.

WHY THE AGGREGATE DEMAND CURVE HAS A NEGATIVE SLOPE

A higher price level reduces

- consumption demand,
- net exports, and
- government (state and local) spending

through

- smaller real money supply,
- higher interest rates,
- lower value of households' financial assets,
- higher (progressive) taxes,
- substitution of relatively cheaper foreign goods for domestic goods, and
- slow growth of sales and property tax revenues.

---

4. Another way of looking at the quantity theory of money as an explanation of the aggregate demand curve is to rearrange the equation of exchange slightly. Dividing through by P and V gives $M_s/P = (1/V)Y$. The term on the left-hand side, M_s/P, is known as the real money supply, because it is the nominal money supply adjusted for changes in the price level. It represents the purchasing power of the money supply. Since the term $1/V$ can be regarded as roughly constant, this equation says that there is a positive relationship between the real money supply and the price level. It also says that for any given nominal money supply, there is a negative relationship between real output and the price level. An increase in the price level reduces the purchasing power of the money supply and therefore the amount of real output that people are able to demand.

aggregate supply curve
A graph showing the amounts of total real output that the producing sector will offer for sale at various price levels.

**FIGURE 3
AGGREGATE SUPPLY CURVES**
(a) An aggregate supply curve with an upward slope, similar to most supply curves. (b) The classical aggregate supply curve, for which the economy is producing at capacity (or full-employment level of output, Y^*). Attempts to increase output will only drive up the price level. (c) The Keynesian version of the aggregate supply curve, which assumes there are enough unemployed resources that output can be increased without driving the price level above P_0.

AGGREGATE SUPPLY

The **aggregate supply curve** shows the various quantities of total real output that the producing sector will offer for sale at various price levels. The equilibrium point on the aggregate supply curve corresponds roughly to NI at factor cost. However, NI at factor cost, like GNP, is computed in money terms and for only one price level, the current one. So NI is just one point on the aggregate supply curve, just as GNP less unplanned inventory investment is only one point on the aggregate demand curve. Points on the aggregate supply curve represent possible values of NI that suppliers are willing to produce and offer for sale.

THE SLOPE OF THE AGGREGATE SUPPLY CURVE. What is the shape of the aggregate supply curve? Economists would like to know the answer to that question! Probably no single graphical construction in economists' vast collection has generated as much argument as the aggregate supply curve. A large part of this dispute has to do with how firms and owners of resources respond to changes in the price level, and how quickly. Time plays an even more important role with respect to aggregate supply than with respect to aggregate demand. Thus, the dispute over the slope often centers on the difference between what the aggregate supply curve looks like in the short run and in the long run and how much time is meant in each of these cases.

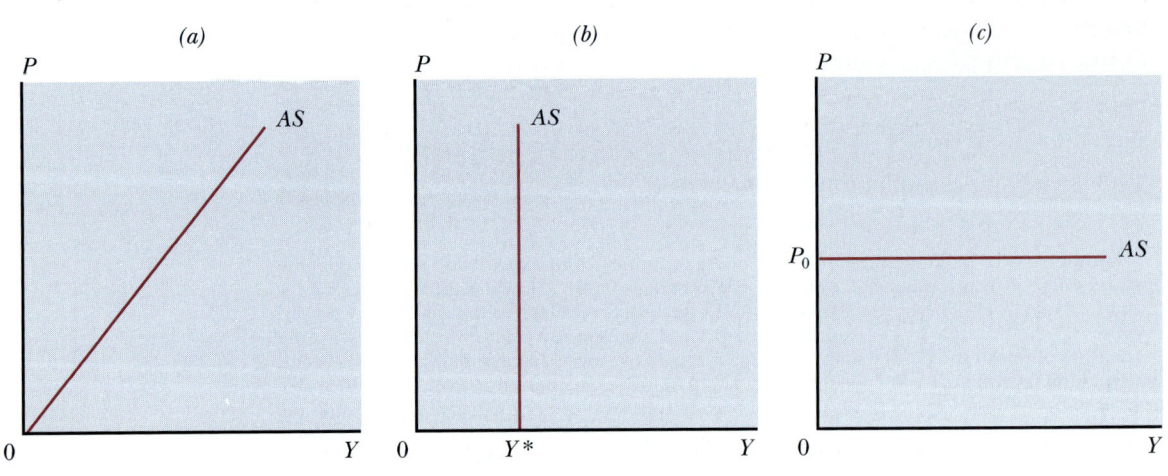

Recalling the market supply curve for an individual product from Chapter 3, you are probably expecting the aggregate supply curve to slope up from left to right, like line *AS* in Figure 3(a). However, like the aggregate demand curve, the aggregate supply curve differs from the supply curves for individual products in some important ways. The problems of adding individual prices and outputs also exist for aggregate supply, so the aggregate supply curve is not simply the sum of the market supply curves for all goods and services. One of the reasons for the upward-sloping microeconomic supply curve for a single product is substitution. (Producers shift to more profitable products when prices of those goods rise relative to the prices of other goods the firm could produce.) This reason, however, has no validity at all in explaining why the aggregate supply curve slopes upward. Total real output on the horizontal axis already includes all possible substitute goods.

Nevertheless, many economists expect the aggregate supply curve to slope upward for some of the same reasons that supply curves for individual goods and services slope upward. As firms in general try to produce more output with given resources, some labor has to work overtime at higher pay, driving up costs and prices. Firms are working their capital harder, so it wears out faster and breaks down more often. Competition among producers for scarce resources drives up wages and interest rates. All of these cost increases, for individual products and for aggregate real output, will be reflected in higher prices.

Another reason for an upward-sloping supply curve, either for a single product or for goods and services in the aggregate, is that the lure of higher prices will induce producers to try to expand output. If firms and entrepreneurs can sell their products for more, and if their overall costs have not risen as much as the prices of what they sell, they can make more profit. Profit is the incentive and the reward to which producers respond. If higher prices do indeed mean higher profits, then the aggregate supply curve will slope upward.

A VERTICAL AGGREGATE SUPPLY CURVE. Before the 1930s, an even simpler view of the aggregate supply curve prevailed. It was seen as a vertical line, running straight up and down. This slope indicates that output does not respond at all to changes in the price level. Classical economists believed that the economy naturally tended toward the level of output that available resources could support. There was really only one level of real output that could occur in a properly functioning economic system, where supply and demand in labor markets assured full employment. This real output level was defined as the full-employment level of output, or capacity output. The **full-employment level of output** is the level of real output associated with full use of all factors of production, especially labor.

Figure 3(b) shows the aggregate supply curve as a vertical line (AS). The level of real output associated with full employment is labeled Y^*. In this model, the price level can vary, but it will have no effect on real output. A fixed real output level and a variable price level imply a vertical aggregate supply curve. Such a curve plays an important role in the classical macroeconomic model.

full-employment level of output
The level of real output associated with full use of all of the factors of production, especially labor.

A HORIZONTAL AGGREGATE SUPPLY CURVE. The British economist John Maynard Keynes, who was introduced briefly in Chapter 4, offered a third view of the aggregate supply curve in the 1930s. He suggested that during periods when large amounts of resources were unemployed, the aggregate supply curve could be horizontal, as in Figure 3(c). It would be possible for firms to increase both individual and aggregate output without driving the price level above P_0. They could produce more simply by putting unemployed resources to work. Firms would not have to pay higher prices to compete for scarce resources. They could simply hire idle workers at the going wage and use their factories' idle capacity. A horizontal aggregate supply curve implies that the economy is inside its production possibilities curve, since there is unemployed labor (and other resources) willing to work at the present wage.

A COMPOSITE VIEW. These three views of the aggregate supply curve are sometimes combined in a composite version with three distinct regions, shown in Figure 4. The horizontal region (sometimes known as the Keynesian region) represents a situation in which there are ample idle resources. Thus, output can be increased without driving up prices. This segment corresponds to the Keynesian aggregate supply curve of Figure 3(c).

In the middle region of the composite aggregate supply curve, there are some unemployed resources. Perhaps they are not the right kind for the mix of additional output that firms are trying to produce. Attempting to expand output in this situation will drive up the price level but will also result in more output. This segment corresponds to the upward-sloping curve of Figure 3(a).

The last segment of the composite aggregate supply curve shows what happens when there are no more unemployed resources available. It is possible to produce more of good A only by cutting output of good B. As producers of A try to bid resources away from other uses, they drive up prices and reduce output of other goods. In this region, the economy is on the production possibilities curve. More of one kind of output can only be obtained by sacrificing output of other goods or services. Attempts to expand total real output will only drive up the price level. This segment corresponds to the classical curve of Figure 3(b).

THE SHORT RUN AND THE LONG RUN. The composite aggregate supply curve is one way to reconcile the conflicting views of how the graph should look. Another way of reconciling these conflicting views is to clarify what is meant by the short run and the long run. Part of the debate between Keynes and both his predecessors (the classical economists) and his successors (monetarists) is a matter of defining terms. Most economists

**FIGURE 4
AGGREGATE SUPPLY CURVE: COMPOSITE VERSION**
This composite aggregate supply curve is made up of a horizontal (Keynesian) region, an intermediate region in which prices and output rise or fall together, and a vertical (classical) region.

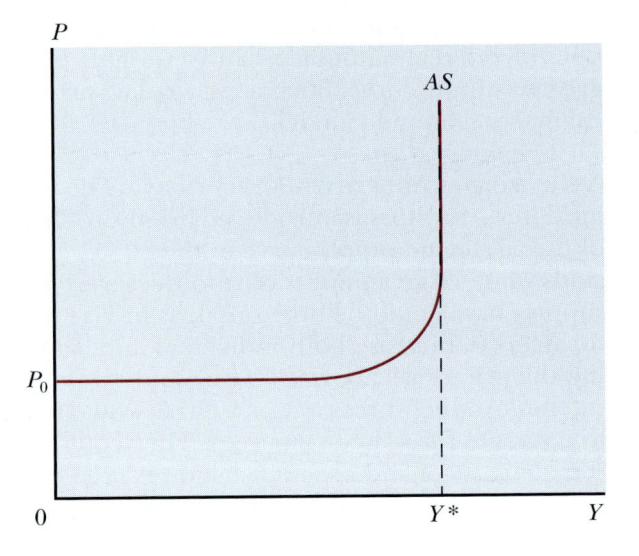

would agree that in the long run, the level of output will tend toward full employment, which corresponds to a vertical aggregate supply curve. They disagree about the curve's shape in the short run, however. Even more important, they disagree about the length of time that separates the short run from the long run. If the long run is six months, a fair amount of unemployment can be tolerated until the economy returns to "normal." If the long run is ten years, people will be less patient. Keynes and his followers pointed to the length and severity of the Great Depression as evidence of how long an economy can deviate from the long-run equilibrium level of output corresponding to full employment of resources.

AGGREGATE EQUILIBRIUM

What happens when we put aggregate supply and aggregate demand together? In Chapter 3, we combined the demand curve and supply curve for a specific good to determine an equilibrium quantity and price. In the same way, the aggregate demand and aggregate supply curves together determine the level of real output and the price level.

Consider the simplest case, a downward-sloping aggregate demand curve and an upward-sloping aggregate supply curve (Figure 5). Equilibrium occurs at Y_1 and P_1. This price and output combination is an equilibrium in the same sense that the intersection of an individual supply curve and demand curve is. If firms collectively try to produce any other level of output, forces in the marketplace will tend to push the economy toward the equilibrium level.

Consider what happens if firms try to produce a real output, Y_2, that is larger than the equilibrium level of output, Y_1. For that level of output, producers will attempt to charge prices that average out to a price level of P_2. But consumers are only willing to purchase that large quantity of output, Y_2, when the price level is much lower, P_3. At a price level of P_2, consumers are only willing to buy a total quantity of Y_3. At the higher output level, Y_2, producers will find themselves with unsold output (unplanned

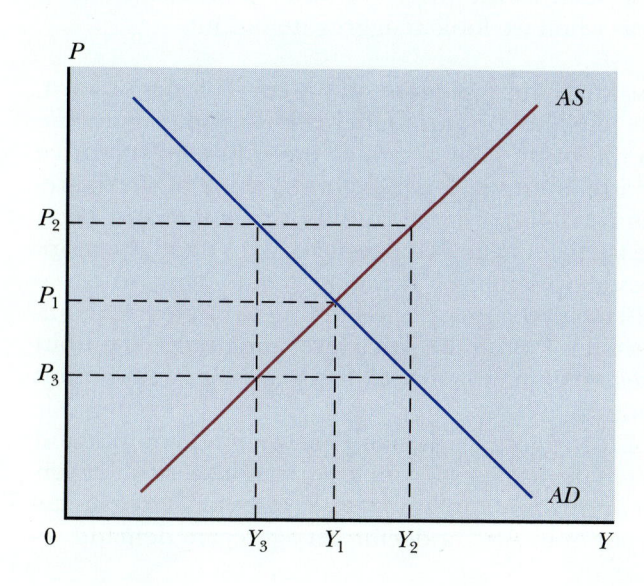

**FIGURE 5
EQUILIBRIUM OUTPUT AND PRICE LEVEL**
Equilibrium occurs at the intersection of *AS* and *AD*. If producers attempt to produce and sell the quantity Y_2, they will have unsold output at the desired price level. As they accumulate unwanted inventory, they will cut production. Real output and the price level will fall to Y_1 and P_1.

inventory investment) and will have to cut prices. As prices fall, the incentive to produce more output is lower. Thus, real output declines, until equilibrium is restored. You may want to go through this process for output levels below equilibrium, such as Y_3, to make sure you understand how equilibrium is restored.

In Figure 5, as in the diagrams for individual markets, the quantity sold and the quantity bought are always equal. Producers may offer quantity Y_2 at price level P_2, but they only sell quantity Y_3 at that price level. Both NI and GNP, however, are equal to $P_2 \times Y_2$. The unsold output is counted as inventory investment, and the workers and owners of capital who produced that output receive factor incomes. The national income accounts balance whether or not the economy is in equilibrium. In the circular flow model, the unplanned investment that firms make in inventory means that they will reduce their inventories in the near future. When that happens, the size of the flow will shrink back to a sustainable level of $P_1 \times Y_1$.

SHIFTS IN AGGREGATE DEMAND AND AGGREGATE SUPPLY

Changes in output and price level can result from shifts in either aggregate demand or aggregate supply. Aggregate demand can shift if any of the underlying conditions changes at every possible price level. These *ceteris paribus* conditions are the size of the money supply, household consumption, government spending, business investment, and net exports. Some of the effects that can shift individual demand curves are also still relevant. These effects are changes in consumer wealth, tastes, population, expectations, and interest rates. Two things that shift individual demand curves are not relevant here. One is the prices of substitutes and complements, which disappear when we aggregate over all goods. The other is changes in income. Since real output is also real income, income is already represented in the model and cannot be an exogenous variable.

Aggregate supply can also shift for two of the reasons that individual supply curves shift. There may be an increase or decrease in the amount of resources available or a change in technology. Other things that affect individual supply curves, such as the prices of other products the firm could produce, disappear when we look at aggregate output.

SHIFTS IN AGGREGATE DEMAND. If the aggregate supply curve slopes upward, we expect both the price level and output to increase when the aggregate demand curve shifts to the right. How much of the shift is in the price level and how much is in real output depends on the slope of the aggregate supply curve. In Figure 6, the original equilibrium is at P_1 and Y_1 on AD_1. A shift of the curve to AD_2 means that people want to purchase more real output at every possible price level. If the aggregate demand curve shifted to AD_3, this would mean that people are willing to buy less real output at every possible price level. Both the price level and total real output will fall. When the aggregate demand curve shifts, prices and real output move in the same direction.

The effect of shifts of the aggregate demand curve on real output and the price level is different if the aggregate supply curve is horizontal or vertical. Along a horizontal aggregate supply curve, increases in aggregate demand drive up real output only. Also, a decline in aggregate demand re-

Chapter 6 Aggregate Demand and Aggregate Supply

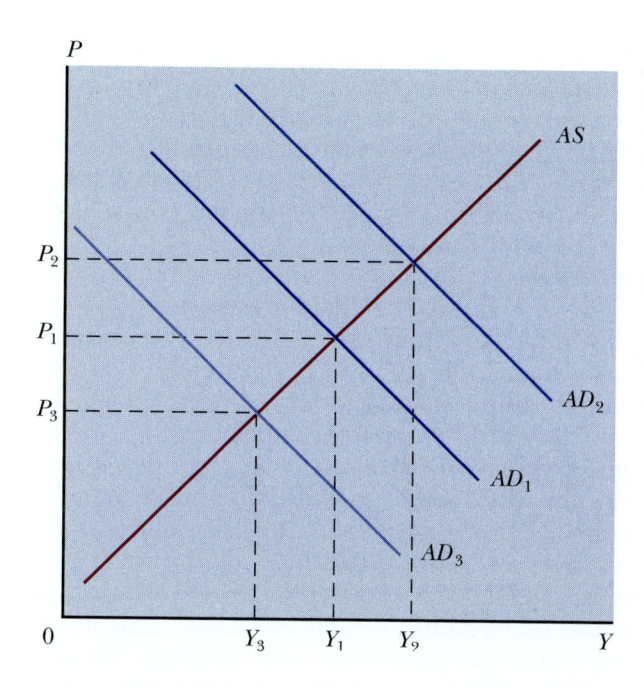

FIGURE 6
SHIFTS IN AGGREGATE DEMAND
An increase in aggregate demand from AD_1 to AD_2 (a shift to the right) drives output and prices up. A decrease in aggregate demand from AD_1 to AD_3 (a shift to the left) drives output and prices down.

duces real output only, with no effect on the price level. With a vertical aggregate supply curve, the price level rises when the aggregate demand curve shifts to the right and falls when it shifts to the left, but real output does not change. You might experiment with the composite aggregate supply curve of Figure 4 to observe these different effects on prices and output.

SHIFTS IN AGGREGATE SUPPLY. Shifts in aggregate supply are shown in Figure 7. For simplicity, we use the upward-sloping aggregate supply curve.

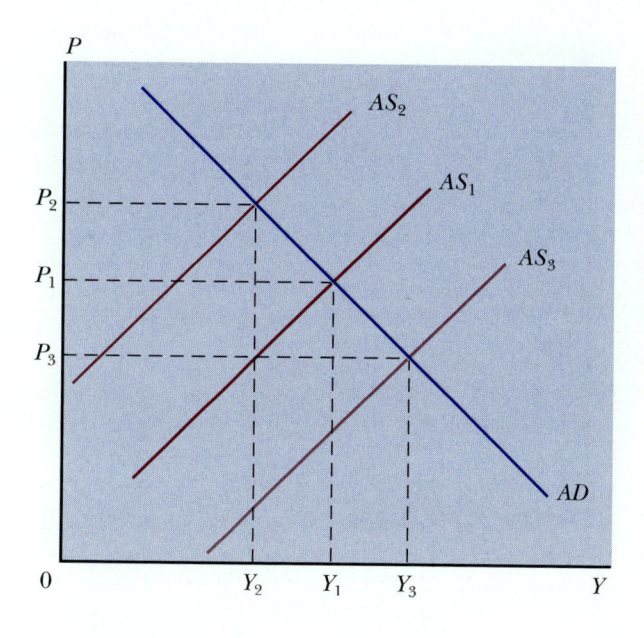

FIGURE 7
SHIFTS IN AGGREGATE SUPPLY
A decrease in aggregate supply from AS_1 to AS_2 (a leftward shift) raises prices and lowers real output. An increase in aggregate supply from AS_1 to AS_3 (a rightward shift) lowers the price level and increases real output.

A shift in aggregate supply to the left (from AS_1 to AS_2) means that producers will be willing to supply a smaller quantity of real output at every possible price level *or* the same real output at a higher price level. Real output falls and the price level rises—the worst of all possible worlds. When aggregate supply shifts to the right (from AS_1 to AS_3), the result is the best of all possible worlds—rising real output and a falling price level.

EMPLOYMENT AND UNEMPLOYMENT

The three macroeconomic goals identified in Chapter 4 are steady growth of total output, price stability, and full employment. Since Y represents real output and P represents the price level, two of the three goals are included in the aggregate supply and demand model. This graphic model can be extended to include the third goal of full employment.

Figure 8 is an **aggregate production function**. This graph shows how much total real output can be produced by various amounts of labor. A production function is normally drawn with labor (the independent variable) on the horizontal axis and real output (the dependent variable) on the vertical axis. The diagram in Figure 8, however, is turned sideways so that the horizontal axis shows real output (Y) and the vertical axis shows the aggregate level of employment of labor (N). Assuming that the size of the labor force is stable, the higher the value of N, the lower the rate of unemployment will be.

There is a positive relationship between the number of workers employed and the level of real output. More workers will produce more output. In Figure 8, output rises as more workers are hired, but as more workers are added, total ouput grows more slowly. The best workers are hired first, and the last workers hired are usually less productive. Also, if the stock of capital is fixed, each worker added has less and less capital with which to work. So extra workers increase total output, but later ones do not add as much as previous ones.

aggregate production function
A graph showing the relationship between total real output and the number of workers employed.

**FIGURE 8
THE AGGREGATE PRODUCTION FUNCTION**
The aggregate production function shows the relationship between the level of real output and the level of employment. The increase in real output gets smaller as more and more workers are hired.

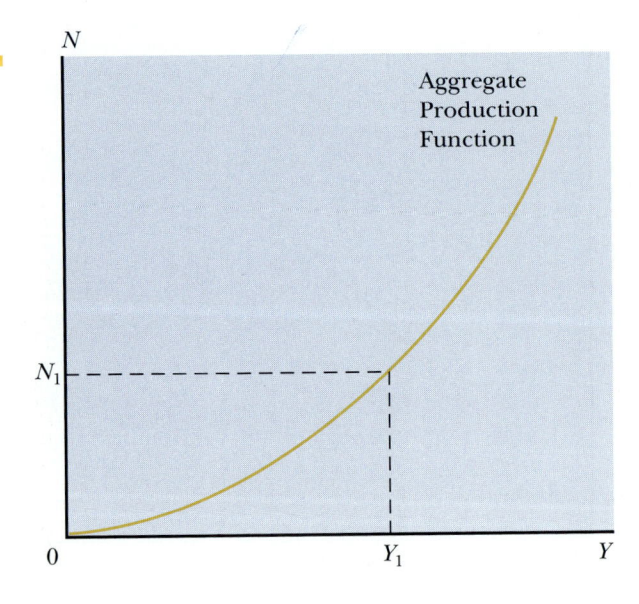

Combining Figure 8 with aggregate supply and demand curves provides a view of output, employment, and prices all at once. This is done in Figure 9. Equilibrium values of the price level and real output are determined to be P_1 and Y_1, where AS crosses AD_1. Tracing real output down to the aggregate production function, we find that N_1 workers must be employed in order to produce that level of real output. Thus, aggregate supply and demand combined with a production function determine not only the price level and real output but also the level of employment and, by extension, the level of unemployment.

If N_1 is less than full employment, then the diagram in Figure 9 suggests how to get to full employment. A shift of either AD or AS to the right will cause the two curves to intersect at a higher level of real output. This shift increases employment and reduces unemployment. For example, a shift from AD_1 to AD_2 will raise output to Y_2, the price level to P_2, and employment to N_2. In this case, statistics would show an increase in both out-

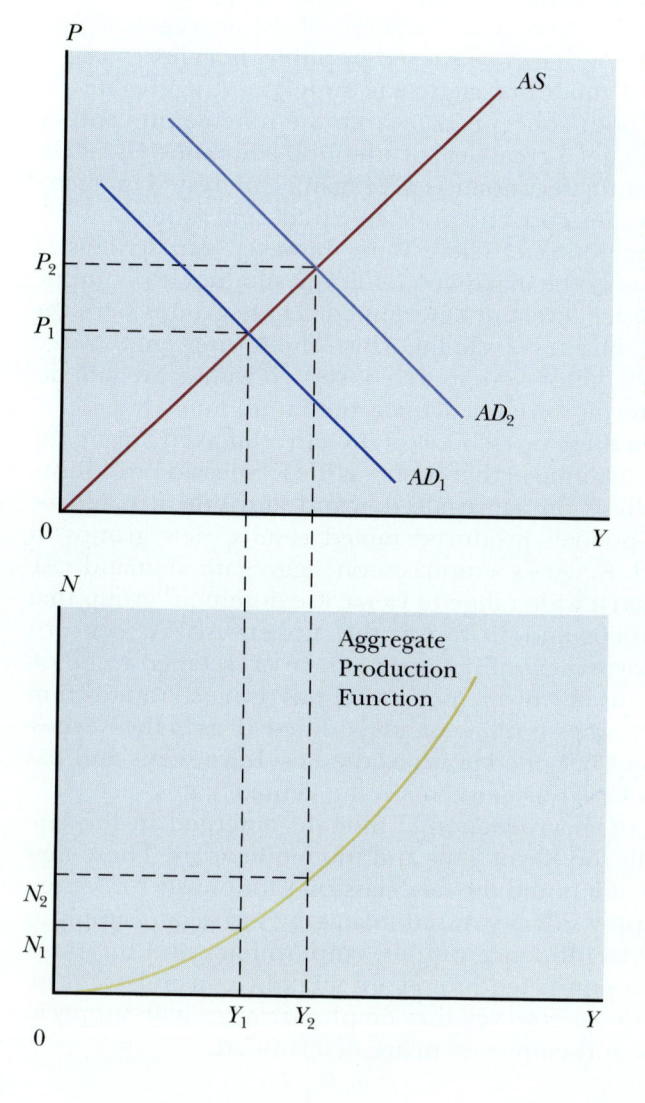

FIGURE 9
OUTPUT, EMPLOYMENT, AND PRICE LEVEL
Combining aggregate supply, demand, and production function in two interrelated graphs shows what is happening to output, employment, and the price level all at once. Shifts of AD or AS affect employment as well as the price level and real output.

put and employment but at the expense of a higher price level (inflation). You can experiment with other combinations to see how changes in aggregate supply and demand affect employment and unemployment.

AGGREGATE SUPPLY AND DEMAND AND COMPETING MACROECONOMIC IDEAS

The aggregate supply and demand model is very useful for looking at macroeconomic policy. It is also helpful in understanding some of the disputes over what policy can and cannot do. The competing ideas of the various groups of macroeconomists can be interpreted using this simple framework. Some of the differences between Keynesians and monetarists, Post-Keynesians and new classical economists, or (in the nineteenth century) the classical school and business cycle theorists can be interpreted as disagreements over how aggregate demand shifts, or whether it can be permanently shifted by government policies. Other disputes can be interpreted in terms of differences over the shape of the aggregate supply curve and whether and how it can be shifted by public policies.

Although the formal model of aggregate supply and aggregate demand is relatively new, both concepts date from the nineteenth century. Macroeconomics did not get a great deal of attention before the Great Depression. Nineteenth-century economists were mainly interested in microeconomic questions of value, cost, and price, free trade and protectionism, and monopoly and competition. There were, however, two schools of thought that disagreed over the macroeconomic questions of how output, employment, and the price level are determined. These groups were the classical school and the business cycle theorists. The former emphasized aggregate supply and the latter were more concerned with aggregate demand, although these terms were not actually used until much later.

The conflict between these two schools of thought climaxed during the Great Depression. The outcome of that clash was the Keynesian revolution, which put a new emphasis on aggregate demand and how it could be shifted. As Keynesian policies produced mixed results, new groups of economists challenged Keynes's emphasis on aggregate demand. Although these groups had a wide range of views, the dominant group that emerged during the 1960s and 1970s was the monetarists. As concern shifted from full employment to inflation, monetarists seemed to be offering better explanations of why the price level was rising so rapidly during the 1970s. Other economists refined and modified ideas in the Keynesian tradition. This group became known as the Post-Keynesians and has been much stronger in Great Britain than in the United States.

Two more schools of macroeconomic thought emerged in the late 1970s to challenge both the Keynesians and the monetarists. These new groups were the supply siders and the new classical economists (or rational expectationists). Supply siders stressed managing aggregate supply as the most effective way to influence output, employment, and the price level. New classical economists tend to regard all policies as relatively ineffective. Like supply siders, however, they emphasize aggregate supply in explaining how output and employment are determined.

The Classical School

Economists use the term **classical school** to refer to a diverse group of economists, from David Hume in the early eighteenth century to A. C. Pigou in the early twentieth century. What these economists had in common was a belief that the economy automatically tends toward a level of output associated with full employment. In their view, the aggregate supply curve is vertical, at least in the long run, and the long run is not very long. Because of that belief, they felt that the main goal of macroeconomic policy should be to control the price level and inflation. The core of classical macroeconomics focused on the management of the money supply to control inflation.

One of the central ideas of the classical school was the quantity theory of money introduced earlier in this chapter (and examined in more detail in Chapter 7). The quantity theory of money was originally developed as an explanation for inflation. Today, changes in the money supply are viewed as one of the major sources of shifts in the aggregate demand curve. The other central idea of the classical school was Say's law.

classical school
A group of economists in the eighteenth and nineteenth centuries who believed that the economy automatically tended toward the full-employment level of output.

Say's Law. Jean-Baptiste Say was a nineteenth-century French economist who was interested in business cycles. His name is associated with **Say's law**, which says that "supply creates its own demand." That is, enough income is created in the process of production to buy everything that is produced. Individual goods can be overproduced if suppliers fail to read correctly the signals from the market. These suppliers will be penalized for producing the wrong things by incurring losses. Meanwhile those who read the market signals correctly will be rewarded with profits. General overproduction for any length of time is not possible.

Say realized that this view was rather simplistic. What would happen if households let part of their income "leak" out of the circular flow in order to save, instead of spending it all on consumption? Say had an answer for that objection. Household saving would flow into banks and be lent to business firms that would inject it back into the income stream as investment. In an economy with small government and foreign sectors, saving (leakages) and investment (injections) would be equal.

Say's law
The idea that supply creates its own demand, a cornerstone of classical economics.

What ensures that saving will be equal to investment? The incentive to save is the interest that can be earned. Interest is the reward for saving. Interest is also the price of investment. The biggest obstacle to borrowing in order to invest is the interest that must be paid. Changes in the interest rate, like changes in any price, ensure that the supply of funds (saving) will be equal to the demand for borrowing (investment). Thus, automatic forces will always push real output (Y) toward the full-employment level, or Y^* in Figure 10. Attempts to increase aggregate demand will only drive up the price level. In Figure 10, an increase in aggregate demand from AD_1 to AD_2 drives the price level up from P_1 to P_2, leaving real output unchanged at Y^*. Say's law is the reason why classical economists believed that the aggregate supply curve is vertical at the full-employment level of real output.

**FIGURE 10
AGGREGATE SUPPLY
AND DEMAND:
A CLASSICAL VIEW**
If the aggregate supply curve (*AS*) is vertical, shifting aggregate demand from AD_1 to AD_2 drives the price level up, from P_1 to P_2, leaving real output unchanged at Y^*. Thus, policies aimed at increasing aggregate demand will not be effective.

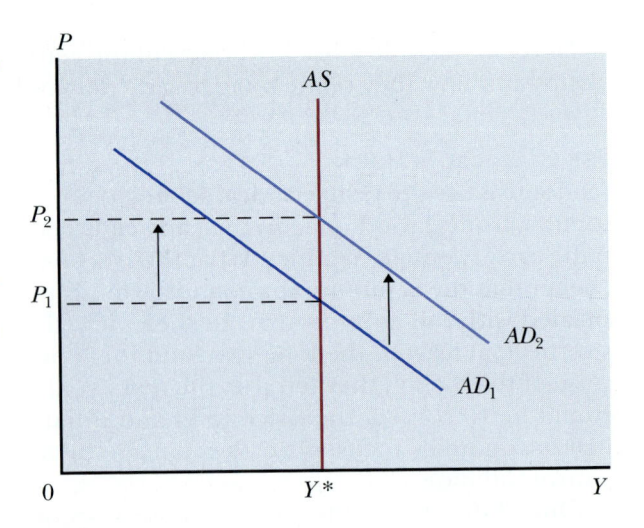

CLASSICAL ECONOMICS AND *LAISSEZ-FAIRE*. Classical economists were the intellectual heirs of Adam Smith and his *laissez-faire* ideas about the effectiveness of free markets. Their prescription for macroeconomic policies could also be described as *laissez-faire*: Leave the macro economy alone, and it will correct itself. According to them, unemployment does occur, but it cannot last very long because the economy automatically tends toward a level of output associated with full employment. With the level of real output determined by the resources available and unemployment viewed as a short-term and self-correcting problem, the classical economists' main macroeconomic concern was the price level. Classical economists in the nineteenth century knew that increases in aggregate demand could drive up the price level. They believed that the government should try to control the money supply in order to keep aggregate demand from shifting to the right and causing inflation.

It is clear from the data presented in Chapter 4 that there were extended periods of falling output and unemployment during the time of the classical school. It is difficult to reconcile these data with an aggregate supply curve that is vertical at the full-employment level of output. However, some of the classical economists' ideas reflected their ordering of macroeconomic goals. Inflation was of greater concern to them than un-

IDEAS OF THE CLASSICAL SCHOOL

- *Output* is determined by available resources (especially labor) and will always tend toward the level associated with full employment. Thus, the aggregate supply curve will be vertical at the full-employment level of output.
- *Employment* is determined by supply and demand in the labor market. Unemployment is generally temporary and can be corrected by a reduction in real wages.
- The *price level* is determined by aggregate demand, or, more specifically, by the money supply, which determines the position of the aggregate demand curve.

employment. Also, minimal government intervention was a goal in itself. They felt that government intervention in the economy, even on behalf of the worthy goal of full employment, was likely to interfere with the more highly valued microeconomic goals of efficiency and freedom.

Finally, classical economists were primarily concerned with the long run, a time period in which the economy is normally at or near the full-employment level of output. They felt that any deviations from full employment and capacity output would be corrected if only people were willing to wait for natural market forces to operate.

THE BUSINESS CYCLE THEORISTS

Nineteenth-century economists who were concerned about large or prolonged deviations from the full-employment level of output were called **business cycle theorists**. Among them were Thomas Robert Malthus and Karl Marx. These economists challenged the classical view that market forces will return the economy automatically to full employment. They thought that view didn't seem to fit the evidence. There were long and painful periods of declining output and widespread unemployment that had to be explained and, if possible, corrected. In addition, cyclical patterns in economic activity were clearly observable, such as the business cycle illustrated in Chapter 4. None of these real-world events were consistent with an aggregate supply curve that was vertical. The business cycle theorists' picture of the economy is captured by Figure 11, which shows a fairly flat aggregate supply curve. In this model, a shift in aggregate demand from AD_1 to AD_2 drives the price level up from P_1 to P_2, but also results in an increase in real output from Y_1 to Y_2.

Business cycle theorists argued that cyclical ups and downs in output, employment, and prices occurred with such regularity and frequency that they seemed to be obeying some natural law of the marketplace. But that law was not Say's law. Unlike the classical economists, the business cycle theorists did not develop a single general theory or model to describe, explain, or predict the recurrent ups and downs in economic activity. Their

business cycle theorists A group of economists in the nineteenth and early twentieth centuries who tried to develop explanations for cyclical patterns in economic activity.

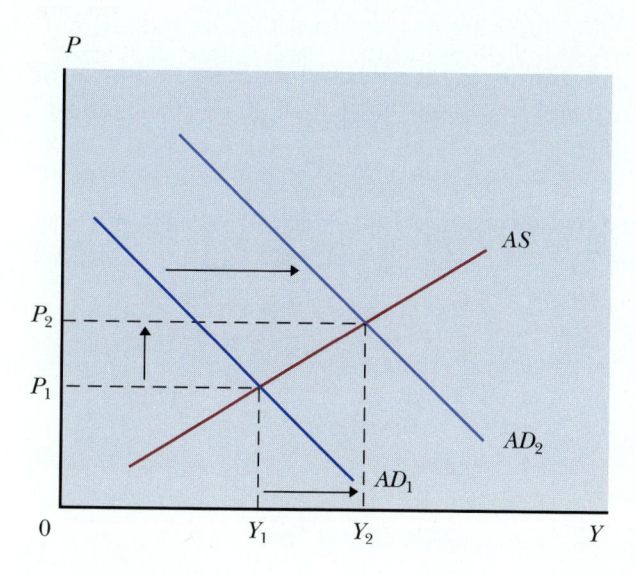

FIGURE 11
AGGREGATE SUPPLY AND DEMAND: THE VIEW OF THE BUSINESS CYCLE THEORISTS
The aggregate supply and demand model can be used to interpret the ideas of business cycle theorists. With a fairly flat aggregate supply curve, a shift of aggregate demand from AD_1 to AD_2 drives the price level up, from P_1 to P_2. It also results in an increase in real output from Y_1 to Y_2.

The Physiocrats (see Chapter 2) felt that saving could cause reductions in the circular flow that would be damaging to the economy. A later French economist, Jean-Baptiste Say, presented a theory that stated that saving (leakages) was no cause for concern. Say, a businessman turned academic, taught political economy at the *Conservatoire des Arts et Metiers*.

Say's law played a central role in classical macroeconomics. This law is based on a simple theory of self-regulating markets. Say's law contends that the aggregate supply of goods and services will always be equal to the aggregate demand for them. Say maintained that the sum of all wages, profits, rents, and interest paid in production (NI) would be equal to the value of the goods produced (GNP) and, therefore, would be sufficient to buy them. The purchasing power in a system is always enough to purchase the goods produced. The simple, popular statement of Say's law is that supply creates its own demand. Household income that does not flow directly back into the income stream in the form of consumption would be channeled as saving through the credit market. It would flow either into investment or into consumption by other households that borrow.

Say never argued that overproduction of some goods and underproduction of others would not occur. He believed, however, that these imbalances would be corrected rather quickly as entrepreneurs adjusted the output mix in order to earn profits by satisfying consumer demands.

Supply side economics, which gained popularity in the 1980s, draws on Say's theory in emphasizing the role of aggregate supply. Many supply siders quoted the following passage from Say:

"The encouragement of mere consumption is no benefit to commerce; for the difficulty lies in supplying the means, not in stimulating the desire for consumption; and we have seen production alone furnishes that means. It is the aim of good government to stimulate production; of bad government to encourage consumption."[a]

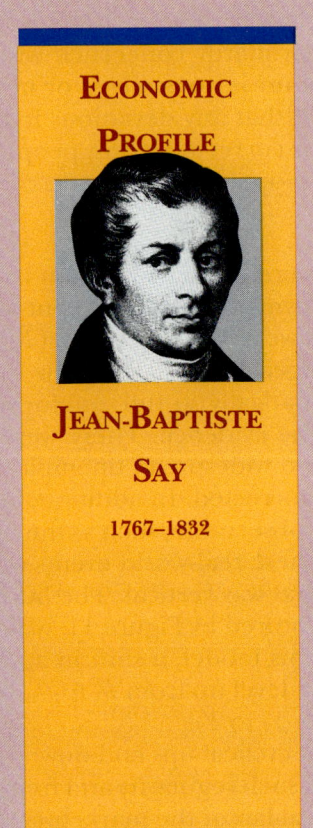

ECONOMIC PROFILE

JEAN-BAPTISTE SAY

1767–1832

---

a. Jean-Baptiste Say, *A Treatise on Political Economy* (Philadelphia: John Grigg, 1830).

major contribution was to point to the role of demand (or what we now call aggregate demand), specifically the behavior of consumption or investment demand, in generating changes in output, employment, and price level. When Keynes tried to explain one of the most severe downturns in economic activity in modern times, the Great Depression, he built on the work of the business cycle theorists.

What values and priorities were implicit in the work of the business cycle theorists? They were more concerned about unemployment and lost output than the classical school was. Business cycle theorists did not ignore inflation, but it was not as urgent a concern to them. Like classical economists, however, most of them (except for Marx) did not prescribe government intervention. Many of them, in fact, shared the classical school's *laissez-faire* attitude about the role of government. In addition, with no real model, it was not easy to devise an appropriate form of government intervention to stabilize the business cycle. That prescription had to await the Keynesian revolution in the 1930s.

JOHN MAYNARD KEYNES AND THE KEYNESIAN REVOLUTION

The greatest challenge to the classical school was the business cycle itself at its worst—the Great Depression. "Wait it out; the economy will correct itself" was not appealing advice in the depths of the Depression. John Maynard Keynes's often quoted answer to the classical economists was "In the long run we are all dead." He insisted that even if the problems of falling output and unemployment could not last indefinitely, they could last long enough to cause great hardship, lost output, and human suffering. Even if the aggregate supply curve was vertical in the long run, its shape could be much flatter, or even horizontal, in the short run. If aggregate supply was relatively constant, shifts in aggregate demand could have significant effects on real output and employment. Economists whose macroeconomic ideas are based on the work of this famous British economist are called **Keynesians**.

The Keynesian challenge to the classical view is one that will take several chapters to develop. Basically, Keynes started with the idea that the aggregate supply curve might be very flat, or even horizontal. In that case, the economy could be in equilibrium, with aggregate supply equal to aggregate demand, at a level of output Y_e that is substantially below the full-employment level of output, Y^*. This situation, pictured in Figure 12, could persist for a fairly long time if there was no government intervention. This view challenged the classical position that equilibrium implied full employment. To the classical economists, the situation Keynes described was a disequilibrium that would set in motion automatic corrective forces.

Keynes also challenged Say's law. He argued that just because enough income is created in the production process to buy the output, that does not necessarily mean that all of the income will be spent. Savings would not be automatically channeled into investment, and the interest rate would not be very effective in ensuring that the two were equal. (We will present a more detailed picture of this challenge in Chapters 7 and 8.) The important conclusion that Keynes drew was that private components of aggregate demand (consumption and investment) might not behave so as to restore full employment. He thought that the government should use its

Keynesian economists Twentieth-century economists who adopted and extended John Maynard Keynes's idea that there could be persistent unemployment without government intervention.

FIGURE 12
AGGREGATE SUPPLY AND DEMAND: A KEYNESIAN VIEW
This model shows an equilibrium situation in which aggregate supply is equal to aggregate demand. Note that the resulting level of output, Y_e, is substantially below the full-employment level of output, Y^*.

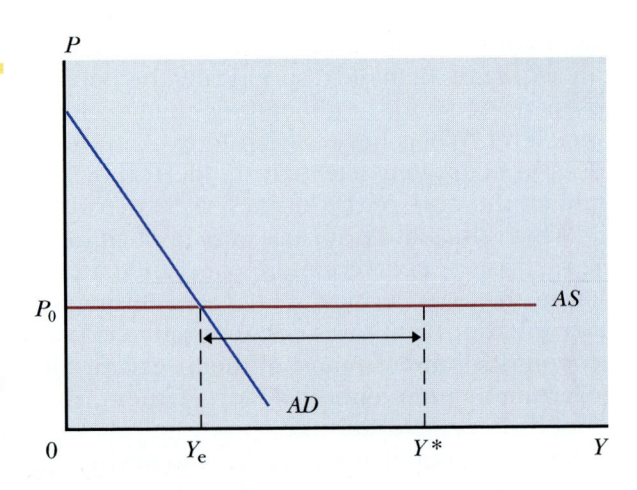

fiscal policy
The use of government spending and taxes to try to influence the levels of output, employment, and prices.

power to spend and tax in order to stabilize private economic activity. The use of government taxing and spending to influence output, employment, and prices is called **fiscal policy**. Keynes saw fiscal policy as a way to shift aggregate demand to the right, increasing output and employment.

Because fiscal policy can be inflationary (depending on the slope of the aggregate supply curve), many people believed that Keynes was more concerned about unemployment than inflation. That is not true. Some of his writings, such as *Treatise on Money* and *How to Pay for the War*, addressed the problem of inflation. In 1936, however, when the *General Theory of Employment, Interest, and Money* was published, unemployment was a very serious concern, and the price level had been falling for several years. What really set Keynes apart from the classical school was not so much his concern for unemployment as his willingness to sacrifice *laissez-faire* principles. Unlike classical economists, Keynes thought that government officials could and should intervene to speed up the process of getting back to full employment.

Again, it is not difficult to draw some inferences about Keynes's values and priorities from what he had to say. He was concerned primarily with unemployment, at least in 1936. He was not willing to let hardship, suffering, and lost output persist while the economy slowly corrected itself. Finally, Keynes was not committed to *laissez-faire* policies and a minimal role for government. He believed that the benefits of intervention in the business cycle would exceed the cost. This argument led to a political revolution with

---

IDEAS OF THE KEYNESIANS

In the short run, if the economy is below full employment,

- *Output* is determined by aggregate demand.
- *Employment* is determined by the level of output.
- The *price level* is unable to fall and unlikely to rise under these conditions, so it can be treated as given.

Chapter 6 Aggregate Demand and Aggregate Supply

respect to the role of government. That change was as important as the intellectual revolution Keynes's ideas caused in the field of economics.

THE MONETARISTS

Keynesian ideas spread rapidly in the 1940s and 1950s. These ideas had so much influence that the impact of Keynes on macroeconomics became known as the Keynesian revolution. Inevitably, there was a counter-revolution. Keynesian economics appeared to be successful in preventing unemployment and major recessions, but neither Keynes nor his followers put much emphasis on the problem of price stability. Some critics questioned whether Keynesian economics was really in any way responsible for postwar prosperity. The most coherent and effective criticisms came from a group of economists somewhat in the classical tradition. This group was named **monetarists** by one of their best known members, Karl Brunner. Using more elaborate theories and statistical evidence than the classical school, monetarists challenged Keynes's theories and policy recommendations.

Although the monetarists are in the *laissez-faire* classical tradition, their name comes from the fact that they admit that at least one kind of government policy can have at least some short-run impact. **Monetary policy** means using changes in the money supply to try to affect levels of output, employment, and prices. Monetarists believe that monetary policy can shift aggregate demand and, in the short run, may affect real output, especially if the changes in the money supply are unexpected.

Monetarists, like classical economists, believe that the aggregate supply curve is vertical in the long run. They do concede that the curve can have a positive slope in the short run, although they expect it to be fairly steep. That is, in the short run, the economy could find itself at a level of output Y_e that is below the full-employment level of output, Y^*, as shown in Figure 13. Expanding the money supply would shift the aggregate de-

monetarists
Twentieth-century economists who criticize Keynesian economics and stress the role of the money supply.

monetary policy
The use of changes in the money supply to try to influence the levels of output, employment, and prices.

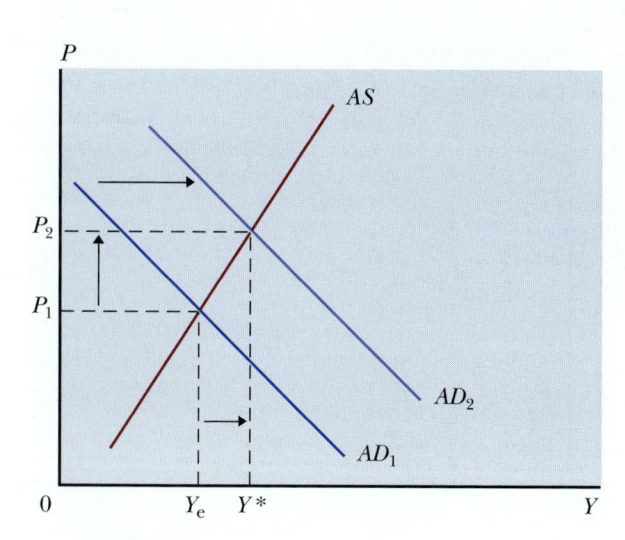

FIGURE 13
AGGREGATE SUPPLY AND DEMAND: A MONETARIST VIEW
If the economy is operating at a level of output Y_e below the full-employment level of output Y^*, expanding the money supply shifts the aggregate demand curve from AD_1 to AD_2. There is a slightly less than vertical slope on the aggregate supply curve in the short run. Thus, the price level rises from P_1 to P_2. Real output also increases slightly, from Y_e to Y^*.

mand curve from AD_1 to AD_2. With a positively sloped aggregate supply curve, the price level in the short run would rise from P_1 to P_2. Real output, however, would also increase from Y_e to Y^*. Like classical economists but unlike Keynesians, monetarists are also concerned about inflation and generally opposed to government intervention. We will look more carefully at their contributions in later chapters.

SUPPLY SIDERS

Both Keynesians and monetarists are primarily concerned with the aggregate demand curve and why it shifts. They both take the aggregate supply curve as given, even if they do disagree about its slope. In the late 1970s and early 1980s, many countries, including the United States, experienced rising prices, falling output, and rising unemployment all at the same time. If you look again at Figure 9, you will see that this combination could not have resulted from shifts in the aggregate demand curve. Something must have been happening to aggregate supply. This was the conclusion of a group of academic economists and policy makers called **supply siders**. This name reflects the fact that they were looking for solutions to problems of inflation and unemployment that would involve shifting aggregate supply to the right.

supply siders
Late-twentieth-century economists and policy makers who want to fight inflation and unemployment by trying to shift the aggregate supply curve to the right.

Figure 14 shows the supply side view. Initially, equilibrium price level P_1 and real output Y_1 are determined by the intersection of a steeply sloped aggregate supply curve (AS_1) and a stable aggregate demand curve (AD_1). Now some event happens to reduce the economy's capacity to produce real output. The most famous such event (called a supply shock) in recent history was the dramatic increase in the price of oil in the mid-1970s. Oil not only is needed for heating and transportation but also enters into the production of many other goods, such as fertilizers, plastics, and medicines. The sudden rise in the price of oil shifted the aggregate supply curve from AS_1 to AS_2, driving the price level up to P_2 and reducing real output to Y_2.

Supply siders are every bit as diverse as the business cycle theorists. They tend, as a group, to be less theoretical than some of the other schools

**FIGURE 14
SUPPLY SHOCKS AND AGGREGATE SUPPLY AND DEMAND**
A supply shock moves the economy away from its initial equilibrium price level, P_1, and real output, Y_1. The shift in the aggregate supply curve from AS_1 to AS_2 drives the price level up to P_2 and reduces real output to Y_2.

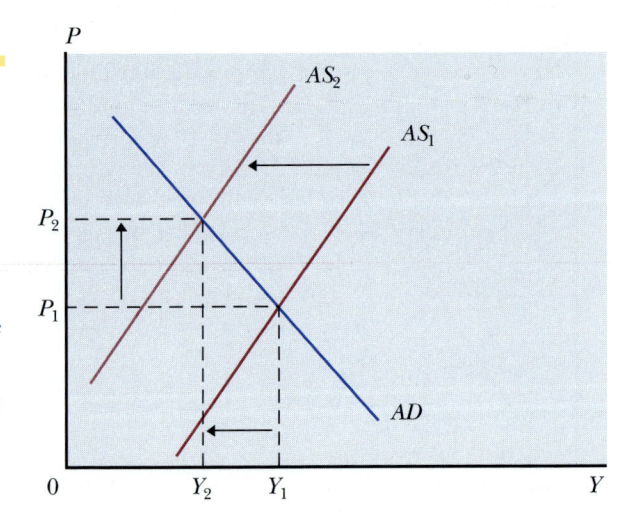

of thought. The theory on which they rely is largely a microeconomic theory of individual incentives. Supply siders are concerned about both inflation and unemployment. Supply siders generally want a strong private economy, but some of them support certain kinds of government intervention. In large part, "Reaganomics" (the economic policies of the Reagan administration from 1981 to 1989) reflected the ideas of the supply siders. We will look more closely at their ideas and experiences in the 1980s with their policy prescriptions in a later chapter.

New Classical Economists

The group of economists known as the **new classical economists** (or sometimes as the rational expectations school) also emerged during the 1970s and 1980s. These economists were displeased with both the usefulness of existing theories and the performance of the economy. They take an even dimmer view of government intervention than the monetarists do. New classical economists regard both monetary and fiscal policies as ineffective because individuals find it in their own self-interest to anticipate government actions and respond in ways that offset the impact of those actions. The new classical models imply that government policies can only be effective when people are taken by surprise. Otherwise, self-interested behavior defeats the effectiveness of government efforts to shift aggregate demand.

New classical economists share with classical economists (and to some extent with monetarists) a good deal of faith in the effective workings of unregulated markets and a preference for a minimal role for government. They believe that the aggregate supply curve is vertical or close to vertical even in the short run, because markets are very efficient and individuals apply new information quickly to their behavior. Their policy ideas and their view of the aggregate supply curve are quite similar to those of the classical school. However, their arguments are more sophisticated, often expressed in elaborate mathematical form. They also differ from the classical school on the issue of aggregate demand. Classical economists believe that policies can shift the aggregate demand curve. However, the shift will only cause inflation, with no effect on real output. New classical economists are skeptical about the ability of policy to shift the aggregate demand curve at all.

New classical economists believe that the aggregate supply curve is vertical in the long run and close to vertical in the short run. They argue that even if government policy makers succeed in shifting aggregate demand, the only effect will be to drive up prices. Unlike classical economists, however, new classical economists believe that monetary and fiscal policy can have some *temporary* effects on both output and price level. These effects will last until the private actors in the economy realize what the government is doing. In the long run (not a very long period of time, in the new classical view), private decisions will determine the level of output and employment. We will explore the ideas of this school in greater detail in a later chapter.

The Post-Keynesians

Every counterrevolution faces loyalists, and the attack on the Keynesian revolution was no exception. The "defenders of the faith" in this case were

> **new classical economists** Late-twentieth-century economists who regard monetary and fiscal policies as ineffective because individuals will anticipate and offset government actions.

Post-Keynesians
A group of late-twentieth-century economists who have refined and extended the work of Keynes. They stress market imperfections such as imperfect information, monopoly power, and inflexible wages and prices.

several groups of economists, both British and American, known as Post-Keynesians.[5] **Post-Keynesians** are economists who have refined and extended the ideas of Keynes in response to real-world experiences as well as challenges from monetarists, supply siders, and new classical economists.

In general, Post-Keynesians are skeptical about the responsiveness of markets, the flexibility of wages and prices, and the speed of the adjustment process. They point to long-term contracts, monopolies, the costs of gathering information, and other real-world considerations that can greatly slow the adjustment process. Thus, their aggregate supply curve, like that of the Keynesians, is relatively flat, and the short run is a fairly long period of time. Like Keynes, they see an important role for government in smoothing out ups and downs and, in particular, in reducing unemployment by shifting aggregate demand. We will examine Post-Keynesian ideas more closely in later chapters.

LIBERALS, CONSERVATIVES, AND POLITICAL ECONOMY

As you may have noticed, some economists support and others are opposed to government intervention to correct unemployment. In general, those who favor a larger role for government in both macroeconomic and microeconomic policy are known as liberals. Those who wish to minimize the role of government and rely on market processes are labeled conservatives.

The old name of economics was political economy, reflecting an emphasis on proposing and evaluating public policy. Although contemporary economists pride themselves on being positive rather than normative, in practice the line between positive and normative is not clearly drawn. Goals, values, and priorities tend to influence economists' thinking, development of models, and interpretation of data.

Keynesians and Post-Keynesians are generally liberal in political philosophy. They are concerned about unemployment, somewhat tolerant of inflation, and inclined to look for solutions through government. Monetarists and new classical economists, on the other hand, tend to be conservative. These two groups have much more faith in market processes and much less trust in the ability of government to improve outcomes. Both of these groups tend to worry more about inflation than unemployment. Supply siders' political philosophy falls somewhere between these two camps, closer to the conservative end. Unlike monetarists and new classical economists, supply siders are concerned about both inflation and unemployment and see some positive but limited role for government. They believe that government can create an environment in which the private sector can work effectively to shift aggregate supply to the right.

As we work through the ideas of these various groups in the next few chapters, keep in mind that even though the theories and models are positive rather than normative, their interpretation and application by particular economists or groups are inevitably tinged by political philosophy.

---

5. A number of American economists who have modified and refined some of their views in response to critics but are still within the Keynesian tradition call themselves "New Keynesians."

Chapter 6 Aggregate Demand and Aggregate Supply

Summary

1. The aggregate demand curve shows the amounts of total real output that consumers will buy at various price levels. This curve slopes down from left to right.
2. A higher price level is associated with less demand for real output. This relationship is due to the effects of changes in price level on tax revenues, interest rates, exports and imports, and households' wealth.
3. Aggregate demand will shift if there is a change in consumption, investment, government spending, or net exports at every price level or if there is a change in the money supply.
4. The aggregate supply curve shows the amounts of total real output that the economy will produce at various price levels. There is much disagreement about whether this curve is horizontal, upward-sloping, or vertical. A composite aggregate supply curve has a horizontal region at low levels of output, followed by an upward-sloping range, and finally a vertical segment as output reaches capacity.
5. An upward-sloping aggregate supply curve results from higher costs of production as firms compete for increasingly scarce supplies of resources. Alternatively, an upward-sloping aggregate supply curve reflects the incentive that higher profits associated with higher prices gives to producers to increase output.
6. The aggregate supply and demand curves, taken together, determine the price level and the level of real output. Adding an aggregate production function also indicates the level of employment.
7. The two competing schools of thought in macroeconomics in the nineteenth century were the classical school and the business cycle theorists. Classical economists thought that the economy tended naturally toward full employment. Thus, the classical aggregate supply curve was vertical. The classical school advocated a *laissez-faire* approach. The business cycle theorists were concerned about the ups and downs of the market economy, which had long periods of unemployment and falling output. Business cycle theorists put more emphasis on the role of what contemporary economists call aggregate demand.
8. Keynes challenged the classical school during the Great Depression. He suggested that the aggregate supply curve could be horizontal, or at least very flat, in the short run. Thus, periods of unemployment could persist for a long time without automatic correction. He advocated government intervention in the form of fiscal policy to shift aggregate demand.
9. The principal competing schools of thought in the late twentieth century are the Keynesians and Post-Keynesians on one side and the monetarists and new classical economists on the other, with supply siders in between. They disagree about the effectiveness of policy and the steepness of the aggregate supply curve.
10. Monetarists criticized Keynesian theory and policy and recommended a return to a more *laissez-faire* approach. However, they believe that shifting aggregate demand by changing the money supply can be an effective policy tool in the short run.
11. Both Keynesians and monetarists focus on aggregate demand. Supply siders advocate shifting aggregate supply. This should result in lower prices and increased output and employment at the same time.
12. New classical economists, like classical economists, see a minimal role for government. The classical school took the position that the private economy will do well enough if left alone. The new classical economists go further. They argue that monetary policy and fiscal policy are generally ineffective because their intended impact on aggregate demand is offset by the rational expectations of households and firms. They also believe that the aggregate supply curve is close to vertical even in the short run.

New Terms

aggregate demand curve
quantity theory of money
equation of exchange

aggregate supply curve
full-employment level of output

aggregate production function
classical school

Say's law
business cycle theorists
Keynesians

fiscal policy   monetary policy   new classical economists
monetarists   supply siders   Post-Keynesians

Questions for Discussion

1. Suppose the President proposes to increase federal spending in order to reduce unemployment. Show the effect of this change on the diagram of Figure 9. What would be the reaction of a classical economist, a Keynesian, a monetarist, and a supply sider?

2. Practice using the aggregate supply and demand curves. What kind of shift would produce a rise in both P and Y? a fall in both? a rise in P and a fall in Y? a rise in Y and a fall in P?

3. How can you shift aggregate demand and/or aggregate supply so that real output increases while prices remain stable?

4. Why does the aggregate demand curve slope down from left to right?

5. Explain how Figure 9 makes it possible to consider all three macroeconomic goals.

6. Identify whether each of these statements is most likely to be made by a classical economist, a Keynesian, a monetarist, a new classical economist, or a supply sider.
   a. "If the government doesn't do something about unemployment, it isn't going to go away any time soon."
   b. "If the government tries to increase employment, all it will wind up doing will be driving up the price level."
   c. "If the government feels it should do something in this recession, it should use monetary policy."
   d. "Whatever the government does, smart people will figure it out in advance and take actions that will wind up offsetting the effect of government policy."
   e. "If we just encourage production by making it worthwhile for business to produce, we will get out of this recession. Demand is not the problem."

7. Assume an upward-sloping aggregate supply curve. How will an increase in foreign demand for exports affect aggregate supply and demand, output, prices, and employment? Use aggregate supply and demand curves and a production function in your answer.

8. How would your answer to Question 7 be different if the aggregate supply curve were vertical? What if it were horizontal?

9. Which variables rise during the upswing of the business cycle? Do any fall? Which ones rise and which ones fall during a downturn?

10. How does Keynes's famous remark "In the long run we are all dead" relate to the debate between classical economists and Keynesians?

11. In what ways are Keynesians and Post-Keynesians liberal? In what ways are monetarists and new classical economists conservative? Why are supply siders harder to classify?

12. In the equation of exchange, suppose V is stable (constant) with a value of 4, and the money supply is $200 billion. What combinations of P and Y are possible? Identify about a dozen combinations, and plot them on a graph. Does your graph look like an aggregate demand curve? Why or why not?

13. Suppose the money supply in Question 12 increases to $300 billion. Identify some new possible combinations of P and Y. Plot the new combinations. Which way has the curve shifted?

14. What kinds of changes can shift the aggregate supply curve to the right? What kinds of changes can shift the aggregate demand curve to the right?

15. Suppose the aggregate demand curve is a straight line. One point on it is represented by a price level of $3 and a quantity of 1,500 units, and another point by a price level of $5 and a quantity of 1,000 units. What quantity of real output is associated with a price level of $4? Can you locate other points on this line?

Suggestions for Further Reading

Backhouse, Roger. *Economists and the Economy: The Evolution of Economic Ideas, 1600 to the Present Day.* Oxford and New York: Basil Blackwell, 1988. Development of economic ideas in a context of economic history; particularly strong in the development of ideas about inflation, employment, and business cycles.

Breit, William, and Roger L. Ransom. *The Academic Scribblers: Economists in Collision*, 2nd ed. Hinsdale, IL: Dryden Press, 1982. Biographical sketches and contributions of a number of famous economists of the past.

Canterbery, E. Ray. *The Making of Economics*, 2nd ed. Belmont, CA: Wadsworth, 1980. History of economic thought; emphasizes interaction of economic conditions, values, and development of economic ideas.

Maddock, Rodney, and Michael Carter. "A Child's Guide to Rational Expectations," *Journal of Economic Literature* (March 1982): 39–51. A fairly nontechnical overview of a highly technical approach to macroeconomics.

Wanniski, Jude. *The Way the World Works: How Economics Fails and Succeeds*. New York: Simon and Schuster, 1978. The best-known popularized version of supply side economics.

APPENDIX: A GLOSSARY OF SYMBOLS

Chapters 4 through 6 have introduced a number of symbols. More will appear in the next few chapters. Here, for handy reference, is a list of symbols you have already encountered.

GNP	gross national product
NNP	net national product
NI	national income
PI	personal income
Y	real output
Y^*	full-employment level of real output
N	level of employment
C	consumption
I	gross private domestic investment
G	government purchases of goods and services
T	taxes
EX	exports
IM	imports
P	price level
M_s	money supply
V	velocity of money
AD	aggregate demand curve
AS	aggregate supply curve

Here are some additional symbols you'll be encountering in the next few chapters.

C_0	that part of consumption that is independent of the level of income
b	marginal propensity to consume (also *MPC*)
M_d	demand for money
t	marginal tax rate
T_0	that part of taxes collected that is independent of the level of income
R	transfer payments
K	capital stock
k	the fraction of money income people want to hold in cash; equal to $1/V$
a	marginal propensity to invest
m	marginal propensity to import
RR	required bank reserves
ER	excess bank reserves
rr	reserve ratio
i_n	nominal, or market, interest rate
r_r	interest rate after correcting for inflation

Determining Output and Employment: Keynesian Macroeconomics and Fiscal Policy

3

> **AFTER STUDYING THIS CHAPTER, YOU SHOULD BE ABLE TO:**
>
> 1. Explain how Say's law led classical economists to conclude that the economy would not go through prolonged periods of overproduction or unemployment.
> 2. Discuss the role of each of these self-regulating markets in ensuring that the economy will tend toward the full-employment level of output:
>   a. the product market,
>   b. the labor market,
>   c. the credit market.
> 3. Use the quantity theory of money to explain how increases in the money supply lead to proportional increases in the price level.
> 4. Discuss the basic ideas of the business cycle theorists.
> 5. Identify and explain the Keynesian criticisms of the classical model.

CHAPTER 7

CLASSICAL MACROECONOMICS AND THE KEYNESIAN RESPONSE

INTRODUCTION

Modern macroeconomic theory cannot be fully understood without looking at how it developed. Before the 1930s, the dominant school of macroeconomic thought was the classical school. There are several reasons to begin the study of macroeconomic theory with the classical school. First, classical macroeconomics represents the best efforts of early economists to develop a theoretical system to explain the aggregate level of economic activity and to predict the effects of changes of various kinds on economic activity.

Second, classical macroeconomics provided the background against which John Maynard Keynes, the great British economist, developed his new ideas. The foundation of classical macroeconomics lay in three ideas: Say's law, the quantity theory of money, and self-regulating markets. Keynes began his "revolution" by attacking each of these in turn.

Finally, each of the three parts of the classical foundation has received renewed attention in the economic debates of the last two decades. New classical economists have stressed the importance of self-regulating markets, which they believe will restore full employment and frustrate attempts by policy makers to change the level of income and output. The roots of the monetarists' ideas are found in the quantity theory of money. Finally, the supply side economics so popular in the 1980s was in many ways a modern version of Say's law.

Classical macroeconomics does not describe a single approach but rather a rich and diverse group of ideas. When Keynes attacked the ideas of the classical school in the *General Theory of Employment, Interest, and Money* (1936), he was attacking the mainstream of nineteenth-century economic thought.[1] In doing so, he ignored some important recent work on the quantity theory of money by economists such as Henry Simons and Irving Fisher, who were working in the classical tradition. The ideas that Keynes criticized were those that drove the macroeconomic policies of his time. His contributions changed the policy approach to recessions and depressions for decades to follow.

---

1. From now on, we will refer to this work as simply *General Theory*.

THE CLASSICAL VIEW OF MACROECONOMICS

The aggregate supply and demand model, although not used until well into this century, is helpful in understanding the ideas of the classical school. Specifically, Figure 1 shows a vertical aggregate supply (*AS*) curve and a downward-sloping aggregate demand (*AD*) curve in the upper panel and the aggregate production function in the lower panel. Classical economists believed that the interaction of labor supply and labor demand determines the real wage and the level of employment. The level of employment (N) then determines how much total real output (Y) will be produced. In Figure 1, N_1 is determined in the labor market (not shown). N_1 is the level of employment capable of producing a real output of Y_1. Output does not vary with the price level because the level of real output is determined by the interaction of labor supply and labor demand. Thus, the *AS* curve is vertical at Y_1. The *AD* curve has no influence on real output. It only serves to determine the price level, P_1. Shifts in aggregate demand will change the price level only.

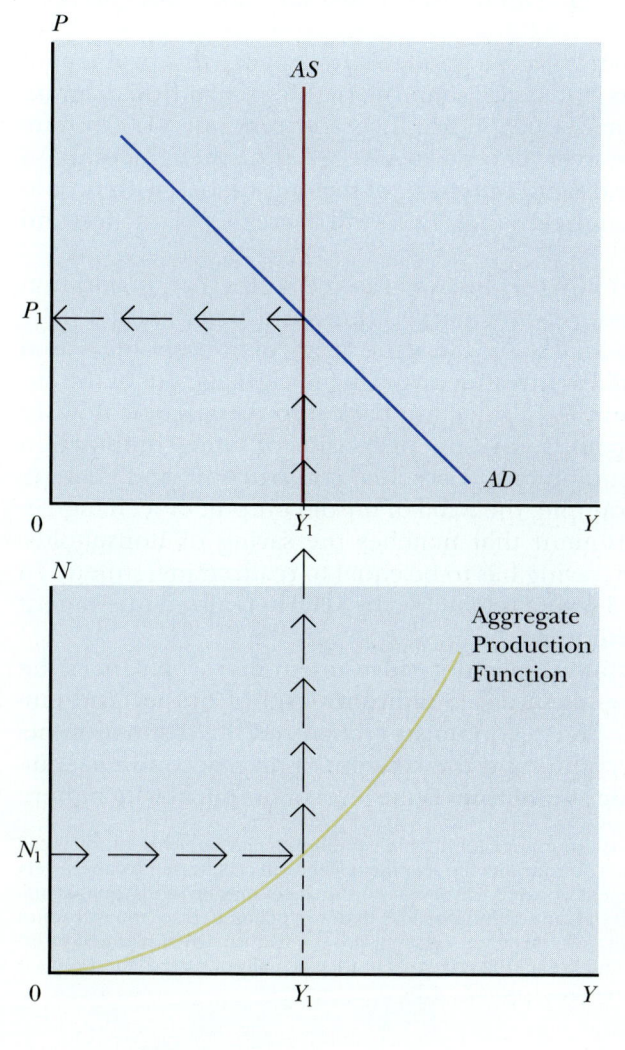

FIGURE 1
A CLASSICAL VIEW OF OUTPUT, EMPLOYMENT, AND PRICES
The level of employment (N_1), established in the labor market determines the level of real output (Y_1), and thus the location of the vertical aggregate supply curve (*AS*). Aggregate demand (*AD*) only affects the price level. It has no influence on output or employment.

Say's Law

Say's law, introduced in Chapter 6, is often phrased as "supply creates its own demand." Say argued that the production of goods and services generates an amount of income equal to the value of the products produced. If firms produce output with a value of $1,000, then they also create incomes for the factors of production equal to $1,000. Since the income created is the same as the value of output, the production process creates the amount of income necessary to purchase the goods and services produced. Say further argued that the only reason people offer their labor or other productive resources in the factor market is to earn income to use for consumption spending. Production generates income, which is all spent to purchase what was produced.

This simple form of Say's law implies that a market economy will not be subject to severe or prolonged periods of overproduction. Say's law would always be true in an economy where there was no saving. However, if people save a part of their incomes, spending can be less than the value of what is produced. This level of spending results in unsold goods. As producers pile up inventories, they cut back on production and lay off workers. Output falls and unemployment rises. Thus, Say's law is not correct if there is any saving.

The circular flow model offers a good way to visualize this problem of overproduction as well as its classical solution. In the circular flow diagram in Figure 2, firms produce $1,000 in products and generate $1,000 in incomes. Households, however, choose to save $200 of their income, so there is not enough spending to purchase all the output. Left with unsold products ($200 worth) on their hands, firms will decrease production and employment.

The classical answer to this problem was to recognize that, in addition to a product market and a factor market, there is a third market—the credit market. The credit market is where the saving of households is used to provide funds for business investment. Saving is a leakage out of the circular flow, but investment is an injection back into the circular flow. In the national income accounts, investment consists of some combination of business plants and equipment, residential construction, and changes in inventories. In our example, the $200 of unsold output, or a change in inventories, is the investment that matches the saving of households. Thus, actual, or realized, saving has to be equal to realized investment. In Figure 2, $200 in realized saving is matched by $200 in realized investment in the form of added inventory.

macroeconomic equilibrium
The level of output at which there is no tendency to change. The amount that buyers wish to buy is exactly equal to what is being produced

Defining unsold output as inventory investment merely balances the accounts. It does not result in an equilibrium level of output and employment. Even in Say's time, economists recognized the distinction between a balancing of accounts and the concept of macroeconomic equilibrium.[2] **Macroeconomic equilibrium** is the level of output at which there

---

2. This distinction between an accounting identity and equilibrium may be clearer if you recall the income statement in Chapter 5. Your income statement will be in accounting balance every year. What comes in is either spent or saved. However, your finances may be in disequilibrium. You may be saving less or borrowing and spending more than you planned. If so, you will adjust your flows next year accordingly. When you are satisfied with the pattern, when planned or expected income, outgo, saving, and borrowing are equal to what actually occurred, then you are in equilibrium as well as in accounting balance.

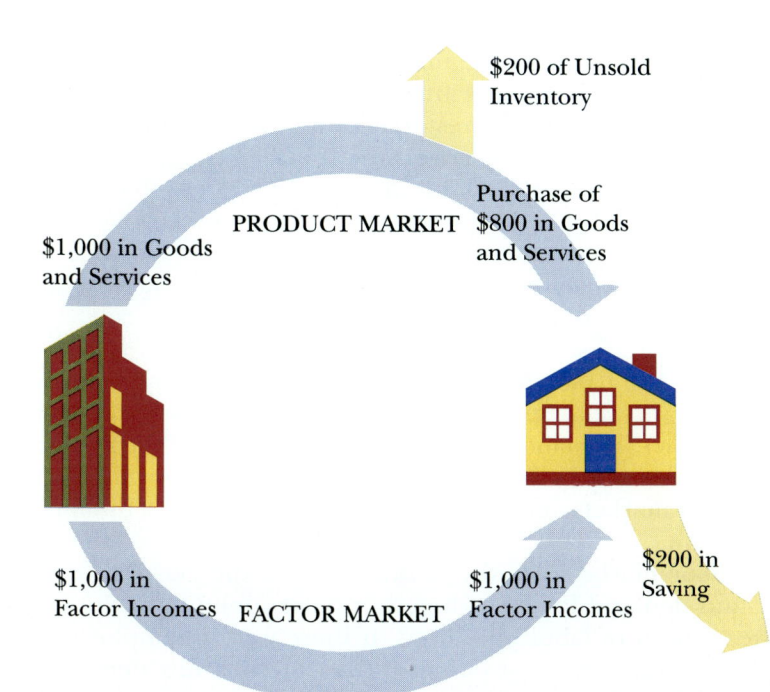

FIGURE 2
SAVING—A PROBLEM?
When business firms produce $1,000 in goods and services, they generate $1,000 in incomes to the suppliers of factors of production. If $200 of this income is saved, only $800 is spent for goods and services. Thus, $200 worth of goods and services remain unsold. In response to inventory buildup, firms cut production. Incomes fall, and unemployment rises.

is no tendency to change. The amount that buyers wish to buy is exactly equal to what is being produced. If firms build up unwanted inventories, their initial response may be to cut prices. However, after cutting prices to unload excess inventories, firms are likely to cut back production in the next period. Then the size of the flow of income and output will shrink.

As long as unplanned and unwanted inventory changes are occurring, the economy is in disequilibrium. Realized saving and realized investment are always equal. In equilibrium, however, planned saving and planned investment must also be equal. The saving desired by consumers must be exactly offset by desired business investment or other planned injections so that the size of the flow is neither shrinking nor growing. Classical economists believed that equilibrium would be reached and maintained at a level consistent with full employment by the actions of three self-regulating markets. These markets are the product market, the labor market, and the credit market. If these three markets functioned properly, Say's law would hold in the sense that the sum of planned spending for consumption and for investment would be enough to purchase all that was being produced.

SELF-REGULATING MARKETS

Classical economists believed that full employment of resources was almost a sure thing in a market economy if markets were allowed to operate freely and given enough time. They did not claim that the economic system would *always* operate at a level of full employment. Occasional problems of overproduction and unemployment would occur. These problems, however, would be quickly eliminated by self-regulating markets.

self-regulating markets Markets that quickly resolve problems of shortage or surplus through price changes, quantity adjustments, or a combination of the two.

Self-regulating markets are markets in which automatic forces move the economy to a new equilibrium whenever there is a shift in supply or demand. Equilibrium will be restored by adjustments in either prices or output, or both, without any government intervention. Classical economists believed that the same kind of corrective forces that restore equilibrium in markets for single products are also at work in aggregate markets. Although temporary shortages or surpluses are possible in either individual or aggregate markets, a lasting general shortage or surplus of aggregate output is not possible.

THE PRODUCT AND LABOR MARKETS. The two primary markets in the circular flow diagram are the product market (upper flow) and the factor market (lower flow). The labor market is the largest part of the factor market. Classical economists believed that flexible prices and wages in the product and labor markets were the first line of defense against unemployment and recession.

The labor market played a central role in the classical model. The supply and demand for labor together determined both the wage level and the amount of labor employed. If there were unemployed workers, the quantity supplied must be more than the quantity demanded. This was a clear indication that the market price (the wage) was too high for equilibrium.

If firms find that they have unsold output, they can dispose of it by cutting prices. The idea of cutting prices when there is a surplus of wheat, autos, or plane tickets is familiar. How do price and wage adjustments work when there is an excess of output in general? Figure 3 shows the usual AD curve and a classical (vertical) AS curve. In this diagram, there is an excess of aggregate supply over aggregate demand at price level P_1, resulting in unsold output. The unsold output is equal to the difference between Y_1 and Y_2. On the diagram, this is the length of line $\overline{AB}$. This diagram seems to suggest that if all firms cut prices, the price level will fall to P_2. Output will remain at the full-employment level, Y_1.

Suppose, however, that firms respond to the piling up of unwanted inventories by cutting output to Y_2 instead of cutting prices. Then employment will fall to N_2. There will be excess labor in the labor market. Competition among workers for jobs will drive down both real and nominal wages (wages with and without adjustments for changes in the price level). With lower wages, a wheat farmer or auto producer will find it possible to produce the same output at lower cost. Firms will choose to hire more workers at the lower wages. Although sellers will have to cut prices to sell the extra output, they can afford to because of lower labor costs. The fall in output is temporary, because flexible wages and prices will always restore output to the full-employment level. In fact, some advisers to President Hoover recommended wage and price cuts in 1930 during the first stage of the Great Depression as a solution to growing unemployment.

You may have noticed a subtle flaw in this reasoning. If all firms cut prices to sell excess output, they will have to cut wages in order to avoid losses. When producers of toothpaste cut the price of their product and the wages of their workers, the wage cut has almost no impact on the market for their product. The firms' workers make up a very small part of the

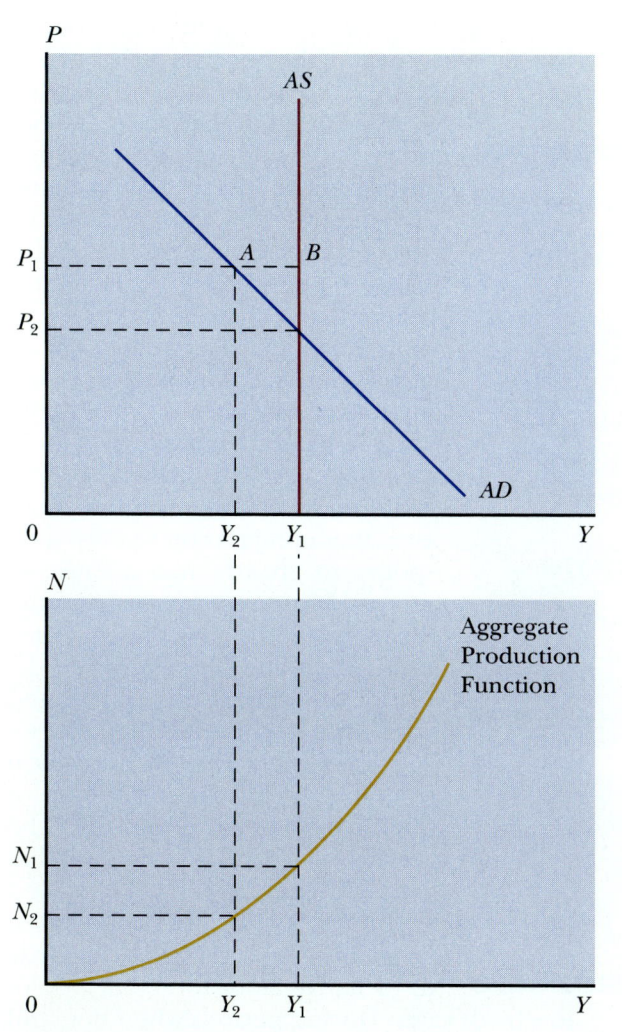

FIGURE 3
EXCESS AGGREGATE SUPPLY
Excess aggregate supply (*AB* in this diagram) will put downward pressure on the price level, either directly or through wages and the labor market. This process continues until full-employment output is restored.

total toothpaste market. What is true of a single good, however, is not necessarily true of aggregate output. If all firms cut wages, the workers (who are also the customers) will have less purchasing power with which to buy the output. Therefore, sales will fall in real terms. (Remember to beware of the fallacy of composition when you think about macroeconomics!)

THE CREDIT MARKET. Flexible wages and prices in the labor and product markets were not the only weapon in the classical armory. A self-regulating credit market was another important part of the classical explanation of why unemployment and unsold output would not persist. Through the credit market, household income that is saved flows into the hands of business firms, which in turn spend it on investment. The interest rate is the incentive to lend and the price of borrowing. Changes in the interest rate assure that planned saving and planned investment spending will be equal.

INTERNATIONAL PERSPECTIVE

IMMIGRATION, EMPLOYMENT, AND UNEMPLOYMENT

Both the classical and Keynesian models assumed that the size of the labor force is known, allowing economists to determine how many jobs are needed to reach full employment. If the population is growing at a moderate pace, then the labor force will also grow at a slow, steady pace. Thus, a labor force of a known size in the short run is a reasonable assumption for both models. The full-employment level of output (Y^*) then depends on the size of the labor force. In the real world, however, labor is free to move from country to country. High employment and rapid growth in one country may induce immigration and thus increase the size of the labor force and the full-employment level of output. Falling output will lead to unemployment, but it may also result in emigration of workers or a slowdown in immigration. Either of these will reduce the impact on domestic unemployment. Thus, unemployment may fall less during the upturn of the business cycle and rise less during a recession if some of the burden of adjustment falls on migration.

The effect of migration on unemployment can be seen using the aggregate supply and demand model. A sharp increase in the labor force due to immigration will shift aggregate supply to the right. This shift allows an increase in aggregate demand with more output as well as some price increase. A fall in the labor force due to emigration will shift aggregate supply to the right. This shift reduces the decline in prices that might otherwise occur during an economic downturn.

Two examples illustrate this point. The first is the pattern of immigration in American history, driven by conditions in both Europe and the United States. The second is the more recent experience in Germany with "Gastarbeiter" (guest workers).

Data from the nineteenth century shows that immigrants were drawn to the United States by prosperity. Peaks in immigration coincided with peaks in the business cycle in 1873, 1882, 1892, 1903, 1907, and 1910. These peaks were followed by downturns in both output and immigration. The pull of prosperity in the United States was often reinforced by pushing effects of pogroms against the Jews in Eastern Europe, bad harvests, or other adverse conditions abroad. Simon Kuznets, a historian of business cycles, has found cycles in immigration of sixteen to eighteen years in length paralleling cycles in economic growth. British economist Brinley Thomas argues, however, that immigration was less a response to growth than a cause of growth. It increased aggregate supply by providing new resources for production and also aggregate demand as immigrants purchased consumer goods with their wages. Thomas's view is in the classical tradition. In this view, the level of output is determined by the resources—especially labor—that are available.[a]

In the 1970s and 1980s, West Germany had a very slow increase in its native labor force because of low birth rates. During periods when demand was strong, West Germany issued special "guest worker" permits to encourage foreign workers to come in to supplement the domestic work force. Most of these workers came from Turkey or, more recently, from Greece. When demand was slack, priority tended to be given to native Germans. Some guest workers would return home until the next peak demand drew them back into the German labor market. With the influx of Germans from what had been East Germany after reunification, there is likely to be little future need for guest workers. Instead, the jobs will go to Germans from the east, who cannot be sent home when they are not needed. Thus, Germany's solution to ups and down in employment opportunities may have been a casualty of reunification.

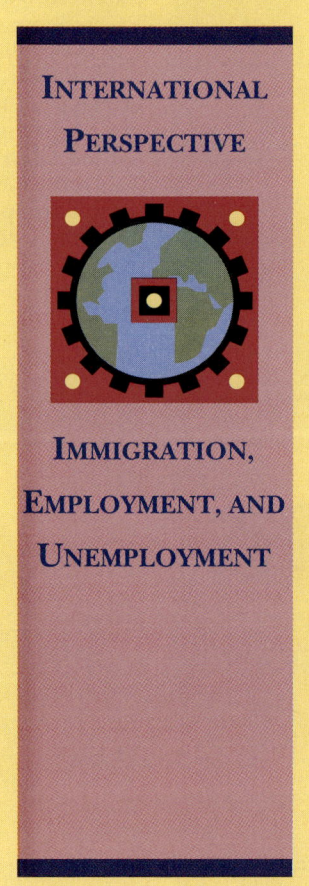

a. Jonathan Hughes, *American Economic History*, 3rd ed. (Glenview, IL: Scott-Foresman, 1990).

Figure 4 shows how the credit market works to make saving available to finance investment. In the classical view, the supply of credit (loanable funds) comes from people's decisions to save. The demand for credit reflects the desire by business firms to borrow for investment purposes. The supply curve has a positive slope. This slope indicates that saving is directly related to the interest rate. People save (give up some spending) only if there is an incentive to do so. The interest rate is the incentive for saving. By saving now, individuals can earn interest and accumulate larger sums of money to spend in the future. When the interest rate rises, saving will increase because the same amount of current saving will provide more future consumption. Thus, a higher interest rate will call forth more saving, or a greater supply of loanable funds. Lower interest rates, on the other hand, will lead to less saving, or a smaller supply of loanable funds. There is less incentive to save instead of consume at lower interest rates.

The demand curve in Figure 4 shows the amount of loanable funds borrowers want at various interest rates. It has the familiar negative slope. The price of borrowing is the interest rate that firms pay to obtain credit. Investment spending increases when the interest rate declines. It decreases when the interest rate rises. Projects or purchases of investment goods that would be profitable at lower rates of interest may not look as attractive at higher interest rates. Thus, planned investment spending will be lower at higher rates of interest.

According to classical economists, the interaction of borrowers and lenders in the credit market should establish an equilibrium interest rate. At this interest rate, the quantity of planned saving will be equal to planned investment spending. This interest rate, i_1 in Figure 4, is deter-

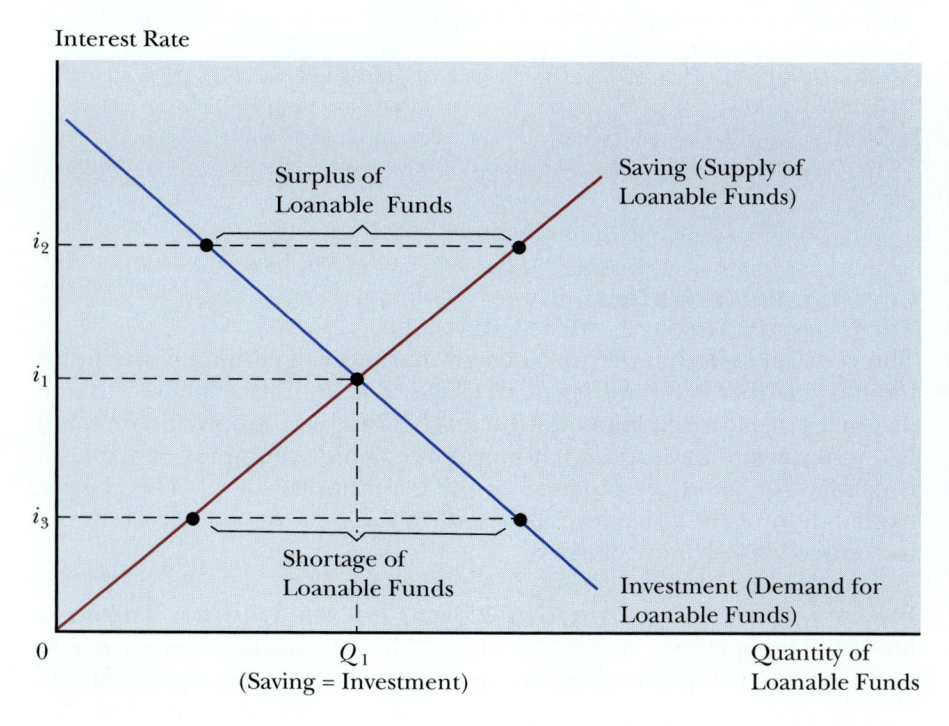

FIGURE 4
THE CLASSICAL VIEW OF THE CREDIT MARKET
In the classical view, changes in the interest rate ensure that the quantity of loanable funds supplied (saving) and the quantity demanded (investment) would be equal. Saving and investment are equal (at Q_1) at i_1, the equilibrium interest rate. There would be a surplus at higher interest rates (such as i_2) and a shortage at lower rates (such as i_3).

mined by the intersection of the saving and investment curves. At higher interest rates, such as i_2, the quantity of loanable funds supplied exceeds the quantity demanded. The surplus of saving over planned investment spending will push the interest rate downward toward i_1. At lower interest rates, such as i_3, the quantity of loanable funds demanded exceeds the quantity supplied. This shortage causes the interest rate to be bid up to i_1 as would-be borrowers compete for the limited amount of credit.

Either the supply curve or the demand curve can shift to create a disequilibrium. Either way, natural forces will restore equilibrium in a self-regulating market. Suppose a fear of recession or a high level of consumer debt causes people to suddenly become more thrifty. The amount of saving will increase at every possible interest rate. That is, the saving curve will shift to the right. The new equilibrium interest rate will be lower than i_1. An increase in saving puts downward pressure on the price of loanable funds. The lower interest rate leads to an increase in the amount of investment spending. Thus, changes in the interest rate ensure that any income not spent on consumption will be channeled into desired investment.

ELEMENTS OF CLASSICAL MACROECONOMIC THEORY

- Employment is determined by the forces of supply and demand in the labor market.
- Output is determined by equilibrium in the labor market.
- The aggregate supply curve is vertical at the full-employment level of output.
- The price level is determined by the supply of and demand for money.
- An economy always tends toward the full-employment level of output because enough income is created during production to purchase the output (Say's law) and self-regulating markets correct temporary disequilibria.
  In the product market, falling prices ensure that all output is sold.
  In the labor market, adjustments in wages clear the labor market.
  In the credit market, changes in interest rates make saving equal to investment.

CLASSICAL AGGREGATE DEMAND: THE QUANTITY THEORY OF MONEY REVISITED

The classical idea that the workings of markets will eliminate unemployment is one that is still widely held. Classical economists believed that individual prices are explained by the market forces of supply and demand. Even they would have agreed, however, that a more complex explanation is needed for the determination of the general price level. The classical explanation of the price level is based on the quantity theory of money, introduced briefly in Chapter 6.

INFLATION, DISCOVERY OF THE NEW WORLD, AND THE QUANTITY THEORY OF MONEY. The quantity theory of money, like many theories in macroeconomics, developed as a way to explain certain economic events. Among the early writers on this theory was the Scottish philosopher David Hume (1711–1776). Hume was interested in the very practical problem of explaining the inflation that followed the discovery of the New World. (Hume had a great influence on Adam Smith, author of *The Wealth of Nations*.)

Gold and silver were the main forms of money in Europe until the nineteenth century. The New World was discovered in the late fifteenth century and colonized by several European nations in the next two centuries. The Spaniards seized the gold and silver of the Aztecs in Mexico and the Incas in Peru and brought it to Europe. As this gold and silver flowed in, Spaniards went on a spending spree. They bid against other potential buyers and drove up the prices of goods and services all over Europe. Hume and other theorists sought to explain the link between the inflow of money and the rising price level.

Although these early theorists did not have the tools of demand and supply, their reasoning can be expressed in those terms. In the supply and demand diagram of Figure 5, an inflow of gold and silver has caused the demand for a specific good, woolen goods, to increase while the supply curve remains unchanged. In the seventeenth century, the newly wealthy Spanish demanded more woolens from both Spanish and British suppliers. Of course, the people who sold woolens then had extra money, so they too demanded more goods of all kinds. As demand for a broad range of products increased, aggregate demand shifted to the right, as shown in Figure 6.

The story didn't end there. People who supplied all kinds of goods found that the prices of their inputs were rising. Higher prices for inputs meant that their costs were rising. For example, the new, higher prices for woolens attracted more people into the business of raising sheep. Com-

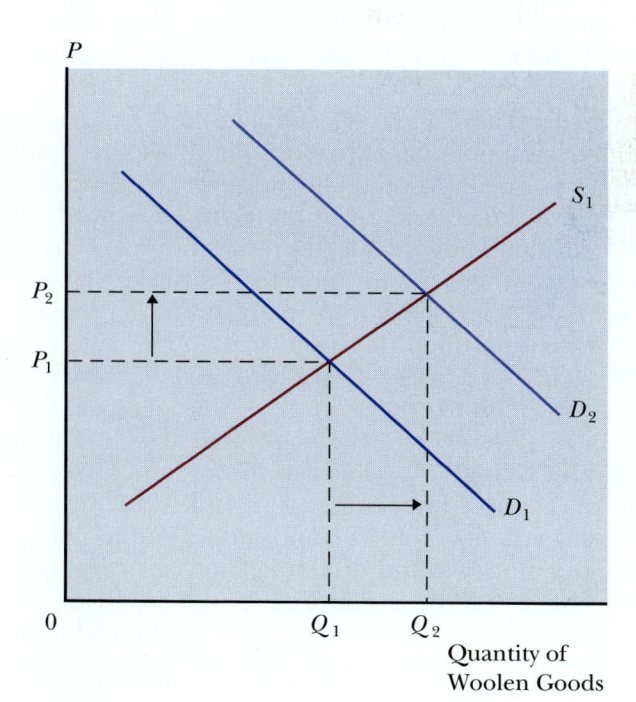

FIGURE 5
A SEVENTEENTH-CENTURY SHIFT IN THE DEMAND CURVE FOR WOOLENS
An inflow of gold and silver from the New World led Europeans to increase their demand for various goods, such as woolen goods. The rightward shift of the demand curve drove up the price of woolen goods from P_1 to P_2. Quantity increased along the supply curve from Q_1 to Q_2 in response to the higher price.

FIGURE 6
ADJUSTING TO AN INFLOW OF MONEY
The general increase in demand for goods drives up both prices and costs. The rise in costs shifts the aggregate supply curve to the left. Both P and Y increase, but equilibrium output ultimately returns to Y_1. When all prices and costs have adjusted (the supply curve has shifted as well as the demand curve), there will have been no change in output but an increase in the price level to P_3.

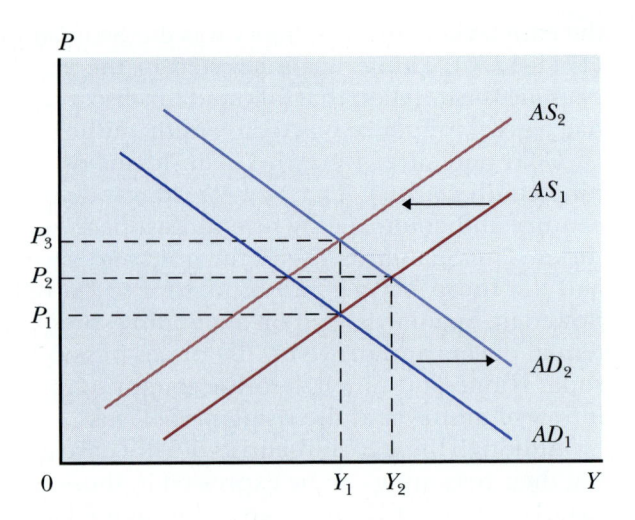

petition for grazing land drove up the lease payments that the sheep herders had to pay, raising the price of raw wool. Eventually these increased production costs caused the individual supply curves for wool and other goods to shift to the left. Thus, aggregate supply shifted to the left, as shown in Figure 6. A leftward shift in aggregate supply means that producers will offer the same amount for sale at a higher price than before because their costs have risen. (We are using an upward-sloping short-run aggregate supply curve here. As you will see shortly, however, the long-run aggregate supply curve will still be vertical. Classical economists tended to concentrate on the long run.)

After both aggregate demand and aggregate supply adjust to changes in the price level, the equilibrium quantity of real output will be the same as before the inflow of money. The inflow of gold and silver to Europe in the seventeenth century did not increase any of the economy's productive resources or improve its technology. Thus, there was no reason why total output would change once the economy adjusted fully to the larger money supply. As long as money was flowing into Spain and from there to the rest of Europe, prices were destined to go on rising. Aggregate demand kept shifting to the right and aggregate supply to the left. Since rising demand spilled over from Spain to other countries, the aggregate demand and supply curves in all of these countries continued to shift. Thus, the money inflow to Spain led to higher price levels throughout Europe.

When would this rise in the price level come to an end? If the inflow of money never stopped, classical economists could see no end to rising prices. However, suppose the money inflow did end. Then, they argued, the increase in the price level would be proportional to the increase in the money stock. A money stock that was twice as large would lead to a price level that was twice as high. A money stock that was four times as large would mean a price level that was four times as high. Land prices and wages would also rise in proportion to increases in the money supply.

Changes in the price level may not be exactly proportional to the rise in the money stock. While the money stock is rising, other things that affect the price level may also be changing. For example, the productivity of labor may rise. Like most economic predictions, those based on the quantity theory are subject to *ceteris paribus* conditions.

The insight that the long-run level of prices is directly related to the money stock was a notable insight of classical economics. To the question "How much will the price level change when the money stock increases?" it gives a reasonably precise answer: The price level changes in proportion to the change in the money stock. However, the quantity theory could not predict how long it would take the price level to change. Furthermore, you should have noticed in Figure 5 that output of a particular good will initially increase when demand increases. (Figure 6 shows that this also holds for goods in general.) Thus, in the short run, changes in the money supply may affect real output as well as the price level. In the long run, real output returns to the level that existed before the added money came into the system.

How much will output increase at the start? How long will it take output to settle back to its old level? The quantity theorists could not really answer these questions. The quantity theory offered a better explanation for long-run changes in the price level than for the short-run effects of changes in the money supply on real output and employment.

INFLATION AND THE NAPOLEONIC WARS. British economist David Ricardo (1772–1823) was responsible for a second important development in the quantity theory of money, this time in response to wartime inflation. Major wars are almost always accompanied by inflation. During wartime, increased production of military goods means that households receive more income as wages. However, there are no additional consumer goods for them to purchase with that added income. When purchasing power increases but output available to purchase does not, the price level will rise.

The Napoleonic Wars (1793–1813) triggered a debate about the role of banks in creating money and fueling inflation. During this period in Britain, notes (paper money) supplied by banks were an important part of the total money supply. As output of military and other goods expanded, a question arose. How much money in the form of notes should banks be allowed to issue? Policy makers were certain that too much new money would result in inflation. Bankers and public officials argued that banks should issue enough money to "meet the needs of trade." That is, banks should supply whatever firms needed to borrow in order to produce goods that had a ready market.

Ricardo pointed out that the amount of money required to meet the needs of trade depends on the price level. The price level, in turn, depends on the money supply. If the price level rises, more dollars will have to be loaned in order to expand output by a given amount. If banks meet this increased demand for loans by issuing more notes, the money stock will become even larger. This increased money stock will drive the price level even higher. At the higher price level, the needs of trade will require more loans and an even larger money supply. The result is an upward spiral, with the stock of bank notes and the price level chasing one another.

To get off this spiral, Ricardo suggested, the Bank of England (the British central bank) should place some limits on the ability of banks to create money by issuing notes. This debate over the effects of issuing bank notes on the price level reinforced Hume's conclusion that controlling the price level depends on controlling the supply of money. Thus, the lesson from wartime inflation was that there was a need for some agency, such as a central bank, to control the money supply in order to control the price level.

THE QUANTITY THEORY OF MONEY BEFORE KEYNES. Both of these historical events raised the question of how the money supply, the price level, and output were related. In the case of the inflow of gold, the money stock was clearly rising more rapidly than real output. Hume and others identified the increase in the money supply as the cause of a rising price level. In the case of wartime inflation, some output was not available for consumption. Resources were being diverted to the war effort. The money supply was at least as large as before, if not larger, but there was less real output available to purchase. Again, the consequence of different rates of growth in the money supply and (available) real output was a rise in the price level.

The government (or the central bank) exerted control over the money supply in the eighteenth and nineteenth centuries, as it does today. Classical economists wanted the government to manage the money supply in such a way as to minimize inflation. Recognizing that output (Y) would grow over time with increases in population and resources, they reasoned that the money supply (M_s) should grow only at the same rate as Y. In that way, inflation would be avoided.

The quantity theory of money underwent some changes in the late nineteenth century because of the work of British economist Alfred Marshall (1842–1924). One of Marshall's most important contributions was to reinterpret the equation of exchange ($M_s \times V = P \times Y$) as a theory of the demand for money. The **demand for money** is the amount of money that people want to hold in the form of currency or checking account balances. The demand for money is not that different from the demand for other goods and services. People demand money because it is useful in making market transactions. Holding money has a price, however. Choosing to hold money means giving up the things that it could buy or giving up the interest that could be earned if it were converted into other kinds of financial assets. Money is also unique in certain respects, especially in its almost total acceptance in transactions for all other goods and services. Thus, although the demand for money is similar to the demand for other goods and services, money plays a special role in a market economy.

Marshall argued that people normally want to hold part of their wealth in the form of money. He assumed that the amount of wealth that individuals choose to hold in the form of currency or checking account balances (as opposed to stocks, bonds, and other financial assets) is positively related to their incomes. The higher a person's income, the higher the average amount of money balances that person will want to hold to meet

demand for money
The amount of money households and businesses wish to hold for making transactions and as a financial asset.

Chapter 7 Classical Macroeconomics and the Keynesian Response   197

day-to-day transaction needs. For the economy as a whole, the total demand for money should be positively related to the aggregate level of income and output.

Marshall observed that the public had to hold whatever amount of money was being supplied. That is, actual M_d had to equal actual M_s. If the money supply is \$1,000, then the public collectively has to hold (demand) \$1,000. Based on this observation, Marshall rearranged the equation of exchange, obtaining

$$M_d = k \times P \times Y = k \times \text{GNP.}$$

Money supply has been replaced by money demand because in equilibrium the two should be equal. The velocity of money, V, has been replaced by k on the other side of the equation, because $k = 1/V$ by definition. Marshall explained k as the fraction of income people desire to hold in the form of cash balances. Like V, the size of k depends on such factors as how often people get paid and have to make payments and what other forms of assets are available. Marshall expected that k, like V, would be fairly stable over long periods of time. If one accepts the classical arguments that Say's law is valid and markets are self-regulating, then Y will be stable at the full-employment level. In that case, Marshall's revised equation of exchange becomes a theory of how the price level is determined.

Suppose there is more money supplied than the amount people want to hold. The money market will be in disequilibrium. That is, $M_d < M_s$. Finding that they have larger cash balances than they wish to hold, individuals will spend more, driving up the price level (P). The rise in the price level will increase the nominal value of output $(P \times Y)$, which determines the amount of money people want to hold. The public will finally be satisfied to hold exactly the amount of money being supplied at the higher price level. Similar forces are set in motion when the money supply is less than the amount people want to hold, or $M_d > M_s$. Reductions in spending as people try to rebuild their cash balances will drive down the price level until the money supply is once again equal to the money demand. Thus, a self-regulating market for money, working through the price level, should assure that the equilibrium condition, $M_d = M_s$, will be satisfied. In equilibrium, money supply and money demand must be equal, and money demand is given by

$$M_d = k \times P \times \overline{Y} = k \times \text{GNP.}$$

The bar over Y in this expression indicates that real output is constant at the full-employment level. The proportional relationship between the money supply and the price level is the same as before. This version of the equation offers an explanation of the price level in terms of money demand and the behavior of households.

A simple example will show how the behavior of households translates an increase in the money supply into an increase in the price level. Assume that the economy is at the full-employment level of output, with 500 units of output being produced ($\overline{Y} = 500$). Also, assume that the fraction of their income that people desire to hold as money is stable and equal to 25 percent of their annual income ($k = 0.25$). Finally, assume that the money supply is initially \$1,000 ($M_{s1} = \$1,000$) and that the annual value of output ($P \times \overline{Y}$) is such that the public is satisfied to hold $1,000 in money ($M_d = M_s$). The initial price level (P_1) can be found by substituting these numbers in

(1) $M_{s1} = k \times P_1 \times \overline{Y}$.

Then we have

$$P_1 = \frac{M_{s1}}{k \times \overline{Y}} = \frac{\$1{,}000}{(0.25)(500)} = \frac{\$1{,}000}{125} = \$8.$$

The equilibrium price level is $8. That is, the average price for a unit of output is $8. The annual value of output is $4,000 ($8 × 500).

What would happen if, as a result of an influx of gold into the economy, the money supply doubled? Substituting the new value of the money supply ($M_{s2} = \$2{,}000$) into equation (1) determines that equilibrium occurs at a new price level, P_2:

$$P_2 = \frac{\$2{,}000}{(0.25)(500)} = \frac{\$2{,}000}{125} = \$16.$$

According to these calculations, a doubling of the money supply (from $1,000 to $2,000) would cause a doubling of the equilibrium price level (from $8 to $16). Therefore, the annual value of nominal output would also double to $8,000 ($16 × 500), even though real output is unchanged.

How and why do prices rise in response to increases in the money supply? Given an initial equilibrium ($M_{d1} = M_{s1}$), an increase in the money supply puts people in the position of having larger money balances than they wish to hold. That is, $M_{s1} > M_{d2}$, relative to the value of total output $P_1 \times \overline{Y}$. Individuals who find themselves with more dollars than they wish to hold will increase their spending for consumer goods and services.[3] Although individuals can decrease their money holdings through spending, the economy as a whole cannot. The excess dollars are passed from person to person. The increased spending, therefore, shifts aggregate demand to the right (see Figure 6). The resulting shortages of goods and services cause price increases. Eventually, wages and other costs also rise, shifting aggregate supply to the left. The level of output returns to the original level (Y_1 in Figure 6) and the price level rises further (to P_3). At the higher price level, the public is willing to hold the entire money supply. The money market is again in equilibrium (quantity supplied equals quantity demanded).

Classical economists favored a strictly *laissez-faire* approach to most markets. Many of them did agree, however, that regulation of the money supply would help control ups and downs in output and employment. If a temporary decline occurred in output, falling prices and wages could be avoided by expanding the money supply. An increase in the money supply could lead to at least a short-run improvement in the level of real output as well as (or instead of) a rise in the price level.

---

3. Some households may choose to purchase financial assets such as stocks or bonds. However, if some households buy existing assets, the other households that sold those assets will increase their spending.

The quantity theory of money, Say's law, and the idea of self-regulating markets provided a complete classical model of macroeconomics. This model explained the level of employment, output, and prices. According to this model, recessions would be temporary and self-correcting. Thus, the role of the government should be limited to careful management of the money supply.

THE BUSINESS CYCLE THEORISTS

In the nineteenth century, the main critics of the quantity theory of money were the business cycle theorists. They called attention to the reality of ups and downs in the economy. The classical model showed with perfect logic that prolonged unemployment was impossible. Actual unemployment seemed to defy the model by lasting for long periods of time. The classical model said that output would always be at, close to, or tending toward the full-employment level. Real-world experience showed that large and prolonged deviations from the full-employment level of output not only were possible, but occurred with alarming frequency.

Business cycle theorists, from Thomas Malthus in the nineteenth century to Wesley Mitchell and Joseph Schumpeter in the early twentieth century, observed regular cyclical patterns in economic activity. They sought to explain these patterns in terms of the nature of the market economy. Unlike the classical school, the business cycle theorists did not offer a complete model of how output, employment, and the price level are determined. Classical economists stressed natural forces that would tend to restore equilibrium. Business cycle theorists were more interested in what happened during the period when the economy was moving from one equilibrium to another. Schumpeter even described economic downturns as periods of "creative destruction." *Creative* meant that the old worn-out capital of declining industries was being replaced by new, improved capital in emerging industries.

The ideas of business cycle theorists such as Schumpeter are noteworthy because they offer a bridge from classical to Keynesian macroeconomics. Two important themes of this school of thought play an important role in Keynes's *General Theory*:

1. *The notion of underconsumption, or inadequate aggregate demand.* Malthus and other business cycle theorists argued that an unequal distribution of income affects the ability of consumers to purchase all that is produced. A small number of wealthy households consume a great deal less than their income and save a large amount. Workers earning very low wages spend most or all of their income. This amount is not enough, however, to purchase the rest of what is produced. If the saving of the wealthy few is not channeled into investment, then leakages from the circular flow will exceed injections. The size of the flow will decrease.
2. *The instability of investment.* If the government and foreign sectors are small and there is not enough consumption, then the burden of purchasing the rest of output falls on business firms. Firms must increase

their demand for funds to invest. Both Schumpeter and Keynes, writing in the 1920s and 1930s, emphasized the fact that investment demand is extremely unstable. Investment depends on changes in technology, development of new industries, interest rates, final demand, and investor psychology. All of these variables are unpredictable and highly volatile. In addition, new plants and equipment last for a long time and continue to produce consumer goods during that time. Once an increase in consumption demand has been filled by investing in new plants and equipment, very little further investment is needed in order to have enough productive capacity for current consumption. As a result, demand for investment goods tends to depend on consumer demand. If consumer demand is growing, new investment is needed to meet that demand. If consumer demand is stable, no new investment is needed. If consumer demand falls, the appropriate level of new investment may be negative as producers work off and wear out excess productive capacity.

Although business cycle theorists identified other influences, inadequate demand from both consumers and investors played the central role in explaining recessions. Business cycle theorists were concerned about aggregate demand, even though they didn't use that term. Both the government and the foreign sector played minor roles in nineteenth-century economics. Thus, the business cycle theorists focused on two major actors in the macroeconomic drama: consumers and investors. In doing so, they laid the groundwork for the Keynesian revolution.

THE KEYNESIAN REVOLUTION

The Great Depression challenged the classical model with the reality of a long depression and high unemployment. In *General Theory*, Keynes attacked the classical model in two important ways. First, he identified some flaws in the model. Second, unlike the business cycle theorists, he offered a well-developed alternative model of the macro economy. This model was the basis for the **Keynesian revolution**, the change in macroeconomic theory and policy that occurred when Keynes's ideas displaced the classical explanation of how output and employment are determined. The Keynesian model begins with aggregate demand and works from there to employment, instead of the other way around.

Keynesian revolution
The change in macroeconomic theory and policy that occurred when Keynes's ideas displaced the classical theory of how output and employment are determined.

KEYNES ON SAY'S LAW

Keynes was critical of Say's law. Classical economists argued that the existence of saving by households and investment by firms does not invalidate Say's law because changes in the interest rate will ensure that planned saving is equal to planned investment at the full-employment level of output. If planned saving is always exactly offset by planned investment, then all output will be sold to willing buyers for either consumption or investment. In that case, overproduction or lasting unemployment is not possible. Keynes argued that even though the interest rate does influence planned saving and planned investment, other important influences can keep the credit market from perfectly matching these two flows.

Keynes identified several reasons why individuals save besides earning interest: (1) to build reserves in case of unforeseen future needs, (2) to develop a nest egg for retirement, (3) to establish a financial base for an increased standard of living in the future, (4) to gain economic independence, (5) to build reserves for speculative purposes, (6) to leave an inheritance, and (7) to satisfy the urge to accumulate. These motives, he argued, generate considerable saving that is relatively independent of the interest rate.

Keynes also argued that the interest rate was only one influence on investment decisions. He argued that firms invest in new plants and equipment only if they expect to make a profit. Based on their expectations of the profit from a given investment project, businesses often borrow even when interest rates are high or refuse to borrow when they are low. According to Keynes, final demand by consumers, the size and age of existing capital stock, and new technology all play more important roles than the interest rate in determining investment.

Since both saving and investment respond more strongly to other influences than the interest rate, Keynes argued, planned saving *could* exceed planned investment at the full-employment level of output. Thus, Say's law would be invalid. According to the classical model, if planned saving exceeds planned investment, the interest rate will fall. Keynes said that a fall in interest rates may have little effect on either saving or investment, but excess saving will lead to a decline in the level of output and income. Thus, if credit markets fail to work as the classical model describes, severe depression and unemployment can persist for long periods in a market economy.

KEYNES ON SELF-REGULATING MARKETS

According to classical theory, temporary overproduction and unemployment in individual markets would be eliminated as unemployed workers competed for jobs and drove down wages. To a firm, falling wages mean lower costs. The firm could profitably cut prices and increase sales. Falling wages and prices would eliminate overproduction and restore full employment.

Keynes also argued that neither the product nor labor market would adjust quickly and automatically to eliminate unemployment and overproduction. He believed that labor unions and large corporations have enough market power to keep wages and prices from falling. Faced with rising unemployment, labor unions would fight to keep wages from declining in order to protect their members who were still working. Without declining wages, business firms would not be willing to cut their prices. Furthermore, when facing overproduction, large corporations are likely to choose to reduce production levels rather than prices. Price cutting risks cutthroat price competition. Keynes felt that in a mature, capitalistic economic system, it would be difficult to reduce either prices or wages. According to him, prices and wages are "sticky downward." Since prices and wages are not fully flexible, there will be no automatic adjustment process in product and labor markets to restore full-employment equilibrium.

Finally, Keynes pointed out that even if wages and prices could fall, the result would not necessarily be to restore output to the full-employment level. Falling prices mean that buyers can purchase more output, but falling wages mean that workers can buy less. In a macro economy, supply

Economic Profile

John Maynard Keynes
1883–1946

John Maynard Keynes was born in Cambridge, England to a prosperous family. His father, John Neville Keynes, was a well-known economist who taught at the university there. The young Keynes grew up in an atmosphere where well-educated people were intensely interested in the public policy issues of the day. All his life, Keynes was able to dominate any group by his great intelligence, witty conversation, and forceful personality.

Keynes divided his life between teaching at Cambridge and active involvement in government and business affairs. He worked for the British Treasury, where he rose rapidly during World War I. In fact, Keynes was a British delegate to the Versailles Peace Conference, which drafted and signed the peace treaty ending World War I in 1919. He was disillusioned by the negotiations at Versailles and the harsh conditions imposed on the losers, especially Germany. In a very critical book, *The Economic Consequences of the Peace*, Keynes argued that the harsh economic conditions imposed on Germany would lead to more problems with that country in the future. This book ended Keynes's employment by the Treasury because he criticized British policy. He returned to Cambridge and turned to business, making a great deal of money with shrewd investments. He also managed the investment funds of King's College at Cambridge, to the college's great benefit.

Keynes was a member of the Bloomsbury Group, which included such literary figures as Lytton Strachey and Leonard and Virginia Woolf. A man of many talents and interests, Keynes married a Russian ballerina, Lydia Lopokova, and was well known for his taste in art and literature. He wrote essays on policy topics and biographical essays on many people, including economists, as well as a treatise on the theory of probability.

Along with his other activities, Keynes did some revolutionary work in macroeconomics. During the 1920s, he wrote the two-volume *Treatise on Money*, which was published in 1930, after the beginning of the Great Depression. The *Treatise* was basically a quantity theory approach to macro problems in the spirit of Keynes's teacher, Alfred Marshall. By the time the *Treatise* was published, Keynes was unhappy with this approach and had begun what he called his "long struggle" to see macro questions from a different perspective. The new view Keynes was working toward was contained in his *General Theory of Employment, Interest, and Money*, published in 1936. This book presented an alternative macroeconomic model aimed at explaining how economies had fallen into the Great Depression and how they could get out of it.

and demand are not entirely independent because they are parts of the same circular flow.

Keynes on the Quantity Theory of Money

Keynes admitted that the quantity theory of money was useful in describing the long-run movement of the economy from one equilibrium to another. He saw the theory as much less useful in the short run. The quantity theory was based on the assumption that, in the equation of exchange, the velocity of money was stable. That is, V was constant. Data from the early 1930s, as well as other periods, showed that this assumption did not hold in the short run.[4] The velocity of money (and therefore k) was especially unstable during the Great Depression. Between 1929 and 1933, V fell sharply, and k increased. (Remember that $k = 1/V$.) A rise in the value of k meant that the amount of money people wanted to hold, relative to GNP, had increased. The quantity theory of money offered no explanation for the sudden increase in the demand for money implied by the sharp drop in V.

Keynes pointed out that a theory that only explains what happens in the long run is not very useful. He reminded his readers that we live in the short run and "in the long run we are all dead." Keynes was more interested in developing a theoretical model to explain short-run economic activity and recommending policies to improve short-run economic conditions.

Keynes questioned the stability of money velocity, which was a basic assumption of the quantity theory. Building on the work of Alfred Marshall, Keynes reasoned that the demand for money was strongly influenced by more than the level of GNP. In addition to demanding money for making transactions, as Marshall claimed, people also want to hold money as a safeguard against changes in interest rates on bonds and other financial assets. If interest rates are low, people will avoid buying bonds and hold more of their wealth in the form of money while waiting for interest rates to rise. When interest rates are low, the opportunity cost of holding money is also low. Thus, very little is sacrificed by holding money instead of bonds or other securities. In addition, people who buy bonds when interest rates are low run a risk of locking in those rates and being stuck with low-yield assets when the rates rise.

When market interest rates are high, people will prefer to hold more of their wealth in interest-earning securities and less in money because the opportunity cost of holding money is high. Much interest is lost by holding money, which earns little or no interest, instead of interest-earning assets. In addition, if interest rates are high compared to the immediate past, people will expect them to fall rather than to rise further. Buying securities when interest rates are high enables the holder to lock in those rates for the life of the assets.

---

4. Some economists before Keynes did not share this simplistic view of velocity. Henry Simons and Irving Fisher recognized its instability, especially over the course of the business cycle. Thus, they advocated an active use of monetary policy to offset changes in velocity and keep the price level and output stable.

asset demand for money Demand for money to hold in order to protect the value of one's assets against changes in interest rates. The asset demand for money is negatively related to interest rates.

transactions demand for money Demand for money in order to make purchases and carry out other day-to-day market transactions. The transactions demand for money is positively related to income.

Keynes called the motive for holding money as an asset the "speculative demand for money." Today economists prefer the term **asset demand for money**, which is the demand for money to hold in order to protect oneself against losses due to changes in interest rates. The asset demand for money is negatively related to interest rates. The motive for holding money identified by Marshall is called the **transactions demand for money**, the demand for money in order to make purchases and carry out other day-to-day market transactions. Transactions demand is positively related to income.[5]

Keynes argued that the interest rate would strongly influence the demand for money. If the interest rate declined, the quantity of money demanded relative to GNP ($P \times Y$ in the equation of exchange) might increase, even if GNP were stable or declining. In the equation of exchange, this change in people's desire to hold money would appear as an increase in k or a decline in V. Thus, changes in V and k during the Great Depression could be explained by including the interest rate as an important influence on the demand for money.

In summary, Keynes criticized the quantity theory because it neglects the role of interest rates and fails to explain short-run changes in V and k. He argued that Say's law was not valid and that long periods of overproduction and unemployment *were* possible. Without Say's law and self-regulating markets, no automatic forces would bring the economy back to equilibrium during a recession. Without a stable velocity of money, even an increase in the money supply might not work. Having criticized the classical view of the way the macro economy worked, Keynes offered a different model. As you will see, in his model, only government intervention could bring the economy out of a downturn as severe and prolonged as the Great Depression.

A PREVIEW OF KEYNESIAN THEORY AND POLICY

During the Great Depression, the U.S. economy experienced severe and lasting unemployment, along with falling prices and a sharp decline in real output. Classical theory could not account for such conditions. In developing an alternative theory, Keynes and his followers focused on the question "What determines the level of employment in a market economy?" They knew that if they could explain employment, the same model would explain unemployment.

KEYNESIAN MACROECONOMIC THEORY

In attempting to identify the cause of employment, Keynes reasoned as follows:

1. The level of employment is directly related to the level of production, or output (Y).
2. In a market economy, planned spending on the output of the business

---

5. Keynes identified a third motive, the precautionary demand for money. This motive drives those who hold cash for "a rainy day" (as an emergency fund). Since this demand, like transactions demand, is related to income, later economists combined it with transactions demand.

sector will determine the level of production. Firms adjust their levels of production to meet demand for their products. Put simply, "supply adjusts to demand." (In contrast, Say's law said "supply creates its own demand.")

3. Since employment depends on production and production responds to spending, the level of employment in a market economy depends on the level of planned spending in the economy.

Note how Keynes reversed the sequence of events from the classical model. In the classical model, the labor market determined employment, and employment determined the level of output. Therefore, the position of the aggregate supply curve is vertical. Recall from Chapter 6 that the aggregate supply curve can be very flat, even horizontal, if many resources are unemployed. The Keynesian model of the Depression economy has ample unemployed resources and a horizontal aggregate supply curve. If aggregate supply is constant (horizontal), then aggregate demand determines the level of output. In turn, the level of output determines the level of employment. Aggregate demand, which determined only the price level in the classical model, has the starring role in Keynes's model. It determines the level of real output. In Figure 7, the price level is given at P_1, and aggregate demand determines the level of output, Y_1. Output, in turn, determines the level of employment, N_1.

Consider how this model might apply to the situation in the 1930s. Unemployment was high because planned spending was too low to generate the level of output (Y^* in Figure 7) that would result in full employment (N^*). Thus, too little spending was identified as the cause of unemployment. To reduce unemployment, planned spending had to increase. In the language of aggregate supply and aggregate demand (a model developed after Keynes), aggregate demand had to shift to the right.

How could aggregate demand be shifted to ensure a level of output that would result in higher employment and lower unemployment? Keynes's answer goes back to the circular flow model. He identified the groups of purchasers (households, firms, government, and the foreign sector) in the spending stream and considered what determines the amount of planned spending by each group. Keynes was very interested in determinants of planned consumption spending and planned investment spending.[6] He concluded that sometimes these two sources of spending will be inadequate to lead the economy to the full-employment level of output. At such times, the government, as a third major spending sector, should step in and boost planned spending (and aggregate demand) to the desired level.

What determines planned consumption and investment spending? According to Keynes, consumer spending (and saving) depends primarily on the level of income. Keynes believed that household spending habits are relatively stable and that households will spend a specific fraction of any increase in income. Investment demand, or planned investment spending, however, is much less stable. Investment depends on such

---

6. Today, with a large and growing foreign sector, economists pay more attention to what determines exports and imports. We will consider the role of the foreign sector more carefully in the next chapter. It did not play much of a role in the original Keynesian model.

put be? What are some possible divisions of that total between P and Y?

3. Keynes argued that k was not stable, especially in the short run. Suppose when you increase the money supply to $1,000 in Question 2, k rises from $1/4$ to $1/3$. That is, people decide to hold a larger fraction of their money income in cash balances. What happens to $P \times Y$ when M_s increases in this case? What does that imply for monetary policy?

4. The variables V and k are not calculated directly but are inferred from the value of M_s and $P \times Y$ (nominal GNP). Given the following data on money supply and GNP (both in billions of dollars), compute V and k for the United States for the years shown.

Year	Money Supply	GNP
1959	$141	$488
1960	143	507
1961	147	525
1962	149	565
1963	155	597
1964	162	638
1965	170	691
1966	174	756
1967	185	800
1968	199	873
1969	206	944
1970	217	993

You can repeat this exercise for other periods with data from the *Economic Report of the President*. What do you conclude about the stability of k and V?

5. Using the data in Table 1, compute the ratio of consumption to GNP and the ratio of investment to GNP for each year. Present the data as a graph. What conclusions can you draw about which form of spending is more stable?

6. Indicate whether each of the following statements about the Great Depression would be likely to be made by a business cycle theorist, a classical economist, or a Keynesian.

a. "Left alone, the economy would have corrected itself."

b. "Unequal distribution of income meant that the rich bought too little and the poor could not buy the rest, leaving a glut of unsold goods."

c. "Instability of investment means that the government has to step in to stabilize demand."

7. Why is the classical aggregate supply curve vertical? Why is the Keynesian aggregate supply curve horizontal?

8. What was revolutionary about Keynes's ideas?

9. According to classical economists, how do interest rates help to ensure that the economy will always return to the full-employment level of output?

10. Suppose that in the last six months real output has fallen by 3 percent, with a sharp rise in unemployment. What would a classical economist recommend as policy? Why? What would a Keynesian recommend?

11. What reason did Keynes give for the instability of money velocity?

12. If you expect interest rates to rise, will you hold money in cash or buy bonds? Why? What if you expect interest rates to fall?

13. Suppose there are 100 million workers in the economy, and full employment is defined as 96 percent of them being employed. Also suppose that each $10 billion in output employs 1 million workers. What is the full-employment level of output? If actual output is $850 billion, what would you expect the unemployment rate to be?

14. Sometimes the Keynesian revolution is described as a switch from "supply creates its own demand" to "demand creates its own supply." Explain this statement.

15. Why, according to Keynes, do self-regulating markets not solve the problem of falling output?

Suggestions for Further Reading

Clarke, Peter. *The Keynesian Revolution in the Making, 1924–1936*. Oxford, UK: Oxford University Press, 1988. Examines the British economic conditions in the 1920s and 1930s as a major influence on the development of Keynes's ideas.

Garraty, John A. "The Big Picture of the Great Depression," *American Heritage* (August/September 1986): 90–97. A good account of one of the most significant economic events of the twentieth century.

Heilbroner, Robert. *The Worldly Philosophers*, 6th ed. New York: Simon and Schuster, 1987. A popular and readable account of the lives and ideas of the great economists.

Hollander, Samuel. *Classical Economics*. Oxford and New York: Basil Blackwell, 1987. Traces the development of the ideas of the classical school.

Lekachman, Robert. *The Age of Keynes*. New York: McGraw-Hill, 1975. The best-known account of the life, times, and contributions of the most famous economist of the twentieth century.

Terkel, Studs. *Hard Times: An Oral History of the Great Depression*. New York: Random House, 1970. A classic retelling of personal experiences of individuals and families during the Depression.

AFTER STUDYING THIS CHAPTER, YOU SHOULD BE ABLE TO:

1. Explain the importance of the consumption function in the Keynesian model of how national income and output are determined.
2. Define:
   a. consumption function,
   b. marginal propensity to consume (*MPC*),
   c. marginal propensity to save (*MPS*).
3. Discuss the role of investment spending in the Keynesian model.
4. Find the equilibrium level of national income from a table or a graph, using each of these methods:
   a. *C* + *I* + *G* + (*EX* − *IM*) equals aggregate expenditure (*AE*);
   b. leakages equal injections.
5. Explain how unplanned changes in business inventories affect the level of income and output.
6. Calculate the value of the multiplier, given either *MPC* or *MPS*.
7. Calculate the change in the equilibrium national income, given the initial change in planned spending and the value of the multiplier.

CHAPTER 8

THE KEYNESIAN MODEL

INTRODUCTION

This chapter develops Keynes's explanation of how national income and output are determined. The Keynesian model explains how it is possible to reach an equilibrium level of income and output that is not the full-employment level.

Keynes did not agree with the classical view that the output level associated with full employment was the only possible equilibrium for the economy. He pointed out that the predictions of classical theory did not match the experience of the 1930s. In the Great Depression, the economy appeared to be at an equilibrium level of national income and output far below that required for the full employment of resources. Keynes did agree with the classical view that the economy would move automatically to an equilibrium level of national income and output. At that level, total planned spending and actual output would be equal. However, Keynes argued that it was quite possible for this equilibrium level to be a relatively low one, associated with a high level of unemployment. The Keynesian model of the economy explained how this could happen.

Keynes argued that supply adjusts to demand. That is, businesses will adjust their level of output to meet the demand as long as there are idle resources to expand production. Demand, or planned spending, plays the key role in determining how much is produced. What determines the spending plans of households and firms? Keynes believed that expenditures, especially consumption expenditures, are strongly influenced by the level of income. All income (wages, salaries, rent, interest, and profit) is received by the owners of the factors of production. There is a continuous flow from income to demand to output and back to income. Planned spending by households and firms determines the level of national income and output, but planned spending itself is influenced by national income. Thus, Keynes recognized that planned spending, output, and national income are *interdependent*. Their values are jointly determined.

In the language of aggregate supply and demand, the Keynesian model has a downward-sloping aggregate demand (*AD*) curve and a horizontal aggregate supply (*AS*) curve. A horizontal slope is one of the possible slopes for the *AS* curve presented in Chapter 6. Recall that the *AS* curve is likely to be horizontal when there are unemployed resources, which happened in the 1930s. At such a time, it is possible to expand output without driving up wages and prices. A horizontal *AS* curve allows the Keynesian model to focus on the position of the *AD* curve because that position determines the equilibrium level of national income and output. The level of real output (*Y*) that results from the intersection of the *AD* curve with Keynes's horizontal *AS* curve does not necessarily ensure full employment.

Keynes, however, did not use the terms *aggregate supply* and *aggregate demand*, at least not in the way they are used today. Instead, the central focus of his model was the relationship between consumption expenditures and disposable income. This relationship is known as the consumption function.

Investment demand also plays an important role in the Keynesian model. The sum of the two sources of planned spending—consumption and investment—is the aggregate expenditure (*AE*) function. This function determines the equilibrium level of national income and output. The multiplier concept is derived from the consumption function and shows how changes in planned expenditures affect that equilibrium level. The addition of government purchases and export and import spending provides a complete Keynesian model of the macro economy. When we have developed all these relationships, we will link the Keynesian model to the aggregate supply and demand framework of Chapter 6.

In this chapter and the next, we make a few simplifying assumptions. First, we will initially ignore the distinctions among GNP, NNP, NI, and PI. We will treat these as though they were all equivalent to *Y*, or real income and output. For the Keynesian model, the only important distinction we will need to make later on is between income before taxes and after-tax, or disposable, income (Y_d). Second, we will assume that the price level is fixed. When the price level does not change, consumption, investment, output, and income have the same values whether they are expressed in current market terms or in real (price-adjusted) terms. For analyzing periods of high unemployment when there is little upward pressure on prices, a fixed price level is a convenient and plausible assumption. (This second assumption will be relaxed toward the end of this chapter.) Third, we will initially ignore government and the foreign sector to concentrate on a simple two-sector economy. The two sectors are households that earn, consume, and save and business firms that produce and invest. Once we have built a working model of this simple economy, we can relax each assumption and bring the model closer to the real world.

THE KEYNESIAN AGGREGATE EXPENDITURE FUNCTION

aggregate expenditure (*AE*) Total planned spending by all sectors for an economy's total output.

The Keynesian model uses a measure of planned spending that is different from aggregate demand. **Aggregate expenditure (*AE*)** is defined as total planned spending by all sectors for an economy's total output. Recall from Chapter 5 that there are four sectors in the economy: households, business firms, government, and a foreign sector. In the upper half of the circular flow, the business sector sells output to each of the four sectors, including business firms that are making investment purchases. Aggregate expenditure for a four-sector economy is the sum of the purchases of all sectors:

$$AE = C + I + G + (EX - IM).$$

Here C is planned consumption spending, I is planned investment spending, G is government purchases of goods and services, and EX and IM are exports and imports, respectively. This breakdown is not the only way of sorting planned spending into components. It is useful, however, because the forces and motives influencing planned spending are different for each of these four sectors of the economy. These four purchasers of output correspond to the four categories of purchasers used in national income accounting and to the four actors in the circular flow model.

In a simple economy with no government and no foreign trade, aggregate expenditure has just two components: consumption and investment. It is useful to start with these two to develop a model of income determination and then add the others to make the model more realistic.

THE KEYNESIAN CONSUMPTION FUNCTION

Recall that Keynes challenged Say's law by arguing that it is demand, or planned spending, that determines how much is produced. Since the largest component of spending is consumption, Keynes began building his model by examining the behavior of consumption. He argued that the amount consumers spend depends mainly on their disposable income. Keynes called this relationship the consumption function and made it a key part of his theory.

The **consumption function** is any equation, table, or graph that shows the relationship between the income of consumers (disposable income) and the amount they plan, or desire, to spend on currently produced final output. Note that this Keynesian function relates consumer spending to disposable income, not national income. The distinction between disposable income and national income is not important here, since we are considering a simple economy with no government and thus no taxes. Later it will be important to distinguish between total output and income (Y) and disposable income (Y_d). Thus, we present the consumption function here in the same form in which it will appear when we add government to the model.

consumption function Any equation, table, or graph that shows the relationship between income of consumers (disposable income) and the amount they plan to spend on currently produced final output.

The general form of the equation for the consumption function is

$$C = C_0 + bY_d$$

where C is consumption expenditures and Y_d is disposable income. This expression says that consumption is positively related to income. That is, consumption rises when income rises and falls when income falls. The expression also indicates that there is a component of consumption (C_0) that is not related to the level of income. In the simple Keynesian model, any variable that is not dependent on income is said to be autonomous, or determined by other variables not included in the model. On a graph, the consumption function is a positively sloped straight line that crosses the vertical axis at C_0.[1] The slope of this line is b.

As an example, assume that the consumption function for a simple economy is expressed as

(1) $C = C_0 + bY_d = \$200 + 0.8Y_d,$

with all values in billions of dollars.

Table 1 shows some specific values for this consumption function. This table was derived by choosing various values for national income ($Y = Y_d$ because there are no taxes). The values for planned consumption spending (C) were then obtained by substituting the values of Y_d into equation (1). That is, the table answers this question: "If disposable income is equal to Y_d, then how much will households spend out of that income on consumption?" For example, if

$Y_d = \$1,200$ billion,

then

$C = \$200$ billion $+ 0.8(\$1,200$ billion$) = \$1,160$ billion.

How were the values for planned saving (S) in the fifth column of Table 1 obtained? Recall from Chapter 4 that saving is that part of income that is not spent. Therefore,

$S = Y_d - C.$

The values for planned saving (S) were obtained by subtracting the values in the third column from those in the first. That is, consumption (C) is subtracted from income (Y_d) to see what is left. Note that saving is negative at very low levels of income. Households will draw on their accumulated savings in order to maintain some minimum level of consumption.

THE MARGINAL PROPENSITIES TO CONSUME AND TO SAVE. Note that the values in Table 1 show a consistent relationship among income, consumption,

TABLE 1
PLANNED CONSUMPTION SPENDING (C) AND PLANNED SAVING (S) AT VARIOUS LEVELS OF NATIONAL INCOME (Y) (BILLIONS OF DOLLARS)

NATIONAL INCOME (DISPOSABLE INCOME), $Y = Y_d$	CHANGE IN DISPOSABLE INCOME, ΔY_d	PLANNED CONSUMPTION SPENDING, C	CHANGE IN PLANNED CONSUMPTION SPENDING, ΔC	PLANNED SAVING, S	CHANGE IN PLANNED SAVING, ΔS
$ 600	$ —	$ 680	$ —	$-80	$—
800	200	840	160	-40	40
1,000	200	1,000	160	0	40
1,200	200	1,160	160	40	40
1,400	200	1,320	160	80	40
1,600	200	1,480	160	120	40
1,800	200	1,640	160	160	40
2,000	200	1,800	160	200	40

1. A linear consumption function is consistent with Keynes's ideas about the relationship between consumer spending and disposable income, discussed in Chapter 7.

Chapter 8 The Keynesian Model

and saving. In the table, every time income increases by $200, consumption increases by $160 and saving by $40. Keynes believed that consumers are creatures of habit. When disposable income changes, he expected consumer spending to change by a constant fraction of the change in income. Keynes called this fraction the **marginal propensity to consume** (*MPC*). It corresponds to *b* in the equation for the consumption function. The marginal propensity to consume (*MPC*) is the ratio of the change in consumption spending (ΔC) to the change in disposable income (ΔY_d):

$$MPC = \frac{\Delta C}{\Delta Y_d}.$$

A related concept is the **marginal propensity to save** (*MPS*), which describes how saving responds to income changes. The marginal propensity to save (*MPS*) is the ratio of the change in saving (ΔS) to the change in disposable income (ΔY_d):

$$MPS = \frac{\Delta S}{\Delta Y_d}.$$

Values of *MPC* and *MPS* are not shown in Table 1 but can be calculated easily from the values given there. For instance, when Y_d increases from $1,000 billion to $1,200 billion, *C* increases from $1,000 billion to $1,160 billion and *S* increases from $0 to $40 billion. Thus, for ΔY_d = $200 billion, ΔC = $160 billion and ΔS = $40 billion. The values of *MPC* and *MPS* are

$$MPC = \frac{\Delta C}{\Delta Y_d} = \frac{\$160 \text{ billion}}{\$200 \text{ billion}} = \frac{4}{5}, \text{ or } 0.8,$$

and

$$MPS = \frac{\Delta S}{\Delta Y_d} = \frac{\$40 \text{ billion}}{\$200 \text{ billion}} = \frac{1}{5}, \text{ or } 0.2.$$

If you calculate *MPC* and *MPS* from other values in Table 1, you will get the same values each time. Table 1 was created using Keynes's assumption that the marginal propensity to consume is constant.

In this example, *MPC* is $4/5$ and *MPS* is $1/5$ of the change in income, and their sum equals 1. In an economy with no taxes, *MPC* and *MPS* will always add up to 1 because all consumer income that is not spent on final goods and services must be saved. (If *MPC* and *MPS* are computed as fractions of changes in disposable, or after-tax, income, then they will sum to 1 even if taxes are included in the model.) When income rises by $500 billion, the additional consumption spending is the marginal propensity to consume times $500 billion. If *MPC* is 0.8, consumption spending rises by $400 billion. The amount *not* spent is (1-*MPC*) times $500 billion, or $100 billion. The amount not spent on consumption is, by definition, saving. Thus, when income rises by $500 billion, the change in saving is equal to the marginal propensity to save times $500 billion. Since all the added income must be either spent or saved, we can conclude that

$$MPS = 1 - MPC, \text{ or } MPC + MPS = 1.$$

If *MPC* is 0.9, then *MPS* must be 0.1. If *MPC* is 0.6, then *MPS* must be 0.4. If $9/10$ or $6/10$ of an increase in income is spent, only $1/10$ or $4/10$ is saved.

---

marginal propensity to consume (*MPC*)
The fraction of any change in income that is consumed. The *MPC* is greater than 0 and less than 1.

marginal propensity to save (*MPS*)
The fraction of any change in income that is saved. The *MPS* is greater than 0 and less than 1.

Figure 1 is a graphic presentation of the numbers in Table 1 and the corresponding consumption function,

$$C = \$200 + 0.8Y_d.$$

The marginal propensity to consume is equal to b, the slope of the consumption function. Recall that the slope of a line is the ratio of the change in the variable on the vertical axis to the change in the variable on the horizontal axis, moving from left to right along the horizontal axis. In Figure 1, the slope is the ratio of the change in C to the change in Y. In symbols, $b = \Delta C/\Delta Y = MPC$. Similarly, the slope of the saving function is $\Delta S/\Delta Y = MPS$. When consumers receive more income, a larger share of it normally goes to consumption than to saving. The marginal propensity to save is usually smaller than the marginal propensity to consume. Thus, the slope of the consumption function is steeper than the slope of the saving function in Figure 1. (If you have difficulty with slopes, you may want to review the appendix to Chapter 1.)

Keynes believed that the marginal propensity to consume would be relatively constant, at least over a modest range of values of income and output. That is, he expected that a rise in disposable income from $1,000 billion to $1,200 billion would lead to the same increase in consumption as a rise in disposable income from $1,200 billion to $1,400 billion. Since Keynes wrote *General Theory*, economists have devoted much attention to examining the behavior of the consumption function. When consumption functions are estimated from annual data for total consumption and

FIGURE 1
PLANNED CONSUMPTION AND PLANNED SAVING
The consumption function shows the relationship between planned consumption and national income. The saving function shows the relationship between planned saving and national income. The slope of the consumption function is equal to *MPC*. The slope of the saving function is equal to *MPS*.

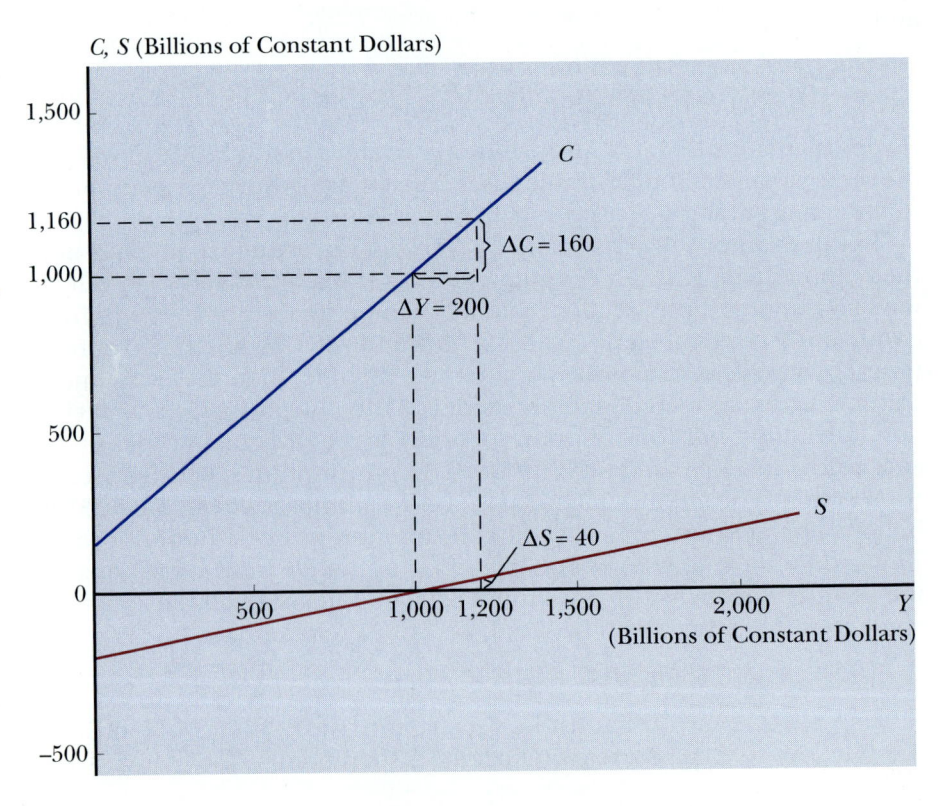

> **KEYNES'S HYPOTHESES ABOUT *MPC* AND *MPS***
>
> - *MPC* and *MPS* are always greater than 0 and less than 1.
> - The sum of *MPC* and *MPS* must always equal 1.
> - *MPC* is the slope of the consumption function, and *MPS* is the slope of the saving function.
> - *MPC* and *MPS* are relatively constant. Their values do not change along the graph of the consumption function.

national income for the United States, they appear to be fairly stable, with a nearly constant marginal propensity to consume. Some of these estimates of the consumption function find a positive value for the constant term (C_0). In Table 1, for example, this constant term is $200 billion. Other estimates of the actual consumption functions appear to be closer to the form $C = bY_d$, which has no constant term. A graph of this function would cross the y-axis at the origin.

Figure 2 plots data for consumption and income in the United States

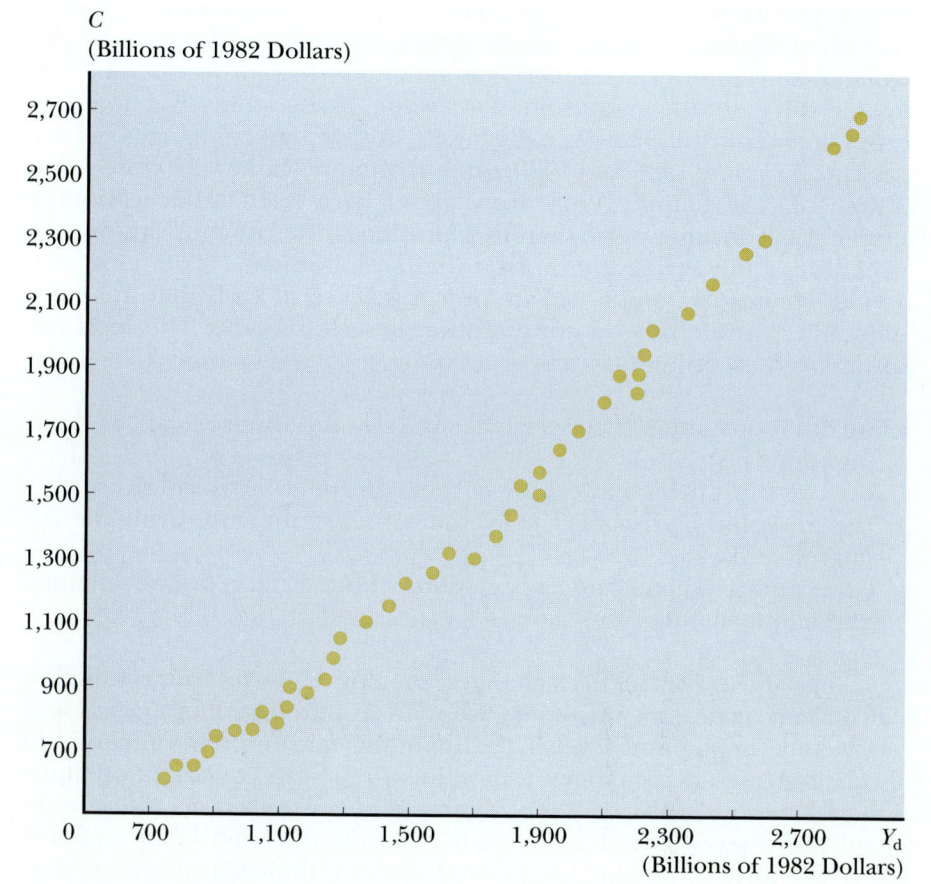

**FIGURE 2
CONSUMPTION EXPENDITURES VERSUS DISPOSABLE INCOME FOR THE UNITED STATES, 1950–1990**
The historical relationship between consumption expenditures and disposable income seems to be very stable, with an *MPC* between 0.8 and 0.9 and a C_0 term that is close to zero.

Source: Council of Economic Advisers, *Economic Report of the President* (Washington, DC: U.S. Government Printing Office, 1991).

from 1950 to 1990. This consumption-income relationship appears to be almost a straight line, with a slope (*MPC*) between 0.8 and 0.9 and no constant term. The ratio of increases in saving to increases in disposable income is relatively low, between 0.1 and 0.2. A low saving rate has concerned many economists who think Americans need to save more in order to speed up economic growth. We will explore this issue further in Chapter 16.

THE CONSTANT TERM IN THE CONSUMPTION FUNCTION. It is easy to understand why consumption might rise as income rises. But where does that constant term, C_0, in the equation for the consumption function come from? If we insert a value of zero for Y_d into the general form of the consumption function, $C = C_0 + bY_d$, this equation seems to say that there is a positive level of consumption, C_0, even when no output is currently being produced and no income is being earned. For Table 1, C_0 had a value of $200 billion. This value indicated that consumers would buy $200 billion worth of goods and services even if there were no production taking place and no income coming into households.

The constant term in the consumption function reflects two important facts. One is that it is possible to consume for a short while even with no current production. An economy could consume inventories and deplete its stock of capital for short periods of time. This process is known as **dissaving**. If an economy was in a crisis situation in which production halted, it could still continue to consume for a while. No economy ever comes to a complete standstill. However, during the revolutionary changes in Eastern Europe in late 1989 and 1990, some economies came very close—that of Romania, for example. What does happen fairly often is that economies temporarily consume more than they produce in wartime by drawing on inventories and wearing out capital without replacing it.

The second fact embodied in the constant term C_0 is that there are many other influences on consumption besides income. The most important of these influences are

1. wealth (consumers' assets such as stocks, bonds, houses, cars, and savings deposits),
2. interest rates (which affect the cost of consumer borrowing),
3. the price level (discussed in Chapter 6 in connection with the *AD* curve), and
4. expectations (including expectations about future prices, income, and employment).

If one of these influences changes, the entire consumption function will shift up or down. Consumers will want to purchase more goods and services at every income level. This shift in the consumption function will also be reflected as a change in the value of C_0 in its consumption equation and the table of values. For example, if consumers acquired more wealth and assets over time and thus felt they did not need to save as much out of any level of income, they would increase their consumption. The value of C_0 might increase from $200 billion to $250 billion. The entire

dissaving
Consuming by drawing on accumulated stocks (inventories) or financial assets.

> **BASIC FEATURES OF THE KEYNESIAN CONSUMPTION FUNCTION**
>
> - Consumption (C) depends on the level of disposable income (Y_d).
>
> - Part of consumption is independent of the level of income. This constant term (C_0) changes in response to changes in such other influences as wealth, interest rates, the price level, and expectations.
>
> - The rest of consumption (bY_d) is positively related to income. The marginal propensity to consume ($MPC = b$) is the fraction of an additional dollar of income that will be spent on consumption: $0 < b < 1$.

consumption function would shift upward as consumers spend more of every possible value of Y_d.

INVESTMENT EXPENDITURE

In a two-sector economy, there are only two kinds of planned expenditures: consumption and investment. Planned expenditures are distinguished from actual expenditures, because sometimes households or firms will find that actual spending does not equal what was planned.

We have already explored what determines consumption. How do we explain the behavior of investment demand (I)? Recall that classical economists believed that the most important determinant of planned investment spending was the interest rate. Keynes did not agree. He argued that profit expectations would be the most important determinant of investment spending. Other important influences on investment are the interest rate, the size and age of the existing stock of capital, changes in corporate taxes, and changes in technology. Some of these influences are subject to drastic and sudden changes.

In order to understand the behavior of investment, you need to recall the breakdown of gross private domestic investment into fixed investment in business plants and equipment, residential construction, and inventories. All three of these components are responsive to changes in both expectations and interest rates, but to different degrees.

Plants and equipment have a long useful lifetime. Thus, there may be a large existing stock to be used up before there will be much replacement. The same is true of residential construction. Also, housing demand is very sensitive to changes in construction costs and patterns of population growth. If a large proportion of the population is twenty to forty years old, there is high demand for new housing as new families are formed. As the population ages, housing demand does not grow as rapidly. Inventories are very dependent on actual and expected final sales. Thus, they tend to fluctuate more in the short run than other types of investment. Unplanned changes in inventories, in fact, play a very important role in moving an economy toward equilibrium. Sudden increases or decreases in inventories signal producers that they need to change their level of output.

In general, all three types of investment fluctuate much more than consumption. Because inventories are more likely than other types of investment spending to exceed or fall short of desired levels, we will assume that other plans are realized. That is, any gap between planned and actual spending will consist of unplanned changes in inventories. This is not always the case, however. In the Soviet Union, actual consumption frequently falls short of planned consumption because stores' shelves are empty and there are no inventories on which to draw.

Keynes assumed that the investment demand curve would shift so frequently that the relationship between planned investment spending and the level of income (or the rate of interest) would not be as important as the causes of its shifts. In the Keynesian model, it is the level of investment spending that matters. For this reason, we will follow Keynes for now and treat investment demand as an exogenous variable, a given value that is determined outside the model.

EQUILIBRIUM IN A TWO-SECTOR MODEL

The consumption function and some measure of investment demand are all we need to develop a two-sector model that determines the equilibrium value of national income and output (Y). Table 2 and Figure 3 add to the consumption function of equation (1) an investment demand of $200 billion, which is autonomous (independent of the level of income). In a two-sector model, consumption and investment represent all of the sources of demand. Figure 3 graphs the data in Table 2 and adds a reference line with a slope of 45°. This reference line locates those points where the value measured on the horizontal axis (total output or income) is equal to the value on the vertical axis (aggregate planned expenditure, or $C + I$).[2] Where the AE (or $C + I$) curve crosses the 45° line, aggregate expenditure is equal to total output. This value of output is, by definition, an equilibrium level. In Figure 3, equilibrium occurs at $Y = \$1,800 = C + I$.

What makes this level of output the equilibrium level? Equilibrium occurs at an output level of $1,800 because no other level can be sustained. At any other level of output, unplanned inventory changes occur. These changes direct business firms to adjust production levels in order to make output equal to aggregate planned expenditure.

Table 3 shows the important role played by unplanned inventory changes. For example, if Y were equal to $1,400 billion, aggregate planned expenditure (AE) would be $1,480 billion. Planned spending for output

TABLE 2
AN AGGREGATE EXPENDITURE (AE) SCHEDULE (BILLIONS OF DOLLARS)

NATIONAL INCOME, $Y = Y_d$	PLANNED CONSUMPTION EXPENDITURE, C	PLANNED SAVING, $Y - C$	BUSINESS INVESTMENT EXPENDITURE, I	AGGREGATE EXPENDITURE, $AE = C + I$
$1,000	$1,000	$ 0	$160	$1,160
1,200	1,160	40	160	1,320
1,400	1,320	80	160	1,480
1,600	1,480	120	160	1,640
1,800	1,640	160	160	1,800
2,000	1,800	200	160	1,960
2,200	1,960	240	160	2,120
2,400	2,120	280	160	2,280
2,600	2,280	320	160	2,440

2. This graphic tool is described in the appendix to Chapter 1. You may want to go back and review that section.

Chapter 8 The Keynesian Model

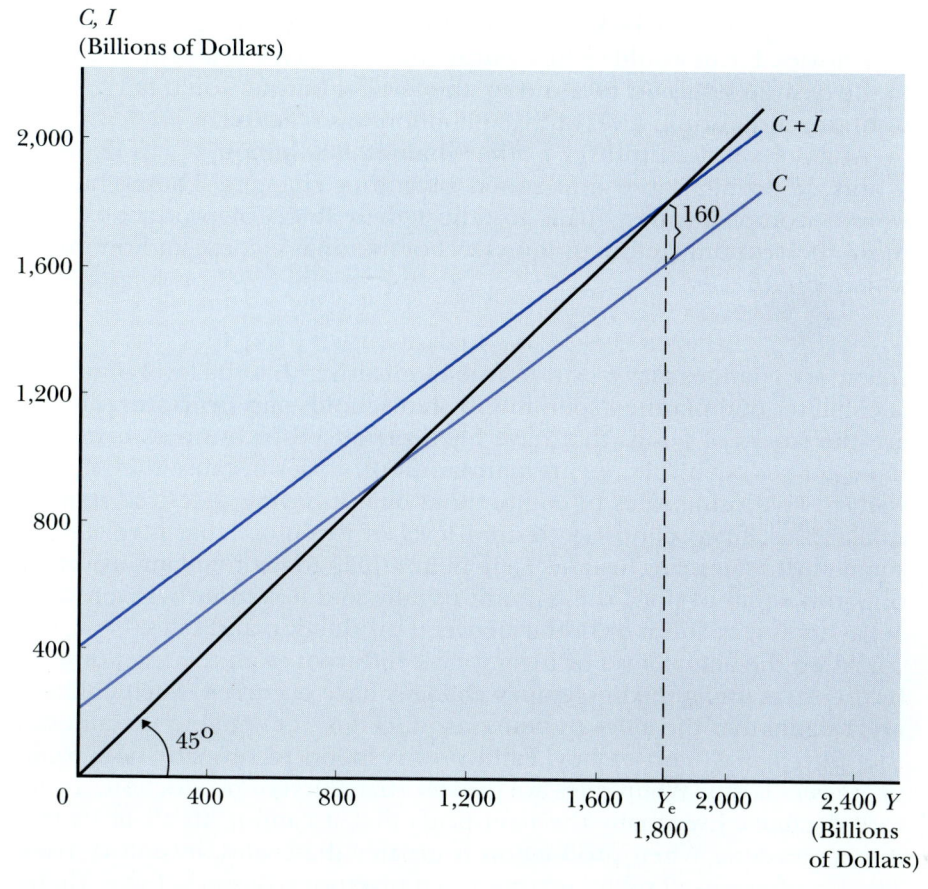

FIGURE 3
AGGREGATE EXPENDITURE AND EQUILIBRIUM OUTPUT Adding investment to the consumption function gives aggregate planned expenditure ($AE = C + I$) at every possible level of output. The 45° reference line shows the points where aggregate expenditure (measured on the vertical axis) equals total output (measured on the horizontal axis). The AE curve crosses the 45° line at the equilibrium level of output (Y_e).

would exceed current production by $80 billion. As firms tried to fill orders, their inventories would begin to decline. They would realize that production is not keeping pace with sales. Firms would respond to unplanned declines in inventories by increasing their levels of output. The expansion in output to rebuild inventories would increase the level of output to the equilibrium level of $1,800 billion.

On the other hand, if Y were equal to $2,400 billion, AE would be only $2,380 billion. In this case, current production would exceed aggregate

TABLE 3
UNPLANNED INVENTORY CHANGES AND THE EQUILIBRIUM LEVEL OF NATIONAL INCOME (BILLIONS OF DOLLARS)

NATIONAL INCOME, $Y = Y_d$	AGGREGATE EXPENDITURE, AE	UNPLANNED INVENTORY CHANGES, $(Y - AE)$	BUSINESS RESPONSE	EFFECT ON NATIONAL INCOME
$1,000	$1,160	$-160	Increase output	Increase
1,400	1,480	- 80	Increase output	Increase
1,800	1,800	0	Maintain output	No change
2,000	1,960	+ 40	Decrease output	Decrease
2,200	2,120	+ 80	Decrease output	Decrease
2,600	2,440	220160	Decrease output	Decrease

planned expenditure by $120 billion, resulting in unplanned buildup of inventories. Firms would reduce output in order to bring inventories back to the desired levels. As they did so, the level of output would fall steadily until the equilibrium level of $1,800 billion was reached.

At any level of output (Y) other than $2,000 billion, a gap between Y and AE would cause unplanned inventory changes. These changes would prompt business firms to adjust their levels of production and move the economy to the unique level of national income and output at which $Y = AE$.

THE CRUCIAL ROLE OF UNPLANNED BUSINESS INVENTORY CHANGES

Inventory changes play a crucial role in ensuring that the level of output is equal to total planned spending by households and firms. **Inventories** are the stocks of goods that have been produced by business firms but have not yet been sold. Firms maintain inventories because they do not want to risk losing sales to competitors by not having a desired item in stock.[3] Most firms choose a desired level of inventory that is related in some way to sales. For instance, a firm may plan to maintain an inventory of goods equal to twice the amount usually sold in a month. Inventories act as a safety cushion or buffer between production and sales.

When the actual level of inventory is different from the level desired by the firm, **unplanned inventory changes** have occurred. Such changes are a signal that the amount being produced is not equal to the amount that purchasers want to buy. Failure to respond to this situation could prove very costly. When sales are greater than current production, inventory declines. Eventually the firm finds that it cannot fill all of its customers' orders. When production is greater than sales, inventory rises. The firm finds itself piling up unwanted inventory. Business firms, therefore, have very strong incentives to respond to unplanned changes in inventories by expanding or contracting their output levels.[4]

LEAKAGES AND INJECTIONS IN A TWO-SECTOR MODEL

The consumption and investment approach is the most commonly used method for explaining what determines the level of output and income. This method finds the value of aggregate planned expenditure and compares it to output to find the equilibrium level. However, there is another approach that will give the same result. The second way is the method of leakages and injections, which derives from the circular flow. Equilibrium national income occurs at the level at which planned leakages from the circular flow (saving in this two-sector model) equal planned injections (or planned investment, excluding unplanned inventory changes). If

---

inventories
The stocks of goods that have been produced by business firms but have not yet been sold.

unplanned inventory changes
Changes that occur when the inventory level rises above or falls below that desired by a firm because the production level is too high or too low relative to current sales.

---

3. What did you do the last time you tried to purchase an item in a store and were told that the item was sold out? You probably went elsewhere to make your purchase. The store that was out of the item not only lost the sale but created a poor image in your mind and gave a competitor the opportunity to gain a customer.

4. The driving force of the Keynesian model is the self-interested behavior of the managers of business firms. Profit-maximizing behavior requires that output be adjusted to the level of demand for the product. This emphasis on self-interested behavior links Keynes to the classical school. In fact, it is also consistent with the recent development of "quick response" as a management strategy. Quick response means that firms are organized so as to react very quickly to unexpected inventory changes.

leakages are greater than injections, the size of the flow is shrinking. If injections are greater than leakages, the size of the flow is increasing. (Think of the level of income as the water in a bathtub, injections as the water flowing in from the faucet, and leakages as water going down the drain.) Only when planned leakages and planned injections are equal is the level of income stable, with no tendency to change. (This concept of equilibrium was introduced in Chapter 4.)

We can use the data in Table 2 to show that the level of income for which $C + I = Y$ is the same level of income at which leakages (planned saving, or S) are equal to injections (planned investment, or I). At the equilibrium level of income ($Y = \$1,800$), consumption is $1,640. Thus, the amount of planned saving (equal to income minus consumption) must be $160. Planned investment takes up the slack in demand not filled by consumption and is also equal to $160. In Table 2, leakages are equal to injections at $Y = \$1,800$. Figure 4 plots the values of investment and saving from Table 2 to locate the equilibrium level of national income (Y or Y_d). This level occurs where leakages in the form of planned saving (S) are equal to injections in the form of planned investment (I). As in Figure 3, in Figure 4 the equilibrium level of output and income is $1,800 billion.

ADDING GOVERNMENT AND THE FOREIGN SECTOR

The simple, two-sector economy with only households and business firms shows how the equilibrium level of national income is determined. A more complete Keynesian model includes all four sectors from the circu-

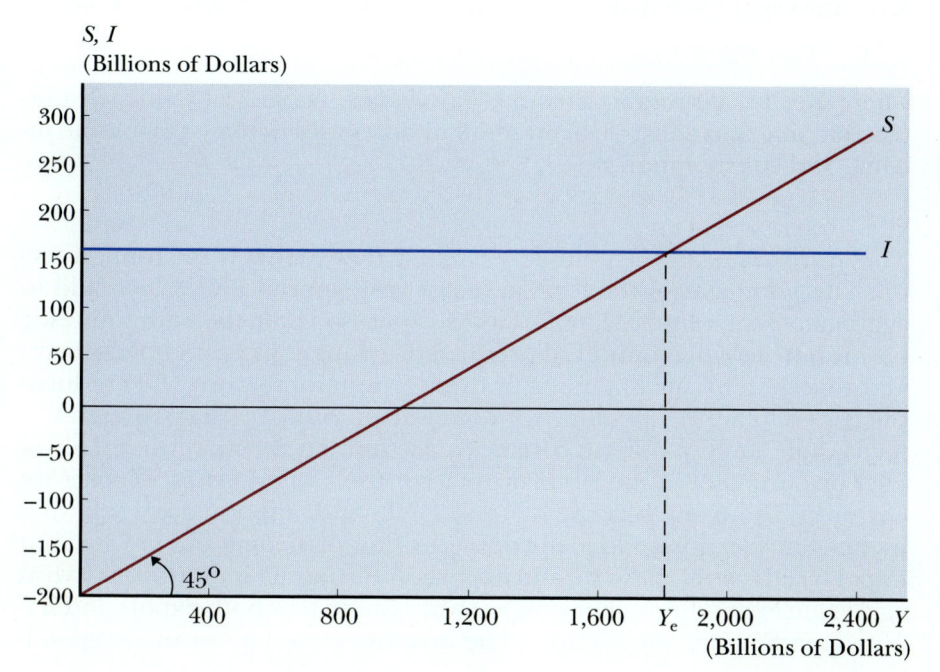

FIGURE 4
DETERMINING EQUILIBRIUM OUTPUT WITH LEAKAGES AND INJECTIONS
Another method to determine equilibrium national income is the leakages and injections approach. In a two-sector economy, the only leakage is saving (S), and the only injection is investment (I). In this case, the two are equal ($I = S$) at a value of $160 billion, which occurs at an income level of $1,800 billion.

lar flow and the national income accounts. Adding government and the foreign sector makes the model more realistic.

GOVERNMENT SPENDING AND TAXES

Adding government to the model causes leakages from the circular flow in the form of taxes (T) and injections of additional spending in the form of government expenditures (G). Government expenditures, like investment expenditures, are assumed to be determined by factors other than income. That is, they are autonomous. There may be some linkage to levels of income and output, but government spending is determined through the political process. Thus, we treat its value (G) as a given constant, like C_0 in the consumption function. When we add government expenditures, aggregate planned expenditure becomes

$$AE = C + I + G.$$

We now have another source of demand for output. Taken by itself, the addition of government expenditures to planned aggregate expenditure would increase the equilibrium level of income and output by a multiplier effect. However, there is a downside to this addition. Government purchases must be paid for, at least in part, by collecting taxes. For simplicity, we assume that taxes are independent of the level of income and that all taxes are paid by consumers.

Taxes constitute a leakage from the circular flow. A part of income received by households is not available to spend on consumption because it has been claimed by the government in taxes. Taxes do not enter the equation for aggregate expenditure directly because they do not represent planned spending for output. Instead, taxes work indirectly. The addition of taxes will reduce disposable income and therefore reduce consumption. (Consumption depends on disposable income.) Taxes (T) are incorporated into aggregate expenditure through the consumption function:

$$C = C_0 + b(Y - T),$$

where $Y - T$ is disposable income (Y_d). A rise in taxes will reduce disposable income and consumption. A fall in taxes will increase disposable income and consumption.

THE FOREIGN SECTOR

The fourth actor in the complete circular flow model is the foreign sector. The purchases of the foreign sector are exports (EX), which add to aggregate expenditure. The foreign sector also competes with domestic business firms when imported products are bought by households, firms, and government. Any spending by these groups for imports (IM) reduces the level of planned spending for domestic output (AE). The foreign sector is quite large for some countries, accounting for more than half of sales or purchases in the circular flow. For the United States, exports are currently about 10 percent of total GNP, and imports are somewhat higher. Since exports add to the domestic flow of income and product but imports reduce this flow, we add exports and subtract imports to arrive at aggregate expenditure. For now, we will assume that both export and import spending are autonomous, like investment and government spend-

International Perspective

The Keynesian Model in a One-Product Economy

The Keynesian model was developed to describe ups and downs of income and output in developed, industrial economies. For such economies, it can be assumed that the components of aggregate expenditure—consumption, investment, government spending, and net exports—are largely independent of each other. The Keynesian model was constructed on the assumption of such independence. In a small economy with a single major export product, however, this assumption may not be valid.

Consider the economy of Ghana, an African country whose main crop is coffee. Coffee represents 60 percent of the value of Ghana's exports and 40 percent of total output. Suppose there is a large drop in Ghana's coffee sales due to changes in tastes abroad. In a developed economy, this fall in net exports would be duly entered in the aggregate expenditure function. It would have ripple effects throughout the economy through the expenditure multiplier and induced declines in consumption.

In Ghana, however, such ripples will be larger and more serious. In addition to the induced decline in consumption, the fall in coffee sales means a loss of revenue to the government. (Taxes on the export crop are often a major source of government revenues in small one-crop economies.) With little capacity to borrow, the government will be forced to reduce government purchases (G). The decline in government purchases has an additional downward multiplier effect on income and output. Furthermore, most of the investment occurring in Ghana is probably linked to the production of coffee. With poor sales prospects for their major crop, investors in Ghana are likely to cut back on their investment spending (I). This fall has a third downward multiplier effect on income and output.

During a boom in coffee sales, the reverse is true. Net export sales have a multiplier effect. They also create a stimulus to government spending from the additional revenue from export taxes and a stimulus to investment in the coffee industry in anticipation of future boom years. These two injections of new spending have their own multiplier effects on consumption and, through consumption, on income and output.

Thus, for such an economy, changes in economic activity are likely to be much more intense than for economies that are more diversified and less dependent on international trade. A modest dip in the level of economic activity in the country or countries to which Ghana exports its coffee could have a major impact on the level of income and output in this small, highly specialized economy. This kind of effect was responsible for a saying heard often for decades after World War II: "When the United States sneezes, the rest of the world catches pneumonia."

in Figure 8. The original equilibrium income of Y_1 ($2,300 billion) no longer holds. At this level of national income, planned spending (AE) is now $2,500 billion and exceeds Y_1 by $200 billion. Unplanned reductions in inventories occur. Business firms respond by increasing output, which increases national income. When all the effects have worked through, how much do you expect national income will have risen?

The final increase in income and output is much greater than the initial $200 billion increase in investment. The new equilibrium point in Figure 8 occurs where AE_2 intersects the 45° line. At that point, national income is at Y_2, or $3,300 billion, which is $1,000 billion higher than the original equilibrium level. Thus, the $200 billion upward shift in aggregate expenditure results in a $1,000 billion increase in equilibrium income and output because of the multiplier effect. The expenditure multiplier measures the impact of a given initial change in aggregate expenditure on equilibrium income and output. This multiplier is an important and powerful tool of Keynesian economic theory.

THE MULTIPLIER AND CHANGES IN INVESTMENT

Suppose that, as a result of changed expectations, firms increase investment expenditures (I) by $200 billion. Aggregate expenditure (AE) initially increases by the same amount. But the process of expanding output and income does not stop there. Additional investment spending creates

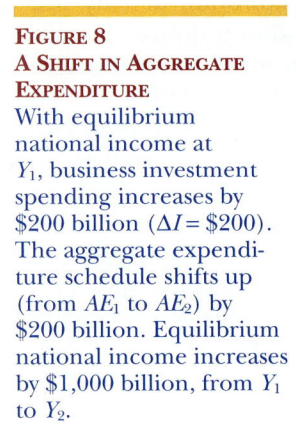

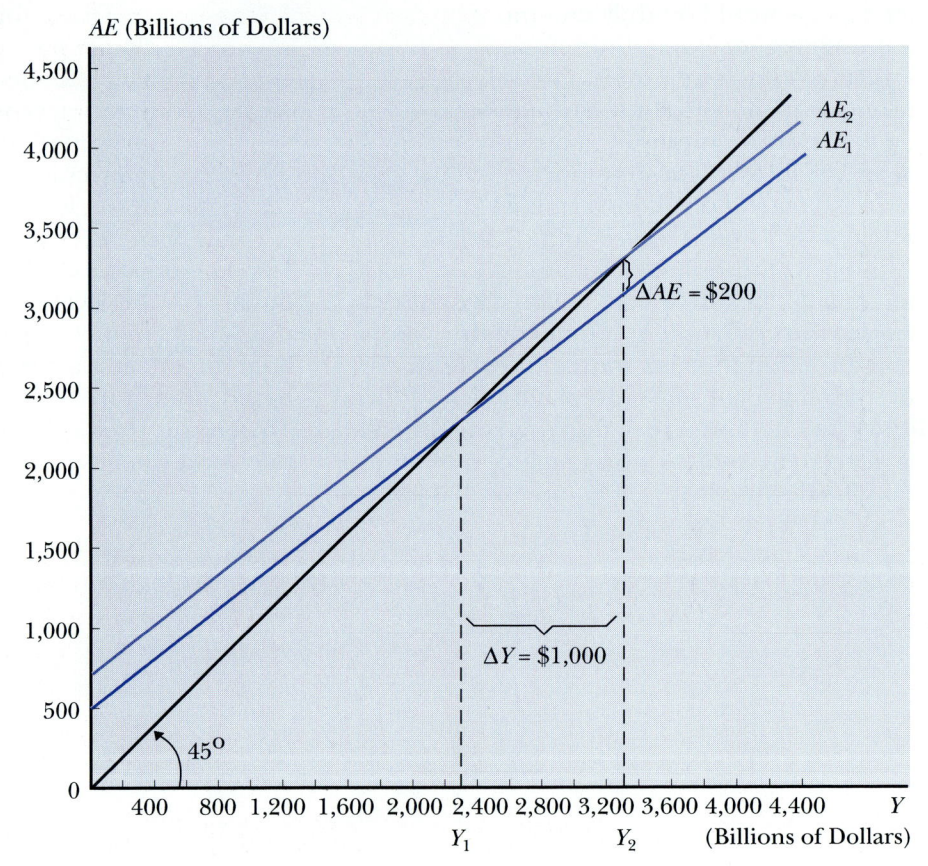

FIGURE 8
A SHIFT IN AGGREGATE EXPENDITURE
With equilibrium national income at Y_1, business investment spending increases by $200 billion ($\Delta I = \$200$). The aggregate expenditure schedule shifts up (from AE_1 to AE_2) by $200 billion. Equilibrium national income increases by $1,000 billion, from Y_1 to Y_2.

additional income for those who produce investment goods. Suppose, for example, the investment consists of building an apartment complex. The plumbers, carpenters, and electricians earn additional income, which they in turn spend to buy groceries, movie tickets, and new cars. Grocers, farmers, theater operators, actors, auto workers, and auto dealers all receive more income, which they in turn spend.

Think about what you have just learned about the relationship between income (Y) and consumption spending (C). When Y changes, C also changes, but by a smaller amount. The marginal propensity to consume describes the relationship between changes in income and the *induced* changes in consumption spending. Thus, an additional business investment of $200 billion causes incomes to increase by $200 billion. This is the round one effect. As a result of receiving this additional income ($200 billion), households will increase their spending by an amount dependent on the marginal propensity to consume. This round two spending will increase aggregate expenditure further. If MPC is 0.8, as in our example, the round two increase in AE will be $160 billion ($200 billion $\times 0.8$). But this spending also becomes additional income to those who receive it, setting off a round three increase in spending. This round-by-round process is shown in Table 5. Each change in output and income causes a change in spending in the next round, which changes output and income. The process continues, with smaller increases in each successive round.

How long does this income-spending process go on? Table 5 traces the process through the first five rounds and then summarizes the remaining rounds. Although in theory the process goes on forever, a shortcut is available to quickly determine the total change in output and income. Note that after round one, each column entry in Table 5 is 80 percent of the entry above it. Thus, the numbers in the columns that show each round of increase in spending and income are declining at a uniform rate of 80 percent—or 0.8, the value of the marginal propensity to consume. There is clearly a relationship between income growth and the size of the marginal propensity to consume. It turns out that the overall effect of the round-by-round changes in national income is shown by

(2) $\Delta Y_f = \Delta AE_1 \times$ expenditure multiplier,

where ΔY_f is the sum of all the changes in the level of national income and

TABLE 5
THE DYNAMICS OF THE MULTIPLIER PROCESS

ROUND	CHANGE IN AGGREGATE EXPENDITURE (BILLIONS)	CHANGE IN NATIONAL INCOME (BILLIONS)
1	$200 (initial change)	$200
2	160	160
3	128	128
4	102.40	102.40
5	81.92	81.92
All following rounds	327.68	327.68
Total	$1,000.00	$1,000.00

expenditure multiplier Measures the impact of a given initial change in aggregate expenditure on equilibrium income and output. The multiplier is equal to $1/(1 - MPC)$.

ΔAE_1 is the initial change in planned aggregate expenditure. The **expenditure multiplier** is defined as

$$(3) \quad \text{Expenditure multiplier} = \frac{1}{1 - MPC} = \frac{1}{1 - b}.$$

It is possible to compute the change in the equilibrium level of national income (ΔY_f) if the initial change in aggregate expenditure (ΔAE_1) and the marginal propensity to consume (MPC) are known. First, we solve equation (3) by substituting the actual value of MPC:

$$\text{Expenditure multiplier} = \frac{1}{1 - 0.8} = \frac{1}{0.2} = 5.$$

Second, we solve equation (2) for ΔY_f by substituting the known values for ΔAE_1 and the expenditure multiplier:

$\Delta Y_f = \$200 \text{ billion} \times 5 = \$1,000 \text{ billion}.$

This result indicates the same change in the level of national income as in Figure 8. This change in output and income is also the value that would result from summing the effects of an infinite number of rounds in Table 5.

The expenditure multiplier applies to a change in any of the components of aggregate expenditure: C, I, G, or $(EX - IM)$. For instance, a $50 billion increase in net exports is subject to the expenditure multiplier of 5 and would, therefore, cause an increase of $250 billion in the equilibrium level of national income. The expenditure multiplier is the same no matter where the change in spending originates. A government dollar multiplies as well as a dollar from the foreign sector. If the C_0 term in the consumption function can shift up or down with changes in consumer wealth or population or other influences, it will have the same kind of multiplier effect. The size of the multiplier, however, is usually somewhat smaller than the value we have been using here, because of a variety of leakages and other effects. The multiplier for the U.S. economy is generally believed to be about 3. That is, over a period of about two years, a given dollar change in the level of autonomous spending will raise equilibrium by about $3.

THE MULTIPLIER AND CHANGES IN CONSUMPTION: A CASE STUDY

The consumption function is one of the most stable components of aggregate expenditure. Government spending is unpredictable, investment is volatile, and exports and imports have swings. Consumers, however, seem to buy food, cars, clothing, and other necessities and conveniences with great regularity. Once in a while, however, consumers take forecasters by surprise. They did so when forecasting output and income with the Keynesian model was in its infancy.

During World War II, output was high and unemployment was low because of massive government spending for the war effort. Since so much output consisted of military goods and so many workers were in the military, few consumer goods were being produced. Consumers worked long hours and earned big paychecks. But they were encouraged to be patri-

Chapter 8 The Keynesian Model

otic and purchase war bonds (save) instead of spending on the limited supply of consumer goods.

Economists had predicted a serious recession at the end of the war as government spending dropped back to normal levels. There was eventually a mild recession, but not until about four years after the war ended. What was wrong with the forecast? The consumption function shifted upward because consumers had amassed large amounts of financial assets in the form of boxes full of war bonds. After the war, they were ready to cash in these bonds to satisfy their pent-up demand for cars, houses, new clothes, and other consumer goods. Most of the decline in planned government spending for national defense was offset by an upward shift in the consumption function. In terms of the Keynesian model, the downward multiplier effect of reduced government spending was offset by the upward multiplier effect of an increase in C_0.

THE PARADOX OF THRIFT

Another application of the expenditure multiplier led to the surprising discovery that an increase in planned saving may not have a positive effect. Americans traditionally have regarded saving as a virtue. Benjamin Franklin said, "A penny saved is a penny earned." How can saving ever be bad?

Keynes questioned the value of increasing saving when an economy is operating well below the full-employment level of output. An upward shift in the saving function implies an equal and opposite downward shift of the consumption and aggregate expenditure functions. The equilibrium level of national income must fall because aggregate expenditure has fallen. As a result, actual saving may not increase at all, even though planned saving is higher. The name given to this phenomenon is the **paradox of thrift**.

paradox of thrift
The fact that attempts by consumers to increase saving cause income and output to decline. Therefore, actual saving may not increase at all.

What causes this unexpected outcome? As people become more thrifty (and thus spend less on consumption at all levels of income), their increased planned saving ultimately causes income and output to decline. Furthermore, the increase in planned saving does not necessarily result in much increase in actual saving. As income falls, households are forced to consume less and save less out of their smaller incomes. It is possible that households may wind up saving no more than before out of a lower level of income and output.

THE KEYNESIAN MODEL AND AGGREGATE DEMAND

Chapter 6 presented a model of aggregate supply and aggregate demand as the framework for the study of macroeconomics. This chapter has developed the Keynesian model in which an aggregate expenditure function determines the level of income and output. The price level receives no attention in the Keynesian model. The price level and real output receive equal billing in the aggregate supply and demand model. How are these two models connected?

The relationship between the aggregate demand (AD) curve of Chapter 6 and the aggregate expenditure (AE) curve of the Keynesian model is shown in Figure 9(a). The AE curve is drawn for a given, fixed price level. Higher price levels are associated with lower aggregate expenditure at every level of income. Chapter 6 suggested many reasons why total demand for goods and services will be lower at higher price levels. Higher price levels discourage consumption by reducing the value of household financial assets. Higher price levels are associated with higher interest rates, discouraging both investment and purchases of consumer durables. Higher price levels also discourage exports and stimulate imports, reducing the net exports ($EX - IM$) component of aggregate expenditure. The same reasons that explain why the AD curve slopes down from left to right also explain why there will be a different AE curve corresponding to

FIGURE 9
DERIVING AN *AD* CURVE FROM A FAMILY OF *AE* CURVES
(a) Each aggregate expenditure function determines a unique equilibrium level of real income (Y). There is a different AE curve for each possible price level. (b) The price level (P) and the unique equilibrium level of output (Y) corresponding to each AE curve are to trace out an AD curve.

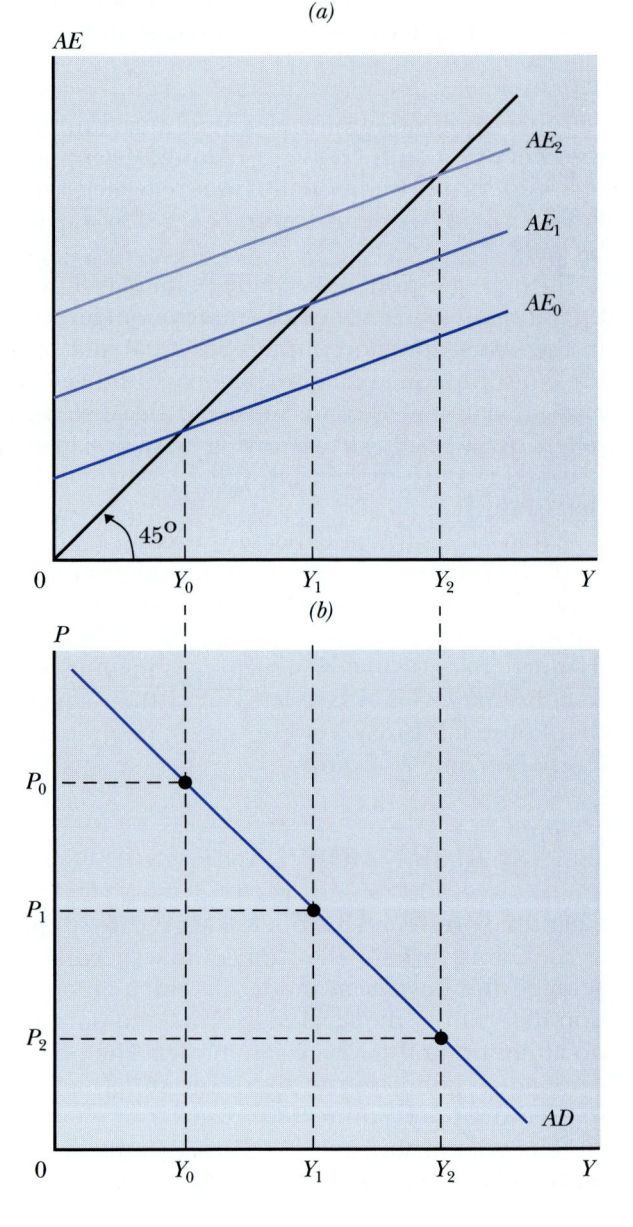

each different price level. Thus, AE_0 is associated with a high price level, P_0; AE_1 with a lower price level P_1; and so forth.

Figure 9(b) derives an AD curve by plotting the various P and Y combinations derived from the set of AE curves in Figure 9(a). For example, along AE_0, price level P_0 is associated with equilibrium real income level Y_0. Remember, the AE curve shows the amount consumers and business firms will plan to spend on consumption and investment at various *income* levels. The AD curve in Figure 9(b) shows the amounts of real output (Y) that will be demanded by households and business firms (and, in a four-sector economy, government and the foreign sector) at various *price* levels.

Both the AE curve and the AD curve represent demand for total output. The AE curve shows the relationship between demand and income. The AD curve shows the relationship between demand and the price level. When we developed individual demand curves in Chapter 3, we defined a demand curve as a price-quantity relationship. The phrase *demand curve* is therefore reserved for those graphs that plot quantity against price. A shift in aggregate expenditure for any reason *other than a change in the price level* will shift the AD curve. An increase in consumer wealth, a change in firms' expectations, a reduction in government spending, a surge in exports, or a shift away from buying imported goods can shift both the AE and AD curves. An upward shift of the AE curve due to any of these events will lead to a rightward shift of the AD curve. A downward shift of AE will shift AD to the left.

Whether you use an aggregate supply and demand model or an aggregate expenditure model, the equilibrium level of national income occurs where total output and planned aggregate expenditure are equal. In the Keynesian model, equilibrium does not mean that the economy will necessarily be at full employment with stable prices. If the economy does reach equilibrium with high unemployed resources (as during the Great Depression) or with rampant inflation (as during the late 1970s), what can be done to alter the situation? The following chapter will discuss the tools government can use to deal with undesirable equilibrium conditions.

Summary

1. In contrast to classical theory, the Keynesian model shows that the macro economy can come to an equilibrium level of national income and output with a high level of unemployed resources.
2. The equilibrium level of national income occurs where output equals aggregate expenditure. In the Keynesian model, the equilibrium levels of national income and aggregate expenditure are interdependent. That is, they are jointly determined.
3. The foundation of aggregate expenditure is the Keynesian consumption function. The consumption function shows how consumption expenditures (C) vary with disposable income (Y_d).
4. The aggregate expenditure function is the sum of four components: consumption expenditures (C), investment expenditures (I), government purchases of goods and services (G), and net exports (EX−IM).
5. The intersection of the AE curve and the 45° line defines the equilibrium level of income. This level does not assure full employment of resources.
6. At nonequilibrium levels of income, differences between aggregate expenditure and income result in un-

planned changes in business inventories. These changes act both as a signal and as an incentive, causing firms to adjust their level of output to the level of spending.

7. Through the multiplier process, any initial change in planned spending will result in a larger change in the equilibrium level of national income.

8. Increases in foreign spending for U.S. exports increase aggregate expenditure and income. Increases in Americans' spending for foreign imports reduce aggregate expenditure and income.

9. The *AE* curve shows the relationship between planned spending and income. The *AD* curve shows the relationship between planned spending and the price level. Shifts in the *AE* curve for any reason except a change in the price level will shift the *AD* curve.

New Terms

aggregate expenditure (*AE*)
consumption function
marginal propensity to consume (*MPC*)
marginal propensity to save (*MPS*)
dissaving
inventories
unplanned inventory changes
expenditure multiplier
paradox of thrift

Questions for Discussion

1. Suppose C_0 is $300 billion and *MPC* is 0.5. Create a table relating *C* and *S* to Y_d for all values of Y_d between 0 and $5,000 billion (by $500 billion intervals).

2. Use the following information to construct a table similar to Table 4:
   - *C* is $200 billion when $Y_d = 0$
   - *MPC* = 0.75
   - *T* = $300 billion
   - *I* = $100 billion
   - *G* = $400 billion
   - *EX* = $50 billion
   - *IM* = $150 billion

3. Use the information in Question 2 to construct a graph of the *AE* curve similar to Figure 8. Indicate the equilibrium level of national income on the graph. What is the dollar value of that equilibrium income?

4. Use the information from Question 2, but change *I* to $200 billion. Determine the new equilibrium income level and the value of the expenditure multiplier.

5. Use each of the following to find the value of the expenditure multiplier:
   a. *MPC* = 0.40
   b. *MPS* = 0.25
   c. *MPC* = 0.67
   d. *MPS* = 0.50
   e. *MPC* = 0.90
   f. *MPC* = 0.75

6. Assume the initial equilibrium level of national income is $4,800 billion and *MPC* = 0.9. What will be the new equilibrium level of *Y* if *I* decreases $100 billion from its initial level?

7. In what direction will each of the following shift the *AE* curve? How will the *AD* curve shift? In what direction will income change?
   a. As a result of U.S. restrictions on foreign goods, there is an exogenous fall in the level of imports (*IM*).
   b. The government launches a new program to improve highways and bridges. That is, government purchases (*G*) increase.
   c. Banks are offering such attractive interest rates that consumers decide to save a larger part of their incomes and spend less.
   d. Business firms decide to change the ratio of inventories to sales from 30 percent to 25 percent. Therefore, there is a planned reduction in inventory investment.

8. Suppose the consumption function is $C = \$300 + 0.85Y$.
   a. What is the value of the multiplier?
   b. What are the values of C_0, *MPC*, and *MPS*?
   c. Determine the level of consumption for Y = $100, $300, $500, $700, $1,000, $1,200, $1,500, $2,000, and $3,000.

9. Discuss what would happen to the consumption function in Question 8 in each of the following situations.
   a. Consumers experience an increase in wealth.
   b. Taxes increase.
   c. Consumers expect prices to rise rapidly in the future.
   d. Interest rates fall.

10. Why did aggregate expenditure and aggregate demand play a more important role in the Keynesian model than in the classical model?

11. In what directions would the *AE* curve and the *AD* curve shift in each of the following cases?
    a. Worried about a recession, business firms reduce their investment spending.
    b. A high birth rate means that families increase their consumption at every level of income to pay for diapers, pediatricians, and day care.
    c. Real income increases.
    d. The government reduces taxes.
12. How is it possible to consume without any income?
13. How do unplanned inventory changes ensure that actual saving and investment are always equal in a two-sector economy, even if planned saving and investment are not?
14. If a rise in the price of the dollar reduced sales of American exports and increased Americans' purchases of imports, what would be the effect on the level of income and output? What about the price level?
15. If a point on the *AE* curve is above the 45° reference line, are unplanned inventory changes positive, negative, or zero? Why?

SUGGESTIONS FOR FURTHER READING

Breit, William, and Roger L. Ransom. *The Academic Scribblers*, 2nd ed. Hinsdale, IL: Dryden Press, 1982. A lively history of some of the great economists discussed in this and earlier chapters, including Marshall and Keynes, as well as Keynes's best-known American disciple, Alvin Hansen.

Dernburg, Thomas. *Macroeconomics: Concepts, Theories, and Policies*, 8th ed. New York: McGraw-Hill, 1989. A somewhat Keynesian intermediate macroeconomics textbook that expands on the Keynesian aggregate expenditure function in a context of aggregate demand and aggregate supply.

Dimand, Robert W. *The Origins of the Keynesian Revolution: The Development of Keynes' Theory of Employment and Output.* Stanford, CA: Stanford University Press, 1988. A recent overview of how Keynes's ideas about output and employment evolved during the 1930s and into the 1940s.

APPENDIX: THE ALGEBRA OF THE KEYNESIAN MODEL

The Keynesian model has been presented in this chapter largely in graphs and numbers. However, the model can be written in algebraic form, providing a formal derivation of the equilibrium level of income and the expenditure multiplier. In this appendix, we derive a series of versions of the Keynesian model, each more complex than the last.

MODEL 1

The simplest Keynesian model is the two-sector model in which there is no distinction between disposable and national income because there is no government. Thus,

$$Y = C + I,$$

where

$$C = C_0 + bY,$$

and

$$I = I_0.$$

So we have

$$Y = C_0 + bY + I_0$$

or

$$Y - bY = C_0 + I_0.$$

Solving for the equilibrium level of Y, we get

$$(1) \quad Y_e = \left(\frac{1}{1-b}\right)(C_0 + I_0).$$

This relationship shows both the equilibrium level of income and the expression for the multiplier.

MODEL 2

The second model adds a government sector, with three activities: government purchases (G), taxes (T), and transfer payments (R). All of these activities are autonomous. With these additions, the model becomes

$$Y = C_0 + b(Y - T_0 + R_0) + I_0 + G_0,$$

or

$$Y - bY = C_0 - bT_0 + bR + I_0 + G_0.$$

Solving for the equilibrium value of Y gives the same multiplier as with the first model. There are now more variables in the expression being multiplied that can shift aggregate expenditures:

$$(2) \quad Y_e = \left(\frac{1}{1-b}\right)(C_0 - bT_0 + bR_0 + I_0 + G_0).$$

The basic multiplier is unchanged, but there are more sources of shifts in the aggregate expenditure function. Note that the impact, dollar for dollar, of a given change in T or R is less than the impact of an equal change in C_0, I, or G because taxes and transfer payments work through the consumption function. This smaller impact is indicated by the fact that T_0 and R_0 are multiplied by the marginal propensity to consume, b, which always has a value of less than 1.

MODEL 3

The third model makes T and R dependent on the level of income, because taxes rise and transfers fall as income rises. That is,

$$T = T_0 + tY$$

and

$$R = R_0 - rY.$$

In these equations, t is called the marginal tax rate and r is called the marginal transfer rate, or the change in transfers per additional dollar of income. We have

$$(3) \quad Y = C_0 + b(Y - T_0 - tY + R_0 - rY) + I_0 + G_0,$$

or

$$Y - bY + btY + brY = C_0 - bT_0 + bR_0 + I_0 + G_0.$$

The solution to the model is given by

$$Y_e = \left(\frac{1}{1 - b + bt - br}\right)(C_0 - T_0 + bR_0 + I_0 + G_0).$$

The multiplier is more complex in this model. If t is greater than r, the multiplier is smaller than in the second model. If t is less than r, the multiplier is larger. This model is applied in the next two chapters to describe the effects of fiscal policy by changing the tax rate.

MODEL 4

The fourth model allows investment expenditures to be at least partly responsive to the level of final demand, rather than being totally autonomous. This change makes investment expenditures, like taxes and transfer payments, a function of the level of income and output. This model uses an investment demand function of the form

$$I = I_0 + aY,$$

where a is defined as the marginal propensity to invest. Incorporating this expression in equation (3) gives

$$Y = C_0 + b(Y - T_0 - tY + R_0 - rY) + I_0 + aY + G_0,$$

or

$$Y - bY + btY + brY - aY = C_0 - bT_0 + bR_0 + I_0 + G_0.$$

Again, solving for the equilibrium value of Y gives the equilibrium condition:

$$(4) \quad Y_e = \left(\frac{1}{1 - b + bt + br - a}\right)(C_0 - bT_0 + bR_0 + I_0 + G_0).$$

The multiplier in this model is larger than the one in the third model because of additional induced investment spending.

Model 5

The last model adds a foreign sector. Exports (EX_0) are independent of the level of income, but imports are not. The import demand function takes the form

$$IM = IM_0 + mY,$$

where m is the marginal propensity to import. This change gives the final form of the model:

$$Y = C_0 + b(Y - T_0 - tY + R_0 - rY) + I_0 + aY + G_0 + EX_0 - IM_0 - mY,$$

or

$$Y - bY + btY + brY - aY + mY = C_0 - bT_0 + bR_0 + I_0 + G_0 + EX_0 - IM_0.$$

The equilibrium condition is

$$(5) \quad Y_e = \left(\frac{1}{1 - b + bt + br - a + m}\right)(C_0 - bT_0 + bR_0 + I_0 + G_0 + EX_0 - IM_0).$$

This multiplier is smaller than the one in the fourth model because of the additional leakage of funds into spending on imports in every additional round of spending.

Equation (5) is a fairly complete form of the basic Keynesian model. The multiplier reflects induced changes in consumption, taxes, transfers, investment, and imports. The aggregate expenditure function can be shifted by autonomous changes in consumption (C_0), taxes (T_0), transfer payments (R_0), investment spending (I_0), government spending (G_0), exports (EX_0), or the autonomous component of export demand (IM_0).

This model can be used as a basis for a microcomputer simulation of economic activity. There are much larger and more complex models that include interest rates, prices, the money supply, and other variables to forecast output and employment. However, you can get an idea of how these variables are interrelated by putting this model on a microcomputer with some initial values for each variable. You can then change one variable and see how the others respond.

AFTER STUDYING THIS CHAPTER, YOU SHOULD BE ABLE TO:

1. Explain the Keynesian argument that active fiscal policy is the only way to assure full employment with stable prices.
2. Distinguish between automatic stabilizers and discretionary fiscal policy, and give examples of each.
3. Define:
   a. fiscal policy,
   b. recessionary gap,
   c. permanent income hypothesis.
4. Describe the use of an appropriate fiscal policy to offset the effects of changes in spending by consumers, businesses, or the foreign sector.
5. Briefly describe these experiences with discretionary fiscal policy in the United States:
   a. the Kennedy tax cut,
   b. the Ford tax rebate,
   c. the Reagan tax cut.
6. Critically analyze the arguments for and against active fiscal policy.

CHAPTER 9

FISCAL POLICY

INTRODUCTION

This chapter discusses the theory and practice of fiscal policy, based on the model in Chapter 8. **Fiscal policy** consists of changes in government expenditures (G) or taxes (T) in order to influence the level of economic activity, inflation, and economic growth. Fiscal policy is not simply any changes in government spending or taxes. Government spending and taxes existed long before the development of Keynesian economic theory. Fiscal policy is *intentional* use of taxing or government spending to affect the level of output, employment, and prices.

Some economists, especially monetarists and new classical economists, consider fiscal policy to have limited benefit and, in some cases, to even be harmful to the economy. Other economists, especially Keynesians, regard active fiscal policy as a valuable tool of the central government. In order to evaluate both sides of this argument, we must look closely at exactly how fiscal policy works in theory and practice.

fiscal policy
Changes in government spending and taxes to influence the level of economic activity, inflation, and economic growth.

WHY FISCAL POLICY?

Both classical and Keynesian economists agree that the economy automatically moves to a level of national income where total output equals aggregate expenditure (or where leakages equal injections). In the Keynesian model, however, such an equilibrium level may not be associated with full employment of resources.

Keynes believed that the equilibrium levels of output reached by major capitalistic economies such as the United States and Great Britain during the 1930s were not acceptable. Levels of unemployment were too high. He argued that governments should respond to such conditions with fiscal policy. That is, government should act so as to increase aggregate expenditure (AE) enough to ensure a socially desirable equilibrium level of income and output.

Aggregate expenditure consists of four components: consumption demand, planned investment spending, government purchases of goods and services, and net exports. An increase in any of these four components can stimulate output and employment. Keynesians, however, do not think it is realistic to expect private demand (consumption and investment) alone to solve the problem of recession combined with high unemployment.

Households and businesses are motivated more by self-interest than by social interest. Individual persons or firms cannot be expected to act in the interest of society as a whole if so acting would conflict with their perceived self-interest. In a recession, social interest calls for households to increase consumption spending and business firms to increase investment spending in the face of stagnant demand for their products. In fact, for individual households or business firms to "swim against the tide," expanding production or consumption while others are contracting, would be futile.

The self-interested behavior of the private sector (households and business firms) usually makes economic fluctuations worse instead of improving conditions. During the Great Depression, for instance, households became more frugal. Also, business firms reduced investment spending because of their uncertainty and pessimistic expectations about future income, employment, and sales. During expansionary periods, expectations of job security, pay raises, and increasing sales and profits are likely to stimulate more private spending, pushing the economy further beyond full-employment equilibrium.

Planned investment (I) is sensitive to changes in profit expectations, input costs, and interest rates. Changes in these influences will shift the investment component of aggregate expenditure. In the Keynesian model, investment is the most volatile component of total spending. It is also the one least sensitive to any direct influence by government policy.

The foreign sector also offers little hope for an automatic cure for prolonged downturns. Export demand (EX) is affected by changes in the price level in the United States relative to those in other countries, exchange rates, economic conditions in foreign countries, trade restrictions, and sometimes even the weather. Imports (IM) are affected by changes in the price level domestically and abroad, exchange rates, trade restrictions, consumer tastes, and the domestic income level. A higher level of income stimulates all kinds of private spending, including spending on imported goods.[1] Net exports ($EX-IM$) are a somewhat volatile but fairly small component of aggregate expenditure.

There are policy tools that government can use to bring about an increase in net exports. Such an increase would shift the AD curve to the right. The government can try to put downward pressure on the price of its currency. Or it can use tariffs and quotas to reduce imports of foreign goods and services. Such solutions were popular in the early years of the Great Depression. They have surfaced as proposed emergency measures in almost every downturn before or since that time. Since these actions

---

1. In Chapter 8, to keep the model simple, imports were treated as autonomous, or independent of the level of income. In a more realistic model, imports depend on the level of income or output.

are taken at the expense of a nation's trading partners, they are referred to as beggar-thy-neighbor policies. One country may increase its level of employment by limiting imports, which will add jobs in producing substitutes. However, the problem is then passed on to the trading partner, who sees a fall in exports and thus in employment. Even if a country were to ignore the negative effects of such policies on its trading partners, their positive effect on the domestic economy would be short-lived. Other countries are likely to retaliate quickly with similar policies. Since policies that can be used directly to affect net exports are rather unappealing and the foreign sector is small, such policies are rarely considered as a potential fiscal policy tool.[2]

Self-interest leads to consumption and investment decisions that aggravate rather than dampen economic ups and downs. Since there is little prospect for help from the foreign sector, Keynesians see government spending as the only hope for stabilization. They argue that only the government can be expected to act in the social interest by using its taxing and spending powers to offset changes in private demand. Keynesian economics also provides an explanation of how income levels can be changed by government intervention. Critics have attacked Keynesians' positive view of the government and their theoretical model. We need to clarify the Keynesian view of fiscal policy before we can critique it.

HOW FISCAL POLICY WORKS

Recall how an economy reaches an equilibrium other than at full employment. Chapter 8 identified changes that could shift saving and consumption, such as changes in wealth, taxes, inflationary expectations, or interest rates. A downward shift in the consumption function due to one of these changes can lead to a fall in output, income, and employment. An upward shift in the consumption function can lead to a rise in output, income, and employment. The effect of tax changes on consumption (C) and the aggregate expenditure (AE) curve is particularly important because tax changes are one of the tools of fiscal policy. Fiscal policy in the form of tax changes can work through the consumption function to affect the level of output, employment, and prices.

Policy makers face an aggregate expenditure function that is very unstable. As consumption spending (C), investment (I), or net exports ($EX-IM$) fluctuate, aggregate expenditure changes. Through the multiplier process, the resulting changes in income, output, and employment are larger than the initial change in C, I, or ($EX-IM$). Shifts in the AE curve are translated into shifts in the AD curve, as you saw at the end of Chapter 8. Shifts in aggregate demand lead to changes in the price level as well as in real output and employment. We will work mostly with the aggregate supply and demand model in this chapter. You should keep in

---

2. The role of the foreign sector in macroeconomic policy is complex. With foreign sales and purchases forming an increased share of U.S. economic activity in recent years, policy makers have become more aware of the effects of domestic policies on exports, imports, and exchange rates, and vice versa. International trade and exchange rates between currencies have a direct relationship with the level of output, prices, and interest rates in the domestic economy.

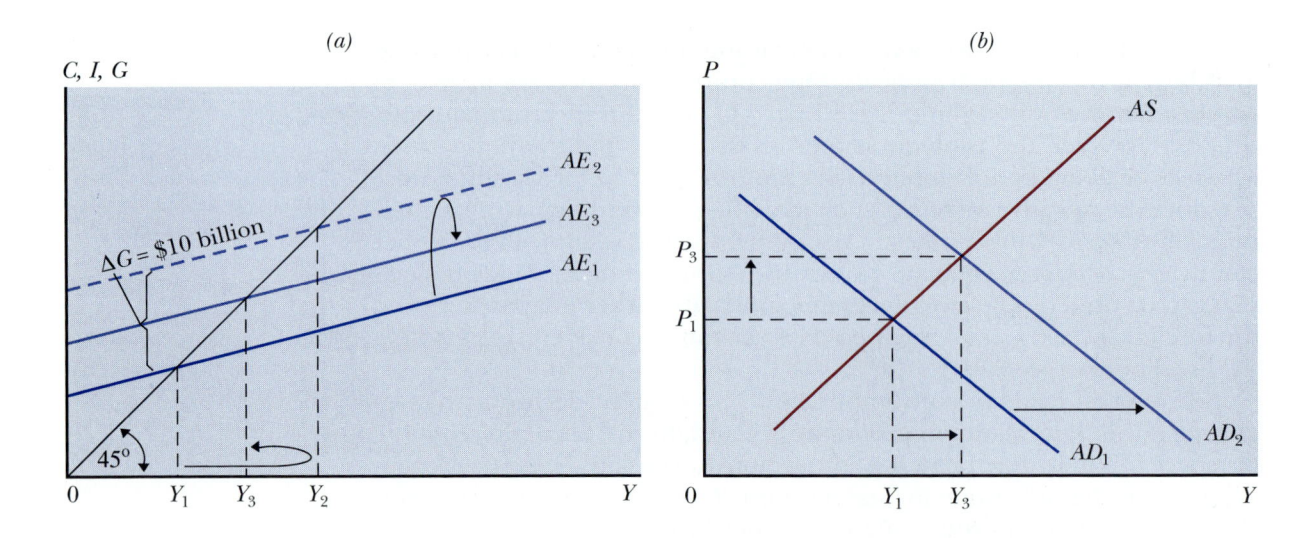

FIGURE 1
AGGREGATE EXPENDITURE, AGGREGATE DEMAND, AND FISCAL POLICY
(a) An increase in aggregate expenditure from AE_1 to AE_2 because of increased government spending will raise equilibrium output from Y_1 to Y_2 if there is no change in the price level.
(b) The shift in AE also shifts the AD curve from AD_1 to AD_2, increasing Y by a smaller amount (from Y_1 to Y_3) and also increasing the price level (from P_1 to P_3). At the higher price level, the economy's AE curve will be AE_3 in part (a), with an equilibrium output level of Y_3.

mind, however, that changes in government spending and taxes shift the AE curve and that shift in turn shifts the AD curve.

Figure 1 shows how an increase in government spending works in both models. In part (a), an increase in government spending (G) by an amount of $10 billion shifts the AE curve from AE_1 to AE_2, increasing the equilibrium level of output from Y_1 to Y_2. In part (b) of the figure, the same increase in government spending shifts the AD curve to the right by a horizontal distance corresponding to $10 billion. With an upward-sloping supply curve (AS), the impact of the added spending is divided between a change in output (from Y_1 to Y_3) and a change in the price level (from P_1 to P_3). Each AE curve is associated with a given price level. Thus, when the price level rises, aggregate expenditure will be lower. As higher prices feed back into the aggregate expenditure function, the economy finds itself on a lower AE curve (AE_3) in part (a), corresponding to a higher price level. The final level of output in both diagrams is Y_3.

Although some forms of fiscal policy may also shift the aggregate supply curve, fiscal policy is mainly directed at aggregate demand. Fiscal policy is designed to shift aggregate expenditure and aggregate demand in the direction that will move the economy toward the desired level of output, employment, and prices. The higher demand must be sustained until conditions change. If government spending (G) increases only temporarily or taxes (T) are reduced temporarily, then when they return to their original level, the AE and AD curves will return to their original positions. Real output and income will also fall back to the original level.

Keynesian economists do not advocate government intervention to offset every shift in aggregate expenditure. They argue that fiscal policy should be used only to offset spending shifts that have substantial and prolonged effects on output, employment, and prices. In reality, specific fiscal policy actions have not been undertaken very often during the last fifty years.

THE GOAL: FULL EMPLOYMENT WITH STABLE PRICES
In order for government to use fiscal policy wisely, policy makers must identify a target level of national income. If this target level is far from the

current equilibrium level, then the government should adjust taxes or spending in the right direction. The usual goal is an equilibrium level of national income that generates full employment with price stability. This level is represented by the symbol Y^*.[3]

In the Keynesian model developed in Chapter 8, the aggregate expenditure function was derived by summing components of planned spending—C, I, G, and $(EX - IM)$—at each level of national income. Consumption expenditures were represented by the equation $C = \$200$ billion $+ 0.8Y_d$. In this consumption function, the marginal propensity to consume (MPC) is 0.8, giving a value of 5 for the expenditure multiplier. The economy in Figure 2 is initially at full employment with stable prices when national income is \$3,500 billion ($Y^* = \$3,500$ billion). Above \$3,500 billion lie inflationary pressures. Below \$3,500 billion lies unemployment. The equilibrium level of output, which in this case is equal to Y^*, is found at the intersection of AE_2 and the 45° line.

The purpose of Keynesian fiscal policy is to assure that the level of spending in the economy is AE_2 (the level that results in Y^*) and not some other level, such as AE_1 or AE_3. If the level of aggregate expenditure is lower than AE_2, unemployment will result. If aggregate expenditure and aggregate demand are above the levels required to bring the economy to full employment, there will be a shortage of workers. Then competition for workers and other scarce resources will result in inflationary pressures.[4]

THE RECESSIONARY GAP

The difference between aggregate expenditure and the full-employment level of output is called the **recessionary gap**. A recessionary gap exists when the equilibrium level of national income is *less* than the desired level Y^*. In Figure 2, a level of planned spending along AE_1 results in a recessionary gap because the resulting equilibrium level of income is only \$3,250 billion. The recessionary gap (measured at Y^*) is equal to the vertical distance between AE_1 and AE_2. This gap, distance DE, measures how much aggregate expenditure must rise in order to bring national income up to the desired level. A recessionary gap exists when buyers are unwilling to purchase as much output as the economy would supply at the full-employment level of output (Y^*). If firms attempt to produce at the full-employment level of output, they will see unplanned increases in inventories and respond with cutbacks in production. Thus, the economy in Figure 2 is in equilibrium at Y_1.

A recessionary gap such as DE calls for expansionary fiscal policy. **Expansionary fiscal policy** consists of cutting taxes, raising transfer payments, or increasing government purchases to try to increase the level of output and employment. For the economy in Figure 2, expansionary

recessionary gap
The difference between aggregate expenditure and the full-employment level of output.

expansionary fiscal policy
Cutting taxes, raising transfer payments, or increasing government purchases to try to increase the level of income and employment.

---

3. In reality, Y^* is a range of values for Y, not a single number.
4. The Keynesian model is less useful when there is inflation because it is based on idle resources, price stability, and a horizontal AS curve. We will use this model mainly to analyze the effects of expansionary fiscal policy during recessions. Fiscal policy can also be used to reduce the level of output. It is not possible to use the Keynesian model to visualize its effects because of the absence of a variable price level. Thus, we will discuss contractionary fiscal policy only in the broader framework of an aggregate supply and demand model.

FIGURE 2
THE RECESSIONARY GAP
The full-employment level of national income, Y^*, is achieved when aggregate expenditure is AE_1. If aggregate expenditure is AE_2, the recessionary gap is DE.

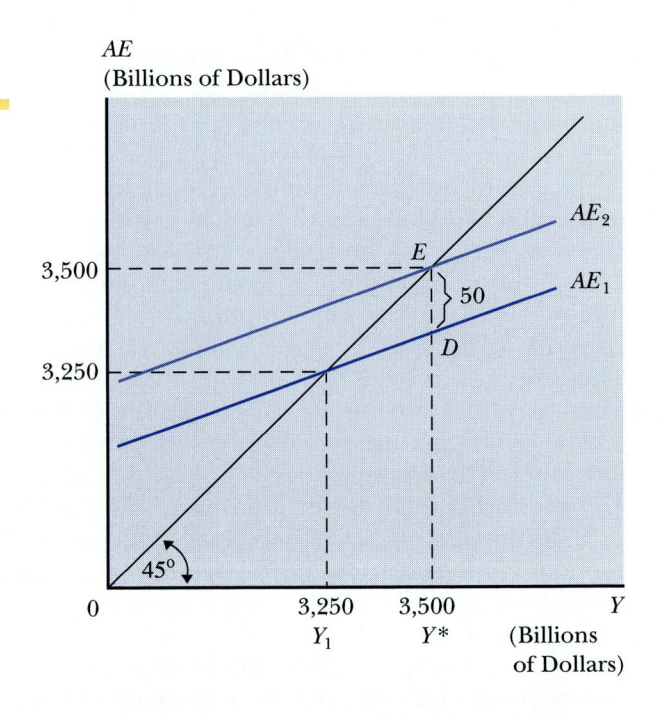

fiscal policy needs to shift the AE curve upward by $50 billion. This shift increases equilibrium income from Y_1 to Y^*, a gain of $250 billion.

How did the economy get a $250 billion increase in equilibrium income from only a $50 billion upward shift in aggregate expenditure? The difference is a result of the multiplier effect discussed in Chapter 8. A $50 billion upward shift in the aggregate expenditure function increases output, income, and consumption through the marginal propensity to consume (MPC). With $MPC = 0.8$, the final change in real output (Y) is equal to the multiplier of 5 times the upward shift in planned spending (AE) of $50 billion. If there is any effect on prices (in the aggregate supply and demand diagram), then the change in real output will be smaller.

CHANGING NATIONAL INCOME USING FISCAL POLICY

The policy challenge is to close a recessionary gap by creating an increase in aggregate expenditure. In Figure 2, an increase in national income of $250 billion (from Y_2 to Y^*) requires an upward shift in aggregate expenditure of $50 billion. To increase spending by $50 billion at each level of national income (to shift from AE_1 to AE_2), government expenditures must increase by $50 billion. Through the multiplier process, a $50 billion change in aggregate expenditure causes national income to change by $250 billion.

Another fiscal policy tool that can be used to shift aggregate expenditure and aggregate demand is a change in taxes (T). Changes in personal taxes affect disposable income. Since consumption spending changes in the same direction as disposable income, the government can use taxes to influence consumption and, therefore, national income. A reduction in taxes will shift the AE curve upward and the AD curve to the right. An increase in taxes will lower the AE curve and shift the AD curve to the left.

International Perspective

Fiscal Policy in the Open Economy

An important limit to the effectiveness of fiscal policy is that much of the intended impact spills over to other nations. When Nation A increases its output level, its citizens demand more imports. Imports are a leakage. Every extra dollar spent on imports instead of domestic goods reduces the multiplier effects of expansionary fiscal policy. For a nation like the United States, in which imports are not a major component of GNP (about 13 percent in 1990), this weakened impact of fiscal policy is not a major problem. But in smaller countries, such as Guyana, Chad, Luxembourg, or Belgium, trade is a large fraction of total spending. In these countries, most of the impact of a fiscal policy may spill abroad, with little effect on the domestic economy.

For the same reason, there is no point in one of the states in the United States trying to pursue an expansionary fiscal policy. (The large and isolated state of Alaska did consider this option to address its local recession in the late 1980s.) If Minnesota runs a budget deficit to try to increase the state's output and employment, a large share of the impact will be felt in Wisconsin, North Dakota, and even as far away as New York and California—all places that supply a substantial amount of Minnesota's "imports."

When expansionary fiscal policy shifts aggregate demand to the right, driving up the price level as well as real output, a second problem emerges in an open economy. At higher prices, a nation's citizens want to buy more cheap foreign goods. At the same time, foreigners are less interested in the nation's high-priced exports. The value of net exports ($EX-IM$) falls. There are fewer injections (EX) and more leakages (IM). A higher price level does even more than a higher level of income to offset the initial expansionary effect of fiscal policy. Prices affect both exports and imports, but rising real income only affects imports.

The same problem plagues contractionary fiscal policy. Falling income will reduce imports, so contractionary fiscal policy is partly offset by reduced leakages. A falling price level will stimulate exports and reduce imports. Again, the effect is to offset some of the contractionary impact of fiscal policy.

Fiscal policy is a powerful tool for affecting output and employment. Some of its effects, however, may spill over to other nations, raising or lowering their incomes and outputs instead of affecting the domestic economy. It is difficult for any nation, especially a small one, to confine the impact of fiscal policy within its borders.

A cut in personal taxes works to close a recessionary gap such as *DE* by increasing consumption, which shifts the *AE* curve upward. How much must taxes be cut to shift *AE* upward by $50 billion in Figure 2? Since the marginal propensity to consume (*MPC*) is 0.8, consumption (*C*) will increase by 80 cents for every dollar increase in disposable income (Y_d) as a result of the tax cut. The change in *C* is equal to the change in Y_d multiplied by *MPC*. In this case, we know the required change in *C* ($50 billion) and the size of the *MPC* (0.8), so we can find the required change in taxes. Taxes must be cut by $62.5 billion at each level of national income in order to change consumption by $50 billion. Once taxes have been cut and the consumption and aggregate expenditure functions have shifted upward, the multiplier process will go to work. Income (*Y*) increases by $250 billion (the multiplier of 5 times the shift in aggregate expenditure of $50 billion). It takes a $62.5 billion decrease in taxes to accomplish the same change in national income as a $50 billion increase in government spending.[5]

Fiscal Policy and the Multiplier

Why is the multiplier for a tax change smaller than the multiplier for a change in government spending? Think about how taxes and government spending enter the income stream. Every dollar of additional government spending immediately contributes another dollar to aggregate expenditure. On the other hand, every dollar not taken by personal taxes is split between saving and consumption. If, for example, the marginal propensity to consume is 0.8, then every $1 reduction in personal taxes contributes 80¢ to increased aggregate expenditure (through an increase in consumption spending) and 20¢ to increased saving. The tax change multiplier is smaller than the government spending multiplier because a portion of a tax decrease leaks immediately out of the spending stream and into saving.

Ignoring the foreign sector for the moment, recall from Chapter 8 that the equilibrium level of national income is given by

$$AE = Y_e = C_0 + b(Y - T) + I + G,$$

where *b* is the marginal propensity to consume (*MPC*) and disposable income (Y_d) is equal to *Y* – *T*. We can rearrange this expression:

$$Y_e = \frac{1}{1-b}(C_0 - bT + I + G).$$

When we arrange this expression this way, we have separated equilibrium income into two components. The first term, $1/(1-b)$, is the multiplier from Chapter 8. The second term, in parentheses, contains all the factors that can shift aggregate expenditure: C_0, *T*, *I*, and *G*.

Note that the investment, government spending, and constant consumption values are all multiplied by the multiplier, but the tax term is also multiplied by –*b*. This difference between the tax term and the oth-

---

5. In this model, we assume that the change in taxes is not accompanied by any change in spending as a result of reduced revenue. If a fall in taxes is accompanied by a fall in government spending, the two will tend to offset each other. There will be only a very small impact on output and employment.

ers reflects two important facts. First, changes in taxes work in the opposite direction from changes in all of the other terms. An increase in taxes reduces aggregate expenditure, and a reduction in taxes increases aggregate expenditure. Changes in all of the other terms move aggregate expenditure in the same direction. Second, because b is always less than 1, the effect on output and employment of a given change in taxes will be smaller than that of a change of equal amount in any of the others. We can express this difference by writing two multipliers:

$$\text{Consumption } (C_0) \text{ Multiplier,}$$
$$\text{Government Expenditure } (G) \text{ Multiplier,} = \frac{1}{1-b}$$
$$\text{and Investment } (I) \text{ Multiplier}$$

and

$$\text{Tax Change Multiplier} = -b\left(\frac{1}{1-b}\right) = -\frac{b}{1-b}.$$

For our example, with $MPC = b = 0.8$, the government expenditure multiplier has a value of 5 and the tax change multiplier has a value of -4.

THE BALANCED BUDGET MULTIPLIER

These different multipliers bring up an interesting possibility. Suppose the government wanted to pursue an expansionary policy but did not want to unbalance the budget or increase an existing deficit. Since a given dollar amount of change in government spending has a greater impact than the same amount of change in taxes, it is possible to have equal changes in both and still have some positive effect on the equilibrium level of income. Suppose the government increases both spending and taxes by an equal dollar amount, say $20 billion, leaving the budget deficit or surplus unchanged. The increase in the level of income (Y) resulting from the change in spending (G) is the expenditure multiplier, $1/(1-b)$, times the change in G. If b is equal to 0.8, as before, then Y will increase by 5 times $20 billion, or $100 billion. Calculating the effect of the tax change is a little more complex. The $20 billion increase in taxes (T) is multiplied by the tax multiplier of -4, which is equal to $-b/(1-b)$. So the reduction in Y resulting from the tax increase is $-$80 billion.

Thus, the net change in Y from these two offsetting actions is $20 billion—exactly the same as the equal-sized changes in G and T. Is this a coincidence? No. If we add the two multipliers, $+5$ and -4, we get 1. Adding the algebraic expressions for the two multipliers also gives 1:

$$\frac{1}{1-b} + \frac{-b}{1-b} = \frac{1-b}{1-b} = 1.$$

The value of the balanced budget multiplier is always 1. An equal increase in government spending and taxes will have some modest impact on output and employment. This effect, however, will be much less than the impact of a change in only one of these two with the other held constant.[6]

---

6. If tax collections depend on the level of income, which they normally do, the balanced budget multiplier is much more complicated to demonstrate.

THE TOOLS OF FISCAL POLICY: GOVERNMENT SPENDING AND TAXES

The tools of fiscal policy are government spending and taxes (and transfer payments, which can be treated as negative taxes). In general, conservative Keynesians prefer tax changes, leaving the size of government production and purchases constant. Liberal Keynesians are more likely to favor changes in government spending. Before we can examine fiscal policy more carefully, however, we need to examine its tools. That is, we need to consider the spending and income of governments, especially the federal government.

In the United States in the last few decades, a large share of the nation's income has been claimed by government, and a substantial share of output has been produced by or for government. Government spending has been growing faster than the economy as a whole. Between 1949 and 1990, the federal government's expenditures rose from 15 percent of national income to 23 percent. State and local governments' expenditures rose from 8 percent of national income to 14 percent. Because government plays such a major role in the economy, changes in its taxing and spending levels can be a very effective tool for influencing the level of income and output.

GOVERNMENT PURCHASES AND TRANSFER PAYMENTS

Total government expenditures—federal, state, and local—account for about one-third of national income in the United States. The federal government alone spent $1,252 billion in 1990. State and local governments added another $765 billion. Some of these funds were spent to produce or to purchase goods and services, such as defense, health care, highways, police, education, and courts.

Table 1 summarizes the major types of spending by all three levels of government. About two-thirds of government spending is for purchases of goods and services. The rest is for transfer payments to individuals who provide no goods or services in exchange. These payments include veterans' benefits, welfare payments, unemployment compensation, and Social Security benefits. Most transfer payments originate at the federal

**TABLE 1
HOW GOVERNMENTS SPEND THEIR INCOMES**

FEDERAL (1990*)		STATE AND LOCAL (1989*)	
Defense	23.9%	Education	29.6%
Social Security	19.9	Public welfare	10.7
Interest payments	14.7	Highways	6.5
Transfers to state		Police	3.1
and local governments	10.4	Health, hospitals	2.3
All other	31.4	All other	47.8
Total	100.0%	Total	100.0%

*Data are for fiscal years.

Sources: Advisory Commission on Intergovernmental Relations, *Significant Features of Fiscal Federalism* (Washington, DC: U.S. Government Printing Office, 1990), and Council of Economic Advisers, *Economic Report of the President* (Washington, DC: U.S. Government Printing Office, 1991).

TABLE 2
REVENUE SOURCES FOR GOVERNMENTS, FISCAL YEARS

FEDERAL (1990)		STATE (1989)		LOCAL (1989)	
Income taxes	47.3%	Income taxes	19.2%	Property taxes	25.8%
Social insurance taxes	35.1	Sales taxes	15.9	Income taxes	3.6
Other*	4.8	Other*	46.5	Sales taxes	2.1
Borrowing	12.6	Federal grants	18.4	Other*	35.6
				State and federal grants	32.9
Total	100.0%	Total	100.0%	Total	100.0%

*Includes estate taxes, excise taxes, user fees, revenues from government enterprises, and miscellaneous sources.

Source: Advisory Commission on Intergovernmental Relations, *Significant Features of Fiscal Federalism* (Washington, DC: U.S. Government Printing Office, 1990), and Council of Economic Advisers, *Economic Report of the President* (Washington, DC: U.S. Government Printing Office, 1991).

level, although some are administered by state and local governments. Defense and Social Security are the two biggest expenditures for the federal government. Education is the largest item in state and local budgets. Interest on the national debt takes a growing share of the federal budget because of continuing large budget deficits.

PAYING FOR GOVERNMENT

Table 2 lists revenue sources for all three levels of government.[7] Taxes are the major income source for governments. Major federal taxes are income taxes and social insurance taxes (Social Security taxes, workers' compensation taxes, and unemployment insurance taxes). The main revenue sources at the state and local levels are sales taxes and property taxes, respectively. Another revenue source for state and local governments is federal grants-in-aid. State and federal grants combined provide 38 percent of local government revenues. Sometimes the federal government uses these grants as fiscal policy tools to stimulate spending by state and local governments.

IMPLEMENTING FISCAL POLICY: AUTOMATIC STABILIZERS

In practice, there are two kinds of fiscal policy. One kind is put into place and left to respond automatically to changes in the level of economic activity. The second kind, used less frequently, is deliberate action to change tax laws or enact new spending programs so as to influence the level of output, employment, and prices.

---

7. Table 2 suggests an implicit division of revenue sources among federal, state, and local governments. Certain revenue sources, such as income tax, may be suited to being collected by the federal government because there are some cost advantages to national collection or because a particular tax is easier to avoid at the local level than at the federal level. Since the benefits of most local government services are linked to the use of property (fire and police protection, street lights, sewer systems, and so forth), there is some logic to using the property tax at that level. Also, it is more difficult to avoid property taxes than other kinds of local taxes. Thus, it is easier for local governments to rely on that revenue source. State governments are responsible for education and highways and rely heavily on sales and income taxes for revenue. This division of revenue sources and responsibilities among the three levels of government is referred to as fiscal federalism.

automatic stabilizers
Changes in tax collections and transfer payments that are automatically triggered by changes in national income and tend to reduce changes in output and employment.

Congressional legislation over the years, much of it enacted during the Great Depression, has created a system of tax collections and transfer payments that change automatically in response to changes in national income. These **automatic stabilizers** partially offset changes in private spending and tend to reduce changes in output and employment. They include changes in income tax collections, agricultural support payments, Social Security and welfare benefits, and unemployment compensation claims. Automatic stabilizers do not require further action by Congress. They are built into the economy.

PROGRESSIVE INCOME TAXES

In the simple Keynesian model of Chapter 8, taxes (T) were independent of level of income.[8] If you have ever filled out Form 1040 to pay income taxes to the Internal Revenue Service, you know that as your income goes up, your taxes go up even faster. The federal income tax is progressive, as are some state income taxes.

An income tax, or any tax, can be regressive, proportional, or progressive. Table 3 shows examples of how each type of tax affects three income earners. A **regressive tax** is a tax that takes a smaller share (percentage) of income as income rises. In the second column of Table 3, Jones pays a higher share of his income (5 percent) than does Brown (1 percent).

regressive tax
A tax that takes a smaller share (percentage) of income as income rises.

Sales taxes on food are somewhat regressive because the proportion of an individual's budget spent on food declines as income rises. Note that a tax can be regressive even if the tax does not decline in absolute dollars as income rises. In Table 3, Brown paid $5,000, and Jones paid only $500. For Brown, however, the tax represented a smaller percentage of income. Many people object to regressive taxes because of the burden they place on low-income families.

A **proportional tax** takes the same share (percentage) of income from all taxpayers. The proportional tax of 5 percent in Table 3 takes the same share of income from each person. However, the dollar amount increases as income increases.

proportional tax
A tax that takes the same share (percentage) of income from all taxpayers.

A **progressive tax** takes a larger share (percentage) of income as income rises. In Table 3, the progressive tax takes not only more dollars from Brown than from Smith or Jones, but a higher share of Brown's income. The federal personal income tax in the United States is a moderately progressive tax, with rates ranging from 15 percent to 31 percent. The range of rates was reduced by the 1986 tax reform and again in 1990, but the tax is still progressive. That is, your federal taxes will go up more than in proportion to your income as your income rises.

progressive tax
A tax that takes a larger share (percentage) of income as income rises.

TABLE 3
COMPARISON OF AMOUNTS PAID UNDER THREE TYPES OF TAXES

	INCOME	REGRESSIVE TAX	PROPORTIONAL TAX	PROGRESSIVE TAX
Jones	$ 10,000	$ 500 = 5%	$ 500 = 5%	$ 500 = 5%
Smith	$ 80,000	$1,600 = 2%	$ 4,000 = 5%	$ 20,000 = 25%
Brown	$500,000	$5,000 = 1%	$25,000 = 5%	$250,000 = 50%

8. You may wish to review the discussion of endogenous and exogenous variables in the appendix to Chapter 1. In Keynesian models, taxes can be either endogenous or exogenous.

If taxes rise or fall more than in proportion to changes in national income and output, then consumption (which depends on after-tax, or disposable, income) will rise or fall *less* than in proportion to changes in national income and output. Suppose, for example, that at an income level (Y) of $3,000 billion, taxes are $300 billion, or 10 percent. Disposable income (Y_d) is then $2,700 billion. Substituting $2,700 billion for Y_d in the equation for the consumption function gives

C = $200 billion + 0.8$Y_d$ = $200 billion + 0.8($2,700 billion)
= $2,360 billion.

The consumption component of aggregate expenditure is $2,360 billion.

What happens if Y increases by $1,000 billion, so the equilibrium level of income is $4,000 billion instead of $3,000 billion? With a marginal propensity to consume of 0.8, you might expect consumption to rise by 80 percent of the income increase of $1,000 billion, or $800 billion. However, consumption will increase by less than $800 billion even if the tax system is not progressive. If taxes take 10 percent of income, a rise in Y of $1,000 billion will raise Y_d by $900 billion. Consumption will increase by 0.8 times $900 billion, or $720 billion. If the tax system is progressive, taxes may increase from 10 percent ($300 billion) at the old level of income to 12 percent ($480 billion) of the new income. In this case, national income rises by $1,000 billion, but disposable income will rise by only $820 billion, from $2,700 billion to $3,520 billion. Substituting this value of Y_d in the consumption function, we find that consumption (C) is now $3,016 billion. This increase of $656 billion, or 28 percent, in C is less than the 33 percent increase in Y. Thus, when income rises, progressive taxes rise more than in proportion to the increase in income. The effect is to dampen consumer demand.

With progressive income taxes, a fall in national income will lead to a more-than-proportional fall in taxes. The disposable income of households will be a larger fraction of total income and output when income falls. Thus, the fall in consumption will be less than proportional to the decline in output and income. Since consumption spending is more stable than the level of output and income, progressive income taxes reduce ups and downs not only in the household standard of living but also in aggregate planned spending during good times and bad.

The mildly progressive corporate income tax is also an automatic stabilizer. Although this tax became less progressive after 1986, revenues from it still increase sharply during economic expansions and fall sharply during contractions. The corporate income subject to this tax consists of profits. Profits are highly sensitive to changes in the level of economic activity.

TRANSFER PAYMENTS

Transfer payments, many of them dating from the Great Depression, also act as automatic stabilizers. Transfer programs include unemployment compensation, Social Security, farm price supports, food stamps, and welfare benefits. All of these programs involve payments for which no production is expected in exchange.

Transfer programs such as food stamps usually set rules that determine who is eligible, rather than specifying a dollar amount to be spent. The

The term *policy maker* keeps cropping up in any macroeconomic discussion. Who are the policy makers for the U.S. economy? The Board of Governors of the Federal Reserve System, the Secretary of the Treasury, the chairman of the Council of Economic Advisers, the director of the Office of Management and Budget, and the director of the Congressional Budget Office are the macroeconomic policy makers. Most of them are highly visible, appearing on the evening news and *Meet the Press* and giving interviews to the *Wall Street Journal*.

The term *policy* in macroeconomics refers mainly to the use of fiscal policy tools (changes in taxes and government spending) and monetary policy tools (primarily changes in the money supply) to influence the level of output. Macroeconomic policy is a responsibility of the federal government. State and local governments have to stick pretty close to a balanced budget. Furthermore, if they tried to pursue an active fiscal policy, most of the benefits would probably spill over to other states.

Fiscal policy is a responsibility that is shared between the executive branch and the Congress. The President's chief policy advisers are the three economists on the Council of Economic Advisers. These economists are appointed by the President. The functions of the Council are to advise the President on the course of the economy, to participate in decision making on economic, budget, and financial policy (international as well as domestic), to oversee preparation of the annual *Economic Report of the President*, and to speak on behalf of the administration to Congress, the public, and the media.[a] The Secretary of the Treasury also plays an important role in recommending tax and spending policies, especially tax policies. The Office of Management and Budget prepares the annual federal budget to transmit to Congress. In the process of developing that budget, important decisions are made about the level and composition of government spending.

Since 1974, Congress has played a more active role in fiscal policy. Congress established the Congressional Budget Office then to provide an independent analysis of the executive branch's budget proposals and propose alternatives. Most fiscal policy requires congressional legislation, and Congress felt the need for a second opinion on the course of the economy and the impact of proposed legislation.

Monetary policy, which we explore in Chapters 12 and 14, is under the control of the Federal Reserve System. This central bank is a quasi-governmental agency in that its members are appointed officials. However, they are much more independent than most bureaucrats. They are not supported out of tax revenues, since the Federal Reserve System earns enough income from its normal operations to be self-supporting. The seven governors are appointed for one-time, fourteen-year terms by the President. Thus, the Board of Governors has a great deal of independence. The President may try to persuade the Fed to cooperate, but the executive branch often finds itself in conflict with the central bank. Coordination of monetary and fiscal policy is one of the most difficult challenges facing any president.

ECONOMIC INSIGHT

WHO MAKES POLICY?

a. Murray L. Weidenbaum, "The Role of the Council of Economic Advisers," *Journal of Economic Education* (Summer 1988): 237–244.

> **AUTOMATIC STABILIZERS AND HOW THEY WORK**
>
> - Progressive income taxes make disposable income (and consumption) more stable than national income. Examples are federal personal and corporate income taxes and personal and corporate income taxes in some states.
> - Transfer payments rise automatically during recessions and fall in expansions. Examples are unemployment compensation, welfare, farm price supports, food stamps, and means-tested programs such as subsidized housing and heat assistance.

number of families eligible for these transfer programs rises during recessions and falls during periods of expansion. During recessions, more people qualify for unemployment benefits, apply for food stamps, go on welfare, and retire early on Social Security. As the economy recovers, some people—even some of those who retired early—go back to work. Transfer payments fall. In addition, farm prices will be higher during expansionary periods so less will be spent on farm price supports. During recessions, farm prices fall, which triggers a rise in support payments.

If you think of transfer payments as negative taxes, you can see that they work in the same way as progressive income taxes in stabilizing output and employment. Instead of changes in tax rates as the level of income in the economy rises and falls, there are changes in the number of persons who qualify for benefits.

DISCRETIONARY FISCAL POLICY

Automatic stabilizers might be considered Keynesian fiscal policy because they lead to changes in transfer payments and tax revenues that offset changes in private economic activity. For small changes in output and employment, automatic stabilizers may be sufficient to cushion the fluctuations until the economy corrects itself. For major swings in aggregate expenditure, however, automatic stabilizers are not enough. In that case, policy makers turn to discretionary fiscal policy. **Discretionary fiscal policy** consists of changes in tax rates, in levels of transfer payments, or in government purchases of goods and services in order to change the equilibrium level of national income.

At the end of World War II, political and business leaders feared that the transition from wartime to peacetime production would send the economy into another depression. In response to these concerns, Congress passed the Employment Act of 1946. The **Employment Act of 1946** was an official adoption of Keynesian ideas about the role of discretionary fiscal policy in keeping the economy on a steady path.[9] This legislation made the U.S. government responsible for achieving and maintaining full employment, steady growth, and stable prices through the use of fiscal

discretionary fiscal policy Deliberate changes in tax rates, transfer programs, or government purchases designed to change the equilibrium level of national income.

Employment Act of 1946 A law requiring the federal government to actively promote full employment, steady growth, and stable prices through the use of fiscal and monetary policy.

---

9. Nobel Prize winner James Tobin argues forcefully that this act is as relevant today as it was in 1946, and that discretionary fiscal policy still has an important role to play. See "High Time to Restore the Employment Act of 1946," *Challenge* (May-June 1986): 4–12.

Economic Report of the President
An annual report to Congress describing the state of the economy and recommending policy.

(and monetary) policy. To provide policy-making advice, Congress created the three-member Council of Economic Advisers.[10] The legislation also requires the President (with the aid of the Council) to prepare an annual economic report, the **Economic Report of the President**. This report, sent to Congress every January, describes the state of the economy and may recommend changes in policy.

Congress changes tax rates, transfer programs, and government purchases almost every year for various reasons. The end of the military threat from the Warsaw Pact was expected to result in a decline in defense spending. The Gulf War, however, made that prospect less likely. New social problems such as AIDS and homelessness put pressure on policy makers to increase spending in those areas. Congress tinkers with the income tax code regularly to change incentives to save, invest, or give to charity. These actions may affect the level of economic activity. They do not, however, constitute fiscal policy, because their primary purpose is not to influence the level of output and employment.

True acts of pure discretionary fiscal policy are relatively rare. We will examine four fiscal policy actions that took place in the last thirty years. All of them involve tax changes. They illustrate the political and economic processes at work in discretionary fiscal policy.

THE KENNEDY TAX CUT

The first major use of discretionary fiscal policy was the Kennedy tax cut of 1964. When John Kennedy ran for the presidency in 1960, he was critical of the lack of active fiscal policy during Eisenhower's terms of office. The U.S. economy had experienced two major recessions in the 1950s. Although the 5.4 percent unemployment rate and 2.2 percent economic growth rate for 1960 look attractive by current standards, they were worse than figures for earlier years. In terms of the Keynesian model of Chapter 8, the economy was in equilibrium in 1960, but national income and output were below the full-employment level. There was a recessionary gap.

Walter W. Heller, the chair of Kennedy's Council of Economic Advisers, and other Keynesian economists had high hopes for what discretionary fiscal policy could do. In his 1967 book, *New Dimensions of Political Economy*, Heller said, "Today's talk of an intellectual revolution and a 'new economics' arises not out of startling discoveries of new economic truths but out of the swift and progressive weaving of modern economics into the fabric of national thinking and policy."[11] Heller expressed confidence that active fiscal policy based on Keynesian theories offered the best hope for solving macroeconomic problems. He was the first to use "fine-tuning" to describe targeting a particular level of output, employment, and inflation and carefully managing taxes and spending so as to try to reach that goal.

A recessionary gap can be eliminated by expansionary fiscal policy, consisting of some combination of an increase in government spending and a decrease in taxes. In 1962, Kennedy proposed both a decrease in

---

10. For an inside look at how the Council functions today, see Martin Feldstein, "How the CEA Advises Presidents," *Challenge* (November-December 1989): 51–55.
11. Walter Heller, *New Dimensions of Political Economy* (Cambridge, MA: Harvard University Press, 1967), viii.

personal and corporate income taxes and an increase in government spending. The proposal was designed to cause an increase in all three domestic components of aggregate expenditure: consumption, investment, and government spending. The shift in aggregate expenditure and aggregate demand would increase national income and output and eliminate the recessionary gap.

Congress was hesitant to intervene in the economy on the basis of Keynesian economic theory. Many members of Congress resisted the proposed tax cut because it would increase the federal deficit. After Kennedy was assassinated, Lyndon Johnson finally succeeded in getting approval for the tax cut in 1964.

Did the Kennedy tax cut work? From Table 4, you can see that the unemployment rate declined and the economic growth rate rose for several years after 1964. These statistics do not prove that discretionary fiscal policy was responsible for the rapid economic expansion between 1964 and 1968. However, Keynesian economists felt that in this case fiscal policy had worked as theory predicted.

THE JOHNSON TAX SURCHARGE

Arthur M. Okun served on the Council of Economic Advisers from late 1964 until the end of the Johnson administration. In 1968, Okun was named chair of the Council.[12] By 1966, as the unemployment rate continued to fall (Table 4), concern had shifted from slow growth and high unemployment to inflationary pressures and labor shortages. Not only was the Kennedy tax cut successful, but spending for both the Vietnam War and President Johnson's War on Poverty provided more stimulus than the economy needed. The

TABLE 4
UNEMPLOYMENT, ECONOMIC GROWTH, AND INFLATION IN THE UNITED STATES, 1959–1971

YEAR	UNEMPLOYMENT RATE (%)	GROWTH RATE OF REAL GNP (%)	INFLATION RATE (CPI) (%)
1959	5.3	5.8	1.7
1960	5.4	2.2	1.4
1961	6.5	2.6	0.7
1962	5.4	5.3	1.3
1963	5.5	4.1	1.6
1964	5.0	5.3	1.0
1965	4.4	5.8	1.9
1966	3.7	5.8	3.5
1967	3.7	2.9	3.0
1968	3.5	4.1	4.7
1969	3.4	2.4	6.2
1970	4.8	−0.3	5.6
1971	5.8	2.8	3.3

Source: Council of Economic Advisers, *Economic Report of the President* (Washington, DC: U.S. Government Printing Office, 1991).

12. By 1970, Arthur Okun was less positive about the use of discretionary fiscal policy in his book *The Political Economy of Prosperity*. It was becoming apparent that an expansionary fiscal policy that succeeded in stimulating economic growth and employment was likely to also result in budget deficits and inflation. Okun was still convinced that well-designed discretionary fiscal policy could improve the performance of the economy.

contractionary fiscal policy
Raising taxes, lowering transfer payments, or reducing government purchases in an attempt to reduce the equilibrium level of output to one that is attainable with available resources.

time had come for the first (and only) experiment in using contractionary fiscal policy to "put on the brakes"—to reduce the level of aggregate expenditure and the equilibrium level of income and output. **Contractionary fiscal policy** consists of decreases in government purchases, decreases in transfer payments, or increases in taxes in order to reduce the equilibrium level of output to one that can be produced with available resources.

The contractionary policy chosen was a one-time 10 percent surcharge on income taxes (with an option for the President to extend it to a second year). Policy makers expected the surcharge to dampen demand and reduce inflationary pressures. The tax surcharge was requested by the President in 1967 but was not passed by Congress until 1968. This policy was later judged ineffective. Unemployment did rise, but the inflation rate did not fall.[13] However, there was a one-time change rather than a sustained increase in taxes, and monetary policy was expansionary at the time. Both of these facts make it difficult to assess whether or not this policy was really effective.

THE FORD TAX REBATE

By the mid-1970s, the economy was plagued with the twin evils of high unemployment and high inflation. During the administration of President Ford, income tax changes were again used as expansionary policy, in the form of a $23 billion tax rebate in 1975. As the Ford tax rebate took effect, planned spending and aggregate demand increased, and the unemployment rate fell. By 1976, unemployment had fallen slightly to below 8 percent from a high of over 9 percent in 1975. Once again, fiscal policy based on Keynesian theory appeared to produce the intended results. However, the improvement was not enough to get Ford re-elected! In fact, because of the temporary nature of the rebate, it had far less impact than the Kennedy tax cut a decade earlier.

THE REAGAN TAX CUT

In 1981, President Reagan proposed and Congress passed a major tax cut. It was not billed as fiscal policy for three reasons. First, the Reagan tax cut, like the Ford tax rebate, came at a time when both unemployment and inflation were very high. Discretionary fiscal policy is designed to address either unemployment (expansionary policy) or inflation (contractionary policy) but not both. Second, the tax cut was accompanied by (somewhat smaller) spending cuts. For maximum impact, a Keynesian would generally recommend cutting taxes without cutting spending in order to combat unemployment. Third, the tax cuts made were intended to affect aggregate supply, an issue that we will examine in Chapter 16. However, any tax cut, especially one that is larger than spending cuts, will shift both aggregate expenditure and aggregate demand. We can consider the Reagan tax cut as an act of expansionary fiscal policy and examine its effects on output and employment.

---

13. Note that we use the inflation rate rather than the price level in assessing economic performance, even though the aggregate supply and demand model uses the price level. This is for convenience. We also tend to use the rate of growth of real output rather than the level of output as a measure of economic growth, even though it is the level of output that is shown on an aggregate supply and demand diagram.

Personal taxes were cut by 25 percent over a three-year period. The first 12.5 percent cut took effect late in 1981, and the second took effect in July 1983. Thus, the largest effects on disposable income occurred from mid-1982 on. The most important part of the business tax cut was accelerated depreciation for new business investment. This change greatly shortened the time period over which new plant and equipment purchases could be depreciated for tax purposes. Most of the original business tax cut was later offset by increases in business taxes enacted in 1982 and 1986.

From a Keynesian standpoint, the timing of the tax cut was appropriate. It came in the midst of a major recession. Unemployment peaked in November of 1982 at 10.8 percent. At the bottom of the recession in late 1982, real GNP had fallen 3 percent from its previous peak in the third quarter of 1981. By mid-1984, unemployment had fallen to 7.2 percent, and real GNP had bounced back to 7.7 percent above the 1981 peak. From 1985 through 1989, unemployment continued to decline to 5.3 percent. Real income also grew, although at a slower rate of about 2 to 4 percent. Thus, whether or not the Reagan administration considered its actions to be discretionary fiscal policy, the tax cut was successful by Keynesian standards in increasing output and employment.

Business Tax Cuts as Fiscal Policy

With several of the tax cuts above, as well as at other times when there was no major change in personal or corporate income tax rates, changes in business income taxes were made in order to stimulate investment. One such change was the **Investment Tax Credit (ITC)**. This credit offers tax savings over and above depreciation for business firms investing in new plants or equipment. Firms can subtract a percentage of the investment made from their tax liability. The ITC was first introduced as part of the Kennedy tax cut in 1964. The ITC has been a political football—being modified, removed, or restored many times. Each time, Congress weighs the revenue loss against the current perceived need to stimulate investment. Business firms complain that the ITC is less effective in encouraging investment when it is uncertain. They say it should be permanent rather than on and off.

Investment Tax Credit (ITC)
Provision offering tax savings over and above depreciation for business firms investing in new plants or equipment. A percentage of the investment made can be subtracted from tax liability.

The 1981 tax cut also provided for accelerated depreciation. This change meant that for tax purposes investors in real assets of all kinds could depreciate them much more quickly than their resale value actually declined. This tax saving was supposed to provide a stimulus to investment. It is not clear how much additional investment resulted. There was, however, a definite decline in revenues from the corporate income tax. In 1986, when tax reform lowered rates across the board for both individuals and corporations, accelerated depreciation was greatly weakened.

The economic justification for both the ITC and accelerated depreciation was to focus some of the stimulus to aggregate demand on investment rather than consumption. Additional investment is an increase in both demand and the productive capacity of the economy. Thus, it shifts both aggregate demand and aggregate supply to the right, reducing the inflationary effect of fiscal policy.

FISCAL POLICY: PROS AND CONS

Advocates of fiscal policy as a way to affect output and employment claim that government spending and taxes can be used to reduce, if not eliminate, the social costs of unemployment and inflation (discussed in Chapter 4). Furthermore, increased government expenditures intended to close a recessionary gap can provide needed social goods, such as schools, parks, and highways. However, discretionary fiscal policy has been criticized since its beginnings in the 1930s. One theoretical criticism is the permanent income hypothesis, which challenges the Keynesian consumption function and the multiplier. Other criticisms of fiscal policy focus on four issues: budget deficits and the national debt, an increase in the size of government, lags, and the use of fiscal policy for political gain. Because deficits and the national debt have been a key issue for the last ten years and promise to continue to be at least until the end of the century, they are discussed separately in Chapter 10.

THE PERMANENT INCOME HYPOTHESIS

Recall that the centerpiece of the Keynesian model is the consumption function, $C = C_0 + bY_d$, from which the expenditure multiplier, $1/(1-b)$ or $1/(1-MPC)$, is derived. In order to increase the level of income and output, the government can cut taxes (raising Y_d directly) or increase government spending. Then rounds of spending, governed by the consumption function, lead to a multiplier effect on output and income. The expenditure multiplier works in both directions. If the consumption function is very stable, the value of the expenditure multiplier derived from the consumption function will also be stable.

The permanent income hypothesis was a central part of Milton Friedman's attack on the Keynesian model. The **permanent income hypothesis** is the view that consumption does not depend on current income alone, but on past income and expected future income as well. Think about your own consumption. Today's spending is not based just on today's income. If you are paid every other week, you don't consume very heavily on payday and not at all for the next thirteen days! Some people may come close to that pattern, but a household's consumption usually depends on its expected income stream over time. Friedman argues that consumption depends on permanent income, which consists of past, present, and expected future income.

Casual observations of how people act seems to support this idea. Seasonal workers, such as farmers and construction workers, may only work six to eight months a year, but they consume at a fairly constant level throughout the year. Striking or laid-off workers usually maintain their consumption if the strike or layoff doesn't last too long. If these households do not have enough liquid assets (cash or other assets easily turned into cash) or access to credit, they may have to curtail consumption. But in general, Friedman argues, consumption is much more stable than actual current income because it is not based on that income alone.

Another way of understanding the permanent income hypothesis is to think about what you would do if you had less income for a short time. You would probably continue to pay those expenses that are fixed in the short run, such as house payments, car payments, and utility bills. You

permanent income hypothesis
The view that consumption does not depend on current income alone but on past income and expected future income as well.

would still eat meals and put gas in the car but might give up seeing new movies and buying tapes or new clothes. You might cut back a little on food by eating out less and spend less on recreation and other nonessentials. In the short run, your options for cutting spending are limited, especially when the income change is temporary. If your income fell permanently, however, you might decide to sell your house and car and move to smaller quarters or make other big changes in your consumption patterns. You might drop out of school, move out of an apartment and back home or into the dorm, or make other large adjustments.

It is more difficult to argue that individuals won't increase their consumption in response to a temporary increase in income. But people will usually increase consumption less with a temporary increase in income than with a permanent increase. Thus, the permanent income hypothesis seems to make good sense in terms of how people behave.

POLICY IMPLICATIONS. The permanent income hypothesis has some important implications for fiscal policy. If consumers fail to respond to a temporary increase in disposable income by spending a large fraction of it, then fiscal policy will have less effect on output and employment. An increase or decrease in government spending or taxes will still have a first-round effect on output and employment. However, unless people are convinced that the change is permanent, subsequent rounds of changes in spending will be very small. Temporary changes in taxes or spending will have little impact on consumer spending, because a one-time tax cut or a one-year spending increase will affect permanent income much less than current income.

Consider, for example, a person who expects to live twenty-five more years. A one-time tax cut of $1,000 increases this person's current income by $1,000. But his or her permanent income increases (ignoring interest) by only $40 a year! The 1964 and 1981 income tax cuts, which were enacted as permanent changes, appear to have had more effect on income and consumption than the 1968 temporary surcharge or the 1975 one-time tax rebate.

PROBLEMS OF MEASUREMENT. The debate on the consumption function cannot be easily settled by statistical testing. In order to test whether the consumption function works better with current income than with permanent income, economists would have to be able to measure permanent income. A household's permanent income at any given time depends on both experience and expectations. As the household acquires more experience, expectations change and so does permanent income. Economists are even less able to measure permanent income for the entire economy than for one household. They can only offer examples that suggest that temporary income changes have less effect on consumption than permanent income changes do.

GOVERNMENT SPENDING

A group of economists from a relatively new branch of economics has criticized fiscal policy on the grounds that such actions tend to increase the size of the government sector relative to the private sector. **Public choice**

public choice economics
A branch of economic theory that attempts to integrate economics and politics by examining the motives and rewards facing individuals in the public sector.

International Perspective

For most of the period since World War II, Britain has had a large and growing public sector with poor economic performance. Unemployment was stubbornly high, growth was slow, and inflation was persistent. In 1979, Margaret Thatcher became Prime Minister and instituted a combination of economic policies very similar to those adopted later by President Reagan in the United States. Reagan cut taxes more than spending. Thatcher cut taxes only moderately, cut some forms of spending, and emphasized reducing the extent and scope of government activities. Unlike Reagan, Thatcher was successful in reducing the size of government. For a time, her policies were very popular. However, cuts in some important local services and the replacement of property taxes with very regressive poll taxes weakened her position and helped to bring about her removal as Prime Minister in 1990.

Thatcher pursued a complex policy with many goals, including privatization of industry and redistribution of wealth. However, we can evaluate the contractionary aspect of her fiscal policies. In terms of a Keynesian model, aggregate expenditure fell in Britain because the fall in taxes was smaller than the reduction in government spending. As a result the AD curve shifted to the left, and unemployment rose while inflation fell. Inflation was nearly 15 percent in 1979. It fell to about 3 percent in 1987, only to finally rise again to 8 percent in 1988. This rate was still well below that when Thatcher took office. Unemployment, about 5.5 percent when she took office, rose to 13 percent in 1983 and was still at 8 percent by 1988. (These numbers are not comparable to those of the United States because of different ways of counting employed and unemployed workers.) While Reagan pursued an expansionary policy in the name of a healthier private sector and a smaller government, Thatcher pursued a contractionary policy—with the expected effects on inflation and unemployment.

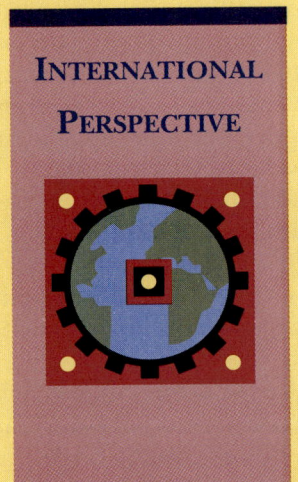

economics attempts to integrate politics and economics by examining the motives and rewards for different types of behavior in the public sector. Public choice economics is the modern form of political economy. Much of public choice economics is microeconomic. However, some work in macroeconomics has been done by public choice theorists.

James Buchanan, a Nobel Prize winner, and his colleague Richard Wagner see rising deficits and resistance to collecting the taxes to pay for spending as logical consequences of the nature of the U.S. political system.[14] Buchanan and Wagner argue that policies that hurt a few citizens very intensely and benefit most others very slightly are not likely to be enacted, even if the total benefits exceed the costs. Conversely, it is politically easy to enact programs that benefit a few very greatly at a small cost to each taxpayer, even if the total costs exceed the total benefits.

Spending programs benefit specific interest groups: welfare clients, hospitals, farmers, defense firms, or industries that compete with imports. A tariff may be designed to protect the shoe industry or the textile industry. Such a policy benefits workers and owners in that industry at the expense of consumers of shoes or textiles. In addition, the costs of many spending programs, such as farm price supports or cost overruns by defense contractors, are borne by taxpayers in general. Taxpayers feel the effects as higher current taxes, more inflation, or higher future taxes to finance deficits. Recessions provide an excuse to fund such programs by borrowing rather than by raising taxes. When the recession ends, the program has acquired a constituency and cannot be axed. Over time, then, the government sector grows relative to the private sector.

Other economists, including Nobel Prize winner James Tobin, argue that the large size of the government sector relative to the private sector is a force for stability. Investment and net exports are quite unstable, as are some components of consumption—especially consumer durables. Government purchases, however, are quite stable. They change slowly from year to year. The share of total output that is bought by or produced by government is much larger now than it was in Keynes's day. With this big, stable sector providing an anchor, the economy is less likely to drift into recession. These economists argue that the growing share of economic activity passing through government is the primary reason why there has not been another Great Depression.

However, in a market system, it is inefficient to make production decisions through government when there are no compelling reasons such as public goods or strong externalities. The market does a better job of allocating resources in response to consumer demand. Thus, if greater macroeconomic stability is due to the larger share of economic activity in the public sector, there will be a difficult tradeoff between stability and efficiency.

LAGS IN FISCAL POLICY

Lags in making policy decisions provide another basis for criticism of discretionary fiscal policy. The **recognition lag** is the length of time required

recognition lag
The length of time it takes to determine that an economic problem exists.

---

14. James Buchanan and Richard E. Wagner, *Democracy in Deficit: The Political Legacy of Lord Keynes* (New York: W. W. Norton, 1977).

to become aware of, or recognize, an economic problem. Statistical measures (unemployment rate, CPI, and GNP) take from one to three months to compile. When these measures become available, they describe economic conditions for the previous month or previous quarter. These measures provide the basis for forecasting whether a recession will continue or end, whether unemployment will rise, fall or remain the same, how fast output will grow, or what the rate of inflation will be. Such forecasts are difficult to make and prone to errors. And an inaccurate forecast can result in the wrong fiscal policy.

Once a problem is recognized, more time passes as the President and Congress choose a fiscal policy solution and enact it into law. Policy makers must decide what kind of action to take—taxes, transfers, or government spending—and at what level. They must decide whose taxes to cut, what kinds of spending programs to undertake, and what section of the country should get the initial benefit. This **implementation lag** is the time it takes after a problem is recognized to choose and enact a fiscal policy in response. Some economists have recommended that Congress give limited power to change tax rates to the President in order to save valuable time.

After a fiscal policy has become law, further time passes before there is any improvement in the economy. Tax changes can be implemented fairly quickly through payroll withholding. Spending programs, on the other hand—especially those involving construction of highways or public buildings—take time to design and carry out. Once the initial round of spending takes place, then the multiplier effects are felt over a period of eighteen to twenty-four months. The **impact lag** is the time that elapses between the implementation of a fiscal policy and its full effect on economic activity.

Taken together, the recognition, implementation, and impact lags add up to a long period of time. It is quite possible that the combined lags can take up so much time that the full impact of a tax cut or an increase in spending will not be felt until after the economy has begun to move out of the recession by itself. In Figure 3, the points labeled R, I_1, and I_2 are,

implementation lag
The time it takes after a problem is recognized to choose and enact a fiscal policy in response.

impact lag
The time that elapses between implementation of a fiscal policy and its full effect on economic activity.

FIGURE 3
LAGS AND DESTABILIZING FISCAL POLICY
Along the course of this business cycle, recognition that the economy is in a recession occurs at point R. Implementation of fiscal policy takes place at point I_1, and its impact on the economy is finally felt at point I_2. Because the expansionary policy was delayed, it causes the economy to take off on the course indicated by the dashed line. The economy has been made less stable.

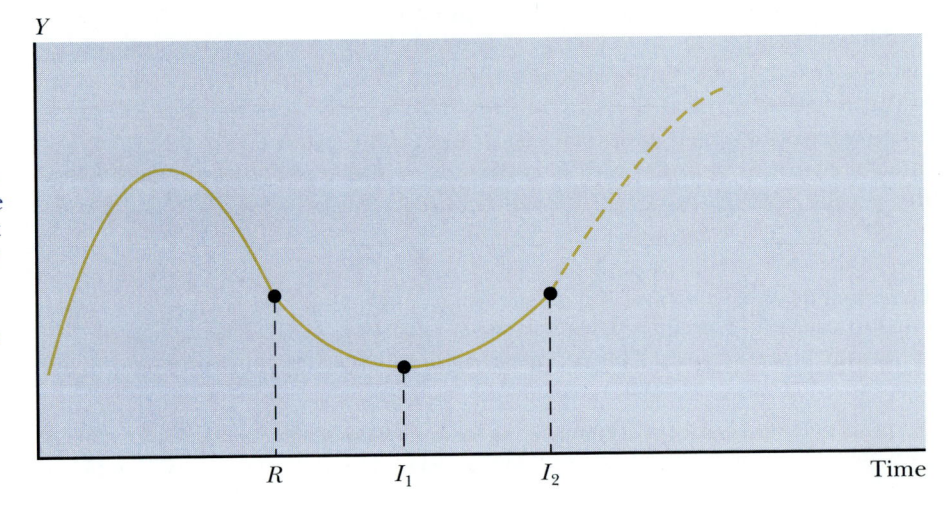

respectively, the end points of the recognition, implementation, and impact lags. As you can see, the delays mean that the policy's effect on economic activity is not actually felt until the economy is well into the recovery phase. The dashed line from point I_2 shows what the path of economic activity is likely to be as a result of poorly timed discretionary policy. The expansionary fiscal policy intended to combat recession will simply fuel inflation. Similar mistiming on contractionary policy could aggravate a recession. Discretionary fiscal policy combined with lags can actually make an economy less stable.

THE POLITICAL BUSINESS CYCLE

Public choice economists have also suggested that discretionary fiscal policy combined with the American political system can create a political business cycle. In many other countries, the political system is parliamentary. The legislative branch and executive branch are united under a prime minister. In such systems the prime minister usually has some say about when elections are called, and campaigns are relatively brief. In the U.S. political system, however, there are only two years between elections. All members of the House of Representatives and one-third of the Senate are elected every two years, and presidents are elected every four years. Consequently, the next election is never very far from the mind of anyone in Congress or the White House.

Under these conditions, the incumbent party has a strong incentive to try to reduce unemployment and inflation so that economic conditions look good at the time of the next election. Such political maneuvering gives the economy a series of short-run policies and rapid reversals to meet political needs, rather than a consistent pursuit of policies with a longer run payoff. Examples of timing spending programs and tax cuts so as to attempt to influence the outcome of an election are not hard to find. In the 1970s, Congress approved automatic changes in Social Security benefits each January based on changes in the CPI. Before that time, these benefits would typically be adjusted just before an election so as to court the elderly vote. Increases in payroll taxes to finance the added benefits would not take place until after the election. The 1981 tax cut is another example. This tax cut had its first substantial effect on withholding in 1982, a congressional election year, and the final impact was felt in the 1984 presidential election year. In fact, it is hard to find a tax cut that took effect in an odd-numbered year or a tax increase that took effect in an even-numbered year!

Some economists have suggested that there may even be a controlled business cycle designed to peak just before elections. This **political business cycle** is the result of the use of fiscal and monetary policy, especially fiscal policy, to influence the outcome of elections. A downturn can follow an election, as long as there is another peak, or at least an upturn, in time for the next election. According to this view, the level and timing of tax and spending changes (and when the Federal Reserve is willing to cooperate, changes in the money supply) tend to respond less to changes in economic activity than to the timing of elections.

American Political Economy, a recent book by Donald Hibbs, offers evidence that favorable or unfavorable economic conditions at the time of

political business cycle
A business cycle that results from the use of fiscal (or monetary) policy to influence the outcome of elections.

an election have a definite effect on the success or failure of the incumbent party.[15] President Reagan saw his party lose many congressional seats in the recession-year election of 1982. Economic conditions had improved by the 1984 presidential election, no doubt contributing to Reagan's landslide re-election. As expansion continued to the end of the decade, low unemployment and only moderate inflation undoubtedly helped Reagan's Vice President, George Bush, win the 1988 election.[16] Although economic conditions can influence political outcomes, there has been little success in using statistics to prove or disprove that politicians can actually create a political business cycle for their own benefit.

> **PROBLEMS WITH FISCAL POLICY**
>
> - Increase in the relative size of government
> - Loss of control over budget deficits
> - Difficulty in making accurate economic projections
> - Lags (recognition, implementation, and impact)
> - Political business cycles

FISCAL POLICY, AGGREGATE DEMAND, AND THE PRICE LEVEL

The analysis of fiscal policy in this chapter has been based on the simple Keynesian model from Chapter 8. That model focuses on aggregate expenditure with a fixed price level. It is adequate when there is severe unemployment, when aggregate supply may be horizontal. When the price level can change, this simple Keynesian model is not as useful. A better model for situations closer to full employment is the blending of the aggregate expenditure and aggregate supply and demand models. Recall that at the end of Chapter 8, we integrated the Keynesian model into the aggregate supply and demand framework.

Figure 4 shows how the slope of the *AS* curve affects the impact of expansionary fiscal policy. Expansionary fiscal policy shifts the *AE* curve upward for all price levels and thus shifts the *AD* curve to the right. Only the shifting of the *AD* curve is shown in Figure 4. If aggregate demand remains in the horizontal range of the *AS* curve (AD_1 and AD_2), all of the impact of expansionary fiscal policy falls on real output. A shift to AD_3 in the upward-sloping range of the *AS* curve means that expansionary fiscal policy will affect both real output and the price level. If the *AD* curve intersects *AS* in its vertical range, the only impact of expansionary fiscal policy will be on the price level. Because classical and new classical econ-

---

15. Donald A. Hibbs, *American Political Economy* (Cambridge, MA: Harvard University Press, 1988).
16. To the extent that Reagan's policies were truly supply side, rather than Keynesian, the impact was likely to be quite slow because such policies depend on work incentives, investment incentives, and productivity, which do not respond very rapidly. Investment in particular, since it requires a long planning horizon, may take some time to respond. We will look more closely at the effect of supply side policies in Chapter 16.

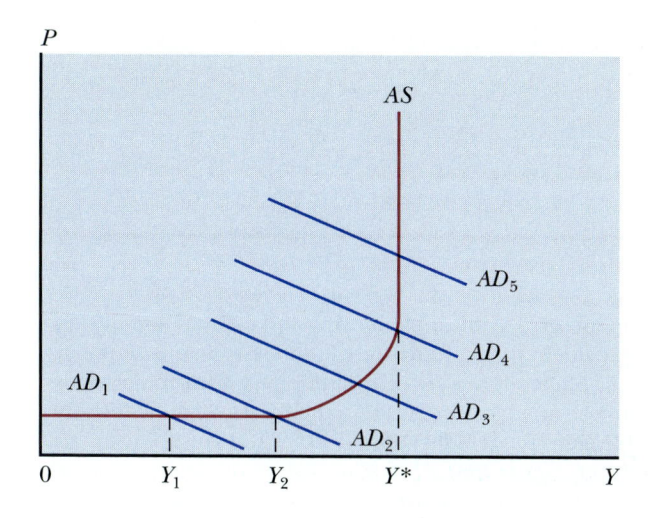

FIGURE 4
AGGREGATE DEMAND, AGGREGATE SUPPLY, AND FISCAL POLICY
Expansionary fiscal policy shifts aggregate demand to the right. A shift in aggregate demand from AD_1 to AD_2 in the horizontal range of AS will increase Y with no effect on P. At higher levels of output, shifts in AD will drive up the price level as well. Once real output reaches Y^*, further increases in AD will only increase the price level.

omists believe the AS curve is vertical, they would not expect fiscal policy to affect real output at all.[17]

For most of this chapter (except in discussing the Johnson surcharge), we have concentrated on expansionary fiscal policy. Higher taxes, lower transfers, or reduced government spending is contractionary fiscal policy. Such policy is rarely undertaken, usually only in response to severe inflation. Contractionary fiscal policy affects both real output and the price level. Which of the two is affected more depends on the range of the aggregate supply curve in which the economy is operating. Contractionary fiscal policy will have its main impact on the price level when equilibrium output exceeds Y^* on the AE diagram. This situation corresponds to aggregate demand curves AD_4 and AD_5 in Figure 4.

Because fiscal policy shifts the aggregate demand as well as aggregate expenditure, it is also known as demand management policy. However, fiscal policy is not the only tool that can shift aggregate demand. Recall from Chapter 6 that one of the factors held constant in drawing the AD curve was the size of the money supply. Thus, changes in the money supply will also shift aggregate demand. After we have looked more closely at debt and deficits in the next chapter, we will explore the effects of money demand, money supply, and monetary policy on the level of output, employment, and prices.

---

17. Actually, classical economists considered fiscal policy ineffective, but new classical economists might expect some temporary effects if the policy was unexpected. We will explore this view further in Chapter 15.

SUMMARY

1. Keynesian fiscal policy is based on three assumptions: (a) Equilibrium output may occur at high rates of unemployment or inflation. (b) Changes in private or foreign-sector spending may move the economy to an equilibrium that is not satisfactory. (c) Only the government can be counted on to change its spending and taxing to move the economy toward a more acceptable equilibrium.

2. A decline in aggregate expenditure that the private sector (households, firms, and foreigners) plans to make can create a recessionary gap. A recessionary gap occurs when aggregate expenditure is too low to purchase an economy's full-employment output.

3. Fiscal policy can be used to close a recessionary gap. Closing a recessionary gap requires increasing government spending, reducing taxes, or both.

4. Automatic stabilizers reduce fluctuations in economic activity without requiring legislation. Discretionary fiscal policy requires deliberate action by the executive branch or by Congress.

5. The Employment Act of 1946 makes the government responsible for achieving and maintaining full employment through the use of monetary and fiscal policy.

6. Major instances of discretionary fiscal policy were the Kennedy tax cut (1964), the Ford tax cut (1975), the Reagan tax rebate (1981–1983), and the Johnson tax surcharge (1968).

7. Advocates of active fiscal policy claim it allows the nation to reduce, if not totally avoid, the social costs of unemployment and inflation.

8. The permanent income hypothesis says that consumption is based on permanent income and income expectations, not just current income. By this hypothesis, the Keynesian expenditure multiplier is unstable and fiscal policy is less effective.

9. Public choice economists argue that active fiscal policy leads to inefficiency because it results in a larger public sector and creates an opportunity for political business cycles.

10. Discretionary fiscal policy is affected by lags in recognition, implementation, and impact.

NEW TERMS

fiscal policy
recessionary gap
expansionary fiscal policy
automatic stabilizers
regressive tax
proportional tax
progressive tax
discretionary fiscal policy
Employment Act of 1946
Economic Report of the President
contractionary fiscal policy
Investment Tax Credit (ITC)
permanent income hypothesis
public choice economics
recognition lag
implementation lag
impact lag
political business cycle

QUESTIONS FOR DISCUSSION

1. Do you think that economists who adhere to classical macroeconomic theory would recommend the use of fiscal policy to eliminate a recessionary gap? Why or why not?

2. Why did Keynes not expect the private sector to offer much help in stabilizing economic activity?

3. Suppose $MPC = 0.9$, $C_0 = \$300$ billion, and I, G, T, and $(EX-IM)$ are each equal to $100 billion. What are the equilibrium values of Y, C, and S?

4. If G in Question 3 rises to $150 billion, *ceteris paribus*, by how much will the equilibrium levels of Y, C, and S change? What would happen to the equilibrium levels of Y, C, and S if T were reduced by $50 billion, *ceteris paribus*?

5. Use the information in Question 3, and suppose Y^* is $5,600 billion. By how much would G have to change to bring the economy to full employment? By how much would T have to change?

6. If the United States changed its political system so that elections were held less often and called by the Pres-

ident at a time that he or she chose, how do you think macroeconomic policy would be affected?

7. Why are economists concerned about the lags associated with fiscal policy actions? What solutions can you suggest?

8. Using the latest issue of the *Economic Report of the President*, list the rates of unemployment, inflation, and real output growth since 1981, the year of the Reagan tax cut. What conclusions can you draw about possible effects of that tax cut as expansionary fiscal policy?

9. What are the costs and benefits of having a larger government sector and a smaller private sector?

10. According to the permanent income hypothesis, which of the following would have the greatest effect on your consumption? Why?
    a. a Christmas bonus
    b. a promotion
    c. a six-week layoff
    d. getting married to someone who is also employed

11. How does the permanent income hypothesis challenge the effectiveness of fiscal policy?

12. Why is fiscal policy less effective in an economy with a large foreign sector?

13. Why does a tax cut have less effect on the level of income and output than an equal change in government spending? What about a change in transfer payments?

14. Classify each of the following as a recognition, implementation, or impact lag.
    a. The numbers on GNP are slow in arriving from the Department of Commerce.
    b. Congress takes a recess to think things over.
    c. A new spending program has finally been put in place, and the dollars are starting to trickle through the economy.

15. How would you identify a political business cycle?

16. Under what conditions will expansionary fiscal policy be inflationary?

SUGGESTIONS FOR FURTHER READING

Blinder, Alan. *Hard Heads, Soft Hearts*. New York: Addison-Wesley, 1987. Blinder looks at fiscal policy from a perspective of efficiency (hard heads) and equity (soft hearts). Chapter 6 examines the 1986 tax reform.

Brookings Institution. *Economic Choices*. Washington, DC: Brookings Institution, annually. This annual review of public policy issues, especially fiscal policy, gives a different perspective from that of the administration, expressed in the *Economic Report of the President*.

Council of Economic Advisers. *The Economic Report of the President*. Washington, DC: U.S. Government Printing Office, annually. Gives a summary and explanation of fiscal actions on an annual basis.

Maynard, Geoffrey W. *The Economy under Mrs. Thatcher*. Oxford and New York: Basil Blackwell, 1988. Looks at fiscal policy in the 1980s in Britain.

Niskanen, William A. *Reaganomics: An Insider's Account of the Policies and the People*. London and New York: Oxford University Press, 1988. Another inside look at making policy in the 1980s written by a member of the Council of Economic Advisers.

Stein, Herbert. *Presidential Economics: The Making of Economic Policy From Roosevelt to Reagan and Beyond*. New York: Simon & Schuster, 1985. A well-written account of the ins and outs of fiscal policy in practice, with thorough coverage of its weaknesses and limitations, by an economist who was a Washington insider for several decades. More recently, Stein has also written *Governing the $5 Trillion Economy* (Oxford and New York: Oxford University Press, 1989).

Willett, Thomas D. *Political Business Cycles: The Political Economy of Money, Inflation, and Unemployment*. Durham, NC: Duke University Press, 1988. A good treatment of political business cycles and other macroeconomic issues from a public choice perspective.

AFTER STUDYING THIS CHAPTER, YOU SHOULD BE ABLE TO:

1. Distinguish between a federal budget deficit and the national debt.
2. Discuss the links between fiscal policy and the national debt.
3. Explain why the national debt grew so rapidly during the 1980s.
4. Define:
   a. high-employment balanced budget,
   b. cyclically balanced budget,
   c. structural deficit,
   d. cyclical deficit.
5. Discuss the pros and cons of running deficits and a national debt.

CHAPTER 10
BUDGET DEFICITS AND THE NATIONAL DEBT

INTRODUCTION

An economy with automatic stabilizers and some use of discretionary fiscal policy will have budget deficits at least part of the time. In the United States, federal budget deficits were one of the most pressing economic issues during the 1980s and will continue to be a concern throughout the 1990s. This chapter focuses on the deficit problem because it is central to current policy discussions.

DEBT AND DEFICITS

It is important to distinguish between national debt, which is a stock concept, and a budget deficit, which is a flow concept. A **deficit** is the amount by which the federal government's expenditures exceed its revenues in a given year (the fiscal year, which runs from October 1st to September 30th). The **national debt** is the cumulative total of all past budget deficits minus all past surpluses. It is the amount owed to lenders by the federal government.[1]

Deficits are nothing new. The United States began its history with a national debt. The Revolutionary War was financed by printing money—before there was a government with taxing power. One of the major problems facing the first Congress in 1789 was the retirement of $79 million in national debt, about two-thirds of it from the Revolutionary War. By the second term of President Andrew Jackson in the 1830s, the entire debt had been repaid.[2]

The U.S. government ran budget surpluses for much of the nineteenth century. However, both the Union and the Confederacy ran large deficits to finance the Civil War. Except for periods during the Civil War and World War I, federal budget deficits were quite small before the 1930s. In 1929, just before the Great Depression, the national debt stood at $16.9 billion, or about 16 percent of GNP. (Because economists expect debt to grow as the economy grows, they usually correct for overall growth

deficit
The amount by which the federal government's expenditures exceed its revenues in a given year (the fiscal year).

national debt
The total of all past budget deficits minus all past surpluses, or the net amount owed to lenders by the federal government.

---
1. Most of the debt is held by the public, but some of it is held by federal agencies and trust funds, including the Social Security Trust Fund.
2. For a good survey of the history of U.S. debt and deficits, see Benjamin Friedman, *Day of Reckoning* (New York: Random House, 1988), Chapter 5.

271

in both by comparing the debt to the size of the economy, measured by GNP.) By 1932, the federal budget had become unbalanced by a sharp drop in output, employment, and the price level. Both Herbert Hoover and Franklin Roosevelt ran for president in that year on a campaign promise to balance the budget.

By 1939, at the outbreak of World War II, the national debt had nearly tripled to $48.2 billion, or 55 percent of GNP. World War II brought a large increase in output but an even larger increase in government borrowing. At the end of the war, the national debt stood at $260.1 billion, or 122 percent of GNP. The debt was reduced slightly in the next few years. Then it began to grow very slowly, much more slowly than GNP. By 1970, the national debt had risen to $380.9 billion. Because GNP had also grown, the national debt was only 38 percent of GNP.

Rapid growth of the debt in the 1970s was matched by rapid growth of nominal GNP. However, these increases reflected inflation more than growth in real output. By 1980, the national debt stood at $908.5 billion, but had fallen in relation to GNP to 34 percent. The 1980s saw a rapid rise in both the national debt and GNP. Between 1980 and 1990, the size of the national debt tripled from less than $1 trillion to over $3 trillion. The estimated 1990 debt of $3,113 billion represents 57 percent of GNP. This figure is the highest since just after World War II. Table 1 shows the behavior of both budget deficits and the national debt over the last two decades. (A few earlier years are also included to provide a benchmark.) Figure 1 plots national debt relative to GNP for the entire post–World War II period.

The current figures for the national debt actually understate certain obligations of the government that could prove costly in the near future. The government has guaranteed not only the safety of deposits in federally insured banks but also mortgage loans, student loans, and other private sector borrowing that could represent serious future liability.

Does Keynesian Fiscal Policy Mean Deficits?

Critics of Keynesian fiscal policy claim that it is at least partly responsible for deficits in the federal budget and increases in the national debt. These economists might be less opposed to Keynesian fiscal policy if budget surpluses offset deficits over the long run. They point out that from 1950 through 1990, budget surpluses totaled less than $20 billion, and budget deficits totaled about $3,000 billion. During what might be considered the heyday of Keynesian policy, the period from 1960 to 1980, the national debt tripled from $290.5 billion to $908.5 billion. (During that period, however, debt as a share of GNP declined from 57 percent to 34 percent.)

In the 1930s, even before Keynes's *General Theory*, there was support for spending more on social projects during economic downturns and cutting back when the economy returned to full employment. However, it is politically very difficult to cut back spending or increase taxes during the expansionary phase of the business cycle. Thus, many economists fear that Keynesian policy provides a ready excuse for the long-run expansion of the relative size of the government sector.

Households and firms are limited in their ability to spend more than their income for any length of time because of the threat of bankruptcy.

Chapter 10 Budget Deficits and the National Debt 273

TABLE 1
NATIONAL DEBT AND BUDGET DEFICITS FOR THE UNITED STATES, 1945–1990

YEAR	FEDERAL DEFICIT (BILLIONS OF DOLLARS)	NATIONAL DEBT (BILLIONS OF DOLLARS)	DEBT/GNP (%)
1945	− 47.6	260.1	122.5
1955	− 3.0	274.4	71.0
1965	− 1.4	322.3	47.9
1970	− 2.8	382.6	38.6
1971	− 23.0	409.5	38.8
1972	− 23.4	437.3	37.9
1973	− 14.9	468.4	36.5
1974	− 6.1	486.2	34.3
1975	− 53.2	544.1	35.7
1976	− 73.7	631.9	37.2
1977*	− 53.6	709.1	36.7
1978	− 59.2	780.4	35.9
1979	− 40.2	833.8	34.1
1980	− 73.8	914.3	34.2
1981	− 78.9	1,003.9	33.6
1982	−127.9	1,147.0	36.5
1983	−207.8	1,381.9	41.6
1984	−185.3	1,576.7	42.7
1985	−212.3	1,827.5	46.3
1986	−221.2	2,130.0	50.8
1987	−152.6	2,345.3	53.4
1988	−155.1	2,707.3	55.4
1989	−152.0	2,866.2	54.8
1990	−123.8	3,113.3	56.5

*The third quarter (July–September) of 1977 was a transition quarter, because the federal fiscal year was changed to start October 1 instead of July 1. The fiscal year for 1977 is July 1, 1976–June 30, 1977, and the fiscal year for 1978 is October 1, 1977–September 30, 1978.

Source: Council of Economic Advisers, *Economic Report of the President* (Washington, DC: U.S. Government Printing Office, 1991).

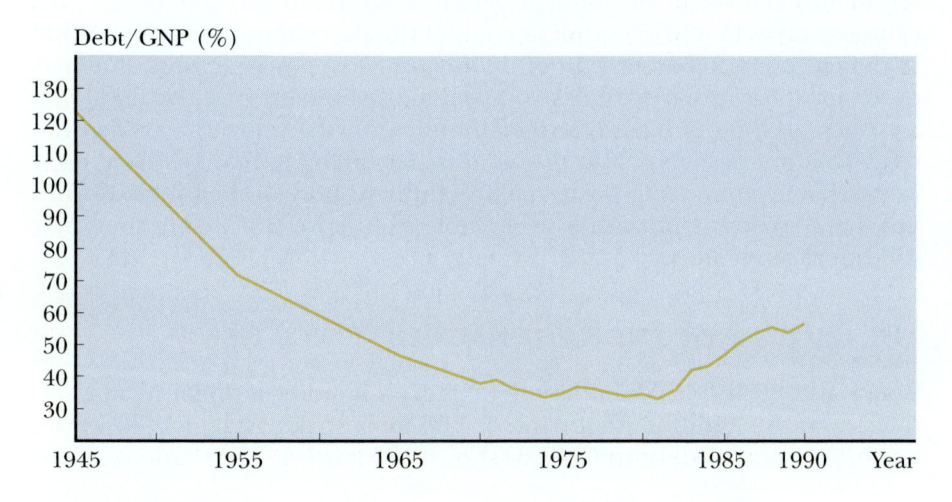

FIGURE 1
THE RATIO OF DEBT TO GNP, 1945–1990
After falling from the end of World War II until 1981, the ratio of the national debt to GNP climbed steadily through the 1980s.

Bankruptcy is a remote possibility for a central government. Sometimes local governments—cities, counties, school districts, and water systems—have been unable to pay their debts and filed for bankruptcy. The difference between a national government and a household, firm, or local government is the power to tax a broad range of persons in order to raise funds to pay off debts. For nations, any threat of bankruptcy comes from abroad. If a national government finances its spending through foreign loans, then it may be unable to come up with the "hard currency" (acceptable foreign currencies) to repay them. This kind of bankruptcy is not a serious concern for the United States at present, but is the heart of the Third World debt crisis (discussed in Chapter 17).

The deficits of the 1970s and 1980s are largely due to political decisions: the expansion of spending programs and several cuts in taxes. Once spending programs are created, they acquire clients and supporters. Thus, it is difficult to reduce or eliminate them. For example, it is difficult to close military bases because nearby towns will lose income and population. On the other hand, voting for higher taxes is politically unpopular. Recent budget deficits were caused not by discretionary fiscal policy but rather by problems in the budget process. The argument about how the government should spend its money—on welfare programs, national defense, or environmental and regulatory programs—often becomes confused with the debate over fiscal policy.

How Fiscal Policy Creates Budget Deficits

Fiscal policy works through changes in government spending or taxes, or both. In most cases, fiscal policy will change the balance of the federal budget, moving it toward deficit or surplus. If the government uses Keynesian fiscal policy to reduce or eliminate a recessionary gap, spending is increased or taxes are decreased. No matter which action is taken, spending will rise relative to taxes, increasing the budget deficit or reducing the surplus. Fiscal policy affects the national debt by changing the size of the budget deficit or surplus. A federal budget deficit increases the national debt, and a surplus reduces it.

Is fiscal policy responsible for the recent long series of federal budget deficits and the huge national debt? Not exactly. The deficits and the debt are mainly the result of political decisions to spend more than the government takes in. Only a small portion of the current national debt is due to deficits incurred as a result of deliberate fiscal policy actions. Furthermore, most Keynesians argue strongly that the benefits of active fiscal policy (increased employment and economic growth) more than offset the costs (budget deficits). The problem is that many politicians have used Keynesian arguments to avoid making difficult budget decisions. Keynes may have created a politically acceptable excuse for increasing spending without raising taxes.

THE GROWTH OF THE NATIONAL DEBT SINCE 1980

Between 1980 and 1990, budget deficits grew steadily in dollar terms, and the size of the national debt tripled. The most striking change, however, was in the ratio of debt to GNP, as shown in Figure 1. That ratio reached

International Perspective

The Other Deficit: The Balance of Trade

Some journalists, as well as some economists, have used the phrase "twin deficits" to identify what they consider to be the most pressing macroeconomic problem in the United States. One of the twins is the federal budget deficit. The other is the trade deficit. The trade deficit is a deficit in the balance of trade or the current account. The balance of trade is the difference between exports and imports of goods. The current account includes the balance of trade as well as trade in services, interest and dividend payments, and a few other items. Both of these accounts are part of the balance of payments, which is discussed in detail in the chapter on international finance. By either measure, a trade deficit means that Americans bought more currently produced goods and services from foreigners than they sold to the rest of the world.

Both the balance of trade and the current account have been mostly in deficit since the early 1970s. The deficits were modest at first, and there were a few surplus years. The current account was in surplus in six of the eleven years from 1971 to 1981. The main reason for these surpluses was the fact that Americans received more interest and dividend payments from the rest of the world than U.S. firms and government paid to foreigners. The balance of trade took a big turn for the worse in the late 1970s, mostly due to higher prices for imported oil. From 1980 to 1985, the balance of trade deficit rose from $25 billion to $122 billion. The current account balance shifted from a modest $1.9 billion surplus in 1980 to a $115 billion deficit by 1985.

The deficit on the balance of trade affects output and employment, because it means that net exports are negative. A negative value for net exports depresses output, employment, and the price level. Part of the reduction in inflation in the early 1980s is generally credited to falling exports and rising imports. Some of the blame for the high unemployment and slow economic growth in the same period fell on the foreign sector for the same reason—falling exports and rising imports. (You may want to check out this process with an aggregate supply and demand diagram.)

Are the two deficits related? Some economists argue that they are. If the budget deficit drives up interest rates, funds will be attracted from abroad to earn high interest. The inflow of funds will cause a demand for U.S. dollars to invest in the United States, driving up the price of the dollar. A high price for the dollar makes exports more expensive and imports cheaper. (We will explore this process in more detail in the international finance chapter.) Thus, interest rates provide a link between the budget deficit and the trade deficit.

As the budget deficit peaked and began to fall in the mid-1980s, real interest rates also began to decline. The price of the dollar fell, and the balance of trade began to improve, although slowly and erratically. By 1990, the balance of trade deficit was $94 billion, still high but smaller than the record $155 billion for 1987. If the budget deficit continues to fall during the 1990s and real interest rates decline as well, foreign investment in the United States should decline. The result will be a further decline in the value of the dollar, an expansion of exports, and a gradual reduction in the trade deficit.

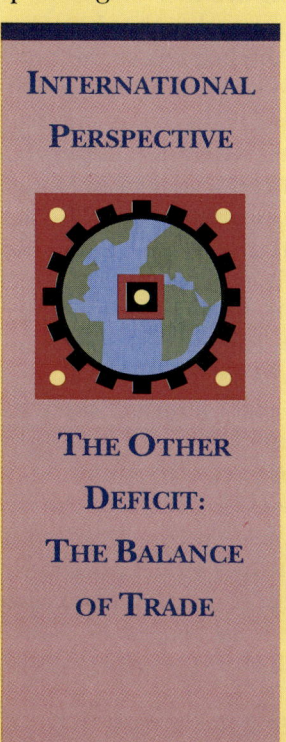

a ten-year low in 1981 at 33.6 percent, only to shoot up to over 56 percent in 1990. The current intense concern about the deficits and debt is not based only on the fact that both are large and growing. More serious is the unpleasant reality that both have risen much more rapidly than total output over the last ten years.

Most of the growth in deficits in the 1980s was not based on Keynesian theory or justified as expansionary fiscal policy. There are various ideas as to exactly what Reagan's advisers had in mind in 1981 when they proposed a 30 percent reduction in personal income taxes and an even bigger cut in corporate profits taxes. (The actual cut was 25 percent.) Some supply siders argued that the increased incentives to work, save, and invest would actually result in increased revenues.[3] That did not occur. A second group (including David Stockman, Reagan's first director of the Office of Management and Budget) argued that the purpose of the tax cut was to cut off the revenue source that was feeding government spending. Lower revenues would force a reduction in spending and in the size of government. A third group claimed that the growth of the deficits was due not to the tax cut but to excessive spending, which they blamed on Congress.

Most observers attribute the deficits of the early 1980s to attempting the impossible—cutting taxes while increasing defense spending. (The latter grew from 5 to 6.5 percent of GNP between 1980 and 1983.) Even attempts to reduce nondefense spending could not bridge the gap. In addition, there were two other contributing factors. One was the recession of 1980–1982, and the other was high interest rates.

THE 1980–1982 RECESSION

The United States entered a recession in 1980, with a sharp drop in GNP during the second quarter. The economy then rebounded, only to see a second sharp decline in output and a rise in unemployment in 1982. Real output fell by 2.5 percent in 1982, and unemployment rose to 9.5 percent in 1982, remaining at that level during 1983. During the recession, the automatic stabilizers did their job. Tax revenues fell even further than they would have with the tax cut alone, and payments for food stamps and unemployment compensation rose. Temporarily, the deficit increased more than it would have under more normal conditions. However, cyclical increases in the deficit are normally corrected by an ensuing expansion. Thus, the recession can only absorb a small part of the blame for the high deficits.

HIGH INTEREST RATES

A second factor contributing to the deficit problem was the fact that both nominal interest rates and real interest rates (nominal rates corrected for inflation) remained high throughout the early 1980s.[4] From 1979 to 1983, the interest rate on a three-month Treasury bill (a very short-term, riskless investment) was over 10 percent. Although interest rates fell in the

---

3. In *Day of Reckoning* (Chapter 10), Benjamin Friedman argues persuasively that the increases in work effort, saving, and so on would have to be much more massive than had ever been observed in order for this supply side idea to work.
4. The relationship between nominal and real interest rates is discussed in Chapter 13.

latter part of the 1980s, the T-bill rate was still higher than it had been for most of the preceding three decades. Interest rates were slow to fall even in nominal terms. In real terms, they have remained high into the 1990s.

When the government borrows money, it must pay interest. Interest must be paid not only on new debt (the deficit) but on all outstanding debt as well (the national debt). In 1980, net interest payments amounted to 8.9 percent of total federal spending. By 1990, interest payments had risen to 14.7 percent of spending. A combination of a larger debt and high interest rates accounted for the increase in the interest payments from $53 billion in 1980 to $171 billion in 1990. This large annual commitment of funds makes it much harder for the President and Congress to cut spending.

GRAMM-RUDMAN-HOLLINGS AND A BALANCED BUDGET

The rapid growth of the national debt alarmed some politicians and created pressure for restricting Congress's unlimited ability to spend. After many years of proposing a balanced budget amendment to the Constitution, which would require a balanced budget on an annual basis, Congress took action by passing the Gramm-Rudman-Hollings Act in 1985. This act set a timetable for reducing the deficit from over $200 billion in 1986 to zero in 1990. Targets were set for each year. However, the President and Congress were required to meet the targets only in the projected budget (based on assumptions about economic conditions), not the actual budget. Failure to meet the targets (not to mention failure to enact a budget at all by October 1st, which often occurs) would automatically trigger painful across-the-board cuts in most federal spending programs.

Clearly, the zero-deficit goal for 1990 was not attained. The size of the deficits did decrease for several years but rose again in fiscal 1990. The deficit reduction plan was revised and extended first to 1993, then to 1996. Each fall still seems to bring a serious crisis as the threat of Gramm-Rudman-Hollings looms over the budget process. Some of the decline in the deficits from 1986 to 1989 was the result of spending cuts and gradual increases in tax revenues from economic growth. Part of the deficit reduction consisted of accounting tricks, sales of assets, and increased revenues in the Social Security Trust Fund. At the end of the 1980s, it seemed that there might be reduced defense spending, the so-called peace dividend, a result of changes in Eastern Europe. This reduced spending combined with rising tax revenues and holding the line on nondefense spending would gradually reduce the deficit. However, the 1990–1991 recession, the war in the Persian Gulf, and the huge cost of the savings and loan bailout sharply increased the 1990 and 1991 deficits and dimmed hopes for reducing deficits in the next few years. (The savings and loan crisis is discussed in a later chapter.)

Both the Gramm-Rudman-Hollings Act and a frequently proposed constitutional amendment requiring a balanced budget involve limits on the freedom of the President and Congress to spend. They also make it more difficult to pursue expansionary fiscal policy or to respond to other needs. Neither policy solves the basic dilemma of how to link the level of public spending to tax revenues while allowing for year-to-year changes based on the state of the economy and the needs of public policy.

SHOULD THE BUDGET BE BALANCED?

The debate over balancing the budget arises from the conflicting needs for appropriate fiscal policy and some degree of budgetary control. This debate is far from new. Before Keynes, the conventional wisdom called for an **annually balanced budget**. In this view, revenues should be equal to expenditures on an annual basis. An annually balanced budget would force Congress to collect taxes to pay for spending programs and thus restrict the growth of government. It would not allow the use of any kind of fiscal policy.

Keynesian economists suggested, instead, a **cyclically balanced budget**. In this case, surpluses during the expansion phase of the business cycle would offset deficits incurred in the recession phase. Over the course of the cycle, the budget would balance. The cyclically balanced budget was a nice idea in theory but hard to apply in practice. For example, a prolonged recession followed by a weak and brief expansion would generate a large deficit and then a small surplus.

Economists who raised such practical objections searched for other approaches to the problem of deficits. Some wanted to throw out the whole idea of balancing the budget and simply let a surplus or deficit emerge from the need to stabilize the economy. This idea was called **functional finance**. The problem with functional finance was that it ignored the issue of putting some limits on government spending.

THE HIGH-EMPLOYMENT BALANCED BUDGET

In the 1960s, a new idea about balancing the budget arose. The **high-employment balanced budget** incorporated the concern about balancing taxes and spending, the need for fiscal policy, and the newly recognized automatic stabilizers. In this view, the actual budget need not be balanced, but tax rates and transfer programs should be set so that the budget would be balanced at the full-employment level of output (Y^*). Those who developed this idea said that the actual deficit or surplus is not important. What is meaningful is what the surplus or deficit would be at the full-employment level of output. The adoption of a high-employment balanced budget as a policy goal was a major victory for Keynesian ideas.

The actual deficit is a poor measure for fiscal policy because it reflects not only decisions about taxing and spending but also the state of the economy. If output (Y) falls far below the full-employment level (Y^*), progressive income taxes and transfer programs will create a deficit as tax revenues fall and transfer payments rise. This deficit is acceptable from a Keynesian standpoint because it helps to stabilize the level of income and output. But if the economy were producing at Y^*, even with no action by Congress, there might not be a deficit. What policy makers need to look at is not the actual deficit but what the deficit would be at Y^*. Figure 2 shows the various levels of taxes (T) and spending (G) that a particular set of tax rates, transfer programs, and spending programs will generate at various national income (Y) levels. At an equilibrium level of income ($Y_e = \$2,500$), the deficit is $70 billion. If the economy were at full employment ($Y^* = \$3,500$), there would be a surplus of $25 billion.

The notion of a high-employment surplus gives policy makers both a

---

annually balanced budget The view that government revenues should be equal to expenditures on an annual basis.

cyclically balanced budget The idea that surpluses during expansionary periods should offset deficits during recessionary periods so that the budget balances over the course of the business cycle.

functional finance The idea that a balanced budget is less important than a stable economy.

high-employment balanced budget The view that tax rates and transfer payments should be set so as to balance the budget at the full-employment level of output Y^*. (The actual budget need not be balanced.)

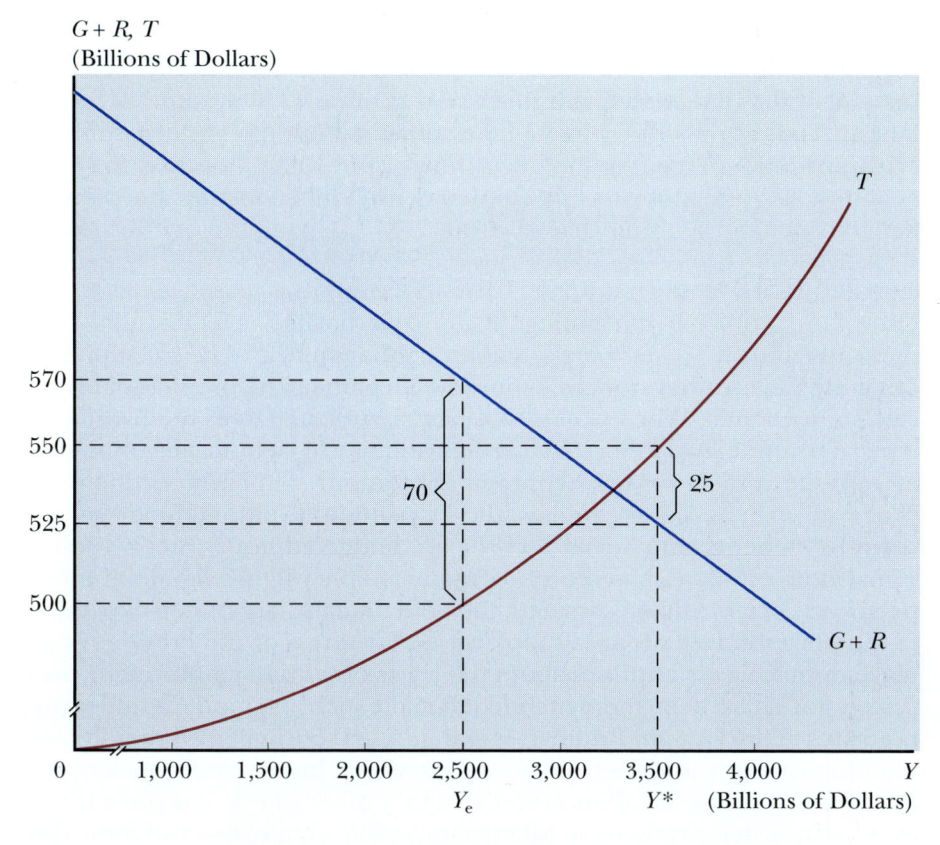

Chapter 10 Budget Deficits and the National Debt

**FIGURE 2
BALANCING THE BUDGET AT THE FULL-EMPLOYMENT LEVEL**
The budget surplus or deficit is equal to government purchases of goods and services (G) plus transfer payments (R) minus taxes (T). When income rises, transfers fall and taxes rise. There is a surplus of $25 billion at the full-employment level of income ($Y^* = \$3{,}500$ billion) but a deficit of $70 billion at the current equilibrium income ($Y_e = \$2{,}500$ billion).

goal to work toward and a measure of the direction of fiscal policy (whether it is contractionary or expansionary). Just because a deficit exists doesn't necessarily mean that the government is pursuing an expansionary fiscal policy. The President and Congress may even be pursuing a contractionary policy. The deficit may simply be the result of automatic stabilizers and recessionary conditions. When economists want to measure the direction of fiscal policy, they look at changes in the high-employment budget surplus or deficit rather than the actual deficit.

THE STRUCTURAL DEFICIT AND THE CYCLICAL DEFICIT
Two new terms were created in the 1980s to distinguish between the part of a deficit related to a downturn of the economy and the part of a deficit that would persist at full employment. The **structural deficit** is the part of a deficit that would persist even if the economy were at the full-employment level. This term is closely related to the concept of a high-employment balanced budget. However, the high-employment balanced budget is regarded as a policy target, but the structural deficit has no such normative meaning. The **cyclical deficit** is that part of a deficit that is due to a downturn in economic activity.

Both these concepts take their meaning from the comparison of potential output to actual output. **Potential output** is another name for the output the economy could produce if all its resources were fully employed. Potential output is thus a number or range of numbers that cor-

structural deficit
The part of a deficit that would persist even if the economy were at the full-employment level of output.

cyclical deficit
The part of a deficit that is due to a downturn in economic activity.

potential output
The output an economy could produce if all of its resources were fully employed.

responds to the full-employment level of output (Y^*) from the aggregate supply and demand and Keynesian models. If the structural deficit is zero, then all of the budget deficit is due to the economy falling short of its potential. That is, there are many idle resources. With unemployment hovering around 5 percent at the beginning of the 1990s, however, the U.S. economy is quite close to full employment. Thus, most of the current deficit is structural rather than cyclical.

THE PROJECTED DEFICIT AND THE ACTUAL DEFICIT

One of the problems with taming the deficit is that its size is difficult to predict and control. The automatic stabilizers that appear to be so helpful in directing the economy toward a more stable path create problems in forecasting the deficit. When Congress enacts a budget, it does not legislate a level of revenue but rather a tax structure that will yield varying amounts of revenue under varying economic conditions. Similarly, entitlement programs such as Aid to Families with Dependent Children, food stamps, veterans' benefits, and Social Security are budgeted not as precise dollar sums but as estimates based on how many people will be eligible. If more people are eligible than estimated, the deficit will be larger than expected.

To make budget proposals look rosier, Congress or the President can make optimistic assumptions about the levels of output, employment, and prices. Both have been more inclined to make such assumptions under the pressures of the Gramm-Rudman-Hollings Act. If output grows rapidly and unemployment is low, then tax revenues will be higher and transfer programs will cost less. If inflation remains low, there will be less pressure to increase transfer payments or salaries for public employees. Inflation also affects the revenue side. With low inflation rates, taxpayers do not find themselves in higher tax brackets because of increased nominal income. For all these reasons, the budget surplus or deficit projected by both the Office of Management and Budget and the Congressional Budget Office is likely to be very different from the actual budget. Output, employment, and inflation rates often differ from what the budget makers assumed.

Another source of error in estimating the deficit is changes in interest rates. With interest payments on the national debt accounting for about 14 percent of federal spending, market interest rates have an important influence on the spending side of the budget. When the Treasury has to sell newly issued bonds, interest rates that are higher than expected will add to the deficit, and lower than expected rates will reduce it.

Long-range projections of the deficit are even more prone to error. They must anticipate changes in output, exchange rates, labor force participation, investment, productivity, and other determinants of government revenues and expenditures. Forecasts of declining deficits in the late 1980s did not anticipate how expensive it would be to bail out failed savings and loans, a major drain on the federal budget in recent years. By 1989, some economists were projecting that in the absence of a recession, the budget deficit would gradually decline if the President and Congress held firm on new spending programs while tax revenues continued to rise with economic growth. The combination of a recession and the unexpectedly large cost of the savings and loan bailout made their predictions far off the mark.

Political factors play a role in forecasts as well. For most of the 1980s, the executive branch (home of the Council of Economic Advisers) was under the control of one political party, while Congress (home of the Congressional Budget Office) had a majority from the other. The forecasts by the CEA were often more optimistic than those of the CBO. The CEA projected higher real growth and lower unemployment. However, a careful comparison to private forecasts shows that, while both the CEA's and the CBO's forecasts are prone to error, neither shows any permanent bias toward erring on the side of optimism or pessimism.[5]

Balancing fiscal policy with controlling the size of the public sector and limiting the size of the deficit is a tough political task. It is made much more difficult by the fact that the actual deficit is not known until after the fiscal year is over.

Obviously, there is a political incentive for the administration to use clever accounting to conceal or reduce the apparent size of the deficit. Presenting the actual deficit as well as the budget in such a way as to make the deficit look smaller is an old practice. Beginning in 1967, the Johnson administration changed the way the budget was presented to a unified format that included Social Security revenues and expenditures. This change was made at least partly to gloss over the deficit by making it appear smaller. When the President and Congress came up with the savings and loan bailout plan in 1989, they put large parts of it "off budget." That is, the bailout is being financed outside the regular budget and is thus not counted in the deficit. When the government sells assets, as it did often in the late 1980s in an effort to at least approach the Gramm-Rudman-Hollings targets for deficit reduction, the proceeds help to reduce the deficit, but only in the current year.

SOCIAL SECURITY AND THE DEFICIT

The federal budget deficits peaked in 1986, then declined steadily in nominal terms before rising again in 1990 and 1991. A large part of the improvement in 1986–1989 was due not to direct Congressional action or better economic conditions, but rather to reforms in the Social Security system, enacted in 1983. Noting that there would have to be increased outlays in the period after the year 2000, as the baby boomers began to reach retirement age, a special presidential commission proposed increasing Social Security taxes to build up a surplus in the Social Security Trust Fund. Since Social Security taxes are collected and benefits are paid out by the federal government, the taxes appear as revenue and the benefits as expenditures in the combined federal budget. Technically, Social Security funds are separate, but the number reported as the overall budget deficit or surplus has included them since 1967.

When the Social Security Trust Fund runs a surplus, those funds are invested in federal government bonds until they are needed to pay benefits. What will happen when the baby boomers start to retire? In theory, other taxes will be increased or other spending decreased in order to provide the revenue to retire those bonds and pay the benefits. In other

---

5. Michael T. Belongia, "Are Economic Forecasts by Government Agencies Biased? Accurate?" *Review of the Federal Reserve Bank of St. Louis* (November/December 1988): 15–23.

TABLE 2
FEDERAL REVENUES, EXPENDITURES, AND DEFICITS WITH AND WITHOUT SOCIAL SECURITY FOR FISCAL YEARS 1980–1990 (BILLIONS OF DOLLARS)

YEAR	FEDERAL REVENUES WITH SS	FEDERAL REVENUES WITHOUT SS	FEDERAL EXPENDITURES WITH SS	FEDERAL EXPENDITURES WITHOUT SS	FEDERAL DEFICIT WITH SS	FEDERAL DEFICIT WITHOUT SS
1980	$ 517.1	359.3	$ 590.9	$240.8	$ 73.8	$118.5
1981	599.3	416.6	678.2	538.6	78.9	112.0
1982	617.8	416.3	745.7	589.7	127.9	173.4
1983	600.6	391.6	808.3	637.6	207.8	246.0
1984	666.5	427.1	851.8	673.6	185.3	246.5
1985	734.1	547.9	946.3	757.7	212.3	209.8
1986	769.1	485.2	990.3	791.5	221.2	306.3
1987	854.1	550.8	1,003.8	796.4	149.7	246.4
1988	909.0	574.7	1,064.1	844.7	155.1	270.0
1989	990.7	727.0	1,144.1	915.1	151.9	188.1
1990	1,031.3	749.7	1,251.7	969.7	123.7*	181.6*

*Estimated.

Source: Council of Economic Advisers, *Economic Report of the President* (Washington, DC: U.S. Government Printing Office, 1991), pp. 398–399.

words, Social Security revenues are being used to finance a part of the regular budget deficit. There will have to be future budget surpluses to repay the "loan" from the Social Security Trust Fund.

There are other special funds and off-budget categories, but Social Security is by far the largest. Table 2 shows federal revenues, expenditures, and deficits with and without Social Security, from 1980 to 1990. As you can see, much of the recent apparent reduction in the deficit is due to increased net revenues in the Social Security system. Social Security revenues have been increasing more rapidly than other federal revenues, while Social Security expenditures have risen more slowly.[6]

The Social Security Trust Fund represents a real policy challenge. It is projected to rise by a large amount in the next thirty years, then drop sharply until about 2050. One option for public policy is to ignore these changes and balance the rest of the budget (which would make the budget deflationary for the next thirty years). Another option, more or less the one that has been pursued for the last twenty-five years, is to treat the federal budget as a single entity. Thus, current Social Security revenues offset deficits in the rest of the budget. In terms of the current impact of federal spending and taxing on the economy, this approach makes a great deal of sense. But unlike other revenues, Social Security revenues carry a deferred commitment to pay benefits. Paying those benefits (by repaying the Trust Fund) will require higher taxes or less spending for other purposes in the future.

In the 1990 *Economic Report of the President*, the Bush administration put forth a proposal addressing the relation of Social Security to budget deficits. This proposal called for continued reduction in the deficit for the

---

6. The use of Social Security revenues to reduce the deficit has received a lot of attention in the last few years. For example, in 1990 Senator Daniel Moynihan proposed reducing the Social Security payroll tax and addressing the deficit in other ways. For two views on this issue, see Lee Smith, "Trim That Social Security Surplus," *Fortune* (August 29, 1988): 84–89; and Alan S. Blinder, "Congress Should Keep Its Hands off This Nest Egg," *Business Week* (July 4, 1988): 20.

combined budget, with a goal of zero deficit by 1994. After that, further deficit reductions would be pursued until the regular budget was in balance. Then there would be a net surplus for the combined budget, reflecting the surplus in the Social Security Trust Fund.

DO DEFICITS MATTER?

The major advantage of being able to run deficits is that they make it possible to use fiscal policy in order to stabilize the level of output and unemployment. However, there are costs associated with running deficits. A number of problems have been attributed to deficits and the growing national debt. Are deficits a problem? Economists differ on this question.

YES: THE GROWTH OF THE PUBLIC SECTOR

When deficits are not controlled, there is no constraint on the size of the public sector. If the government had to finance all its spending out of tax revenues, it would have to weigh the pleasure citizens derive from spending programs against their pain in paying taxes. The necessity to tax would be a constraint on spending. With deficits, legislators can adopt a "spend now, pay later" approach. And "later" is likely to be after they have left office. When the cost of spending programs is not immediately apparent as higher taxes, both legislators and citizens may underestimate the cost of government programs. The expansion of government programs may then take too large a share of total resources. Being able to spend without taxing, at least in the short run, means that added spending has zero opportunity cost for politicians.

YES: HIGHER INTEREST RATES AND INTEREST PAYMENTS

When the government runs a deficit, it borrows by issuing bonds, just as corporations do. In selling bonds, the government competes for funds in the credit market, driving up interest rates for all borrowers. The real interest rate measures the actual cost of repaying a loan in dollars at the time the loan is repaid. The real interest rate is the market interest rate minus the expected rate of inflation. Through the 1980s, this rate remained high relative to the past.

The large deficits of recent years have made many economists concerned that competition from the federal government in the credit market and the resulting high interest rates have discouraged borrowing for private investment. This effect is known as **crowding out**. In fact, the high interest rates have attracted foreign funds to the United States, which have limited the crowding out of private investment.

crowding out
The negative effect on borrowing for private investment due to competition from the federal government in the credit market.

The high interest rates, especially in the early 1980s, also increased the fraction of federal spending going to interest payments on the national debt from 8.9 percent in 1980 to 14.7 percent in 1990. With more and more funds diverted to interest payments, Congress has less choice about the use of funds or about budget cutting. Cutting the size of the deficit in any given year has almost no impact on the interest liability. Only surpluses that actually reduce the debt and/or lower interest rates would reduce this large piece of the budget.

Economic Insight

The Third Deficit?

A group of U.S. economists told a Joint Economic Committee hearing in 1989 that the budget deficit was causing a reduction in public investment in two areas critical to the nation's future. Those two areas are physical infrastructure and children. They named this failure to invest the "third deficit."

During the 1980s, budget makers had to hold the line on nondefense spending because of a political commitment to higher defense spending without any increase in taxes. As a result, funding for existing nondefense programs was scarce, and that for new programs almost nonexistent. This failure to spend in certain key areas may have a long-term impact on productivity and economic growth, according to these economists. One group of neglected expenditures, in their view, includes spending for highways, bridges, mass transit, airports, water supply, and waste disposal. All of these things are highly important to industry as well as to households. The other area of concern of these economists is investment in education for low-income children and youth. Not enough is being done in teaching basic skills, dropout prevention, and job training.[a]

Total government spending grew by 79 percent (not adjusted for inflation) between 1981 and 1990. The areas identified by the concerned economists grew much more slowly. Their first area of concern fits into the budget category of transportation and community and regional development. Their second concern matches with the budget heading of education, training, employment, and social services. Spending in these categories grew by only 11 percent between 1981 and 1990. Such a small nominal increase translates into a large decrease after correcting for inflation. These two categories now constitute a much smaller share of the budget.

The debate on the "third deficit" highlights the fact that the budget is an expression of priorities and values as well as a fiscal policy tool. In the 1980s, there appeared to be a strong consensus for lower taxes and more defense spending. These choices were combined with increasing interest payments on the national debt, growth in a few transfer programs, and a growing determination to contain the size of the deficit. Cuts had to come somewhere. Some of the tradeoff has clearly come out of the kinds of nondefense spending that this group of economists has identified.

---

a. This argument, put forth by a group of economists at the Economic Policy Institute, was summarized in "Pay Now or Pay Later," *Washington Post National Weekly Edition* (July 31–August 6, 1989): 5.

Maybe: A Burden on Our Grandchildren?

The burden of the debt usually means the problems that will arise when it is repaid. President Eisenhower was the first to worry publicly about passing a burden of debt to our grandchildren. Often the size of the national debt is given per person. People who worry about the burden of the debt on the next generation point out that every child born today assumes a national debt burden of more than $11,000.[7]

How valid is this concern? Does a free-spending generation pass on a heavy burden to the next? Not necessarily. Basically, the burden of the national debt falls on the generation in which the debt is incurred. These people are the ones who give up consumption in order to make resources available for government spending. Deficit financing of government spending, just like taxation, takes resources away from the private sector and transfers them to the government. The loss of current consumption is borne by the generation that lent to the government, not their grandchildren. During World War II, the government ran large deficits to finance the war effort. The cost was borne by those who were working, paying taxes, and buying war bonds between 1941 and 1945. They paid by consuming fewer goods and services, because the output mix was skewed toward military production.

Sometimes the national debt is incurred in ways that benefit the next generation. Fighting World War II created benefits for the next generation in terms of the kind of world they inherited. If the government had not borrowed money to fight the war, you might have been born into a totalitarian society. Future generations may benefit from debt incurred through expansionary fiscal policy. If the government borrows to expand the productive capacity of the economy and put idle resources to work, then future generations will inherit a larger capital stock and enjoy a higher output. They will benefit from the borrowing and spending activity that created the debt. When the time comes to repay the debt, it can be repaid more easily out of the higher national income that will result from the productive use of borrowed funds in an earlier time.

Running deficits can create some future problems, however. If funds are borrowed by the government during a period when the economy is close to full employment, such as the last half of the 1980s, then resources may have been diverted away from productive investment. As the government drove up interest rates in the credit market, some private borrowers who wanted funds to build housing, factories, and shopping centers were priced out of the credit market. (We will look more closely at the relationship between deficits, interest rates, and private investment in Chapter 13.) Thus, future generations may be worse off as a result of current borrowing, because of the productive capital that was not created during this period.

When and if the government repays part of the debt, some citizens will be taxed to repay the maturing bonds owned by others. If most bond holders are rich, repaying the debt will mean some redistribution of income from the poor to the rich. In addition, if the government must cut spending programs in order to use tax revenues to repay the debt, the people

---

7. To be accurate, that burden should be adjusted for inflation, so that it is expressed in terms of constant purchasing power.

> **THE COSTS OF THE NATIONAL DEBT**
>
> - The private sector output given up at the time the debt was incurred
> - Lack of constraint on the growth of the public sector
> - Higher interest rates that discourage private investment and reduce the future capital stock
> - Future repayment of debt held by foreigners
> - Income redistribution when the debt is repaid

who would benefit from those spending programs will essentially be "taxed" to pay back the debt.

Finally, Americans no longer simply owe the debt to themselves. High interest rates in the United States during most of the 1980s attracted foreign lenders. Many of them bought U.S. government bonds. About 20 percent of the national debt owed to individuals is owed to foreigners, mostly Japanese. Currently, about $30 billion in interest payments on the national debt is sent abroad. When those bonds are redeemed, the United States will have to transfer real goods and services away from domestic uses in order to pay back the bond holders.[8] Repaying the debt to foreigners is a burden that will fall on future generations.

NO: RICARDIAN EQUIVALENCE

Economist Robert Barro has argued that the choice of deficit spending versus tax financing doesn't matter.[9] According to Barro, rational consumers will recognize that debt financing simply means higher future taxes to pay off the debt. Thus, any increase in their current spending because of higher disposable income would be offset by a reduction in current spending because of anticipated lower future disposable income. That is, they will consume less and save more because of anticipated higher future taxes. This concept is called Ricardian equivalence.

Few economists accept Barro's argument that the impact of tax and debt financing is exactly the same, and there has been little real-world evidence to support the theory. However, Barro does offer a useful insight: The difference in impact between different methods of government financing may be smaller than expected.

NO: THE REAL DEFICIT ARGUMENT

Another argument that minimizes the importance of deficits is the real deficit argument. Some economists, most notably Robert Eisner, claim that the deficit that matters is not the nominal deficit but the real deficit.[10]

---

8. In addition, if a lot of foreign-held debt is redeemed at once, the loss of foreign funds could create a shortage of loanable funds in credit markets and drive up interest rates for domestic borrowers of all kinds, including the government.
9. Robert Barro, "Are Government Bonds Net Wealth?" *Journal of Political Economy* (December 1974): 1094–1118; "The Ricardian Approach to Budget Deficits," *Journal of Economic Perspectives* (Spring 1989): 37–54.
10. Robert Eisner, "Budget Deficits: Rhetoric and Reality," *Journal of Economic Perspectives* (Spring 1989): 73–93. Eisner also suggests a number of other adjustments to the deficit, such as separating out investment-type expenditures and not counting sales of government assets.

The **real deficit** measures the federal budget deficit as the change in the real (inflation-adjusted) value of the national debt from one year to the next. During a period of inflation, the real value of the debt falls. Thus, a budget deficit during an inflationary period could occur at the same time as a fall in the real value of the national debt. If the deficit is measured as the change in that real value, what was a deficit by usual measures might turn out to be a surplus!

This may sound like lying with statistics. We can make the argument more concrete with some numbers. Suppose the national debt at the beginning of a year is $200 billion, and the current-year deficit is $10 billion. Prices rise by 10 percent. At the end of the year, the $210 billion in debt (including $10 billion in new debt from the current deficit) is worth, in real terms, only $210 billion/1.10 = $190.9 billion. The deficit of $10 billion disappears when it is measured in real terms. By such a measure, the deficit should be equal to the change in the value of the outstanding debt. That adjustment turns a $10 billion deficit into a surplus of $9.1 billion!

The deficits of the 1980s do look a little less frightening when measured either in real terms or as a fraction of GNP. The sleight-of-hand trick in the preceding paragraph cannot convert the deficits of the 1980s into surpluses, but it does bring them down to less alarming levels. Table 3 shows what happens to the nominal deficit and the change in national debt when they are measured as the real deficit and as a fraction of GNP.

The data in Table 3 don't change the fact that the deficit grew in the 1980s—in nominal terms, in real terms, and as a percentage of GNP. Furthermore, however the debt and deficits are measured, the basic problem remains. The ability to run unlimited deficits frees politicians from the need to raise the money in taxes for programs they want to fund. That political reality has contributed to the growth of government beyond what

> **real deficit**
> A measure of the federal budget deficit as the change in the real (inflation-adjusted) value of the national debt from one year to the next.

TABLE 3
NOMINAL DEFICIT AND REAL DEFICIT FOR THE FISCAL YEARS 1980–1990

YEAR	NOMINAL DEFICIT (BILLIONS OF DOLLARS)	CHANGE IN NATIONAL DEBT* (BILLIONS OF DOLLARS)	REAL DEFICIT† (BILLIONS OF DOLLARS)	NOMINAL DEFICIT/GNP (%)
1980	73.8	69.5	81.6	2.7
1981	78.9	75.5	84.4	2.6
1982	127.9	134.4	135.0	4.0
1983	207.8	211.8	204.4	6.1
1984	185.3	169.0	158.3	4.9
1985	212.3	199.4	177.0	5.3
1986	221.2	236.8	206.3	5.2
1987	150.4	151.9	128.1	3.4
1988	155.1	161.9	133.5	3.0
1989	152.0	139.1	110.1	2.9
1990	220.4	220.1	162.6	2.3

*Increase in the debt from the end of the previous year to the end of the current year, held by the public. Social Security revenues are subtracted from the revenue side, and that part of the debt held by the Social Security Trust Fund is not counted as part of the total national debt.

†Change in the national debt divided by the GNP deflator (equal to 100 in 1982).

Source: Council of Economic Advisers, *Economic Report of the President* (Washington, DC: U.S. Government Printing Office, 1991).

taxpayers might choose if they were paying the bill directly. In that sense, deficits are still a matter for concern.

NO: THE STATE AND LOCAL SURPLUS

The total impact of government taxes and spending on output involves the combined actions of all governments—federal, state, and local. Local governments usually come quite close to balancing their budgets. State governments rather consistently ran surpluses throughout the 1980s. From 1980 to 1990, these surpluses totaled $511.0 billion, or about 52 percent of the federal deficits during that period.

To some extent this argument mixes apples and oranges. State governments are quite different from the federal government. For one thing, states are much more limited in their ability to run long-term deficits. Many of them are constrained by their constitutions. Even those that do not have balanced budget requirements find their bonds harder to sell if they keep running deficits. Even if states could run deficits for long periods, there is no way to integrate those deficits into fiscal policy. Congress can influence state and local spending through changes in federal grants but cannot exercise any direct control over state and local budgets. As a tool of fiscal policy, only the federal budget is under the control of the policy makers.

Furthermore, the states' surpluses appear to have been temporary. A large part of them was due to retirement contributions. As state employees begin to retire in larger numbers in future years, those surpluses will shrink. Declining federal defense spending has hit certain states hard. Falling incomes and declining property values in some states have turned budget surpluses into deficits and forced tax increases. In most states, there are increased pressures to build prisons, combat homelessness, take care of Medicaid patients, and replace parts of the infrastructure (especially roads and schools). These demands on the states, which have been receiving smaller and smaller amounts of federal aid, mean that their surpluses are projected to be smaller in the 1990s. State and local budget surpluses may help to mitigate federal deficits, but they seem likely to be of less help in the near future than they were in the last decade.

SUMMARY

1. The United States has run large budget deficits for the last decade. As a result, there has been a large increase in the national debt, both in nominal terms and relative to GNP.

2. Fiscal policy can lead to a larger national debt if deficits exceed surpluses. Most deficits are at least partly due to politicians' reluctance to raise taxes or cut spending.

3. The growth of the national debt in the early 1980s was the result of the 1981 tax cut, increased defense spending, the 1981–1982 recession, and high interest rates.

4. The Gramm-Rudman-Hollings Act of 1985 represented an attempt to force Congress and the President to reduce the deficit by targeted amounts over a period of several years.

5. Differing ideas about when or whether to balance the federal budget include the annually balanced budget, functional finance, the cyclically balanced budget, and the high-employment balanced budget. A surplus or deficit for the high-employment balanced budget is used as a measure of the direction of fiscal policy.

6. The cyclical deficit is that part of the deficit resulting from a gap between actual and potential output. The structural deficit is the deficit that would still persist even if the economy were at the full-employment level of output.

7. The actual deficit is difficult to control because it depends on economic conditions. In forecasting the expected deficit, politicians may use optimistic assumptions to make it look smaller.

8. Increased Social Security revenues with only modest increases in benefit payments offset part of the federal budget deficits in the 1980s. Such revenues bring with them the obligation to pay benefits in the future.

9. Deficits are a matter of concern because they may increase the size of government, drive up interest rates, and impose a burden on future generations because of lost productive investment and higher debt to foreigners.

10. One argument that deficits do not matter is based on the idea of Ricardian equivalence—that people will save more in anticipation of higher future taxes. Another argument stresses the real deficit, or changes in the inflation-adjusted value of the debt. State and local surpluses also partly offset the federal deficit.

New Terms

deficit
national debt
annually balanced budget
cyclically balanced budget
functional finance
high-employment balanced budget
structural deficit
cyclical deficit
potential output
crowding out
real deficit

Questions for Discussion

1. What is the real deficit? What are the risks of using this measure instead of the nominal deficit?

2. Suppose the consumption function is $C = \$300$ billion $+ 0.9Y_d$ and the values of I, G, and $(EX - IM)$ are each $\$100$ billion. Taxes (T) and transfer payments (R) are dependent on the level of income according to $T = -\$40$ billion $+ 0.15Y$ and $R = \$500$ billion $- 0.1Y$. Since you know that $Y_d = Y - T + R$, the new consumption function is $C = \$300 + 0.9(Y + \$40 - 0.15Y + \$500 - 0.1Y)$, where all figures are in billions. Use this relationship to determine the equilibrium value of Y. What is the actual surplus or deficit in the government budget? If $Y^* = \$4,000$ billion, what is the high-employment surplus or deficit? Does this indicate that fiscal policy is expansionary or contractionary?

3. Given the following relationships, develop a table that shows the surplus or deficit in the government budget at Y values (in billions) of $\$500$, $\$1,000$, and $\$1,500$. At what level of Y will the government's budget balance?

   $G = \$150$
   $T = -\$25 + 0.2Y$
   $R = \$125 - 0.1Y$

4. Does Keynesian fiscal policy necessarily mean deficits?

5. Will the federal borrowing in the 1980s impose a burden on future generations? Why or why not? How is it different from federal borrowing during the 1930s?

6. What would happen to the real deficit if there was high inflation but no change in the nominal deficit?

7. Suppose businesses in the United States adopt early retirement plans on a large scale. As a result, a much higher proportion of workers decide to retire at sixty-two (when they are first eligible for Social Security benefits) rather than at sixty-five. What would happen to the federal budget deficit?

8. Why does the actual deficit almost always turn out to be very different from the projected deficit?

9. What is a structural deficit? A cyclical deficit? Which is of greater concern?

10. Why is the high-employment surplus or deficit rather than the actual surplus or deficit used to determine the direction of fiscal policy?

11. Why do some politicians advocate an annually balanced budget? What problems would this policy create?

12. Why do some economists say the budget deficit should be measured as the combined federal, state, and local deficit? What problems would this create?

13. Which measure of the deficit would you use for each of the following purposes?

    a. determining the direction of fiscal policy
    b. measuring the inflation-adjusted deficit
    c. estimating the deficit that would persist even at full employment
    d. determining the part of the deficit due to unfavorable economic conditions

SUGGESTIONS FOR FURTHER READING

Aaron, Henry J., Barry P. Bosworth, and Gary Burtless. *Can America Afford to Grow Old?* Washington, DC: Brookings Institution, 1989. A close look at the demographics, economics, and politics of the Social Security system.

Blinder, Alan. *Soft Heads, Hard Hearts*. New York: Addison-Wesley, 1987. This readable book by a well-known contemporary economist takes a critical look at budget deficits and other current issues, such as trade policy and welfare, from a moderately liberal perspective.

Friedman, Benjamin. *Day of Reckoning*. New York: Random House, 1988. A critical look at U.S. policies in the 1980s that led to the increase in federal budget deficits and an outline of policies to address those concerns in the 1990s.

Savage, James D. *Balanced Budget and American Politics*. Ithaca, NY: Cornell University Press, 1988. A historical and political look at the controversy over balancing the federal budget.

MONEY, FINANCIAL MARKETS, AND MONETARY POLICY

4

AFTER STUDYING THIS CHAPTER, YOU SHOULD BE ABLE TO:

1. Explain why money replaces barter as a society becomes more complex and specialized.
2. List the four functions of money and briefly discuss the meaning of each one.
3. Identify the desirable properties of money.
4. List and explain the motives for holding money.
5. Define each of the following kinds of monetary assets:
   a. bank notes,
   b. greenbacks,
   c. commodity money,
   d. full-bodied money,
   e. fiat money,
   f. certificates of deposit,
   g. checkable deposits,
   h. time deposits,
   i. near money.
6. Explain the differences between M1, M2, and M3.
7. Describe the relationship between changes in the money supply and aggregate demand.

CHAPTER 11

MONEY: WHAT IT IS AND WHY PEOPLE HOLD IT

INTRODUCTION

Consumption, investment, government spending, and net exports—the key variables in the last three chapters—are the real flows of goods and services in the circular flow diagram. However, the circular flow diagram also shows flows of money payments and even a credit market. Starting in this chapter, we will expand this model to include money, financial instruments, banks, and financial markets.

The word *money* means different things to different people. The variety of meanings often leads to misunderstandings between economists and noneconomists. Here are some ways in which economists *don't* use the word money:

1. How much money (income) did you earn last year?
2. Most of his money (wealth) is tied up in bonds.
3. It's almost impossible to get mortgage money (credit) in today's market.
4. This country does not have enough money (resources) to increase both military and social spending.

When economists use the word *money*, they usually mean items (cash and checking account balances) that are generally accepted as a means of payment. For example, "if I didn't keep some money on hand, I'd have to use my credit card every time I wanted to buy a candy bar."[1]

Money is not income, wealth, credit, or productive resources, although it is sometimes confused with each of those. This chapter discusses what money is, how it has evolved, and what the U.S. money supply consists of

---

1. Adapted from Ira Kaminow, "The Myth of Fiscal Policy: The Monetarist View," *Business Review*, Federal Reserve Bank of Philadelphia (December 1969).

in the 1990s. We will also look at what money does and how people decide how much money to hold.

Recall from Chapter 6 that we assumed a given money supply in drawing the aggregate demand curve and identified changes in the money supply as one of the factors that can shift that curve. Changes in the money supply were used to explain changes in the price level in the classical model in Chapter 7. The last three chapters, however, have put money on hold while developing the Keynesian explanation of how the levels of output and employment are determined. The simple Keynesian model assumes a fixed price level and a large quantity of idle resources. We will develop a more general model that applies when the economy is at or near full employment and the price level can rise. In such a model, changes in the supply and demand for money, as well as changes in consumption or investment demand or fiscal policy, can shift the aggregate expenditure and aggregate demand curves.

WHAT IS MONEY?

It is difficult to define money without knowing what it does. Let's start with a working definition: Money is something that people accept as payment for a good or service. (Later, after looking at the properties of money, the functions of money, and the reasons for holding money, we will be able to give a more precise definition.) This working definition draws attention to a basic requirement for anything that serves as money. It must be generally acceptable to those who are exchanging goods and services in markets.

If you go into a store and buy some socks or rent a video, chances are you pay with dollar bills, or Federal Reserve notes. Paper money has been used in the United States for nearly 300 years, since colonial times. The paper by itself is worth only a few cents, but you know you can exchange the bills for goods and services in stores, restaurants, and theaters. Other people are willing to accept these pieces of paper in trade for goods and services because they know they can, in turn, spend the money and pass it on to someone else. If you believed that no one would take the money, you wouldn't be interested in having it. If everyone thought the money was worthless, no one would take it. Then it really would be worthless because it couldn't be used to buy anything. Money has value because it is accepted as the means of exchange.

BARTER AND THE INVENTION OF MONEY

Your professors make a living by providing you with high-quality teaching services. They teach, not out of altruism, but because they want to get things in return, such as housing, food, books, and vacations. Professors, like other workers, sell their services in the resource market in order to make purchases in the goods market. And professors, like most people in modern industrial economies, specialize in producing just one or a few goods or services but want to purchase many different ones.

In societies that have only a few goods, trade can be carried out fairly easily. Certain tribes of pygmy hunters in Zaire trade ivory from their elephant hunts for the metal they need to make arrows and spears. They also trade for a few agricultural goods. Because most of their trade is in metal and tusks, prices are measured not in money but in terms such as arrow tips per tusk. Money is not needed here because few goods are traded. People can easily arrange to trade what they have for what they want. This type of direct trade of goods and services is called **barter**.

barter
Direct exchange of one good or service for another without the use of money.

Consider a barter economy in which a potter wants to buy a pizza. Such trades require a **double coincidence of wants**. That is, each trader must find a trading partner who wants what he or she offers and offers what he or she wants. If the potter goes to the market and the pizza maker wishes to exchange a pizza for a ceramic bowl, all is well. But what if the pizza maker isn't interested in pottery and wants a shirt instead? The potter then has to find someone who wants to trade a shirt for a bowl before going to trade with the pizza maker. In addition, a pizza or a shirt may not be equal in value to a bowl, raising the problem of making change. Barter is costly in terms of the time and effort required to find a trading partner.

double coincidence of wants
The necessary requirement for barter that each trader has what the other wants and wants what the other has.

A large or highly specialized economy cannot function by barter. A better system eliminates the need for the double coincidence of wants by finding one commodity that everyone will accept in trade. The most common solution to the problems of barter is to use money. This solution is extremely efficient because using money saves on the search and transactions costs that are involved in bartering. Although money has other uses, carrying out transactions is its most important role.

Even in modern industrial economies, people still engage in barter. Newspapers sometimes report creative barter transactions made to avoid taxes. Barter is common among friends and neighbors. Lawn mowing is traded for babysitting or the use of tools for some help with a fix-up project. Doctors have been known to perform operations in exchange for a two-week vacation at a beachfront condominium. Most transactions in the United States and other developed countries, however, are made with money rather than by barter.

THE FUNCTIONS OF MONEY

medium of exchange
A function of money in simplifying transactions by allowing people to exchange the goods and services they produce for money and then exchange money for other goods and services they want.

Because barter can be inconvenient, money developed as a means for trading in goods and services. That is, money serves as a **medium of exchange**. As a medium of exchange, money simplifies transactions by allowing people to exchange the goods and services they produce for money and then exchange money for other goods and services they want. People receive their wages in the form of money and use it to buy clothes, food, housing and other items. In the jargon of economics, money reduces transactions costs. This function is so important that it is the first part of our definition of money: In order for something to be money, it must be used to carry out transactions.

unit of account
A function of money in providing a measuring unit in terms of which goods can be valued and thus readily compared with each other.

A second function of money is to serve as a **unit of account**, a way to compare the costs, values, or prices of various goods.[2] In this sense, money is the equivalent of such measures as lengths or weights. If people did not

---

2. Because money does so many things, it's difficult to separate its function as the medium of exchange from that as a unit of account. It might help to think in terms of the bit, which is a rare example of a unit of account that is not also a medium of exchange (a coin or bill in circulation). Two bits equal 25 cents. The Spanish dollar used in the New World for some time consisted of pieces of eight. Each eighth of such a dollar was a bit.

have prices and money as a way of making comparisons, they would have to keep track of the value of each good in terms of all other goods. The price of an apple might be ⅔ of an orange, or ¹⁄₅₀₀ of a pair of shoes. In fact, in a barter economy that had only 100 goods, there would be 4,950 prices without money. (Imagine being an accountant in a barter economy!) Having money to serve as a unit of account reduces those 4,950 prices to 100 prices.[3]

The third function of money is to serve as a **standard of deferred payment**, allowing people to make contracts that extend into the future. As a standard of deferred payment, money gives borrowers and lenders a medium in which to express the repayment of debt in the future. If you work for someone today, you may be paid two weeks later. If you charge something on your credit card, you are agreeing to make a future payment. (If you don't know that, read the fine print on the back of the card!) In this way, money allows an economic link to the past and the future. It is easier to specify a repayment in terms of money than as a list of a number of goods and services.

The fourth and final function of money is to serve as a **store of value**, or financial asset. As a store of value, money provides a general form of purchasing power that can be held in order to buy goods and services in the future. A decision to store your wealth as automobiles works well only if you happen to need a car in the future or can easily and quickly find a car buyer when you need cash. Not knowing what their future needs will be, people usually want to store some wealth in a form that can serve as a medium of exchange. Then they will be able to easily convert their wealth into goods and services. The ease with which an asset can be converted into the medium of exchange is called **liquidity**. Money is the ultimate liquid asset because it already is the medium of exchange. In its function as a store of value, money competes with other (substitute) financial assets such as savings bonds or certificates of deposit. These assets offer interest but do not serve as a medium of exchange.

This list of functions makes it possible to replace the working definition of money with a more precise definition. Money is what money does. That is, anything that performs all four of the functions just listed is money. **Money** is any financial asset that serves as a medium of exchange, a unit of account, a standard of deferred payment, and a store of value.

Desirable Properties of Money

Money can take all kinds of forms. What should be used for money? Fishhooks? Stones? Shells? Beads? Tobacco? All of these have served as money at some time. Some of the desirable properties of money can be inferred by considering the forms of money that have been used for long periods and those that haven't made the grade. Experience suggests that money should have a stable value, be somewhat scarce (but not too scarce), and be portable, durable, uniform, divisible, acceptable, and transferable. Let's explore each of these properties.

---

standard of deferred payment
A function of money in providing borrowers and lenders a medium for the repayment of debt in the future.

store of value
A function of money in providing purchasing power in a general form that can be held in order to buy goods and services in the future.

liquidity
The measure of how quickly a financial asset can be converted into the medium of exchange.

money
Any financial asset that serves as a medium of exchange, a unit of account, a standard of deferred payment, and a store of value.

---

3. For 100 items, each having 99 prices in terms of the others, you might think there are 9,900 prices. But half of these can be eliminated. The price of apples in terms of oranges is just the reciprocal of the price of oranges in apples. That leaves 4,950 prices—still a lot to keep track of!

STABILITY OF VALUE. Stability of value means that purchasing power doesn't change very rapidly. If the value of a currency is stable, one currency unit (such as a dollar) buys about the same amount of goods and services, even though the prices of some items may rise or fall in response to changes in supply and demand in individual markets. A stable value is of key importance in making people want to use money and accept it. Inflation means that money is losing purchasing power. If further inflation is expected, money is a poor store of value.

Stability of value is especially important if money is to function as both a store of value and a standard of deferred payment. Money whose value is being eroded by inflation is not a satisfactory standard for determining loan repayment. The money repaid will have less value than the money borrowed. If you fear that the value of your money is in danger of being rapidly eroded by price increases, you may be tempted to switch some of your store of value into land, buildings, fine art, rare coins, diamonds, or gold. These other assets are real goods whose value rises when prices increase. Owning them thus partly protects you against inflation. The amount of money you hold as a store of value will depend on what you expect to happen to its future value. Stability of value depends on controlling the money supply (as you learned when we discussed the quantity theory of money in Chapter 7).

If several forms of money are available, the one whose value is most stable will be hoarded and disappear from circulation. People will choose to hold the more stable form of money as a store of value and attempt to use the money whose value is unstable as a medium of exchange. Sellers, however, will be reluctant to accept such money. If they do, they will try to pass it on quickly. This behavior has been observed so often that it has the status of a law. Gresham's law says, "Bad money drives out good [out of circulation]."[4]

Confederate money in the closing days of the Civil War offered a good example of Gresham's law at work. A more recent example occurred in Poland and Yugoslavia. In those two countries, U.S. dollars were hoarded and highly valued by those who could get them. Thus, dollars largely disappeared from circulation. The local currencies—the zloty and the dinar—circulated rapidly because, unlike dollars, both were a poor store of value. Zlotys and dinars were more acceptable as a unit of account and a medium of exchange. Reforms in 1990 stabilized the purchasing power of the zloty and the dinar and made them more acceptable as a store of value.

SCARCITY. Scarcity of money is a key property. The general level of prices tends to increase directly with the quantity of money in circulation. Sand, for example, meets many of the other criteria for money but is too easy to scoop up in large quantities. Scarcity was one reason for the popularity of precious metals as money in the past. Today, governments try to maintain the scarcity of the money supply by limiting the quantity of money they produce.

---

4. Gresham's law dates back to the fifteenth century but is commonly attributed to Sir Thomas Gresham, the founder of the Royal Exchange in Great Britain in the nineteenth century.

International Perspective

Yap Island Money

Yap, one of the Caroline Islands, lies in the western Pacific Ocean, north of the equator and the island of New Guinea and east of the Philippines. The fame of Yap lies in its stone money, called *fei*, first described in anthropological literature early in this century. The *fei* are large wheel-shaped stones, with holes in the center to allow them to be carried on poles. The stones range in size from one foot to eight feet in diameter. They aren't portable or divisible, but they are not easily counterfeited. A new stone had to be brought from Palau or Guam by raft or canoe, costing a certain amount of human time and effort. These costs ensure the scarcity of Yap's stone money.

Each stone is quite valuable. Together they represent most of the island's financial wealth. As you can imagine, the stones aren't used in everyday transactions. The usual currencies are tridacna shells, used for large transactions, and mother-of-pearl, used for smaller transactions. The stones are mainly used as a store of value, a unit of account, and a standard of deferred payment rather than as the common medium of exchange. They are still thought of as money, however. The larger stones are well known, and possession can change hands without the location being changed. Indeed, even stones that are now under the sea (lost in shipment between islands) maintain their value, and their ownership (though not their locations) can be changed. The stone in the Smithsonian Institution is probably still a part of the Yap money supply!

Yap's experiences with modern currencies explains why the stones have retained their monetary role. The Spanish first claimed Yap, but after defeat in the Spanish-American War, they sold the island to Germany in 1899. After Germany's defeat in World War I, Yap was transferred as a League of Nations trust territory to Japan. The Japanese controlled it until the end of World War II, when it came under the jurisdiction of the United States. All these nations introduced their currencies to Yap. Upon the introduction of U.S. currency, a Yap chief said, "First Spanish money no good, then German money no good, now Japanese money no good. Yap money always good!"[a]

---

a. "The Trust Territory: Its 2,130 Islands Form a New U.S. Domain in the Pacific," *Life* (25 April 1949): 100.

PORTABILITY. Medieval Swedish copper coins and the stone money of the Island of Yap were both very heavy. In general, however, portability is an important attribute of money. Portable forms of money—usually gold—have been very useful in crises. Some people, such as refugees fleeing political upheaval or persecution, discovered how critical portability is when they had to convert their assets to a form that could be carried and concealed.

DURABILITY. Durability is another important quality of money. Perishable commodities such as apples or fragile commodities such as glass would not serve well as money. Paper money is not extremely durable, but it is easy to replace. You can turn in a tattered U.S. dollar bill for a new one at a bank, which then turns in the old bill to the Federal Reserve. The tattered bill is destroyed, typically after a useful lifetime of about sixteen months. Coins, in contrast, have a useful lifetime of about twenty years.

UNIFORMITY. Uniformity is an essential quality of money that rules out many commodities. Variations in quality complicated the use of tobacco as money in the South during colonial times. Cows can be fat or thin, healthy or sick, and their value as money would vary accordingly. The advantage of paper money or precious metals is that it is easy to verify uniformity. The purity of gold and silver can be tested by weight or vouched for by a stamp of approval, as on coins.

DIVISIBILITY. Divisibility of money is essential in making transactions. It has to be possible to make change. Small denominations and coins are needed for this purpose. Divisibility as well as portability makes cows, houses, and other large, heavy assets very unsatisfactory forms of money. Divisibility helps to account for the popularity of both gold and silver as money.

ACCEPTABILITY. Another important property of money in its function as a medium of exchange is acceptability. To be useful, money must be acceptable; people must be willing to take it in payment for goods and services. A person will accept money only because of the belief that others will also accept it.

If the substance used as money is also a commodity with nonmonetary uses (such as gold), its value as a commodity sets its minimum value, which gives it some general acceptability. If the money is not itself a commodity but is always redeemable in a commodity, the acceptability and value of the commodity transfer to the money. Such money is known as **representative money**. The gold certificates and silver certificates used as currencies in the United States until 1933 and 1963, respectively, were representative monies. Bank deposits were representative money if the bank promised to redeem them in gold. The acceptability of representative money depends on whether people believe it will be redeemed as promised.

Modern money, however, is normally neither a commodity nor redeemable as a commodity. It is usually **fiat money**, which is whatever the government declares to be money. What gives such money its value and acceptability? Part of the answer lies in the term **legal tender**. By law, cer-

representative money
Money that is redeemable in a commodity (or commodities), such as gold.

fiat money
Money that is not a commodity and is not redeemable in any commodity.

legal tender
Money that, by law, must be accepted by private parties and governments in payment of debts and obligations.

tain forms of money (currency in the United States) are "legal tender for all debts, public and private." That phrase is printed on all U.S. bills. If something is legal tender, all persons are required to accept it in payment of debts. Governments must also accept paper money for the payment of taxes if it is designated as legal tender. Since most households have a fairly large tax obligation, this guarantee is one good reason to accept legal tender in exchange for goods or services of real value. Even people who don't have to pay taxes can feel confident that this money will be of value and acceptable to others.

FORMS OF MONEY

An incredible variety of items have served as money throughout history. All monies have had at least some of the desirable properties of money but in different degrees. Milk—a very nondurable item (but liquid!)—has been used as money. Cattle and slaves have also served as money, though they are neither very homogeneous nor divisible. Even cannons have been used as money, despite the fact that they are not very portable.

Various precious metals, such as gold and silver (and copper, though it is not as rare), have frequently served as money. The value of coins made from precious metals can be reduced by clipping, chipping, or shaving, either by private citizens or by the issuing governments. Precious metals can also be combined with less expensive (base) metals. In the Middle Ages, it was not uncommon for a monarch to call in all the coins, melt them, add base metals, recast them, and redistribute twice as many coins. The increased number of coins drove up the prices of goods and reduced the value of each coin. This **debasement of money** made the value of coins suspect. How much gold (or silver) was really in a coin?

During World War II, prisoners of war in German detention camps used cigarettes as money. They received cigarettes as part of their rations from the Red Cross and elsewhere. There were more cigarettes than people wanted to smoke, so they were traded for other goods. The supply was well known, so cigarettes gradually became recognized as a form of money with a fairly stable value. Toward the end of the month, before new cigarette rations arrived, many of the cigarettes had been smoked. The value of a cigarette in terms of most other goods, such as chocolate bars, tended to rise until a new shipment came in.

Money in the form of coins has been around for a long time. Originally, coins were made out of precious metal, and the stamp of the royal authority (often complete with a flattering profile) certified to their value. Such coins were **full-bodied money**, with a value in other uses equal to their monetary value. Modern coins are **token money**. Their value as money is greater than the value of the metal they contain. Currency and checks, mostly issued by banks, are somewhat more recent than coins but still have a long history.

In the United States, money consists of coins, currency, and checkable deposits. **Currency** is paper money with a specified value. In the United States, official currency is now issued solely by the central bank (the Federal Reserve System). In the past, paper money has been issued by the Treasury (gold and silver certificates), private banks, and even state governments. In some countries, private banks continue to issue currency.

debasement of money
The practice of reminting coins of gold or silver with base metals added, thus increasing the number of coins, driving up the prices of goods, and reducing the value of each coin.

full-bodied money
Money that has a value in other uses equal to its monetary value. Coins made of precious metals are the best examples.

token money
Money whose monetary value is greater than its commodity value. Modern coins, for example, are worth more as money than the metal they contain.

currency
Paper money with a specified value, issued by the government or central bank.

checkable deposits Balances in accounts at depository institutions on which checks can be drawn.

Traveler's checks, a form of money issued by U.S. banks, are a safe and acceptable medium of exchange that is very close to currency. **Checkable deposits**, the principal component of the money supply, consist of balances in checking accounts at banks and other depository institutions. All of these forms of U.S. money have the desired properties of money.

BANKS AND MONEY

Banks play an important role in the creation of money. Modern banking evolved from the services provided in the Middle Ages by goldsmiths. Goldsmiths made jewelry and decorative objects and kept a stock of gold for their own use. Because they maintained safe storage facilities, goldsmiths began storing other people's gold. They issued receipts for the gold left with them. Depositors often found it more convenient to use those receipts as money than to retrieve the gold. The receipts began to circulate as currency, fully redeemable in gold. Goldsmiths were thus the earliest bankers.

The emergence of banks resolved several problems with existing forms of money. Coins were bulky, inconvenient to carry in large amounts, and easy to steal. Paper money, on the other hand, needed some guarantee of its value. One form of guarantee was its convertibility into coins. Thus, banks could provide safe storage for and convenient access to coins and could issue currency that had some guarantee of value. Another need fulfilled by banks was the need for a credit market—a way of transferring money balances from those individuals who did not wish to use them at the moment to those who did. Your local bank or savings and loan still offers these basic banking services today.

BANK NOTES, CHECKING ACCOUNTS, AND OTHER FORMS OF MONEY

By the late eighteenth century, bank notes like the receipts issued by goldsmiths had become a substantial part of the money supply in England and many other countries. Such bank notes carried a promise to give the bearer the specific sum of gold stated on the face. Sometimes banks failed because they could not meet their obligations to redeem these notes in gold as promised.

Governments also issued notes redeemable in gold or silver on demand. Like banks, governments were sometimes unable to keep their promise to redeem this paper money for gold or silver. During the Civil War, the U.S. government issued notes called **greenbacks** that were not redeemable in gold. The Confederate States of America also issued nonredeemable notes. When the war was going well for the Union forces, greenbacks traded at close to their face value in gold. Greenbacks fell in value during periods when the war was going badly for the North. Confederate notes became virtually worthless toward the end of the war. It became clear that the Confederacy would lose, and the notes would not be redeemed. Confederate notes are now popular collectors' items, but you would have a hard time getting anyone to accept them in payment!

Until 1862, most U.S. banks were chartered by individual states. The National Banking Act (1863) imposed a federal tax on bank notes issued by

greenbacks Paper money issued by the U.S. government during the Civil War that was not redeemable in gold.

International Perspective

Money Around the World

Most countries have coins in various denominations as well as currency. In many countries, as in the United States, a decimal system is used. The currency is divided into 100 units, as the U.S. dollar is divided into 100 cents. The British currency was one of the last major currencies to change to a decimal system. Before the 1970s, there were 12 pence to a shilling and 20 shillings to a pound. The pound is now divided into 100 pence as a result of currency reform, and the shilling has ceased to be coined.

Many currencies have only one unit. There is the peso in Mexico, the yen in Japan, the franc in France and Switzerland, the mark in Germany, and the lira in Italy. Often the unit has a historic name. The franc is a name going back to the Dark Ages, when the tribe inhabiting the area that is now France was the Franks. The bolivar in Venezuela is named for a Latin American hero, Simon Bolivar. The krone of several Scandinavian countries simply means "crown," indicating that it is issued by the king or queen. The pound sterling originally was worth one pound of sterling silver. Sometimes the name is changed in a currency reform. In 1986, Brazil called in its cruzeiros and replaced them with a new currency, the cruzado, at a ratio of 1 cruzado for 1,000 cruzeiros.

The basic currency unit may be very large or very small. That is, it may take a large number or a small number of currency units to buy a newspaper or a loaf of bread. In most cases, the size of the currency unit says nothing about the currency's value or stability. The yen is a small currency unit but has a stable and rising value. The pound sterling is a large currency unit but has much smaller purchasing power relative to other currencies than it had ten, twenty, or forty years ago. Sometimes a currency unit changes from large to small as a result of severe inflation. For example, in early 1989, it took 78,000 australs to buy a car in Argentina. A year later, 78,000 australs bought dinner for four at a nice restaurant in Buenos Aires.[a]

The value of the currencies of the major industrial countries is determined by supply and demand in the international marketplace. Here are the values of a few of the major currencies in terms of U.S. dollars in early 1991.

Currency	Price in U.S. Dollars
Japanese yen	0.0076
German mark	0.6782
French franc	0.1994
Canadian dollar	0.8604
British pound	1.9675

You can check on currency prices in most major daily newspapers.

a. *Washington Post National Weekly Edition* (4–10 March 1990): 20.

state-chartered banks. This act was an attempt to force banks to obtain federal charters and come under federal regulation. Instead, it virtually drove bank notes out of existence and encouraged the development of checking accounts as a substitute for gold and bank notes in the United States.

Checking accounts, or **demand deposits**, first appeared in fifteenth-century Italy. They have some advantages over bank notes. There is no problem of making change, because a check can be written for the exact amount. Checking accounts are easier to protect from theft than cash because you can stop payment on checks if your checkbook is stolen. Checking accounts have one important drawback, however. The person who accepts a check has no easy way to verify that the check will be accepted by the bank on which it is written. If the check writer doesn't have enough funds on deposit, the check will "bounce"—right back to the person who accepted it in payment. Thus, especially if you are young, move around a great deal, or don't have satisfactory identification, your check is not always as widely accepted as currency or coins.

In the last twenty years, the variety of accounts offered by banks has increased. The federal government eliminated many of the regulations on the kinds of accounts banks could offer and the interest rates they could pay. The revolution in banking began when interest rate ceilings were suspended in the 1970s. Banks had to compete more aggressively for deposits in order to have funds to lend. Instead of offering toasters and other premiums, they offered new kinds of accounts with higher interest rates. The first new type of account to develop was the **certificate of deposit** (**CD**). CDs are deposits with financial institutions for specific periods, with higher interest rates than savings accounts and a penalty (often substantial) for early withdrawal. They function well as a store of value, but they are not very liquid.

In the early 1980s, for the first time since the 1930s, bank depositors could have an account that offered both interest on deposits and check-writing privileges. These accounts were introduced under various names, such as negotiated order of withdrawal (NOW) accounts and money market accounts. Many of these new accounts allow unlimited check writing and electronic transfers of funds. Even ordinary checking accounts began to pay interest once deregulation made it possible.

MEASURING THE MONEY SUPPLY

Because of these changes, economists had to rethink exactly what to count in measuring the money supply. Until the late 1970s, there were two widely used definitions of the money supply. One definition included currency plus demand deposits at commercial banks. The second definition added savings accounts. Which measure would an analyst use? The answer depended on which one seemed to do the best job of explaining people's behavior. Usually the two measures would move together. Sometimes, when there was switching between checking and savings accounts, one measure might rise while the other fell.

Before the development of such options as CDs and money market accounts, there was a wide gap between demand deposits, which are considered money by even the strictest definition, and savings accounts,

---

demand deposits
Bank deposits on which checks can be written (also known as checking accounts).

certificate of deposit (CD)
A deposit made with a financial institution at a specified interest rate for a given (fixed) period of time.

which cannot be used directly for transactions. Changes in the banking system have filled this gap with NOW accounts, credit union share draft accounts, automated funds transfers between accounts, and money market deposit accounts. There is a much wider variety of checkable deposits offered by all types of depository institutions.

Before 1980, there was a clear line that separated money from near money. A financial asset—coin, currency, CD, or bond—was either a medium of exchange (money) or an interest-earning asset (near money). With a whole new array of interest-bearing checking accounts, the dividing line became blurred. Economists have had to decide where these new kinds of deposits fit into the various definitions of the money supply.

Liquidity is the most important criterion for deciding what financial assets are a part of the money supply. Since money is highly liquid, the amount of liquidity that a financial asset has is useful for deciding whether it should be considered money or near money. **Near money** is a financial asset that is a close but not perfect substitute for money as a medium of exchange.

Today, the **M1 money stock** is defined as the total of those kinds of financial assets that function as a medium of exchange. It includes currency in circulation (outside banks), traveler's checks, demand deposits at commercial banks, and other checkable deposits (NOW accounts, credit union share draft accounts, and demand deposits at thrift institutions).

The **M2 money stock** is equal to M1 plus small time and savings deposits, money market accounts at banks and other financial institutions, and a few other specialized monetary assets. Time and savings deposits are those on which you can earn interest and on which you cannot write a check. Money market accounts with banks or mutual fund companies are deposits invested in short-term liquid assets (such as Treasury bills), on which the owner can write a limited number of checks. A still broader measure, the **M3 money stock**, is equal to M2 plus large time deposits, repurchase agreements, and a few other items. Table 1 gives exact definitions and current magnitudes of these three widely used measures.[5]

THE MONEY SUPPLY AND THE EQUATION OF EXCHANGE

The equation of exchange, $M_s \times V = P \times Y$, was introduced in Chapter 7. Of the three measures of the money supply, how do economists decide which to use for M_s in this equation? This decision is important because the equation is used to predict changes in the price level and real output (and as we will see later, changes in interest rates as well). The choice is not easy. Suppose you decide to use M1 for the money supply in the equation of exchange. Everything not a part of M1 is then near money. However, savings and time deposits at banks, which are a part of M2 but not M1, are very good substitutes for checking accounts. With an automatic teller card, it is possible to withdraw cash from a money market account just as easily as from a checkable deposit.

Clearly, there will always be some near money that is close to the money

near money
Assets that are very similar to the kinds of assets included in the money stock. Near money is usually highly liquid.

M1 money stock
The total of all financial assets in the United States that function as a medium of exchange: currency, traveler's checks, demand deposits, and other checkable deposits.

M2 money stock
The total of M1 and small-denomination time and savings deposits at all financial institutions, money market accounts, and a few other items.

M3 money stock
The total of M2 and large-denomination time deposits, repurchase agreements, and a few other items.

---

5. There are other measures of the money supply that become more inclusive, all the way up to a measure called L (for liquidity) that includes a broad array of assets. The definitions for these other measures are given in the *Federal Reserve Bulletin*.

**TABLE 1
MONEY STOCK MEASURES
AND COMPONENTS,
OCTOBER 1990
(BILLIONS OF DOLLARS)**

MEASURES	
M1	$ 820.1
M2	3,320.1
M3	4,088.2

MAJOR COMPONENTS	
Currency	$ 244.0
Demand deposits	276.8
Other checkable deposits	291.0
Savings/time deposits	1,172.3
Money market accounts	376.3

M1 money stock: currency held by the public plus commercial bank demand deposits, traveler's checks of nonbank issuers, and other checkable deposits (which include NOW and ATS accounts, credit union share draft accounts, and demand deposits at thrifts).

M2 money stock: M1 plus small-denomination savings and time deposits at all depository institutions, money market deposit accounts and money market mutual funds (except those owned by institutions), overnight repurchase agreements at commercial banks, and overnight Eurodollars.

M3 money stock: M2 plus large-denomination savings and time deposits at all depository institutions, term repurchase agreements at commercial banks and savings and loans, term Eurodollars, and money market mutual funds (institutions only). (There is another correction for interbank deposits.)

Source: *Economic Indicators* (Washington, DC: U.S. Government Printing Office, January 1991).

concept you choose. If you use M2 in the equation of exchange, you will find that deposits at savings and loan associations, which are not included in M2, are not very different from similar accounts at commercial banks. If you choose M3, which includes negotiable CDs, you will find that short-term U.S. government obligations, such as Treasury bills, are fairly good substitutes for those CDs because there are active resale markets for Treasury bills.

In order to use the money supply as a policy tool or a forecasting tool for prices, employment, and real output, it is important to agree on the best measure. Some economists use the one that is the most accurate in predicting the money value of GNP. That measure is usually M2. M2 is also more stable than M1. When individuals look for higher-yielding assets, they often switch to some of the interest-bearing accounts included in M2. Such changes make M1 fluctuate a great deal more than M2.

Other economists argue for M1 because it corresponds to money's function as the medium of exchange. M2 incorporates more of money's function as a store of value, which is important both in the Keynesian model and in modern monetarist explanations of what determines interest rates, the price level, and real output. By the late 1980s, the preference among model builders and policy makers had shifted from M1 to M2, but not all economists agreed with the change.

DEMAND FOR MONEY

Now that you have a working definition of what money is, what it does, and what the money supply consists of, we can use the equation of exchange to see the effects of changes in money supply and demand on output, employment, and the price level. The demand for money developed here is based on the quantity theory of money introduced in Chapter 7. The supply of money is closely linked to the banking system, which we will describe in the next chapter. Changes in the supply and demand for money can shift the aggregate demand curve introduced in Chapter 6. By shifting that curve, they affect the levels of output, employment, and prices.

MOTIVES FOR HOLDING MONEY

Two of the four functions of money—as the medium of exchange and a store of value—relate directly to its uses by individuals and business firms. People hold money because it is convenient for market transactions. They also may hold money as one of many forms in which to store wealth.

Economists believe that individuals decide how much money to hold in the same way they decide which goods and services to buy. That is, they compare the satisfaction obtained from holding money with the satisfaction obtained from holding alternative assets. Money is useful for two important purposes: making transactions and storing purchasing power for future use.[6] Whenever money is used to carry out transactions or held in anticipation of transactions in the near future, those funds are satisfying the transactions demand for money, or the desire for cash balances to meet day-to-day spending needs. Recall from Chapter 7 that the transactions demand for money is positively related to income.

The classical quantity theory of money was based on the role of money as a medium of exchange, or the transactions demand for money. If people hold money mostly for making transactions, the amount they wish to hold is related to the volume of transactions they expect to make. For an individual, the amount of money held for transactions is proportional to income. For the economy as a whole, the amount of money demanded for transactions is proportional to the aggregate volume of transactions, which is roughly equal to GNP (or $P \times Y$).[7] Recall that the equation of exchange can be written as either

$$M_d = k \times P \times Y = k \times \text{nominal income}$$

or

$$M_s \times V = P \times Y,$$

where $k = 1/V$. Classical economists expected that k and V would be con-

---

6. Money also provides some degree of security against unexpected events that might require an outlay of cash. Money held for such purposes is said to satisfy the precautionary demand for money. Since both the transactions demand and the precautionary demand for money depend on the level of nominal income ($P \times Y$), they are often lumped together under transactions demand.
7. It is not exactly the same because there will be transactions in used goods, illegal goods, and financial assets that are not reflected in GNP. But if the relationship between the volume of these transactions and GNP is a fairly constant ratio, GNP is a good approximation for the dollar value of transactions.

Economic Insight

The Underground Economy

The underground economy in the United States consists of a mix of barter and cash transactions, some legal and some not. Many people who transact business in the underground economy are trying to avoid payment of income taxes and Social Security taxes. Some want to avoid losing welfare benefits. Others, such as drug dealers, are more worried about the police than the Internal Revenue Service. Transactions are more difficult for the government to uncover if they are made by barter or in cash instead of by check.

The underground economy is a major source of demand for currency instead of checkable deposits. Cash transactions can be used to avoid taxes. Wages are often paid in cash to retired persons on Social Security who would lose some benefits if their earnings were reported. Some workers who get tips in cash don't want to pay income tax or Social Security taxes on those earnings. Cash wages to illegal aliens can help them avoid deportation.

One measure of the size of the underground economy is the growth of currency (Federal Reserve notes) relative to other forms of money. Currency rose from 23 percent of the money supply in 1970 to 30 percent in 1983. High Social Security taxes, a progressive income tax, and high inflation made the underground economy attractive during that period. Several factors combined to reduce the demand for cash by the end of the 1980s: lower marginal tax rates, lower inflation rates, and more intensive monitoring of large cash transactions by tax officials. By 1990, these factors had dropped the currency ratio slightly to 28 percent of the money supply, suggesting a modest decline in underground activity.

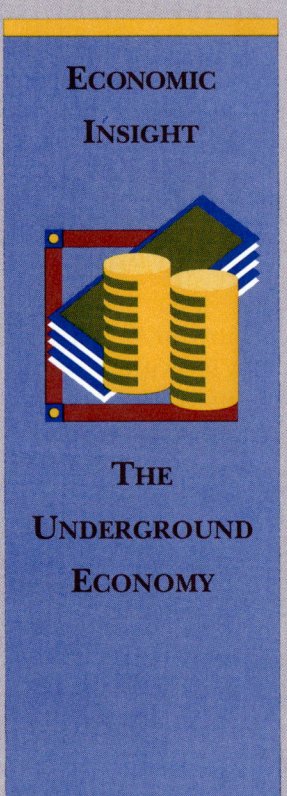

Chapter 11 Money: What It Is and Why People Hold It

stant, or at least stable, because transactions demand reflects patterns of earning and spending that do not change very rapidly.[8] Think about your own spending and earning. The money you receive—from a part-time job, from scholarships, or from your parents—comes in at regular intervals and you spend it at a rather steady and predictable pace.

During the Great Depression, however, there was a large decline in the velocity of money that took many economists by surprise. In the 1930s, people wanted to hold more money at every level of GNP. In the equation of exchange, this change in preferences meant that k increased and V fell. When people attempted to increase their money holdings, they engaged in fewer transactions and, on average, held each dollar longer. As they spent less, both GNP ($P \times Y$ in the equation of exchange) and V declined. Keynes attempted to explain changes in people's desired cash balances in terms of other reasons for holding money besides transactions demand.

INTEREST RATES, RISK, AND THE ASSET DEMAND FOR MONEY

Despite the advantages of money for transactions and precautionary purposes, individuals don't choose to keep all of their wealth in cash or checking accounts. There are costs associated with holding money. A major cost is the opportunity cost of the interest that could be earned by holding other assets instead of money.[9] Keynes explored the manner in which yields on other assets can affect the demand for money. Specifically, he identified a third kind of demand for money. He labeled it the speculative demand for money, but it is now more often called the asset demand for money (as we discussed in Chapter 7). The asset demand for money is the amount of money people wish to hold as a store of value in preference to other kinds of financial assets. This demand for money depends on the interest rates on other kinds of financial assets. The asset demand is negatively related to the interest rate.

Keynes further clarified the relationship between the interest rate and the demand for money. He pointed out that it is not only the current interest rate that affects the decision to hold money, but also how that rate compares to past and expected future rates. Suppose that for the past decade the yield on bonds had averaged 6 percent, but this year it dropped to 4 percent. You would tend to prefer cash balances to bonds because the opportunity cost is lower. But there is another reason to stay away from bonds. If you think that 6 percent interest is "normal" and the 4 percent yield is temporary, then you expect the yield on bonds to go back up to 6 percent in the near future. If you buy bonds now, not only will you get a low yield, but you will be risking a capital loss. A bond that you purchase for $1,000 at 4 percent with a very long maturity period (twenty years or more) will be worth only $667 when the interest rate rises to 6 percent.[10]

---

8. Late nineteenth-century economists and early twentieth-century economists in the classical tradition, such as Irving Fisher and Henry Simons, did not share this view. They were concerned about the instability of velocity, especially in the short run, and although they would agree with this equation, they would not regard either k or V as constant.

9. Another cost comes from the fact that money's value, or purchasing power, rises and falls with changes in the price level. Holding money is costly during periods of rising prices. We will explore this concern in more detail in Chapter 13.

10. If the maturity period were shorter, the individual could hold the bond to maturity to collect the face value. We will explore bond prices and interest rates in Chapter 13.

WHY PEOPLE HOLD MONEY	
MOTIVE	**CHARACTERISTICS**
Transactions demand for money	• To meet day-to-day expenses
	• Reflects money's function as the medium of exchange
	• Positively related to level of income
Asset demand for money	• As a store of wealth or as one asset among many
	• Reflects money's function as a store of value
	• Negatively related to interest rate

Suppose the Federal Reserve System (described in Chapter 12) tries to increase aggregate demand by increasing the money supply. The increased money supply will reduce interest rates and should result in more investment spending. However, if interest rates are already low relative to past experience, a larger money supply may have little effect. Banks, firms, and individuals will just increase their holdings of cash. Thus, the larger money supply will have little effect on lending, interest rates, and investment. Velocity will fall, as it did during the Great Depression. We will explore this issue further in Chapter 14.

EXPECTED PRICE LEVEL CHANGES AND THE DEMAND FOR MONEY. A more general theory of money demand can build on both the classical quantity theory and Keynes's asset demand. Such a theory includes three important influences on money demand: real output/income (classical transactions demand), interest rates (Keynes's asset demand), and the price level (including changes in both actual and expected prices).

Changes in price expectations influence the demand for money. Consider how changes in the price level affect the purchasing power of money. When prices rise, a dollar buys less. When prices fall, it buys more. People will be concerned that a rising price level will cause money holdings to decline in value. If the price level was expected to rise, this would provide an incentive for people to shift part of their assets out of money and into other kinds of financial assets that are less vulnerable to losing value through inflation. They might try to purchase real assets (such as land, coins, or houses) whose value rises with the price level. Or they may purchase financial assets with yields high enough to offset the expected loss of purchasing power. As people try to exchange their money for other kinds of assets, such as bonds, desired money balances fall relative to GNP ($P \times Y$ in the equation of exchange). Velocity (V) increases, or k declines.

An expected drop in the price level would have just the opposite effect. As money increases in purchasing power and is expected to increase further in the future, people will expect the value of their money holdings to rise. As they cut spending, GNP falls. Since the money supply is unchanged, the equation of exchange must be balanced by a decline in V or a rise in k.

THE STABILITY OF VELOCITY. The combined influence of interest rates and price expectations on the demand for money explains why k and V vary in the short run. It is easy to verify that this was the case in the 1930s when V fell and k rose. After the stock market crash of 1929 and the many bankruptcies of the early 1930s, many people wanted to hold a larger fraction of their assets in the form of money. The interest rates on bonds and other financial assets were very low. In 1933, the yield on a three-month Treasury bill was only 0.5 percent, compared to about 6–7 percent in recent years. Furthermore, the price level was falling in the early 1930s and was expected to fall further.

Velocity, measured by comparing GNP to M1, declined sharply again in the late 1980s. However, this time the decline in velocity was not tied to a recession. A gradual decline in interest rates played some role. The decline in velocity was also related to changes in financial markets and the emergence of new forms of near money. These changes made M1 a less satisfactory measure of the money supply as more close substitutes appeared for its components. An imperfect measure of the money supply would give an imperfect measure of velocity, since $V = \text{GNP}/M_s$.

How often and how much does the velocity of money change? Figure 1 on page 310 plots two values of V ($V_1 = \text{GNP}/M1$ and $V_2 = \text{GNP}/M2$) as well as the interest rate on a Treasury bill for the period from 1970 to 1990. You can see from this diagram that V_1 is less stable than V_2, but that both seem to be related to the interest rate. We will consider the stability of velocity and its implications in Chapter 14.

DETERMINANTS OF VELOCITY

The velocity of money (V) is determined by

- Interest rates — Higher interest rates increase velocity. Lower interest rates reduce velocity.
- Price expectations — Inflationary expectations increase velocity. Deflationary expectations reduce velocity.
- Institutional changes — Different forms of money or payment periods will change spending habits and affect velocity.

MONEY DEMAND, MONEY SUPPLY, AND AGGREGATE DEMAND

The money supply is largely under the control of the central bank, which uses tools that are described in Chapter 12. Until now, we have treated the amount of money in the economy as an exogenous variable or a given number. Money demand, however, is subject to many influences, including (1) the interest rate, which determines the demand for money as a store of value, (2) the level of income, which determines transactions demand, and (3) the price level and price expectations. Money demand is positively related to the level of money income $(P \times Y)$.[11]

---

11. In the equation $M_d = k \times P \times Y$, nominal money demand ($M_d$) is a function of nominal income $(P \times Y)$. If the equation is written as $M_d/P = k \times Y$, real money demand (M_d/P) is a function of real income (Y).

FIGURE 1
VELOCITY OF MONEY, 1960–1990
Velocity is equal to GNP divided by the money supply (M1 or M2). In the last thirty years, V_1 has increased, but with ups and downs around the upward trend. Presently the value of V_1 (GNP/M1) is in the range of 5.5–7. The value of V_2 (GNP/M2) is around 1.5–2.0.

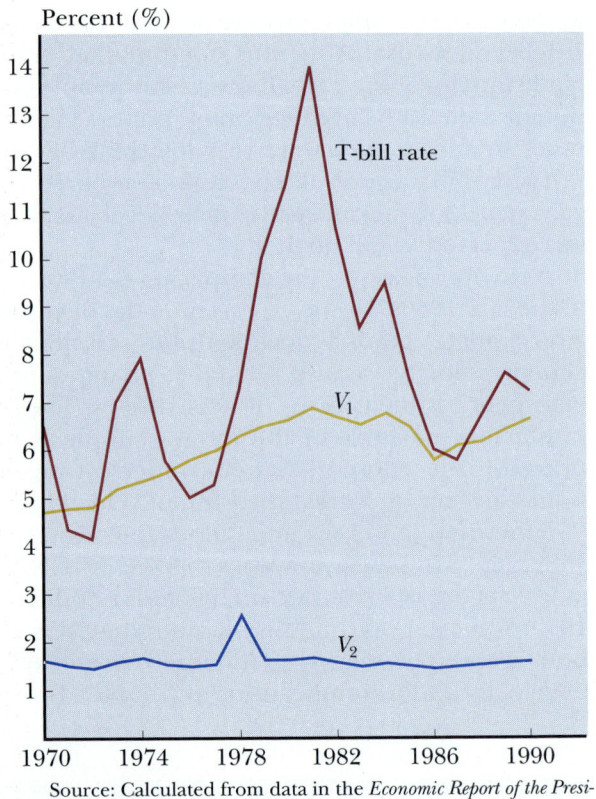

Source: Calculated from data in the *Economic Report of the President*, 1991.

EQUILIBRIUM IN THE MONEY MARKET

Figure 2 shows the relationship of money demand and money supply to nominal income. An increase in $P \times Y$ will increase the amount of money demanded along the curve M_{d1} in Figure 2. Equilibrium occurs at that

FIGURE 2
MONEY SUPPLY, MONEY DEMAND, AND INCOME
Here the money supply is considered as given, or independent of the level of money income. Money demand is positively related to the level of money income, *ceteris paribus*. A change in some other factor, such as interest rates, will shift the money demand curve from M_{d1} to M_{d2}.

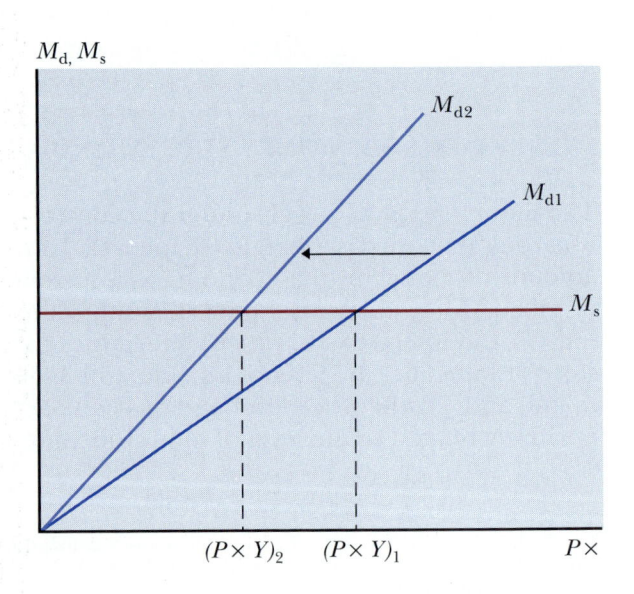

Chapter 11 Money: What It Is and Why People Hold It   311

level of $P \times Y$ at which the quantity of money demanded is equal to the quantity supplied, which occurs at $(P \times Y)_1$ in Figure 2.

Suppose interest rates fall. With a lower opportunity cost of holding money, people will choose to hold larger cash balances at every level of income. The demand curve for money shifts to M_{d2} in Figure 2. Since V and k measure the relationship between money demand and money income, another way of saying the same thing is that velocity has fallen. At income level $(P \times Y)_1$, there is a shortage of money balances. Money demand exceeds money supply.

How does this economy return to equilibrium? As people try to build up their cash balances, the decline in spending reduces the level of income and output to $(P \times Y)_2$. At that lower income level, individuals will demand smaller cash balances. Note that the money market is back in balance, but money income has fallen.

Not all of the burden of adjustment falls on output and the price level. As individuals try to build up their money balances, less is available to lend. Interest rates begin to rise as borrowers compete for a limited supply of funds. As interest rates rise, some individuals will settle for smaller holdings of money as an asset. They will choose to use money to purchase financial assets offering attractive interest rates. These higher interest rates will shift the money demand curve back toward M_{d1} in Figure 2. Changes in interest rates will cushion some of the impact of increasing demand for money on output and the price level.

Suppose, instead, the money supply increases. In Figure 3, this development is shown as a shift in the horizontal money supply curve from M_{s1} to M_{s2}. Note that there is now too much money in the system. Quantity supplied exceeds quantity demanded. When the money supply increases, how do individuals respond? If money demand is unchanged, people have larger money balances than they want. When people have excess money balances, they have only two choices about what to do with the money:

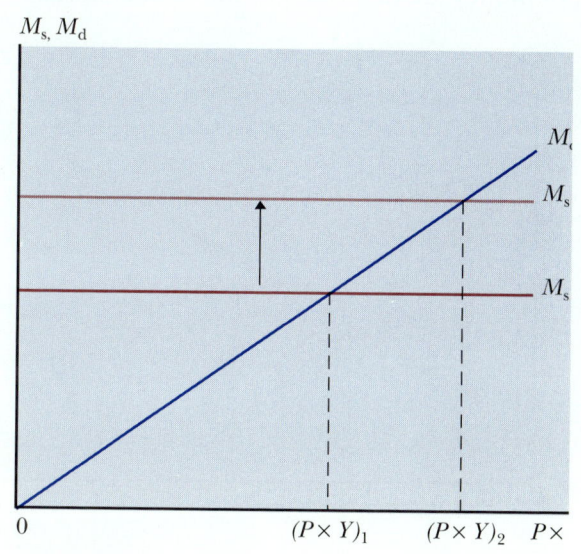

FIGURE 3
AN INCREASE IN THE MONEY SUPPLY
An increase in the money supply shifts the money supply curve from M_{s1} to M_{s2}. The result is an increase in the level of money income from $(P \times Y)_1$ to $(P \times Y)_2$ as households spend their excess cash balances and drive up income and the price level.

spend it or lend it. (If they choose to leave the money in their bank accounts, the bank will lend it to someone.) Spending it drives up output and prices. The economy moves along the money demand curve to a larger quantity of money demanded at a higher level of $P \times Y$. Lending the money drives down interest rates. At lower interest rates, people will be willing to hold larger cash balances (lower velocity of money). A combination of a lower velocity and a higher level of $P \times Y$ will ensure that the larger money supply brings the equation of exchange back into balance.

THE MONEY MARKET AND AGGREGATE DEMAND

Recall from Chapter 6 that the aggregate demand curve reflects the idea that a given money supply will buy various combinations of P (price level) and Y (real output). If we add aggregate demand to the analysis above, we can determine how much of the impact of a change in money demand or supply will be on real output and how much on prices. There are other factors that affect the slope and position of the aggregate demand curve, but money supply and demand are both important. If M_s increases and that increase is not entirely offset by a decline in V, there will be an increase in aggregate demand for goods and services. The AD curve shifts to the right, as shown in Figure 4. The result is an increase in P or Y or both. The exact combination depends on the slope of the AS curve. In Figure 4, the price level rises from P_1 to P_2, and real output rises from Y_1 to Y_2. The supply and demand for money are reflected in aggregate demand and therefore affect output, employment, and prices.

The addition of money to the aggregate supply and demand model identifies another source of shifts in aggregate demand besides fiscal policy or changes in consumption or investment habits. The fiscal policy tools used to shift aggregate demand are under the control of Congress and the executive branch. The money supply is under the control of the banking system, mainly the Federal Reserve System. In order to understand how this tool for shifting aggregate demand can be used, you need to know more about the banking system and how it works. The Federal Reserve System and the creation of money are described in the next chapter.

FIGURE 4
MONEY AND AGGREGATE DEMAND
An increase in the money supply (or a decrease in the demand for money) creates a surplus of money. As it is spent on consumption or invested, aggregate demand shifts to the right (from AD_1 to AD_2) and drives up the price level (from P_1 to P_2) and real output (from Y_1 to Y_2).

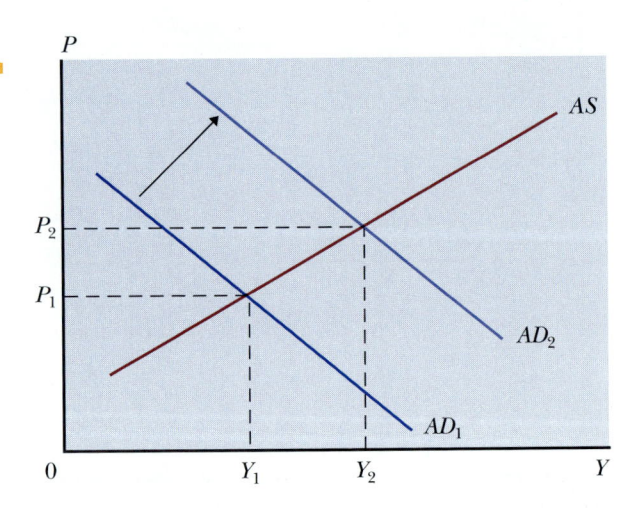

Chapter 11 Money: What It Is and Why People Hold It

Summary

1. People accept money because it can be exchanged for other things they want. Money is desirable and useful only to the extent that it is accepted.
2. Barter is extremely costly and inefficient. The use of money allows people to carry out market transactions more economically.
3. The functions of money include its use as a medium of exchange, unit of account, standard of deferred payment, and store of value (asset). A variety of items have been used as money.
4. Desirable properties of money include stability of value, transferability, portability, durability, acceptability, recognizability, divisibility, and scarcity.
5. Several different measures of the money stock are used today in the United States. Whatever measure is used, money will have close substitutes, called near money. To draw the line between money and near money, economists usually try to determine which measure of the money stock works best for the problem they are working on.
6. Banking developed from goldsmiths' acceptance of deposits for safekeeping. Over time, the goldsmiths began to issue written promises to return a certain amount of gold. These promises were an early form of paper money.
7. Bank notes gradually replaced gold and were in turn replaced by checking accounts. It is not necessary for paper money or checking accounts to be redeemable in gold. For money to work well, it simply has to be generally acceptable.
8. The demand for money is expressed by the equation $M_d = k \times P \times Y$, another form of the equation of exchange, $M \times V = P \times Y$. Transactions demand for money is related to the level of income. Money is also demanded as an asset. Asset demand for money is higher when the interest on other financial assets is low.
9. Changes in the money supply affect output and prices through money demand. Excess money balances will be spent or lent, increasing aggregate demand and driving up prices and/or output.

New Terms

barter
double coincidence of wants
medium of exchange
unit of account
standard of deferred payment
store of value
liquidity
money
representative money
fiat money
legal tender
debasement of money
full-bodied money
token money
currency
checkable deposits
greenbacks
demand deposits
certificate of deposit (CD)
near money
M1 money stock
M2 money stock
M3 money stock

Questions for Discussion

1. In terms of the desirable properties of money, why have precious metals (gold and silver) been such popular choices for money? Why would each of the following be a poor choice: peanuts, seashells, glass, diamonds, teeth, cows, and trees?
2. Do you sort out your money on hand into transactions money, precautionary money, and asset money? Why do you think economists make these distinctions?
3. Part of the U.S. money supply (M1) is currency, and part of it is checkable deposits. Why might the ratio of currency to checkable deposits change? That is, why might people prefer to keep more of their money in currency or more of it in checkable deposits?
4. Draw a line labeled "Liquid" at one end and "Not very liquid" at the other end. Place the following financial assets along the line from most liquid to least liquid:

currency, twenty-year bonds, money market accounts, NOW accounts, savings accounts, checkable deposits, certificates of deposit, real estate, and Treasury bills (short-term obligations that mature in less than a year). Explain how this continuum relates to the problem of defining the money supply.

5. In each case, solve for the missing term in the equation of exchange.
   a. $M_s = \$500$, $V = 3$, $Y = \$750$, $P = $ _____
   b. $M_s = \$600$, $P = 3$, $Y = \$500$, $V = $ _____
   c. $M_s = \$800$, $V = 2$, $P = 0.75$, $Y = $ _____
   d. $V = 4$, $Y = \$1,400$, $P = 1.5$, $M_s = $ _____

6. Using the equation of exchange and the quantity theory of money, explain how each of the following would affect the money value of GNP.
   a. Workers get paid more often. (*Hint*: What happens to the average balance in their checking accounts?)
   b. A big promotional campaign persuades individuals to buy more government bonds. Thus they hold smaller cash balances.
   c. An evening TV program convinces people that rampant inflation is coming back soon.

7. Classify each of the following as transactions demand, precautionary demand, or asset demand for money.
   a. lunch money in your wallet (cash)
   b. money set aside in your checking account to pay next week's bills
   c. a coin bank in the kitchen for emergencies
   d. the proverbial stock of money kept in the mattress because of fear of banks
   e. funds in a NOW account that will be put into bonds when interest rates rise

8. In the *Federal Reserve Bulletin*, find the most recent figures for the sizes of M1, M2, and M3. List the components (for example, currency and checkable deposits) of each. What is the largest component of the money supply?

9. What are the benefits of holding cash? What are the costs or risks?

10. Take a bill from your wallet and answer the following questions:
    a. How do you know it is legal tender?
    b. Whose signatures are on it?
    c. By whom and in what city was it issued?

11. How would each of the following affect people's demand for money?
    a. lower interest rates
    b. higher price level
    c. higher expected inflation rate
    d. lower real income

12. Why did the velocity of money fall so sharply during the Great Depression?

13. Why, according to Keynes, is the relationship between current interest rates and "normal" interest rates important in determining how much money to hold as an asset?

14. "If you have excess money balances, your only choices are to spend the money or lend it." What does this statement mean? Can people collectively get rid of excess money balances?

15. If it is not possible for people as a group to get rid of excess money balances (Question 14), how is equilibrium restored in the money market when people have more money than they currently wish to hold?

SUGGESTIONS FOR FURTHER READING

Galbraith, John K. *Money: Whence It Came, Where It Went.* New York: Bantam Books, 1976. A delightfully readable account of money by one of the most talented writers in economics.

Mayer, Thomas, James S. Duesenberry, and Robert Z. Aliber. *Money, Banking and the Economy*, 4th ed. New York: W. W. Norton, 1990. A very up-to-date look at money and the monetary system.

Polanyi, K., M. Arenseberg, and H. W. Pearson, eds. *Trade and Markets in the Early Empires.* Chicago: Regnery Gateway, 1971. Looks at the history of money.

Radford, R. A. "The Economic Organization of a P.O.W. Camp." *Economica* (November 1945): 189–201. Many times reprinted, a classic article that looks at the use of cigarettes as money in an actual situation.

AFTER STUDYING THIS CHAPTER, YOU SHOULD BE ABLE TO:

1. Explain how banks create money.
2. Explain why a central bank is necessary.
3. Describe the structure and functions of the Federal Reserve System.
4. Define each of the following terms related to the money creation process:
   a. reserves,
   b. required reserve ratio,
   c. excess reserves,
   d. discount rate,
   e. open market operations,
   f. currency drain,
   g. money multiplier.
5. Explain how the Fed uses each of following tools to influence the money supply and interest rates:
   a. open market operations,
   b. the reserve ratio,
   c. the discount rate.
6. Calculate the maximum possible change in checkable deposits that would result from each of the following:
   a. an open market operation,
   b. a change in the reserve ratio.
7. Describe the federal funds market and explain how the Fed influences the federal funds rate.

CHAPTER 12

MONEY CREATION AND THE FEDERAL RESERVE SYSTEM

INTRODUCTION

You know that changes in the money supply shift the aggregate demand curve. In Chapter 11, we explored the mechanism by which this shift takes place. Increases in the money supply mean that people's money balances are larger than they wish to hold. As they attempt to get rid of the excess money by spending or lending, they drive up consumption and investment demand, shifting the aggregate demand curve to the right. The opposite happens when the money supply shrinks.

Left unanswered in Chapter 11 were the questions of exactly where money comes from and how the supply can be changed. This chapter provides the answers to these questions by explaining the source of the money supply. The key players in the creation of money are the central bank and all depository institutions, including commercial banks and thrift institutions (savings banks, savings and loan associations, and credit unions). We will refer to all depository institutions as banks to simplify the discussion.

Recall from Chapter 11 that the M1 money supply consists of coins, currency (Federal Reserve notes), and checkable deposits. Coins, issued by the U.S. Treasury, are a very small part of the money supply. Federal Reserve notes are issued by the Federal Reserve System, and checkable deposits are held by depository institutions. Thus, money creation (except for the small amount of money in coins) is under the control of the depository institutions and the central bank.

The United States was one of the last modern industrial countries to

Federal Reserve System (Fed)
The central bank of the United States.

establish a central bank. The **Federal Reserve System (Fed)**, established in 1914, is the central bank of the United States. In addition to regulating banks, the Fed exerts control over the size of the money supply. This chapter will discuss the events leading up to the creation of the Fed and the tools it uses to influence the money supply.

WHAT BANKS DO

As you learned in Chapter 11, goldsmiths were responsible for the development of the first paper currency and were also the first modern bankers. Goldsmiths issued notes as receipts for gold deposits, and the notes began to circulate as currency. It didn't take the goldsmiths very long to discover that they had few day-to-day requests from depositors to redeem these notes for gold. They could safely lend out some of the depositors' gold (as well as their own), earning interest and eventually paying interest on deposits.

Suppose a prosperous medieval baron deposited 100 florins in gold with a goldsmith, accepting a paper receipt, or note, in exchange. This paper note, redeemable in gold, could serve as money. In fact, in some ways the note served better as money than the 100 gold florins because it was just as acceptable but much easier to carry. The goldsmith could lend someone else 50 florins of the baron's gold, which would also be money.

The deposit of 100 florins expanded the money supply by 50 florins. The original deposit of 100 florins was still money but so was the 50 florins lent by the goldsmith. This kind of transaction by goldsmiths is the origin of fractional reserve banking, a fundamental principle of all modern banking systems. **Fractional reserve banking** is the practice of holding a fraction of money deposited as reserves and lending the rest. This practice is the basis for money creation in most market economies.

fractional reserve banking
The practice of holding a fraction of money deposited as reserves and lending the rest.

The development of banking was as great an innovation as the development of money. By replacing barter, money solved the problem of meeting the double coincidence of wants in order to make trades. When banking came into being, it was no longer necessary to hunt for an individual who was willing to lend as much as the borrower wanted to borrow for the desired time and on acceptable terms. Just as money simplified the problem of matching traders, banks simplified the problem of matching lenders with borrowers. The most important function of a bank is to be a wholesaler in the lending business, gathering up small sums from depositors and lending larger amounts to borrowers. Banks pay some interest to depositors, charge more interest to borrowers, and make their profit and pay their expenses out of the difference.

It is risky for individual lenders to deal with individual borrowers because a lender loses the entire amount of the loan if the borrower fails to repay. If individuals lend through a bank rather than directly, they are "buying" a piece of the whole range of loans made by the bank. Although one or two borrowers may default, most of the loans will be repaid.

THE BANK'S BALANCE SHEET

A bank is a business firm, just like a grocery store or a shirt factory. It is in business to earn a profit for its owners, who are stockholders. The balance

Chapter 12   Money Creation and the Federal Reserve System   317

sheet of any firm provides a picture of its financial situation. The balance sheet of a bank lists its assets in order of liquidity (from most liquid to least liquid), its liabilities, and its net worth. Table 1 is a balance sheet for Amacher National Bank. The first thing you should notice is that the balance sheet balances. That is, assets equal liabilities plus net worth. A balance sheet must always balance. The fact that it balances says nothing about how well the bank is doing. To determine the bank's condition, we must look at some individual assets and liabilities.

For Amacher National, reserves are the most liquid asset. **Reserves** are bank assets that can be used to pay depositors when checks are presented for payment. Reserves consist of currency on hand (vault cash) and deposits at the central bank. It is important for a bank to keep enough reserves to meet the day-to-day withdrawals of customers. However, a bank does not want to keep any more reserves than necessary because reserves do not earn interest, and loans do.

The interest-earning assets of Amacher National are government bonds and loans to the public. Note that the bank's assets are others' liabilities. Government bonds are liabilities of the U.S. Treasury, and loans are liabilities of the households and businesses who borrowed the money. The fixed assets of Amacher National consist of the bank's building, furnishings, and other equipment. This kind of asset is the least liquid on the list because it is the most difficult to convert to cash.

The largest liability for Amacher National is its checkable deposits of $50,000. A small volume of savings or other deposits and some loans that the Fed has made to this bank (which will be explained later in the chapter) make up the rest of the bank's liabilities. The net worth of $8,000 represents the value of the bank to its stockholders.

The balance sheets of banks and savings and loans (thrifts) have received a great deal of public scrutiny in the last few years. During the late 1980s, there were many depository institutions whose assets came to have much less value than their liabilities, leaving these institutions with negative net worth. We will examine this banking crisis in more detail in the next chapter. For now, we are mainly interested in the balance sheet as a tool to describe the process of money creation.

reserves
Bank assets that can be used to pay depositors when checks are presented for payment, consisting of currency on hand and reserve deposits at the central bank.

T-ACCOUNTS AND MONEY CREATION

The items on a bank's balance sheet play an important role in the money creation process. Rather than relisting all assets and liabilities, it is simpler

ASSETS		LIABILITIES	
Vault cash	$ 1,000	Checkable deposits	$50,000
Reserves at the Fed	19,000	Other deposits	5,000
Government bonds	15,000	Loans from the Fed	2,000
Loans to the public	20,000		
Fixed assets	10,000	TOTAL LIABILITIES	$57,000
TOTAL ASSETS	$65,000	NET WORTH	$ 8,000
		TOTAL LIABILITIES AND NET WORTH	$65,000

TABLE 1
BALANCE SHEET FOR
AMACHER NATIONAL BANK

T-accounts
Partial balance sheets showing changes in assets and/or liabilities resulting from a transaction or group of transactions.

to look at only those that change. We will use a partial balance sheet, called a **T-account**, that shows changes in assets and/or liabilities resulting from a transaction or group of transactions. The only items listed on a T-account are those that have changed. If the balance sheet balances at the start, then as long as the changes on the T-account offset each other, the balance sheet will still be in balance after the transaction is completed.

Table 2 shows how T-accounts are used to record changes in Amacher National's balance sheet for two sample transactions. Suppose Susan Smith came in with $100 in cash to deposit in her checking account, and the bank took the deposit and put it in the vault. There would be a $100 increase in assets (vault cash, or reserves) and a $100 increase in liabilities (checkable deposits). The balance sheet would still be in balance. In the second transaction, Amacher National sells a $1,000 bond and uses the proceeds to make a loan. The balance sheet would still be in balance after this transaction because the increase in one kind of asset (the loan) would be exactly offset by the decrease in another (the bond).[1] T-accounts are useful for following the process of money creation in banks.

Note that the plus and minus signs in the T-accounts refer to increases and decreases, not to assets or liabilities. The +$100 represents an increase in reserves in transaction 1, and the –$1,000 refers to a reduction in bonds in transaction 2.

The way today's banks create money is not very different from the way medieval goldsmiths increased the money supply—by making loans with the gold others had deposited for safekeeping. The goldsmiths discovered that on any given day, most depositors did not withdraw much of their gold. A fractional amount was all goldsmiths had to hold to meet daily demand. Although gold has ceased to play much of a role in the money supply, banks still lend part of the reserves created by deposits. Banks' checkable deposits serve as money, just as the notes issued by the goldsmiths served as money.

How much can Amacher National lend? The balance sheet in Table 1 shows that this bank already has $20,000 in loans outstanding. The balance sheet also shows that the bank has reserves of $20,000 (including vault cash) and checkable deposits of $50,000. To keep things simple, we

TABLE 2
SAMPLE TRANSACTIONS AND T-ACCOUNTS

TRANSACTION 1:
Susan Smith puts $100 in cash in her checking account; Amacher National Bank adds the $100 to its reserves.

ASSETS		LIABILITIES	
Reserves	+$100	Checkable deposits	+$100

TRANSACTION 2:
Amacher National Bank sells a bond and makes a loan.

ASSETS		LIABILITIES
Loans	+$1,000	
Bonds	–$1,000	

---

1. There would really be two sets of changes on the asset side. When the bond was sold, bond holdings fell and reserves rose. When the reserves were lent, reserves fell and loans rose.

Chapter 12   Money Creation and the Federal Reserve System   319

will assume that banks keep reserves only to back up checkable deposits. Amacher National's reserves are 40 percent of its checkable deposits. This is a fairly high level of reserves. This bank can probably lend more without worrying about meeting the demands of depositors.

Assume that Amacher National has decided to reduce reserves to only 20 percent of deposits. Twenty percent of the $50,000 in checkable deposits is only $10,000. Thus, Amacher National can expand its loans by $10,000. Remember, reserves do not earn interest, but loans do. When the next promising borrower comes in, the bank will make a $10,000 loan. The bank will probably not give the borrower cash but will simply credit the borrower's checking account, increasing the bank's checkable deposits (liabilities) by $10,000. The T-account for this transaction is shown in Table 3.

The balance sheet of Amacher National is still in balance, and the bank has increased the money supply by $10,000 in new checkable deposits. It looks as if Amacher National could lend still more because the note at the bottom of the T-account points out that reserves are still $20,000 and checkable deposits are $60,000. The bank only needs to keep $12,000, or 20 percent, in reserves to back up $60,000 in checkable deposits.

Amacher National did not lend more than $10,000 because the loan officer knew that Joe's Barber Shop intended to spend the money. Those funds will not stay in the firm's checking account very long. Joe will spend them on equipment for his shop, and Joe's supplier will probably deposit Joe's check in another bank. When a check drawn on one bank is deposited in another, the first bank loses reserves and checkable deposits. The bank that receives a check drawn on another bank finds its reserves and checkable deposits increasing. The receiving bank's ability to make loans and expand the money supply will increase. If Joe's supplier deposits the check in Ulbrich Savings Bank, the T-accounts for the two banks will be as shown in Table 4 on page 320.

After this transfer of reserves, Amacher National is "all loaned up." It cannot make any more loans until it somehow acquires more reserves. However, Ulbrich Savings can make new loans. If this bank also keeps a 20 percent reserve behind checkable deposits, then it needs only $2,000 in reserves behind the $10,000 in new checkable deposits. Ulbrich Savings can safely lend the other $8,000 of newly acquired reserves.

MAXIMUM EXPANSION OF THE MONEY SUPPLY

Amacher National lent $10,000 in **excess reserves**, which are reserves above the level required by law. Then Ulbrich Savings Bank expanded its lending by $8,000. It's not hard to see that Ulbrich's lending will create new reserves for a third bank, which will in turn lend and create new reserves

excess reserves
Reserves above the level required by law.

TABLE 3
T-ACCOUNT FOR A LOAN TRANSACTION

AMACHER NATIONAL BANK MAKES A LOAN TO JOE'S BARBER SHOP.

ASSETS	LIABILITIES	
Loans +$10,000	Checkable deposits	+$10,000

Note: Total reserves = $20,000; total checkable deposits = $60,000.

TABLE 4
T-ACCOUNTS FOR A TRANSFER OF RESERVES FROM ONE BANK TO ANOTHER

AMACHER NATIONAL BANK	
ASSETS	LIABILITIES
Reserves −$10,000	Checkable deposits −$10,000

Note: Total reserves = $10,000; total checkable deposits = $50,000.

ULBRICH SAVINGS BANK	
ASSETS	LIABILITIES
Reserves +$10,000	Checkable deposits +$10,000

for a fourth bank, and so on. How long will this process continue? If we know what ratio of reserves to deposits banks wish to maintain, we can identify the upper limits of the money expansion process.[2]

Any bank can expand its loans as long as it has excess reserves. The banking system as a whole can expand loans as long as there are excess reserves in the system. Thus, expansion of the money supply must stop only when there are no more excess reserves in the banking system. The only way to get rid of excess reserves is for banks to lend them.

Suppose all banks in the system hold reserves of 20 percent of checkable deposits, either voluntarily or because they are required to do so by law. Each bank wants to lend out any excess reserves (ER) in order to earn interest. The money creation process will stop only when there are no more excess reserves. That is, no more money will be created when all bank reserves (BR) in the entire banking system have been converted to required reserves (RR). The **reserve ratio** (rr) is the fraction of deposits that banks are required to hold in reserves. Banks' required reserves are thus $rr \times D$, where D = checkable deposits. The banking system (as well as any individual bank) is fully loaned up when RR equals BR, or

(1) $RR = BR = rr \times D.$

Dividing equation (1) by rr gives

(2) $D = \dfrac{1}{rr} \times BR.$

The steps in the money expansion process are shown in Table 5. This table shows the change in deposits, reserves, and loans for the first five banks as well as the totals for the process. Note that the bottom line satisfies equation (2). That is, newly created checkable deposits are equal to the initial excess reserves multiplied by the deposit multiplier, $1/rr$. The **deposit multiplier** is the ratio between the maximum increase in the money supply and a given increase in excess reserves. It equals the reciprocal of the reserve ratio.[3] The deposit multiplier depends only on the ratio of required reserves to checkable deposits.

reserve ratio
Fraction of deposits that banks are required to hold in reserves.

deposit multiplier
Ratio between the maximum increase in the money supply and a given increase in excess reserves. It equals the reciprocal of the reserve ratio.

---

2. The maximum money supply may not be reached because no one can force a bank to make loans from its pool of excess reserves. If there are no loan customers that look worthwhile, a bank can simply hold some excess reserves. We will consider this effect a little later.
3. This term should not be confused with the Keynesian expenditure multiplier discussed in Chapter 8.

BANK	CHANGE IN CHECKABLE DEPOSITS	CHANGE IN BANK RESERVES	AMOUNT THE BANK LENDS
Amacher National	$ —	$ —	$10,000
Ulbrich Savings	+10,000	+2,000	8,000
C	+8,000	+1,600	6,400
D	+6,400	+1,280	5,120
E	+5,120	+1,024	4,096
All others	+20,480	+4,096	16,384
Total	$+50,000	$+10,000	$40,000

TABLE 5
INCREASE IN MONEY SUPPLY WITH INITIAL EXCESS RESERVES OF $10,000 AND A RESERVE RATIO OF 20 PERCENT

According to equation (2), checkable deposits (*D*) can change only if the reserve ratio (*rr*) changes or if all bank reserves (*BR*) change. Using the symbol Δ to represent "change in," we have:

$$\Delta D = \frac{1}{rr} \Delta BR = \Delta M_s.$$

Thus, the change in checkable deposits will be equal to the reciprocal of the reserve ratio (*rr*) multiplied by the change in bank reserves (Δ*BR*). In our example, *rr* = 0.20, so the value of 1/*rr* is 5. If the Δ*BR* equals $10,000, then Δ*D* = 5 × $10,000 = $50,000.

Expansion of checkable deposits can occur only when there are excess reserves. If all reserves are being held to meet the desired ratio of reserves to deposits, then there are no excess reserves available. In that case, the money supply cannot increase.

WHY EXPANSION MAY BE LESS THAN THE MAXIMUM

The actual expansion of the money supply may be less than the maximum that existing bank reserves can support. One reason why this may occur is that the public may decide to hold more of its financial assets in currency and less in checkable deposits. Individuals may make this choice because of concerns about bank safety or because they are using cash transactions to avoid income taxes or to hide illegal activities (such as drug dealing).

A **currency drain** is an increase in cash held by the public that causes a dollar-for-dollar decline in bank reserves. Since currency is part of reserves when it is in the banking system, a currency drain means a reduction in bank reserves. If reserves decline, the banking system cannot support as many checkable deposits. For every dollar of currency flowing out of the banks and into circulation, bank reserves (*BR*) fall by $1. With a 20 percent reserve ratio (*rr*), $5 of potential new deposits are eliminated.

A second reason why expansion of the money supply may fall short of the maximum lies with banks. Banks may choose to hold more reserves than are legally required. Usually banks like to keep reserves down to the required minimum because reserves earn no interest. But if economic conditions are depressed, loan prospects are risky, or interest rates on loans are so low that the only direction they can go is up, banks may choose to hold some excess reserves until conditions improve. In addition, during recessionary times, banks may choose to hold some reserves in case there are large withdrawals during a run, or bank panic. Even if

currency drain
An increase in cash held by the public that causes a dollar-for-dollar decline in bank reserves.

banks are willing to lend, households and firms may not be anxious to borrow. If households and firms are already heavily in debt or have gloomy expectations, they may be reluctant to borrow from banks.

CONTRACTING THE MONEY SUPPLY

The process of contracting the money supply is the expansion process in reverse. Suppose that, for some reason, Amacher National Bank lost reserves. Perhaps a customer withdrew currency from her account in the amount of $2,000. If Amacher National Bank was all loaned up before this withdrawal, this loss of reserves will put the bank below the required reserve level. Amacher has lost $2,000 in reserves and $2,000 in deposits. With a 20 percent reserve ratio, the bank was holding only $400 in reserves behind that deposit. The shortfall of $1,600 must be made up by not making loans or by selling bonds. As Amacher works to rebuild its reserves, however, it gains reserves at the expense of the other banks in the system. Table 6 shows the first few stages of this process. The deposit multiplier is the same here as for the expansion process. Thus, the initial loss of $2,000 in reserves will lead to a maximum contraction of the money supply of $10,000 if no banks had any excess reserves before the first transaction.

BANKS AND THE CENTRAL BANK

This description of the money expansion and contraction process raises two important questions. Where do reserves come from, and who sets the reserve ratio? Deposits and withdrawals of currency by the public are one source of changes in bank reserves, but these flows are relatively small in the U.S. banking system. The major source of bank reserves, including cash in the form of Federal Reserve notes, is the central bank, the Federal Reserve System. The Fed not only creates reserves but also sets and changes the reserve ratio.

CENTRAL BANKING IN THE UNITED STATES

The Federal Reserve System was created by Congress in 1914 in response to two perceived needs. The public wanted Congress to regulate banks in order to prevent them from making risky loans that threatened the safety of deposits. There was also a demand for a lender of last resort to rescue basically sound banks that were threatened with failure and bankruptcy because of temporary economic conditions. Later, a third goal was established: managing the size of the money supply so as to promote economic growth, high employment, and a stable price level. This goal is now the Fed's most important function, but it was not part of the original design of the system. It has only become significant since the Great Depression.

TABLE 6
DECREASE IN MONEY
SUPPLY FOLLOWING
A LOSS OF RESERVES
OF $2,000

BANK	CHANGE IN CHECKABLE DEPOSITS	CHANGE IN BANK RESERVES	REDUCTION IN BANK LENDING
Amacher National	$ —	$–2,000	$–1,600
Ulbrich Savings	–1,600	–1,600	–1,280
Bank C	–1,280	–1,280	–1,024

Chapter 12 Money Creation and the Federal Reserve System

The U.S. Constitution gave the federal government the power to "coin money and regulate the value thereof." It said nothing, however, about establishing banks. Two early attempts to establish a central bank failed. Alexander Hamilton, the first Secretary of the Treasury, was the mastermind behind the creation of the Bank of the United States in 1791. Located in Philadelphia, the bank was privately owned but chartered by the federal government. Its role was to supervise other banks, promote bank safety, and serve as a lender of last resort. Its charter expired in 1811. In 1816, the Second Bank of the United States was created. When its charter was not renewed in 1836 for political reasons, the United States no longer had a central bank.

Banking Problems in the Nineteenth Century

The nineteenth century was marked by frequent bank panics in the United States. **Bank panics** are sudden waves of fear that banks will not be able to pay off their depositors. In the nineteenth century, banks made loans by issuing their own bank notes rather than creating checkable deposits. These notes were supposed to be redeemable in gold. Banks did not maintain enough reserves to redeem all their notes at the same time. As long as the note holders believed they could redeem their notes, very few would actually do so on any given day. The day-to-day demand for redemption in gold could easily be met.

During bank panics, some banks only had problems of liquidity. That is, they did not have enough reserves to meet current demand. Most of the loans they had made would eventually have been repaid, but not quickly enough to meet depositors' current withdrawals. Other banks had more serious problems of solvency. These banks had so many bad loans that the value of their assets was less than the value of their deposits.

For banks that followed unsound lending practices, there usually came a day when too many notes were presented for redemption. The bank's reserves would be too low to redeem all of them. When this happened at one bank, people sometimes panicked and tried to redeem notes at other banks as well. At the height of the bank panics, many sound and well-managed banks were unable to redeem the large numbers of notes presented in a single day. These banks failed, or closed, even though they were basically sound. People who had deposited money in failed banks lost it, and people who needed loans could not get them. Even the banks that didn't fail had to greatly reduce their lending to build reserves against a run of withdrawals.

A run could occur at a perfectly sound bank. All that was needed was a rumor of possible failure that was believed by enough people. To prevent sound banks from going under in a panic, a lender of last resort was needed. A **lender of last resort** is a source of funds for rescuing sound banks by lending them as much as they need to meet temporary high demand from depositors. If sound banks could obtain funds from a lender of last resort, depositors would be less likely to panic. Thus, panics would be less likely to occur in the first place and would be less severe when they did occur.

Does this description of bank panics sound like the banking crisis of the late 1980s? There are some similarities between the two crises and some important differences. Because of federal deposit insurance (discussed later

bank panics
Sudden waves of fear that banks will not be able to pay off their depositors.

lender of last resort
A source of funds for rescuing sound banks by lending them as much as they need to meet temporary high demand from depositors.

in this chapter), few depositors in the 1980s crisis suffered losses. The numerous bank failures of the 1980s represented problems of solvency, not liquidity. These banks had made ill-advised loans and investments. When the value of those investments fell, many banks became insolvent. We will examine the banking crisis in more detail in the next chapter.

EARLY ATTEMPTS AT CONTROL

Without a central bank to regulate unsound banking practices in the nineteenth century, some larger private banks tried to fill the void. A major bank, or group of banks, that was concerned about overissuing of notes and unsound loan practices at Bank A could exert pressure by presenting Bank A's notes to be redeemed in gold. This action drained gold from Bank A and slowed down its issuing of notes. (Such a process was carried out with some success by the Suffolk Bank and its affiliated banks in New England.) Such actions by private banks did not work very well or last very long. Private banks did not have the power to examine another bank's books and lending practices or to force it to stop making bad loans. They lacked the legal authority to regulate other banks and weren't financially strong enough themselves to withstand a major panic. Also, state governments' oversight of banks was generally ineffective and varied widely from state to state.

The logical conclusion seemed to be that only the federal government had the effective power to regulate banks, as well as the financial resources to act as the lender of last resort. However, political battles over whether to give central banking powers to the federal government went on for nearly a century. One reason for the resistance to a central bank was the fear that the centralized power would be used to benefit rich and powerful bankers. The Bank of the United States, originally chartered by the federal government, had tried to restrain the excesses of other banks. Many people felt that the Bank of the United States had used governmental power to benefit the bank's owners, their friends, and business associates. These feelings led to the failure of the first two attempts to establish a central bank.

Another source of resistance to a central bank was disagreement about the importance of sound money and the dangers of inflation. Conservative bankers wanted to limit the expansion of loans for fear it would lead to inflation. If that happened, the value of the loan repayments they received would fall. Rapid money growth and inflation did not seem like problems to some other groups, however. The people who wanted loans—for example, farmers on the Western frontier or small businesses in the East—looked on the expansion of loans as a good thing. People who were in debt had their interest payments fixed in dollar terms. In times of rising prices, they had increasing incomes with which to make their payments. In times of falling prices, they had to make these fixed payments out of a falling income. Borrowers and debtors were afraid that a central bank would pursue a conservative policy that would make life more difficult for them.

THE NATIONAL BANKING SYSTEM

During the Civil War, Congress tried again to make banks safer. The **National Banking System**, established in 1863, allowed banks to apply for federal instead of state charters (formal permission to incorporate and

National Banking System Agency that chartered and regulated national banks during the latter half of the nineteenth century, before the Federal Reserve System.

operate). Banks that receive their charters from the federal government are called **national banks**. A **state bank** is chartered and regulated by one of the states.

The agency that is charged with chartering and regulating national banks is the Comptroller of the Currency in the Department of the Treasury. State banks are regulated by various agencies and commissions in the different states. After 1863, state banks continued to exist alongside national banks. Since state regulation was rather weak and ineffective, the National Banking Act did not substantially improve the stability of banks. Furthermore, there was still no lender of last resort.

national banks
Banks chartered by the federal government and subject to its rules and regulations.

state banks
Banks chartered and regulated by individual states, as opposed to the federal government.

THE FEDERAL RESERVE ACT

The panic of 1907 and the recession that followed convinced Congress to hold hearings on banking problems. After a series of compromises designed to quiet some of opponents' fears, the Federal Reserve Act was passed in 1913. The Federal Reserve System, modeled after the British central bank (the Bank of England), began operating in November 1914. The Federal Reserve System was intended to be an agency that regulated banks and served as a lender of last resort.

STRUCTURE AND FUNCTIONS OF THE FEDERAL RESERVE SYSTEM

The Federal Reserve System was structured to allay fears people had about concentrating financial power at the federal level. The United States is divided into twelve Federal Reserve districts, each with its own Reserve Bank (see Figure 1).[4] The purpose of having districts was to keep the management of the Federal Reserve Banks in closer touch with the people, instead of concentrating power in Washington, DC or New York City.[5] In addition, the board of directors of each district bank was to contain specific numbers of representatives of the banking industry, agriculture, and the general public in order to prevent domination by bankers.

The district banks play an important role in clearing checks from bank to bank. Suppose you write a check for $100 on your account at Student Union Bank in Boston and send it to a firm in Georgia. The firm deposits your check in its account in Citizens and Southern Bank. Citizens and Southern records an entry of $100 in the firm's account and sends the check to the Atlanta Federal Reserve Bank, which credits the Citizens and Southern reserve account with $100 and forwards the check to the Boston Federal Reserve Bank. The Boston Fed takes $100 out of the reserve account of Student Union and transfers it to the account of the Atlanta Fed.

---

4. You can easily determine which district bank issued a Federal Reserve note. To the left of the portrait on the face of each bill is a seal that gives the name of the district bank. The letter in the middle of the seal corresponds to the number that appears four times near the corners. For example, a bill from the Federal Reserve Bank of Dallas, Texas will have the letter K in the seal and four 11's near the corners. Dallas is the 11th Federal Reserve district, and K is the 11th letter of the alphabet.
5. It was also thought that each district could experiment with different policies, which would allow everyone to learn which strategies worked best. This idea never really worked out, as it became apparent that monetary policy had to be coordinated at a national level.

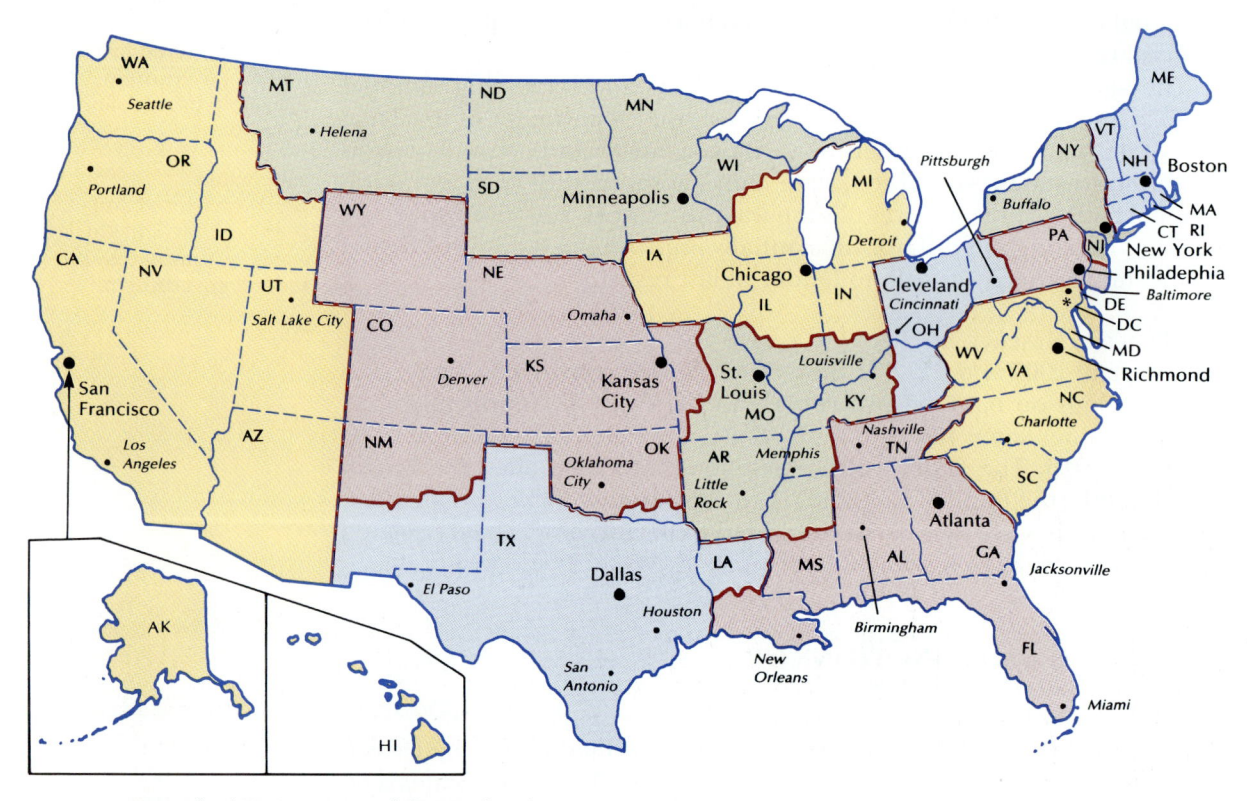

* Board of Governors of the Federal Reserve System
• Federal Reserve Bank Cities
· Federal Reserve Branch Cities

Source: Board of Governors of the Federal Reserve System, *Federal Reserve Bulletin*, June 1990.

FIGURE 1
THE FEDERAL RESERVE SYSTEM
There are twelve Federal Reserve districts, each with its own bank. Most of these banks have branches. The Board of Governors of the Federal Reserve System is located in Washington, DC.

Board of Governors
Central governing body of the Federal Reserve System.

Finally, the check is returned to Student Union, which loses $100 in reserves (an asset) and deposits (a liability). Complex as this process sounds, it is more efficient than what happened before the Fed existed. Checks were passed from bank to bank to bank until they returned to the point of origin, often months later.

When the Federal Reserve System was created, national banks were required to be members. State-chartered banks were allowed but not required to join. The incentives for state banks to join voluntarily were the privileges of borrowing from the Fed and of having direct access to its interbank check-clearing services. Both of these privileges were limited to member banks. In 1980, the law was changed to place all depository institutions under the control of the Fed.

To provide for some central control, a **Board of Governors** was established as the governing body of the Federal Reserve System. The seven governors are appointed by the President for fourteen-year, staggered terms. There can be no more than one governor from any of the twelve districts. Most governors have a background in law, banking, or economics.

International Perspective

Central Banking in Europe and the United States

Most countries have central banks. In fact, the United States was one of the last developed, industrial countries to establish a central bank. All central banks attempt to control the money supply, provide services to banks, manage monetary policy, issue currency, and perform other central banking functions. However, most other central banks have an easier job than the Fed.

The setup of the Fed reflects the fact that the United States is a federal country. The nation is made up of states with some degree of independence. (There are not very many other federal countries. Among the few are Canada, Australia, Brazil, and West Germany.) In countries with unitary (nonfederal) systems, there is less need to provide representation for states and regions in policy making and no need for regional banks of the central bank. In the United States, the transition from state to federal regulation of banking required some compromises that were not made in most other countries.

A typical name of a foreign central bank is the Bank of England or the Bank of Italy. The first central bank of the United States was called the Bank of the United States. When this country took another stab at central banking, a new name was needed. The central bank was named the Federal Reserve System to reflect its federal nature and what was originally regarded as its primary function, storing and supplying reserves.

In European countries, the central bank's task of supervising banks and carrying out monetary policy is easier because there are only a few large banks with many branches. The United States has a large number of individual banks, many of them not members of the Federal Reserve System. Branch banking and interstate banking are recent developments in this country, partly because of the suspicions of Westerners about the power of large Eastern banks. In Europe, large banks with branches have a long history. Some extend back into the Middle Ages. Many less developed countries that were formerly colonies of European nations (especially of France or Britain) have banking systems and central banks that were copied from those of the colonial power.

Finally, European governments do not face one major political problem that confronts the President and Congress in the United States. Control of monetary policy is assigned to an agency that operates independently of both the executive and legislative branches of the U.S. government. Central banks in most other countries are a part of the government and are under its control. This arrangement makes it much easier to coordinate monetary and fiscal policy.

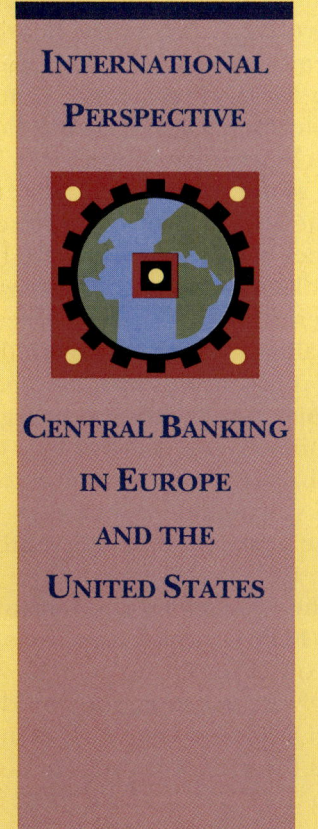

Because the governors serve such long terms, it is rare for even a two-term President to appoint more than a bare majority of the board. These long terms give the Fed a degree of political independence from the executive branch. Technically, the Fed is outside both executive and legislative control, operated by the Board of Governors. The Fed is accountable to its regional boards, its stockholders, and the banks, but there is no effective way for the President or Congress to exercise any control except by the appointments to the Board. Political insiders in Washington have labeled the chairperson of the Fed's Board of Governors, currently Alan Greenspan, as the second most powerful person in Washington.

In the late 1970s, the Federal Reserve System was losing members because member banks were subject to higher reserve ratios than most nonmember banks, whose reserve ratios were set by state regulators. Although the Fed offered member banks access to borrowing and check-clearing services, smaller banks could obtain these services indirectly through correspondent relationships with member banks. With high market interest rates, the opportunity cost of holding reserves was very high. Legislation in 1980 eliminated this disadvantage of belonging to the Federal Reserve System by phasing in uniform reserve ratios for the same type of deposits for all banks, whether or not they were member banks.[6] This action stemmed the loss of membership and helped the Fed to retain more control over the banking system and the money supply.

Federal Open Market Committee (FOMC)
Committee that supervises the conduct of the Fed's monetary policy.

Within the Fed, the most powerful group is the **Federal Open Market Committee (FOMC)**, which supervises the conduct of monetary policy. This committee consists of the Board of Governors plus the presidents of five district banks, always including the president of the New York Federal Reserve Bank. The FOMC meets regularly to make decisions about changes in bank reserves and the money supply. All district bank presidents, not just those currently on the FOMC, attend these meetings.

Are Banks Safer under the Federal Reserve System?

Bank safety was one of the primary reasons for establishing the Federal Reserve System. The first test of the Fed was the Great Depression. Based on the number of bank failures, the Fed flunked. Two deposit insurance agencies, the Federal Deposit Insurance Corporation (FDIC) and the Federal Savings and Loan Insurance Corporation (FSLIC), were created in the 1930s. These two insurance corporations were designed to protect bank depositors, not banks or bank stockholders, from insolvency. Originally deposits were insured up to $2,500, but the ceiling was raised several times and is currently $100,000. The insurance is required for all members of the Federal Reserve System and is financed by premiums paid by the member banks. Both the FDIC and the FSLIC (which were merged in 1990) supervise member banks for safety and compliance with federal banking regulations. The bank insurance system seemed to work well until the late 1980s when a number of bank failures shifted the burden of protecting depositors to the federal government. We will consider this issue in more detail in Chapter 13.

---

6. Although all depository institutions and all types of accounts are treated alike, there is a distinction based on size. The reserve ratio is higher for banks with deposits of over $40 million.

Thus, national banks are subject to a great deal of oversight because they must belong to the Federal Reserve System and carry deposit insurance. The Fed supervises its member banks, the Comptroller of the Currency supervises national banks, and the FDIC supervises its member banks. Some state-chartered banks, however, are supervised only by their state's banking commission and any state or private deposit insurance group to which they belong.

Recall that there are two sources of bank failure. One is a liquidity problem—a lack of ready cash to meet excessive withdrawals by the public. The insurance of deposits by the FDIC and FSLIC and the existence of the Fed as a lender of last resort have largely resolved that problem. The other problem is one of solvency—the value of a bank's assets is not enough to cover outstanding liabilities, such as deposits. A bank becomes insolvent if it has too many assets in loans that may never be repaid. When a bank becomes insolvent, it will go out of business or be taken over by another bank in a merger. Such a merger is often forced by the insuring agency.

The FDIC and the Comptroller of the Currency also regulate kinds of investments that banks can make. This regulation provides stockholders and depositors some protection against insolvency. Even in a regulated industry such as banking, it is important to allow unsuccessful firms to fail and leave the industry if the market system is to function effectively. However, a very high failure rate, such as occurred in the late 1980s, overstrains the capacity of the regulatory authorities and the resources of the insurance corporations.

There were some spectacular failures of major banks in the late 1970s and early 1980s. For example, Franklin National Bank in New York City, Continental Illinois in Chicago, and Penn Square in Oklahoma failed. Failures of state-chartered banks in Ohio, Nebraska, Mississippi, and Maryland in 1984 and 1985 led to demands for reform to provide greater protection for depositors. After a two-year wave of failures (79 banks in 1984 and 120 in 1985) and a number of shotgun mergers, many of the surviving state-chartered banks became members of the FDIC or FSLIC.

In the late 1980s, bank failures were far less spectacular but much more numerous, threatening the soundness of the two deposit insurance corporations. A number of banks—especially savings and loans—developed some serious solvency problems. On their balance sheets, the value of assets had fallen below the value of liabilities, leaving them with negative net worth. Some of these banks were suffering from mismanagement by own-

FUNCTIONS OF THE FED

- Preventing bank crises and panics by serving as the lender of last resort
- Supervising banks
- Providing currency and check-clearing services
- Providing banking services to the Treasury
- Conducting monetary policy

ers who made loans to themselves and their friends on the basis of property with inflated values. Others ran into regional economic problems. Banks that served rural, agricultural communities saw the value of loan collateral drop sharply with falling prices for farmland and high bankruptcy rates among farmers. Similar problems affected banks in Texas and Oklahoma that had made many loans to oil companies. A number of big urban banks had to write off bad loans to less developed countries or extend them with a risk of never being repaid. In 1990 and 1991, several major New England banks failed as the recession and falling real estate prices hit that region harder than the rest of the country. We will explore the origins of this banking crisis and its consequences in the next chapter.

THE BALANCE SHEET OF THE FEDERAL RESERVE SYSTEM

Like all banks, the Federal Reserve System has a balance sheet that lists its assets, liabilities, and net worth. Table 7 shows a simplified balance sheet for the Fed for 1990. Note that member banks' reserves are assets to those institutions but liabilities of the Fed. Federal Reserve notes, now the only legal form of U.S. currency, are another major liability of the Fed. Treasury deposits are a relatively small entry on the liability side. One of the original but now less important functions of the Fed is to be a bank to the U.S. Treasury. The Treasury also keeps funds in commercial banks. The main assets of the Fed are government bonds of various maturities, which are used in open market operations. The Fed also holds gold certificates, issued by the Treasury when it acquires gold. A small amount of the Fed's assets consists of loans outstanding to banks.

On a balance sheet, the best measure of financial health is net worth, or assets minus liabilities. For a corporation, net worth represents the value of ownership rights of stockholders. Who owns the Fed? Member banks do, and they earn a guaranteed return on their shares. Any earnings in excess of that guaranteed return go to the U.S. Treasury, since the Fed is both a privately owned firm and an agency of the government.

In Chapter 11, we used T-accounts to show the effect of single transactions for Amacher National Bank. A T-account can also be used to describe the transactions of the Fed. The main transactions of interest are those that relate changes in member bank reserves, because bank reserves determine bank lending and the size of the money supply. Thus, the most

TABLE 7
FEDERAL RESERVE BALANCE SHEET, OCTOBER 1990
(MILLIONS OF DOLLARS)

ASSETS		LIABILITIES	
Government securities	$237,763	Reserves of banks	$ 34,546
Loans to banks	591	Federal Reserve notes	255,866
		Treasury deposits	7,607
Gold certificates	11,060	Other liabilities	10,628
Other assets	65,653	TOTAL LIABILITIES	308,641
		NET WORTH	6,426
		TOTAL LIABILITIES	
TOTAL ASSETS	$315,067	AND NET WORTH	$315,067

Source: Board of Governors of the Federal Reserve System, *Federal Reserve Bulletin* (Washington, DC: U.S. Government Printing Office, January 1991).

important items on the balance sheet are government securities, loans to banks, and reserves of banks.

Table 8 shows two sample transactions and T-accounts for the Fed. In transaction 1, the Fed buys a $10,000 government bond from Amacher National Bank. In transaction 2, the Fed makes a $20,000 loan to Ulbrich Savings Bank. When the Fed buys the bond, we assume that Amacher National is paid by a credit to its reserve account at the Fed. When the Fed makes the loan to Ulbrich Savings, we assume that Ulbrich requests that the funds be paid in Federal Reserve notes.

THE FED AND THE MONEY SUPPLY

Actions concerning bonds, reserves, loans to banks, and Federal Reserve notes are the tools of monetary policy. The Fed uses the money supply and interest rates to affect output, employment, and the price level. The Fed has three methods of influencing the money supply: open market operations, changes in the reserve ratio, and changes in the discount rate. Open market operations involve buying and selling bonds to affect banks' reserves. Changes in the reserve ratio affect their excess reserves. The discount rate affects the borrowing done by the banks.

OPEN MARKET OPERATIONS

The Fed's most frequently used tool is open market operations, although it is the most recent of the three to develop. **Open market operations** are purchases and sales of government securities (bonds) by the Federal Reserve on the open market in order to affect bank reserves.[7]

Open market operations are a very flexible tool. The impact on reserves can be precisely determined to be as large or small as desired. Open market operations can be reversed if necessary and can be done without any fanfare. As a result, the Fed relies most heavily on open market operations for monetary policy.

Open market operations are carried out at the open market desk at the Federal Reserve Bank of New York. Bonds are bought and sold through brokers in New York City. The New York district bank has this responsibility because New York is the financial center of the country. The

open market operations Purchases and sales of government bonds on the open market by the Fed in order to affect bank reserves.

TRANSACTION 1:
The Fed buys a bond from Amacher National.

ASSETS	LIABILITIES
Government bonds +$10,000	Reserves of banks +$10,000

TRANSACTION 2:
The Fed makes a loan to Ulbrich Savings.

ASSETS	LIABILITIES
Loans to banks +$20,000	Federal Reserve notes +$20,000

TABLE 8
SAMPLE TRANSACTIONS AND
T-ACCOUNTS FOR THE FED

7. The term *bond* is used here to refer to all U.S. Treasury securities. In reality, a large part of open market operations is carried out in short-term Treasury obligations, or T-bills.

open market desk, however, does not buy and sell on the basis of its own decisions. It carries out the overall directives of the FOMC.

How do the Fed's open market operations affect bank reserves? Suppose Bank A has reserves of $1,000,000 that it holds in the form of deposits with the Fed. The Fed buys $100,000 worth of government bonds from Bank A. The Fed now owns the government bonds and pays for them by writing on its books that Bank A has $100,000 more in deposits (reserves) with the Fed. Thus, Bank A's reserves are now $1,100,000. These changes are shown on the T-accounts of Bank A and the Fed in Table 9. Suppose the Fed buys a bond from an individual or a business firm. The seller is a customer of some bank, so the check received from the Fed will be deposited in a bank. The bank will then clear the check through the Fed, and the bank's reserves with the Fed will increase by the amount of the sale. No matter where the Fed buys bonds, bank reserves increase by the amount of the Fed purchase. Conversely, open market sales of securities by the Fed decrease the reserves of banks by the amount of the sale. Through open market operations, the Fed can directly affect the reserves of banks.

FIRST-ROUND EFFECTS OF OPEN MARKET OPERATIONS. Assume that the level of required reserves is 20 percent of checkable deposits and that all of Bank A's reserves were required reserves prior to the purchase of $100,000 in government bonds by the Fed. As shown in Bank A's T-account in Table 9, this transaction affects its reserves. The bank's interest-earning assets in the form of government bonds have fallen by $100,000. Its reserves have risen by $100,000. Now its excess reserves, total reserves *minus* required reserves, are $100,000.

This change in the makeup of Bank A's assets is only the first-round effect of the open market operation. What will Bank A do with these excess reserves? It now has fewer interest-earning assets because it sold the $100,000 bond to the Fed. When the next customer asks for a $100,000 loan, it will be granted if that customer is a good risk. Further, the bank may be a little more eager to make loans on easier terms. The bank may even be willing to lend at a lower interest rate. The new loan of $100,000 is shown in Table 10 as an increase in both checkable deposits (liabilities) and loans (assets) of Bank A.[8]

Bank A had new deposits of $100,000 and new reserves of $100,000. Of these new reserves, 20 percent of new deposits, or $20,000, were required reserves. Why didn't Bank A lend more money? Because, as mentioned earlier in this chapter, the loaned money is likely to be withdrawn from the bank very soon. Borrowers usually do not take out loans just to

TABLE 9
EFFECTS OF AN OPEN MARKET OPERATION ON BANK A AND THE FED

BANK A			THE FED			
ASSETS		LIABILITIES	ASSETS		LIABILITIES	
Reserves	+$100,000		Government bonds	+$100,000	Reserves of banks	+$100,000
Government bonds	−$100,000					

8. If you were drawing up a T-account for the borrower, that person's T-account would show an increase in checkable deposits as an asset and a loan to be repaid as a liability.

TABLE 10
T-ACCOUNT FOR BANK A'S LOAN EXPANSION OF $100,000

ASSETS		LIABILITIES	
Loans	+$100,000	Checkable deposits	+$100,000

let the money sit idle in a checking account. For instance, a builder will take out a loan to finance the construction of a new office building and will use the funds to pay for materials and hire construction workers. When the borrower's checks are deposited in other banks, they will be presented for payment to Bank A. When checkable deposits are withdrawn, reserves will decline by the same amount.

The lesson for a single bank is clear. It can safely lend only its excess reserves because it can afford to lose these reserves and still meet the reserve ratio. As long as a bank lends only reserves that are in excess of its required reserves, it will be able to meet its reserve requirement, even if all the loaned funds leave the bank.

OPEN MARKET OPERATIONS AND THE DEPOSIT MULTIPLIER. What happens to the funds that the borrower pays out? Bank A will lose reserves and deposits, but another bank will gain both, just as before. The new reserves the Fed has created will remain in the banking system until the Fed withdraws them (perhaps by an open market operation in the opposite direction).[9] These reserves can be passed around from bank to bank, but banks cannot create new reserves. As long as they are in the banking system, they can support additional checkable deposits and thus a larger money supply. The amount of additional deposits they can support depends on the reserve ratio, according to the relationship developed earlier in this chapter:

$$\Delta D = \frac{1}{rr} \Delta BR = \Delta M_s.$$

The change in checkable deposits (ΔD) from the $100,000 open market operation ($\Delta BR = \$100,000$) with a reserve ratio ($rr$) equal to 0.20 is $100,000/0.20, or $500,000. How did this happen? Initially, member bank reserves increased by $100,000. Since the reserve ratio was unchanged, all of these additional reserves were excess reserves, available for lending. As loans and deposits expand, however, the excess reserves gradually become required reserves behind newly created checkable deposits. This process continues until all of the new reserves are serving as required reserves.

CONTRACTING THE MONEY SUPPLY. Open market purchases of bonds by the Fed are expansionary. When the Fed purchases bonds, it pays for them by increasing member banks' reserves. If the Fed wishes to contract the money supply or prevent banks from expanding the money supply, it will offer to sell bonds to the banks. Very small changes in their yield[10] will

---

9. Certain actions by the U.S. Treasury, foreigners, and the public can reduce member bank reserves. We will neglect these for the moment.
10. A slight fall in the price will raise the yield, which is equal to interest income divided by price paid. We will explore this relationship further in the next chapter.

make it extremely profitable for banks to purchase these bonds. The Fed thus has no trouble finding buyers. (If banks do not wish to buy, their customers will, and the effect on reserves is the same.) When the Fed sells bonds, it accepts payment by decreasing the bank's reserve account.

As a result of the sale of government bonds by the Fed, bank reserves fall. The deposit multiplier works on this reduction in reserves in the same way it works on an expansion of reserves. The money supply that can be supported by existing reserves is smaller than before. If banks were fully loaned up before this transaction, there would be a decrease in the money supply.

CHANGING THE RESERVE RATIO

The second tool used by the Fed is its power to set and change the reserve ratio. Items that a bank can count toward meeting the required reserve consist of two assets. One is the currency and coins the bank has on its premises, called vault cash. The second, and larger, consists of funds the bank has on deposit with its district Reserve Bank. The Fed requires depository institutions to hold reserves equal to certain fractions of the different kinds of deposits they have.[11] One reason why banks collapsed during panics before the Fed was created was that their reserves were too small or not readily available. In practice, reserves now have little to do with the safety of checking and savings account deposits. Their safety is ensured by the federal deposit insurance. However, reserves do ensure that banks will have some ready funds to meet withdrawals.

THE RESERVE RATIO AND BANK LENDING. The reserve ratio is less important as a way to ensure a cushion of liquidity and solvency than as a means for the Fed to control the ability of banks to lend and create money. To see how this works, assume that banks have to hold reserves equal to 20 percent of their checkable deposits. Suppose Bank A has exactly the required reserve level: deposits of $1,000,000 and reserves of $200,000. If people withdraw $100,000 from their checking accounts (checkable deposits), Bank A will have only $100,000 left in reserves supporting checkable deposits of $900,000. Required reserves behind that level of deposits are $180,000. Thus, Bank A's reserves are now $80,000 below the level required by the Fed. The bank must make up these reserves or face fines by the Fed. When Bank A, and other banks, are forced to contract lending to make up reserves, the money supply will shrink.

A change in the reserve ratio increases or decreases banks' ability to lend money. With a given level of reserves, an increase in the reserve ratio from 20 percent to 25 percent would create a reserve shortage and make bankers less willing to lend. A reduction in the reserve ratio from 20 percent to 15 percent would convert some required reserves to excess reserves and make bankers more willing to make loans. (Normally changes in the reserve ratio are much smaller than that, no more than 0.5 percent at a time.)

---

11. Historically, the Fed had different reserve ratios for different types of deposits and different sizes of banks. Nonmember banks and other depository institutions had still different reserve ratios set by their regulatory agencies. All this was changed in 1980. Now reserves vary only with the kind of account and not with the type or size of the depository institution. All checkable deposits, whether at commercial banks, savings banks, or credit unions, have the same reserve ratio. The Fed can adjust the requirements within a range of 8–14 percent. Reserve ratios are graduated by total volume of deposit.

International Perspective

The International Monetary Fund and the World Bank

There are two international financial institutions that perform certain banking functions for nations. One is mostly concerned with the international market for national currencies. The other is primarily a lending institution that makes long-term loans in order to promote economic growth in less developed countries.

Representatives of the major nations met in Bretton Woods, New Hampshire in 1944 to make plans for international monetary coordination in the postwar period. The result of that meeting was the creation of the International Monetary Fund (IMF) and the International Bank for Reconstruction and Development (World Bank). The first problem that the delegates were concerned about was the international monetary system. The gold standard had died, and nations wanted to maintain stable currency prices. Most delegates thought that stable currency prices would require a "manager." There would also be a need for a place where nations could go to borrow foreign currency when they had temporary shortages and needed to pay for imports. That is, the "manager" would also be a lender of last resort for countries.

The IMF was intended to be that manager, supplying liquidity to nations to meet temporary crises. The IMF supplies liquidity by lending currencies of other countries that can be used to meet international obligations. Since 1973, when the major industrial nations shifted from fixed currency prices to floating exchange rates, the role of the IMF in international finance has been much less important.

The World Bank's primary role is as a long-term lender and technical adviser to developing nations. It was created to assist in the reconstruction of Europe after World War II and to help former colonies to get on their feet. Today, the World Bank receives contributions from the developed nations and borrows money in financial markets in order to make long-term, low-interest loans to less developed nations. The loans are used for such developmental projects as roads, dams, electric power plants, and water systems. As these loans are repaid, the World Bank recycles the funds to other nations and other projects.

Neither the IMF nor the World Bank is a bank in the sense of creating money. Since gold ceased to play a monetary role, there has been no true international money, although the U.S. dollar has functioned as such to some degree for most of the last forty years. The IMF does operate as a bank in lending to nations in need of foreign currencies, and the World Bank plays a banker's role as a wholesaler of loanable funds. Without a single world government to create and direct a worldwide central bank, the IMF and the World Bank represent as much international central banking as we are likely to have.

Both open market operations and changes in the reserve ratio affect the amount of checkable deposits by changing excess reserves. The difference between the two tools is that changes in the reserve ratio leave the amount of reserves the same but convert some required reserves to excess reserves, or vice versa. A reduction in the reserve ratio increases the size of the money supply that can be supported by any given amount of bank reserves. An increase in the reserve ratio reduces the size of the potential money supply.

The impact of a change in the reserve ratio is shown on a T-account for Bank A in Table 11. Suppose the Fed reduces the reserve ratio from 20 to 10 percent. Bank A's reserves are still $200,000, but required reserves have fallen to $100,000, and excess reserves have risen to $100,000. With $100,000 in excess reserves, Bank A can be expected to expand its lending, just as it did when an open market sale of a bond to the Fed increased its reserves. Table 11 traces the response by Bank A, which is similar to its response to the open market operation. Whether excess reserves result from an open market operation or a change in the reserve ratio, they are still something of a "hot potato." They move from bank to bank and can be eliminated only by being turned into required reserves.

What happens when the reserve ratio is raised? If excess reserves are initially zero, an increase in the reserve ratio will result in a reserve deficit. Checkable deposits will fall as banks are forced to contract loans. The maximum money supply that any given volume of reserves can support will be smaller because the deposit multiplier will be smaller.

THE RESERVE RATIO AND THE DEPOSIT MULTIPLIER. A change in the reserve ratio changes the maximum size of the money supply, not by changing bank reserves (BR), but by changing the deposit multiplier ($1/rr$). The deposit multiplier is the reciprocal of the reserve ratio. When the reserve ratio changes from 20 percent to 10 percent, the deposit multiplier increases from 5 to 10. Thus, a reduction in the reserve ratio has a double impact on the money supply. First, it converts some required reserves into excess reserves. Second, it increases the size of the deposit multiplier. An increase in the reserve ratio works in the opposite way. The higher reserve

TABLE 11
BANK A RESPONDS TO A CHANGE IN THE RESERVE RATIO FROM 20 PERCENT TO 10 PERCENT

BANK A BEFORE THE CHANGE IN THE RESERVE RATIO:

ASSETS		LIABILITIES	
Reserves	$200,000	Checkable deposits	$1,000,000
Loans and government bonds	800,000		

After the change in the reserve ratio, Bank A makes a loan of $100,000. When the borrower spends the funds, Bank A loses reserves and deposits to another bank.

ASSETS		LIABILITIES	
Reserves	$100,000	Checkable deposits	$1,000,000
Loans and government bonds	900,000		

Chapter 12 Money Creation and the Federal Reserve System

ratio creates a shortfall of excess reserves and also reduces the size of the deposit multiplier.

A change in the reserve ratio is more complex than open market operations because of this double impact. Because it is such a powerful tool, changes in the reserve ratio are made rarely and in small amounts. Even a change of a fraction of 1 percent can have a very large (and somewhat uncertain) impact on the economy and can be very unsettling to banks. In the last two decades, the Fed made adjustments to the reserve ratio an average of three times a year, most of them affecting only one or two types of deposits.[12]

DISCOUNTING AND THE DISCOUNT RATE

One additional way for banks to make up a shortage of required reserves is to borrow from the Fed. This lending power is the Fed's third tool of monetary control. It derives from the role of the central bank as a lender of last resort. A bank borrows from the Fed by putting up some of its assets as backing, or collateral, for the loan. Only certain kinds of assets held by banks are eligible to serve as collateral. A loan is made when the bank discounts such an asset with its district Reserve Bank.

The term *discounting* refers to the method by which the Fed charges interest on a loan to a bank. Discounted loans can be made by banks to their customers as well as by the Fed to a bank. This type of loan simply deducts the interest in advance. Normally, if you borrowed $10,000 for a year, you would receive $10,000 and expect to repay $11,000 or more. The difference between the principal (the amount borrowed) and the total repaid is the interest. With a discounted loan, the principal would still be $10,000, but the borrower might receive only $9,000. The interest is subtracted at the beginning instead of added during or at the end of the term of the loan.

Borrowing from the Fed by banks is called "using the discount window." The interest rate the Fed charges banks is called the **discount rate**. Changing the discount rate is one of the tools of monetary policy. The higher the rate charged, the less eager banks are to borrow. The lower the rate, the more willing banks are to increase reserves by borrowing. The Fed may deny use of the discount window to banks that have made unwise loans. The discount rate is almost always below other interest rates at which banks could borrow.

discount rate
The interest rate the Fed charges on loans to banks.

THE DISCOUNT WINDOW AND CHANGES IN THE RESERVE RATIO. Recall what happens when an increase in the reserve ratio leaves banks with too little reserves. Banks are forced to contract their deposits by selling some interest-earning assets or eliminating loans. Such a forced contraction is a very difficult situation for both banks and their loan customers. It takes time to make the transition to the new conditions. For this reason, the Fed may choose to cushion the impact of a decline in bank reserves by keeping the discount window open—by standing ready to make loans to banks as needed.

---

12. A list of these changes is given by Michelle R. Garfinkel and Daniel L. Thornton in "The Link Between M1 and the Monetary Base in the 1980s," *Review*, Federal Reserve Bank of St. Louis (September-October 1989): 35–52.

With an open discount window, instead of immediately calling in loans and selling bonds, banks can borrow reserves from their district Bank. What they borrow is deposits with that Federal Reserve Bank. An increase in the Fed's lending activity means an increase in member bank reserves. However, banks have taken out loans with the Fed that they will eventually have to repay. They will still have to make the adjustment by reducing their assets, but they have bought some time in which to adjust more gradually.

Each Federal Reserve Bank sets a discount rate at which the depository institutions of its district can borrow. Since the Board of Governors must approve the rate, the rates are usually the same in all twelve districts. Normally the discount rate is slightly below the market interest rate. To keep banks from borrowing from the Fed at low rates and lending to customers at high rates, the district banks ration the borrowing privilege, and banks are warned by Fed officials about abusing the discounted loans. Many people are under the impression that the Fed sets market interest rates, but the discount rate is the only rate the Fed sets directly. We will discuss how the Fed has an indirect effect on the general level of market interest rates in Chapter 14.

The discount rate functions as a signal more than as a direct tool of monetary control. An increase in the discount rate indicates to banks that the Fed wants to cool down the economy by reducing bank lending. A decrease signifies the Fed's desire to stimulate the economy. Changes in the discount rate also alter the profitability of borrowing from the Fed in order to relend. Raising the rate makes it more expensive to borrow. In that case, banks are expected to borrow less and hold larger excess reserves in order to avoid borrowing. A lower rate makes borrowing from the Fed more attractive and encourages banks to hold fewer excess reserves. They know they can easily borrow from the Fed if necessary.

Raising and lowering the discount rate is not as powerful a tool as changes in the reserve ratio or open market operations. Its impact is harder to measure than the others, since the magnitude of the effect depends on bankers' reaction to the change. If this tool were used too often, it would lose its effectiveness as a signal of the Fed's policy direction.

THE FEDERAL FUNDS MARKET. Banks can borrow reserves from each other as well as from the Fed. These loans between banks are made in the **federal funds market**. If Bank A has excess reserves, it can lend some of these (for one day at a time) to Bank B. The rate charged is the **federal funds rate**. If the annual rate is 12 percent, it costs the borrowing bank approximately $1/30$ of 1 percent for a one-day loan. Such loans can be renewed, but a bank can get its loaned funds back after one day if it so desires.

The Fed does not directly set the federal funds rate, but it does set a target range for that rate, such as plus or minus $1/8$ of 1 percent around 12 percent. Then, if the federal funds rate drops to $11\frac{7}{8}$ percent, the Fed will sell bonds to drain reserves from the banking system. As excess reserves of member banks fall relative to the demand for them, the federal funds rate will be driven up. Similarly, if the rate rises to $12\frac{1}{8}$ percent, the Fed will buy bonds to inject reserves into banks. The supply of reserves increases relative to demand, driving the federal funds rate back down

federal funds market
The market in which banks borrow reserves from each other.

federal funds rate
The interest rate charged in the federal funds market.

toward 12 percent. Many economists think that this indirect control of the federal funds rate plays a very important role in monetary policy and in how well the policy works. The federal funds rate is usually slightly above the discount rate because banks prefer to borrow from other banks rather than from the Fed.

OTHER TOOLS OF THE FEDERAL RESERVE SYSTEM

The Fed has a few more specialized tools. From time to time, the Fed has been authorized to set maximum repayment periods and minimum down payments for consumer credit. It can also set the fraction of stock purchases that a buyer can finance with credit (the margin requirement). These tools, called selective credit controls, are not used very frequently. They have become less useful in the last few decades with the growth of alternative sources of funds (nonbank financial institutions) to which borrowers can turn.

The Fed can also use **moral suasion**. That is, it can try to convince banks to do what it favors. For example, the Fed may think that the money supply is growing too quickly. The Board of Governors will urge banks not to make as many new loans in order to hold down the rate of growth. Since the Fed regulates banks and controls their access to the discount window, banks have to pay some attention to such requests. Although the Fed has some success in persuasion, this approach is generally less effective than open market operations as a way of controlling the money supply.

moral suasion Attempts by the Fed to convince depository institutions to do what the Fed favors.

The way in which the Fed has used its monetary policy tools has cre-

FEDERAL RESERVE TOOLS

TOOL	WORKS THROUGH	PLUSES AND MINUSES	FREQUENCY OF USE
• Open market operations	Changing bank reserves	Flexible Broad impact	Used frequently
• Changes in the reserve ratios	Changing excess reserves	Broad impact Extremely powerful	Used rarely
• Changes in the discount rate	Changing the amount of borrowing banks will do	Useful as signal Affects interest rates	Used relatively infrequently
• Selective credit controls	Changing terms of consumer loans and borrowing to buy stock		Used infrequently
• Moral suasion	Persuading banks to change amount of lending	Limited in effectiveness	Used occasionally

ated disagreements among economists as well as politicians. The debates of the nineteenth century over how freely banks should lend are still alive. There is still support for easy money, unlimited credit, and inflation among those who are in debt and want to be able to borrow more and pay it back with cheaper dollars. There are also several groups of hard-money backers, ranging from those who simply want monetary growth carefully controlled to those who would like to return to full-bodied money, usually a gold standard. Developments in banking and financial markets in the last fifteen years have changed the nature of banking in the United States in ways that have yet to be fully seen. The next chapter will take a closer look at some of these changes as part of a broader examination of financial markets and interest rates.

Summary

1. The banking system in the United States is based on the principle of fractional reserve banking, first applied in the Middle Ages by goldsmiths.

2. Depository institutions make loans, which expands the money supply. The upper limit on such expansion is determined by the amount of reserves banks must keep to back up deposits.

3. The Federal Reserve System was created in 1913 to limit the damage to the economy from bank panics in the nineteenth and early twentieth centuries. It was designed to serve as a regulator and lender of last resort to member banks.

4. There are twelve Federal Reserve districts in the United States, each with a Federal Reserve District Bank. The central authority is the Board of Governors in Washington, DC. A main concern of the Fed is monetary policy, which is carried out by actions that influence interest rates, credit conditions, and the money supply.

5. The Fed has three main tools it can use in implementing monetary policy: open market operations, changes in the reserve ratio, and lending at the discount rate.

6. Open market operations are purchases and sales of government bonds by the Fed on the open market. Open market operations go on daily.

7. The reserve ratio determines the amount of reserves banks must hold as a fraction of checkable deposits. Required reserves must be held in the form of vault cash and deposits in a Federal Reserve Bank.

8. Both changes in the reserve ratio and open market operations work by changing banks' excess reserves. Excess reserves are total reserves minus required reserves. As excess reserves expand, banks can increase their loans and, thus, the money supply. Reductions in excess reserves tend to force contractions of loans and the money supply.

9. Banks can borrow from the Fed at the discount rate to cushion reductions in reserves.

10. Both the reserve ratio and the discount rate are changed infrequently. Open market operations are the main tool of monetary policy.

New Terms

Federal Reserve System (Fed)
fractional reserve banking
reserves
T-account
excess reserves
reserve ratio
deposit multiplier
currency drain
bank panics
lender of last resort
National Banking System
national banks
state banks
Board of Governors
Federal Open Market Committee (FOMC)
open market operations
discount rate
federal funds market
federal funds rate
moral suasion

Questions for Discussion

1. Why are there twelve Federal Reserve districts? In which district are you? What is the Board of Governors?

2. Which of the following items appear on the Fed's balance sheet? For each item that appears on the balance sheet, indicate whether it is an asset or a liability.
   a. government bonds
   b. reserves of banks
   c. deposits by the Treasury
   d. deposits by the public
   e. loans to banks
   f. currency

3. Which of the following items appear on a bank's balance sheet? For each item that appears on the balance sheet, indicate whether it is an asset or a liability.
   a. government bonds
   b. reserves
   c. deposits by the Treasury
   d. deposits by the public
   e. loans to the public
   f. currency

4. What are the three main tools of the Fed? Which one is used most often? Why?

5. Suppose the reserve ratio is 20 percent. If an extra $2 billion in excess reserves are injected into the banking system through an open market purchase of T-bills by the Fed, by how much can checkable deposits rise? What would your answer be if the reserve ratio were 10 percent? Does the total of checkable deposits have to rise?

6. Would it make a difference in your answers to Question 5 if the increase in excess reserves came about because the Fed lowered the discount rate and thus induced banks to borrow $2 billion?

7. Suppose bank reserves are $100 billion, the reserve ratio is 20 percent, and banks are fully loaned up (that is, excess reserves are zero). Now suppose the reserve ratio is lowered to 10 percent and banks once again become fully loaned up. What is the new level of checkable deposits? Do this problem again, but assume the reserve ratio rises to 25 percent.

8. List the steps by which a sale of government bonds by the Fed affects output and the price level through aggregate supply and demand.

9. If the Fed sells bonds, what is likely to happen to each of the following?
   a. bank reserves
   b. interest rates
   c. the money supply
   d. output and/or prices (money GNP)

10. How did the inflation of the 1970s add to the pressure for bank deregulation in the early 1980s?

11. Why do banks borrow from one another instead of from the Fed?

12. How are the effects of changes in the reserve ratio on bank lending and the money supply different from the effects of open market operations?

13. How does the Fed's role differ from what was originally envisioned?

14. Why did it take the United States so long to establish a permanent central bank?

15. List all of the actions the Fed can undertake to try to increase lending, the money supply, and the level of economic activity.

Suggestions for Further Reading

Goodhart, Charles. *The Evolution of Central Banking.* Cambridge, MA: MIT Press, 1988. Explains why and how central banks evolved, drawing on the experiences of several countries.

Greider, William. *Secrets of the Temple.* New York: Simon and Schuster, 1987. A critical look at the working of the Federal Reserve System.

Mayer, Thomas, James S. Duesenberry, and Robert Z. Aliber. *Money, Banking and the Economy,* 4th ed. New York: W. W. Norton, 1990. An excellent intermediate book with thorough coverage of theory, institutions, and history.

AFTER STUDYING THIS CHAPTER, YOU SHOULD BE ABLE TO:

1. Discuss the effects of deregulation on banks.
2. Explain the relationship between:
   a. bond prices and bond yields,
   b. real and nominal interest rates,
   c. risk and interest rates.
3. Describe each of these nonbank financial markets or institutions:
   a. the stock market,
   b. the bond market,
   c. mutual funds,
   d. pension funds,
   e. insurance companies.
4. Discuss the effect of interest rates on investment spending, output, and income.

CHAPTER 13
FINANCIAL MARKETS AND INTEREST RATES

INTRODUCTION

Financial markets are shown as the outer flow in the bottom half of the circular flow diagram in Figure 1. The role of financial markets, or the credit market, is to gather funds from households and other savers and channel them to borrowers (households, government, or business firms) or to firms that sell ownership rights (stock). The prices at which funds are borrowed in the credit market are interest rates. Ownership claims convey a right to a share in the profits of the firm.

The last two decades have seen dramatic changes in financial markets. There are more kinds of institutions offering more kinds of deposits, financial instruments, and services. The 1980s saw bank deregulation, the invention of junk bonds, and a stock market crash. There was also a banking crisis that continues into the 1990s.

The Fed is interested in lending, borrowing, and interest rates mainly as a channel of monetary policy. But it cannot ignore the close links between the market for stocks and the market for loanable funds. This chapter describes the workings of financial markets in the wake of all the changes that have occurred since the 1970s.

BANK DEREGULATION IN THE 1980s

The functions of banks and the rules under which they operate have changed dramatically in the last two decades. The typical commercial bank of the early 1970s offered checking accounts (which paid no interest), passbook savings accounts, and a few other financial services, such as safe deposit boxes, traveler's checks, and loans. In 1970, there were no money market accounts, no NOW accounts, and no certificates of deposit (CDs). Handy automatic teller machines (ATMs) dispensing cash and accepting deposits were yet to be developed. Interest rates on passbooks were regulated, and interest on checking accounts had been forbidden since the 1930s. Banks that wanted to compete for deposits offered trading stamps, free gifts, and other rewards instead of higher yields. Interstate banking was forbidden. In many states, even branch banking (multiple offices for

FIGURE 1
THE CIRCULAR FLOW WITH A CREDIT MARKET
The credit market gathers savings from households and channels them into business and government investment. The major participants in this market include banks, savings and loan institutions, credit unions, the stock market, the bond market, mutual funds, insurance companies, and pension funds.

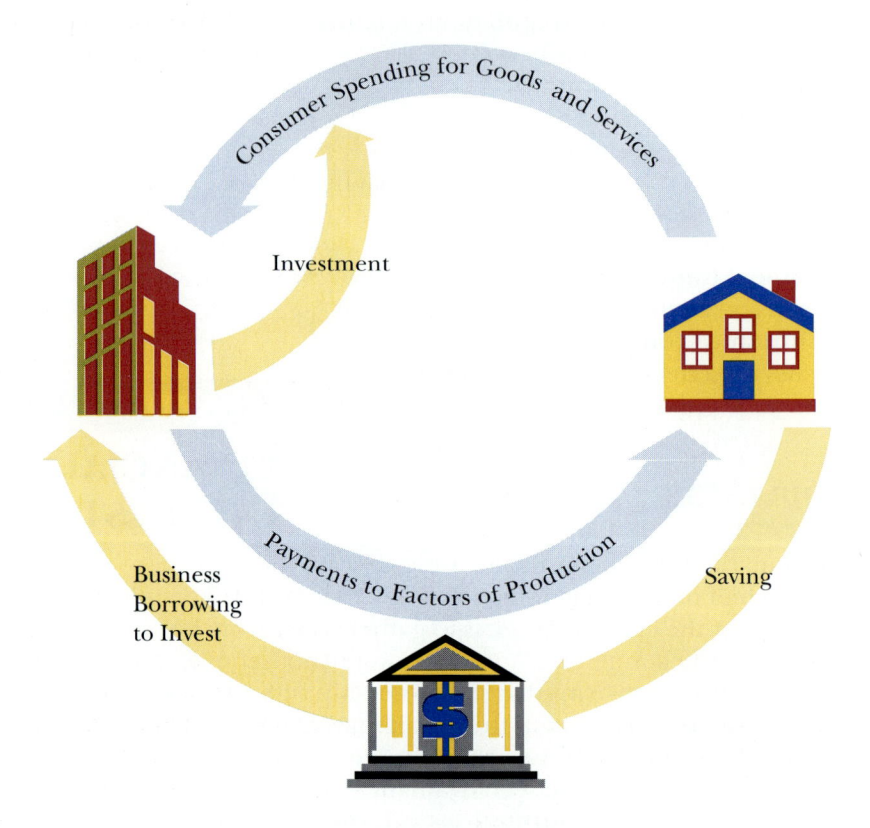

a single bank) was forbidden. Thus, unlike many foreign countries, the United States had no large nationwide or even regional banks. Around 1975, all of these rules and practices began to change.

DEVELOPMENTS IN THE BANKING INDUSTRY
High inflation rates and high market interest rates in the 1970s were the stimulus for some major changes in the banking system. One such change occurred in New England. State-chartered and state-insured savings banks, not subject to federal regulations on interest on deposits, pioneered a new type of savings account that allowed depositors to write negotiated orders of withdrawal. These NOW accounts were the first interest-bearing checking accounts in forty-five years. Funds started flowing out of national banks in New England into these accounts. Finally, those banks were allowed to compete by offering this type of account, but with an interest rate no higher than the regulated passbook rate. NOW accounts later spread nationwide.

Competition from money market mutual funds, offered by nonbank financial institutions, became a serious threat to the banking system in the 1970s. Money market mutual funds are financial instruments with high yields, fairly low minimum balances (ranging from $500 to $5,000), and high liquidity. For the first time, someone with only a few thousand dollars, or even less, could earn the kind of high rates that had required a

$10,000 minimum. Although money market mutual fund accounts, unlike bank deposits, were not insured, the funds were invested quite safely in commercial paper (short-term business borrowing) and T-bills. Some of these accounts also allowed check writing. Banks offered no comparable type of deposit to compete with money market mutual funds. The result was a massive loss of deposits from banks and savings and loans.

A third important development during the 1970s was the loss of member banks by the Federal Reserve System. Although the Fed offered its member banks check-clearing services and borrowing privileges, the banks also had to meet higher reserve ratios than most state banks. Since reserves earn no interest, higher required reserves meant that member banks were losing interest earnings. Thus, banks began exchanging their federal charters for state charters. Fewer banks were under the direct control of the Fed, making it more difficult for the Fed to carry out monetary policy.

LEGISLATIVE CHANGES

The result of these developments was the passage of two major pieces of legislation that were intended to bring about bank deregulation. **Bank deregulation** is a policy enabling banks to compete more aggressively with nonbank financial institutions by reducing the regulations affecting them. The first deregulatory act was the Depository Institutions Deregulation and Monetary Control Act (DIDMCA) of 1980. This act put all depository institutions—commercial banks (with either state or national charters), savings banks, savings and loan associations, and credit unions—under the control of the Fed. All gained access to Fed services and became subject to the same reserve ratios for the same types of deposits. This act also provided for gradual phasing out of interest ceilings on deposits and authorized all banks to offer interest-bearing checking accounts. The role of savings banks and savings and loan associations was expanded. These banks formerly offered mostly passbook savings accounts and invested almost exclusively in home mortgage loans. Under DIDMCA, they were allowed to offer a full range of accounts and invest in a greater variety of loans and assets.

In 1982, Congress passed the Garn–St. Germain Act to expand the range of accounts that could be offered by banks. This act allowed banks, including thrift institutions, to issue checkable, interest-bearing deposit accounts similar to the money market mutual funds available from nonbank institutions. These accounts are known as money market accounts, super NOW accounts, or other names. They generally pay slightly lower interest rates than money market mutual funds, but they offer the advantages of deposit insurance and convenient access at local branches and ATMs.

Another provision of the Garn–St. Germain Act opened the door to interstate banking. National banks had been forbidden by the 1927 McFadden Act to engage in interstate banking unless so authorized by state law. Failures of thrift institutions in the early 1980s were so numerous that the Federal Savings and Loan Insurance Corporation (FSLIC) had to find many merger partners to take over the assets of failed banks. Often the most attractive candidates were from out of state. The Garn–St. Germain Act allowed an out-of-state bank to take over a failed bank if it was the only candidate.

bank deregulation
A policy enabling banks to compete more aggressively with nonbank financial institutions by reducing the regulations affecting them.

Bank deregulation was intended to benefit depositors, banks, and the Fed. The two federal laws made it possible for banks to offer a wider range of services and more attractive interest rates to small depositors and middle-income households. Although interest rates on all assets had fallen by the end of the 1980s, depositors still had a choice among a much wider variety of accounts than before. Armed with these new types of accounts, banks could compete more effectively with nonbank institutions in attracting deposits. The Fed gained better control over the money creation process.

Partly as a result of the Garn–St. Germain Act and partly as a result of new technology, both branch banking and interstate banking increased during the 1980s. A number of states had severe restrictions on both of these practices. The use of ATMs made it increasingly difficult for these states to determine exactly what constituted branch banking. Bank holding companies were created to get around prohibitions on interstate banking, leading to further demands by banks that state legislatures relax these prohibitions. Finally, the wave of bank failures in the 1980s put pressure on legislatures to allow the development of larger (and presumably safer) banks. The combined impact of these developments was that many states did relax restrictions on both branch banking and interstate banking. This move allowed the development of larger banks with more diversified assets and greater economies of scale. In many small towns, the bank is now a local unit of a statewide or even interstate bank.

Why did Congress suddenly decide to deregulate the banking industry after decades of regulation? Most of the federal bank regulations originated in the 1930s to prevent bank failures. Banks did not object to regulation as long as they had no serious competition from other firms offering deposit accounts. Regulation kept banks from competing with each other to attract deposits by offering interest on checking accounts. They could lend the funds deposited in checking accounts without having to pay depositors any interest.[1] Consumers, whether they liked it or not, were being protected from bank failure at the sacrifice of higher yields and a greater array of accounts and services. It was really the inflation of the 1970s that brought an end to regulation of interest rates. Inflation drove up market interest rates and widened the gap between what banks were allowed to pay and what other depository institutions were willing to pay. Banks lost deposits to these other institutions, where depositors could earn higher rates, a process known as disintermediation. Deregulation enabled banks to fight back and regain some of the lost deposits.

THE BANKING CRISIS

Although the benefits of deregulation were soon apparent, the costs were slower to appear. Freed from interest rate ceilings, banks began to compete aggressively for deposits. With fewer restrictions on the kinds of assets they could hold, some thrifts—especially savings and loans—began to make riskier investments. When the 1981–1982 recession hit, banks took a double hit. Interest rates fell on the loans they were making, while funds

---

1. Some payments were made to depositors, in the form of free checks, free access to other bank services, or sometimes premiums or gifts for new deposits. These payments were an indirect form of interest.

INTERNATIONAL PERSPECTIVE

FINANCIAL MARKETS IN JAPAN

Each country's system of banks and financial markets is unique, but most have some features in common. Japan's financial system provides an interesting comparison to that of the United States.[a]

Japan has had a central bank, the Bank of Japan, since 1882. Like the Fed, the Bank of Japan issues currency, serves as a bankers' bank and a depository bank for the government, and conducts monetary policy. The banking system consists of city and regional banks, *sogo* banks, *shinkin* banks, and postal savings. There are only twelve city banks, which hold 20 percent of all deposits of financial institutions and lend to large corporations. (The Japanese government also invests directly in business ventures.) The sixty-four regional banks, located in medium-sized cities, hold individual deposits (mostly time deposits for one year or more). Thus, one major difference is the smaller number of what are called commercial banks in the United States.

Sogo banks are roughly equivalent to U.S. savings banks or savings and loans. *Shinkin* banks are the Japanese equivalent of credit unions. These banks are much more numerous than the city and regional banks and serve the needs of individuals. However, Japanese households also maintain large deposits in postal savings (deposits at the post office). Such deposits were important in the United States at one time but no longer exist. Like the United States, Japan has deposit insurance. However, the government protects the Japanese deposit insurance system from large demands by imposing strict collateral requirements on most loans in order to ensure bank solvency.

Bank deregulation hit Japan at about the same time as the United States and for a similar reason. The development of medium-term government bond funds with higher yields than bank deposits led to an outflow of households' and small firms' funds from the banking system. Interest rates were then allowed to rise. More generous funding of the deposit insurance system and stricter collateral requirements have helped Japan to avoid bank failures.

Partly for cultural reasons and partly because there is no Social Security system, Japanese households save a much larger share of their incomes than American households do. Thus, the banking system plays an even larger role in overall financial markets in Japan than it does in the United States.

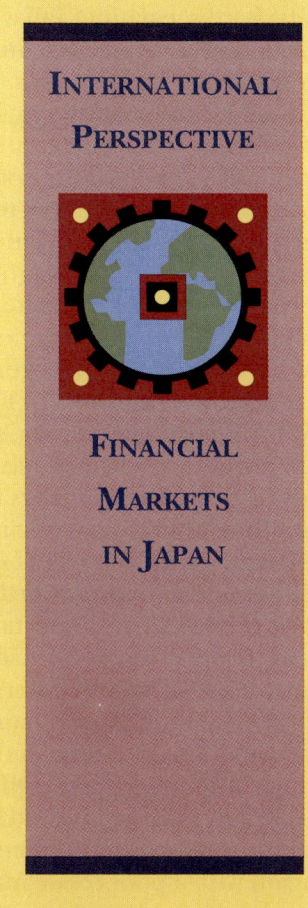

---

a. This description is based on Yoshio Suzuki (ed.), *The Japanese Financial System* (Oxford: Clarendon Press, 1987).

spread
The difference between the average interest rate earned on loans and the average interest rate paid on deposits.

in CDs were locked in for periods from one to seven years at the old high interest rates. In addition, many of the banks' loans were in default.[2]

Banks earn an income by charging more interest on loans than they pay on deposits. Banks' earnings fall when there is a decline in the **spread**, the difference between the average interest rate earned on loans and the average interest rate paid on deposits. Banks will then be tempted to make riskier loans in order to earn higher interest rates and restore earnings. In the early 1980s, market interest rates dropped sharply. The average interest rate on banks' loan portfolios responded very quickly, because banks hold a large amount of short-term assets, such as T-bills and commercial paper (very short-term business loans). As these assets matured, banks tried to replace them with higher-earning ones, even though most of those involved greater risk. In spite of such efforts, average bank earnings on investments fell. It took somewhat longer, however, for banks to bring about a change in the average interest paid on deposits, because many deposits were long-term CDs. For some banks, the spread was not enough to cover operating expenses, so they suffered losses (negative net earnings). Since the net worth of banks grows or shrinks depending on their earnings, negative net earnings reduced many banks' net worth.

At the same time, there was a decline in the market value of banks' assets. Banks in Texas, Oklahoma, and Louisiana had made many loans to oil companies. These assets became worthless when the price of oil dropped sharply. Because oil is such an important part of economic activity in these three states, the drop in its price had widespread effects. The prices of houses in Houston and other oil centers dropped sharply, threatening mortgage holders (usually savings and loans) with losses. As owners defaulted, the houses they abandoned to the bank usually had a resale value less than the balance due on the mortgage. Office buildings in large cities in these three states, especially in Houston, had few tenants. When rental income was not enough to meet mortgage payments, developers abandoned buildings to the bank, again with a poor resale market. In addition to these problems, defaults on loans to Third World countries hit some of the larger banks.

Savings and loans had also taken advantage of the freedom created by deregulation combined with the safety net of deposit insurance to make some very risky loans. Banks that were close to insolvency were tempted to make such loans. If the loans paid off, at high interest rates, the bank could become solvent again. If the gamble failed, depositors were protected by deposit insurance.

To understand the nature of the insolvency problem, consider the simple balance sheet of Petroleum Savings and Loan in Table 1. As you can see, this bank has $100 million in assets, consisting of reserves, mortgages, and commercial loans. It has $94 million in deposits as liabilities and a net worth of $6 million. This bank exceeds the current capital requirements imposed on banks by regulatory agencies. Its capital is 7 percent of its loans ($6 million divided by $85 million).[3] Capital requirements are being raised but will rise to only 3 percent of loans by 1995.

2. A loan is in default when the lender fails to make regularly scheduled payments of principal and interest.
3. Bankers and investors, unlike economists, use the word "capital" when talking about money. Therefore, the word is used in that sense in this chapter.

ASSETS		LIABILITIES	
Reserves	$ 15	Deposits	$ 94
Mortgages	40		
Commercial loans	45		
TOTAL ASSETS	$100	TOTAL LIABILITIES	$ 94
		NET WORTH	$ 6
		TOTAL LIABILITIES AND NET WORTH	$100

TABLE 1
BALANCE SHEET OF PETROLEUM SAVINGS AND LOAN (MILLIONS OF DOLLARS)

Suppose a soft housing market results in foreclosures on a number of Petroleum Savings and Loan's mortgages. The bank takes over some of the houses and sells them to pay off the mortgages. Assume that the bank forecloses on $10 million in mortgages, but distress sales of those properties bring in only $5 million. The value of the mortgage part of the bank's portfolio of assets drops to $30 million. The bank adds the $5 million received from property sales to its reserves. At the same time, suppose some of the bank's commercial loans do not pay off. A few borrowers go bankrupt and are able to pay only a small fraction of what they owe. The value of commercial loans drops to $38 million. Now the bank's balance sheet looks like Table 2.

This bank is still liquid—in fact, its reserves have increased. However, it is no longer solvent—the value of its liabilities is greater than the value of its assets. Unless matters improve quickly, this bank will have to file for bankruptcy. Its assets will be sold to pay the claims of depositors. After the bank pays off $88 million worth of deposits, the remaining $6 million (of deposits up to $100,000) will be paid by the Federal Deposit Insurance Corporation (FDIC) if this bank is a member.

The experience of Petroleum Savings and Loan is typical of what happened to many depository institutions in the 1980s. From 1980 to 1988, 879 commercial banks and 517 savings and loan associations were closed because of solvency problems. In comparison, 80 commercial banks and 43 savings and loans closed during the 1970s, and 58 commercial banks and 43 savings and loans closed during the 1960s. Clearly something had happened to the banking system. Commercial banks that failed from 1980 to 1988 represented 6 percent of those existing at the beginning of the decade. The failure rate for savings and loans during the same period was

ASSETS		LIABILITIES	
Reserves	$ 20	Deposits	$94
Mortgages	30		
Commercial loans	38		
TOTAL ASSETS	$ 88	TOTAL LIABILITIES	$94
		NET WORTH	-$ 6
		TOTAL LIABILITIES AND NET WORTH	$88

TABLE 2
REVISED BALANCE SHEET OF PETROLEUM SAVINGS AND LOAN (MILLIONS OF DOLLARS)

13 percent.[4] Although the vast majority of both commercial banks and savings and loans remained healthy, those that failed rolled up huge losses. The payoffs to depositors far exceeded the financial resources of the deposit insurance agencies, the FDIC and the FSLIC.

BAILOUT LEGISLATION

Response to the crisis in the banking industry was slow to emerge. Legislation was finally passed in 1989. The Financial Institutions Reform, Recovery and Enforcement Act (FIRREA) merged the FDIC with its savings and loan counterpart, the FSLIC. It also set up a new agency, the Resolution Trust Corporation (RTC), to deal with the problems of insolvent banks, including the sale of their assets. The insurance premiums banks pay for deposit insurance were increased, and banks were made subject to higher capital-to-loan ratios to provide a larger cushion for solvency.[5] These higher ratios mean that the bank's stockholders have more to lose from risky loans, and the concerns of stockholders should force banks to be more cautious and thus less likely to be insolvent in the future. However, these changes still leave the taxpayers facing a bill for the bailout that is currently estimated at $130–176 billion, including some $40 billion spent prior to passage of the law.

The process of restoring health to the banking industry will take many years. Housing demand and prices are expected to be stable or declining in the 1990s, as the smaller generation following the baby boom reaches the stage of family formation. Since savings and loans are still heavily committed to mortgages, a weak housing market may endanger some institutions that are currently healthy. In 1990, the Bank of New England, the flagship of a bank holding company that controlled several large New England banks, declared bankruptcy as a result of declining real estate prices in Massachusetts and Connecticut. By the end of the century, however, the United States should have a leaner, safer banking industry, with fewer small banks and more conservative portfolios of assets than in the go-go years of the 1980s.

THE LOANABLE FUNDS MARKET AND INTEREST RATES

market for loanable funds
The market in which transactions between borrowers and lenders determine the interest rate and equate quantities of loanable funds offered to quantity demanded.

Banks are only one group of players, although a very important group, on the lending side of financial markets. The other major lenders in the loanable funds market are stockbrokers, bond dealers, insurance companies, pension funds, credit unions, and mutual funds. The borrowers are business firms, households, and government. The **market for loanable funds** is the market in which transactions between borrowers and lenders determine the interest rate, which ensures that the quantity of loanable funds offered is equal to the quantity demanded. The price in this market is the interest rate.

---
4. Data from Dwight M. Jaffee, "Symposium on Federal Deposit Insurance for S&L Institutions," *Journal of Economic Perspectives* (Fall 1989): 3–10.
5. For a description of this legislation and the events leading up to it, see Dwight M. Jaffee, "Symposium of Federal Deposit Insurance for S&L Institutions," *Journal of Economic Perspectives* (Fall 1989): 3–10.

Chapter 13 Financial Markets and Interest Rates

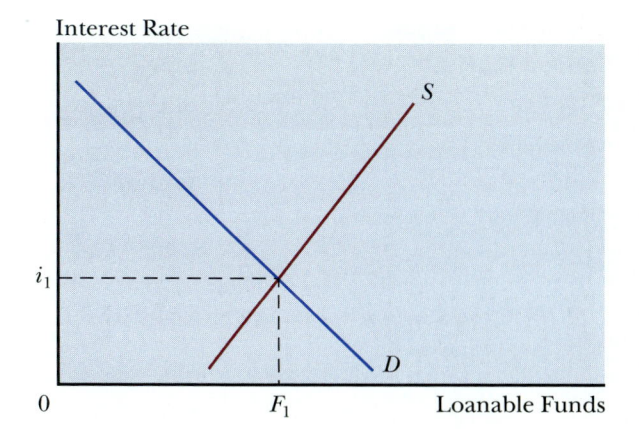

**FIGURE 2
THE MARKET FOR LOANABLE FUNDS**
The demand curve for loanable funds slopes downward because at lower nominal interest rates, borrowers want to borrow more. The upward-sloping supply curve shows that at higher nominal interest rates, lenders are willing to lend more. At the equilibrium interest rate i_1, the amount borrowers want to borrow equals the amount lenders want to lend (F_1).

The demand for loanable funds (to invest) is negatively related to the interest rate, as shown in Figure 2. More will be borrowed at lower rates, *ceteris paribus*, and less at higher rates. The supply of loanable funds, which consists of savings plus newly created money, rises with the interest rate. The interest rate is the price of loanable funds. Like any price, this rate rises and falls to clear the market and make quantity demanded equal to quantity supplied. The interest rate is a very important macroeconomic variable because it affects business investment decisions, household purchases of consumer durables, demand for the U.S. dollar, and the cost of servicing the public debt.

THE RANGE OF INTEREST RATES

We have been using the term *interest rate* as if there were a single interest rate paid by all borrowers in the market. In fact, there is a whole complex of interest rates. A few of these are

- interest rates on home mortgages and car loans,
- interest rates on bonds (ranging from the lowest on T-bills to the highest on junk bonds),
- interest rates that banks pay the Fed (the discount rate) and each other on borrowed reserves (the federal funds rate), and
- interest rates banks pay on checking and savings accounts and CDs.

The interest rate for a loan depends on who the borrower is and how much risk the borrower poses, as well as on how long the repayment period is. Short-term loans usually carry lower rates than long-term loans. Risky borrowers pay more than safe, dependable borrowers. Table 3 lists interest rates from 1981 to 1990 on a variety of loans, including bonds. The lowest rate is usually the discount rate, followed by the T-bill rate and the rate on municipal bonds. Interest rates on municipal bonds are low because the interest is exempt from federal income taxes. In general, the interest rates included in the table rise and fall together. In the late 1970s

Year	Government Bonds			Corporate Bonds		Mortgages (New Homes)	Discount Rate (New York Fed)
	T-Bills	Three-Year	Municipals	Aaa	Baa		
1981	14.0%	14.4%	11.2%	14.2%	16.0%	14.7%	13.4%
1982	10.7	12.9	11.6	13.8	16.1	15.1	11.0
1983	8.6	10.5	9.5	12.0	13.6	12.6	8.5
1984	9.6	11.9	10.2	12.7	14.2	12.4	8.8
1985	7.5	9.6	9.2	11.4	12.7	11.6	7.7
1986	6.0	7.1	7.4	9.0	10.4	10.2	6.3
1987	5.8	7.7	7.7	9.4	10.6	9.3	5.7
1988	6.7	8.3	7.8	9.7	10.8	9.2	6.2
1989	8.1	8.6	7.2	9.3	10.2	10.1	6.9
1990	7.5	8.3	7.3	9.3	10.4	10.1	7.0

*For bonds, the figure is current yield rather than the interest rate, which is equivalent. Corporate and municipal bonds are graded by bond-rating services according to the degree of risk from Aaa downward. The lowest investment grade recommended for purchase by individuals is Baa. The highest-rated bonds pay the lowest rates of interest because there is little risk of default on either interest payments or principal.

Source: Council of Economic Advisers, *Economic Report of the President* (Washington, DC: U.S. Government Printing Office, 1991).

Table 3
Interest Rates, 1981–1990*

and the beginning of the 1980s, they all rose to levels that were very high compared to past experience. Home mortgage rates, which had been in the 6–8 percent range, rose to 14 percent and higher. T-bills, which had been paying interest at a rate ranging from 4 to 6 percent in previous decades, peaked at 14 percent in 1981.

Risk and Interest Rates

Although all the interest rates rise and fall, the differences among them will vary over the course of the business cycle. During downturns, some private borrowers may have a higher risk of default as their businesses teeter on the edge of bankruptcy. As private borrowers begin to look riskier relative to the government, lenders will be more reluctant to lend to them and be more inclined to buy safer assets such as T-bills. The rate that lenders charge private borrowers rises relative to the T-bill rate. The difference between interest rates charged to the safest borrowers and those charged to less safe borrowers for the same length of time is called the **risk premium**. Risk premiums vary from borrower to borrower, but they generally rise during recessions and fall during expansions.

With so many interest rates, it is difficult to choose one to serve as an indicator of how the market is doing. Generally the interest rate on T-bills is used as the market indicator. The T-bill rate is the interest rate the U.S. government, the safest borrower of all, pays on its short-term borrowing.

Real and Nominal Interest Rates

Why did interest rates rise so sharply in the late 1970s and early 1980s? To answer this question, we need to distinguish between the real rate of interest and the nominal rate of interest. The rate that people observe, or the market rate, is nominal. The **nominal rate of interest** is the rate of interest actually charged, without any correction for inflation. The real rate of interest is not observed. The **real rate of interest** is the nominal rate of

risk premium
The difference between interest rates charged to the safest borrowers and those charged to less safe borrowers for the same length of time.

nominal rate of interest
The rate of interest actually charged, without correction for inflation (also known as the market rate of interest).

real rate of interest
The nominal rate of interest minus the expected rate of inflation.

Taken together, banks and nonbank financial institutions make up the credit market at the bottom of the circular flow diagram (see Figure 1). The principal nonbank financial institutions are stockbrokers and the stock market, bond dealers and the bond market, mutual funds, insurance companies, and pension funds. There are other players in financial markets, but these major ones should be enough to give you a sense of how financial markets work. Stockbrokers and bond dealers purchase and sell one type of financial asset. Mutual funds, insurance companies, and pension funds are more like banks in that they collect funds at "retail" and invest in diversified assets.

STOCKS, STOCKHOLDERS, AND THE STOCK MARKET

The **stock market** is a financial market in which ownership claims on corporations are bought and sold.[10] Most daily trades involve just one stockholder selling shares to another. However, new stock is also issued. Individuals make investment funds available to corporations by purchasing the newly issued shares of stock. The performance of the market is measured daily in terms of several indexes of stock prices as well as the daily volume of shares traded. We are primarily interested in the stock market as an economic device for attracting loanable funds to corporations and allowing individuals to share the risks of losses in the hope of gain.

stock market
A financial market in which ownership claims on corporations are bought and sold.

STOCKS AND STOCKHOLDERS

Only corporations can issue stock. A share of **stock** is an ownership claim in a corporation. Stockholders, who own shares of stock, have a claim on the profits of the corporation after all expenses are paid. Stockholders are therefore risk takers. They are taking the chance that there will be no profits and thus no earnings. If the corporation goes bankrupt, the value of their stock will fall sharply, perhaps to zero. Then they will lose their capital as well as their earnings. If the corporation succeeds, however, stockholders gain both by an increase in the value of their shares and by higher earnings. Some of a corporation's net earnings are paid as dividends to stockholders. Other parts of net earnings are reinvested to increase future earnings. Such reinvestment normally increases the net worth of the corporation and therefore increases the value of a share of stock.

stock
An ownership claim in a corporation.

Stockholders also enjoy voting rights in the corporation. They can attend the annual meeting to vote on the board of directors and comment on company policy. Few stockholders take advantage of this privilege. Some, however, have chosen to vote their shares to change a corporation's leadership, to redirect its market strategy, and sometimes even to involve it in social policy. In the 1980s, the focus of many corporate annual meetings was shifted by a minority of stockholders to issues such as environmental awareness, disinvesting in South Africa, and increasing opportu-

---

10. The stock market is too complex to describe fully in just a few pages. If you are interested in this fascinating subject, there are many books that can provide you with more detailed information and many newspapers and magazines that can help you watch the market.

Economic Insight

Stock Market Crashes and Economic Activity

In October 1987, the major indexes that measure the average price of a stock on the New York Stock Exchange all dropped sharply, the largest decline since the 1929 stock market crash that marked the beginning of the Great Depression. The Dow-Jones Industrials average dropped 30 percent in about three weeks. Standard and Poor's 500 index fell about 22 percent. The most widely used indicator, the Dow-Jones Industrials, had broken 2,000 points earlier in the year only to fall from its September level of 2,571 to a December low of 1,910. It took almost two years, until August 1989, for the market to recover to pre-crash levels. The 1929 stock market crash was even more severe. The market fell by 34.8 percent from its peak in September 1929 to the end of that year. It continued to fall until it hit its low point in 1932, with the average price of a share down 89 percent from its peak value.

How does a stock market crash affect the rest of the economy? The links between the stock market and overall economic activity run through four channels. First, when stock prices fall, it is more difficult for firms to raise equity capital in order to invest. Thus, a weak stock market discourages investment. Second, stocks are part of the assets of households. When the value of household assets falls, households experience a decline in wealth and respond by cutting back consumption. Both these actions will shift the AD curve to the left, reducing output and the price level. Third, investors often borrow in order to finance their stock purchases. When the value of the stocks that serve as collateral for their loans falls, they have to come up with some cash to reduce the size of the loan in line with the lower value of their stocks. The reduction in loans also tends to reduce output and prices.

Finally, the market both reflects and creates expectations about the current and future condition of the economy. A stock market crash may reflect generally negative expectations, or it may create them. Negative expectations tend to reduce lending, borrowing, and spending, thus having the effect of lowering economic activity.

Because the stock market is one of the dozen leading indicators used to predict downturns and upturns in economic activity, the crash in 1987 was widely heralded as a forecast of an impending recession. As you may have noticed, there was no recession during the following year. Both nominal and real GNP continued to rise and unemployment continued a slow decline for almost three years. A major reason for this positive outcome was that the Fed rushed to pump loanable funds into financial markets. In fact, stock market declines are not very reliable as a forecaster. During the period from the end of World War II until 1990, there have been eight major stock market declines, of which only three were associated with a recession.

In 1929, stocks were one of the few financial assets available to small investors. Today, individuals have access to many types of assets, and stocks make up a smaller part of their portfolios. Thus, the impact of the 1987 crash on consumption was much weaker. In addition, requirements about borrowing to buy stocks are much stricter now than they were in the 1920s. Fewer stock buyers were caught in 1987 with large loans on stocks that had fallen in value. Finally, the consensus of observers after the 1987 crash was that the market decline did not reflect general pessimism about the economy.

When the average price of a stock, or prices of stocks in general, rise more rapidly than is justified by the underlying value of the companies issuing the stock, a correction eventually takes place. Stock prices will fall to more realistic levels. Many large institutional investors (such as mutual funds and pension funds) have programmed trading plans that respond automatically to price changes. These investors may thus tend to overreact and buy or sell too much. The stock market showed large swings in the 1980s, largely because these large buyers and sellers dominated the market and had a great influence on prices.

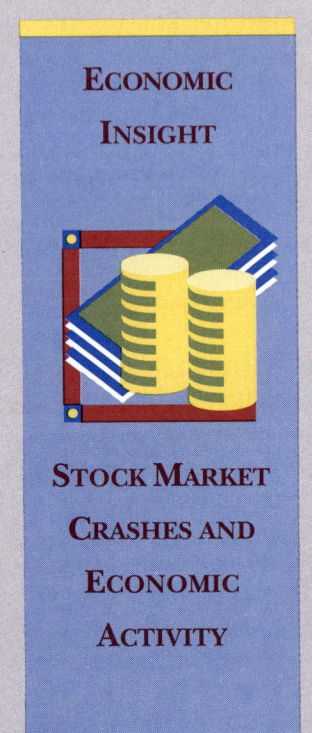

nities for minorities and women. Other stockholders are more interested in such bread-and-butter issues as new product development, marketing strategy, and profitability.

THE STOCK MARKET

The organized stock market in the United States has its primary center in the New York Stock Exchange, where ownership shares of large corporations are traded. Other exchanges are the American Stock Exchange and the Pacific Stock Exchange. Stocks that are not traded as frequently or that are issued by smaller corporations are traded through brokers in the over-the-counter market. Buyers may also invest through foreign exchanges, such as the London or Tokyo stock exchange.

The average price of a share on the New York Stock Exchange is considered a leading indicator, forecasting downturns and upturns in the business cycle. There are several indexes that provide a handy guide to the performance of the market on any particular day. The Dow-Jones Industrials and Standard and Poor's 500, for example, follow the prices of a fixed group of stocks and measure the change in the average price.

Although individuals see the stock market as an opportunity for gain through sharing corporate risk, the most important economic function of the stock market is to provide equity funds for corporations. Equity refers to ownership. In contrast, debt, or borrowed funds, has a fixed interest rate and must be repaid at some future date. Stock ownership provides a way to share the risks of new ventures, new technology, new products, or expanding in an uncertain market among a large number of individuals holding shares in the corporation.

BONDS AND THE BOND MARKET

The second major financial market is the **bond market**, in which the debt instruments of governments and corporations are traded. Sometimes governments and corporations borrow by taking out a loan from a bank or other financial institution at a specified interest rate. Such loans involve formal agreements about regular payments of capital and interest until the sum is repaid. More often, however, governments and corporations issue bonds. A **bond** is a debt instrument issued by a corporation or a government agency and having a fixed face value, annual interest payment, and maturity date. The face value is the dollar amount for which the bond can be redeemed at maturity. The maturity date tells how long a time period will elapse between when the bond is issued and when it is redeemed.

WHO ISSUES BONDS?

Corporations issue bonds in order to raise money to invest. The federal government issues bonds in order to finance the deficit in the federal budget. As you learned in Chapter 12, such bonds are a major asset of the Federal Reserve System and its member banks. These bonds are attractive because they are safe, offer reasonably good yields, can be readily marketed if necessary, and have a wide range of maturities. In addition, federal agencies such as the Federal National Mortgage Association issue bonds

bond market
A market in which the debt instruments of governments and corporations are traded.

bond
A debt instrument issued by a corporation or a government agency and having a fixed face value, annual interest payment, and maturity date.

municipal bond
Any bond issued by a state or local government to finance a capital project.

(called agency bonds) in order to help finance mortgage loans and for other purposes. State and local governments also issue bonds in order to finance capital projects, such as school buildings and sewer systems. These bonds are called **municipal bonds** regardless of whether they are issued by a state, city, county, or school district. They are attractive to investors because the interest on them is not subject to federal (and sometimes state) income tax.

Governments are major borrowers. In 1989, about 25 percent of all the funds raised in the U.S. credit market went to finance the borrowing of federal, state, and local governments. Some critics of government borrowing argue that competition from the government makes it harder for private firms to sell their bonds or to borrow. If funds are limited, the federal government will have its demand satisfied first because it is a safer borrower. Private borrowers may have to settle for borrowing less at higher interest rates. When government borrowing drives up interest rates and chokes off some private borrowing, crowding out has occurred.

junk bonds
High-yield, high-risk securities that are usually issued to finance a takeover of one corporation by another.

The 1980s saw the emergence of a popular but very risky type of bond, called **junk bonds**. Junk bonds are high-yield, high-risk securities that are usually issued to finance a takeover of one corporation by another. During the wave of corporate mergers and takeovers in the 1980s, a large number of these bonds were issued to raise the cash to buy the stock of the corporation being acquired. When the dust settled, the newly merged firm was saddled with a very large burden of debt at a very high interest rate. A number of the merged corporations wound up in bankruptcy. Holders of junk bonds suffered severe losses as scheduled interest and principal payments were not made and the market value of their bonds fell sharply.

Bonds versus Stocks

Bonds other than junk bonds are usually considered a safer investment than stock because bonds have a prior claim on a corporation's assets. Bond prices do fluctuate with changes in interest rates but are generally more stable than stock prices. Interest payments on bonds are safer and more certain than dividends from stock shares.

The annual interest rate is fixed when the bond is sold, but the yield is not. The yield on a bond is the annual income from it (the annual interest payment plus any change in its market price) divided by the current selling price of the bond. Since the selling price of the bond can go up or down, the yield varies with that price. When interest rates are high, buying bonds is a way to lock in high yields. Even if you have to sell the bonds before they mature, you will get some of the high yield in the form of a **capital gain**, an increase in the market price of the asset (bond). If your bond is yielding 12 percent when newly issued bonds are paying only 9 percent, buyers will bid up the price of your higher yielding bond.

capital gain
An increase in the market price of an asset.

The advantage of bonds when interest rates are high becomes a disadvantage when interest rates are low. If you buy bonds when interest rates are low, not only are you getting a low yield, you may also suffer a capital loss if interest rates rise. When interest rates are low, two other assets are more attractive than bonds: stocks and money. Stocks are more attractive because the dividend and the potential for capital gains look better when bonds are offering low yields. Money is more attractive because its opportunity cost (the bond interest forgone) is lower and the risk of capital loss on bonds is higher if interest rates go back up.

BOND YIELDS, INTEREST RATES, AND BOND PRICES

There is a fairly simple relationship between the price of a bond and its yield. Higher bond prices mean lower yields, and vice versa. An example will illustrate this relationship. Assume that the federal government issues bonds maturing in ten years with a face value of $10,000 and an annual interest payment of $900. At this price, their yield is 9 percent. Now suppose the Fed engages in open market operations, buying so many of these bonds that their price rises by $100. (In the bond market, like any other market, an increase in demand with no change in supply will drive up the price.) This price increase will reduce the current yield on these government bonds to 8.91 percent ($900/$10,100).[11]

Because financial markets are interrelated, lower interest rates on government bonds will spread to other assets. Imagine that both government and low-risk corporate bonds are priced at $10,000 with yields of 9 percent. Most buyers would not prefer one to the other. But if the price of a government bond rises to $10,100, its yield will fall, as in the example just given. Corporate bonds, whose yield remains at 9 percent, then become more attractive than government bonds, and buyers will shift from government to corporate bonds. As buyers demand more corporate bonds, their prices will also be driven up, and yields will fall.

NONBANK FINANCIAL INTERMEDIARIES

There are some nonbank financial institutions that also collect funds from households and pass them on to borrowers and to firms raising equity capital (issuing stock). Recall that one of the major reasons for bank deregulation was the competition for both loan customers and depositors from nonbank financial institutions. Although these nonbank competitors cannot provide a substitute for money as a medium of exchange, they can provide good substitutes for money as a store of value. Individuals who hold deposits in banks can shift those deposits to other specialized financial assets, such as shares of mutual funds. Individuals may also own financial assets that are serving several purposes, such as deposits in pension funds and life insurance policies. These financial assets are a store of value, but also provide funds for retirement income or to take care of dependents in case of death.

Pension funds, insurance companies, and mutual funds are known as **institutional investors**. Because these investors deal in much larger volumes than the individual investor, their purchases and sales can affect the market price of a stock or bond. If institutional investors become more cautious and switch from stocks to bonds, the stock market suffers a decline. If institutional investors become bullish (optimistic about stocks), stock

institutional investors Large investors, including insurance companies, pension funds, and mutual funds, whose purchases and sales have an impact on the prices of investment assets.

---

11. The Fed usually sells T-bills, which are bonds with a very short maturity. Then prices will not fall nearly that far because the owner always has the option of holding the T-bill until it matures, which is very soon. On a bond with a long time to maturity, however, large price swings such as this one are observed when interest rates change.

Mutual Funds

Mutual funds compete directly with banks for the deposits of households and small businesses. Like banks, mutual funds invest in a variety of assets. The most common assets held by mutual funds are stocks and bonds. A **mutual fund** is a financial institution that pools money from many individuals in order to invest in a diversified portfolio of assets. Through a mutual fund, a small investor could own a small share of a wide array of assets instead of taking the risk of owning stock or a bond of one corporation. Mutual funds charge a small fee for their management services, but often offer an excellent return with minimal risk. Although deposits at mutual funds are not insured, most of them are not risky.

As mutual funds became more popular, a whole array of options developed. You can buy shares in a fund that specializes in municipal bonds, or small corporations, or socially responsible companies. You can invest in a fund that stresses safety, or income, or risky growth. International portfolios, diversified by both industry and country, are available through mutual funds. An especially popular type of fund during the late 1970s was the money market mutual fund, which was invested in short-term government bonds (T-bills) and commercial paper (short-term business loans) and offered check-writing privileges. It was mainly competition from these funds that led to deregulation of bank interest rates in the early 1980s.

mutual fund
A financial institution that pools money from many individuals in order to invest in a diversified portfolio of assets.

Insurance Companies

There are many insurance companies and types of insurance policies covering homes, automobiles, health care, disability, and death. These companies accumulate investment funds in reserves against expected future losses. The insurance companies with the largest sums to invest are the life insurance companies. Life insurance companies sell two types of policies that accumulate a cash value while they are in effect. (Thus, the cash value is an asset on a household's balance sheet.) The first type is whole, or universal, life insurance, which pays off when the policyholder dies or can be cashed in for some sum during the policyholder's lifetime. The other type of policy is an annuity, which involves making current payments in return for an income later on, usually after retirement. Both types of policies provide life insurance companies with large cash reserves, which are invested in a variety of assets. Earnings on these assets, along with premiums paid by policyholders, provide enough funds to pay off present and estimated future claims as well as the costs of operation and profit for stockholders.

Insurance companies often invest in major construction projects such as office buildings and shopping centers. They also invest in stocks and bonds and make short-term loans, called **commercial paper**, to business firms. (Banks also hold a large amount of commercial paper.) Insurance companies are often a source of venture capital, which is funding for starting new businesses or developing new and unproven products or technologies.

commercial paper
Short-term loans by financial institutions to business firms.

Pension Funds

Pension funds are very similar to insurance companies in that they take in large amounts of cash that they hold and invest. The cash reserves are used for payments to pensioners. Pension funds do not have stockholders. Usually pension funds are connected to an employer or a union, although some large ones cover a broad industry. For example, the Teachers' Insurance and Annuity Association (TIAA) is a large pension fund that covers many school and college teachers across the country. Because workers normally pay into the fund for many years before collecting benefits, pension funds have very large sums available to invest. They are generally quite cautious in their investments, preferring a safe low yield to a riskier higher one.

THE BORROWER'S SIDE: INVESTMENT AND INTEREST RATES

We have examined the motives of lenders and the structure of financial markets. Now we need to complete the picture by looking at why firms and individuals borrow. (We looked at government borrowing in an earlier chapter.) We know that many households borrow in order to finance the purchase of houses, cars, and consumer durables. This section concentrates on borrowing by businesses for investment purposes. Bear in mind, however, that much of what we say about business borrowing also applies to borrowing by households and state and local governments. Like business firms, these actors borrow to buy durable assets that will yield a stream of services in the future.

The Investment Demand Schedule

A business firm makes a decision to invest by comparing the expected rate of return on the investment to the market interest rate. Assume that a manufacturing firm is considering three investment projects for the coming year: (1) an automated welding machine that costs $20,000, (2) a computerized accounting system that costs $60,000, and (3) a forklift that costs $30,000. The firm has calculated the expected revenues and costs of operation for each piece of equipment over its useful life to the firm. These calculations also took into account the initial cost and salvage value. With this information, the firm's accountants have calculated that the expected rate of return on investment is 14 percent for the welding machine, 22 percent for the accounting system, and 8 percent for the forklift.

Based on this information, we can construct an investment demand schedule for the manufacturing firm. An **investment demand schedule** ranks all possible investment projects for a firm in order of decreasing expected rate of return. The investment demand schedule for this firm is shown in Figure 4. The schedule looks like a set of steps rather than a smooth line because the firm is considering three separate projects, each of which requires a lump sum expenditure.

For the economy as a whole, aggregate business investment spending will also depend on how the interest rate compares to the expected rate of return on investments. An investment demand schedule that sums the schedules of every firm in an economy is a smooth line, as shown in Fig-

investment demand schedule
A graph that ranks possible investment projects for a firm in order of decreasing expected rate of return.

FIGURE 4
AN INVESTMENT DEMAND SCHEDULE FOR A FIRM
Three possible investment projects for a manufacturing firm are ranked according to their expected rates of return. The firm decides which investment to undertake by comparing their expected rates of return to the market interest rate.

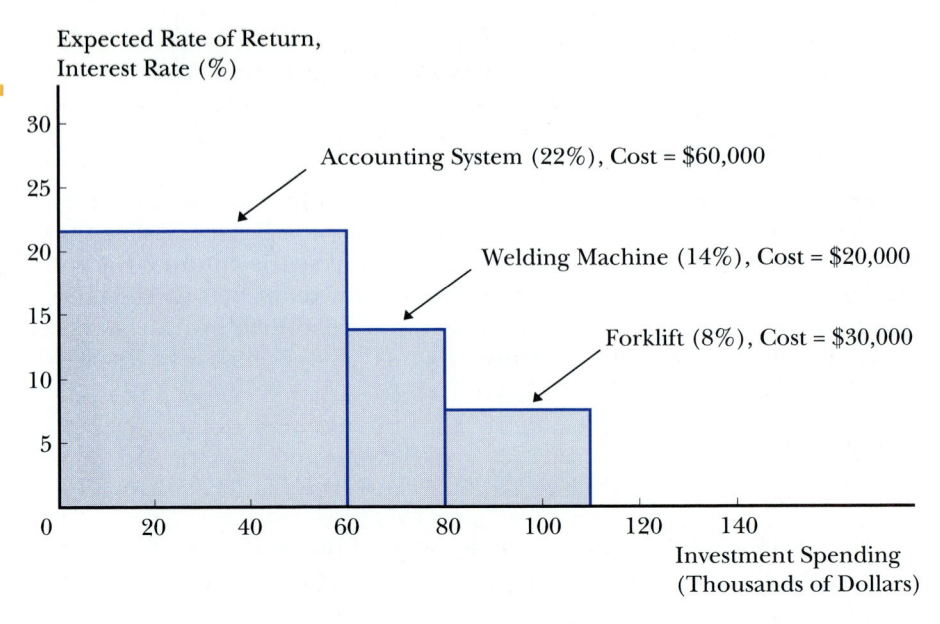

marginal efficiency of investment (MEI) curve
A graph that sums the investment demand schedules for all firms in an economy. It ranks all investment possibilities for all firms according to their expected rates of return.

ure 5. The economy's investment demand schedule in Figure 5 is also known as the **marginal efficiency of investment (MEI) curve**. This diagram ranks all investment possibilities for all firms according to their expected rates of return.

Given the *MEI* curve for an economy, the market interest rate will determine the amount of investment spending. Every investment with an expected rate of return equal to or exceeding the market interest rate will be undertaken. For instance, at an interest rate of 20 percent, the level of

FIGURE 5
AN INVESTMENT DEMAND SCHEDULE FOR AN ECONOMY
Aggregate investment spending depends on the interest rate, *i*. If *i* is 20 percent, then total investment will be $50 billion. If *i* declines to 12 percent, investment will increase to $100 billion. Investment demand is negatively related to the interest rate.

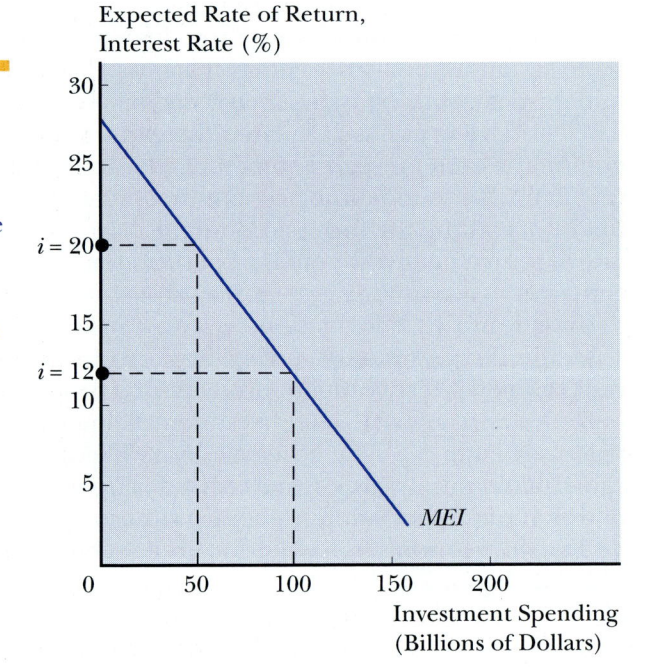

investment spending for the entire economy will be $50 billion in Figure 5. There are $50 billion worth of investment projects with an expected rate of return exceeding 20 percent. At an interest rate of 20 percent, the firm in Figure 4 would invest in the accounting system because its expected rate of return (22 percent) exceeds that interest rate. Neither the welding machine nor the forklift would be purchased. At an interest rate of 12 percent, the firm would invest in the welding machine as well as the accounting system. For the entire economy, a 12 percent interest rate would result in $100 billion of investment spending.

Investment demand and interest rates are negatively related. When interest rates rise, investment spending declines. When interest rates decline, investment spending rises. Higher interest rates raise the cost of investing so that only the most desirable investments will be undertaken. Less promising projects may become cost-effective at lower interest rates.

Note that the interest rate is relevant whether the firm is borrowing or not. When a firm borrows funds to invest, it wants to be sure that it will earn enough to pay all costs and interest, with some profit left over. If the firm is using its own funds to finance a project, there is still an opportunity cost. The firm must consider whether investing those funds in financial assets (bonds or other corporations' stock, for example) instead would offer a higher return than investing in new physical capital.

INVESTMENT SPENDING AND NATIONAL INCOME

This discussion of the borrower's side completes the picture of the loanable funds market. Investment demand, household demand for auto and mortgage loans, and borrowing demands of all levels of government combine to create a downward-sloping demand curve for loanable funds, as shown in Figures 2 and 3. The supply of loanable funds is positively related to the interest rate. Higher yields will induce lenders to make more funds available through financial markets. Lower yields will make them more likely to hold cash and wait for more attractive yields.

Financial markets are linked to aggregate supply and aggregate demand through changes in planned investment, which is a highly volatile component of aggregate demand. Other borrowing decisions (by households and governments) are also translated into changes in aggregate demand. Recall from the Keynesian model in Chapter 8 that a change in consumption, investment, government spending, or net exports causes a shift of the aggregate demand (*AD*) curve and a change in the equilibrium level of national income. Thus, if interest rates fall in financial markets, more firms will borrow or issue bonds in order to invest. The resulting increase in investment spending will shift the *AD* curve to the right. The increase in aggregate demand increases the equilibrium level of national income, employment, and prices. An increase in the interest rate has the opposite effect. Investment declines, the *AD* curve shifts to the left, and national income and output, employment, and the price level all decline.

Monetary policy has an important influence on interest rates, lending and borrowing, and investment, both directly through banks and indirectly through other players in financial markets. The next chapter will explore some of the problems in making monetary policy have the intended impact on output, employment, and the price level.

SUMMARY

1. The Depository Institutions Deregulation and Monetary Control Act (DIDMCA) of 1980 made all depository institutions members of the Federal Reserve System. It also greatly reduced the differences among types of depository institutions.

2. Bank deregulation combined with conditions in the oil industry and the real estate market, among other things, resulted in the failure of a number of savings and loans and banks in the 1980s.

3. The real rate of interest is the nominal, or market, rate of interest adjusted for the expected rate of inflation. When lenders guess wrong about inflation, the real rate of interest they earn can be negative. The real rate, not the nominal rate, governs money demand and investment decisions.

4. The rates of interest on various assets are all related, but they differ because of differences in risk and maturity.

5. A higher inflation rate will shift the demand curve for loanable funds to the right and the supply curve to the left, driving up the market interest rate.

6. The two major financial markets are the stock market and the bond market. Buyers and sellers exchange ownership shares in corporations in the stock market and debt instruments of governments and corporations in the bond market.

7. Bonds are generally less risky than stocks. The yield on a bond is inversely related to its current market price. When a bond's price rises, its yield falls.

8. The major nonbank financial institutions, or institutional investors, are mutual funds, insurance companies, and pension funds. These institutions gather funds from households and other sources and invest them in stocks, bonds, or major construction projects. They also invest in commercial paper and provide capital for new business firms.

9. Business firms compare the expected rate of return on an investment to the market rate of interest in deciding whether to undertake that investment. The ranking of investments by their expected rates of return is a firm's investment demand schedule. For the economy as a whole, the investment demand schedule is the sum of the demand schedules of all firms and is called the marginal efficiency of investment (*MEI*) curve.

10. Changes in the interest rate affect the level of investment by shifting aggregate expenditure and aggregate demand so as to influence output, employment, and the price level.

NEW TERMS

bank deregulation
spread
market for loanable funds
risk premium
nominal rate of interest
real rate of interest
yield
expected yield
risk
stock market
stock
bond market
bond
municipal bond
junk bonds
capital gain
institutional investors
mutual fund
commercial paper
investment demand schedule
marginal efficiency of investment (*MEI*) curve

QUESTIONS FOR DISCUSSION

1. How do banks and financial institutions today differ from what they were in 1979?

2. Suppose you were the manager of Petroleum Savings and Loan, and you knew that federal regulators were aware of your problems and would soon be checking your books and deciding whether to close your bank down. What might you do? How is your self-interested behavior likely to make the problem worse?

3. In terms of a balance sheet, what does it mean to say that a bank has become insolvent?

4. A one-year bond issued today will pay $1,000 at maturity. Calculate the yield on this bond for prices of $999, $975, $950, $925, $900, $850, and $800.

5. Suppose the equilibrium real rate of interest is 3 percent and that people always try to earn this rate. If they believe inflation will be 5 percent, what should the nominal rate of interest be? What if they believe inflation will be 12 percent? Suppose they believe inflation will be 12 percent, but it turns out to be 15 percent. What is the actual real rate of interest that people will receive? (*Hint:* When people try to earn the equilibrium real rate in every period, the difference between the expected real rate of interest and the actual real rate is the expected inflation rate minus the actual inflation rate.)

6. Is it possible for the real rate of interest to rise while the market rate is falling? How would this happen?

7. In Table 3, why is the interest rate on Baa corporate bonds always higher than the rate on T-bills?

8. You own a bond with a face value of $1,000 and a yield of 6 percent. That is, it pays interest of $60 a year. Now the nominal rate of interest rises to 8 percent. In order for your bond to yield 8 percent, to what level must its price rise or fall?

9. What would happen to the price of the bond in Question 8 if the market interest rate fell to 5 percent?

10. What are the two major financial markets? What does each deal in? How are they related?

11. What is the difference between a stock and a bond? Which would you prefer to own if you were willing to take risks in hope of profits? Which would you prefer if you wanted safety and interest income?

12. What are institutional investors? Why are they so important in financial markets?

13. Using the investment demand schedule in Figure 5, assume that *i* declines from 20 percent to 15 percent. How would the amount of investment spending change?

14. Why is the level of investment for a firm or an economy negatively related to the interest rate? Does it make any difference whether the firm borrows or uses its own funds?

15. How would a decline in the interest rate affect aggregate demand?

SUGGESTIONS FOR FURTHER READING

Cargill, Thomas F., and Gillian G. Garcia. *Financial Reform in the 1980s.* Stanford, CA: Hoover Institution Press, 1986. Reviews the history of financial changes and their impact on monetary policy from a monetarist perspective.

Kane, Edward J. *The S&L Insurance Mess: How Did It Happen?* Washington, DC: Urban Institute Press, 1989. A good history of how the savings and loan problem evolved and evaluation of the bailout policy.

Lewis, Michael. *Liars' Poker: Rising through the Wreckage on Wall Street.* New York: W. W. Norton, 1989. A novel that describes the action in the New York bond market and how the major firms created new markets in the 1980s.

Mishkin, Frederick S. *The Economics of Money, Banking, and Financial Markets,* 2nd ed. Glenview, IL: Scott, Foresman, 1989. A textbook with a thorough treatment of financial markets.

AFTER STUDYING THIS CHAPTER, YOU SHOULD BE ABLE TO:

1. Explain the Keynesian view of the monetary transmission mechanism.
2. Discuss the effect of interest rates on investment and money demand.
3. Evaluate interest rates and monetary aggregates as alternative targets for monetary policy.
4. Recount the main monetary policy actions of the Federal Reserve System.
5. Explain how each of the following raises questions about the effectiveness of fiscal policy:
    a. the stability of the multiplier versus the stability of the velocity of money,
    b. crowding out.
6. Discuss the advantages and disadvantages of the three ways of financing government spending:
    a. by taxes,
    b. by borrowing,
    c. by printing money.
7. Identify the major areas of agreement between economists.

CHAPTER 14

MONETARY POLICY IN THEORY AND PRACTICE

INTRODUCTION

In the last three chapters, we have discussed money, the banking and financial systems, the Federal Reserve System, and the role of interest rates. Now we can take a closer look at how monetary policy works in the aggregate supply and demand model. Although monetary and fiscal policy focus attention on different aspects of demand management, both work by shifting aggregate demand (*AD*). Monetarists and Keynesians, or economists in the broad classical and Keynesian traditions, disagree about the effectiveness of monetary policy and about how it works to influence the levels of output, employment, and prices. This chapter looks at how monetary policy works in theory and practice and then summarizes the arguments from both sides about its effectiveness.

HOW MONETARY POLICY AFFECTS AGGREGATE DEMAND

There are two approaches to explaining how monetary policy affects aggregate demand. Monetarists stress demand for cash balances (transactions demand) and the equilibrium between money supply and money demand. Keynesians emphasize the role of interest rates (asset demand for money). These explanations do not necessarily contradict one another. Both mechanisms can work at the same time to translate changes in the money supply into shifts in aggregate demand. Those shifts lead to changes in output, employment, and the price level.

When the money supply and monetary policy are added to the simple Keynesian model, it becomes more realistic in two important ways. Interest rates become another exogenous variable, and the expanded model allows for changes in the price level. Interest rates play a modest but important role in the Keynesian model, because they influence consumption and investment decisions. The price level was ignored in the simple version of the Keynesian model, in which output was so far below the full-employment level that the *AS* curve could be treated as horizontal. Since changes in the price level are closely linked to changes in the money supply, it was difficult to use that model to explore the impact of contractionary as well as expansionary fiscal policies. The more complete model, including money and interest rates, enables us to consider the use of both monetary and fiscal policies in both expansionary and contractionary directions.

MONETARY THEORY BEFORE KEYNES

To discuss the role of money in the Keynesian model, we need to review some of the ideas of the classical economists on the subject of money. Recall that the classical economists made the quantity theory of money the center of their macroeconomics. According to the quantity theory, when the money supply (M_s) expands, both individuals and private banks find that they are holding larger money balances than they want. Demand for money to hold for transactions depends mainly on money income, as shown by the money demand equation,

$$M_d = k \times P \times Y.$$

Figure 1 shows the demand for money as a function of money income. The graph is a straight line with a positive slope of k and an intercept of zero.[1] Since the money supply is given (determined by the Fed), it can be represented as a horizontal line, such as M_{s1}. Now suppose the money supply increases to M_{s2} in Figure 1. At the current level of money income, $(P \times Y)_1$, money supply exceeds money demand. People attempt to spend

FIGURE 1
MONEY SUPPLY AND DEMAND
An increase in the money supply from M_{s1} to M_{s2} will create an excess supply of money. As people try to spend the money, they drive up nominal income from $(P \times Y)_1$ to $(P \times Y)_2$. At the higher level of income, people are satisfied to hold larger money balances.

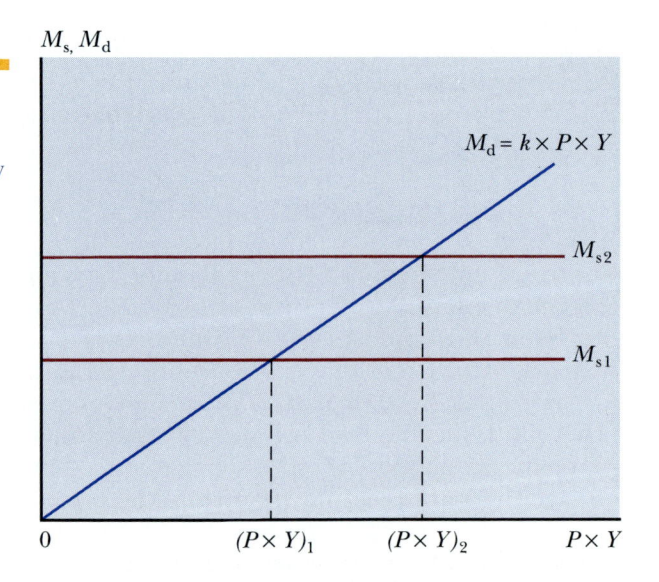

1. It is also possible to plot money demand as a function of real income, Y, rather than money income, $P \times Y$. If money demand is plotted versus real income, then changes in P can also shift the demand curve.

their excess cash balances. As they do, the level of money income will tend to rise. This process will continue until people are satisfied with their larger cash balances as a fraction of a larger money income, $(P \times Y)_2$. Thus, classical economists saw changes in the money supply as affecting spending directly, rather than working indirectly through interest rates.

A KEYNESIAN VIEW OF MONETARY POLICY

The classical view of how changes in the money supply lead to increases in demand was generally accepted before the 1930s. Keynes, however, stressed the effects of monetary policy working through changes in interest rates. An increase in the money supply will reduce interest rates, at least initially, because more funds will be available for banks to lend, if people do not immediately anticipate an offsetting rise in the price level.[2] (Inflationary expectations will be slower to change during a recession or depression.) The lower interest rates will stimulate investment demand. Changes in investment demand shift the *AD* curve, causing changes in output and income. Thus, according to Keynes, monetary policy works by influencing interest rates, which influence investment, which then affects output and income. The process of translating money supply changes into changes in demand, output, and the price level is called the **transmission mechanism**. Figure 2 shows this process. Let's consider each step in more detail.

FROM MONEY TO INTEREST RATES. Recall that there are only two things that individuals can do when they have more money than they wish to hold: spend it or lend it. (If you leave money in a checking or savings account, the bank will lend it for you.) Classical theory puts a strong emphasis on spending as the way to get rid of the extra money. The Keynesian model puts an equally strong emphasis on lending.

When the Fed creates money by buying bonds, most of it enters the marketplace in the form of additional excess bank reserves. Banks will want to lend these reserves in order to earn interest.[3] To entice borrowers, banks may have to offer lower interest rates. In fact, the process of monetary expansion itself will tend to lower interest rates, at least in the

transmission mechanism The process of translating money supply changes into changes in demand, output, and the price level.

FIGURE 2
THE MONETARY TRANSMISSION MECHANISM: A KEYNESIAN VIEW
Keynesians think that monetary policy affects output and income mainly through interest rates. If the Fed buys bonds, the money supply increases, and interest rates fall. Lower interest rates stimulate investment, driving up aggregate expenditure. Higher aggregate expenditure causes output and income to rise through the multiplier effect.

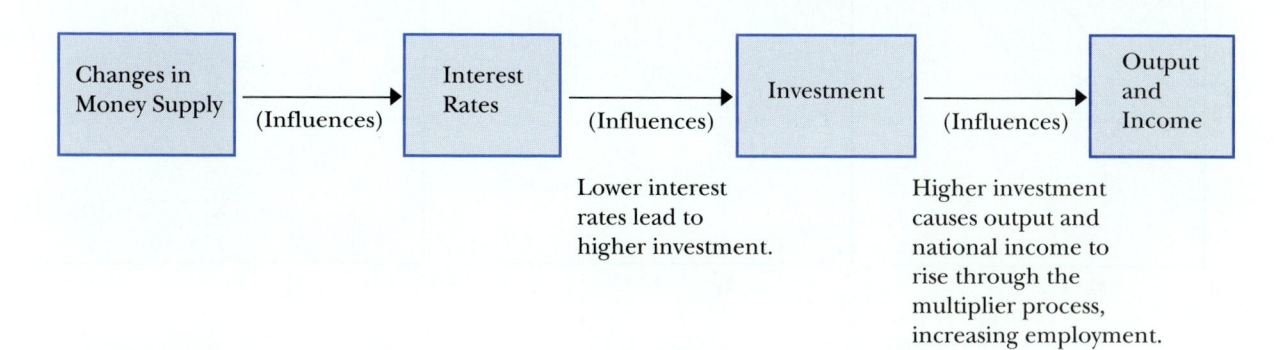

Changes in Money Supply → (Influences) → Interest Rates → (Influences) → Investment → (Influences) → Output and Income

Lower interest rates lead to higher investment.

Higher investment causes output and national income to rise through the multiplier process, increasing employment.

2. If the increase in the money supply means that people expect more inflation, the inflationary expectations component of the market interest rate will rise. Thus, any effect of monetary expansion on interest rates is likely to be temporary.
3. If the Fed buys a bond from an individual, it's also very possible that that person will want to reinvest (lend) the money received.

FIGURE 3
THE MONETARY TRANSMISSION MECHANISM AND AGGREGATE DEMAND
(*a*) The process of transmitting changes in the money supply into changes in output and the price level begins in the market for loanable funds. Increased loanable funds depress the interest rate and increase investment demand from $100 billion to $125 billion. (*b*) The increased investment demand shifts aggregate expenditure upward, from AE_1 to AE_2. (*c*) The increase in aggregate expenditure shifts aggregate demand to the right, from AD_1 to AD_2.

short run. Recall the relationship between bond prices and bond yields. When the Fed uses open market operations to expand the money supply, it buys bonds. The increased demand for bonds drives their prices up and their yields down. As the lower yields on bonds spread to other assets and other financial markets, interest rates in general tend to fall.

Modern macroeconomists have tried to build their theories and models on a solid foundation of microeconomics. That is, they have sought to develop models that are firmly anchored in the self-interested behavior of individuals. In the Keynesian model, the response of banks and individuals to money creation is based on how they respond to changes in interest rates as the opportunity cost of holding money. If open market operations by the Fed result in banks holding more excess reserves than they would like to, bankers will be eager to lend those excess reserves even at lower interest rates. If individuals find themselves with larger cash balances than they need, they will make some of them available for lending in order to earn interest. Both of these actions will increase the supply of loanable funds and tend to put downward pressure on the market interest rate.

FROM INTEREST RATES TO INVESTMENT DEMAND. The next step in the transmission mechanism is from interest rates to investment demand. Recall from Chapter 13 that the relationship between investment demand and the interest rate is shown by the *MEI* curve. In Figure 3(*a*), the *MEI* curve, representing private investment demand, is the only source of demand for borrowing.[4] When the supply of loanable funds increases due to expansion of the money supply, the interest rate falls from 15 percent to 12 percent and the quantity of loanable funds demanded for investment purposes increases from $100 billion to $125 billion.

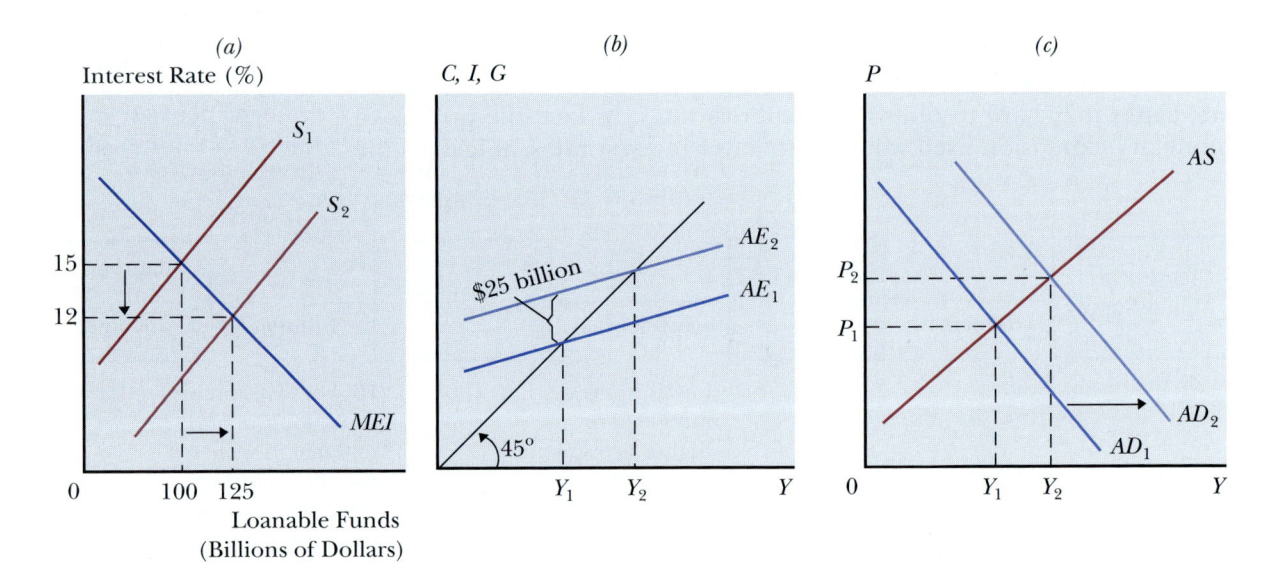

---

4. Investors are not the only possible borrowers. Two other components of aggregate demand may also respond to lower interest rates. Consumers borrow to finance the purchase of houses, cars, and appliances. (Recall from Chapter 8 that one of the things that can shift consumption is a change in the interest rate.) Also, state and local governments borrow to finance capital projects, such as schools and roads. They also may borrow more at lower interest rates.

Since investment is an important component of aggregate expenditure, the *AE* curve will shift from AE_1 to AE_2 as shown in Figure 3(*b*). The vertical shift will equal the $25 billion increase in investment demand. (Actually, the whole family of *AE* curves shifts upward. We have shown only one pair.) The upward shift in the *AE* curve will shift the *AD* curve to the right as shown in Figure 3(*c*), increasing output and the price level.

PROBLEMS WITH THE TRANSMISSION MECHANISM

Thus, monetary policy works through interest rates and investment demand to influence the levels of output and prices. In the Keynesian view, however, there are several things that could go wrong in the process of translating changes in the money supply into changes in output.

BANK LENDING AND EXCESS RESERVES. The first thing that could go wrong is that banks might choose to hold excess reserves. Banks are more likely to make that choice during a recession, when interest rates are already low and the potential borrowers look risky. If the Fed buys bonds from the public rather than banks, the individuals who sell the bonds might choose to hold cash. If interest rates are low, individuals find that the opportunity cost of holding money instead of interest-bearing assets is also low. Thus, currency drains and excess bank reserves can reduce the expansionary effect of open market operations on the money supply.

Keynes believed that both excess reserves of banks and increased money holdings by households were very likely in response to an increase in the money supply under recessionary conditions of low interest rates and pessimistic expectations. He thought that the demand for excess reserves by banks and for cash balances by households would be very sensitive to interest rates, at least during recessions.

HOW SENSITIVE IS MONEY DEMAND TO INTEREST RATES? Even if banks or individuals lend some of the newly created money in the form of bank loans or purchases of other financial assets, it is possible that the interest rate might not fall very much, or at all. Figure 4 shows two views of the negative relationship between money demand and interest rates. The demand curve in both cases slopes down from left to right because interest

FIGURE 4
MONEY DEMAND, MONEY SUPPLY, AND INTEREST RATES
(*a*) If money demand is very sensitive to interest rates, expanding the money supply lowers interest rates only from i_0 to i_1. (*b*) If money demand is less sensitive to interest rates, changes in the money supply have more effect on interest rates, dropping then from i_0 to i_2.

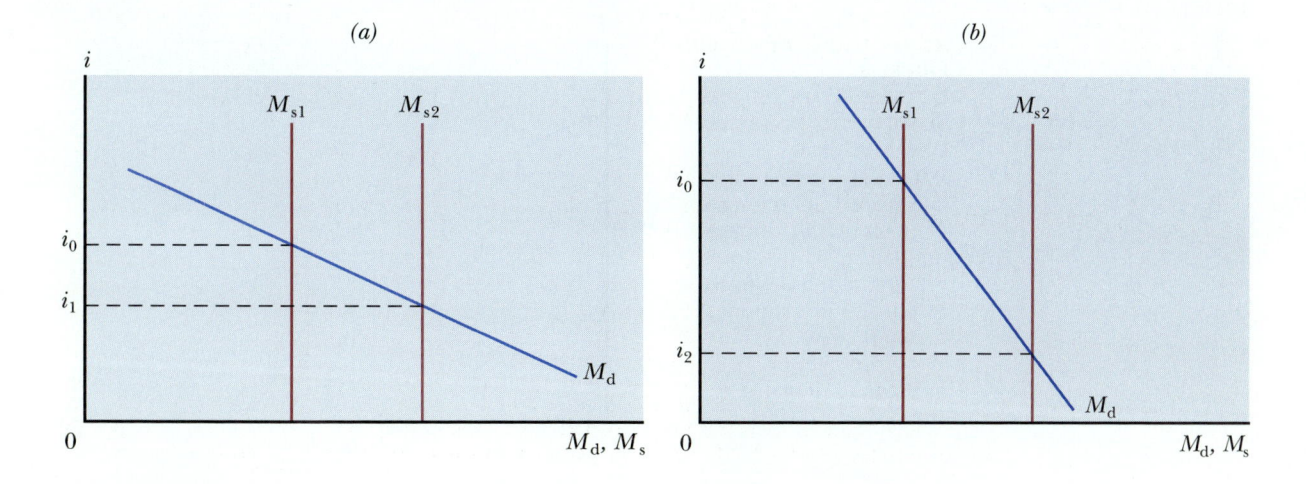

is the opportunity cost of holding money, and when that cost is lower, more money will be demanded. The real issue between Keynesians and monetarists is not the negative slope but the steepness of the money demand curve.

Part (*a*) of Figure 4 shows a Keynesian money demand curve. Here the quantity of money demanded is very sensitive to interest rates (interest-elastic). Part (*b*) shows a monetarist money demand curve. In this case, the quantity of money demanded does not respond very much to interest rates (interest-inelastic). In both parts of the figure, the money supply expands by the same amount, shifting from M_{s1} to M_{s2}. Interest rates fall much more in part (*b*) than in part (*a*).

Why does a given expansion of the money supply bring about a smaller decline in interest rates, when money demand is highly sensitive to interest rates? A very small drop in interest rates is enough to induce banks and households to hold much more cash and fewer other financial assets, such as loans and bonds. The responsiveness of money demand to interest rates is a major point of disagreement between Keynesians and monetarists.

INVESTMENT DEMAND AND INTEREST RATES. Even if interest rates did fall, investment demand might not be very responsive to the lower rates. In Figure 5, the investment demand curve labeled I_1 is relatively flat. A small decline in interest rates leads to a big change in investment demand along this curve, from I_A to I_C. The investment demand curve labeled I_2 is relatively steep. Here the same fall in interest rates increases investment demand only from I_A to I_B. Keynesians argue that the investment demand curve is more like I_2, which shows interest rates having little influence on investment demand. According to this view, investment demand is more dependent on changing expectations and other influences than on interest rates. Shifts in investment demand are so frequent that the steepness of the investment demand curve isn't really very important.

It is very difficult to measure the responsiveness of investment demand to changes in the interest rate. Both investment demand and interest rates are highly sensitive to changes in demand, expectations, and other eco-

FIGURE 5
INTEREST RATES AND THE SLOPE OF THE INVESTMENT DEMAND CURVE
When the interest rate falls from 16 percent to 15 percent, the change in quantity of investment is larger along the more responsive investment demand curve, I_1, than along the steeper investment demand curve, I_2.

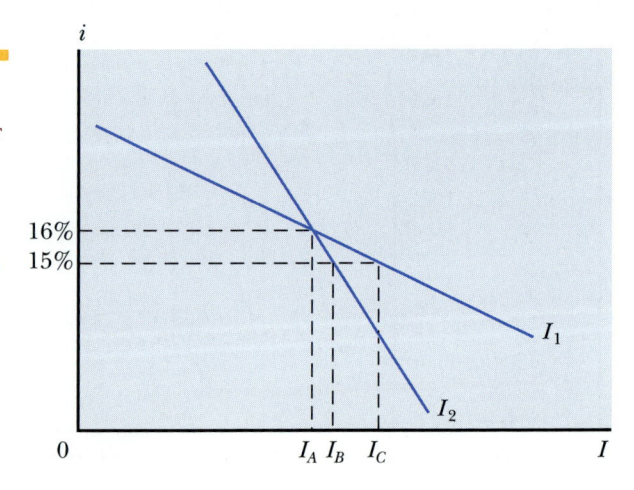

nomic conditions that vary over the course of the business cycle. Thus, investment demand and interest rates may move in the same direction because of other influences that offset or hide any negative relationship between the two. There has been no conclusive proof one way or the other.

EMPIRICAL EVIDENCE ON MONEY DEMAND

The relative importance of money income and interest rates in determining money demand is an issue that may be resolved using empirical tests. In a famous article from 1973, Stephen Goldfeld estimated the money demand function.[5] He found that a 1.0 percent change in money income leads to a 0.19 percent change in money demand (transactions demand) in the short run (three months) and a 0.68 percent change in the long run (two years). Thus, money demand is positively related to money income, but the response is rather small in the short run. According to Goldfeld, the demand for money is negatively related to both short-term and long-term interest rates. However, the effect of interest rates on money demand is less powerful than the effect of money income. For example, Goldfeld found that a 1.0 percent increase in the interest rate on time deposits led to a reduction in money demand (asset demand) of 0.045 percent in the short run and 0.16 percent in the long run. In general, his evidence clearly shows that interest rates do influence money demand, but not as much as Keynesians would expect.

Recent tests using data from the 1980s show a greater impact of interest rates on money demand. In tests done for the National Bureau of Economic Research by Dennis Hoffman of Arizona State University and Robert Rasche of Michigan State University, a 1.0 pecent increase in interest rates generated a reduction in long-run money demand of 0.5–0.6 percent, much higher than what Goldfeld found.[6] Thus, the modern version of money demand as a function of both income and interest rates appears to hold up well under empirical testing.[7]

IS MONETARY POLICY EFFECTIVE?

Suppose banks do not lend, or the public holds cash, or interest rates do not fall very much, or investment demand does not respond to lower interest rates. If any one of these occurs, it might require a very large increase in the money supply to bring about much of a change in aggregate expenditure, output, and employment. Thus, the possibility that money demand is very sensitive to interest rates while investment demand is not is, in the Keynesian view, a serious drawback to monetary policy. In this view, monetary policy should play a supporting role for fiscal policy, keeping credit available and interest rates low when fiscal policy is expansionary and keeping credit tight when fiscal policy is contractionary. Keynesians argue that you can lead investors to money, but you can't make them

---

5. Stephen M. Goldfeld, "The Demand for Money Revisited," *Brookings Papers on Economic Activity* (Washington, DC: Brookings Institution, 1973).
6. Dennis Hoffman and Robert H. Rasche, "Long-Run Income and Interest Elasticities of Money Demand in the United States," National Bureau of Economic Research Working Paper No. 2949, April 1989.
7. The appendix to Chapter 15 describes how economists conduct empirical tests, using real-world data and statistical tests to support or disprove economic theories.

International Perspective

Monetary Policy, Interest Rates, and the Rest of the World

Both the Keynesian and monetarist models of monetary policy are based on a closed economy. That is, they ignore the rest of the world. However, the fraction of U.S. output entering international trade has grown in recent decades. Flows of money and financial assets between countries have also expanded. It has become increasingly clear that neither monetary policy nor fiscal policy can ignore the rest of the world.

Suppose the Fed is pursuing an expansionary policy. According to the monetarist model, there will be an excess supply of money. As people try to spend it, their purchases will drive up both real output and the price level, in some combination. In an open economy, however, some of their purchases will be imported goods rather than domestic products. As the price level starts to rise, sales of exports will fall, and imports of relatively cheaper foreign goods will rise. A fall in exports and a rise in imports mean that the aggregate demand curve shifts to the left. This shift reduces the impact of expansionary monetary policy on output and the price level. Some of the extra money is, in effect, exported, increasing demand in the rest of the world as well as at home.

In the Keynesian model, monetary policy works mainly through interest rates. As interest rates start to fall in an open economy, domestic firms will want to borrow more in response to the lower rates. Lenders, however, are more likely to want to make loans in other countries where higher interest rates are offered. Some of the newly created money goes abroad in search of higher interest rates. In addition, the inflow of funds from abroad shrinks as domestic interest rates fall. The net increase in loanable funds is fairly small, and there is little effect on investment.

The same problems occur with contractionary monetary policy in a Keynesian model. Spending falls, but some of the decline is in spending for imports, rather than domestic goods and services. Thus, there is less impact on aggregate demand, output, and the price level. Higher interest rates will attract an inflow of foreign funds, frustrating any attempts to reduce investment demand.

Thus, although Keynesians and monetarists disagree about the process, they concur that monetary policy is less effective in an open economy. Regardless of whether monetary policy works directly through spending or indirectly through interest rates, it will be less effective in an economy that is very open (has a lot of economic interactions with other countries). Small countries, such as Guyana, Taiwan, the Netherlands, and Costa Rica, find it virtually impossible to pursue an independent monetary policy because most of the effects leak out of the economy instead of staying at home.

spend. If fiscal policy is successful in inducing investors and other spenders to borrow, however, then it is important that funds be available to them. Keynesians do not deny that monetary policy is important, but they think it clearly takes a back seat to fiscal policy, especially during recessions. To Keynesians, money matters, but not very much.

Monetarists share the view of classical economists about the importance of the interest rate to investment decisions. Keynesians are firmly grounded in microeconomic behavior with respect to money demand and interest rates. But monetarists have the solid microeconomic foundation in their view of what determines investment demand. Recall that, in the classical model, the interest rate ensured that investment demand and the supply of savings would always be equal. Interest is the price that firms must pay for the use of funds now rather than later. Firms compare that interest rate to the rate of return on the investment, whether they are borrowing funds or using their own funds that could be earning interest.

The debate over the role of interest rates in affecting lending and borrowing is not just theoretical. It has important policy implications. If the Keynesian view is correct, then monetary policy is relatively ineffective, especially during recessions. If the monetarist view is correct, monetary policy is much more important and powerful as a tool to influence the price level and real output.

There is no simple test of whether Keynesians or monetarists are more nearly correct about the impact of monetary policy. One interesting comparison, however, is shown in Figure 6, which plots the percent change in

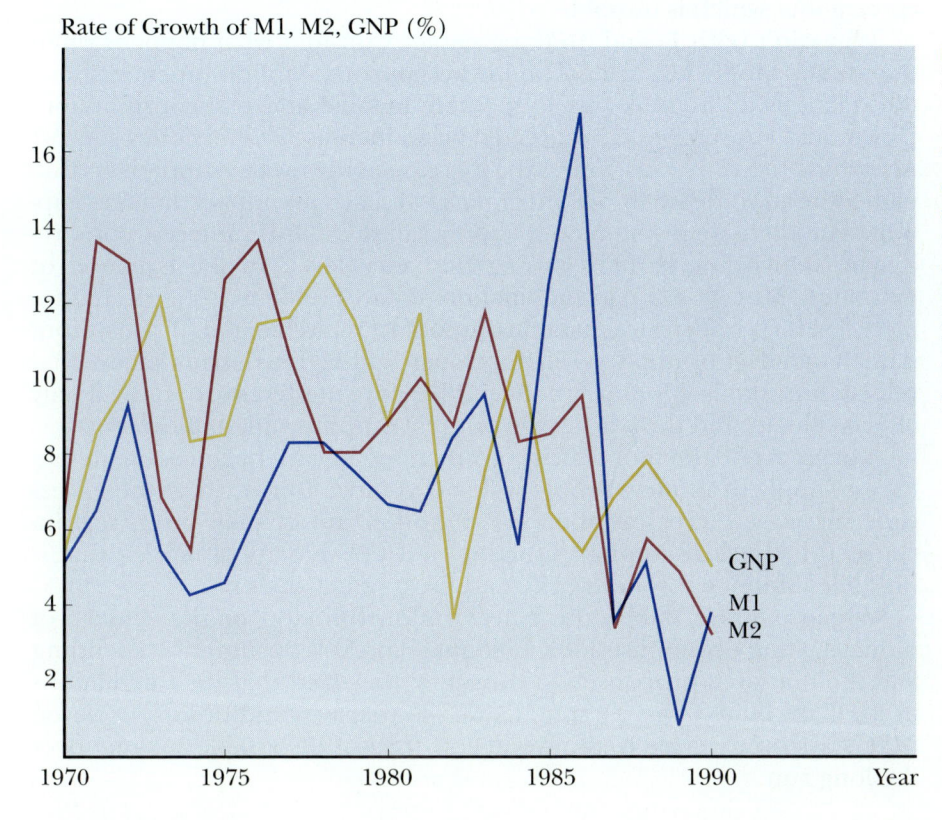

FIGURE 6
CHANGES IN M1, M2, AND GNP, 1970–1990
This figure plots changes in the M1 and M2 measures of the money supply versus changes in nominal GNP for a twenty-year period. Note that the relationship between M1 and GNP has become weaker in recent years.

money supply (both M1 and M2) versus the percent change in nominal GNP for the period 1965–1989. Note that the relationship of M1 and GNP was much closer in the earlier part of the period than in more recent years. M2 tracks GNP a little better than M1 does for the entire period. This graph does not prove anything, but it does at least suggest that monetary policy has some influence on GNP. Since the relationship is not extremely close, the graph suggests that other factors besides monetary policy are also influencing GNP.

VELOCITY OR THE EXPENDITURE MULTIPLIER: WHICH IS STABLE?

Monetarists argue that monetary policy is more effective than fiscal policy because of the way households respond to changes in the money supply and changes in real income. They argue that households respond in predictable ways to changes in the money supply. That is, the velocity of money (V in the equation of exchange) is stable. Monetarists also claim that the marginal propensity to consume (MPC) is not stable. Therefore, the Keynesian consumption function and expenditure multiplier are not stable. Since fiscal policy depends on multiplier effects, this attack on the consumption function raises questions about the effectiveness of fiscal policy.

Velocity and the marginal propensity to consume cannot both be stable. If V is stable, MPC is unstable, and so is the expenditure multiplier. Keynesians and monetarists agree that both cannot be stable. They disagree about which is unstable.

Why can't both V and MPC be stable? Consider what happens when the money supply increases. The Keynesian consumption function shows the relationship between real disposable income and real consumption. How would consumption be affected by an increase in the money supply? According to Keynesians, unless the increase in the money supply is accompanied by an increase in real income, it will have no impact on consumption. The increase in the money supply will drive down interest rates, reducing velocity or perhaps raising the price level. In the equation of exchange, $M_s \times V = P \times Y$, a combination of lower velocity (V) and a higher price level (P) will ensure that real output (Y) is unchanged. If real output is unchanged, consumption will not change either. Keynesians believe that velocity is unstable. Monetary policy is therefore ineffective, because it only affects velocity and the price level, not real output (and employment).

Not so, argue the monetarists. An increase in cash balances creates an excess supply of money. People will spend more to get rid of the excess cash balances, increasing their consumption out of their given real income. It is the consumption function, not the velocity of money, that is unstable. Monetary policy works, and fiscal policy does not.

Which is more stable, the consumption function or the velocity of money? When economists look at annual data for consumption spending and the marginal propensity to consume, they find that the fluctuations in MPC are quite large. Despite its year-to-year ups and downs, however, MPC stays pretty close to an average of 0.89 of disposable income over the long run.

Velocity averages about 6 (relative to M1). It rose steadily in the 1970s, then fluctuated. Velocity is positively related to real income, prices, and interest rates. Like the marginal propensity to consume, velocity is highly unstable over the short run. The measurement of velocity for recent years has been complicated by changes in the measurement of the money supply and the introduction of new kinds of financial assets (such as money market accounts). Until recently, velocity appeared to show a steady upward trend in the long run. However, it tends to rise during expansions and fall during recessions and appears to be fairly sensitive to interest rates.

What can we conclude from this debate about the stability of velocity, the stability of the expenditure multiplier, and the relative effectiveness of monetary and fiscal policy? No definite conclusions emerge. Both the Keynesian expenditure multiplier and the velocity of money are fairly unstable in the short run, especially over the course of the business cycle. An unstable Keynesian expenditure multiplier makes the effects of fiscal policy less certain. An unstable velocity of money that is sensitive to interest rates seems to support the Keynesian view and to make monetary policy less effective.

MONETARY POLICY IN PRACTICE

Keynesians argue that monetary policy works mainly through interest rates. As a result, some economists argue that the target of monetary policy should be controlling interest rates. Monetarists place less emphasis on interest rates and more on the direct effects of changes in the money supply on spending. They believe that the Fed should emphasize controlling the size of the money supply. Interest rates and the money supply are alternative targets for monetary policy, and there has been an ongoing dispute about which works better.

This dispute is important for two reasons. First, the Fed's impact on market interest rates is limited and temporary. If the Fed tries to reduce interest rates by expanding the money supply, there will eventually be upward pressure on the price level. Inflationary expectations will spread. Since these expectations are an important influence on interest rates, market interest rates will rise.

The second reason why the dispute is important is that the Fed cannot pursue both targets at once. If the Fed tries to control interest rates, it must adjust the money supply to whatever level is needed to maintain the desired rates. If interest rates rise above the desired level, the Fed must buy bonds and increase bank reserves to stimulate lending and bring interest rates back down. If interest rates fall below the desired level, the Fed must cut back on the money supply to try to bring them back up. If the Fed tries to control the money supply, then it cannot control interest rates. When the Fed chooses one target, it loses control of the other.

MONEY SUPPLY OR INTEREST RATES?

The Fed can direct its attention to controlling the growth of the money supply or to controlling the level of interest rates. Monetarists usually favor controlling the size of the money supply and its rate of growth.

> **KEYNESIANS VERSUS MONETARISTS ON MONETARY POLICY**
>
> Keynesians believe:
>
> - Money demand is sensitive to interest rates.
> - The velocity of money is unstable.
> - Investment is insensitive to interest rates.
> - Monetary policy is not very effective in changing aggregate demand, output, and employment.
>
> Monetarists believe the opposite:
>
> - Money demand is insensitive to interest rates.
> - The velocity of money is stable.
> - Investment responds to changes in interest rates.
> - Monetary policy is effective in influencing aggregate demand, output, and employment in most cases.

Keynesians usually prefer an interest rate target. This choice reflects the Keynesian belief that interest rates exert an important influence on business activity.

In addition, some Keynesians argue that it is difficult, if not impossible, for the Fed to control the growth of the money supply within narrow limits. This argument is based on the fact that the Fed does not exercise direct control over the money supply. The Fed affects the money supply indirectly through its control of bank reserves and currency (Federal Reserve notes). Banks' decisions about excess reserves and individuals' decisions about cash balances will affect how large a money supply a given monetary base supports.

THE MONEY SUPPLY AS TARGET. The Fed can influence bank lending by influencing bank reserves, but it cannot directly control lending and the money supply. Recall the deposit multiplier ($1/rr$) from Chapter 12. This multiplier determines the maximum money supply and the maximum expansion or contraction that could result from a given change in bank reserves. A slightly different concept is the **money multiplier**, a ratio which gives the relationship of the actual money supply to the monetary base. The **monetary base** consists of the currency in the hands of the public plus reserves held by banks. (Currency in people's hands is part of the monetary base because it becomes bank reserves if it is deposited in banks.) Thus, the monetary base is used either as cash holdings for the public or as reserves to support bank deposits.

The money supply can be defined by the relationship

$$M_s = m \times B,$$

where M_s is the money supply, B is the monetary base, and m is the money multiplier. The money multiplier is then

$$m = \frac{M_s}{B}.$$

money multiplier
The ratio of the actual money supply to the monetary base.

monetary base
The currency in the hands of the public plus reserves held by banks.

Thus, the money multiplier (m) is closely related to the deposit multiplier ($1/rr$) in the equation $D = (1/rr) \times BR$, developed in Chapter 12. However, B includes currency as well as bank reserves (BR). Thus, instead of being determined by the Fed, as the deposit multiplier is, the money multiplier is influenced by the decisions of banks and individuals whether to hold cash or reserves or to lend.

Different money multipliers correspond to the different measures of the money supply. For example, suppose M1 = $400 billion, M2 = $1,000 billion, and B = $200 billion. Then the M1 money multiplier is

$$m_1 = \frac{M1}{B} = \frac{\$400 \text{ billion}}{\$200 \text{ billion}} = 2,$$

and the M2 money multiplier is

$$m_2 = \frac{M2}{B} = \frac{\$1,000 \text{ billion}}{\$200 \text{ billion}} = 5.$$

Both the size and the stability of the money multiplier are important because the Fed can control the monetary base, but it cannot control the money supply directly. Changes in the money supply are caused by changes in the monetary base, the money multiplier, or both.

If the Fed wants to increase the monetary base, it can use open market operations to buy government bonds. If the Fed buys the bonds from a bank, their market value is automatically added to the bank's reserves. If the Fed buys the bonds from a private citizen, the citizen will ultimately deposit the Fed's check in a bank. In either case, the monetary base (B) will rise by the amount of the purchase. If m is constant, M_s will increase by m times the change in B. For example, a $1 billion increase in B would cause M_s to rise by $2 billion if m were 2, by $3 billion if m were 3, and so on.

If the money multiplier is not constant, however, changes in its value can affect the money supply even with no change in the monetary base. Suppose B is $200 billion and m is initially 2.5. Then M_s equals $500 billion (2.5 × $200 billion). A fall in m of only 0.1, to 2.4, means that M_s becomes $480 billion (2.4 × $200 billion), a fall of $20 billion. Thus, a very small change in m has a large effect on M_s.

The Fed controls B, which is one source of change in M_s. The other source of change, variations in m, is only partly under the Fed's control. A portion of an increase in B could go to extra holdings of currency, so there would be less of an increase in bank reserves. In this case, the public's decision to hold more currency and coins instead of checkable deposits would keep M_s from rising as much as it otherwise would. If an increase in B goes entirely to reserves, banks could decide not to lend all these reserves. In either case, an attempt to make M_s rise by a certain amount by increasing B could be frustrated in part by an offsetting fall in m.

Monetarists argue that the money multiplier is fairly stable over periods of a few quarters and that most changes in the money supply are therefore caused by changes in the monetary base. Thus, to monetarists, controlling the money supply is very important. Controlling the monetary base can allow the Fed to control the money supply fairly well.

Table 1 gives the values of m for two measures of the money supply, M1 and M2, for the period 1970–1990. In each case, *m* was calculated by dividing the money supply by the monetary base. The numbers in each column seem quite close. But note that the spread from the lowest value of the M1 multiplier (in 1980) to the highest (in 1972) is 0.32/2.70, or about 12 percent. For the M2 multiplier, the maximum spread is 32 percent. During the 1980s, however, the M2 multiplier was more stable than the M1 multiplier. Because the money multiplier is less than perfectly stable, the Fed usually sets its targets in terms of the growth of the money supply and adjusts the monetary base rather than the other way around.[8]

Another problem in targeting the money supply is choosing among the different measures of that supply. The Humphrey-Hawkins Act of 1978 requires the Fed to report its monetary growth targets for the year to Congress, and Congress interprets that target as M1. With more kinds of financial institutions and deposits, the Fed has shifted its monetary target from M1 to M2. This change was made partly because the link between the monetary base and M2 (see Table 1) seems to be slightly more stable and partly because M2 seems to be more closely linked to the level of economic activity (money income, or $P \times Y$). In any case, the target is not a

TABLE 1
MONEY MULTIPLIERS, 1970–1990

YEAR	M1 MONEY MULTIPLIER	M2 MONEY MULTIPLIER
1970	3.02	8.84
1971	3.01	9.40
1972	3.02	9.76
1973	2.96	9.66
1974	2.85	9.42
1975	2.80	9.97
1976	2.78	10.51
1977	2.78	10.78
1978	2.76	10.69
1979	2.74	10.64
1980	2.70	10.71
1981	2.73	11.15
1982	2.74	11.30
1983	2.77	11.61
1984	2.73	11.72
1985	2.83	11.70
1986	3.00	11.65
1987	2.92	11.28
1988	2.87	11.14
1989	2.80	11.28
1990	2.66	10.90

8. The link between the monetary base and M1 in the 1980s was affected to some degree by reforms that brought all depository institutions under the Fed's control and provided for uniform reserves. For a discussion of this relationship, see Michelle R. Garfinkel and Daniel L. Thornton, "The Link between M1 and the Monetary Base in the 1980s," *Review*, Federal Reserve Bank of St. Louis (September-October 1989): 35–52.

precise number or a specific rate of growth but a range of growth rates for the various monetary aggregates: the monetary base, M1, M2, and related measures.

INTEREST RATES AS TARGET. Until the late 1970s, the Fed paid more attention to interest rates than to the money supply. Letting interest rates rise too high could discourage investment and cause a recession. The decision to target interest rates instead of the money supply was reinforced by the fact that the Treasury has to borrow by selling U.S. government securities to the public. The government budget deficit is financed through these bond sales, and the Treasury prefers low, stable interest rates to high, unstable ones.

The Fed attempts to control interest rates by keeping the federal funds rate (the interest rate banks charge each other when lending and borrowing reserves) within a certain range. If, for example, Bank A needs $1 million in reserves to meet the reserve requirement, it can borrow them from Bank B and pay that bank interest at the federal funds rate. Bank B notifies the Fed to transfer $1 million from its reserve account to Bank A's account.

The Fed targets a range for the federal funds rate, such as 7–7.5 percent. If the demand for reserves rises, driving up the federal funds rate, the Fed will buy government bonds. The prices of bonds will rise, and their yields fall. As lower interest rates spread from bonds to other assets, the federal funds rate is kept from rising above 7.5 percent. If demand for reserves falls, and the federal funds rate seems likely to fall below 7 percent, the Fed will sell government bonds. Open market sales of bonds will depress bond prices and put upward pressure on interest rates.

An interest rate target requires the Fed to keep adjusting the monetary base to whatever is demanded in the market for loanable funds. Thus, the Fed cannot control both the money supply and interest rates at the same time. The Fed was widely criticized by monetarists in the 1970s for giving interest rate targets priority over money supply targets. In an abrupt shift, the Fed changed its priorities from interest rates to the money supply in the fall of 1979. This change, under the leadership of chairman Paul Volcker, was regarded as a milestone in monetary policy and a victory for monetarist ideas. The policy of focusing on the money supply remained in place until 1982, but pressure on the Fed during the recession then forced it to moderate that policy. In addition, changes in the banking system made it more difficult to forecast and control relationships between the size of the monetary base and the money supply in the 1980s. Since 1982, the Fed has been using a mix of targets: a range of growth rates for the several measures of the money supply and a range of market interest rates.

GNP TARGETING

In recent years, there has been an attempt by the Fed to shift from targeting interest rates or the money supply to **GNP targeting**. This policy calls for the Fed to aim at some level of nominal GNP by influencing a number of variables that affect it. These variables include the measures of the money supply as well as total credit and interest rates. However, even

GNP targeting
A monetary policy that calls for the Fed to aim at some level of nominal GNP by influencing a number of variables that affect GNP.

if changing GNP is the ultimate goal, the Fed must choose intermediate targets that are within its control to try to attain that goal. Those targets are still some combination of money supply and interest rates.[9]

LAGS IN MONETARY POLICY

Lags present another problem in implementing monetary policy. Monetary policy is affected by the same kinds of lags that affect fiscal policy: recognition, implementation, and impact lags. The recognition lag is probably about the same length for both monetary and fiscal policy. Unlike fiscal policy, however, monetary policy has a very short implementation lag. The Federal Open Market Committee (FOMC) meets regularly and makes decisions about changes in the money supply. Because of the Fed's independence from Congress and the executive branch, it can move quickly without asking anyone's permission.

In discussions of monetary policy, the recognition and implementation lags are combined and known as the inside lag. The impact lag—known as the outside lag in monetary policy—can be quite long. In the 1960s, it was estimated that it took one to two years for money supply changes to be fully reflected in prices and output. By the 1980s, the lag appeared to be getting shorter. The inflation of the late 1970s had made lenders and borrowers more sensitive to the need to acquire and use current information to form correct expectations about inflation. Shorter lags also reflect increased competition in financial markets as a result of bank deregulation.

The length of the outside lag depends on how quickly people recognize and respond to a change in the money supply. It takes time for banks to increase or decrease their lending or for individuals to adjust their spending. In general, it is estimated that, because of the outside lag, it takes at least two quarters for monetary policy to have half its ultimate impact and eighteen to twenty-four months for the full effect to be felt.

Lags are an important concern because they can cause monetary policy to have the wrong effect, just as they can for fiscal policy. From 1945 to 1982, cycles of economic activity have been brief, with the average recession lasting only eleven months. A policy that cannot be implemented quickly and have a rapid impact may be worse than no policy at all.

SECTORAL EFFECTS

Monetary policy does not affect all sectors of the economy equally. When monetary policy is tight, those economic activities that depend on borrowing are affected more heavily. Business investment in plants and equipment, housing, consumer durables (especially automobiles), and state and local government capital projects are very dependent on borrowing and sensitive to changes in monetary policy. Consumers, the auto industry, and the construction industry resent being singled out to bear more than their share of the battle against inflation when monetary policy is tightened. Adjustable-rate mortgages (ARMs) and other innovations in home financing have somewhat lessened the impact of monetary pol-

---

9. For a more detailed discussion of GNP targeting, see Michael D. Bradley and Dennis W. Jansen, "Understanding Nominal GNP Targeting," *Review*, Federal Reserve Bank of St. Louis (November-December 1989): 30–40.

Chapter 14 Monetary Policy in Theory and Practice

icy on housing. However, this and other parts of the private sector are still sensitive to changes in interest rates and the availability of funds.

In the 1980s, the foreign sector became more sensitive to monetary policy. A tight monetary policy that drives up interest rates will attract funds from abroad and drive up the price of the dollar (see the International Perspective). When the price of the dollar rises, exporters find it harder to sell their goods abroad. Also, some firms in this country find that foreign competitors can more easily undersell them. Thus, the international sector of the economy has become increasingly sensitive to monetary policy.

POLITICAL PROBLEMS

Even though the Fed is technically independent, it is not immune to political pressures. The best-known instance of political pressure on the Fed was when it helped to finance the government deficit immediately after World War II. In recent years, Congress has put pressure on the Fed to keep interest rates low, often in response to the construction and auto industries and others who want low interest rates. The Fed was often pressured by Congress or the President to ease monetary conditions in election years. The Fed is also under pressure from banks, which would like to be able to lend freely (and borrow freely from the Fed) during times of high loan demand.

All of these forces tend to push the Fed in the direction of monetary expansion. It was only after some painful experience with the resulting inflation that the Fed was able to fight back and tighten monetary conditions in the late 1970s and early 1980s. The Fed now resists pressure to expand the money supply for political reasons, especially to make incumbents look good at election time.

RULES VERSUS DISCRETION

Many economists, especially monetarists, have not been happy with the Fed's performance. They blame the Fed for both recessions and inflation, as the course of monetary policy zigzags between expansion and contraction. The Fed has come under criticism in recent years for monetary tightness during the Great Depression. The same criticism was levied at the Fed during the 1980–1982 recession. A proposed regulation requiring the Fed to chart a course of growth in the money supply at some predetermined, steady rate is called a **monetary rule**. Such a regulation would replace discretionary monetary policy.

monetary rule
A proposed regulation requiring the Fed to make the money supply grow at some predetermined, steady rate.

The most commonly suggested form of monetary rule is to allow the money supply to grow at about the same rate as, or just a little faster than, real output over the long run, keeping inflation at a tolerable rate of 1–2 percent a year. This rule would call for a growth rate of 4–5 percent a year for the money supply. When output growth slows down because of a recession, monetary policy would be mildly inflationary. (If M_s is growing at 4–5 percent a year and velocity is stable, then $P \times Y$ must grow at the same rate. If Y is growing more slowly, P must take up the slack.) If the economy is overheated and demand is fueling growth of, say, 7 percent a year, monetary policy would be contractionary. Proponents of such a rule argue that attempting to respond to imperfect information from the marketplace, with the added hindrance of lags, is worse than having no monetary policy at all. Nobel Prize winner Milton Friedman is probably the best-known advocate of having a monetary rule.

The Fed is not likely to adopt such a binding rule voluntarily. It has, however, tried to stabilize the monetary growth rate and give more emphasis to the money supply as target rather than interest rates in recent years. Although monetarists are still unhappy with the Fed's performance in the last decade, especially with rapid monetary growth in the early 1980s, this change in targets represented a victory for monetarist ideas.

Another proposed "rule" is to return to a gold standard. Being on a gold standard requires a nation to have enough gold to redeem its currency in gold on demand. The stock of gold would place limits on the size of the money supply, and the Fed's discretionary policy role would be greatly reduced. The United States went off the gold standard in 1934 and is not likely to return, but some conservatives find the idea of an automatic limit on monetary expansion very attractive.

MONETARY POLICY UNDER THE FED, 1914–1990

When the Federal Reserve System was established in 1913, one of its primary functions was to keep the United States in compliance with the international gold standard. Complying meant that the Fed had to allow the size of the U.S. gold stock held by the Treasury to set an upper limit on the size of the money supply, in some fixed ratio. Such a requirement severely limited the Fed's freedom to expand the money supply.

The first problem confronted by the Fed was helping the federal government finance its deficit during and after World War I. The Fed cooperated in keeping interest rates low and buying any government bonds that could not find a buyer. These actions were inflationary. When the Fed recognized that the ratio of money to gold was getting too high, it began to contract the money supply. That action played a role in bringing about the 1920–1921 recession.

THE FED AND THE DEPRESSION

The biggest controversy over the Fed's policy centers on its actions from 1929 to 1937. The money supply fell by 25 percent from August 1929 to March 1933, in part because of widespread bank failures. Such a wave of failures was exactly what the Fed was intended to prevent. The Fed, aided by large inflows of gold, did keep the discount rate low during the early years of the Depression. It was the money supply, not the monetary base, that fell sharply. The monetary base remained stable while the ratio of currency to deposits rose (as people withdrew cash from the banking system) and the ratio of deposits to reserves fell (as banks held more excess reserves). Widespread bank failures led to large cash withdrawals from banks. Thus, the same monetary base supported fewer deposits. Banks saw few good loan prospects, and interest rates were low. Therefore, they chose to hold large excess reserves. Cash withdrawals combined with excess reserves meant that the money multiplier was smaller.

The most vocal critics of the Fed's actions in this period have been Milton Friedman and Anna Schwartz, who did a thorough study of these actions.[10] They argued that the Fed was too passive, failing to pump up reserves to offset what was happening in the private sector. The Fed did not shrink the monetary base but did not allow it to expand either. However, the Fed was constrained with respect to the size of the money supply by the gold standard until 1934. The most controversial policy decision by the Fed during the Depression took place after the United States went off the gold standard. The Fed chose to raise reserve requirements in 1936, trying to "mop up" excess bank reserves. This action was widely blamed for sparking an economic downturn in 1937.

Peter Temin argued that Friedman and Schwartz came down too hard on the Fed.[11] The money supply can change from either the supply side or the demand side. The return on investment was low during the early years of the Depression. If there is low return on investment and weak consumption demand, interest rates will fall. That fall will lead both individuals and banks to hold onto more cash and make less available to borrowers. The opportunity cost of holding currency and excess reserves will be low because of demand factors, which are largely outside the control of the Fed.

The Fed did not cause the Depression, but perhaps a more aggressive expansionary monetary policy would have made it shorter and milder. Bear in mind, however, that the Fed had had only seventeen years of experience when the Depression occurred. Also, some of its actions prior to 1935 were restricted by its need to comply with the gold standard.

THE ACCORD

During and after World War II, the Fed's main task was helping the Treasury finance the enormous debt incurred during the war at acceptably low interest rates. The Fed abandoned monetary targets in order to hold down interest rates. The result was inflation, because every time the Fed bought Treasury obligations to keep interest rates down, it expanded bank reserves. In 1951, the Fed and the Treasury reached an agreement. This agreement, called **The Accord**, stated that the Fed was no longer obliged to hold interest rates low to assist with the Treasury's debt financing. In 1952, the Fed was finally free to turn its monetary policy in the direction of stabilizing economic activity.

For most of the rest of the 1950s, the Fed used free reserves as its target. **Free reserves** consist of bank excess reserves less bank loans from the Fed. If free reserves were large, the Fed took that as a signal of too much slack in the credit market. The Fed defined its role during this time as "leaning against the wind." That is, the Fed was determining the direction of economic activity and trying to steer the economy back toward a middle ground of steady growth, stable prices, and high employment.

The Accord
The 1951 agreement between the Fed and the Treasury that the Fed was no longer obliged to hold interest rates low to assist with the Treasury's debt financing.

free reserves
A bank's excess reserves less its loans from the Fed.

MONETARY POLICY IN THE 1960S AND 1970S

The inflation rate began to creep up in the late 1960s and rose faster in the 1970s. From 1965 to 1979, the CPI rose 130 percent. For most of this

---

10. Milton Friedman and Anna J. Schwartz, *A Monetary History of the United States* (Princeton, NJ: Princeton University Press, 1963).
11. Peter Temin, *Did Monetary Forces Cause the Great Depression?* (New York: W. W. Norton, 1976).

credit crunch
The 1966 shortage of loanable funds caused by the sudden slowing of monetary growth rates by the Fed.

period, monetary policy was expansionary. The one major exception was the 1966 credit crunch. The **credit crunch** was a shortage of loanable funds caused by the sudden slowing of monetary growth rates by the Fed. The Fed abruptly reduced the rate of growth of M1 from 4.6 percent in 1964 and 1965 to 0 percent in mid-1966. This reduction was a response to what it perceived as a threat of inflation. The housing industry ground to a halt. Savings and loan associations lost deposits to higher interest assets elsewhere as interest rates rose sharply in response. The Fed reversed its course and continued monetary expansion through the end of the 1960s. Inflation rates (predictably) began to rise.

The 1970s began with a financial crisis, a sharp drop in the stock market combined with the failure of Penn Central. That railroad was a major borrower from commercial banks. The Fed earned some of its highest marks ever for monetary policy during this crisis. It announced that the discount window was open and lowered reserve requirements. As the 1970s wore on, inflation took hold, pushed by the OPEC oil price hike. The Fed responded with a more restrictive monetary policy, which probably contributed to the 1974–1975 recession.

By the late 1970s, after flip-flopping between targeting the money supply and targeting interest rates, the Fed began to move more in a monetary direction, while keeping an eye on interest rates. An abrupt change of direction in October 1979 was later named the "Saturday night special." Instead of interest rates, the Fed decided to make the growth of the various measures of the money supply, especially M1, the focus of its policy actions. The Fed cut the monetary growth rate sharply at the end of 1979, which drove interest rates to all-time highs. This action contributed to the recession (and drop in the inflation rate) of the early 1980s. The 1979 shift marked a firm choice of money supply targets over interest rate targets.

RECENT MONETARY POLICY

Through most of the 1980s, the Fed was chaired by Paul Volcker. Volcker and the Fed emerged as heroes with a fairly restrictive monetary policy. This policy was credited with helping to reduce both the inflation rate and nominal (but not real) interest rates. Part of the decrease in inflation and interest rates, however, was the result of a decline in velocity rather than a slowing of the growth of the money supply. Monetary policy in the 1980s was complicated by rapid growth in the federal debt, an influx of foreign lending, changes in bank regulations, and more numerous bank failures. In 1982, the Fed backed off from its 1979 decision to focus solely on money supply targets and began to pursue interest rate targets as well. In addition, M1 competed with other measures of money and credit for the role of primary money supply target.

In 1987, Volcker was succeeded by Alan Greenspan as chairman of the Fed. A combination of changing leadership and experience has changed the Fed's operating style and priorities. The experience of the 1970s and early 1980s made the Fed much more concerned about inflation and much more aware of the effects of high interest rates on the economy. Bank deregulation, increasing involvement of foreigners in U.S. money and credit markets, and the gradual weakening of the close link between

M1 and GNP have made the Fed much more uncertain about the effects of its actions on the economy.[12]

GOVERNMENT BORROWING, CROWDING OUT, AND MONETARY POLICY

As you have seen at several points in this brief history of monetary policy, monetary and fiscal policy are closely related. Financing government borrowing is one area in which the two policies must be coordinated. In the 1980s, the most important links between fiscal and monetary policy had to do with the effects of government deficit financing on interest rates and private investment and the Fed's response to crowding out.

Monetarists argue that increased government spending (G) may not have much effect on aggregate expenditure (AE) or aggregate demand (AD) because it is likely to be offset by a decline in private investment. How does this happen? If government spending is financed by borrowing, this drives up interest rates. Higher interest rates discourage private investment. Thus, the increase in G is offset by a fall in gross private domestic investment (I).

As you learned in Chapters 10 and 13, reductions in private borrowing and investing because of increased government borrowing, which drives up interest rates, is called crowding out. In extreme cases, total spending may not increase at all. The simple Keynesian model has no crowding out. In that model, the interest rate does not rise when G increases. Instead, AE rises by the full amount of G, with the usual effect on output and employment due to the expenditure multiplier.

Figure 7 shows how crowding out occurs, using supply and demand curves for loanable funds at various rates of interest. Assume that the initial demand curve, D_0, reflects only demand for private investment. Ini-

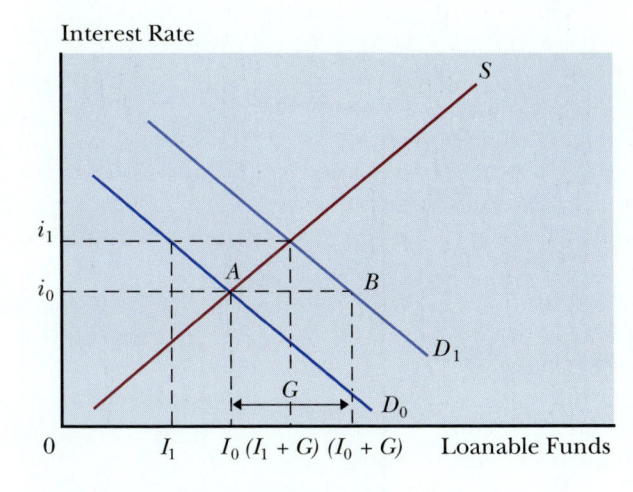

FIGURE 7
SUPPLY AND DEMAND FOR LOANABLE FUNDS AND CROWDING OUT
Increased demand for loanable funds to finance government spending shifts demand from D_0 to D_1. Increased demand drives up interest rates and reduces private borrowing. Total borrowing rises to $I_1 + G$, but private investment falls from I_0 to I_1.

---

12. Council of Economic Advisers, *Economic Report of the President* (Washington, DC: U.S. Government Printing Office, 1990), 83–84.

tially the government is not borrowing at all. The interest rate is i_0, and the volume of lending and borrowing is I_0. Suppose the government adds its demand (to finance an increase in G with no additional taxes). The combined demand curve shifts to D_1. The horizontal distance between the two demand curves at the initial interest rate is AB, the amount of increased G financed by borrowing. The interest rate rises to i_1. At that interest rate, private borrowers (still represented by D_0) only want to borrow I_1. Total demand for loanable funds (as well as the total expenditure function AE) has risen, but actual lending increases only by the difference between I_0 and $(I_1 + G)$. That amount is much smaller than the increase in G.

THE KEYNESIAN CASE

How much crowding out actually occurs? Figure 8 diagrams two extreme cases: one with a horizontal supply curve of loanable funds in part (*a*) and one with a vertical supply curve in part (*b*). The horizontal version represents the extreme Keynesian view, perhaps appropriate to conditions like those of the Great Depression. In this case, banks have excess reserves but are reluctant to lend to risky private borrowers. However, they will lend freely to the government because they are certain of being repaid. Thus, government borrowing has no effect on interest rates because there are funds available at the existing rate. No crowding out occurs. Aggregate expenditure will rise by the full amount of G, the distance between I_0 and $(I_0 + G)$, and the interest rate will not change. There will be a large shift of aggregate demand to the right, driving up output and prices—the normal result of fiscal policy in the Keynesian model.

THE MONETARIST CASE

Part (*b*) of Figure 8 represents an extreme monetarist view. In this case, banks are already all loaned up when the government issues new bonds. Government borrowing can occur only at the expense of private borrowers. These borrowers include not only business investors but also state and

FIGURE 8
THE SUPPLY CURVE FOR LOANABLE FUNDS
(*a*) In the Keynesian view, there are ample loanable funds available at the current interest rate. When G increases, no crowding out occurs, interest rates do not rise, and aggregate expenditure increases by the full amount of G. Aggregate demand shifts to the right (from D_0 to D_1). Real output and/or the price level rises. (*b*) In the monetarist view, the rise in G is fully offset by a decline in I as interest rates rise sharply. Aggregate expenditure is unchanged, and there is no effect on aggregate demand, real output, or the price level.

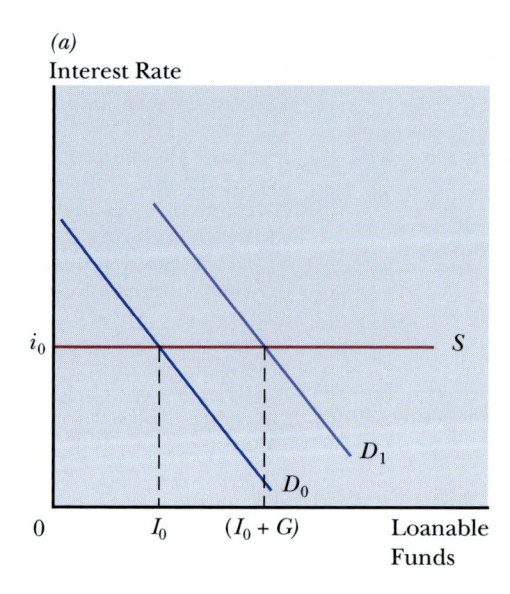

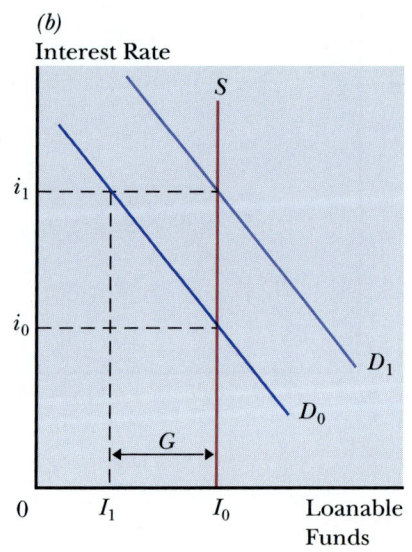

local governments (borrowing to build schools and sewer plants) and consumers (borrowing for houses, autos, and stereo systems). The rise in G is offset by an equal fall in I from I_0 to I_1 as interest rates rise from i_0 to i_1. Thus, part (b) shows total crowding out. Expansionary fiscal policy has no effect on the level of real output. There is no shift in aggregate expenditure because the upward shift caused by rising G is offset by an equal and opposite fall in I. Aggregate demand is unchanged.

THE INTEREST RATE AND THE SUPPLY OF LOANABLE FUNDS

The slope of the supply curve for loanable funds depends on how sensitive the demand for money is to changes in interest rates. Money that households do not wish to hold becomes available to lend in the loanable funds market. If money demand is very responsive to interest rates, the supply curve for loanable funds will be relatively flat. Only a small rise in interest rates will be needed to induce individuals to switch from holding money to lending it. A supply curve for loanable funds drawn by a Keynesian would be very flat, although not as flat as the curve in Figure 8(a). Interest rates hardly change at all when the government enters the market as a borrower.

The monetarist supply curve for loanable funds is vertical, or nearly so. Monetarists do not expect money demand to be very responsive to the interest rate. When interest rates rise, the funds lent to government are exactly offset by a reduction in business borrowing, with no increase in aggregate expenditure or aggregate demand.

Who is right? Both sides are partly correct. According to the empirical tests cited earlier, money demand is moderately responsive to changes in interest rates. If money demand is responsive to interest rates, higher interest rates will call forth more loanable funds as banks lend excess reserves and individuals cut down on their cash balances. Thus, under normal circumstances, there should be partial but not total crowding out.

The experience of the 1980s did not provide a good test of the crowding out hypothesis, because of the effect of foreign lending. A part of both government and private borrowing was financed by foreign funds flowing into the United States. This flow of funds reduced direct competition between government borrowing and business borrowing for the same pool of funds. Instead, the inflow of foreign funds drove up the price of the dollar and made U.S. exports more expensive and U.S. imports cheaper. Thus, instead of the crowding out of investment, there appears to have been some crowding out of net exports.

THE INTEREST RATE AND INVESTMENT DEMAND

It is not only the slope of the supply curve for loanable funds but also the slope of the marginal efficiency of investment (*MEI*) curve that determines how much crowding out takes place. The slope of this demand curve represents the responsiveness of investment demand to interest rates. Recall that Keynesians think investment is influenced more by aggregate demand, expectations, and other factors than by interest rates. Monetarists expect investment to be affected more by interest rates.

These two views are pictured in Figure 9. An upward-sloping supply curve for loanable funds is paired with a very steep or unresponsive

International Perspective

The Budget Deficit and the Exchange Rate

The huge U.S. government budget deficits in the 1980s appear to have resulted in very little crowding out of investment. Between 1981 and 1985, foreign investment in the United States rose sharply, attracted by high interest rates, an appealing business climate, and other factors. As a result, international capital flows provided funds for investment.

When foreigners purchase U.S. bonds, stocks, or whole firms or make bank deposits, they must first convert their currency (yen, pounds, francs, Canadian dollars, or whatever) into U.S. dollars. As foreigners demand more dollars, the price of the dollar, or the exchange rate, rises. Between 1981 and 1985, the price of the U.S. dollar rose 60 percent.

Was this development good or bad? Both. A higher price for the dollar is great if you want to visit Europe or buy a foreign car. American dollars will buy more foreign currency and thus more foreign goods. A more expensive dollar is also good news on the inflation front. Relatively cheap imports will keep the CPI from rising as rapidly. If, however, you are an exporter or compete with imported products, a higher dollar price presents problems. When dollars are expensive, American goods are expensive, and foreign goods are relatively cheap. It is hard to sell goods abroad or to compete at home. Exports fell steadily as the dollar rose during the early 1980s. Slow growth of real output and employment was blamed on the high price of the dollar, the flood of imported goods, and the decline in U.S. exports. Thus, some of the pressures for protection against competition from imports in the first half of the 1980s reflected the high price of the dollar.

The rising tide of foreign investment in the United States and the rising price of the dollar both halted in 1985. These changes occurred partly because there were better investment opportunities elsewhere and partly because federal deficits stablized and began to fall, reducing interest rates. Between 1985 and 1990, the price of the dollar fell 38 percent. If the lower price for the dollar holds in the 1990s, the United States can expect more exports, fewer imports, more jobs—and higher prices. In economics, there is no free lunch and no unmixed blessing. The inflow of foreign investment in U.S. stocks, bonds, and bank accounts bring both costs and benefits and so does a slowdown in such investment.

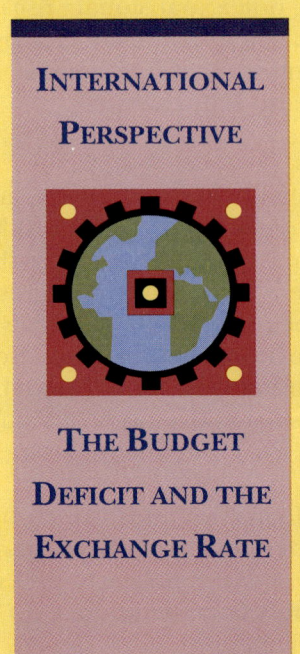

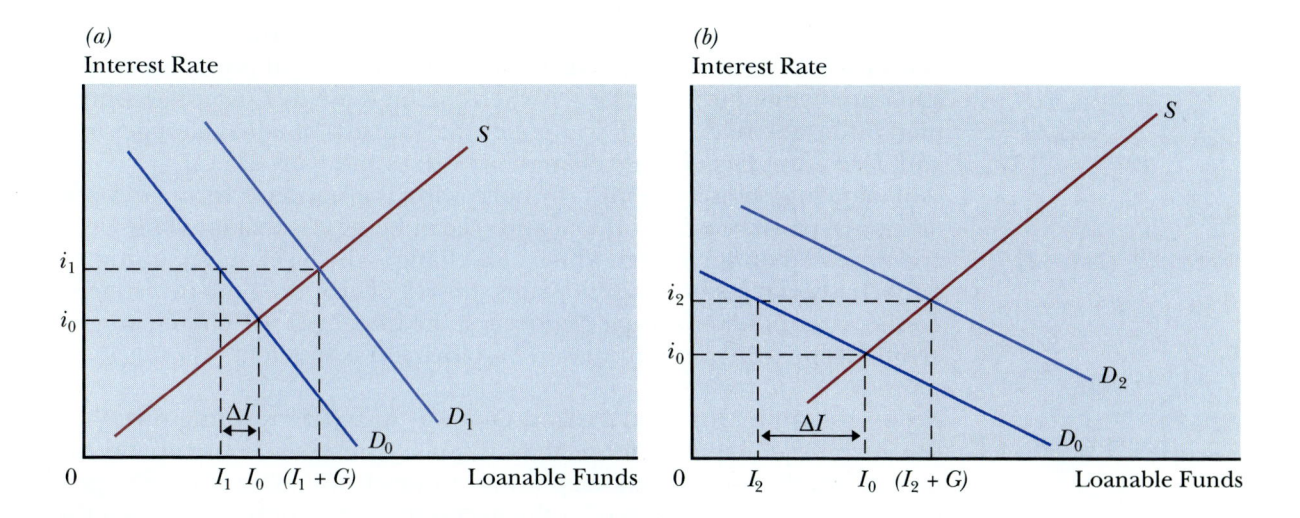

(Keynesian) investment demand curve in part (a) and a very flat or responsive (monetarist) investment demand curve in part (b). In both cases, crowding out is measured by the decline in private investment. When demand shifts from D_0 to D_1 in part (a), very little crowding out occurs. Interest rates rise, but investment demand is not affected much. More crowding out occurs in the monetarist model in part (b) when demand shifts from D_0 to D_2. If an increase in government spending is partly offset by a decline in investment, then the resulting shift in aggregate expenditure and aggregate demand will be smaller. There will be less impact on output, employment, and the price level.

The debate over crowding out is not yet resolved. Empirical tests have not proved whether increased government borrowing has much effect on interest rates and, as a result, on the amount of private borrowing. In the early 1980s, real interest rates did remain high when the government borrowed heavily to finance record deficits. However, very little crowding out of investment was observed because the high interest rates attracted an inflow of foreign funds. This inflow of foreign funds not only increased the supply of loanable funds but also drove up the price of the dollar from 1980 to 1985. In effect, it crowded out net exports to some degree. As the level of government borrowing stabilized and began to fall during the late 1980s, the price of the dollar fell. There was some increase in net exports, due to a reduction in imports at first and later some increase in exports as well.

HOW SPENDING IS FINANCED

Borrowing is not the only way to finance an increase in government spending (G). There are three ways: raising taxes, borrowing, and printing money. Each of these methods affects aggregate demand differently. Only raising taxes is pure fiscal policy. The other two methods involve a blend of monetary and fiscal policy.

Tax financing of G may be slightly expansionary, according to the Keynesian model. As you learned in Chapter 9, the government expen-

FIGURE 9
CROWDING OUT AND THE INVESTMENT DEMAND CURVE
(a) When government borrows, interest rates rise from i_0 to i_1, but private investment falls only from I_0 to I_1.
(b) Investment is very sensitive to interest rates. Government borrowing drives interest rates from i_0 to i_2. There is a large fall in private investment from I_0 to I_2.

ditures multiplier $[1/(1-b)]$ is a little larger than the tax multiplier $[-b/(1-b)]$. However, the effect of expansionary fiscal policy on output and employment is much larger when the increase in G is not accompanied by higher taxes (T). Fiscal policy that consists of equal changes in G and T requires a very large change in both to have any effect.

Financing an increase in G by borrowing is a standard Keynesian policy prescription. On the other hand, G can be held constant while taxes are increased or decreased, which also changes the level of borrowing. In either case, expansionary policy runs the risk of crowding out investment. To the extent that crowding out occurs, the impact of the change in government spending on output and employment is smaller.

ACCOMMODATING MONETARY POLICY. One way to avoid crowding out when the government spends more than it collects in taxes is to expand the money supply. In order to keep interest rates from rising when the government borrows, the Fed buys the excess government bonds. When the Fed buys bonds, bank reserves increase, and the money supply expands. Monetary expansion that is undertaken to help the Treasury finance deficits without driving up interest rates very much is called **accommodating monetary policy**. Monetarists argue that expansionary fiscal policy supported by accommodating monetary policy is not fiscal policy at all, but monetary policy. If an increased deficit leads to increases in output and employment, they believe, the higher output is caused by monetary expansion, not fiscal policy. It is clear that when an increased deficit is financed with a larger money supply, it is difficult to tell whether changes in output, employment, and the price level are the effects of monetary or fiscal policy.

DO FINANCING METHODS MATTER? Economist Robert Barro of the University of Rochester argues that the method of financing government spending has no impact on private spending.[13] People will perceive that increased government spending now, financed by borrowing, will mean increased taxes in the future to pay off the debt. If they are consuming on the basis of permanent income, as Friedman argues, then they will reduce their consumption because of the expected future increased taxes. Thus, the effect of higher government spending will be to increase current income, decrease future income, and leave permanent income unchanged.

Barro's argument is based not only on the permanent income hypothesis but also on the macroeconomic idea that people have rational expectations. That is, they make economic decisions using all available information and they avoid repeating previous errors. That people have rational expectations is a central idea of the new classical school. According to this view, people may not be misled into changing their behavior in response to temporary policy changes. The policy implications of rational expectations, an approach to macroeconomics that has been strongly advocated by Robert Lucas and Thomas Sargent, will be explored further in the next two chapters. Barro's view that financing methods do not have

---

accommodating monetary policy Monetary expansion that is undertaken to help the Treasury finance deficits without driving up interest rates very much.

---

13. Robert Barro, "Are Government Bonds Net Worth?" *Journal of Political Economy* (November/December 1974): 1095–1117.

any effect on output and employment has produced a great deal of debate, but so far has not won wide acceptance among either Keynesians or monetarists.

Does Policy Do Any Good?

The question of whether policy can help reflects a final basic difference between Keynesians and monetarists. Keynesians believe that policy makers should be concerned about the short run. The long run, or the period in which the economy may adjust to some full-employment equilibrium, is very long. In the interim, there may be an unacceptable amount of suffering from unemployment, inflation, or both. Most monetarists share the classical view that the economy should be left to correct itself, but they go one step further. Monetarists believe that activist policy, especially fiscal policy, may do more harm than good. How is a policy maker to know what to do if economists can't agree among themselves?

DO ECONOMISTS EVER AGREE?

Although monetarists and Keynesians disagree about macroeconomic theory and policy, they agree about a number of things. More than two decades ago, Milton Friedman said, "We are all Keynesians now." That is, most economists use a modified Keynesian framework to discuss macroeconomic issues. Since that time, mainstream economists would tend to add, "We are also all monetarists now." The model of the loanable funds market that was used in Chapter 13, for example, incorporates both monetarist and Keynesian views. The aggregate supply and demand model is broad enough to encompass not only Keynesian and monetarist views but others as well.

Here is a list of some points of agreement between Keynesians and monetarists:

1. The money supply can affect output as well as prices, although the effects on output may be only short-run.
2. Velocity is more stable in the long run than in the short run.
3. The demand for money depends on both income and interest rates, although income has a stronger effect.
4. Expectations about income, prices, and interest rates are an important influence on consumption and investment.
5. Fiscal policy can have some effects on real output in the short run. The long-run effects are much less certain.
6. Both inflation and unemployment beyond a certain minimum are undesirable.
7. Lags may distort the intended effects of monetary and fiscal policy.
8. Some crowding out is a likely result of a deficit-financed increase in government spending.

Note all the qualifiers in this list: "may," "to some degree," "some," and "in the short run." Monetarists and Keynesians disagree about the slope of the aggregate supply curve, the importance of crowding out, and the relative length of the long run and the short run. But even when they dis-

Summary

1. The Keynesian view of monetary policy is that it works by lowering interest rates. In turn, lower interest rates stimulate investment and increase aggregate expenditure and aggregate demand. However, Keynesians do not think that monetary policy is always very effective at lowering interest rates or that lower interest rates are very effective in stimulating investment.
2. Monetarists believe that monetary policy works directly by creating a money supply that exceeds money demand. The excess money is spent, driving up prices and/or output.
3. The effectiveness of monetary policy depends on how sensitive money demand is to interest rates and how responsive investment demand is to changes in interest rates.
4. The Fed can attempt to control either the money supply or interest rates, but not both. In recent years, more emphasis has been placed on targeting the money supply.
5. Monetary policy suffers from lags, regional effects, and political pressures. Because of these problems with monetary policy, some economists support a monetary rule that would set a fixed rate of growth for the money stock.
6. Monetarists believe that the velocity of money is stable (at least in the long run) and the expenditure multiplier is not. Keynesians argue the opposite. Stable velocity means monetary policy is more effective. A stable expenditure multiplier means fiscal policy is more effective.
7. Velocity rises during business expansions and falls during recessions. It has had a long-term upward trend in the last twenty years.
8. Fiscal policy will not be effective if government borrowing drives up interest rates and crowds out private borrowers.
9. If an increase in government spending is financed by higher taxes, the taxes reduce the impact of fiscal policy. Financing government spending by printing money makes it hard to separate the effects of fiscal and monetary policy.

New Terms

transmission mechanism
money multiplier
monetary base
GNP targeting
monetary rule
The Accord
free reserves
credit crunch
accommodating monetary policy

Questions for Discussion

1. The monetarist transmission mechanism accepts "spend it" as the explanation of what happens to an increase in the money supply. The Keynesian transmission mechanism follows the "lend it" route. Explain the difference.
2. If $MPC = 0.75$, what change in Y would occur if i decreased from 20 percent to 15 percent? Use Figure 3 to determine your answer.
3. Let $i = 15$ percent and $MPC = 0.9$. Further, suppose the economy is in equilibrium and $Y = \$2,000$ billion. If $Y^* = \$2,200$ billion, what change in i would be necessary to bring the economy to the full-employment level of national income? Use Figure 3 to determine your answer.
4. Let B be $200 billion. If m is 3 and then rises to 3.2, what is the change in M_s? What is the dollar change in M_s if B rises from $200 billion to $225 billion, and m is constant at 3?
5. Why do Keynesians think that monetary policy is

likely to be less effective than fiscal policy?

6. If money demand is sensitive to changes in interest rates and investment demand is not, how would that affect the relative effectiveness of monetary and fiscal policy? What if money demand is not sensitive to interest rate changes but investment demand is?

7. Why can't the Fed control both the money supply and interest rates at the same time? Discuss the advantages and disadvantages of each target.

8. Which sectors are most affected by changes in monetary policy? Why?

9. How might each of the following have differed if the Fed had been following a 4 percent monetary growth rule?
   a. the 1936–1937 recession (during the Depression)
   b. the postwar interest rate agreement with the Treasury
   c. the 1966 credit crunch

10. If you were in charge of the Fed and concerned about inflation, would you pursue an interest rate target or a money supply target? Why?

11. Why can't both velocity and the expenditure multiplier be stable at the same time? If the demand for money is sensitive to interest rates, how is velocity affected?

12. If the government is pursuing an expansionary fiscal policy, which of the following conditions will make that policy more effective and which will make it less effective? Why?
   a. Money demand is very sensitive to interest rates.
   b. Investment demand is very sensitive to interest rates.
   c. Monetary policy is accommodating.

13. If the Fed is pursuing an expansionary monetary policy, which of the following conditions will make that policy more effective and which will make it less effective? Why?
   a. Money demand is very sensitive to interest rates.
   b. Investment demand is very sensitive to interest rates.
   c. Fiscal policy is also expansionary.

14. If the government tries to increase the level of output by increasing G, what difference does it make how that increase is financed?

15. According to Barro, why should the financing method in Question 14 make no difference?

SUGGESTIONS FOR FURTHER READING

Burns, Arthur. *The Anguish of Central Banking*. Washington, DC: American Enterprise Institute for Public Policy Research, 1980. Monograph on monetary policy by a former chair of the Board of Governors.

Federal Reserve Bank of St. Louis. *Review*. Published six times yearly. Follows the Keynesian-monetarist debate closely, from a strongly monetarist perspective.

Friedman, Milton, and Walter Heller. *Monetary versus Fiscal Policy*. New York: W. W. Norton, 1969. A classic debate by two influential economists.

Greider, William. *Secrets of the Temple: How the Federal Reserve Runs the Country*. New York: Simon and Schuster, 1987. A critical and highly controversial look at how the Fed has conducted monetary policy in recent years.

Mayer, Thomas, James S. Duesenberry, and Robert Z. Aliber. *Money, Banking and the Economy*, 4th ed. New York: W. W. Norton, 1990. Chapters 20 through 25 offer a thorough evaluation of recent monetary policy.

AFTER STUDYING THIS CHAPTER, YOU SHOULD BE ABLE TO:

1. Discuss how decisions made by individuals may lead to undesirable aggregate outcomes.
2. Describe the shape of the Phillips curve and explain what makes it shift.
3. Describe the stagflation of the 1970s and the challenge it posed to both Keynesian and monetarist models.
4. Define:
   a. the natural rate of unemployment,
   b. demand-pull inflation,
   c. cost-push inflation.
5. Evaluate the Post-Keynesian policy of wage and price controls as a method for dealing with stagflation.
6. Identify the major differences among the six schools of macroeconomic thought.

CHAPTER 15

INFLATION AND UNEMPLOYMENT: CHALLENGES TO DEMAND MANAGEMENT

INTRODUCTION

Thomas Schelling, a Harvard economist, has developed some very creative approaches to analyzing the aggregate results of individual choices. In one of his many books on this subject, *Micromotives and Macrobehavior*, he offers a wide range of examples of the unfortunate effects when individuals make choices without considering the choices of others.[1] His examples include choosing seats at a concert, picking a route when commuting to work, and buying or selling a house in a racially mixed neighborhood. The outcomes are likely to be an empty front section at a concert, overcrowding on some roads and little use of others, or panic selling and housing segregation. Schelling shows that outcomes are usually less satisfactory for everyone than would be the case if individuals were somehow able to devise strategies to cope with the effects of interdependence.

Consider, for example, what might happen in an economy where everyone had pessimistic expectations and decided to save more as a hedge against recession. With such expectations, it is likely that some of the added savings would not be reinvested. As a result of increased saving (and lower consumption), demand and income would both fall. Increased planned saving would be offset by less actual, or realized, saving out of lower income. (This effect is the paradox of thrift discussed in an earlier chapter.) Fear of recession and a self-interested response to that fear would help to cause a recession.

If a group is small enough—such as a family, a club, a small town, or a class—its members are aware of their interdependence. Their individual contributions to an outcome are each large enough to make a difference. As a group gets larger, however, it matters less what any one person does because each has such a small effect on the aggregate outcome. Thus, individuals make self-interested decisions without considering the effects of interdependence. The outcome may be unsatisfactory for everyone.

This problem of an aggregate outcome that is unsatisfactory to every-

---

1. Thomas Schelling, *Micromotives and Macrobehavior* (New York: W. W. Norton, 1978).

one, or at least to a majority, is the central concern of macroeconomics. The sum of individual and collective decisions can lead to a rate of inflation and a level of unemployment that few people find satisfactory. Citizens call on government to offset the effects of these choices and to provide a better outcome. The demand management (fiscal and monetary) policies discussed in the last eight chapters suggested some ways to act collectively through government in order to offset some of the undesirable effects of self-interested private decisions.

We began our discussion of macroeconomics by identifying three important macroeconomic goals: economic growth, price stability, and full employment. We can complete our discussion of price stability and full employment (and their mirror images, inflation and unemployment) at this point, because both of these goals are closely linked to demand management. (Economic growth is closely linked to aggregate supply, so we will discuss that goal in the next two chapters.)

Until this point, we have looked at demand management policies under the assumption that policy makers had a clear sense of direction, either to reduce unemployment or to contain inflation. In this chapter, we consider some of the problems of using either monetary or fiscal policy during a period of stagflation, when inflation rates and unemployment rates are both high. We will also look at wage and price controls as an alternative policy tool to contain inflation without creating unemployment. Finally, we will conclude our discussion of demand management policies by looking again at the various schools of macroeconomic thought. Although each group has a slightly different approach, they basically fall into two camps. One group, consisting of Keynesians and Post-Keynesians, believes that the actions of the private sector (households and business firms) lead to unsatisfactory outcomes that must be corrected by government. The other group, which consists of the descendants of the classical school (the monetarists, new classical economists, and supply siders), believes that correction can be left to market forces. Both groups may agree that outcomes are unsatisfactory at any given moment. However, the first group calls for corrective action, and the second group relies on existing corrective forces.

STAGFLATION AND THE PHILLIPS CURVE

According to the simple Keynesian model, too low a level of aggregate planned expenditure results in unemployment. When aggregate planned expenditure is too high, relative to full-employment output (Y^*), the result is inflation. In this model, it is not possible to experience both inflation and unemployment at the same time. The stagflation of the 1970s presented a major challenge to Keynesian thinking.

The monetarist model is somewhat better suited to describing stagflation. In this model, inflation results when the money supply grows faster than real output. During the 1960s, monetarists developed an explanation of the relationship between inflation and unemployment called the natural rate hypothesis. The stimulus for this work came from a diagram describing the historical relationship between changes in wages (or price level changes) and changes in unemployment. That diagram was

Chapter 15 Inflation and Unemployment 401

developed by British economist A. W. Phillips. Later work by Edmund Phelps, who explained Phillips's results using the natural rate hypothesis, contradicted the prevailing Keynesian view of the inflation-unemployment relationship. These new approaches were used by economists to explain the stagflation of the 1970s.

IS THERE AN UNEMPLOYMENT-INFLATION TRADEOFF?

The simple Keynesian model is based on a horizontal aggregate supply curve. The more general version of the Keynesian model uses a composite aggregate supply curve with a horizontal region at low levels of output and an upward-curving region where the economy approaches full employment. At that point, the aggregate supply curve becomes vertical. With such a composite aggregate supply curve, as shown in Figure 1, a movement of the aggregate demand curve from AD_1 to AD_2 increases output (and employment) with no change in the price level. A shift from AD_3 to AD_4 drives up prices with no change in output. A shift from AD_2 to AD_3 increases output (and employment) and the price level.

When economists look for an explanation of the relationship between unemployment and inflation, they usually begin with the aggregate supply and demand curves, which determine output and the price level. Changes in employment and unemployment are very closely linked to changes in production, or real output. The inflation rate is a measure of the rate of change in the price level.

It is important to distinguish between a one-time change in the price level and inflation. A sustained and continuous rise in the price level is inflation. The aggregate supply and demand model explains the price level, not the inflation rate. It takes a single shift in aggregate supply or aggregate demand to change the price level. There must be continuous shifts to produce sustained inflation.

In the 1950s and 1960s, economists generally believed that there was a consistent negative relationship between the inflation rate and the unem-

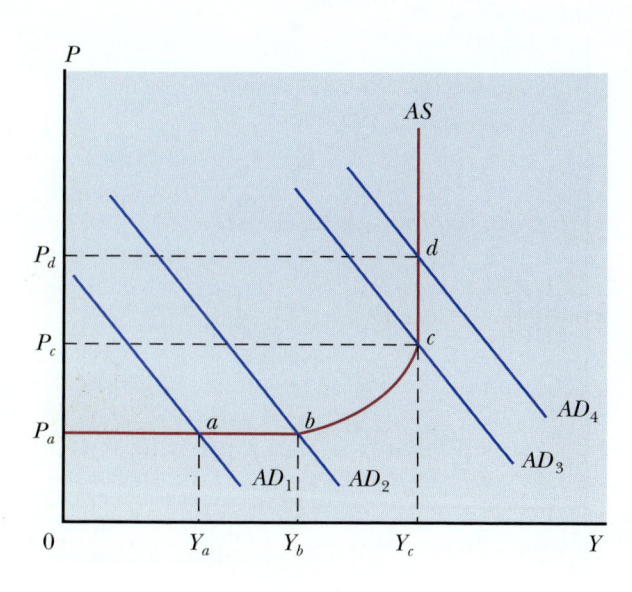

FIGURE 1
AGGREGATE DEMAND AND AGGREGATE SUPPLY: A COMPOSITE VIEW
When aggregate demand shifts in the range from Y_a to Y_b (from AD_1 to AD_2), only output and employment rise. Prices are unchanged. From Y_b to Y_c, further rightward shifts in aggregate demand (to AD_3) increase both prices and output (and employment). Beyond Y_c, rightward shifts in aggregate demand (to AD_4) only drive up the price level.

ployment rate. That kind of relationship between inflation and unemployment is shown in Figure 2. The vertical axis measures the inflation rate, and the horizontal axis measures the unemployment rate. The curve in Figure 2 corresponds closely to the composite aggregate supply curve in Figure 1. The zero inflation rate and the levels of unemployment at points a' and b' correspond to output levels Y_a and Y_b in Figure 1. These points lie on the horizontal section of the inflation-unemployment tradeoff curve in Figure 2. When aggregate demand shifts from AD_1 to AD_2 in Figure 1, unemployment falls from a' to b' in Figure 2, with no inflation (no change in the price level). A shift to point c in Figure 1 and point c' in Figure 2 means a decline in unemployment but a rise in the price level (or inflation). Output level Y_c in Figure 1 is defined as the full-employment level of real output, corresponding to an unemployment rate of 4 percent. This amount of unemployment was generally accepted as the definition of full employment during the 1950s and 1960s.

Note that, according to Figures 1 and 2, increases in the price level and the unemployment rate cannot occur together as a result of shifts in aggregate demand. A rightward shift of the aggregate demand curve will reduce unemployment or raise the price level, or some combination of the two. A leftward shift of the aggregate demand curve will increase unemployment or lower the price level (or the inflation rate), or both.

The actual unemployment and inflation rates for 1961 to 1970 are shown in Figure 3. With one exception, these points seem to lie on or fairly close to a smooth curve, like the one in Figure 2. Until the late 1960s, a relatively stable composite aggregate supply curve, combined with changes in aggregate demand, seemed to offer an accurate description of the relationship between unemployment and inflation. This curve was consistent with the general Keynesian model.

FIGURE 2
INFLATION AND UNEMPLOYMENT WHEN AGGREGATE DEMAND SHIFTS AND AGGREGATE SUPPLY IS STABLE
The inflation and unemployment rates at a', b', c', and d' correspond to the points of intersection of AD_1, AD_2, AD_3, and AD_4 with AS in Figure 1.

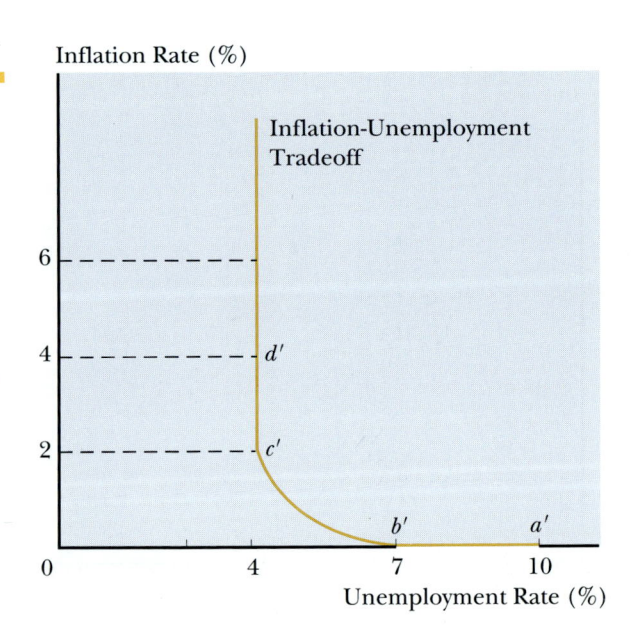

Chapter 15 Inflation and Unemployment

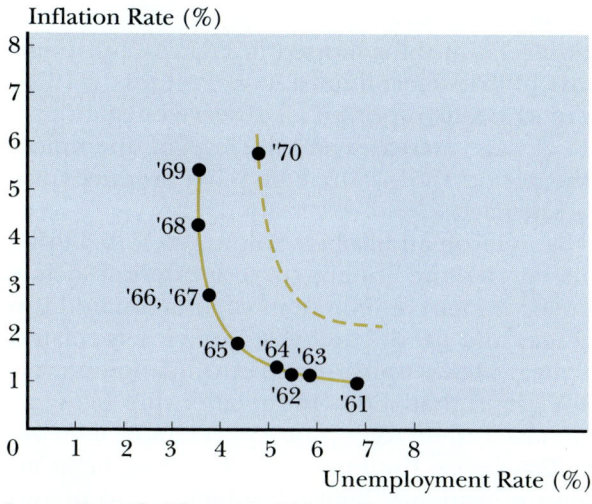

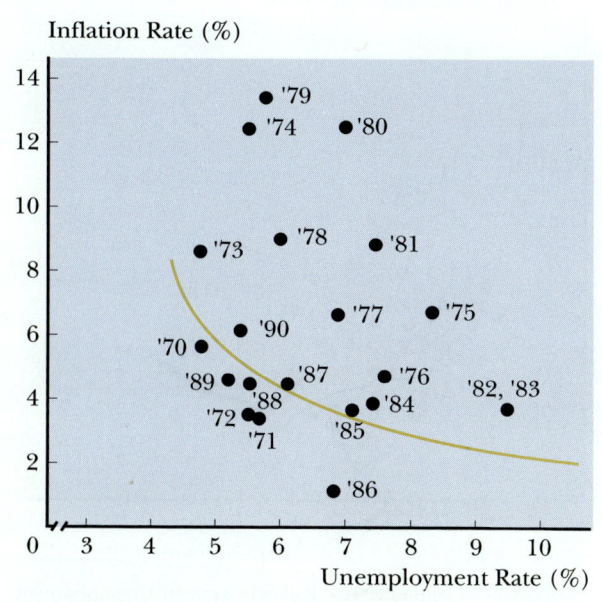

**FIGURE 3
INFLATION AND UNEMPLOYMENT IN THE U.S. ECONOMY, 1961–1970**
The data for this period seem to show a consistent negative inflation-unemployment relationship, except for 1970. Later evidence suggested a shift to the right of the Phillips curve beginning in 1970 (the dashed line).

Source: Council of Economic Advisers, *Economic Report of the President* (Washington, DC: U.S. Government Printing Office, 1982).

Figure 4 plots the unemployment and inflation rates for 1970 to 1989. Note that a negative relationship between the two rates is not apparent here. In fact, during the late 1970s, inflation and unemployment seemed to have a positive relationship. Most observers attribute the change in the relationship between inflation and unemployment to shifts in the aggregate supply curve. By the 1980s, aggregate supply seemed to have stabilized somewhat, restoring the inflation-unemployment link. However, the relationship was still not as close and consistent as it was two decades earlier.

**FIGURE 4
INFLATION AND UNEMPLOYMENT IN THE U.S. ECONOMY, 1970–1990**
The data for this period seem to suggest a much less consistent relationship between unemployment and inflation than in earlier periods. Most observers attribute the lack of a relationship to shifts in aggregate supply. It is possible to trace two patterns, one for the 1970s and one for the period 1982–1990.

Source: Council of Economic Advisers, *Economic Report of the President* (Washington, DC: U.S. Government Printing Office, 1991).

THE DEVELOPMENT OF THE PHILLIPS CURVE

The unemployment-inflation relationships plotted in Figures 2 through 4 had their origin in the work of British economist A. W. Phillips. In 1958, Phillips published a paper in which he reported an observed negative relationship between the rate of wage increases and the level of unemployment in Great Britain for the period 1861–1913. Figure 5 reproduces one of the graphs from Phillips's article.

In the early 1960s, Paul Samuelson and Robert Solow, two Nobel Prize winners in economics, reinterpreted the Phillips curve as offering society a choice, or tradeoff, between various combinations of inflation and unemployment. Since both wages and production costs are closely related to prices, Phillips's original diagram was transformed into an inflation versus unemployment curve. A graph that shows the relationship between the rates of inflation and unemployment for a country over a specified period of years is called a **Phillips curve**. Phillips curves have also been interpreted as offering a menu of tradeoffs between inflation and unemployment. For example, along the Phillips curve in Figure 5, a society could opt for low unemployment such as that at point A and pay the price of rapid increases in prices. On the other hand, it could keep price increases low, as at point B, at the cost of higher unemployment.

Phillips presented evidence suggesting that a tradeoff existed between inflation and unemployment, but he offered no theoretical explanation. Early explanations for the Phillips curve focused on how changing conditions in the labor market influenced prices. When aggregate demand is increasing, business firms expand output and increase employment. As

Phillips curve
A graph showing the relationship between the rates of inflation and unemployment for a country over a specified period of years.

FIGURE 5
A PHILLIPS CURVE
This Phillips curve was created by A. W. Phillips with data for Great Britain from 1861 to 1957. Note the negative relationship between the rate of change of nominal wages and the unemployment rate. The curve is not very steep at high rates of unemployment (say, 10 percent) but is quite steep at low rates of unemployment (say, 1 percent). Thus, reducing employment from 10 percent to 9 percent would not cost much in extra wage inflation, but reducing unemployment from 2 percent to 1 percent would result in a lot of extra wage inflation.

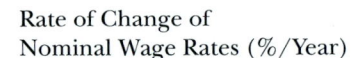

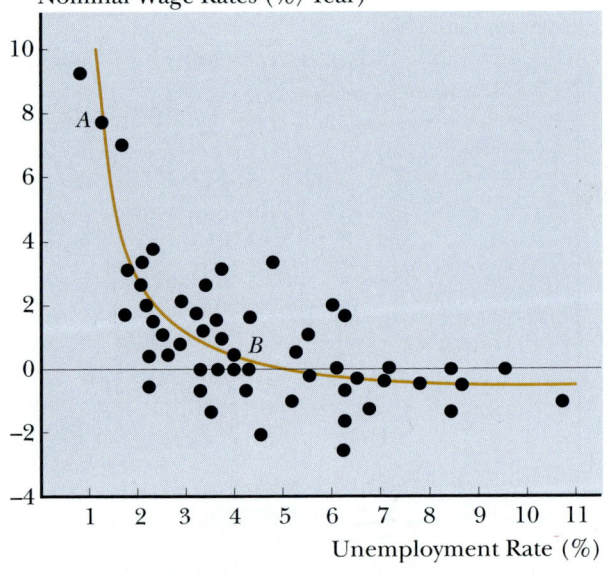

Source: A. W. Phillips, "The Relation between Unemployment and the Rate of Change of Money Wage Rates in the United Kingdom, 1861–1957," *Economica* 25 (1958): 283–300.

the unemployment rate falls, the labor market becomes tighter. It becomes increasingly difficult to hire qualified workers at the prevailing wage rates. Business firms must, therefore, offer higher wages to attract new workers. Because aggregate demand is increasing, those higher wages can be passed along to consumers in the form of higher prices. Thus, falling unemployment rates are associated with continuous increases in the wage rate and the price level, or inflation.

THE PHILLIPS CURVE IN THE 1960s. In the 1960s, the idea that the Phillips curve represented a menu of choices for economic policy makers was reinforced by the behavior of inflation and unemployment rates. Take another look at Figure 3, which is a Phillips curve for the U.S. economy using unemployment and inflation data for 1961–1970. Recall that the 1964 Kennedy tax cut was intended to reduce the unemployment rate. As Figure 3 shows, from 1965 through 1969, lower unemployment rates were traded for higher inflation rates. This choice of a specific unemployment-inflation target at which fiscal policy could be directed was called "fine tuning" the economy during the Kennedy-Johnson years.

SHIFTS IN THE PHILLIPS CURVE. In 1970, the U.S. economy moved to a higher level of unemployment and a higher rate of inflation, as you can see in Figure 3. One explanation for this unexpected change was that something had caused the tradeoff between unemployment and inflation to worsen. That is, the Phillips curve had shifted to the right (the dashed line in Figure 3). Early explanations for this shift of the Phillips curve focused on random supply shocks and changes in the makeup of the labor force. Several supply shocks affected the U.S. economy in the early 1970s, increasing the price level without lowering the unemployment rate. These shocks included the devaluation of the dollar with respect to other currencies in 1971 and again in 1973 and the series of dramatic increases in the price of OPEC oil beginning in 1973. Although these shocks affected both aggregate demand and aggregate supply, we will focus on the effects on aggregate supply.

Devaluation meant that the dollar bought fewer units of foreign currency. As a result, the dollar price of imports increased.[2] Higher import prices contributed to general price increases in the economy. Because the physical volume of imports declined very little, however, there was no reduction in the unemployment rate. The rise in oil prices had an even wider effect on the U.S. economy. Gasoline prices quadrupled between 1973 and 1980. In addition, because petroleum and its derivatives are used for many other purposes, including heating and as raw materials, rapidly rising prices for imported oil set off price increases throughout the economy.[3]

---

2. For example, suppose that a German exporter sold Volkswagen vans for 32,000 DM (Deutsche Marks). At an exchange rate of $1 for 4 DM, a U.S. importer could have purchased a van for resale in the United States for $8,000. If $1 bought only 3 DM after devaluation, the U.S. importer would have to pay $10,666 for the same van.
3. The opposite effect occurred in the 1980s. A sharp drop in the price of crude oil from about $35 to under $15 a barrel appeared to shift the aggregate supply curve to the right and contributed to the drop in the inflation rate.

International Perspective

Inflation and Unemployment in Eastern Europe

With the move away from command economies in Eastern Europe, one of the most striking developments has been the emergence of both inflation and unemployment as serious macroeconomic problems. In Poland, for example, the early months of 1990 saw a 70 percent rise in the price level, along with a sharp decline in wages and rising unemployment. What has happened? Did the restructuring of these economies toward greater decentralization and use of markets shift the aggregate supply curve back to the right, resulting in severe stagflation?

No. The stagflation in Eastern Europe can be interpreted in an aggregate supply and demand framework, but not as a sudden decrease in aggregate supply at the time of the change. For many years, the economies of Eastern Europe suffered from repressed inflation and disguised unemployment. An inefficient system of production failed to produce enough output to keep pace with the normal growth of aggregate demand. When aggregate demand exceeds aggregate supply at a given price level, the price level is normally expected to rise. However, price controls in Eastern European countries kept the price level from rising. Instead, there was a chronic gap between aggregate supply and aggregate demand at the artificially low price level maintained by the state. That gap showed up as empty shelves, chronic shortages of consumer goods, long lines, and long waiting lists for telephones, apartments, and other goods and services. When prices were allowed to adjust, they rose quickly. As output begins to expand under a more efficient system, prices should stabilize. In the meantime, shelves are full again at the higher, more realistic prices.

The rising unemployment in Eastern Europe also represents a surfacing of what used to be disguised. The Communist governments guaranteed a job and a paycheck for everyone who was able and willing to work. Those workers were not necessarily productive, however. (A standing joke in Eastern Europe went like this: "The government pretends to pay us, and we pretend to work.") Incentives to work and to manage and use workers effectively were missing because of the lack of market signals. Now that some production is being privatized, most of the new owners and managers get to choose how many workers to employ and what to pay them. They may even be allowed to fire those who do not earn their keep.

Many Eastern Europeans are fearful about the transition to a market-based economy where there is no job security. The tradeoff between a higher standard of living and job security is one that workers in market-based economies have always faced. It is one of the costs of a productive market system.

Total spending on imports increased, resulting in a fall in net exports ($EX - IM$) and a leftward shift of the aggregate demand curve. According to the Keynesian model, this reduction in total spending should have resulted in a decrease in national income and output and an increase in unemployment. The increase in oil prices clearly had price effects as well as output effects. Those price changes could not be accounted for in a simple Keynesian framework.

Price increases resulting from random economic shocks cause the inflation rate associated with any given unemployment rate to be higher than before the shocks. That is, the Phillips curve shifts to the right, and the aggregate supply curve shifts to the left. Such shifts are depicted in Figure 6. Point A represents the inflation-unemployment combination on the Phillips curve in part (b), corresponding to point A' on the aggregate supply curve in part (a) prior to the random shocks. Point B is the inflation-unemployment combination after the shocks. The movement from A to B implies a shift in the Phillips curve from PC_1 to PC_2. Thus, random economic shocks provide one plausible explanation for why the Phillips curve shifted in the 1970s.

Another explanation for the higher unemployment rates and inflation rates in the 1970s focuses on the changing makeup of the U.S. labor force. From 1960 to 1980, the proportion of women and young people in the labor force rose significantly. These new and less experienced workers had higher unemployment rates and also increased the size of the labor force as a fraction of the total population. Thus, the unemployment rate rose relative to the level of output, because of the changing makeup of the labor force. In this case, higher rates of unemployment will be observed at each inflation rate. In contrast, the explanation based on random shocks suggested a higher inflation rate at each unemployment rate. In both cases, however, the Phillips curve shifts up and to the right.

THE INSIDER-OUTSIDER MODEL AND THE PHILLIPS CURVE. Another explanation of the worsening inflation-unemployment tradeoff received considerable

FIGURE 6
SHIFTS IN AGGREGATE SUPPLY AND THE PHILLIPS CURVE
When aggregate supply shifts to the left, as in part (a), it is possible to have rising prices and rising unemployment at the same time. This outcome is depicted as a shift in the Phillips curve in part (b) from PC_1 to PC_2. Points A' and B' correspond to points A and B.

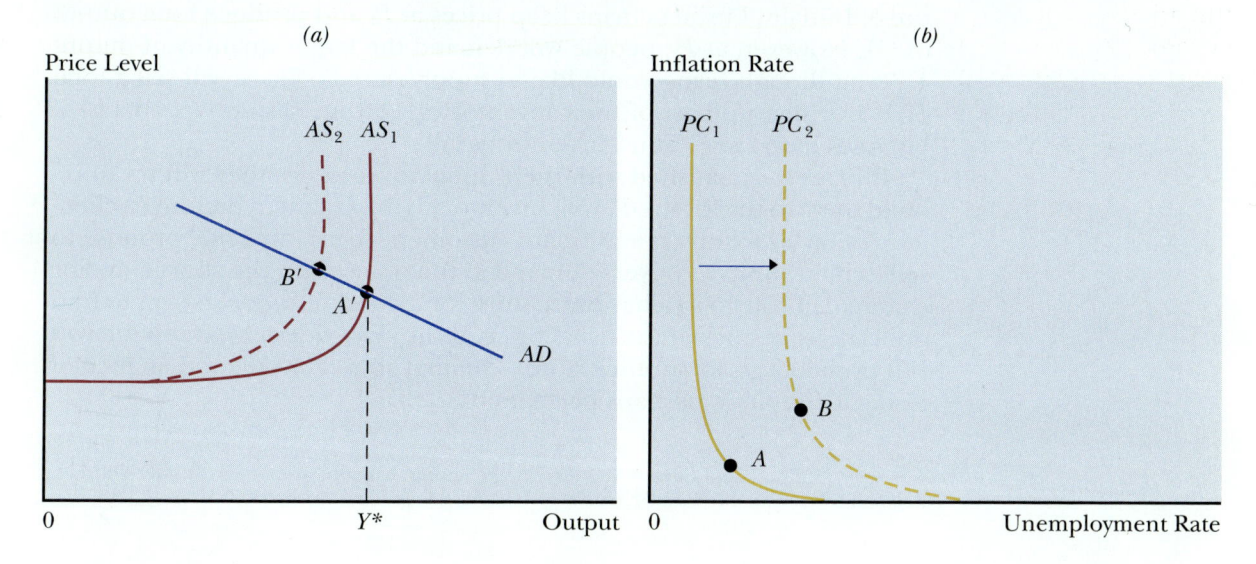

insider-outsider model
An explanation of labor market behavior that assumes that insiders (employed union members) will negotiate for higher real wages for themselves at the expense of jobs for outsiders, thus worsening the inflation-unemployment tradeoff.

attention in the 1980s. This model is based on the power of insiders (employed union members) relative to outsiders (nonunion members).[4] The **insider-outsider model** rests on the assumption that, with a union, those already employed (insiders) will bargain for a higher wage even at the expense of employment for those on the outside. During economic downturns, some workers are laid off and become outsiders. When economic activity increases, insiders will bargain for a higher real wage in preference to more jobs. If this kind of bargaining is widespread, the upturn in economic activity will be accompanied by more inflation and less reduction in unemployment than would otherwise be the case. The insider-outsider model is in the Keynesian and Post-Keynesian tradition of market power and market imperfections. It offers an explanation for stagflation that was missing in the simpler Keynesian model.

CRITICISMS OF THE PHILLIPS CURVE

Some economists were dissatisfied with all of these explanations for the worsening tradeoff between unemployment and inflation. Monetarists, in particular, were skeptical about whether there really was a stable tradeoff between unemployment and inflation and a resulting menu of policy choices. They countered with another view of the Phillips curve, developed by Milton Friedman in his presidential address to the American Economic Association in 1967. Friedman argued that any tradeoff was purely short run, that no real tradeoff between inflation and unemployment existed in the long run. The basis of Friedman's argument lay in expectations. To understand his criticism, we need to look closely at the role of expectations in determining the response to a change in aggregate demand.

CORRECT VERSUS MISTAKEN EXPECTATIONS

Suppose the government attempts to reduce unemployment by increasing the money supply. The increase in the money supply shifts the demand for output to the right, as shown by the shift from AD_1 to AD_2 in Figure 7. Initially, business firms keep prices at P_1 and produce total output of Y_1. However, at P_1, people will demand the larger quantity of output Y_2, even though firms would like to supply only Y_1. Firms will sell a total of Y_2 by using up part of their inventories. Output has not yet changed, but sales have risen. Thus, inventories fall.

If firms were satisfied with their initial inventories, they will try to rebuild them to that desired level. Inventory is important in building a clientele. In order to attract and retain customers, firms implicitly promise to sell as many units as buyers demand at the price set in the short run. For example, if you go to a hardware store for a doorknob, you expect to find doorknobs in stock at the usual price. If the store doesn't have them, you will probably go to another store. The first store runs a good chance of losing a customer, perhaps permanently.

---

4. Assar Lindbeck and Dennis Snower, "Wage Setting, Unemployment and Insider-Outsider Relations," *American Economic Review Papers and Proceedings* (May 1986): 235–239.

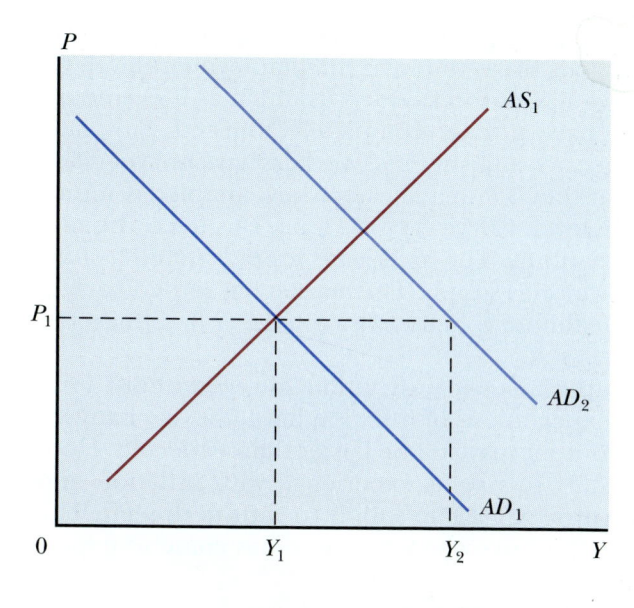

FIGURE 7
EXPANSIONARY FISCAL POLICY SHIFTS THE AGGREGATE DEMAND CURVE
When government spending increases, there is a shift in aggregate demand. At the old price level, firms sell Y_2 units, but only Y_1 units are produced. The unplanned reduction in inventories induces producers to expand output. Increased demand for inputs puts upward pressure on prices.

When demand shifts to the right, as in Figure 7, many firms will experience falling inventories. They will order new inventories from their suppliers or begin to produce more themselves. Output will start to rise. Prices will also start to rise. Any business firm that holds its prices at P_1 will find inventory falling steadily. As firms replenish their inventories by buying more inputs or semi-finished goods, they find themselves competing for limited supplies. Market forces drive up the prices of inputs. Suppliers will be charging higher prices. The aggregate supply curve will start to shift to the left, from AS_1 to AS_2 in Figure 8.

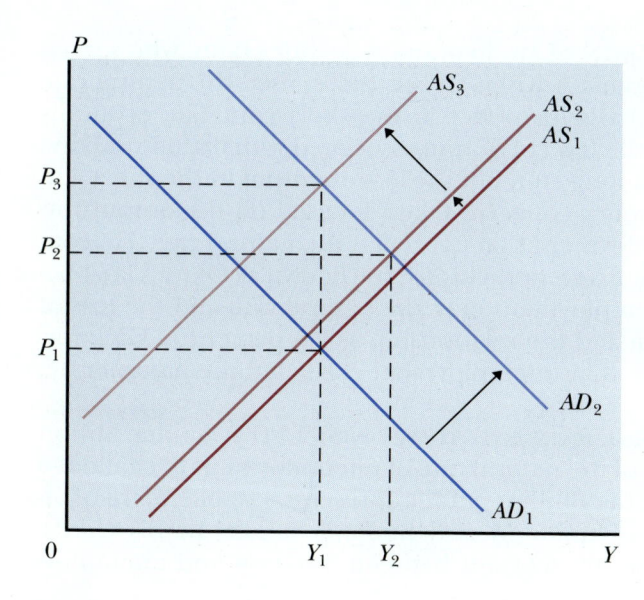

FIGURE 8
AGGREGATE SUPPLY SHIFTS WITH INFLATION
As sellers respond to higher demand with more output and higher prices, the price level rises to P_2. Y_2 is beyond the long-run productive capacity of the economy. Competition for resources continues to drive up prices until the short-run aggregate supply curve reaches AS_3. There it intersects the aggregate demand curve at the full-employment level of output, Y_1, and the new higher price level, P_3.

In Figure 8, the quantity of real output demanded at a higher equilibrium price level, P_2, exceeds the economy's full-employment level, Y_1. The aggregate supply curve has not shifted left as much as it eventually will because expectations have not yet completely adjusted. Suppliers have not yet made their full price adjustments. Workers have not yet made the full wage demands that they will make when they completely anticipate the new, higher price level. Curve AS_3 in Figure 8 reflects the ultimate equilibrium of the economy. The aggregate supply curve has fully adjusted to the new, higher money supply. The market has settled back to the initial output (Y_1), but the new, higher price level (P_3) reflects the higher money supply.

It might well be that output first expands, as in Figure 7, without a rise in the price level because expectations of inflation have not yet changed. For some time, aggregate output may still be larger than expected. However, the price level will start to rise as experience with inflation and inflationary expectations cause aggregate supply to shift to the left. The final equilibrium in Figure 8 occurs when everyone has come to expect the new, higher price level.

THE NATURAL RATE OF UNEMPLOYMENT

Another attack on the Phillips curve was based on the idea of a natural rate of unemployment. The **natural rate of unemployment** is the rate of unemployment determined by frictional and structural factors. It is the rate toward which the economy tends to return. The natural rate of unemployment corresponds (approximately) to the structural and frictional unemployment discussed in Chapter 4. These kinds of unemployment are due to changes in the number, location, and job skills of people in the labor force and to changes in the demand for labor. For example, if the demand for aluminum workers increases and the demand for steelworkers falls, there will be temporary unemployment while workers shift from one industry to another. The full-employment level of output, Y^*, is the level corresponding to the natural rate of unemployment.

natural rate of unemployment
The rate of unemployment that is determined by frictional and structural factors and toward which the economy tends to return.

THE NATURAL RATE AND OKUN'S LAW. Economist Arthur Okun, who served on the Council of Economic Advisers in the 1960s, used the natural rate of unemployment as a basis for policy in the short run. The economy might indeed return to the level of output associated with the natural rate of unemployment in the long run, but the loss of output in the short run represented a serious policy concern. Okun focused on the output forgone in spells of unemployment that exceeded the natural rate. He concluded that there was a consistent relationship (known as Okun's law) between the excess of unemployment over the natural rate and the loss of potential GNP. He estimated the relationship as 2.5 percent of GNP forgone for every 1 percent that unemployment exceeded the natural rate.

FRIEDMAN AND THE NATURAL RATE HYPOTHESIS. Nobel Prize winner Milton Friedman used the idea of the natural rate of unemployment to challenge the Keynesian view that the Phillips curve represents a stable menu of attainable combinations of inflation and unemployment. In his words, "There is always a temporary tradeoff between inflation and unemployment; there is no permanent tradeoff."[5] Friedman stated that there may be a short-run tradeoff between inflation and unemployment because of mistaken expectations, but in the long run the Phillips curve is vertical at the natural rate of unemployment.

Friedman argued that workers' expectations about inflation influence their decisions in the labor market. Those decisions in turn collectively determine the level of employment and wage rates. The short-run tradeoff between inflation and unemployment will exist only if the actual inflation rate turns out to be different from what workers expected it to be. If inflation is fully anticipated (as it is more likely to be in the long run), no tradeoff will occur. The current rate of unemployment might change in the short run in response to monetary and fiscal policies, but the natural rate of unemployment would not be affected.

Workers' expectations are not the only reason why policy actions may be more effective in the short run than in the long run. Consider a discretionary fiscal policy action, such as an increase in government spending to reduce the unemployment rate. The resulting rightward shift of the aggregate demand curve causes temporary shortages at the current price level. Excess aggregate demand begins to pull the price level upward. Rising prices result in rising profits for business firms, which respond by increasing output. In order to produce more output, more workers must be hired. The newly employed workers take jobs at the prevailing wage rate. Even though prices have begun to rise, wage rates do not respond at once to the changed conditions. The price increases are initially perceived as changes in particular prices, not in the general price level. Even after people recognize that there is an increase in the general price level, wages are slow to adjust because many wage rates are determined by contracts that are renegotiated only once every two or three years. There is some lag between rising prices and the upward adjustment of wage rates. This lag allows firms to earn more profits.

Thus, in the short run, unemployment declines and the inflation rate rises, as the Phillips curve suggests. By increasing spending, the government buys a reduction in the unemployment rate at the cost of an increase in the inflation rate. But, Friedman argues, the new inflation-unemployment combination is not stable. The decline in the unemployment rate is achieved only because workers expect no inflation. Workers will eventually realize that prices in general have risen and are continuing to rise, reducing the purchasing power of their wages. They will adjust their expectations about inflation and demand higher wages to restore the purchasing power of their earnings. Higher wages will cut business profits back to their original levels. Business firms will reduce output to the old level at the new higher price level, and the unemployment rate will rise to its original level. If aggregate demand is maintained at the new, higher level by expansionary fiscal policy and continued growth in the money supply, the economy will remain at the new, higher inflation rate. Unemployment will remain at the natural rate. These rates represent a stable combination of inflation and unemployment because they are based on expected and actual inflation being the same.

---

5. Milton Friedman, "The Role of Monetary Policy," *American Economic Review* (May 1968): 1–15.

Friedman concluded that after all adjustments to inflation are complete and the labor market is in equilibrium, unemployment will return to the natural rate. The inflation rate can be at any level, depending on whether aggregate demand continues to shift to the right. Thus, in the long run, the Phillips curve will be vertical at the natural rate of unemployment.

THE NATURAL RATE, AGGREGATE DEMAND, AND AGGREGATE SUPPLY. The natural rate hypothesis can also be described using aggregate supply and aggregate demand curves. In Figure 9, the economy is initially in equilibrium at point A, at output level Y_1 and price level P_1. Again, no inflation is expected. Assume the government wishes to increase output to Y_2 in order to reduce unemployment from, say, 6 percent to 4 percent. Expansionary fiscal policy shifts the aggregate demand curve from AD_1 to AD_2. Both real output (Y) and the price level (P) rise as the economy moves to point B.

However, the upward slope of the short-run aggregate supply curve, AS_1, is based on incorrect expectations about inflation. Workers are willing to supply more labor and firms more output only because they do not realize that the higher wages and prices are general, rather than specific to their labor or their product. Once workers realize that the price level as a whole is rising and the purchasing power of their wages is falling, they will demand higher nominal wages. Costs will rise, eroding the temporary profits of business firms. As the cost-profit relationship returns to its original level, firms will want to produce the same real output at the new higher prices, represented as a shift in the short-run aggregate supply curve from AS_1 to AS_2.

At the new equilibrium, at point C in Figure 9, output has returned to the old level, Y_1, corresponding to the natural rate of unemployment, but the price level is higher, at P_3. The economy is once again operating on the long-run vertical aggregate supply curve, AS^{lr}, corresponding to the natural rate of unemployment.

FIGURE 9
AGGREGATE SUPPLY AND DEMAND AND THE NATURAL RATE OF UNEMPLOYMENT
A rightward shift of the aggregate demand curve can temporarily increase employment and output with some rise in prices. Eventually, however, the aggregate supply curve will shift to the left. There will be no long-term increase in output or employment, just higher prices.

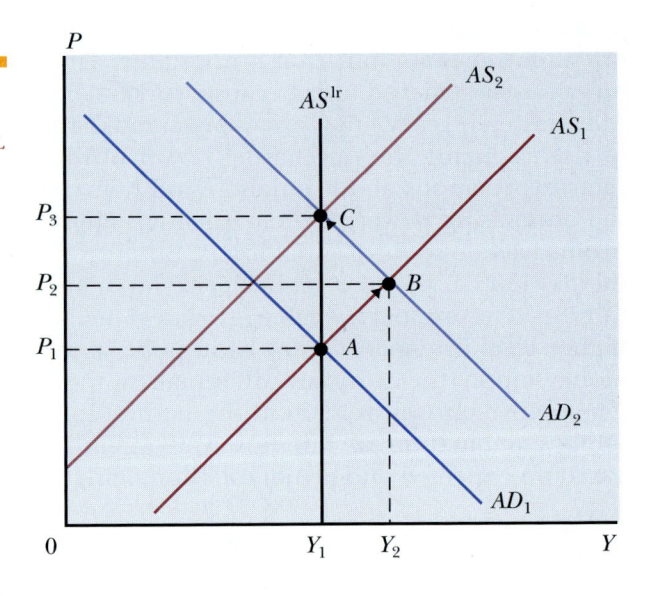

Chapter 15 Inflation and Unemployment 413

If government uses expansionary monetary or fiscal policy again, the same thing will happen. Real output will always return to the full-employment level, Y^*, corresponding to the natural rate of unemployment but at a higher price level. This "Christmas tree" pattern of changes in Y and P is illustrated in Figure 10. The heavy arrows trace the path of output and prices in response to successive doses of expansionary fiscal (or monetary) policy shifting the aggregate demand curve up and to the right. Thus, attempts to reduce unemployment below its natural rate using demand management policies may have temporary success but will ultimately only drive up the price level.

This emphasis on expectations and aggregate supply was developed largely from the ideas of the new classical school about rational expectations. We have discussed those contributions briefly in earlier chapters and will encounter them again in the next chapter when we explore aggregate supply more fully. Both new classical economists and monetarists expect policy actions to affect the price level but not to have much impact on real output in the long run. New classical economists believe that expectations adjust very rapidly and thus the short run is a very brief period of time. In their view, the economy returns very quickly to the long-run aggregate supply curve, on which policy actions will have no effect on real output and employment.

DEMAND-PULL AND COST-PUSH INFLATION

The inflationary process described in the preceding section is the result of shifts in aggregate demand. **Demand-pull inflation** is inflation that

demand-pull inflation
Inflation that starts as a result of a rise in aggregate demand, usually due to expansionary monetary or fiscal policy.

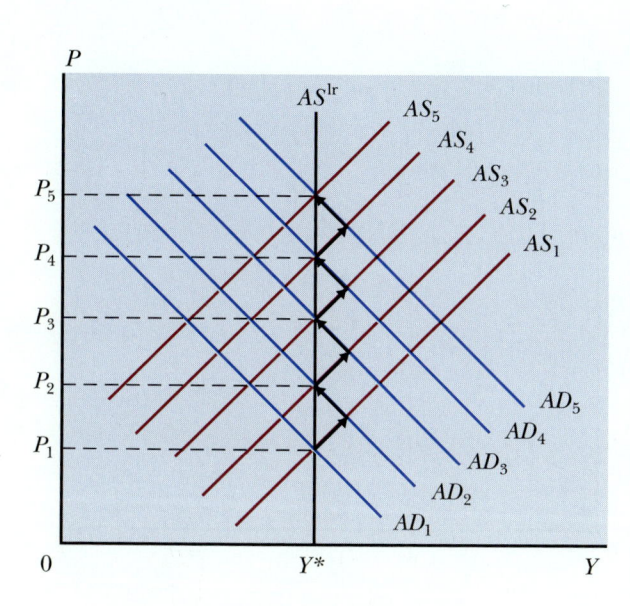

FIGURE 10
THE NATURAL RATE OF UNEMPLOYMENT AND REPEATED SHIFTS IN AGGREGATE DEMAND AND AGGREGATE SUPPLY
The arrows trace a path of shifts of the short-run aggregate demand curve to the right followed by shifts in the aggregate supply curve to the left as workers and other owners of inputs react to higher prices and wages. Output always returns to the level associated with the natural rate of unemployment (Y^*). There is, however, a series of temporary increases in output (and decreases in unemployment) and continued increases in the price level.

starts as a result of a rise in aggregate demand, usually due to expansionary monetary or fiscal policy. Increases in the money supply, which shift the *AD* curve rightward, are one possible source of demand-pull inflation. Expansionary fiscal policy is another, and that's why inflation is often blamed on government deficits. An increase in the federal budget deficit can shift the *AD* curve rightward and set off inflation, although there is no precise link between deficits and inflation. (The record-breaking budget deficits of the 1980s were associated with very low inflation rates.) However, the private sector can also initiate demand-pull inflation if consumers or businesses increase demand. Regardless of how inflation begins, it cannot be sustained for very long without monetary expansion. The velocity of money can't rise indefinitely. There is a limit to how fast money can change hands. So if there is no monetary expansion, demand-pull inflation will eventually grind to a halt.

Another type of inflation is initiated by a rise in costs, which decreases aggregate supply. **Cost-push inflation** is inflation that starts as a result of a leftward shift of the *AS* curve because of wage or price increases. We have already considered some shocks to the economy that had this effect, such as devaluations of the dollar in 1971 and 1973 and the OPEC oil price hikes. Shocks can come from within the economy, too. Unions blame business firms, and business firms blame unions for inflation. Is there any truth to these claims?

Figure 11 illustrates cost-push inflation. Assume that nationwide union contracts have, on the average, resulted in wage increases that are higher than can be justified by increases in productivity. The wage increases raise costs to businesses, and they try to pass these higher costs on to the consumer as higher prices. The resulting shift from AS_1 to AS_2 leads not only to a higher price level (P_2) but to lower output (Y_2), which means higher unemployment.

What happens next depends on the government's response. If policy makers are more upset about the rise in unemployment than the rise in

cost-push inflation
Inflation that starts as a result of a decrease in aggregate supply due to wage or price increases.

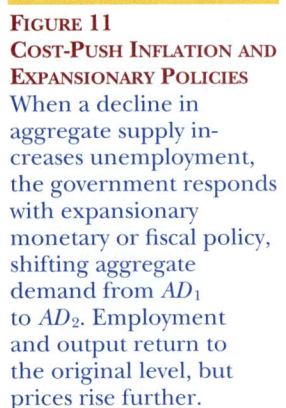

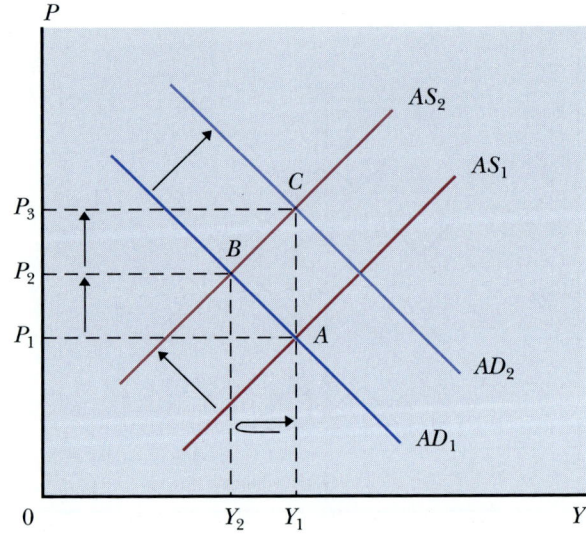

FIGURE 11
COST-PUSH INFLATION AND EXPANSIONARY POLICIES
When a decline in aggregate supply increases unemployment, the government responds with expansionary monetary or fiscal policy, shifting aggregate demand from AD_1 to AD_2. Employment and output return to the original level, but prices rise further.

inflation, they will try to "cure" the unemployment by shifting aggregate demand from AD_1 to AD_2 through expansionary fiscal or monetary policy. This shift will drive up prices further. The unemployment rate will return to where it started as output returns to Y_1. The process may end there, or it may repeat itself. If the process is repeated, with continual expansion of the money supply, stagflation is likely to result.

Sometimes business firms are portrayed as the villains in this drama. They seem to start the process by charging higher prices to their customers. It really doesn't matter how the process gets started. The important thing is that inflation cannot be sustained without expansionary monetary or fiscal policy.

How can you tell if inflation is demand-pull or cost-push? Once it gets started, it's hard to trace its roots. But if you look at Figures 9 through 11, you can see that demand-pull inflation starts with increases in both output (Y) and prices (P), followed by a fall in Y and a further rise in P. On the other hand, cost-push inflation starts with a fall in Y and a rise in P. Only when policy makers respond by shifting aggregate demand does Y go back up and P rise further.

THE POST-KEYNESIANS

The discussion of theoretical and policy approaches to dealing with stagflation has been cast in terms of just two rival views, those of the Keynesians and those of the monetarists. In the 1970s, another school of thought, called Post-Keynesianism, began to attract attention. Post-Keynesians are economists in the Keynesian tradition who believe that market power and institutional rigidity keep macroeconomic markets from arriving at full-employment equilibrium. The primary source of Post-Keynesian ideas was Cambridge University in England. The leading figure in the group was the British economist Joan Robinson (1903–1983), who was a colleague of Keynes.

EFFECTS OF MARKET POWER

When market power is concentrated, Post-Keynesians argue, firms often cut output instead of prices when demand is weak. Cutting output when aggregate demand declines leads to more unemployment rather than a falling price level. When aggregate demand increases, firms with market power are likely to raise prices instead of output. Thus, since prices are flexible upward but not downward, it is possible to experience chronic unemployment along with inflation during periods of expanding demand. This behavior of prices should make demand management policies effective— a very Keynesian conclusion. However, policies to expand demand will reward the powerful firms with higher prices and profits. Post-Keynesians are concerned with the distributional effects of such policies. Expansionary policies appear to benefit monopolistic firms. Contractionary policies put the burden on workers in the form of higher unemployment.

Lester Thurow of the Massachusetts Institute of Technology shares some of the views of the Post-Keynesians on issues such as the role of income distribution, market imperfections, and the importance of economic power in determining the effects of monetary and fiscal policy. He argues that differences in distributional preferences will guarantee disagreement among economists in the near future.[6] He and others believe that the existence of different schools of macroeconomic thought, each holding to different theoretical models and empirical conclusions, is really the result of differences in distributional preferences.

Groups hurt by inflation are different from those hurt by unemployment, although there is some overlap. Those who benefit from active fiscal policy are different from those who benefit from a *laissez faire* approach. Those who gain from supply side policies may or may not overlap with those who benefit from easy or tight monetary policies. Recall that tight monetary policy falls heavily on housing, investment, and industries that export and compete with imports. Supply side policies benefit high-income groups, those making certain favored investments, and entrepreneurs. Benefits to the poor or to average workers may trickle down as the result of increased output, investment, and productivity.

WAGE AND PRICE CONTROLS

Post-Keynesians have made useful contributions to the recent debates on macroeconomic theory and policy. Here we are interested in their approach to stagflation. The focus on market power and income distribution makes the Post-Keynesians the only major school of economic thought to advocate the use of wage and price controls to contain inflation during periods of expanding demand.

Wage and price controls are government-imposed restrictions on increases in prices or wages in order to contain inflation. They were used during World War II, when aggregate demand increased and the United States was hitting the limits of its productive capacity. Most market-oriented economists—monetarists, supply siders, classical and new classical economists, and many Keynesians—are critical of such controls because of the problems they create.

Figure 12 illustrates the problem of controls in the market for a single product. The controlled price, (P_c), is set below equilibrium. The controlled price reduces the quantity supplied from Q_e to Q_s and increases the quantity demanded to Q_d. The result is an excess demand at that price. Market signals are prevented from calling forth an increase in quantity supplied to eliminate the shortage. Instead, the limited supply, Q_s, must be rationed among consumers using lines, coupons, or other means. These methods are less efficient than using prices to determine what mix of goods to produce and to ensure that goods go to those who want them most, measured by the prices they are willing to pay.

During periods of excess demand for goods and services in general, changes still occur in relative demand and supply of particular goods and services. Demand for shoes may increase relative to demand for toothpaste, or the cost of building houses may rise faster than the cost of pro-

wage and price controls
Government-imposed restrictions on increases in prices or wages in order to contain inflation.

---

6. Lester Thurow, *The Zero-Sum Society* (New York: Penguin Books, 1981) and *Dangerous Currents: The State of Economics* (New York: Random House, 1984). Thurow and other U.S. economists in the Keynesian tradition (especially at Harvard and MIT) who do not subscribe to all of the Post-Keynesian views often call themselves New Keynesians.

Chapter 15 Inflation and Unemployment

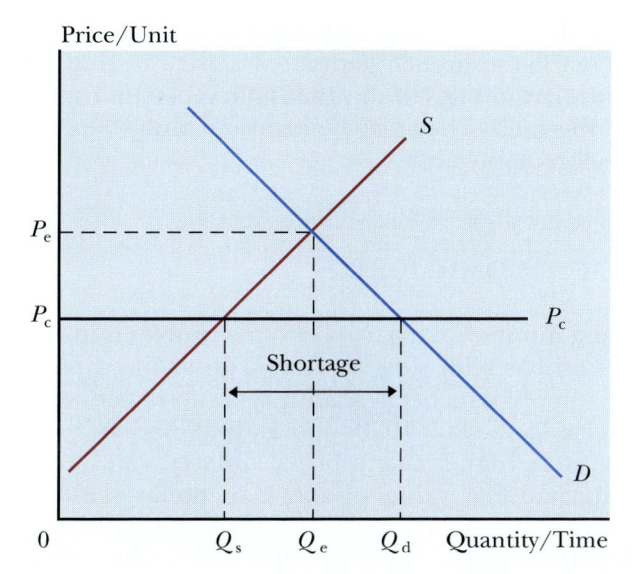

**FIGURE 12
EFFECTS OF WAGE-PRICE CONTROLS**
In the market for an individual product, a price ceiling of P_c reduces quantity supplied from Q_e to Q_s and increases quantity demanded to Q_d. A shortage results.

ducing haircuts. Under controls, the same limits on raising prices (and wages) apply across the board, making relative price adjustments very difficult. This lack of flexibility is a major defect in the use of controls.

Given the drawbacks, why do Post-Keynesians advocate controls? One reason has already been suggested. When government uses demand-expanding policies, the resulting distribution of income may favor the most powerful elements—the largest firms and the strongest unions. Such changes in income distribution can be minimized when wage and price controls are used in conjunction with demand-expansion policies. Post-Keynesians also favor controls when deflationary policies are in effect. Again, distributional effects are part of the reason. However, Post-Keynesians also see controls as having a psychological effect on inflationary expectations. If people observe a lower rate of inflation—which controls will provide, at least for a time—they may revise their expectations more rapidly and speed up the adjustment process.

Probably the most effective criticism of wage and price controls is that they are not a substitute for demand management policies. If demand management policies are expansionary, then controls will merely suppress inflation for a time. If demand management policies are anti-inflationary, they will eventually work with or without controls and without the distortions in market signals that controls create.

In spite of their drawbacks, controls have a great deal of political appeal. They were last used in the United States during the early 1970s by the Nixon administration. Inflation did slow briefly, but monetary and fiscal policy remained expansionary. As soon as the controls were lifted, prices skyrocketed, just as they did after World War II. Controls can be a complement to demand management policies but not a substitute for them.

During the 1970s, some sophisticated approaches to controls were developed that tied allowable increases in prices and wages to tax breaks and penalties and used market incentives to attempt to control price in-

tax-based inflation policy (TIP)
A sophisticated approach to wage and price controls that ties allowable increases in prices and wages to tax breaks and penalties and uses market incentives to attempt to control price increases.

creases. The best known of these plans was called **tax-based inflation policy** (**TIP**). This modified market approach generated a great deal of interest in 1970s. Declining inflation rates in the 1980s put most innovative anti-inflationary ideas on the shelf. They may be revived if and when the inflation rate becomes unacceptably high.

THE CLASH OF MACROECONOMIC IDEAS

The United States has had a number of macroeconomic problems in the last twenty years. The period has seen slow economic growth and poor productivity. In addition, there have been several recessions and very large federal budget deficits. In the late 1970s and early 1980s, both unemployment and inflation were higher than normal. Interest rates were at record highs. The international value of the U.S. dollar skidded through the late 1970s. It rose sharply from 1981 to 1985 and then took an abrupt fall from 1985 to 1989. By the end of the 1980s, the value of the dollar had stabilized and even risen slightly.

The macroeconomic models used in the 1960s and early 1970s were not adequate to deal with these problems because both the Keynesian model (as well as the Post-Keynesian alternative) and the monetarist model were focused on demand management. Problems of productivity, slow growth, and stagflation have to be explained in terms of the behavior of the aggregate supply curve. We will explore those relationships in more detail in the next chapter.

The issue of whether or not to call for government to improve on market outcomes is the touchstone that most strongly differentiates the various schools of economic thought. The six schools that we have identified—classical, monetarist, supply side, new classical, Keynesian, and Post-Keynesian—can be divided into two broad groups. Here is a rundown of where each group stands:

1. *The classical group.* This group includes four schools of thought that in various ways call for a minimal role of government: classical economists, monetarists, new classical economists, and supply siders.

    Classical economists argued that unsatisfactory outcomes are only temporary. Market forces would correct such mistakes, just as market forces lead commuters to less congested freeways to save valuable time or make it attractive for a couple to move into a racially mixed neighborhood because the price of housing is relatively cheaper there. Although there are no classical economists today, their ideas persist in three schools of thought.

    Monetarists agree with the classical view that market forces do move the economy in the right direction but recognize that these forces operate at uncertain speeds. However, monetarists also believe that the corrections proposed by Keynesians are likely to prove less satisfactory than waiting for the problem to resolve itself.

    Supply siders argue that government intervention has been misdirected. The proper role of government is to provide adequate incentives to work, earn, save, and invest through appropriately targeted tax-

Economic Insight

Is the Business Cycle Dead?

The question of whether the business cycle is dead recurs during every period of extended prosperity. The long recovery of the U.S. economy from 1982 to 1990 was no exception. An article in the *Washington Post* was just one of many that asked whether the business cycle had gone out of business.[a] Drawing on the work of several economists, *Post* writer Jodie Allen cited such changes as more responsive financial markets, a leaner and stronger manufacturing sector, more rapid assimilation of information, and better policy (mainly monetary). Unfortunately, the 1990–1991 recession began before the end of the year in which Allen wrote this upbeat assessment.

In fact, the fluctuations in economic activity during the entire period since World War II have been mild by historical standards. A number of reasons have been offered for this experience. First, some economists credit the greater stability to automatic stabilizers and stabilization policy, both monetary and fiscal. Second, others point to the fact that the United States is a more open economy (a higher ratio of trade to GNP), and shocks are now dampened by spillovers to the rest of the world. Still others claim that a larger government sector has been a source of stability. Fluctuations may be milder, but there have been two recessions in the last decade: the rather severe (but brief) recession of 1981–1982, and the 1990–1991 recession. The business cycle has been declared dead before, usually—like this time—just on the eve of the next recession.

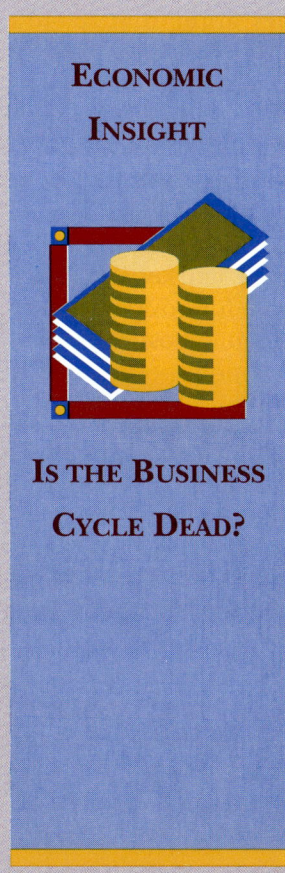

a. Jodie Allen, "Has the Business Cycle Gone the Way of the Dodo?" *Washington Post National Weekly Edition* (15–21 January 1990): 25.

ing and spending policies. In addition, supply siders argue that government should not tamper with market incentives.

New classical economists put little faith in any kind of government action. They argue that self-interested individuals quickly anticipate and often offset the effects of any demand-expanding policies. Unsatisfactory macro outcomes will be quickly changed because rational individuals will act in their own self-interest. These economists argue that government intervention often makes things worse and that the role of government should be reduced.

2. *The Keynesian group.* Both Keynesians and Post-Keynesians believe that unsatisfactory outcomes can persist for long periods of time and that the corrective market forces are weak and ineffective. Thus, they see an active role for government in moving the economy to a more satisfactory outcome. Post-Keynesians put more emphasis than Keynesians do on monopoly power and distributional effects of inflation and unemployment.

This list brings us back to a basic macroeconomic question raised in Chapter 4. Should the government be asked to try to stabilize economic activity? Should—or can—the government do anything to control unemployment and inflation? If so, what actions should it undertake, and how effective will they be? These are questions to which the two groups of economists give very different answers. The four schools that are part of the classical group share a faith in the effectiveness of market processes, the importance of incentives, and the self-correcting nature of the economy, at least in the long run. Both Keynesians and Post-Keynesians see a larger role for government and more evidence of market failure of various kinds. They also share a concern about the short run as well as the long run.

The differences among the various schools of thought can be grouped into four major areas, as shown in Table 1:

1. what determines the level of output and employment,
2. the role of interest rates,
3. the goals and values that can be inferred from the theories, and
4. the general thrust of policy recommendations.

THE AGGREGATE SUPPLY CURVE

Chapters 7–15 concentrated on the aggregate demand curve. This emphasis on demand reflects the dominance of Keynesian and monetarist ideas in economics. Both of those schools focus attention on the pros and cons of demand management strategies. The only attention we have paid to the aggregate supply curve has been to see how its shape affects the outcome of changes in aggregate demand.

Shifts in the position of the aggregate supply curve received little attention until the late 1970s. At that point, some economists started looking more closely at the determinants of the aggregate supply curve, both its position and its slope, as a possible explanation for stagflation. As we

School of Thought	Determination of Output and Employment	Role of Interest Rates	Goals and Values	Policy
THE CLASSICAL GROUP				
Classical	Output tends toward the full-employment level. Supply creates its own demand.	Interest rates fluctuate to make saving and investment equal.	Minimum government, price stability, and steady growth.	None (*laissez-faire*).
Monetarist	Output is determined by planned spending in the short run but tends toward the level associated with the natural rate of unemployment in the long run.	Interest rates influence investment spending, may frustrate fiscal policy through crowding out, and have a modest influence on money demand and velocity of money.	Minimum government, price stability.	Monetary policy with stress on stable monetary growth, minimal fiscal policy.
Supply Side	Output is determined mainly by the location of the aggregate supply curve.	Interest rates are not central. High interest rates can discourage capital formation.	Growth, productivity, full employment, low inflation, reliance on private sector.	Deregulation, tax policy stressing work and investment incentives.
New Classical	Output tends to move rapidly toward the level associated with the natural rate of unemployment.	Interest rates affect demand for financial assets (including money) fairly quickly and have some effect on investment.	Use and respect market processes, minimum government.	Only fiscal and monetary surprises affect output and then only temporarily.
THE KEYNESIAN GROUP				
Keynesian	Output is determined by planned spending. Output level is not necessarily at or near full employment.	Interest rates have little influence on investment. Interest-elastic demand for money makes monetary policy ineffective.	Full-employment, role of government as a stabilizing force.	Fiscal policy primarily, with monetary policy in a supporting role.
Post-Keynesian	Output can deviate from the full-employment level for long periods. Demand plays a central role.	Interest rates (and other prices and wages) tend to adjust slowly.	Pessimistic about market processes, perceive a lot of institutional barriers to quick adjustments, see government as a stabilizer.	Wage-price controls, activist fiscal policy, control the concentration of economic power to reduce wage and price rigidities.

TABLE 1
DIFFERENCES AMONG SIX SCHOOLS OF THOUGHT IN MACROECONOMICS

have seen, supply siders emphasize policy tools to shift the aggregate supply curve. New classical economists have looked more closely at the curve's slope and concluded that it is vertical, or nearly so, in the short run as well as the long run. Economists in general have begun to pay more attention to the behavior of aggregate supply. Aggregate supply, productivity, and economic growth are the subject of Chapter 16.

SUMMARY

1. The aggregate outcome of individual decisions may not be satisfactory to everyone or even to a majority. The purpose of macroeconomic policy is to avoid or change that kind of outcome.

2. The Phillips curve shows the various combinations of inflation and employment that an economy has experienced in a specific period of time. Early Phillips curves showed a negative relationship, leading economists to view the Phillips curve as a menu of policy choices between inflation and unemployment.

3. Experience in the last two decades has led economists to doubt that the Phillips curve offers a stable menu of policy choices.

4. Friedman developed the natural rate hypothesis to explain why there is no long-run tradeoff between inflation and unemployment.

5. When expectations about inflation are correct, expansionary policy will have only a temporary effect on output, driving up the price level only and restoring the natural rate of unemployment.

6. Post-Keynesians are concerned about market power and the distributional effects of inflation and unemployment. They advocate some temporary use of wage and price controls as a complement to contractionary monetary and fiscal policies.

7. There are six schools of macroeconomic thought. The classical group includes the classical, monetarist, new classical, and supply side schools. The Keynesian group consists of Keynesians and Post-Keynesians. The two groups differ primarily in their views of the shape of the AS curve and their goals, values, and policy recommendations.

8. The Phillips curve appears to show a tradeoff between inflation and unemployment, but the relationship shifted in the 1970s. Friedman argues that the long-run Phillips curve is vertical at a level of output corresponding to the natural rate of unemployment.

9. Demand-pull inflation is started by a rightward shift of the AD curve, with the AS curve shifting in response. Cost-push inflation is begun by a shift of the AS curve to the left, with policy makers responding by shifting the AD curve to the right.

NEW TERMS

Phillips curve
insider-outsider model

natural rate of
unemployment

demand-pull inflation
cost-push inflation

wage and price controls
tax-based inflation policy (TIP)

Chapter 15 Inflation and Unemployment

QUESTIONS FOR DISCUSSION

1. Why, according to Schelling, are aggregate outcomes more likely to be unsatisfactory as the group size increases?

2. According to the simple Keynesian model, the economy can't experience both inflation and unemployment at the same time. Why not?

3. What difference does it make for a Phillips curve whether aggregate supply is stable or not?

4. What difference does it make to monetary and fiscal policy if the long-run Phillips curve is vertical?

5. If the Phillips curve has shifted to the right, what does that suggest about the direction and relative size of shifts in aggregate supply and aggregate demand?

6. What is the natural rate hypothesis? Why does it imply that policy is ineffective in the long run?

7. How can you tell cost-push inflation from demand-pull inflation by looking at shifts in the *AD* and *AS* curves, ?

8. In what way are Post-Keynesians similar to Keynesians? How do the two schools differ?

9. How would a Keynesian deal with stagflation? A monetarist? A Post-Keynesian?

10. What are the costs and benefits of using wage and price controls?

11. Identify some of the distributional effects of expansionary and contractionary policies.

12. Why do economists disagree over macroeconomic policy recommendations?

13. If there were high unemployment and low inflation, what would each of the six schools of thought recommend? How would the policy recommendations differ if both unemployment and inflation were high?

14. What is the role of interest rates according to each of the schools of thought?

15. Trace the adjustment process in Figure 7, beginning with a decrease in the money supply.

SUGGESTIONS FOR FURTHER READING

Blinder, Alan. *Hard Heads, Soft Hearts*. New York: Addison-Wesley, 1987. A very readable, fairly Keynesian look at policy options with a concern for distributional effects. Chapters 2 and 3 look at unemployment, inflation, and demand management.

Eichner, Alfred (ed.). *A Guide to Post-Keynesian Economics*. New York: M. E. Sharpe, 1979. A collection of essays by major Post-Keynesians outlining the central ideas of that school.

Klamer, Arjo. *Conversations with Economists: New Classical Economists and Opponents Speak Out on the Current Controversy in Macroeconomics*. Totowa, NJ: Rowman and Allanheld, 1984. Informal dialogues between new classical economists and their critics on the current state of macroeconomics.

Schelling, Thomas. *Choice and Consequence*. Cambridge, MA: Harvard University Press, 1984. One of several unusual works by an economist with a unique perspective on the collective effects of individual choice.

Sheffrin, Steven M. *The Making of Economic Policy*. Cambridge, MA: Basil Blackwell, 1989. Discusses the current state of stabilization policy and the areas of consensus that have emerged in the last two decades.

Thurow, Lester. *Dangerous Currents: The State of Economics*. New York: Random House, 1984. Looks at the state of macroeconomic theory and why policy has not been successful, from a liberal Keynesian viewpoint.

acquiring and responding to information works more slowly, the upward-sloping aggregate supply curve may be the better model. That process could be slow for two reasons.

First, information is not free. It takes real resources to generate and acquire information. It also takes time to distribute information. These lags became much shorter in the 1980s (aptly labeled the start of the "Information Age") because of increasing use of telecommunications networks, personal computers, and other information technology. However, information is still not widely available on an instantaneous basis.

Second, people may learn from their mistakes, but they do not always learn immediately or adapt fully. For example, they may expect next year's rate of inflation to be the same as this year's, rather than adjusting their forecasts upward or downward on the basis of changes in the money supply, the unemployment rate, and other relevant information. On the other hand, they may keep in mind an average of the last few years' data, to which they add some current information about changes in policy and market conditions in order to form expectations about next year. People will adjust their behavior in the right direction but not completely. They may not correctly anticipate the actual rate of inflation. Individuals acquire, process, and act on relevant economic information in their own self-interest, but they never have information that is entirely accurate or complete. This view of how expectations are formed is summarized by the concept of **adaptive expectations**.[1]

adaptive expectations Expectations about the future that are formed by economic actors on the basis of current and past experience and that adjust slowly to changing conditions.

The experience of the late 1970s and early 1980s was consistent with the view that individuals' expectations are adaptive. That experience also suggested that people adapt more quickly as the payoff from acquiring and using accurate information gets higher. Throughout the 1950s and 1960s, inflation rates were low and steady, so past experience was a good guide to the future. Conditions changed in the mid-1970s. Many people—mortgage lenders, investors, workers, and producers—were surprised by the high rates of inflation. They saw their real wages and the value of their assets fall because they had not correctly anticipated the inflation. By the end of the 1970s, cost-of-living adjustment clauses in contracts, variable-rate mortgages, and other developments allowed markets to react more quickly to changes in the inflation rate. In terms of Figure 2, the short-run aggregate supply curve shifted upward more quickly and also became steeper as many price adjustments became automatic.

In the 1980s, as the rate of inflation began to fall, the opposite problem surfaced. With many contracts fixed, the real rate of interest rose sharply because the market rate included too high an inflation premium. Wage contracts had to be quickly renegotiated because they were based on higher inflation rates.[2] Within a year or two, however, people were incorporating lower expected rates of inflation in their economic decisions.

The rational expectations (new classical) view of how market partici-

1. An even simpler model is called extrapolative expectations. This model suggests that people expect the current period to be just like the preceding one.
2. An example of a delayed response to inflation was the introduction of indexing into the federal income tax with the 1981 law, to take effect in 1985. By the time indexing took effect, inflation rates had dropped sharply. With the reduction in the number of rates from fourteen to three in the 1986 tax reform, indexing was eliminated.

pants behave is an extreme one. It requires individuals to obtain large quantities of information quickly, sort out the relevant information, and process it through a sophisticated economic model about how changes in some variables will impact on others. However, even though this model represents an extreme, it is helpful in understanding the long run. When the payoff for obtaining and using correct information is high enough, people will make the effort to seek it out and act on it to the greatest extent possible. When the costs of ignorance and the benefits of possessing accurate information rise, the speed of reaction will also rise. Furthermore, it is not necessary that each and every market participant acquire and respond to information. It is only necessary that the search for and use of information take place at the margin.

While economists have been arguing over adaptive versus rational expectations, psychologists have been studying how people actually form expectations. Their work suggests that expectations typically consist of a mixture of recent past experience, current experience, and some projections of future events. That is, they are closer to adaptive than to rational expectations. Work with psychologists may help economists clarify how expectations are formed and how rapidly they adjust.

AUCTION MARKETS AND CONTRACT MARKETS

Even if expectations are rational, the aggregate supply curve will not be vertical if the process of changing wages, prices, and interest rates is slow. When aggregate demand increases, a slow response of wages, prices, and interest rates means that output may expand for a fairly long period of time before the short-run aggregate supply curve shifts up. A decline in aggregate demand may lead to long periods of low output and high unemployment until prices finally respond. This possibility is stressed by Post-Keynesians.

Although people may have accurate information, some time may pass before they are in a position to act on it. In some cases, it may not be desirable to act at all because the cost of responding is too high. Acting on accurate information may require changing jobs, selling assets, or other drastic actions. Thus, some people may choose to wait until the rate of inflation falls back to what they had expected. Often the costs of responding depend on the kinds of product markets and resource markets in which individuals are buying and selling. People will be more likely to relocate, for example, if their houses can be sold quickly at acceptable prices and if new jobs at satisfactory wages are easy to find.

Markets characterized by good information, many buyers and sellers, and rapid adjustments of price to changing conditions are known as **auction markets**. Typically, auction markets have many buyers and sellers making frequent transactions. You may have been to an estate auction, an antique auction, or a livestock auction. At these auctions, a fixed stock of goods is offered for sale, one item at a time. The price moves up the demand curve until one buyer pays the final price bid. Price bears all the burden of adjustment, and price changes rapidly.

Other markets are **contract markets**. In these markets, buyers and sellers enter into long-term agreements at fixed prices. The contract protects both buyer and seller from risks of price changes or other uncertainties.

auction markets
Markets characterized by good information, many buyers and sellers, and rapid adjustments of price to changing conditions.

contract markets
Markets characterized by few buyers and sellers, imperfect information, long-term contracts, and sluggish price adjustments.

Typical transactions in contract markets are long-term fixed-rate mortgages, tenure appointments for college faculty members, apartment leases, labor union contracts, and business or government contracts for major construction projects. Contracts of pro athletes or college football coaches reflect past performance. Such contracts may run for several years and be very expensive to change if the player or coach fails to live up to expectations. Prices move slowly in contract markets because it takes time for old contracts to expire. During that time, the cost of violating a contract can be very high.

If auction markets are typical, then prices will adjust quickly to changes in demand at both the micro and macro level. That is, a relatively small increase in aggregate demand will drive the price level up quickly with little effect on real output. The aggregate supply curve will be vertical, or nearly so. If contract markets are more typical, then price adjustments will be slow and the aggregate supply curve flatter. In the long run, even contract markets become auction markets because no contract lasts forever.[3] Rent controls expire. The 99-year leases in Hong Kong end in 1997 and will not be renewed. The typical contract is much shorter and more flexible.

Thus, rational expectations and auction markets suggest that the long-run aggregate supply curve is vertical or at least very steep. Adaptive expectations and contract markets suggest that the short-run aggregate supply curve could be fairly flat and that the short run itself may be a fairly long period of time.

EXPECTATIONS, MARKETS, AND AGGREGATE SUPPLY

• IF expectations are rational	People are correctly informed about current conditions and form appropriate expectations about the future.
and markets are efficient (auction),	Prices adjust quickly to changing conditions.
THEN the aggregate supply curve is vertical in the long run and very steep in the short run.	Demand management policies have little if any effect on real output.
• IF expectations are adaptive	Information is acquired gradually, and expectations adjust slowly.
and markets are contractual (contract),	Prices cannot change rapidly because it is too difficult to change them.
THEN the aggregate supply curve is upward sloping, at least in the short run (which can be fairly long).	Demand management can have a significant impact on short-run output.

---

3. In long-term contracts, the benefits to one side will be capitalized, that is, reflected in the value of the property the contract concerns. For instance, houses with guaranteed low utility costs will sell for a higher price than comparable houses not offering that benefit. However, this doesn't help the utility company!

ECONOMIC GROWTH: SHIFTING THE AGGREGATE SUPPLY CURVE

Although economists disagree about the slope of the aggregate supply curve, they agree about what makes it shift. Economists know that the long-run aggregate supply curve will shift to the right in response to increases in the capital stock, improvement in the size and/or quality of the labor force, additional natural resources, improvements in productivity, or technological advances. Increases in resources or productivity will shift the aggregate supply curve to the right. Encouragement of production through reduced taxes or regulations that lower costs to firms will also shift the curve to the right. Anything that shifts the aggregate supply curve to the right is a source of economic growth. That is, the shift will produce a rise in real per capita income, the measure of a nation's standard of living. Thus, what causes economic growth can be visualized in graphic terms as the factors that increase aggregate supply.

The aggregate supply curve can also shift to the left, indicating negative growth, or a decline in a nation's standard of living. Factors that can shift the curve to the left include resource depletion, a decline in the size and/or quality of the labor force, and public policies (taxes or regulations) that discourage productive activity.

Long-term economic growth requires steady rightward shifts of the aggregate supply curve. Economic growth has been a major concern in the United States for at least thirty years. Economists are constantly examining the growth rate of the U.S. economy to make sure that the standard of living is rising, or that Americans are economically more successful than the Soviets or as successful as the Japanese. Economists are also concerned that output expand fast enough to create enough jobs for a growing labor force. The antigrowth voices of the early 1970s became muted when Americans started realizing the costs of not growing in terms of inflation, unemployment, and a lower standard of living, if population grew faster than real output. During the 1980s and into the 1990s, the continuing debate has not been over *whether* to grow but rather *how* to grow. Economists try to determine what strategies are most successful for shifting the aggregate supply curve to the right.

GROWTH IN INVESTMENT AND SAVING

Between 1960 and 1990, real output increased 150 percent in the United States. Some of that growth was a result of increased resources, specifically labor and capital. Gross investment in constant dollars was 173 percent higher in 1990 than it was in 1960. However, recall from Chapter 5 that a large (and increasing) part of gross private domestic investment goes to replacement of worn-out capital. After correcting for depreciation, real net investment was only 64 percent higher in 1990 than it was in 1960. Thus, the real growth rate of investment was much lower than the rate of economic growth.

Because investment is so volatile, year-to-year comparisons must be treated carefully. Figure 3 plots both gross and net investment expenditures as percentages of GNP for 1950 to 1990. The growth of gross in-

FIGURE 3
GROSS AND NET PRIVATE INVESTMENT IN THE UNITED STATES AS A SHARE OF GNP, 1960–1990
Note that investment dropped sharply relative to GNP during recessions, especially in 1975 and 1982.

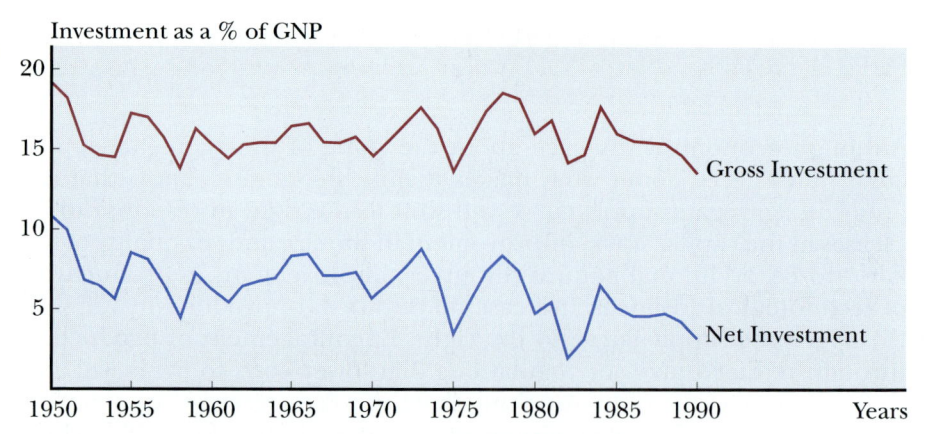

Investment as a % of GNP

Gross Investment

Net Investment

Source: Council of Economic Advisers, *Economic Report of the President* (Washington, DC: U.S. Government Printing Office, 1991).

vestment over that whole period was greater than the growth of total GNP but was very erratic. Net investment is investment in new plants, equipment, and housing as opposed to replacement of worn-out facilities and equipment. It actually fell relative to GNP. Note that in recession years, such as 1975 and 1982, investment declines even more than GNP, reducing the stock of capital available for future economic growth.

PRIVATE SAVING. Private saving is the major source of funding for investment to expand future output. Saving by households and business firms, which provides the funds for investment, has not kept pace with the growth of GNP in recent years. From 1980 to 1990, business and household saving rose 64 percent in current dollars, while GNP increased by 100 percent. In addition, much of the saving in the 1980s was absorbed in financing the large federal budget deficits. The combination of low private saving and negative saving in the public sector resulted in a substantial inflow of funds from abroad to cover the shortfall.

savings rate
The ratio of combined business, household, and government saving to GNP.

The most commonly used indicator of what is happening to saving is the **savings rate**, or saving by households, business, and government combined as a percentage of GNP. The current U.S. rate is low compared to past experience and to savings rates in many other industrial countries. However, saving has fallen in other industrial countries as well in the last two decades. From 1960 to 1980, the United States saved 19.6 percent of GNP, somewhat below the average for seventeen industrial countries, which was 23.4 percent. (Japan, at 35 percent, had the highest ratio.) Demographic factors such as the maturing of the baby boomers contributed to the low savings rate in the United States. As individuals grow older, they enjoy higher incomes and finish paying for houses and educating their children. Their savings rates will rise. Such a rise should occur in the United States in the next two decades.

The savings rate fell throughout the 1980s in both the United States and other industrial countries. By 1988, the U.S. savings rate was 15.1 percent, compared to an average of 20.3 percent for other industrial countries. This decline was fueled less by demographic changes than by a fall in government saving. Federal deficits combined with state and local government surpluses reduced the overall savings rate by about 2 percent of GNP.[4] The national savings rate was the focus of much attention in the 1980s as economists tried to explain why it was so low and policy makers tried to invent creative ways to induce households to save more.

Gross private domestic investment and saving each accounted for about 12 percent of GNP in 1990. Inflows of funds from abroad were an important source of investment financing in the 1980s because domestic saving was not sufficient to both meet private investment demand and fund federal budget deficits. In 1988, more than $200 billion in foreign investment flowed into the United States, including $58 billion in direct investment. (Direct investment consists of developing or acquiring ownership of office buildings, factories, and other tangible assets.) Even after allowing for an outflow of $82 billion for investment abroad, the net foreign funding of private and public sector borrowers in the United States in 1988 came to $112 billion.

One of the major sources of foreign funds was Japan, which invested more than $40 billion in the United States in 1988–1989. A large part of Japanese investment was in the auto industry. Some of these investments were joint ventures, and others were entirely Japanese-owned. Between 1982 and 1988, investments by Toyota, Suzuki, Honda, Mazda, Mitsubishi, Fuji, and Nissan created 32,000 jobs and the capacity to produce 2.4 million cars a year in seven plants in the United States and three in Canada. Although some Americans resented the invasion of the Japanese and other foreign investors, others were happy to have new plants and job opportunities in their communities.

PRIVATE AND PUBLIC INVESTMENT. Business investment in new equipment is a key source of economic growth. Additional equipment gives each worker more capital with which to work and thus increases productivity. New equipment embodies new technology, which also increases productivity. Thus, the slowdown in investment in the 1970s and 1980s led to a search for policies that would stimulate investment. Tax incentives of various kinds were proposed and implemented. In the 1981 tax law, accelerated writeoffs of new investment greatly reduced corporate income taxes. Those revenues were partly restored by reforms in the 1986 tax law. Since 1986 there has been a great deal of interest in restoring to the tax code the special treatment of capital gains, which are currently taxed as ordinary income. Capital gains are "profits" that result from the sale of assets at a higher price than they cost. Many policy makers argue that favorable tax treatment of capital gains would stimulate more sales of business firms and corporate stock.

A higher level of investment was seen as the cure for stagflation because it would shift the aggregate supply curve to the right. Such a shift would increase employment without more inflation. Although stagflation is no longer the main problem, investment is still very important. The pattern of the last few years has been one of slow growth, steady inflation of

---

4. Data from Andrew Dean et al., "Savings Trends and Behavior in OECD Countries," *OECD Economic Studies* (Spring 1990): 7–58.

4–5 percent, and unemployment that is perhaps just a little above the natural rate. Higher investment would address all of these concerns, so the focus on increasing investment can be expected to continue in the 1990s.

The policy emphasis in the last decade has been on private capital as a way to increase economic growth. However, the role of infrastructure as capital should not be overlooked. Most of this capital is in the state and local public sector, where the growth of the capital stock has slowed considerably from earlier decades. The transportation network of highways and airports on which private business depends is provided in the public sector. Investment in human capital also requires local public sector investments in schools and health care facilities.

Growth in the Labor Force

Another source of economic growth is a larger and/or more skilled labor force. Increases in both the size and the quality of the labor force can contribute to economic growth. If only the size increases, as occurred during the 1970s, real GNP may increase but there will be little if any increase in real per capita GNP, which measures improvements in the standard of living. A more skilled and productive labor force, which has more capital and better technology to work with, is the essential ingredient for an increase in real per capita GNP.

The Size of the Labor Force. During the 1970s, the labor force grew by 29 percent. A large part of that increase reflected the entry of the baby boom generation into the labor force. Another large part of the increase was due to the increased participation of women, many of whom were entering the labor force for the first time. Thus, labor force growth was much more rapid than before, but the average level of workers' skill and experience fell. This fall slowed the growth of GNP and the rightward movement of the aggregate supply curve.[5]

In the 1980s, the labor force grew much more slowly. From 1980 to 1990, it grew by only 16 percent, much less than the 22 percent growth of the preceding decade. In 1970, 16 percent of the population was between sixteen and twenty-four years old, the age group that makes up most of the new entrants to the labor force. By 1990, those in that age group made up only 13.4 percent of the population. Thus, if labor is to make a contribution to economic growth in the 1990s, the emphasis must shift to the quality of the labor force, or the labor force must be expanded by immigration or by a higher labor force participation rate.[6]

Investment in Human Capital. Investment is traditionally defined as the creation of new capital in the form of tangible productive assets, such as buildings, machines, and roads. The notion of capital is, however, broader

---

5. As the labor force ages in the next century, there is a risk that productivity will decline because there will be more older workers with obsolete skills.
6. The 1990 *Economic Report of the President* considered the labor force an important enough issue to devote an entire chapter (Chapter 5) to the subject. Immigration in the 1980s averaged 580,000 persons per year, a large proportion of them of working age. Many of them are unskilled. These immigrants generally filled slots in the lower end of the labor market and did very little to address the increasing need for skilled workers (although immigrants to the United States in 1990 included 48,000 Chinese graduate students, hardly unskilled!).

than just physical tools. Capital is anything used to increase the flow of output. Human capital thus includes "investment" in health, vigor, education, or training—anything that will increase the productivity of the individual worker.

Both individuals and firms can invest in human capital. An individual's decision to seek additional education is very similar to an entrepreneur's decision to purchase a new piece of equipment. In both cases, the investment is productive if the return (discounted) exceeds the cost (also discounted).

The largest investment in human capital in the United States is in the public schools, which offer "free" education through grade 12. This education is supplemented by post-secondary education in colleges, universities, technical schools, and vocational training programs, adult literacy and retraining programs, and on-the-job training. Estimates by Jacob Mincer in the 1970s indicated that as much as half of human capital in the United States was derived from on-the-job training.[7]

The United States invests heavily in education at all levels but most heavily in elementary and secondary schools. In 1959, expenditures per pupil were $1,635 (measured at 1982–1983 prices). By 1988, this figure had risen to $2,239, a real increase of about 36 percent. This amount compares favorably with educational expenditures in other developed nations. Of other major industrial nations, only Switzerland spends more per pupil. Canada, Japan, Australia, and the other nations of Western Europe all spend less.[8] The median amount of education (years of schooling completed) of persons twenty-five years old and over has also risen steadily in the United States, from 10.5 years in 1960 to 12.7 years in 1987. In 1987, 76 percent of the adult population had at least a high school diploma. The United States spends about 6.3 percent of GNP on education at all levels, compared to about 10 percent of GNP on business investment in plant and equipment.

The U.S. educational system has come under much criticism for failing to produce a well-educated labor force. Public schools were among the scapegoats for the slow economic growth in the 1970s and early 1980s. Parents, taxpayers, and educators pointed to falling SAT scores and high dropout rates. Employers complained about lack of basic skills in writing and computation. The result has been a careful examination of how effectively resources invested in education are being used. At the elementary and secondary levels, a number of states have enacted reforms in order to use those resources more effectively. Those reforms include tougher attendance laws, stricter teacher certification, basic skills testing for students, and other measures designed to improve the quality of public education. A few business leaders have even offered to provide college funds for those who make it through twelfth grade in certain inner city schools. That guarantee has lowered the dropout rate in those schools. All of these steps are attempts to improve the quality of human capital. The result would be an increase in aggregate supply and in the U.S. standard of living.

---

7. Jacob Mincer, *Schooling, Experience, and Earnings* (New York: National Bureau of Economic Research, 1974).
8. Comparative international data is taken from John Hood, "Education: Money Isn't Everything," *Wall Street Journal* (2 February 1990): A-10.

ECONOMIC INSIGHT

DEFENSE SPENDING AND THE CIVILIAN ECONOMY

The Gulf War has raised once again the question of whether military spending is responsible for the slower growth rate of the United States compared to those of other industrial countries. For example, Lloyd Dumas argues that "owing to the disproportionate allocation of scientific and engineering talent to military research, the rate of commercial innovation has declined appreciably since the late 1960s. Rising prices and deteriorating relative quality have made U.S.-produced goods increasingly noncompetitive in both world and domestic markets, forcing production cutbacks and plant closures in the United States and creating additional inflationary pressures."[a]

This statement is stronger than many observers would make. It does, however, highlight a concern about the role of military spending in the economy. Does defense spending displace infrastructure investment or funding for human capital? Does more for military research and development mean less for private industry?

The first question is a difficult one to answer. In the United States, 5.5 percent of GNP went to defense spending in 1990, a slightly higher share than the average for all industrialized countries as reported by the World Bank.[b] It is not clear how those funds would have been spent if defense outlays were reduced. The result might have been lower deficits or lower taxes rather than more spending on infrastructure and human services.

The second question is a little easier to address. Research and development (R&D) spending, public and private, accounts for about 2.8 percent of GNP. This figure is comparable to levels in West Germany (prior to reunification) and Japan (both at 2.8 percent). It exceeds the share of GNP that goes to R&D in France and the United Kingdom (both at 2.4 percent). However, a large share of that R&D spending in the United States was devoted to military research and technology, with very limited spinoffs in terms of civilian production. Nondefense R&D spending in the United States amounts to about 2 percent of GNP compared to 2.8 percent for Japan and 2.6 percent in West Germany (before reunification). With defense R&D eliminated, the gap in R&D spending between the United States and France or the United Kingdom was also much narrower—2 percent of GNP in the United States compared to 1.8 percent in both those countries.

The distinction between military and civilian R&D spending would be less important if there were substantial spillover benefits between the two. The one great success of military R&D that was translated into profitable civilian applications is the transistor. However, other examples are hard to find. In fact, Hewlett-Packard argues that defense is now a net user of civilian-created technology in electronics, rather than the other way around.[c] The military is generally more interested in performance than in price. The civilian market is sensitive to both concerns. Thus, for example, machine tool manufacturing in the United States has been stimulated by military demand, but the result has been an industry that has been more attentive to high performance than to cost. The more price-sensitive civilian sector of the market has gone to the Germans and the Japanese.

Some of the greatest military innovations with spinoffs to the private sector have not been in technology but in management. Cost-benefit analysis, operations research, and planning-programming-budget systems originated in the military and spread quickly to private industries. Overall, however, it is difficult to evaluate whether high levels of defense spending, with or without the Gulf War, have increased, reduced, or had no impact on U.S. economic growth.

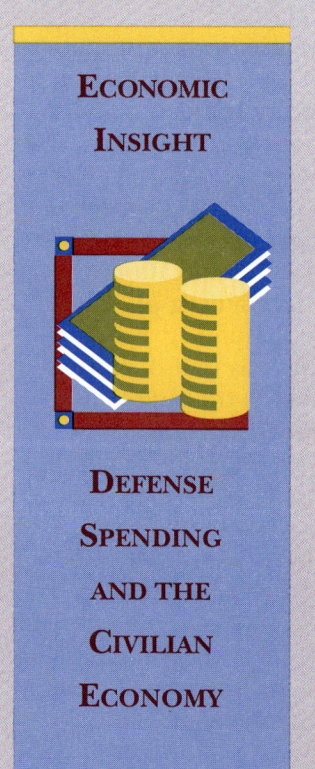

---

a. *The Political Economy of Arms Reduction*, Selected Symposium 80, American Association for the Advancement of Science, 1982.
b. World Bank, *World Development Report 1990* (New York: Oxford University Press, 1990).
c. Jacques S. Gansler, *Affording Defense* (Cambridge, MA: MIT Press, 1989).

GROWTH IN NATURAL RESOURCES

The last category of inputs that can shift the aggregate supply curve is natural resources. In the late 1960s, a group of doomsayers called "The Club of Rome" used a computer simulation model to predict massive shortages of natural resources by the end of this century. Many economists are not very concerned about resource shortages because they have observed how market forces have dealt with such problems in the past. The market has several mechanisms to address problems of declining resource availability. When high-grade sources are exhausted, lower-grade sources are substituted. When a given resource becomes scarce, its price rises. Users then turn to natural or synthetic substitutes. Higher prices also stimulate searches for new sources of supply. Finally, technological change has helped to lower extraction costs and make lower-grade deposits worth exploiting.

Economists V. Kerry Smith and John V. Krutilla have examined experience with natural resources over the last hundred years. They do not lightly dismiss concerns over increased resource scarcity, but they found the record of the past to be encouraging.[9] Higher prices typically called forth the kinds of responses just described.

With one exception, increased resource prices did not have much to do with the slowdown of the last two decades. That exception was oil, whose price rose tenfold in just seven years, leading to a temporary leftward shift of the aggregate supply curve. Even in that case, with a dramatic price increase of a widely used natural resource, producers and consumers adapted. More fuel-efficient cars, alternative energy sources, insulation, modified production methods, and other responses minimized the long-run effect on the economy. The higher price also ultimately called forth additional oil supplies, shifting the aggregate supply curve back to the right to some extent.

RESEARCH AND DEVELOPMENT

Increased productive resources are not the only source of increases in aggregate supply. If new ways of using resources can create more output, then those technological changes can also shift the aggregate supply curve to the right. New technology may be embodied in new capital or in a change in methods of production. Research and development, or R&D, consists of efforts to develop new products and new production methods and put them to use.

Technological change is a two-step process. The first step requires investment in research into new products and new methods. This step results in inventions. The second step is to translate those inventions into something that is commercially feasible and cost-effective. This second step is **innovation**, or the translation of new methods and products into actual production and marketing. A special issue of *Business Week* devoted to innovation suggested that Americans excel at the invention phase, but the Japanese are much more successful in making the transition from invention to innovation and exploiting the profit potential of new ideas.[10]

innovation
The translation of inventions into products and processes that are commercially feasible and cost-effective.

---

9. V. Kerry Smith and John V. Krutilla, "Economic Growth, Resource Availability, and Environmental Quality," *American Economic Review Papers and Proceedings* (May 1984): 226-230.
10. "Innovation in America," *Business Week* (special issue), 1989.

Technological change is difficult to measure in the aggregate. It is possible to measure changes in spending on research and development and new equipment, which embodies the latest technology. There is no easy way, however, to measure the extra output due to the new technology. The United States does spend heavily on research and development. About 2.8 percent of GNP goes to research and development, much of it funded by the federal government and carried out by industry and universities. In the 1970s and 1980s, however, about 25 percent of U.S. spending on research and development was directed to defense-related research, which has limited applications to other markets. Other countries (especially Japan) have put much more effort directly into industrial research.

Research and development spending usually requires investment in new capital that embodies the newly developed technology. Thus, research and development spending and new capital spending go hand in hand to shift the aggregate supply curve to the right and promote economic growth.

REAL BUSINESS CYCLES

A growing economy typically exhibits some instability, because innovations resulting from research and development and investment spending do not occur at a steady pace. Thus, such an economy would be expected to exhibit business cycles, as described in Chapter 4. The Keynesian model explains such cyclical fluctuations in output, employment, and the price level in terms of shifts in aggregate demand in both directions, combined with a relatively stable aggregate supply curve that gradually moves rightward over time.

Another explanation of cyclical fluctuations, in the classical tradition, was developed in the 1980s. Its roots go back to such early twentieth-century economists as Wesley Clair Mitchell (who first measured business cycles) and Joseph Schumpeter. This explanation holds that cyclical economic fluctuations result from changes in aggregate supply rather than in aggregate demand. The cyclical pattern is called the **real business cycle**. If changes in aggregate supply as a result of technology shocks and other disturbances occur irregularly in large bursts, they can generate cyclical fluctuations in output.[11]

real business cycle A cyclical pattern of economic activity resulting from changes in aggregate supply (rather than aggregate demand).

The supply-induced explanation of fluctuations was a response to the experience of the 1970s and early 1980s. At that time, supply influences, such as a less experienced labor force and higher oil prices, appeared to shift the aggregate supply curve to the left. Such a shift would result in the usual decline in output and employment that indicates a recession. Unlike most recessions, however, there would be no fall in the price level (or the inflation rate), as would normally be the case. In a supply-induced recession, in contrast to a demand-induced recession, real output can fall while the price level rises. A subsequent shift of the aggregate supply curve

---

11. A temporary shock, such as a drought, earthquake, crop failure, or short-term oil price hike, will produce a temporary backward shift in the *AS* curve. In contrast, long-term resource depletion, technological change, or capital accumulation or depreciation produces longer-term shifts.

to the right would expand both employment and real output. What happened to the price level during such an expansion would depend on whether aggregate demand also shifted to the right during that period.

In general, a real business cycle—one based on shifts in aggregate supply—would tend to imply rising price levels or higher inflation rates during recessions and lower price levels or lower inflation rates during expansions. This pattern is somewhat consistent with the experience of the 1970s but does not generally describe cyclical fluctuations for longer periods. Evidence to support a real business cycle on a regular and recurring basis has been weak.[12] The major cyclical fluctuations of the last century can be explained in terms of aggregate demand, as has been done by both Keynesians and monetarists.

THE PRODUCTIVITY DILEMMA

New and better capital and methods of production are one of the most important sources of increased labor productivity. **Productivity** is the measure of real output per worker hour. Like the price level, productivity changes are measured by an index. Table 1 shows the increase in productivity by decade for the United States.

productivity
A measure of real output per worker hour.

According to studies by economist Edward Denison, increases in labor productivity accounted for about two-thirds of U.S. economic growth from 1929 to 1982.[13] (The remainder was due to an increase in the size of the labor force.) Increases in the productivity of labor resulted from having more capital with which to work as well as such important factors as education and technological change.

The slow growth of productivity in the last two decades is a dramatic change from earlier periods. The problem is not unique to the United States. A similar slowdown in productivity growth has plagued all of the developed industrial countries. The concern over productivity, slow growth, and the combination of rising prices and rising unemployment

TABLE 1
U.S. PRODUCTIVITY GROWTH, 1950–1990

Period	Productivity Index*	Average Annual Increase (%)
	1950 = 50.2	
1950–1960	1960 = 65.9	+2.8%
1960–1970	1970 = 87.3	+2.9%
1970–1980	1980 = 99.2	+1.3%
1980–1990	1990 = 111.9	+1.2%

*1977 = 100.

Source: Council of Economic Advisers, *Economic Report of the President* (Washington, DC: U.S. Government Printing Office, 1991).

---

12. The pros and cons of this highly technical subject are discussed in Charles I. Plosser, "Understanding Real Business Cycles," *Journal of Economic Perspectives* (Summer 1989): 51–78, and N. Gregory Mankiw, "Real Business Cycles: A New Keynesian Perspective," *Journal of Economic Perspectives* (Summer 1989): 79–89.
13. Edward F. Denison, *Trends in American Economic Growth 1929–1982* (Washington, DC: Brookings Institution, 1985).

led to many efforts to explain what was occurring and to devise suitable policies to get the economy moving again.[14] Former Prime Minister Margaret Thatcher's program of "Thatcherism," a uniquely British set of supply side policies, was perhaps the most dramatic political response to concerns about productivity.

One type of policy to increase productivity consists of various types of incentive, bonus, or profit-sharing schemes to encourage labor to work harder and become more skilled. Under such plans, workers are paid for output rather than input. Their pay is based on what they produce, rather than being an hourly wage or annual salary. Economist Alan Blinder has reviewed a number of studies on productivity incentives and concluded that at least some evidence suggests that such incentives do increase productivity.[15]

The explanations for the productivity slowdown are not hard to find. Although the labor force has grown, there has been some (short-term) decline in its quality as a result of a fall in the average age, training, and experience of workers, a situation that will gradually improve during the 1990s. The rates of saving and investment have remained stubbornly low. The pace of technological change has been slow. A great deal of research and development spending has been directed toward defense rather than commercial innovations. Finally, there have been problems with the cost and availability of some natural resources. All of these factors either failed to shift the aggregate supply curve to the right fast enough or, in some cases, pushed it to the left. The search was on for supply side policies.

POLICIES TO SHIFT AGGREGATE SUPPLY

It is virtually impossible to devise a policy to shift aggregate supply that does not also shift aggregate demand. Unlike the supply and demand curves for individual products, the aggregate supply and demand curves are not entirely unrelated. A tax cut, for example, may encourage work and investment, which shifts the aggregate supply curve to the right. However, it also stimulates spending on consumption and investment, which shifts the aggregate demand curve to the right. In the late 1970s and early 1980s, a group of economists, policy makers, and business journalists proposed that the United States adopt policies that would be aimed at shifting aggregate supply to the right more than aggregate demand. The result was supposed to be larger output and employment at the same or lower prices.

Supply side economics, unlike Keynesian theory or monetarism, does not consist of a clearly defined theoretical model. In the narrow sense, supply siders are a group of economists advocating a specific group of policies relating to deregulation, tax incentives, and work incentives. In designing those policies, supply siders emphasize certain microeconomic foundations of aggregate supply. In a broader sense, all economists are supply siders in that they believe that factors that can shift the aggregate supply

---

14. Issues of productivity growth are discussed in detail in a symposium edited by Stanley Fischer in the *Journal of Economic Issues* (Fall 1988): 3–98.
15. Alan S. Blinder (ed.), *Paying for Productivity: A Look at the Evidence* (Washington, DC: Brookings Institution, 1990).

International Perspective

Is the United States Exporting Tax Policy?

In the 1980s, U.S. economic policy seemed to be out of step with much of the rest of the world. European countries were committed to demand management policies, and the United States was pursuing supply side policies. In recent years, however, just as supply side policies fell out of favor in the United States, they became more popular in European countries. As more conservative politicians came into power in France, Denmark, and the United Kingdom, a less progressive tax system aimed more at incentives and less at redistribution of income became a U.S. "export." Similar tax reforms were also undertaken in New Zealand and Canada.

The reasons that led these countries to re-examine the incentive effects of their tax systems are twofold. First, most of the countries of Western Europe, as well as Canada and New Zealand, were dissatisfied with their economic performance in the 1980s. Growth rates in the twelve member countries of the European Community, as well as in New Zealand, have been lower than growth rates in the United States and Japan for the last ten years. Unemployment is high in most European countries. Most of them have had higher rates of inflation than the United States. Canada's growth has kept pace with that of the United States, but Canada has suffered from slightly higher unemployment and inflation.

Second, the changes in the U.S. tax system legislated in 1981 and 1986 have had important implications for the major trading partners of the United States. As a result of lower marginal tax rates, the United States has become a more attractive place to work, earn, live, and invest. Some other industrial countries have seen an outflow of highly skilled workers to the United States, such as college professors, medical doctors, entertainers, and artists. There has also been a flow of investment from Europe into the United States. Other industrial countries have felt pressured to lower their marginal income tax rates in order to compete with the United States for investment and skilled workers and to increase rates of growth of output and employment. Canada reformed its income tax in 1988, reducing the number of brackets from ten to three. However, marginal rates dropped very little for most families.[a] In New Zealand, tax reform enacted in 1987 lowered the top rate from 66 percent to 33 percent and reduced the number of brackets to only two.[b]

Prime Minister Margaret Thatcher in Great Britain went even further than reformers in the United States, Canada, and New Zealand. As her government reduced dependence on the income tax, some responsibilities were shifted from the central government to the local government, just as was done in the United States. In the United States, however, some of the responsibilities fell on state rather than local governments. State governments rely on income and sales taxes, but local governments in both the United States and Britain rely mainly on property taxes. Since there is no state government in Britain, the burden shifted to the property tax. The Thatcher government attempted to take some of the pressure off the property tax by reinstituting an old and very regressive tax called the poll tax. The poll tax generated a tax revolt in Britain far more widespread than the property tax revolt in the United States a decade earlier. Other countries have confined their tax reforms to reducing the progressivity of the income tax, and most are watching the reforms in Britain with interest.

American economists have generally found little evidence that supply side policies had a significant impact on saving, investment, or productivity. However, some of the countries of Western Europe have jumped on the tax incentive bandwagon for fear they will be left behind.

---

a. "Will Canada's Tax Reform Have a Supply Side Effect?" *Wall Street Journal* (3 September 1988): 15.
b. "New Zealand's Painful Economic Cure," *Wall Street Journal* (11 October 1988): 17.

curve are important for long-term economic growth. In fact, a Keynesian or a monetarist is often an advocate of some supply side policies.

Supply siders insist that economic incentives are important and that the driving force behind economic decisions is the self-interested behavior of individuals. Recall the importance of incentives and response to the role of interest rates in money demand, bank lending, and business investment decisions on the aggregate demand side of the market. The responses of individuals in their roles as workers, managers, investors, and savers to changes in the reward structure of their environment is also important for aggregate supply. Supply siders point out that the government has a great deal of influence on this reward structure.

THE TAX WEDGE AND WORK INCENTIVES

Supply siders are concerned about the effects of taxes, especially income taxes, on incentives and economic activity. Higher taxes taxes drive up costs of production and consumer prices.[16] Taxes to support government activity create a **tax wedge**, which is the gap between prices paid by consumers and the prices (incomes) received by sellers (factor owners). Thus, the tax wedge discourages both consumption and production. If the government borrows instead of raising taxes to finance additional spending, this action raises the cost of borrowing to private firms. The rise in the cost of borrowing drives up their costs and discourages private-sector investment. Either way, supply siders argue, the growth of government contributes to rising costs.

Supply side economists argue that the growth of the tax-transfer system reduces incentives to work, save, invest, and innovate, all of which contribute to productivity. High marginal tax rates discourage individuals from putting forth extra effort and encourage tax avoidance. Under a progressive income tax system (and the U.S. federal income tax was fairly progressive until 1986), increases in nominal income push workers into higher marginal tax brackets. As a result, a significant portion of the return to increased effort and productivity is taxed away. Consequently, workers are likely to opt for more leisure (longer vacations, increased absenteeism, less moonlighting, and earlier retirement).

Consider Ms. A, a skilled accountant earning $35 an hour. She is considering either putting in an extra four hours for a client on Saturday morning or spending that time cleaning her carpets. If she works, her gross income will be $140. A commercial carpet cleaner charges $100. Without considering taxes, it makes sense for her to work four hours, pay the carpet cleaner, and come out $40 ahead. Resources would be efficiently allocated. The value of her time as an accountant is higher than the value of her time as a carpet cleaner. However, taxes may change her decision. If her marginal income tax rate (federal plus state) is 40 percent, then after taxes she will earn only $84. It would be cheaper to clean her own carpets. A lower tax rate would induce her to use her time where it is most productive—as an accountant, not as a carpet cleaner. These con-

---

tax wedge
The gap between prices paid by consumers and the prices (incomes) received by sellers (factor owners).

---

16. The extent to which taxes fall on consumers, rather than on producers or factors of production, depends on the kind of tax and the amount of market power possessed by the producers. However, most economists would agree that the tax wedge has some impact on both producers and consumers.

cerns about the incentive effects of high marginal tax rates were reflected in the 1981 tax cut and the 1986 tax reforms. Both of these policy actions sharply reduced marginal income tax rates for individuals.

Supply siders also argue that transfer payments discourage productive work. Unemployment compensation programs encourage workers to stay unemployed until their benefits are exhausted. Welfare programs, including not only cash transfers but also food stamps, subsidized housing, and Medicaid, discourage people from taking low-wage jobs. The wages they could earn may barely offset the loss of welfare payments plus other benefits. Consider Mr. B, who currently receives $120 a week in welfare benefits. A job becomes available, which would require Mr. A to work forty hours a week at the minimum wage of $4.25 an hour. If he takes the job, he loses his welfare benefits. He will earn $170 a week instead of $120. The "tax" on his earnings will be $120/$170, or about 71 percent. Is it worth working forty hours a week to earn $50 more? (After Social Security and other taxes, Mr. B's net earnings increase may actually be negative.) This argument was popularized by Charles Murray in his book *Losing Ground* in the early 1980s. He argued that welfare actually discourages people from investing in human capital.[17] Workfare programs in some of the states and finally on the national level in the late 1980s were designed to overcome this problem by allowing people who go off welfare to accept jobs to keep more of their earnings.

Clear evidence is hard to find, but there is some support for the argument that marginal tax rates affect those at the bottom of the ladder. There is also some weak support for a similar effect on those in high tax brackets. Economists Gary Burtless and Robert Haveman, summarizing a variety of studies of the effects of taxes and transfers, conclude that the loss of welfare benefits was a deterrent to work effort in some experimental programs to test work incentives. They also found that possible loss of Social Security benefits had a negative effect on work effort among the elderly.[18]

Taxes, Saving, and Investment

Supply siders also raise the tax issue with respect to saving and investment. An individual's reward for saving depends on both the interest rate and the marginal tax rate on the next dollar of income. For any given interest rate, there is less incentive to save additional dollars at a higher marginal tax rate. Less credit will be available to borrowers. Thus, a progressive income tax discourages saving and indirectly, through the higher cost of borrowed funds, discourages investment.

Supply siders also apply this argument to entrepreneurial or management risk taking. In deciding whether to expand productive facilities or to implement new technologies, owners or managers must weigh the risks that are involved against the expected profits *after taxes*. The higher the marginal tax rate, the smaller the expected profit will be, and the less eager investors will be to assume risks. As a result, less new technology is adopted, and both output and productivity growth are retarded.

---

17. Charles Murray, *Losing Ground: American Social Policy, 1950–1980* (New York: Basic Books, 1984).
18. Gary T. Burtless and Robert H. Haveman, "Taxes and Transfers: How Much Economic Loss?" *Challenge* (March-April 1987): 45–51.

There is not much evidence from the 1980s to support this view of supply siders. Despite two major reductions in the marginal income tax rate, neither saving nor investment responded very strongly during the 1980s.[19] The 1981 tax law even contained some tax breaks for special savings accounts, such as All Savers Certificates and Individual Retirement Accounts (IRAs). Despite these incentives, the share of after-tax income that people saved continued to fall. Investment did not show much response either.

In the late 1980s, a modified supply side argument became popular. Some economists and policy makers argued that the special tax treatment of capital gains, eliminated in the 1986 tax reform, should be restored. (Recall that capital gains are earnings that result from an increase in the market value of an asset over its purchase price.) Under a highly progressive tax system, capital gains are likely to push their recipient into a higher tax bracket and generate more tax liability than they would have if they were received over several years instead of all at once. Special tax treatment (a lower rate) for capital gains is believed to be an incentive to invest in riskier ventures and thus provide capital for innovation and growth. However, there is no conclusive evidence about the effect of this tax break on investment.

OTHER EFFECTS OF TAXES ON OUTPUT

Supply siders also argue that progressive taxes cause resources to be allocated inefficiently. Resources flow to certain sectors of the economy, such as real estate, that enjoy tax advantages. All depreciation, taxes, and interest expenses are deductible on real estate investments. Individuals in high marginal tax brackets find that their after-tax yields are higher from investing in real estate than in other assets. Thus, supply siders argue that too many financial resources flow into the real estate market, instead of more productive uses. The 1986 tax reform eliminated some but not all of the special tax provisions for certain types of investments.

Finally, supply siders stress that high marginal tax rates cause too many scarce resources to be devoted to avoiding taxes. Time spent looking for tax loopholes (by individuals and their hired attorneys and accountants) could be used more productively.

REGULATION AND DEREGULATION

Supply siders are also very critical of government regulations in environmental and health and safety areas that increase costs of production and drive up prices without increasing output. In addition to the direct costs of compliance, these regulations place a heavy burden of paperwork on industry. Although the purposes of the regulations might indeed be desirable, they divert real resources from producing goods and services to complying with regulations and filing forms. These higher costs shift the aggregate supply curve to the left. Deregulation should shift it back to the right.

Deregulation was a central feature of the policies of the Reagan administration. Some regulations were repealed. Others were simply not enforced. Experiments with deregulation in the 1980s in the airline indus-

---

19. Supply siders point out that a large part of the tax cut was offset by increased Social Security taxes and higher state and local taxes in many cases. Thus, some of the expected benefits did not occur.

try, telephone service, and banking, however, generated mixed results. The enthusiasm for deregulation appears to have peaked in the mid-1980s. The policy is currently being reassessed.

PUBLIC POLICY TOWARD RESEARCH AND DEVELOPMENT

Since the federal government plays a major role in the allocation of research and development funds, it has an important direct influence on the activities of invention and innovation. In addition to direct expenditures, the federal government also finances the education of many scientists and engineers, protects property rights to inventions through the patent system, and offers special tax breaks for research and development spending in the private sector.

Profits are the incentive to engage in research and development. The outcome of a research and development effort will be more profitable if the resulting product reaches the broadest possible market. One effort to increase the return to research and development, therefore, has concentrated on opening foreign markets to new U.S. products and better protecting patents and copyrights on a worldwide basis (protecting rights in "intellectual capital").

SUPPLY SIDE ECONOMICS IN THE 1980S

For the most part, what President Reagan did in his first term was a textbook application of supply side economics. Congress and the President reduced some social welfare programs and enacted a three-stage, 25 percent cut in personal income taxes in 1981. Accompanying the tax cuts were some incentives to save and invest. Also, efforts were made to reduce the burden on business of complying with government regulations. The goal was to shift aggregate supply to the right, increasing saving, investment, productivity, output, and employment while reducing inflation.

It is difficult to evaluate supply side policies because it is impossible to conduct *ceteris paribus* experiments. Tight monetary policy combined with lower inflation rates drove real interest rates to record highs. The worldwide recession from 1980 to 1982 led to falling output and employment and probably deserves some of the credit for lower inflation rates. Since recovery from a recession is generally associated with rising productivity, it is hard to know how much productivity was affected by the Reagan program. The most noteworthy changes were the drop in the inflation rate and the steady recovery and expansion since the 1981–1982 recession. The massive budget deficits that followed the tax cut are also at least partly the result of these supply side policies.

In addition, the supply side program was often criticized on distributional grounds. Critics argued that the package of tax cuts and incentives was "welfare for the rich," who received the biggest tax cuts and benefited the most from saving and investment incentives. Defenders of these policies countered that the rich were paying the most to begin with. In addition, as a group they tend to include the most productive workers (measured by their high salaries) and the individuals most willing and able to save and invest. Thus, any program aimed at encouraging work effort, saving, and investment has to focus on incentives for individuals with higher incomes. But, the defenders argued, the resulting economic growth, lower inflation rates, and higher productivity will eventually benefit everyone.[20]

Supply side ideas have declined in popularity in the last few years. There has been a lack of hard evidence of their effectiveness. There has also been concern about the distributional effects of higher taxes on the poor (especially Social Security) combined with tax breaks for the rich.

IS INDUSTRIAL POLICY THE ANSWER?

Supply side economics is a politically conservative growth strategy, relying on private market forces. In the last few years, a competing growth strategy has been proposed. This politically liberal strategy, known as **industrial policy**, consists of government programs to identify and encourage promising industries and to ease the decline of old industries. Japan has often been cited as an example of the successful use of industrial policy. European countries also pursue similar strategies.

industrial policy
A growth strategy consisting of government programs to identify and encourage promising industries and to ease the decline of old industries.

The tools of industrial policy usually include subsidies, tax incentives, government-sponsored research and development, low-interest loans, and other devices designed to promote an industry or group of industries. Often restrictions on imports or promotion of exports is part of the policy. The basic goal is to identify promising industries and help them to develop to the point where they can continue to grow and prosper on their own. In some cases, industrial policy is proposed as a way to avoid the pain of structural change in declining industries by propping them up and helping them to survive. In other cases, industrial policy attempts to ease the transition for labor and capital out of declining industries and into other areas with more promising futures.

The primary goal of industrial policy is competitiveness. Much of the interest in industrial policy was spurred by the decline in exports and the rise in imports in the United States in the 1980s. To a large extent, the change in the balance of trade (exports minus imports of goods and services) was a result of the rise in the price of the U.S. dollar from 1981 to 1985. As the price of the dollar declines, some of the problem of competitiveness may be resolved.

The United States already has an industrial policy of sorts, although it is not deliberate and coordinated. Existing tax, subsidy, and regulatory policies, as well as government spending for research and training programs, favor certain industries at the expense of others. Concentration of research in agriculture, defense, and space programs favors industries in those areas and suppliers to those industries. The minimum wage, by *not* favoring industries that use large amounts of unskilled labor, has tipped the balance in favor of industries using more capital and/or skilled labor. The Investment Tax Credit and accelerated depreciation, until modified in 1986, favored capital-intensive industries. The list is endless. The point

---

20. The notion that benefits to the rich will eventually spill over to lower income groups is known among development economists as the trickle-down theory. Those who suggest direct aid to the poor to help them earn and be more productive, with benefits spilling over to higher-income groups, call their approach the bubble-up theory.

International Perspective

Industrial Policy in Japan and the European Community

Japan and the European Community (EC) offer good examples of positive and negative industrial policy. Japan pursues a more positive policy of identifying and promoting industries that seem to have growth potential. Since Japan has the best record of economic growth of any industrial country since World War II, other countries have shown much interest in its policies. As a general rule, the nations of the EC have pursued a more negative approach. This approach consists of protecting and supporting declining industries, trying to get them back to a competitive level.

The key to Japan's program is the Ministry of Trade and Industry (MITI), which selects the industries to assist. Methods used in the 1950s and 1960s included organizing cartels, providing loans at low interest rates to targeted industries, and controlling imports. In the 1970s and 1980s, the government did offer aid to declining industries in the form of tax breaks and loan guarantees. Overall industrial policy in Japan has been directed much more at supporting promising industries through accelerated depreciation allowances, tax benefits, research support, and loans. The U.S. government usually makes such benefits available to all firms, but Japan is more selective in deciding which industries to favor. Critics have argued, however, that the MITI is not always successful in identifying which industries to promote. It has backed some losers and missed some potential winners, such as the auto industry. Although the Japanese strategy is mostly positive, selected industries, such as agriculture, are heavily protected.

The EC's primary strategy has been to slow structural changes that cause losses and unemployment in declining industries. Low-interest loans and import restrictions play a key role. Agriculture has benefited from subsidies and import controls, despite its comparative disadvantage. Other declining industries that have been singled out for special treatment are shipbuilding, steel, textiles, and footwear. One exception to the EC pattern has been Italy, which has relied heavily on antitrust policy, deregulation, and reducing the size of the public sector in order to make its industries more competitive within as well as outside the EC. At the same time, Italy is promoting small and medium-sized industries with technical assistance and low-cost loans in order to enable them to compete with larger firms in both Italy and the EC.[a] Italy's strategy, intended to position Italian industry to compete when the EC becomes a single integrated market after 1992, is more forward-looking than those of some of its neighbors. It will be difficult to support, subsidize, and protect specific industries against competition within a unified twelve-nation market with uniform product standards, no trade barriers, and free flow of goods and productive resources.

American policy makers interested in industrial policy have been attracted to the Japanese positive model because of Japan's high growth rate. However, policy proposals and practice in the United States seem to more closely resemble the EC model. They have emphasized protection from foreign competition and focused on rebuilding declining industries rather than developing promising new ones.

---

a. "Italy's Industrial Policy Challenged by 1992," *Wall Street Journal* (27 June 1988): 15.

is that every nation has an industrial policy. The real question is whether it is pursued as a deliberate strategy and the results are evaluated to see if the industries the nation wishes to help are indeed the ones benefiting.

The foremost advocate of industrial policy in the United States has been economist Robert Reich, who laid out such a strategy for the United States in his 1983 book, *The Next American Frontier*. Among his recommendations were replacing the income tax with an expenditure tax (to encourage saving), increased federal spending for research and science training, tax incentives for human capital investments, and aid to declining industries to encourage conversion to other areas.

Critics of industrial policy point out that it involves second-guessing the market. The government, rather than the market, is selecting the industries to develop, using its judgment instead of the judgment of consumers, entrepreneurs, and owners of productive resources. In addition, industrial policy creates a field day for lobbyists and special interest groups trying to make a case that their industry is most deserving of any special benefits.

The debate over industrial policy began in the 1980s when it was put forth as a liberal answer to conservative strategies of tax cuts, deregulation, and reduced government spending. This debate will continue well into the 1990s.

SUMMARY

1. There are four shapes for the aggregate supply curve: horizontal, vertical, upward sloping, and composite. Each shape has different implications for the effects of a change in aggregate demand on prices, output, and employment.

2. If the long-run aggregate supply curve is vertical, shifts of the aggregate demand curve can affect output in the short run but only the price level in the long run.

3. An upward-sloping aggregate supply curve may be the result of imperfect information or a limited ability to adapt to changing conditions. If expectations are rational and markets work well, the aggregate supply curve is vertical, at least in the long run.

4. The aggregate supply curve can be shifted by changes in the quantity and quality of resources available or by changes in technology.

5. Increases in capital, including human capital and improvements in technology, increase worker productivity. Productivity growth in industrial countries has been slower in recent decades than in earlier periods.

6. Supply side economics is a group of policies intended to shift the aggregate supply curve to the right. These policies include work incentives, saving and investment incentives, and deregulation. The Reagan administration implemented a supply side program in the 1980s.

7. Industrial policy is an alternative to supply side economics. It also emphasizes tax and production incentives but aims to promote and encourage a specific industry or a group of industries.

Chapter 16 Aggregate Supply and Economic Growth

New Terms

adaptive expectations
auction markets
contract markets
savings rate
innovation
real business cycle
productivity
tax wedge
industrial policy

Questions for Discussion

1. How can a tax cut be both a demand side (Keynesian) and a supply side policy? Does it make any difference what kinds of taxes are cut?
2. Why is the shape of the *AS* curve important?
3. What determines the slope of the *AS* curve?
4. Economists who believe in rational expectations assume that individuals will acquire and process all relevant information to make economic decisions in their own self-interest. If you watch key variables and expect the inflation rate to rise, how will that affect your consumption, saving, and work behavior?
5. Sketch the four versions of the aggregate supply curve shown in Figure 1 and show how a leftward shift of *AD* (a reduction in aggregate demand) affects prices and output in each case.
6. Which of the following can be classed as auction markets and which as contract markets?
   a. the stock market
   b. the mortgage market
   c. the labor market
   d. the market for new houses
   e. the market for tickets to a baseball game
7. Why are both rational expectations and auction markets necessary in order to have a vertical *AS* curve in the short run?
8. What is industrial policy? How is industrial policy different from supply side economics?
9. How would each of the following affect measured productivity?
   a. new and better capital equipment for many workers
   b. a sharp rise in the labor force participation rate
   c. higher prices for natural resources in general
10. What are some of the factors that can increase labor productivity?
11. Ms. Karcher is retired and receiving Social Security benefits, but she is considering working part-time. If she works part-time, she will pay about 15 percent of her earnings in federal income tax, 4 percent in state income tax, and 7.3 percent in Social Security tax. What is her marginal tax rate on earnings? If she works twenty hours a week, she will earn a gross income of $100. What is her net income and her net hourly wage? Should she take the job?
12. Mr. Stewart is trying to decide whether to work on Saturday for three hours at an hourly rate of $20 or to spend the three hours cleaning his garage. He can hire two neighborhood boys to clean the garage, but they charge $35. What should he do if his combined tax rate (federal income tax, state income tax, and Social Security tax) on the additional income totals 30 percent? What if the combined tax rate totals 50 percent?
13. Does business investment shift aggregate supply or aggregate demand? How do you think increased business investment will affect prices and real output?
14. Were supply side policies successful in the 1980s? Why or why not?
15. According to Smith and Krutilla, why have natural resources not been a serious limit to growth?

Suggestions for Further Reading

Aschauer, David A. "Does Public Capital Crowd Out Private Capital?" *Journal of Monetary Economics* (September 1989): 171–188. Explores the relationship between public and private capital as both complements and substitutes in promoting economic growth. Aschauer concludes that public sector capital does make a significant contribution to growth.

Blinder, Alan S. (ed.). *Paying for Productivity: A Look at the Evidence.* Washington, DC: Brookings Institution, 1990. Examines the potential for increasing workers' productivity through various types of pay incentives.

Council of Economic Advisers. *The Economic Report of the President.* Washington, DC: U.S. Government Printing Office, annual. Policies to promote growth are always emphasized. The 1990 edition has a thorough discussion of growth policy.

Dertouzos, Michael L., et al. *Made in America: Regaining the Productive Edge.* Cambridge, MA: MIT Press, 1989. Examines the productivity decline and offers proposals for improvement.

Hicks, Donald A. *Is New Technology Enough? Making and Remaking the Basic Industries.* Washington, DC: American Enterprise Institute, 1988. Looks at whether technology will help basic manufacturing industries survive. Includes case studies of machine tools, steel, automobiles, textiles, ceramics, and fiber optics.

Perry, George. "Reflections on Macroeconomics." *American Economic Review Papers and Proceedings* (May 1984): 401–407. Discusses the shapes of the *AS* curve and some reasons why it has an upward slope.

Sheffrin, Steven M. *The Making of Economic Policy.* Cambridge, MA: Basil Blackwell, 1989. Chapter 3 discusses real business cycles.

Stein, Herbert, "Should Growth Be a Priority of National Policy?" and Heller, Walter, "Activist Government: Key to Growth?" *Challenge* (March/April 1986). Two former chairs of the Council of Economic Advisers, one from the Nixon administration in the 1970s and one from the Kennedy and Johnson administrations in the 1960s, debate the growth policy issue.

AFTER STUDYING THIS CHAPTER, YOU SHOULD BE ABLE TO:

1. List and discuss the characteristics of less developed countries.
2. Define:
   a. per capita income,
   b. dependency ratio,
   c. the crude birth rate,
   d. the crude death rate.
3. Explain what development economists call the vicious circle of poverty.
4. Compare and critically evaluate the economic development theories of Karl Marx and W. W. Rostow.
5. Contrast the following strategies for economic development:
   a. big push versus leading sectors,
   b. *laissez-faire* versus government-directed development.
6. Describe the problems that population growth and international debt create for development and discuss possible remedies.
7. List the proposals of the New International Economic Order (NIEO).

CHAPTER 17

ECONOMIC DEVELOPMENT AND THE THIRD WORLD

INTRODUCTION

Growth is a matter of concern for developed, industrial countries like the United States. However, it is closer to a life-or-death matter for many less developed countries (sometimes referred to as LDCs).[1] The problems facing these countries encompass the whole operation of the economy. The term *economic growth* used in Chapter 16 is too narrow to describe the goal of most of the poorer nations of the world. Economic development is a total process of transformation. It means not only raising current standards of living but also building a solid foundation of human and physical capital, technology, infrastructure, and economic institutions that will support continued improvement in the future. This chapter takes a closer look at conditions in less developed countries, using some of the economic concepts developed in earlier chapters to explain some of the reasons for differences in the levels of development.

It is easy to blame the poor countries themselves for their failure to attain a high standard of living, or to blame the rich for the problems of the poor. One development economist, writing from the perspective of analysts in the industrial world, identifies two explanations:

One says that we are so rich and they so poor because we are so good and they so bad; that is, we are hardworking, knowledgeable, educated, well-governed, efficacious,

---

1. In the jargon of development economists, the name for less developed countries has changed frequently. The changes have in part reflected the increasing political power of these countries. In the 1950s and 1960s, the term "underdeveloped countries" was most commonly used. (Before that, they were often called "backward countries.") In the late 1960s and early 1970s, the term "less developed countries" emerged. In the late 1970s, the term "Third World" was in vogue. In the early 1980s, U.N. publications used the terms "low-income countries," "middle-income countries," and "industrialized countries" to designate the levels of development. In most recent U.N. publications, the term "developing countries" is used. These countries often refer to themselves as the Group of 77.

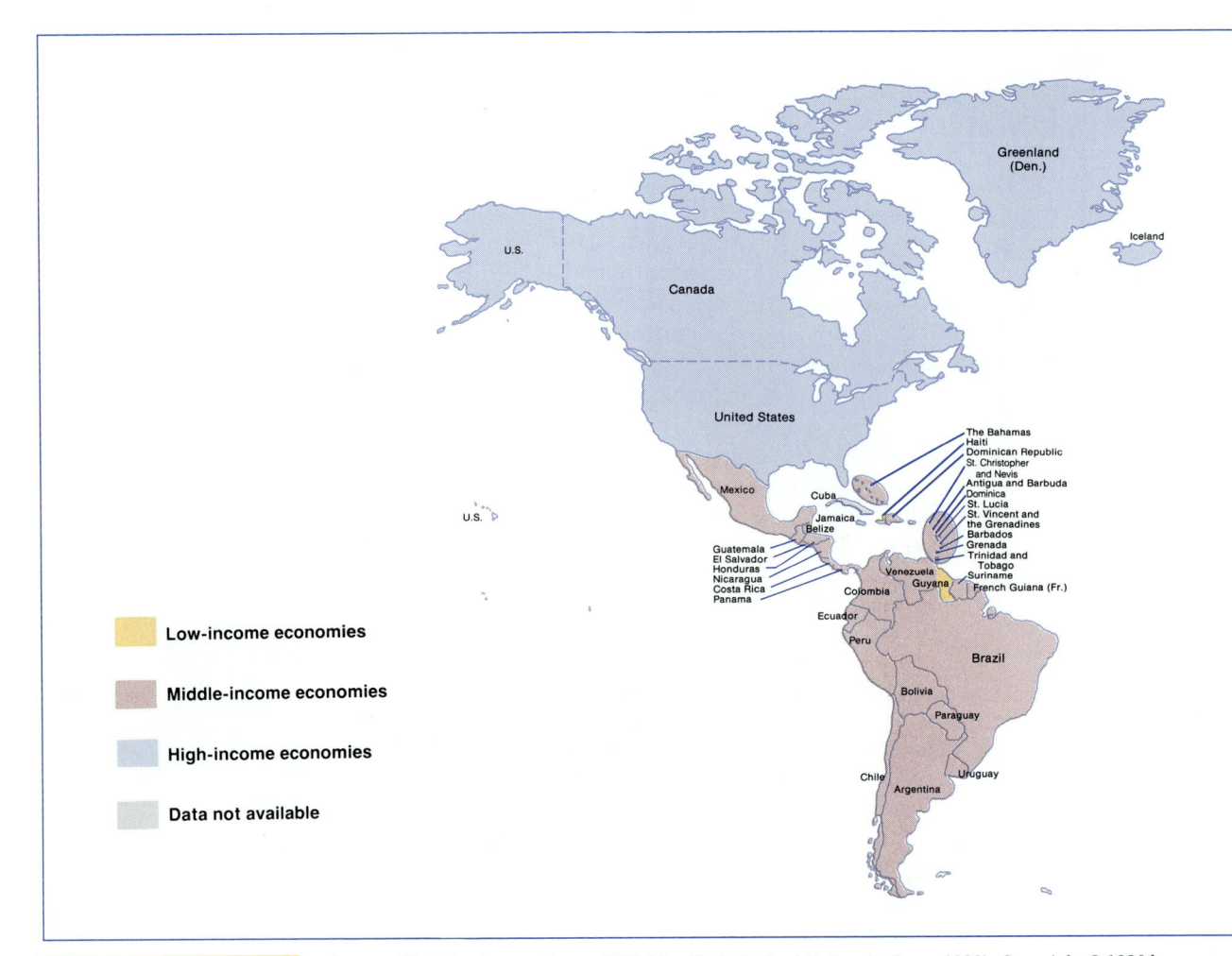

**FIGURE 1
WORLD BANK ECONOMIC
CLASSIFICATIONS**
Although it is common to divide the world's nations into three eonomic groups, there is no agreement as to name and which countries belong in each group. The World Bank has developed its own classification system and terminology suitable to its needs.

Source: *World Development Report, 1990* (New York: Oxford University Press, 1990). Copyright © 1990 by the International Bank for Reconstruction and Development/The World Bank.

and productive, and they are the reverse. The other says that we are so rich and they so poor because we are so bad and they so good; we are greedy, ruthless, exploitative, aggressive, while they are weak, innocent, virtuous, abused, and vulnerable.[2]

Neither of these "good guys, bad guys" versions fully captures the extent to which relations between rich and poor countries affect the growth and development of both partners. This quotation does suggest, however, that the industrial world has a role to play. We will explore the role the developed, industrial countries can play in assisting the development process.

CHARACTERISTICS OF LESS DEVELOPED COUNTRIES

Although less developed countries are diverse, they share a number of important characteristics. The most obvious characteristic of a less devel-

2. David S. Landes, "Why Are We So Rich and They So Poor?" *American Economic Review Papers and Proceedings* (May 1990): 1.

Chapter 17 Economic Development and the Third World 457

oped country is low per capita income. This criterion is used to sort nations out into various stages of economic development. Accompanying low per capita income, however, are several other important characteristics that contribute to the persistence of poverty.

LEVEL OF PER CAPITA INCOME

The World Bank considers any country with a GDP of less than $500 per capita (in 1988 U.S. dollars) as a low-income country. GDP differs very little from GNP for most countries. GNP measures all the output produced by a country's citizens, at home or elsewhere. GDP measures all production that takes place within the country, whether by citizens or foreigners. Forty-two countries were categorized as low-income countries in 1989. Another thirty-seven countries were classed as lower middle-income, with per capita GDP ranging from $570 (Bolivia) to $2,160 (Brazil). Seventeen countries were classed as upper middle-income, with a range from $2,290 (South Africa) to $5,420 (Libya). Only twenty-five countries made the list of high-income countries, including both industrial market economies and high-income oil exporters. Among this prosperous group, per capita incomes ranged from $6,200 (Saudi Arabia) to $27,500 (Switzerland). Figure 1 identifies the World Bank's low-, middle-, and high-income economies.

Table 1 presents the World Bank's most recent figures for per capita gross domestic product (GDP) and growth rates of GDP for selected countries at various income levels. (Because of recent changes in Eastern European countries and because data from those countries tends to be unreliable and incomplete, we have left them out of the table. We will discuss

TABLE 1
BASIC INDICATORS OF ECONOMIC DEVELOPMENT FOR SELECTED COUNTRIES

	PER CAPITA GDP, 1988	YEARLY GROWTH RATE OF PER CAPITA GDP, 1965–88
LOW-INCOME COUNTRIES	$280	3.1%
Bangladesh	170	0.4
Uganda	280	−3.1
India	340	1.8
Lesotho	420	5.2
Indonesia	440	4.3
LOWER MIDDLE-INCOME COUNTRIES	$1,380	2.6%
Philippines	630	1.6
Egypt	660	3.6
Paraguay	1,180	3.1
Chile	1,510	0.1
Mexico	1,760	2.3
UPPER MIDDLE-INCOME COUNTRIES	$3,240	2.3%
South Africa	2,290	0.8
Hungary	2,460	5.1
Argentina	2,520	0.0
Portugal	3,650	3.1
HIGH-INCOME COUNTRIES*	$17,080	2.3%
Saudi Arabia	6,200	3.8
United Kingdom	12,810	1.8
Kuwait	13,400	−4.3
France	16,090	2.5
Federal Republic of Germany	18,590	3.2
United States	19,840	1.6
Japan	21,020	4.3

*Note that Kuwait's per capita income will fall in the next few years because of the Gulf War, but it had been falling before 1990. Also, the unification of the two Germanys will reduce per capita income.

Source: Adapted from *World Development Report, 1990* (New York: Oxford University Press, 1990). Copyright © 1990 by the International Bank for Reconstruction and Development/The World Bank.

developments in the centrally planned economies of Eastern Europe in a later chapter.)

Table 1 both exhibits and conceals a great deal of diversity. The oil-exporting countries in the high-income category are subject to the fluctuations of the world oil market and must eventually find other economic activities to replace their dwindling oil reserves. Although Bangladesh is very poor and its growth in per capita GDP has been slow because of a high birth rate, it has made progress in agricultural production. Thus, it probably has more hope of development than some of the poor and largely desert nations of sub-Saharan Africa. Some of the middle-income countries, notably Mexico, although better off than the poorer countries, are saddled with heavy debt burdens. Measures to resolve that problem, as well as to contain inflation, have brought the growth process to a virtual standstill not only in Mexico but in several other Latin American nations as well.

The figures in Table 1 must be used with caution. Per capita GDP is not very reliable for comparison purposes. The problems of accurately measuring income and production are even greater in less developed countries than in developed ones. Less developed countries cannot use sophisticated methods of gathering and processing data. In addition, a much larger share of output in these countries does not pass through the market. In rural areas especially, a family is likely to grow its own food, build its own house, and make its own clothes. This output is difficult to estimate and value at market prices. Finally, a major problem is the use of exchange rates to convert figures into a common currency, the U.S. dollar. Fluctuations in the value of the dollar can create impressions of faster or slower growth than actually took place.[3]

Growth rates are very important over time. The spread in growth rates among the four groups in the table is quite narrow. Compare the 2.3 percent per year for the lower middle-income group to the 3.1 percent for the low-income group. However, this narrow spread in rates of growth does not imply that income gaps are closing. First, the averages conceal the fairly wide country-to-country variation within each group, including some rates that are negative. Second, starting from a lower base of per capita income, it is possible for one country to grow at a faster rate than another and still fall further behind in absolute dollars. If country A starts at $100 per capita and grows at 5 percent a year while country B starts at $1,000 and grows at 3 percent a year, at the end of ten years, country A will have a per capita income of $163, and country B will have a per capita income of $1,344. The gap between the two will have widened from $900 to $1,181.

Even very small differences in growth rates can matter a great deal. Consider the growth rate of 2.3 percent for the lower middle-income group versus 3.1 percent for the low-income group. A country starting out at a per capita income of $1,000 will see its income rise to $1,243 in ten years at a 2.3 percent growth rate. The same per capita income will rise to $1,450 in ten years at the higher growth rate of 3.1 percent.

---

3. An effort to develop more meaningful estimates was undertaken in the 1970s. A composite market basket of goods was chosen and priced in each country, with a comparison to the United States as a standard. This process was quite complex and has not been repeated. The estimates were published by Irving B. Kravis in *World Product and Income: International Comparisons of Real GDP* (Baltimore, MD: Johns Hopkins Press, 1982).

convergence hypothesis
The prediction that income differences among countries will shrink over time because of the transfer of technology and innovation.

The issue of whether income differences among countries are growing or shrinking has long fascinated economists. The prediction that these gaps will narrow over time through the transfer of technology and innovation is called the **convergence hypothesis**. Economist William Baumol looked at the historical evidence on convergence from 1870 to 1979. He found the strongest convergence among the industrialized countries, with much less convergence between rich and poor countries. Other economists, however, have criticized his findings for not covering enough countries or for being biased by the strong convergence of the last thirty years.[4]

POPULATION, BIRTH RATE, AND THE DEPENDENCY RATIO

One of the most striking differences between less developed and more developed countries is in the area of population. The population is characterized by the birth rate, the population growth rate, and the age distribution of the population. The study of population characteristics is called demography. Table 2 shows some important differences in population characteristics between less developed and more developed countries.

crude birth rate
Number of births per thousand of population.

dependency ratio
The percentage of the population not of working age (under fifteen or over sixty-five).

The **crude birth rate** is the number of births per thousand of population. As Table 2 shows, there is a large difference in the crude birth rates of poor and industrialized countries. An important consequence of a high birth rate is a high **dependency ratio**, or the percentage of the population not of working age (under fifteen or over sixty-four). Low-income countries have much higher dependency ratios. Almost half of the population of low-income countries is not of working age, compared to less than 33 percent in the industrial economies. A high dependency ratio means that a smaller proportion of the population is available to engage in productive labor. More resources must be used to meet the needs of dependent persons (a few of them elderly, but mostly children) for food, clothing, shelter, medical care, and basic education. Those resources will not be available to promote economic development through building factories

TABLE 2
POPULATION CHARACTERISTICS AT VARIOUS LEVELS OF DEVELOPMENT

	CRUDE BIRTH RATE, 1988*	CRUDE DEATH RATE, 1988*	POPULATION GROWTH RATE, 1980–88	PERCENTAGE OF POPULATION AGED 0–14, 1988
Low income	3.1	1.0	2.8	35.7
Lower middle-income	3.0	0.8	2.3	38.0
Upper middle-income	2.6	0.8	1.8	33.4
High-income countries	1.4	0.9	0.7	20.5

*Births per 100 people and deaths per 100 people per year.

Source: Adapted from *World Development Report, 1990* (New York: Oxford University Press, 1990). Copyright © 1990 by the International Bank for Reconstruction and Development/The World Bank.

4. William J. Baumol, "Productivity Growth, Convergence, and Welfare: What the Long Run Data Show," *American Economic Review* (December 1986): 1072–1085. A later article by J. Bradford DeLong questioned whether Baumol has really proved convergence. See "Productivity Growth, Convergence, and Welfare: Comment," *American Economic Review* (December 1988): 1138–1154.

and power plants, providing worker training, and developing transportation systems.[5]

There are many reasons for high birth rates. Women marry soon after puberty in many poor countries, because they have few economic alternatives except marriage. They produce children early because children, especially sons, are useful as labor and for old-age insurance. These economic motives are reinforced by cultural patterns that frown on failure to marry and have children.

Population growth due to high birth rates may have positive consequences. A larger population can result in more specialization and economies of scale. Julian Simon has been one of the few voices in favor of population growth as a development strategy. In his book *The Ultimate Resource*, Simon argues that the negative aspects of growth and development—pressure on limited food supplies, land, and energy, slow growth of per capita income, and increasing pollution—are vastly overstated. An additional person is a productive resource who will ultimately add more to production than society had to invest in his or her care, feeding, and education up to maturity.[6] Most economists, however, consider a large number of dependent children as a drag on economic development. We will explore the population problem in more detail later in this chapter.

Table 2 also shows that people in poorer countries have a shorter life expectancy. Life expectancy reflects health, nutrition, and infant mortality factors. A shorter life expectancy means that the productive work life of the average adult is not as long. The consequence of the short life expectancy and the high birth rate in less developed countries is a large number of children with relatively few adults to support them. This age distribution is a major barrier to achieving the goal of increasing output and raising the standard of living.

THE DEATH RATE AND THE POPULATION EXPLOSION. Recent health care advances have greatly lowered the death rate in most poorer countries. It has remained almost constant in industrialized countries. The crude death rate fell from 1965 to 1987 in the low-income and lower middle-income countries: from 1.6 per 100 to 1 per 100 in low-income countries and from 1.4 to 0.8 in lower middle-income countries. The **crude death rate** is the number of deaths per hundred of population. The consequence of the declining death rate and the high and stable birth rate has been a population explosion in many less developed countries. This population growth means that these countries must grow rapidly in productive capacity just to stay *even* in per capita income.

crude death rate
Number of deaths per thousand of population.

The effect of the population explosion on per capita income is easily seen by referring to Figure 2. The figure shows the average annual growth rate of GDP in low-income, lower middle-income, upper middle-income, and high-income countries. But the picture is very different for growth in per capita GDP, also shown in Figure 2. The poorest countries have managed to stay ahead of population growth, largely because of a slowdown in birth rates in China and India. (Outside of those two countries, the pop-

---

5. For a thorough discussion of this issue, see Allen C. Kelley, "Economic Consequences of Population Change in the Third World," *Journal of Economic Literature* (December 1988): 1685–1728.
6. Julian L. Simon, *The Ultimate Resource* (Princeton, NJ: Princeton University Press, 1981).

FIGURE 2
GROWTH OF GDP, POPULATION, AND PER CAPITA GDP
Average annual growth of GDP has been more rapid in all three groups of developing countries than in the high-income economies. However, rapid population growth has soaked up most of the additional output.

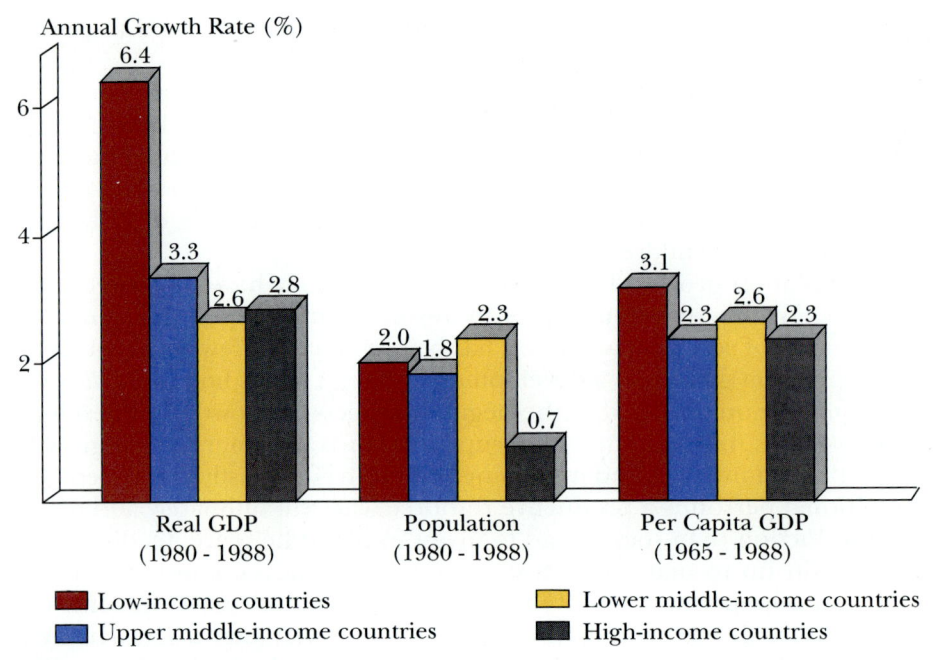

Annual Growth Rate (%)

Real GDP (1980-1988): Low-income 6.4, Upper middle-income 3.3, Lower middle-income 2.6, High-income 2.8
Population (1980-1988): Low-income 2.0, Upper middle-income 1.8, Lower middle-income 2.3, High-income 0.7
Per Capita GDP (1965-1988): Low-income 3.1, Upper middle-income 2.3, Lower middle-income 2.6, High-income 2.3

■ Low-income countries
■ Upper middle-income countries
■ Lower middle-income countries
■ High-income countries

Source: *World Development Report, 1990* (New York: Oxford University Press, 1990). Copyright © 1990 by the International Bank for Reconstruction and Development/The World Bank.

---

ulation growth rate for the low-income countries has been 2.8 percent.) High rates of population growth have meant that both groups of middle-income countries have slower than average growth rates of per capita GDP.

INVESTMENT IN HUMAN CAPITAL. Most low-income countries invest very little in human capital, or the health, education, and skills of their citizens. Labor that is healthy and well-educated is more productive. Investment in humans can do as much to increase productivity as investing in machines, bridges, and power plants. Of course, one reason why low-income countries invest little in human capital is that they have little to invest. One of the reasons they have little to invest is that they have had such low levels of investment in human and other kinds of capital in the past. This trap is called the **vicious circle of poverty**. There is little investment because there is a low level of income, and there is a low level of income because there has been little investment.

Table 3 gives some indications of the levels of investment in human capital at different levels of development. Investment in health care is reflected in the number of people per physician. There are many more persons per physician in less developed countries than in high-income countries. Another important area of investment is in education, which is measured in Table 3 by school enrollment data. Low school enrollments in the low-income countries reflect the need for everyone to work to support the family in a subsistence economy. Education is a luxury that the family can rarely afford, especially for more than one child. Girls are less likely than boys to be enrolled in school. The effect of low school attendance is an uneducated and therefore less productive work force.

vicious circle of poverty
A trap in which many low-income countries are caught—there is little investment because of a low level of income, and a low level of income because of little investment.

TABLE 3
INVESTMENT IN HUMAN CAPITAL AT VARIOUS LEVELS OF DEVELOPMENT

	NUMBER OF PEOPLE PER PHYSICIAN, 1984	SCHOOL ENROLLMENT RATE, 1986 (%)* PRIMARY	SECONDARY	HIGHER EDUCATION
Low-income countries	5,580	104	37	3
Lower middle-income countries	3,030	104	54	16
Upper middle-income countries	1,220	104	67	20
High-income countries	940	102	93	39

*Figures exceed 100 percent because older children and adults are enrolled in primary school.

Source: Adapted from *World Development Report, 1990* (New York: Oxford University Press, 1990). Copyright © 1990 by the International Bank for Reconstruction and Development/The World Bank.

AGRICULTURE

One characteristic of most less developed countries is the large share of resources devoted to agriculture. Some of this agriculture is large-scale and relatively modern, producing export crops such as cocoa, coffee, and bananas. Most of it, however, is basically subsistence agriculture. Simple, labor-intensive technology is used to produce food for individual families rather than crops to be sold for cash. Rural overcrowding, small land holdings that preclude modern economical cultivation, and low agricultural yields per acre are typical. A dominant role for the agricultural sector is strongly linked to low levels of per capita income. In order to escape poverty, a country must have some resources left over after feeding itself, either directly (by producing enough food for home use and export) or indirectly (by exporting enough nonfood items to import needed foodstuffs).

Table 4 shows some important differences in the agricultural sector at various levels of development. In the low-income group, about one-

TABLE 4
ROLE OF AGRICULTURE AT VARIOUS LEVELS OF DEVELOPMENT

	SHARE (%) OF GDP FROM AGRICULTURE, 1988	SHARE (%) OF MERCHANDISE EXPORTS FROM AGRICULTURE, 1988
Low-income countries	33	23
Lower middle-income countries	14	30
Upper middle-income countries	10	13
High-income countries	3	12

Source: Adapted from *World Development Report, 1990* (New York: Oxford University Press, 1990). Copyright © 1990 by the International Bank for Reconstruction and Development/The World Bank.

INTERNATIONAL PERSPECTIVE

NEGATIVE DEVELOPMENT IN ARGENTINA

Just because a country becomes highly developed doesn't mean it stays that way. At different times in history, Egypt, Rome (Italy), Greece, and Babylonia (now Iraq) were highly developed by the standards of their time. All are relatively poor today.

Argentina, which was once one of the richest countries in the world, offers a twentieth-century example of negative development. In 1900, New Zealand and Argentina, with growth fueled in part by agricultural exports to Europe, had the two highest GNPs in the world. Wage rates in Argentina in 1910 were 25 percent higher than in Paris and 80 percent higher than in Marseilles. Europeans were migrating to Argentina in large numbers. Over the fifty-year period before 1914, Argentina's economy grew by an average rate of 5 percent per year, an achievement that still ranks as one of the highest and longest episodes of long-term economic growth. At the turn of the century, the Argentinean rancher played much the same role in French plays as the vulgar Texas oil tycoon did in *Dallas*.

In 1987, Argentina had a per capita GNP of $2,767, and that of New Zealand was $10,000. New Zealand was labeled (by the World Bank) as a high-income country, and Argentina was labeled an upper middle-income country. Between 1965 and 1988, Argentina's real per capita GNP did not grow at all. New Zealand's average growth rate was 0.8% per year.

What happened? Argentina taxed its exports heavily. Very little was invested. Argentines spent—Buenos Aires became the center of high living. Elvio Baldinelli, an Argentine trade expert, explained it well: "Argentina despised its export industries and taxed them very heavily, yet lived off them very well until markets closed and prices fell." Norman Gall wrote in *Forbes* magazine that Baldinelli's lament and the explanation for the decline of Argentina can be summed up in one sentence: "To succeed in the modern world, a country needs economic policies that encourage, not hamper, economic initiative."[a]

Economic development is not something that is achieved and then enjoyed forever. The decline of the Roman Empire, the decline of Britain in the 1960s and 1970s, and the rapid rise and fall of some of the oil-rich countries suggest that attention to the causes of economic growth are important for even the most developed countries.

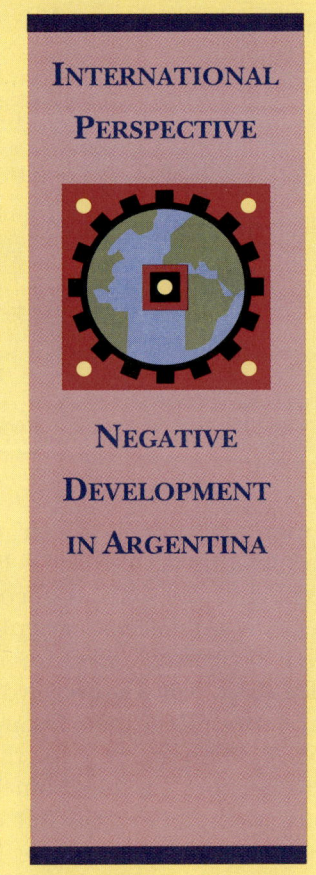

---

a. Norman Gall, "The Four Horsemen Ride Again," *Forbes* (28 July 1986): 96.

third of GDP is derived from agriculture. In both low-income and lower middle-income countries, the agricultural sector is a major source of exports. In low-income countries, an average of 70 percent of the population is in agriculture, compared to 44 percent in middle-income countries and 7 percent in high-income countries. In the United States, only 2 percent of the labor force produces enough to feed the entire nation, with a surplus for export. In general, agriculture tends to be much more productive in upper middle-income and high-income countries. In those countries, agriculture is highly mechanized and a small part of the population produces an abundant harvest, including some for export. The table shows a consistent pattern of declining reliance on agriculture as a nation becomes wealthier.

As a producing sector, agriculture faces certain problems in both developed and less developed countries. Supply is unpredictable, depending on the weather. Demand is not very responsive to price changes. Thus, a bumper crop will lead to a big price drop. A poor harvest will command high prices, but high prices are little comfort to farmers with little or nothing to sell. These problems are more serious when agriculture is a large share of GDP. For this reason, reducing dependence on agriculture is a goal of every development program.

A major contributor to improved agricultural output in a number of less developed countries in the last two decades was the development of high-yield dwarf varieties of rice and wheat. This agricultural innovation, known as the **Green Revolution**, was undertaken by the Rockefeller Foundation, initially in Mexico and then in other countries. This project had to overcome obstacles such as lower resistance to pests in the new varieties. The new strains also required changes in techniques toward farming methods requiring more fertilizer, irrigation, and use of machinery. Nevertheless, the Green Revolution led to a rapid increase in production of these two basic foodstuffs in some less developed countries.

Green Revolution
An agricultural innovation consisting of the development of dwarf, high-yield varieties of wheat and rice that have enabled some less developed countries to improve food production.

CLIMATE

Almost all the poorest countries are in tropical climates. Conversely, all the industrialized countries are in temperate climates. This relationship between climate and development is so strong that it seems unlikely to be a coincidence. In fact, the gap between levels of development between the regions is sometimes referred to by development economists as the "North-South problem." Some development economists have suggested that warmer climates produce lower human effort, more diseases, and unfavorable agricultural conditions. There is no winter to wipe out large numbers of disease-bearing pests and parasites. In addition, many tropical countries are largely jungle or desert, neither of which is hospitable to agriculture.

DUALISM

A final characteristic of almost all less developed countries is the coexistence of two societies in the same country—one modern, urban, and market-oriented and the other made up of rural peasants who are illiterate, largely employed in agriculture and with very little of their economic activity passing through the market. This coexistence is called **dualism**.

dualism
The coexistence of a modern, urban, market-oriented society and a rural, agriculture-based, traditional peasant society, characteristic of most less developed countries.

The cities in less developed countries contain many poor people, but also have modern transportation and plumbing, manufacturing and service jobs, culture, a concentration of educated people, and a modern market economy. Birth rates are lower and in most cases women have access to education and market opportunities. Rural areas, in contrast, tend to maintain simple, traditional lifestyles with centuries-old farming methods, early marriage with many children, and much home production with few market transactions. The majority of the population in the rural areas lives in poverty or near poverty, generating little saving and investment, little improvement in human capital, and little interest in innovation.

Dualism can be a major handicap to development. The urban population in a dual economy is too small to provide a market for manufacturing and services or to generate enough saving and investment in human and physical capital.

MODELS OF ECONOMIC DEVELOPMENT

The study of economic development has resulted in few elegant theoretical models. The field has tended to attract practitioners and field economists rather than theorists. There are, however, a few models or theories that attempt to describe and predict various aspects of the development process. These models have, at times, been the basis of policies aimed at encouraging development.

The basic elements of the development process are the same as those outlined in Chapter 16 for economic growth in developed countries. The production possibilities curve and the aggregate supply curve must both be shifted to the right. To do that, either existing resources must be used more effectively or additional resources must be created or acquired. Technology and cultural change are the keys to better resource use. Additional resources can come from within, through sacrificing consumption today to invest in physical and human capital for tomorrow, or from other countries.

CLASSICAL ECONOMICS AND ECONOMIC DEVELOPMENT

The original theorist of economic development was also the person who is regarded as the founder of market economics. The complete title of Adam Smith's *Wealth of Nations* (1776) was *An Inquiry into the Nature and Causes of the Wealth of Nations*. In that book, Smith set forth the classical principles of economic development. These principles rested on a *laissez-faire* governmental policy (nonintervention) toward private industry and commerce. The division of labor and the resulting increase in productivity were limited only by the size of the market. Smith advocated free trade as a way to promote this division of labor by exploiting each nation's comparative advantage in production.

Some of Smith's successors in the classical tradition were less optimistic about the development process. David Ricardo developed the theory of diminishing marginal productivity. This theory suggested that as an economy grew, additional resources would add less and less to total output. Thomas Robert Malthus is best known for his dismal predictions about the race between population and the food supply. He saw population growth as the surest way to slow down or even reverse the growth of per capita output and the rise in the standard of living.

Karl Marx as a Development Economist

Karl Marx is best known as the intellectual founder of communism, but he also described a sequence for economic development. Marx saw all society passing through a series of historical stages: (1) primitive society (tribal communism), (2) slavery, (3) feudalism, (4) capitalism, (5) socialism, and, finally, (6) communism. At this final stage, Marx argued, scarcity would no longer exist, and workers would produce without material incentives. His contributions to economic development were in three areas. First, he discussed problems of income distribution as economies developed. Second, he described a pattern of relationship between capitalistic economies and the peripheral nations that is still cited today by Third World critics of the industrial nations. Third, the Soviet model of Marxism has been copied by a number of less developed countries as a development strategy.

Marx and his early followers predicted that a class struggle would emerge between the workers (the proletariat) and the capitalists. According to the labor theory of value, widely held among economists in the early nineteenth century, capitalists would pay workers only the minimum amount necessary to subsist. Wages would always tend toward the subsistence level because capitalists, seeking to maximize profits, would pay the minimum amount necessary. Marx labeled the difference between the value of the goods produced by labor and the subsistence wage the workers received **surplus value**. This surplus value, which accrued to capitalists, represented their exploitation of workers. It was this exploitation, Marx believed, that would eventually lead to the overthrow of capitalism by the workers.

This prediction did not hold up well in subsequent years. Industrialization did spread throughout the Western world in the aftermath of the Industrial Revolution. However, the pattern of capitalist exploitation of the working masses did not emerge. In fact, the material well-being of workers increased rapidly with spreading industrialization.

Marx's second contribution, a view of the relationship between the capitalistic countries and the Third World, was closely related to his view of income distribution. With workers living at the subsistence level, markets for the products of capitalism would have to be found in other countries. The capitalist machine would also need the foodstuffs and raw materials from the Third World. By keeping Third World countries dependent on the capitalist nations for manufactured goods and exploiting their agriculture, capitalists could siphon off income and wealth from them.

Although this view of the relationship between developed and less developed countries is simplistic, many citizens in less developed countries continue to believe it. However, keep in mind that, according to the theory of comparative advantage, both parties are better off as a result of specialization and trade. Contacts with the developed world have brought new methods, ideas, products, capital, and opportunities to the Third

surplus value
The difference between the value of the goods produced by labor and the subsistence wages the workers received.

World. The relationship is much less one-sided than Marx would have us believe.

The third, more indirect, contribution of Marx was to encourage a socialist, state-directed approach to development to avoid the supposed evils of capitalism. Marxist ideas continue to hold sway in a decreasing number of nations today, including Cuba, Albania, Angola, and China. These countries have nationalized the means of production in order to ensure that economic growth is for the benefit of the workers rather than capitalists. To date, these nations have had little success in accelerating growth. Some countries have engaged in land reform under the umbrella of Marxism. Large land holdings have been broken up in order to create co-operative farms or give small holdings to the peasants. These co-operative farms have generally shown low productivity because workers have little incentive to produce. The distribution of land to peasants (private ownership) has generally been more successful in increasing output.

W. W. Rostow: The Stages of Economic Growth

W. W. Rostow, in a book entitled *Stages of Economic Growth*, responded to Marx's theory with a different development theory in the same historical tradition.[7] Based on the experience of the modern industrial countries, Rostow argues that all countries go through five stages of economic growth. He believes that it is possible to classify countries according to their current stage. This classification enables researchers to look for the barriers that have kept some countries from advancing into the next stage in their development process.

The first stage is the traditional society, in which economic decisions are made on the basis of custom and obligation. The second stage develops the preconditions for takeoff. In this stage, cultural barriers to development are overcome, advances in agriculture take place, and an entrepreneurial class of risk takers begins to emerge. Takeoff is the third stage, during which there is a large increase in the rate of saving. Increased saving finances capital investment in the leading sectors (the industries that are developing most quickly). The leading sectors grow rapidly, and their growth pulls other sectors along. The takeoff is, of course, the key to emerging as an industrialized country. The Industrial Revolution in Western Europe and the United States marks the takeoff in these countries.

The final two stages are the drive to maturity and high mass consumption. During the drive to maturity, lagging sectors of the economy catch up to the leading sectors. The takeoff is consolidated into sustained growth. The fifth stage, high mass consumption, describes the present level of development in the United States and Western Europe. In this stage, the economy settles into a steady pace of growth that provides a high level of consumption for most members of the society.

Rostow's theory of stages implies that all countries follow a (roughly) similar path to development. Critics of the theory have pointed out that although the stages might describe the development process of the pres-

---

7. W. W. Rostow, *Stages of Economic Growth*, 2nd ed. (New York: Cambridge University Press, 1971).

ent industrialized nations, the present less developed countries will not necessarily follow the same sequence. The dualism in the typical less developed country, for example, makes it very different from seventeenth-century England, where the level of technological development was similar in all sectors of the economy.

Economist Simon Kuznets, a Nobel Prize winner, has pointed out that there are many differences between conditions in today's less developed countries and the preindustrial phase of today's developed countries.[8] Among the most important of these differences is agricultural production. Per capita agricultural output in today's less developed countries is about one-fourth the level it was in preindustrial stages of the present developed countries. Another significant difference is that population is still growing much more rapidly in less developed countries than it was in today's developed countries at a similar stage in their development. Social and political obstacles are also more formidable in many less developed countries. Thus, some of the preconditions are not yet met in the majority of less developed countries, and little progress is being made in getting ready for takeoff.

THE BIG PUSH STRATEGY

Broad theories are less helpful in prescribing policies than specific strategies are. One specific approach is the **big push strategy**. It calls for a major thrust on all fronts in the economy by government or by private enterprise with the government's support. This strategy is based on the classical notion that growth in the output of an industry is limited by the extent of the market. At low levels of economic development, it is futile for any one industry to expand its output to a larger scale. It would be unable to sell its added product. But if all industries expand in a big push, the inputs needed for the production of one commodity become the demands for other industries' output. Also, the incomes generated will create a large demand for the final products. The big push must be orchestrated by the government, its proponents argue, because no single entrepreneur or group of entrepreneurs has the incentive to expand production unless there is expansion in other industries at the same time.

big push strategy
The development strategy calling for a major thrust on all fronts in the economy by government or by private enterprise with government inducement.

THE LEADING SECTORS STRATEGY

Albert O. Hirschman, a development economist with a great deal of field experience, takes a different tack from the big push strategy.[9] Hirschman supports a **leading sectors strategy** for economic growth. He argues that a country should concentrate on developing successful sectors that will then influence other sectors in the chain of production through backward and forward linkages.

For example, if there is a successful sardine fishing industry, it could be linked forward to a canning operation, which in turn could be linked forward to a packing and shipping industry. Backward linkages could develop effective demand for cans and shipping cartons, stimulating a min-

leading sectors strategy
The development strategy calling for concentration on a few successful sectors, which will then pull along other sectors in the development process.

---
8. Simon Kuznets, *Economic Growth and Structure* (New York: W. W. Norton, 1965).
9. Albert O. Hirschman, *The Strategy of Economic Development* (New Haven, CT: Yale University Press, 1958).

ing industry and a paper industry. In this view, if the government is to be involved in the development process, it should concentrate its efforts on encouraging those sectors or industries that maximize the number of potential linkages. Private entrepreneurs would then take over in response to the demand created through the linkages. The role of the government would be limited. The market would play the primary role in allocating productive resources.

GOVERNMENT AND THE DEVELOPMENT PROCESS

The theories and strategies just discussed prescribe a variety of roles for government. The Marxist extreme calls for state ownership of resources and direction of production. Adam Smith would recommend a *laissez-faire* approach. The big push strategy calls for a strong government role. The leading sectors approach relies more on the private sector.

Development policies of some less developed countries and policies advocated by some development economists call for governments to direct the development process. Many of these views grew out of the experience of the 1930s and 1940s, when the Soviet Union was able to grow very rapidly by applying severe authoritarian techniques.[10] As a result of the apparent Soviet success, some economists began to argue like this:

No policy of economic development can be carried out unless the government has the capacity to adhere to it. . . . Quite often, however, democratic governments lose equanimity and determination in the face of opposition. . . . This is the dilemma of most democratic governments. It is here that socialist countries . . . have an immense advantage: their totalitarian structure shields the government from the rigorous and reactionary judgments of the electorate. . . . Another advantage of the socialist countries is their passionate conviction and dedication to the objective of economic growth—which contrasts visibly with the halting and hesitant beliefs and actions of most democracies. The firm and purposive sense of direction . . . is in pointed contrast to the extensive revisions and changes in policies and methods which are prompted by minor setbacks in most democratic governments and which produce a sense of drift and helplessness. The political economy of development appears to pose a cruel choice between rapid (self-sustained) expansion and democratic processes.[11]

The idea that development requires authoritarian leadership has been dealt a severe blow by recent events in Eastern Europe and by troubles in the Soviet economy. However, this notion was challenged earlier in an empirical study by U.S. government economist G. William Dick.[12] He divided the independent less developed countries into three classifications: authoritarian, semicompetitive, and competitive. An authoritarian country is headed by one political party. A competitive country has two or more political parties competing for power, with free elections at regular intervals. A semicompetitive country has one majority party and several mi-

---

10. This drastic approach to development is sometimes called the Stalinist model.
11. Jagdish Bhagwati, *The Economies of Underdeveloped Countries* (New York: McGraw-Hill, 1966), pp. 203–204.
12. G. William Dick, "Authoritarian versus Nonauthoritarian Approaches to Economic Development," *Journal of Political Economy* (July/August 1974).

nority parties or one political party that conducts legitimizing elections. In any case, there is much less extensive control of individual choices in a semicompetitive country than in an authoritarian country. Dick examined the growth rates of real per capita GDP in each of the less developed countries. He found that the authoritarian countries generally had lower growth rates than the competitive countries. Growth is a complex process that cannot be reduced to a single factor, but the main lesson of Dick's empirical study is that rapid growth and democracy may be linked.

Most approaches to development are at neither the totalitarian nor the *laissez-faire* extreme. Government is usually expected to play some role. One important role it can play is to create a set of taxes and regulations that is favorable to development of private enterprise. Another important role for government is the development of human capital through health and education. Government also needs to provide infrastructure, such as roads, water systems, and airports. Finally, it is important for government not to become an obstacle to development by dissipating scarce and valuable resources on political goals or as favors to special interest groups.

Property Rights and Development

Although there are no definitive theories of development, there is ample evidence that private ownership of property and competition can play important roles. Private property, the ability to buy and sell and exchange the products of one's labor, is an essential condition for individual incentives to work, save, invest, and take risks. When governments restrict property rights, they can reduce these work and investment incentives, slowing the economic growth process. (We discussed the role of private property and property rights in Chapter 2 when the stage was being set for the study of economics.)

Governments influence the amount of competition that exists. Government monopolies, or government-sponsored monopolies, can prevent competition from developing. Monopolies have less incentive to expand output, innovate, or take risks because there are no competitors nipping at their heels. Many African countries that were formerly under British rule inherited colonial policies that created government monopolies in many export industries, licensing of private sector producers, and state enterprises that spawned huge bureaucracies. With established public monopolies, or government-created private monopolies, it is difficult to create the kind of competitive environment in which economic growth is more likely to take place.

A 1988 study by Gerald Scully explored the role of the economic and political environment in development. Scully classified 115 economies on the basis of political rights, individual rights, and use of a free market. He found that those that most strongly emphasized political and individual rights and the use of markets had been growing at a rate 2.7 times as fast as those that did not.[13] Thus, the institutions of democratic capitalism appear to make a significant contribution to the development process.

---

13. Gerald W. Scully, "The Institutional Framework and Economic Development," *Journal of Political Economy*, 1988, 96(3): 652–662.

MILITARY SPENDING AND DEVELOPMENT

The war in the Persian Gulf in early 1991 was a dramatic reminder of another obstacle to development. In many less developed countries, a large share of public expenditure is diverted into military uses. Several African countries have been fighting guerrilla wars for a long time. Other ongoing battles are in Sri Lanka, the Philippines, and Central America. Iraq and Iran ended a long and bloody conflict not long before Iraq invaded Kuwait. The result of the Gulf War has been a sharp drop in both population and income for Iraq and Kuwait. It will take a long time to rebuild infrastructure and restore levels of output in both those countries.

According to the World Bank, world military expenditures in the 1980s accounted for about 5 percent of total world income. Developing countries spent $173 billion on defense in 1987, which accounted for 5.1 percent of GNP and 19.2 percent of central government budgets in those countries.[14] Defense takes a much larger share of GNP in some countries. Pakistan, with a per capita GNP of only $350, spends 6.4 percent of GNP on defense. Yemen spends almost 10 percent.

In addition to the absolute amount of resources used, another problem created by defense spending in less developed countries is that much of that spending is for imported arms. These imports use scarce foreign exchange needed in industrial and agricultural development. Even if these countries do not actually go to war, their military spending is taking resources badly needed in other sectors. If military spending increases the likelihood of war, there is an additional potential loss of lives and infrastructure.

THE ROLE OF DEVELOPMENT ASSISTANCE

Still another role for government in development is a flow of economic aid from governments of already developed countries. The United States and Canada received substantial aid, both public and private, in their earliest days. Israel is often cited as a modern-day developmental miracle. It has received massive infusions of foreign capital of all kinds—physical, financial, and human. Japan and the Soviet Union, on the other hand, developed almost in isolation. Thus, although aid can be helpful, it apparently is not essential to development.[15]

The United States concentrates its official development assistance through the **Agency for International Development (AID)**, which is part of the State Department and is in charge of U.S. aid to foreign countries. A publication of AID states:

Programs to assist these people reflect an American tradition of sharing and helping the needy as well as enlightened national self-interest. In part, foreign aid is an expression of the American people's sense of justice and compassion. It also plays an important role in the continuing effort to achieve an enduring structure of world peace. This role is essential to the quest for global tranquility, freedom and progress. There are many things, however, that foreign aid cannot do. Experience has shown that it cannot right all social wrongs or solve every economic problem in

Agency for International Development (AID)
An agency that is part of the U.S. State Department and is in charge of U.S. aid to foreign countries.

---

14. World Bank, *World Development Report 1990* (New York: Oxford University Press, 1990), p. 17.
15. Agency for International Development, *AID's Challenge in an Interdependent World* (Washington, DC: Office of Public Affairs, 1978), p. 3.

International Perspective

How Americans Feel About Development Assistance

A report published in 1987 by The Overseas Development Council describes the attitudes of U.S. citizens toward economic development and U.S. development assistance.[a] This very comprehensive survey was carried out by the Strategic Information Research Corporation and turned up some surprising conclusions. Here are the pollsters' findings:

- Americans are aware of the problems of poverty and underdevelopment that face the Third World and do not believe that much progress has been made in improving Third World living conditions over the last decade.
- Americans have strong negative perceptions of Third World *governments*, but not of the *people* of those countries.
- A majority of Americans favor U.S. efforts to assist Third World countries with development.
- Policy makers perceive public support for U.S. economic assistance to be weak and fluctuating.
- Most Americans are poorly informed about U.S. foreign policy, the Third World, development issues, and U.S. relations with developing countries.
- Most Americans are aware in very general terms of the existence of economic relationships between the United States and the Third World and believe such relationships to hold potential mutual benefits.
- The perceived tradeoff between promoting *domestic* well-being and helping those *overseas* limits public support for specific U.S. trade, aid, and financial policies to promote Third World growth or alleviate poverty.
- Most Americans recognize that the United States has political or strategic interests in the Third World, but many are concerned about U.S. overinvolvement in the affairs of developing countries.
- The major reason for public support for economic assistance is a humanitarian concern or a sense of responsibility. Economic or political self-interest rationales are generally less compelling.
- Americans consider economic assistance a legitimate tool to use in pursuing U.S. political or strategic objectives, but they are concerned that this result is not always achieved.
- In some cases, public preferences about the U.S. aid program appear to be at odds with official policy.
- Americans express a strong preference for those types of U.S. economic aid aimed at delivering help directly to poor people.
- Economic aid is widely perceived to be ineffective or wasted. However, this opinion does not dissuade many Americans from supporting assistance efforts.
- The American public makes little distinction between private and official aid.
- A small—but not insignificant—proportion of Americans have been personally involved in efforts to eliminate poverty and stimulate development in the Third World. A larger active constituency may, however, exist.
- Personal experience or personal approaches are most likely to motivate Americans to become actively involved in efforts to promote development or to alleviate poverty in Third World countries.

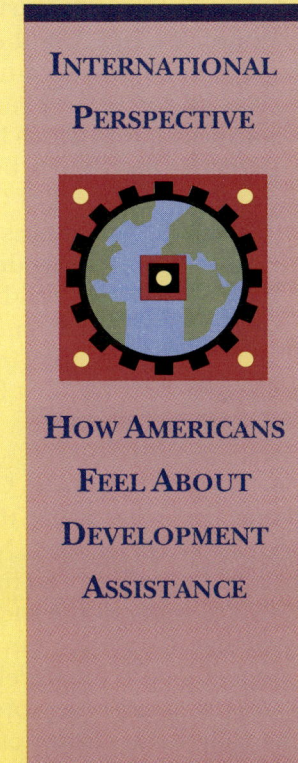

---

a. Christine Contee, *What Americans Think: Views on Development and U.S.–Third World Relations* (New York: InterAction and The Overseas Development Council, 1987).

a developing country. It cannot bring about instant progress. Some economists even claim that it has not been very effective in promoting economic development. Economic aid must be considered as a complement to other elements of foreign policy.[16]

The United States is a major contributor to the development programs of low-income countries. In 1988, the United States contributed 24 percent of all the aid given by Western industrialized countries and gave far more than any one of the other countries. However, as a percentage of GNP, thirteen countries gave a much larger share to low-income countries than the 0.25 percent contributed by the United States. France, for example, gave more than 1 percent of GNP to development aid.

At the end of the 1980s, pressures for renewed and expanded foreign aid came mainly from the fledgling democracies of Eastern Europe. They looked to the West for aid in rebuilding their economies. East Germany received aid mainly from West Germany before and after reunification. Poland, Hungary, Romania, and Czechoslovakia looked to Japan, the United States, Canada, and Western Europe for equipment, technical assistance, and other forms of aid.

THE NEW INTERNATIONAL ECONOMIC ORDER

New International Economic Order (NIEO)
A proposal by the Group of 77 calling for changes in international economic institutions to redistribute income from richer nations to poorer nations through trade preferences, increased aid, and other measures.

Economic aid and trade are two of the major issues underlying a call by many Third World countries for a **New International Economic Order (NIEO)**. This proposal calls for a change in international economic institutions in order to redistribute income from richer nations to poorer nations. In particular, it calls for developed nations to assume more responsibility for speeding up the development process.

The NIEO was proposed by a group of less developed countries in the United Nations called the Group of 77. Among its proposals were increased foreign aid and preferential tariff treatment and reduced regulations to allow less developed countries to export more to the developed nations. It also proposes that developed nations support price stabilization programs for tropical agricultural products, much like the farm price support programs in the United States and Europe. To this point, the success of the NIEO has been small. One outcome has been increased attention to the problems of less developed countries in trade negotiations in the 1970s and the 1980s.

HELP FROM THE PRIVATE SECTOR: MULTINATIONALS

In addition to aid from government to government, many countries' development efforts benefit from direct foreign investment by private firms and individuals, which supply scarce capital. Both private loans and multinational corporations (MNCs) transfer capital to these countries. Private loans have contributed to the debt problem, discussed later in this chapter.

A multinational corporation is a firm with headquarters in one country and one or more branch plants in other countries. Multinational corporations are headquartered in every developed, industrial country and a few less developed ones. Most of them have their branch plants in in-

---

16. The debate over the effectiveness of economic aid is summarized in Robert Cassin et al., *Does Aid Work? Report to an Intergovernmental Task Force* (New York: Oxford University Press, 1986). This report, written for the World Bank, provides some good data and a review of the arguments.

dustrial countries. There has been a foreign corporate presence in most less developed countries at least since World War II, and in many cases going back to the beginning of the century.

The impact of multinational corporations on development is hotly disputed. Multinational corporations often choose locations in less developed countries for access to raw materials or to local and regional markets for products they cannot easily export from home, because of either distance, perishability, or trade barriers. They do bring in capital, provide job opportunities, and increase foreign exchange. However, the good jobs are often filled by foreign nationals, not local workers. A multinational corporation may have no meaningful linkages to the rest of the host economy. It will then fail to act as a leading sector that spreads development to other sectors. A multinational corporation may be the largest taxpayer, largest export earner, and major employer in a small country. Thus, it may wield more real power than the host government. Multinational corporations can play a useful role in economic development. Any benefit they bring, however, may not be enough to overcome the many obstacles that developing nations face.

One of the major concerns about multinational corporations is that they tend to transplant technology developed in their home country, usually a nation with abundant capital and skilled labor, but scarce unskilled labor. Critics point out that these firms rarely adapt their methods of production to make the best use of local resources. This process is called technology adaptation, and its result is **appropriate technology**. In addition, they do not usually make their technology available to other companies in related fields in the less developed countries. Thus, there are none of the linkage effects necessary to promote development.

appropriate technology Methods of production that have been adapted to take advantage of the mix of resources available in less developed countries.

TIME BOMBS IN THE DEVELOPMENT PATH

There are two major problems that developing countries must address. The first is control of population growth. The second is the huge debt that many of them have compiled in recent years.

THE POPULATION BOMB

As you saw earlier in this chapter, even countries experiencing economic growth can see their per capita income decline if their population is growing at a faster rate than income. Yet discussions of managing population growth are very sensitive. Many countries regard foreign advice concerning birth rates as inappropriate.

In 1800, the world's population is estimated to have been about 1 billion. In 1988, it was 5.1 billion. By the year 2000, it will have swelled to 6 billion. The world's population is growing by 250,000 people per day, or 90 million people per year. The problem for development is that more than 90 percent of that projected growth will occur in the less developed countries.

Table 5 shows estimates of expected populations and population growth rates for the world's most populous countries. It is important to note that no developed industrial country can be found in the list of countries with rapid population growth.

Fastest-Growing Nations	Population in 2000 (millions)	Average Annual Growth Rate, 1987–2000 (%)	Slowest-Growing Nations	Population in 2000 (millions)	Average Annual Growth Rate, 1988–2000 (%)
Oman	2	3.9	Hungary	10	−0.2
Rwanda	10	3.8	West Germany	61	0.0
Ivory Coast	18	3.8	Denmark	5	0.0
Yemen Arab Republic	13	3.6	Belgium	10	0.0
Jordan	6	3.6	Austria	8	0.1
Libya	6	3.6	Italy	58	0.1
Syria	18	3.6	Greece	10	0.2
Malawi	12	3.5	Finland	5	0.2
Zambia	11	3.5	Ireland	4	0.3
Uganda	24	3.5	Britain	59	0.3
Kenya	34	3.4	Switzerland	7	0.4
Tanzania	37	3.4	Sweden	9	0.4
Iraq	26	3.4	Portugal	11	0.4
Togo	5	3.3	Spain	41	0.4
Congo People's Republic	3	3.3	France	59	0.4
			Japan	129	0.4
Niger	11	3.3	Norway	4	0.4

Source: Adapted from *World Development Report, 1990* (New York: Oxford University Press, 1990). Copyright © 1990 by the International Bank for Reconstruction and Development/The World Bank.

TABLE 5
PROJECTED POPULATIONS AND GROWTH RATES OF FASTEST- AND SLOWEST-GROWING NATIONS

demographic transition
The bridging of the developmental gap from falling death rates to falling birth rates, resulting in slower population growth.

DEFUSING THE POPULATION BOMB. Understanding why populations grow provides a clue to a solution. During the Industrial Revolution in Western Europe and the United States, populations grew rapidly but not at the explosive rates of today's less developed countries. There were somewhat different reasons for those increases. As the standard of living began to rise during the Industrial Revolution, the birth rate increased, and death rates slowly began to decline. After incomes increased to higher levels, the birth rate also declined. Today, medical advances, inoculations, and many life-lengthening techniques have spread throughout the world, reducing death rates even in less developed countries. As a result, those countries have high birth rates and declining death rates and, therefore, an exploding population.

Birth rates didn't decline in the developed world until most countries had attained relatively high levels of per capita income. In most nations, death rates fell first as better health care, better nutrition, and higher standards of living lengthened lifespans. After a time, birth rates fell. A nation that has bridged the developmental gap from falling death rates to falling birth rates, thus slowing population growth and reducing the dependency ratio, has made the **demographic transition**.

Less developed countries are feeling pressure from both within and abroad to try to influence their birth rates even though income levels are still low. In the present developed countries, the demographic transition occurred naturally. Most efforts to deliberately encourage or even enforce population control have occurred in Communist countries, although India has made some strong efforts toward voluntary sterilization and birth control. In China, the Communist authorities have instituted a get-tough campaign that denies many state-supplied benefits to couples with more than one child. This "planned" approach has slowed China's population growth rate to 1.3 percent. It has had many unintended side effects, however, including claims of female infanticide and a very high number of late-term abortions.

POPULATION AND POVERTY. Economists must be careful in their analysis of the problems of overpopulation. After all, the existence of large numbers of people by itself has little to do with poverty. Many stories of famine and the problems of the population explosion are reported from areas of the world such as Africa, by a reporter standing in the middle of the most densely populated city in one of the poorest countries in the world. The implication is clearly that there is a link between population density and poverty. Yet the report will probably be produced in and certainly broadcast from New York City or Washington, D.C., two of the richest *and* most densely populated places on earth. Clearly, people aren't starving because of dense population. They are starving because they are poor. As we saw above, population growth and slow economic growth may be interrelated, but the relationship is not causal. If the less developed countries could speed up economic growth, fast food franchisers would be bidding for prime spots in their large cities.

THE DEBT BOMB

One of the elements of the vicious circle of poverty is a low level of investment. It seems logical, then, that one way to break this circle would be for both the public and private sectors in less developed countries to borrow from the developed world. For many years, the World Bank operated with this goal in mind. The World Bank made low-interest loans to less developed countries to build roads, dams, and power plants. The modest amount of borrowing from private-sector financial institutions was mainly short-term commercial credit and was not viewed as a serious developmental problem.

This pattern began to change in the 1970s, as more and more private banks lent to both governments and private firms to undertake projects in less developed countries. These projects were expected to boost GNP enough to allow the borrowing country to make the interest and principal payments and still be better off.

By 1982, problems had begun to surface. Not all of the loans were being used for capital investment that would generate income to make repayment. Many of the loans went to finance current consumption (especially oil imports) or ill-conceived investment projects. Loans to Mexico were singled out as being used unwisely, because funds often lined the pockets of corrupt politicians. The crisis became apparent in the U.S. banking community. Some banks had made so many risky loans to developing countries that default could lead to bank failure. Some nations were unable to service their debts (to meet scheduled payments of interest and/or principal). As a result, banks were increasingly reluctant to extend or renew existing loans to those countries (to say nothing about making new loans).

By 1987, the total external public debt of Third World countries exceeded $911 billion. Brazil topped the list in debt size, with a total debt of almost $90 billion. Seven countries had annual payments of principal and interest amounting to more than 10 percent of GNP, with Jamaica heading the list at 17 percent. Private debt was large (over $1 billion) in eighteen of the ninety-seven less developed countries. Most of the debt, however, is public sector debt, usually foreign aid loans, for which terms are generally favorable and renegotiable.

There really is only one long-term solution to the Third World debt problem, although it may have several aspects. The solution is that of any debtor: consumption must be cut, and income must be generated to repay the debt. The debtor nations must improve their trade balances to earn income to repay or refinance the loans. This can be done by decreasing imports, allowing more foreign investment, and setting realistic exchange rates. Another solution that has been proposed is a debt-equity swap, whereby debt is exchanged for ownership of local assets. First proposed by American bankers and public officials, the idea was not well received in debtor countries.

Growth in both the debtor nations and the industrial market economies that buy their exports will aid the process of bringing debt under control. As developed nations grow, they demand more imports from the less developed countries. These imports allow the less developed countries to earn foreign currency needed to repay their debt.

In the past few years, negotiations between governments and banks have worked out interim solutions for some of the nations most deeply in debt. Some have worked out agreements for partial or deferred payments. No actual major default has occurred, but banks are increasingly cautious about lending without firmer guarantees of repayment.

A DEVELOPMENT SUCCESS STORY: THE NEW ASIAN TIGERS

The most remarkable story in economic development in recent decades is a group of Asian countries that have been reclassified from less developed countries to newly industrializing countries (NICs). These four countries—Hong Kong, Taiwan, South Korea, and Singapore—have been nicknamed "The Asian Tigers." They have grown rapidly in the last twenty years in a climate of private enterprise, hard work, minimal regulation, and open trade.[17] Two more Asian countries, Thailand and Indonesia, may be repeating the success of the other four.

All four of these nations have seen rapid growth of both GNP and exports with low inflation rates and high employment. There is a consistent pattern of high levels of saving and investment relative to GNP and a strong emphasis on development of exports and export markets. In some ways, all four have followed the Japanese model. In other ways, each of them is unique. What they have in common is average growth rates from 1981 to 1988 ranging from 5.4 to 9.9 percent, per capita GNPs ranging from $3,600 (South Korea) to $9,070 (Singapore), and bright prospects for the future. All of them have deliberately embarked on a strategy involving a strong private sector and a government that plays a supporting rather than directing role in the growth process. These development success stories make a powerful case for a market-oriented approach to development.

17. Lawrence A. Veit, "Time of the New Asian Tigers," *Challenge* (July-August 1987): 49–55.

Chapter 17 Economic Development and the Third World   479

SUMMARY

1. Less developed countries are characterized by low per capita income, high population growth, dualism, and a large part of productive activity in the agricultural sector. A tropical climate and a culture that is not favorable to economic activity are common in these countries.

2. Low-income countries invest little in human capital, that is, in the health, vigor, and education of the population. An unhealthy and uneducated labor force is relatively unproductive.

3. Marx offered a historical model of economic development in which countries advance through stages from primitive society to communism. He emphasized the role of income distribution and the relationship between capitalistic countries and peripheral countries. He felt that state ownership and control would promote economic development.

4. Rostow's theory of economic development sees each country passing through stages of growth. It is based on how development occurred in the present developed countries.

5. The big push strategy suggests that government can speed the process of economic development through a major coordinated thrust on all fronts of the economy. The leading sectors strategy strongly suggests that if effort is concentrated in some key sectors and linkages are developed, those sectors will pull along the other sectors.

6. The United States has traditionally aided less developed countries. Much U.S. aid is channeled through the Agency for International Development (AID). U.S. aid is large in an absolute sense, but other Western nations contribute a larger share of GNP than does the United States.

7. The New International Economic Order (NIEO) is a call for a new international economic system that gives preference to less developed countries in international trade and involves greater aid from the industrial countries.

8. Multinational corporations also channel capital to less developed countries, but the effects on development are mixed.

9. Population growth creates problems for economic development because of the diversion of resources into caring for those too young or too old to be productive workers.

10. The debt of developing countries is an increasingly serious problem for those countries and for the U.S. banks that have been granting development loans.

11. Evidence from the newly industrializing countries (NICs) of Southeast Asia suggests that market forces are positively linked with economic growth. Government can play an important role in providing infrastructure and investment in human capital.

NEW TERMS

convergence hypothesis
crude birth rate
dependency ratio
crude death rate

vicious circle of poverty
Green Revolution
dualism
surplus value

big push strategy
leading sectors strategy
Agency for International
 Development (AID)

New International
 Economic Order
appropriate technology
demographic transition

QUESTIONS FOR DISCUSSION

1. Does development change the cultural environment or does the cultural environment cause economic development?

2. What role do you think the United States should play in world development?

3. If you were to advise the government of a less developed country on steps to take toward development, what would be your top four priorities? Why?

4. Suppose you visited a less developed country and the local officials told you that they were pursuing a big push

strategy instead of a leading sectors strategy. How could you tell if this was true?

5. In recent years, there has been a great deal of television coverage concerning drought and famine in Africa. Is this an agricultural problem or an economic development problem?

6. Why is the study of demographic trends so important in the study of economic development?

7. What is the New International Economic Order (NIEO)? How would it help less developed countries?

8. What do development economists have in mind when they speak of linkages?

9. What is the vicious circle of poverty?

10. What are Rostow's preconditions for takeoff?

11. Suppose you were in charge of development for a less developed country and were approached by a multinational corporation interested in locating in your country. What kinds of concerns might you have?

12. Suppose the multinational corporation in Question 11 was in the business of printing books to ship abroad. What kinds of linkages might be involved?

13. What role should government play in the development process? How does this differ from what governments actually do?

14. Which of the following pieces of data are useful in determining whether countries are less developed countries? Why?
GNP (or GDP)
per capita GNP
population growth rate
death rate
literacy rate
share of GNP derived from agriculture

15. Who are the Asian Tigers and what are they doing right?

Suggestions for Further Reading

Bianchi, Andres, Robert Devlin, and Joseph Ramos. *External Debt in Latin America: Adjustment Policies and Renegotiation.* Boulder, CO: The United Nations Economic Commission for Latin America and the Caribbean, 1985. A description of the magnitude of the debt problem with some calm and reasoned solutions.

Hagen, Everett W. *The Economics of Development*, 4th ed. Homewood, IL: Irwin, 1986. A thoughtful and thorough textbook that emphasizes differences in the problems facing the various developing countries.

Kang, T. W. *Is Korea the Next Japan? Understanding the Structure, Strategy, and Tactics of America's Next Competitor.* New York: Free Press, 1989. A book that examines the reasons for Korea's rapid economic development in the 1980s.

McCord, William, and Arline McCord. *Paths to Progress.* New York: W. W. Norton, 1986. Two field sociologists argue that Third World countries must make profound cultural, political, and social changes if they are to experience economic development.

Meier, Gerald (ed.). *Pioneers in Development.* Oxford and New York: Oxford University Press, 1988. Examines major contributions to understanding the process of economic development.

Reynolds, Lloyd G. *Economic Growth in the Third World.* New Haven, CT: Yale University Press, 1985. A book that contains good statistical surveys on forty countries.

Rostow, Walt Whitman. *Rich Countries and Poor Countries: Reflections on the Past, Lessons for the Future.* Boulder, CO: Westview Press, 1987. This collection of essays on the world economy includes some comments on the development process from one of the best-known twentieth-century development economists.

Schumacher, Ernest Friedrich. *Small Is Beautiful: Economics as If People Mattered.* New York: Harper & Row, 1976. A somewhat dated, but still popular book that questions the value of economic growth and stresses the importance of developing appropriate technologies.

The World Economy

6

AFTER STUDYING THIS CHAPTER, YOU SHOULD BE ABLE TO:

1. Describe the benefits of free trade.
2. Distinguish between absolute and comparative advantage, and discuss the gains from trade based on comparative advantage.
3. Identify the effects of a tariff and a quota.
4. Discuss the arguments for trade protection.
5. Explain why firms build foreign plants and what the economic effects are.

INTRODUCTION

CHAPTER 18
INTERNATIONAL TRADE

Except for the international perspectives, this book has generally ignored the rest of the world in order to concentrate on how the U.S. economic system operates. Yet the world is increasingly an important part of the American economy. You may drive a Japanese car, drink coffee from Brazil, eat Mexican tomatoes and Honduran bananas, or take pictures with a German camera. Chances are there is a plant of a foreign-owned multinational corporation close to where you live.

Even for a country as large as the United States, where trade with other countries is a relatively small fraction (about 10 to 12 percent) of GNP, international trade has become increasingly important. The percentage of output and sales entering into international trade has doubled in the last 15 years. Foreign competition is important to major industries such as textiles, steel, and autos. Immigration (both legal and illegal), foreign investment in the United States and American investment abroad, and the ups and downs in the value of the dollar are all issues in the news.

International economics is usually separated into two parts: international trade and international finance. International trade deals with the microeconomic questions of who produces what and who trades with whom and why, as well as with multinational firms, tariffs, and quotas. International finance examines the determinants of exchange rates between national currencies, the balance of payments, and the relationship between domestic macroeconomic concerns and the foreign sector.

This chapter covers international trade and the next chapter looks at international finance. You need to recognize, however, that trade and finance are closely related. For example, changes in the price of the dollar affect U.S. imports and foreign demand for U.S. exports. An inflow of investment from abroad can affect output, employment, and interest rates in the United States.

WHY NATIONS TRADE

The reasons for international trade are really no different from the reasons for trade between individuals who live in the same country. It is important to realize that in most cases international trade takes place between individuals and firms. When we speak of trade between the United States and Japan, we are really talking about trade between individuals

Chapter 18 International Trade   483

and firms in these countries. These individuals and firms trade for the same reasons that individuals and firms within a country trade. Trade takes place because of the availability of a better product or a better price or because of an opportunity for profit. Exactly what determines the patterns of trade between nations and how much each nation benefits have been important concerns to economists as long as there have been nation states and economists.

Before Adam Smith, the dominant view was that government should direct many spheres of economic activity, especially international trade. This view, called mercantilism, put heavy emphasis on control of shipping, maintaining colonies, discouraging imports, and promoting exports. Two famous economists are responsible for developing the arguments for a policy of free trade. One was Adam Smith, whose *Wealth of Nations* in 1776 made a strong case for freedom in every sphere of economic activity. The other was David Ricardo, a distinguished nineteenth-century British economist and member of Parliament who was very interested in the practical question of what trade policy England should pursue. He developed the principle of comparative advantage in his classic 1814 book, *Principles of Political Economy and Taxation*.

THE BENEFITS OF EXCHANGE

It is easier to envision the processes at work in international trade by focusing first on exchange rather than production. Consider Heather and Peter, who are both stamp collectors. Like most stamp collectors, they expand their collections by trading duplicates of stamps they have. Let's say that Heather has the complete 1938 Presidential series and several extras. Peter has some gaps in that series, but has some extra Canadian stamps that he would like to trade and that Heather would like to have. They work a deal. She trades three Presidential stamps for five Canadian stamps. As an outside observer, you might say that the trade was one of "equal values." That may be true in a market sense, but the stamps weren't of equal value to Peter and Heather. Heather wanted the Canadian stamps more than she wanted the extra Presidential stamps, and Peter felt just the opposite. They both were better off as a result of the trade.

Economists who look at international trade emphasize the **gains from trade**, or the increase in economic well-being that comes from specialization and exchange. The emphasis on exchange is one aspect of the theory of international trade that makes it different from the rest of microeconomics. However, we have to back up one step from exchange to production. Rarely do people trade solely out of existing stocks of goods. People produce in order to trade. The explanation of how people and nations decide what to produce for trade is based on the concepts of absolute advantage and comparative advantage.

gains from trade
The increase in economic well-being resulting from specialization and exchange.

ABSOLUTE ADVANTAGE

Suppose Heather and Peter are sister and brother, and their parents want the 12 windows in the house washed and the 24 square yards of leaves raked. Heather and Peter estimate their output as shown in Table 1. If this brother and sister divided the tasks equally, they would each have to wash half the windows (6 for Heather, which would take her 1½ hours, and 6

TABLE 1
AN EXAMPLE OF
ABSOLUTE ADVANTAGE

	WINDOWS PER HOUR	SQUARE YARDS OF LEAVES PER HOUR
Heather	4	6
Peter	2	8

for Peter, which would take him 3 hours) and rake 12 square yards of leaves (which would take Heather 2 hours and Peter 1½ hours to complete). At the end of a long afternoon, Heather would have worked 3½ hours, and Peter would have worked 4½ hours. On the other hand, if they each specialized in what they do better, Heather could have all of the windows washed in just 3 hours and Peter could have all of the leaves raked in 3 hours. There would be a clear gain of a valuable ½ hour for Heather and 1½ hours for Peter.

Both Heather and Peter are better off if they specialize, because each has an **absolute advantage**. Heather is more efficient than Peter at washing windows, and Peter is more efficient than Heather at raking leaves. It's not difficult to convince anyone of the benefits of specialization and trade when there is a clear absolute advantage for each partner.

absolute advantage
The ability to produce something using fewer resources than other producers use.

COMPARATIVE ADVANTAGE

Suppose, however, that one partner is better at both. Assume that Heather is better at *both* window washing and leaf raking. The production rates for Heather and Peter in this case are shown in Table 2. Is there still an opportunity for specialization and trade? If they continue to divide the tasks equally, Heather will spend 1½ hours on her 6 windows and 2 hours on 12 square yards of raking. She's through in just 3½ hours. Poor Peter, however, has to spend 6 hours on windows and 3 hours on leaves, for a total of 9 hours of work. Can Heather do something to make Peter better off without spending any more of her own time working?

Suppose they specialize. This time it's not as obvious who should specialize in what. The concept of opportunity cost provides an answer. When Heather rakes 6 square yards of leaves, she's giving up 4 clean windows she could have "produced" in that time. A clean window costs her 1½ square yards of raking. For Peter, a clean window costs 4 square yards of raking. Clearly, Heather's window washing is cheaper than Peter's in terms of alternatives. Heather has a **comparative advantage** in window washing because her opportunity cost is lower in that activity than in the other one. Peter also has a comparative advantage in raking, even though he has an absolute disadvantage in both activities. His opportunity cost of raking leaves is only ¼ of a clean window per square yard, and Heather's

comparative advantage
The ability to produce something at a lower opportunity cost than other producers face.

TABLE 2
AN EXAMPLE OF
COMPARATIVE ADVANTAGE

	WINDOWS PER HOUR	SQUARE YARDS OF LEAVES PER HOUR
Heather	4	6
Peter	1	4

is ⁴⁄₆, or ⅔. So Peter should specialize in that activity in which he has a comparative advantage, that is, in which his opportunity cost is lower.

Heather and Peter implement a policy of specializing on the basis of comparative advantage. Heather washes all the windows, which takes her 3 hours. Peter rakes all the leaves, which takes him 6 hours. By specializing on the basis of comparative advantage, both of them are better off! They have produced the same "output" (clean windows and a leaf-free yard) with considerably less input. Heather saved ½ hour, and Peter saved 3 hours. Both parties gained from specialization.

FROM INDIVIDUALS TO NATIONS. The same principles that determine specialization for two individuals in simple situations apply to more complex situations involving individuals and firms in groups, regions, or nations. Trade between nations is also based on comparative advantage. By specializing, both parties can gain from trade. For simplicity, economists usually use a two-country, two-commodity example. The same analysis applies to situations involving more countries or more commodities.

Suppose there are two countries called Inland and Outland. Before they discover one another, they are producing the products shown in Table 3. Outland, like Peter, is able to produce less of both commodities. This lack of absolute advantage may be due to Outland's resources being less efficient, or Outland may just be a smaller or poorer country with fewer resources. The reason for absolute advantage or absolute disadvantage makes no difference for comparative advantage and the gains from trade.

The output numbers for Inland and Outland in Table 3 represent points on their production possibilities curves. (To keep things simple, both production possibilities curves are assumed to be straight lines as in Chapter 3.) One more piece of information is needed in order to draw the straight-line production possibilities curve for each country. Assume that each country is devoting two-thirds of its resources to steel and one-third of its resources to cloth. This assumption makes it possible to calculate the end points of their production possibilities curves.

If Inland specializes in cloth, the country can produce 225 bolts. If it specializes in steel, it can produce 75 tons. If Outland specializes in cloth, the country can produce 180 bolts. If it specializes in steel, it can produce 30 tons. These points give the production possibilities curves in Figure 1.

Which country should specialize in what product or mix of products? The answer lies in the two countries' opportunity costs. For Inland, the opportunity cost of producing 75 tons of steel is 225 bolts of cloth not produced, or 3 bolts of cloth per ton of steel. For Outland, the same calculation says that 1 ton of steel costs 6 bolts of cloth. Inland's steel is cheaper

COUNTRY	STEEL (TONS)	CLOTH (BOLTS)
Inland	50	75
Outland	20	60
World Total	70	135

TABLE 3
PRODUCTION POSSIBILITIES WITHOUT TRADE

FIGURE 1
PRODUCTION POSSIBILITIES CURVES FOR INLAND AND OUTLAND

The production possibilities curve illustrates the gains from specializing on the basis of comparative advantage. Each country moves from pretrade production and consumption (point A), to output with specialization (point B) and then to consumption after trade (point C).

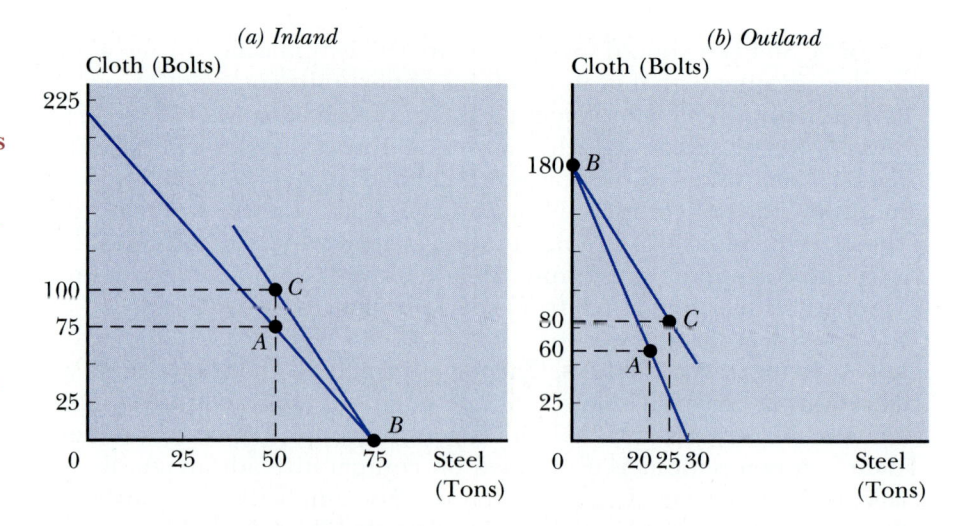

in terms of cloth forgone. Measuring the cost of cloth in terms of steel, on the other hand, gives these results: One bolt of Inland cloth costs $\frac{1}{3}$ of a ton of steel, and one bolt of Outland cloth costs only $\frac{1}{6}$ of a ton of steel. Measured in terms of opportunity costs, Outland's cloth is cheaper. The result of specialization is shown in Table 4.

Total world output has increased, without using additional resources, by 5 tons of steel and 45 bolts of cloth. Are the two countries better off?[1] Not yet. After all, they could have been producing those combinations anyway. It is only after trade that they can be better off.

THE TERMS OF TRADE. At what rate will Inland and Outland trade steel for cloth? Inland will not accept less than 3 bolts of cloth for a ton of steel, because this country can do that well producing its own cloth. Outland will not offer more than 6 bolts of cloth per ton of steel, because more than that would make it cheaper not to specialize. Anywhere between 3 and 6 bolts of cloth per ton of steel should be a mutually acceptable trading ratio. Let's make it 4 bolts of cloth for 1 ton of steel. This ratio is called the **terms of trade**. The exact terms of trade will lie somewhere between the parties' opportunity costs. Exactly where the terms of trade falls between those limits depends on the relative strength of demand for both products in both countries.

terms of trade
The ratio at which one product is exchanged for another.

TABLE 4
PRODUCTION BEFORE AND AFTER SPECIALIZATION

	BEFORE SPECIALIZATION		AFTER SPECIALIZATION	
	STEEL	CLOTH	STEEL	CLOTH
Inland	50	75	75	0
Outland	20	60	0	180
Total	70	135	75	180

1. To be sure that they are better off without knowing anything about their tastes and preferences, we need to be sure that each country has at least as much of one good as before and more of the other.

There are numerous after-trade combinations of steel and cloth that could make both countries better off. One possibility is to let Inland take all of its gains from trade in extra cloth, keeping its steel consumption at the original level of 50 tons and trading away the other 25 tons to Outland for 100 bolts of cloth. That exchange leaves Outland with 25 tons of imported steel and 80 bolts of domestic cloth, a consumption combination that represents more of both goods. The results of trade are summarized in Table 5.

These new consumption points are shown in Figure 1. Point C in part (a) shows Inland consuming 50 tons of steel and 100 bolts of cloth. Point C in part (b) represents a consumption combination of 25 tons of steel and 80 bolts of cloth for Outland. In each graph, this point lies along a "terms of trade" line, or a **consumption possibilities curve**, beginning at point B (total production with specialization) and having a slope of $\frac{1}{4}$ (1 steel to 4 cloth). Each country is able to get beyond its production possibilities curve by separating production (at point B) from consumption (at point C). The gains from trade are the same kinds of improvements in well-being that a country gets from having additional economic resources. Point C in each case represents one of many trade and consumption combinations that makes that partner better off.

consumption possibilities curve
A line showing the consumption combinations attainable through trade.

THE BASIS OF COMPARATIVE ADVANTAGE. What makes Inland better at producing steel and Outland better at producing cloth? For some products, the reasons are obvious. Climate determines the cheapest place to produce bananas, potatoes, and other agricultural products. Mineral resources determine other production patterns. Some products use a high proportion of unskilled labor relative to capital and other inputs. These products will be produced in countries with relatively large amounts of low-cost, unskilled labor. Other products require relatively more skilled labor, capital, or fertile land. These products will be produced in countries where those resources are abundant.

Still other products follow what economist Raymond Vernon called the **product cycle**. When the product is introduced, it will be exported by the country in which it was developed. But as the product and the production process become standardized, production will eventually migrate to other countries with a suitable resource mix. Automobiles, whose production technology was developed in the United States, are now produced almost everywhere. Textile was originally developed in England, but the production of simple cotton textiles (the most standardized part of the industry) has migrated around the globe in search of the inexpensive, low-skill labor that is used heavily in their manufacture.

product cycle
A series of stages, from development to standardization, through which a new product passes.

	BEFORE SPECIALIZATION		AFTER SPECIALIZATION		AFTER TRADE	
	STEEL	CLOTH	STEEL	CLOTH	STEEL	CLOTH
Inland	50	75	75	0	50	100
Outland	20	60	0	180	25	80
Total	70	135	75	180	75	180

TABLE 5
GAINS FROM TRADE

Sometimes the explanation for comparative advantage lies in historical accident. A product starts being produced in country *A* because that is where it was invented, or because its citizens want such a product. Country *A* develops the skills and resources needed to produce that product, including related industries that supply inputs or use the product in making other goods. If *A*'s resources are suited to the production of the good, *A* is likely to have a comparative advantage that it can retain for some time. If the world market is not large, there may be room only for a few suppliers who take advantage of cost savings in large-scale production. The first producer may enjoy a lasting advantage for that reason.

All these factors may explain the existence of comparative advantage. The important point is that it is possible for both partners to increase output and economic well-being by specializing on the basis of comparative advantage, no matter how that advantage originated.

OTHER BENEFITS FROM TRADE

There are at least two other important benefits from trade besides the increased output from comparative advantage. One is competition. The other is economies of scale.

Trade increases the number of competing firms from whom consumers can buy, widening their range of choices of goods and suppliers. This benefit of trade can be very important if the domestic industry has only a few firms. For example, car buyers in the United States have a wide range of choices because of international trade, although there are only a few domestic producers. As a result of foreign competition, domestic producers have responded to demands of some car buyers for smaller, more fuel-efficient cars.

Access to a large world market instead of a smaller domestic one may enable firms to operate at a more efficient scale. Producers of mainframe computers, aircraft, and heavy machinery need a very large market in order to produce at a scale that results in the lowest possible costs per unit.

THE WHY AND HOW OF PROTECTION

With all of these good reasons for free trade, why are some U.S. firms and industries protected from foreign competition? Many arguments are offered by firms that have to compete with imports, but most of these arguments come down to one reason—income distribution. A country as a whole benefits from free trade, but not everyone benefits equally.

Protection of domestic industries is accomplished with two main tools: tariffs and quotas. A **tariff** is a tax on imported goods or services. The tariff can be specific (based on weight, volume, or number of units) or *ad valorem* (figured as a percentage of the price). The average U.S. tariff is less than 5 percent. Many items bear no tariff at all, and a few items have large tariffs.

A **quota** is a quantity limit. It specifies the maximum amount of a good or service that can be imported during a given time period (usually a year). Quotas can be global (limiting total imports of widgets from all foreign suppliers to 1,000 widgets per year) or geographic (assigning quotas

tariff
A tax on imported goods or services.

quota
A limit on the amount of a good or service that can be imported during a given time period.

to specific countries). Quotas also can be combined with tariffs in a **tariff quota**. In this case, a certain amount of a good from one country is allowed to enter another country without a tariff. For amounts in excess of that limit, a tariff is applied.

EFFECTS OF A TARIFF

Figure 2 illustrates the effects of a tariff. In this figure, Inland produces, consumes, and imports cheese. The domestic supply curve is S_d. The domestic demand curve is D_d. Because Inland is a small country, its purchases of imported goods do not affect the world price of those goods. Inland can buy all the cheese it wants at the world price, P_w. At P_w, domestic producers are producing A pounds and consumers are buying B pounds. The difference between production and consumption is imports of $B - A$ pounds of cheese.

P_t is the price of imported cheese after Inland imposed a tariff equal to T. Since the tariff drives up the price, consumers buy less. Cheese consumption falls to C. Domestic producers move up along their supply curve to E. They get a bigger share of the smaller market. Imports decrease from $B - A$ to $C - E$.

Who gains? Domestic producers, including their owners, workers, and suppliers. These firms can charge a higher price and have a larger market share, which benefits everyone connected with them. Government also gains some tariff revenue. Who loses? Domestic consumers are paying more and getting less, so they lose. Foreign producers have lost sales. Also, the country imposing the tariff has given up some of the benefits of free trade noted earlier—more output, competition, and economies of scale. Since foreign cheese producers are more efficient than most of Inland's domestic cheese producers, this country is switching from more efficient to less efficient producers.

EFFECTS OF A QUOTA

Quotas are similar to tariffs. In fact, they can be represented by the same diagram. The main difference is that quotas restrict quantity, and tariffs

tariff quota
A combination of a quota and a tariff that allows a certain amount of a good or service to be imported without paying a tariff and imposes the tariff on further imports.

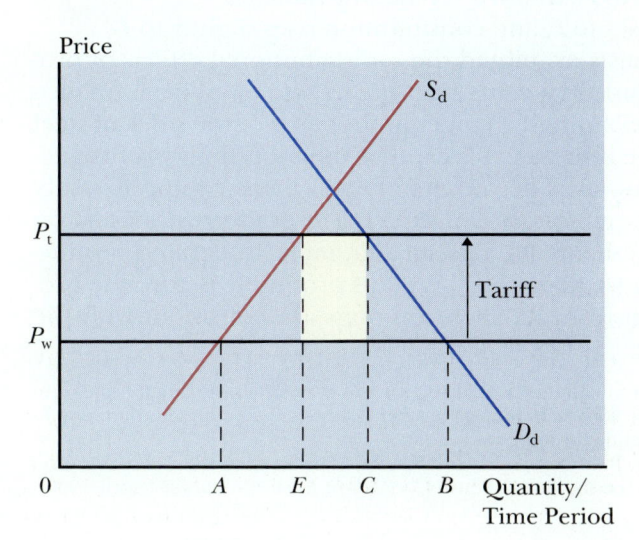

**FIGURE 2
EFFECTS OF A TARIFF OR QUOTA**
A tariff $T = P_t - P_w$ or an equivalent quota $C - E$ raises prices for domestic consumers (from P_w to P_t), reduces imports (from $B - A$ to $C - E$), lowers consumption (from B to C), and increases domestic output and sales from (A to E).

TARIFFS VERSUS QUOTAS	
A TARIFF	**A QUOTA**
• Raises prices	• Raises prices
• Reduces imports and consumption	• Reduces imports and consumption
• Increases domestic output	• Increases domestic output
• Produces government revenue	• Creates monopoly profits for those with import licenses
• Lets imports rise when demand increases	• Makes prices rise when demand increases

work through prices. If, in Figure 2, the government imposed a quota in the amount of $C - E$ on cheese, the effects on price, domestic production, consumption, and imports would be the same as those of the tariff $T = P_t - P_w$. There are a couple of important differences, however.

First, a tariff raises revenue for the government, in the amount of the shaded area in Figure 2. A quota generates no government revenue.[2] All the benefits of a quota go to protected domestic producers and to those importers who manage to get the scarce and valuable import permits used to implement quotas. Permit holders can buy the good at the low foreign price and resell it at the higher domestic price. The difference between the price the importer pays the foreign supplier and the price the importer can charge the domestic consumer $(P_t - P_w)$ times the number of units imported is a monopoly profit that comes from having a license to import. Note that this monopoly profit is equal to the revenue the government would have received under a tariff.

Second, suppose demand increased in the country. With a tariff, the quantity of imports would increase. With a quota, only the price would increase. Originally, the tariff T and the quota $C - E$ had the same effect on prices and quantities. As Figure 3 shows, however, when demand shifts from D_d to D'_d under a tariff, imports rise to $H - E$ and consumption rises to H. With a quota, price rises to P_f. Imports remain the same ($C - E = G - F$). Domestic production rises to F, and consumption rises slightly to G.

Several U.S. economists examined the redistributional effects of protectionism in the steel industry, using techniques borrowed from finance and accounting.[3] They examined changes in the value of the stock of steel companies to determine if these firms capture the monopoly profits generated by tariffs and quotas. The owners of steel firms captured a substantial portion of the economic rent created by trade restrictions on steel. Not all firms gained equally. The smaller, more integrated producers gained the most. Those firms that were less profitable before the protection gained the most from it. These findings are consistent with the analysis presented here.

---

2. In the 1980s proposals were made that would require the government to auction the right to import under a quota to the highest bidder. If this kind of policy was adopted, then quotas could also be used to raise revenue for the government.
3. Stefanie Lenway, Kathleen Rehbein, and Laura Sparks, "The Impact of Protectionism on Firm Wealth: The Experience of the Steel Industry," *Southern Economic Journal* (April 1990): 1079–1093.

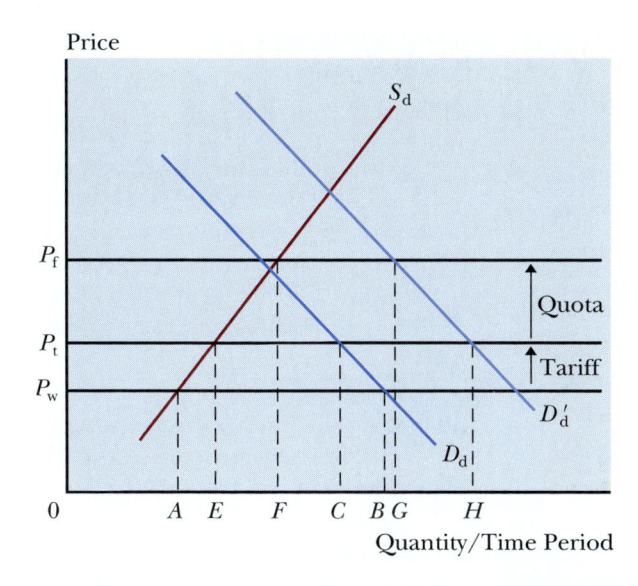

FIGURE 3
EFFECTS OF A TARIFF OR QUOTA WHEN DEMAND INCREASES
Under a tariff, an increase in demand increases the quantity of imports (from $C - E$ to $H - E$) and consumption (from C to H) but leaves the price unchanged (at P_t). With a quota, increased demand leads to a rise in price (from P_t to P_f) and in domestic production (from E to F). Consumption rises slightly (from B to G). Imports are unchanged ($G - F = C - E$).

Most economists prefer free trade to either tariffs or quotas. If they have to choose, they usually consider a tariff less harmful than an equivalent quota. A tariff does allow imports to increase in response to increases in demand. Also, at least some of the tariff revenue goes to the government, which uses it to further the general welfare. Also, a tariff is more visible and therefore easier to eliminate. A quota is less obvious and more likely to remain in place indefinitely.

NONTARIFF BARRIERS TO TRADE

In addition to tariffs and quotas, there are other kinds of government barriers to trade. Domestic laws or policies other than tariffs and quotas that interfere with the free exchange of goods and services across national borders are called **nontariff barriers**. Some of these barriers are intentional. One example is *domestic preference laws* requiring the government to favor domestic suppliers when making purchases for government agencies and programs. Other nontariff barriers are laws or regulations enacted for domestic reasons that make it more difficult for foreign suppliers to compete. For example, it may be difficult for a foreign supplier to comply with U.S. safety standards and labeling requirements. A common form of nontariff barrier is requiring excessive paperwork that adds to costs and reduces profits for foreign suppliers and domestic importing firms. In France, a shortage of customs inspectors constitutes a nontariff barrier because it creates long delays and thus discourages imports.

Sometimes nontariff barriers work the other way. Some U.S. laws and regulations make it more difficult for domestic firms to sell abroad. If American products must meet higher safety standards, for example, the American firm may not be able to compete with foreign producers who do not have to incur those costs.

Another type of nontariff barrier is antidumping codes. Dumping con-

nontariff barriers Trade restrictions other than tariffs and quotas.

Economic Insight

U.S. Barriers to Imports

In May 1989, the United States took action against Japan, Brazil, and India for unfair trade practices. The U.S. government demanded that these countries end unfair practices and threatened retaliatory tariffs on selected goods from their countries if action was not forthcoming. Reporting on this development, *U.S. News & World Report* noted that President Bush suggested to one of his economic advisers, "Maybe we ought to take action against a whole bunch of countries—including ourselves."

The United States is a very open market, but there are numerous barriers to trade that its trading partners regard as unfair. These barriers include "voluntary restraints" on automobiles, customs user fees on boats, planes, and trucks, Superfund taxes on petroleum products, quotas on cheese, ice cream, and sugar, a 35¢ per gallon tariff on orange juice, steel restraints, antidumping laws, and consumer preferences for American products. Professor Gary Hufbauer estimates that tariffs, quotas, and nontariff barriers cost American consumers more than $80 billion annually.

Antidumping laws can be a bureaucratic and legal nightmare. A 1989 hearing before the International Trade Commission (ITC) offers a case study. In 1989, Torrington Company, a Connecticut-based maker of ball bearings, claimed firms in eight European countries were engaging in unfair trade practices (dumping). Torrington reportedly budgeted $1 million for the legal battle. The ITC ruled in Torrington's favor that bearings were being dumped in the U.S. market at 60 percent below their home market value. U.S. producers of power tools and machinery were not happy with this ruling. They pointed out that there was a shortage of such bearings in the United States and that Torrington was producing at capacity. They thought the ruling disadvantaged them in export markets because the price of ball bearings they use went up significantly.

Buy American mandates create another barrier that foreign countries claim is unfair. These legal requirements are most commonly found in the defense industry, road construction, and mass transit. Such preferential treatment generally gives American suppliers a price advantage over foreign suppliers. A recent European Community publication refers to these preferences as "permanent discrimination in favor of U.S. products."

Criticism of U.S. barriers to imports by U.S. trading partners conveniently ignores the fact that their barriers are just as irksome to U.S. firms trying to export. As you can see, however, and as Professor Hufbauer reports, the costs of U.S. barriers are significant to American consumers.

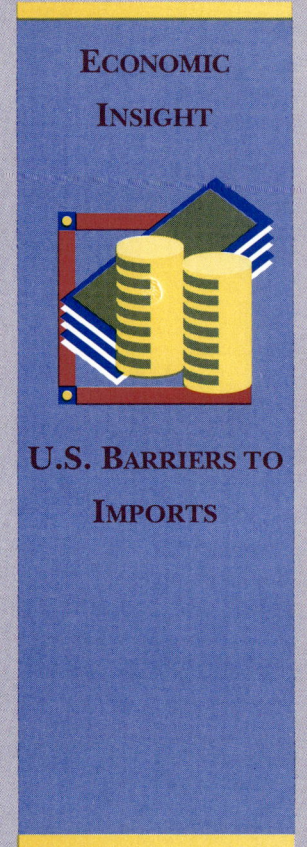

Source: Clemens P. Work with Robert F. Black, "Uncle Sam as Unfair Trader," *U.S. News & World Report* (12 June 1989): 42–44.

sists of selling a good at a lower price in a foreign country than in the firm's home country. Firms may dump abroad to get rid of surpluses, to take advantage of differences in elasticity of demand (price discrimination), or to establish a foothold in a competitive market. Most countries, including the United States, have antidumping regulations that forbid this practice as unfair competition. If a foreign firm is accused of dumping (usually by a competing firm in the importing country), the International Trade Commission will hear the case and may impose a duty on the dumped good to counteract the price difference. American firms often claim dumping is being done in order to make selling in the United States more difficult for foreign competitors.[4]

U.S. COMMERCIAL POLICY

The set of actions that a country undertakes to deliberately influence trade in goods and services is its **commercial policy**. For most of its history, the United States has had high tariffs and other trade restrictions. The highest U.S. tariff ever was imposed by the Smoot-Hawley Act of 1930, an average charge of 53 percent.

Since 1934, the United States has greatly reduced tariffs and other trade barriers by negotiating treaties with other countries. Trade barriers were reduced under a series of Congressional acts, beginning with the Reciprocal Trade Agreements Act of 1934. Regular trade negotiations led to reductions in tariffs by the United States and its major trading partners. The latest complete series of trade negotiations, which took place from 1974 to 1979, was called the Tokyo Round. After the tariff cuts agreed to in that round were finally implemented, the average U.S. tariff was only about 4.2 percent. The Tokyo Round also involved some agreements on reducing nontariff barriers. In 1986, a round of negotiations called the Uruguay Round began. In December 1990, the talks broke down over trade in agricultural products. The European countries were unwilling to lower their agricultural supports and the protection necessary to maintain them.

commercial policy
The set of actions that a country undertakes to deliberately influence trade in goods and services.

THE POLITICS OF PROTECTION

Reducing tariffs does not result in free trade. Quotas still protect autos, steel, textiles, and other industries. Nontariff barriers are still an important impediment to free trade. As the value of the dollar rose from 1981 to 1985, making imports cheap and exports expensive for the United States, pressures for protection rose. These pressures fell, however, as the dollar declined in 1986 and 1987. Critics of free trade point to the success of Japan and Korea, which experienced economic growth with very restrictive trade barriers. The battle between free trade and protectionism is an ongoing one.

Most demands for protection come from industries that once had a

---

4. For a clear, nontechnical review of the different types of nontariff barriers, see Cletus C. Coughlin and Geoffrey E. Wood, "An Introduction to Non-Tariff Barriers to Trade," *Review*, Federal Reserve Bank of St. Louis (January/February, 1989): 32–46.

comparative advantage but lost it when other industries developed even greater relative efficiency. Such demands also come from industries where monopoly or oligopoly conditions allowed them to ignore the need to improve technology and productivity. Shoes, clothing, steel, and, most recently, automobiles are U.S. industries that have asked for protection because they have lost a comparative advantage. Part of the problem with steel and automobiles is that they have been slow to modernize and to respond to changes in consumer preferences.

It is easy to identify gainers and losers from tariffs and quotas. Consumers lose. Foreign producers lose sales. Domestic competitors gain. One loser who does not show up in Figures 2 and 3 is the U.S. exporter. When one country raises tariffs, other countries are likely to do so in response, and the first country's exports fall. Thus, political support for free trade should come from a coalition between exporting firms and consumers, with help from wholesalers and retailers of imported goods. However, such a diverse group is not easy to organize and hold together.

Firms that gain from protection spend large sums of money in lobbying to get or keep a tariff or quota. Consider a tariff on shoes. As a consumer, you may find that the tariff only costs you a few more dollars a year, so it's hardly worthwhile to lobby against the tariff. But if you are a worker whose job in a shoe factory depends on protection or a shoe manufacturer losing sales to imports, you will work much harder to get and keep protection. Even though the total benefits of free trade would exceed the costs, complaints from a few big losers tend to generate far more noise and attention than the lobbying for free trade. If the losers are concentrated in certain regions, the American system of representation by states and districts makes it easier for them to develop "client" relationships with their members of Congress.

COMMON ARGUMENTS FOR PROTECTION

When workers and owners from import-competing firms go to Washington to lobby for protection, they use some tried and true arguments for protection. Some of these arguments have some economic validity. Others have strong political or emotional appeal, but weak economic foundations. We will discuss the most common arguments for protection in this section and then turn to two very sophisticated ones.

INFANT INDUSTRY ARGUMENT

One theoretically valid argument for protection is the infant industry argument. An infant industry is a new industry that is not yet ready to compete with established foreign producers. Given some time (and sheltered conditions) to master the technology, establish a reputation, train workers, and reach economies of scale, the infant industry may eventually be competitive. Comparative advantage can change over time. Temporary protection could give an infant industry the chance to acquire a comparative advantage and "catch up" with established foreign firms.

This argument is only valid if the protected industry will be competitive in time. There is no reason to protect industries that will never be competitive, wasting scarce resources that could be better used elsewhere. There should be no need to protect industries that will quickly become competitive, because entrepreneurs (and lenders) should be able to see past the early losses to profits. The only industries that really qualify are those that generate some kinds of external benefits to society that they are unable to recoup in the early years. Thus, the few deserving infant industries are those that are not profitable by simple cost and revenue calculations, but are worth protecting because they meet two tests:

1. They will eventually be able to compete in the market without protection.
2. They generate benefits to society that are worth the cost of a tariff.

What kinds of external benefits might an infant industry create? Examples include developing roads and power sources that are then available to other industries, training a labor force that may migrate to other firms, or producing a low-cost input that other industries can use. Benefits such as these are likely to be created in less developed countries. It's difficult to make a convincing case for protecting an infant industry in a developed country such as the United States. Even in less developed countries, this argument is easily abused by overstating external benefits and underestimating how long it will take for the industry to be competitive.

NATIONAL DEFENSE ARGUMENT

Another common and economically valid argument for protection is national defense. The product of this industry may be needed in wartime, the argument goes, but the domestic producer can't compete with cheaper foreign producers. Without protection during peacetime, the firm may not be here when war comes and foreign supplies are cut off. This argument gained merit after the War of 1812. England had been the United States's main trading partner and then became an enemy who successfully blockaded the U.S. coast. Again, during World War II, German interference with shipping created problems in obtaining some needed supplies.

However, this argument make less sense for the United States today. The government stockpiles strategic raw materials, and most products needed in wartime are those in which the United States has a comparative advantage, such as heavy machinery, sophisticated electronics, and aircraft. Economists Leland Yeager and David Tuerck argue that the national defense argument only applies in the case of another World War II, what they describe as a "prolonged non-nuclear war of attrition."[5] But, they argue, the more likely kinds of wars—the kind the Pentagon seems to be preparing for—are either "brush fire" wars, such as Panamanian invasion of 1990 and other localized battles, which do not affect U.S. access to supplies, or else all-out nuclear war, in which case there would be no time to resupply. Even the 1991 Gulf War, which was too large to be called a "brush fire," did not affect U.S. access to shipping and supplies.

---

5. Leland B. Yeager and David G. Tuerck, *Foreign Trade and U.S. Policy* (New York: Praeger, 1976).

BALANCE OF PAYMENTS ARGUMENT

Most other arguments for protection have more emotional or political appeal than economic logic. Proponents of protection argue that a balance of payments deficit (or at least that part of the deficit that is accounted for by exports and imports) could be reduced by imposing tariffs and importing less. Up to a point, this argument is correct, but only in the short run. Over time, tariffs encourage the development of domestic industries producing import substitutes, usually products in which the nation has a comparative disadvantage. This policy encourages inefficient use of scarce resources. Furthermore, tariffs usually lead to retaliatory tariffs on the exports of the country imposing the tariff.

EMPLOYMENT ARGUMENT

The employment argument suggests that reducing imports can create jobs producing import substitutes. However, the cost of doing so is high. Protectionism encourages misallocation of resources and tends to lead to retaliation. The tariff-imposing country may gain jobs in import-competing industries and lose them in more efficient exporting industries. Employment may also be lost if domestically produced items cost more or are of inferior quality. Thus, less is demanded and jobs are lost.

CHEAP FOREIGN LABOR ARGUMENT

The cheap foreign labor argument popular among protectionists goes something like this: "We're just as efficient as the foreign competition—we use the same machinery and technology and produce at least as high a quality product. However, U.S. labor costs are at least $7.00 an hour, and firms in some foreign countries have to pay only $1.00 an hour. How can we possibly compete?"

There are several possible answers. One is that cheap labor often means lower productivity. Another is that labor, especially unskilled labor, may be cheap in some countries, but other inputs such as capital and skilled labor are relatively expensive. A country such as the United States should concentrate on producing those products that use relatively more of its abundant (and, therefore, relatively less expensive) resources, capital, and skilled labor.

SOPHISTICATED ARGUMENTS FOR PROTECTION

Two sophisticated arguments from the highly mathematical literature of trade theory are valid arguments for trade restriction. These arguments are so advanced that they rarely appear in beginning economic textbooks. We include them here because we don't want to leave you with the impression that all economists favor free trade in all situations. This section will introduce you to the very basic ideas behind these arguments. You can learn more through the suggestions for further reading if you are interested.

OPTIMAL TARIFF ARGUMENT

If the price elasticity of demand for imported goods is greater than zero and the price elasticity of foreign supply is less than infinite, the imposition of a tariff raises the price of the foreign good by less than the amount of the tariff. The tariff causes the foreign supplier to lower prices in order to maintain sales. The country imposing the tariff then experiences a gain in its terms of trade, because the price of its imports has fallen while the price of its exports remains the same.

This effect on the terms of trade gives rise to the concept of an optimal tariff. An **optimal tariff** is a tariff that maximizes a nation's net gain from altering its terms of trade. At one extreme, if the supply of imports were perfectly inelastic, the optimal tariff would be infinite because the importing country would be a pure monopsonist. At the other extreme, where the import supply was perfectly elastic, the optimum would be zero.

The optimal tariff argument is valid within its restrictive assumptions. The main assumption is that the foreign countries do not retaliate. If other countries see their terms of trade deteriorate and retaliate with an optimal tariff of their own, the flow of trade diminishes. After a series of retaliations and counter-retaliations, world welfare will be diminished. All countries will be at lower consumption levels. Another problem is that application of optimal tariffs would be very difficult in practice. It would require that policy makers know the elasticities of demand for the traded goods. It is difficult to determine these elasticities, and they change over time.

The optimal tariff argument suggests using a country's monopsony power to provide a gain to it by imposing a tariff that causes the rest of the world to suffer a loss. It is likely that such a gain would be only a short-term one, as the rest of the world would soon retaliate.

optimal tariff
A tariff that maximizes a nation's net gain from altering its terms of trade.

THE THEORY OF THE SECOND BEST

The **theory of the second best** is an argument in favor of tariffs as distortions needed to offset other distortions. Monopoly, government policies, and externalities often cause a divergence between private and social costs and benefits, and governmental policy may not be able to eliminate this divergence in order to pursue the first-best policy of free trade. Then a second-best policy of tariffs may be useful to introduce new distortions that eliminate the existing distortions.

theory of the second best
A theory that a second-best policy of tariffs may be useful to introduce new distortions that eliminate existing distortions.

The theory of the second best can be used to justify import restrictions on a selective basis when external effects make the private costs to a domestic producer higher than the social costs to the country. Consider, for example, an excise tax on a domestically produced good, automobile tires. This tax raises the cost of producing tires because that cost will include the portion of the tax that is a transfer from tire producers to the government. As a result, domestic production of tires is lower, and imports of tires are higher than they would be without the excise tax. The country is importing tires at a higher social price than it would cost to produce them at home. An import duty equal to the excise tax would increase the domestic production of tires to the point where the marginal social cost of imported tires and the marginal cost of domestic production are equal.

If government-created cost differences or foreign trade restrictions affected all industries equally, they would not affect comparative costs and distort the efficient pattern of specialization and trade. It is only when these factors affect different industries differently that there may be a distortion of relative prices that justifies some kind of protection. For example, the minimum wage has more impact on costs for industries that use large amounts of unskilled labor than for industries that use primarily highly skilled labor and capital. Thus, the minimum wage raises the costs of the first type of industry more than the second.

The theory of the second best is not limited to trade theory. It recognizes that whenever market prices fail to reflect real opportunity costs, a second-best policy may be appropriate. You should remember, however, that the first-best policy is free trade.

FAIR TRADE AND THE MAINTENANCE OF THE U.S. MARKET

If there are so few valid economic arguments for protection, why does protection exist? There is a group of politically appealing arguments labeled **fair trade**. The concept of fair trade is often described as a "level playing field." If foreign countries erect tariff barriers, nontariff barriers, or quotas that limit U.S. firms' exports to those countries, protectionists argue that the United States should do the same. For example, if the Japanese make it very difficult or expensive for their citizens to buy U.S. automobiles or beef, protectionists say that Americans should treat Japanese exports the same way.

One version of the fair trade argument is called maintenance of markets. Some protectionists argue that it is more costly to operate in the U.S. market than in other markets. U.S. firms pay high corporate taxes, face strict environmental and safety standards, and have to comply with employment regulations such as affirmative action, minimum wage, and overtime pay. Many foreign producers, especially in less developed countries, do not incur similar costs. They can participate in the U.S. market without incurring the costs of maintaining it. This issue has received considerable attention recently because of the proposed free trade area between the United States and Mexico. Mexico has lax environmental standards and few employment regulations.

These fair trade arguments are usually put forward by organized lobbies for industries that are losing sales to foreign competitors. The appeal makes sense to the average voter, because it is couched in terms of fair play and equal treatment. Coupled with arguments against trading with Communist countries and other political enemies, the case for "fair trade" looks even more appealing. International trade differs from domestic trade in that the political dimension carries much more weight. Political concerns help to explain why the economically sound practice of free trade is rarely implemented.

Advocates of protection on the basis of fair trade or maintenance of the U.S. market offer two policy solutions. The more traditional one is a tariff on foreign goods. This tariff would be equivalent to the restrictions placed on U.S. exports by other countries or to the excess cost of maintaining the U.S. market. Computing the appropriate tariff in either case would be a difficult task. For some European nations, with large government sectors and restrictive laws governing employment, the appropriate tariff might actually be negative.

fair trade
The idea that the United States should impose trade barriers equivalent to those that its trading partners place on U.S. exports.

Economic Insight

The United States and Free Trade Pacts

In November 1989, Canadian voters approved the U.S.–Canada Free Trade Agreement (FTA). The FTA called for a ten-year phase-in of complete free trade. Before the pact, about 75 percent of the markets between the two countries had free trade. Autos have been freely traded since 1965. The beneficiaries of this agreement were predicted to be primarily Canadian consumers and U.S. producers, because Canadian tariffs were about three times higher than U.S. tariffs. For example, two months after the agreement was signed, some Harley-Davidson motorcycle models sold for $2,000 less in Canada than they had before the pact.

Freer access to U.S. markets has contributed to a surge of business investment in Canada. The Royal Bank of Canada has reported an increase in plant and equipment investment of more than 28 percent since the signing of the agreement. Canada's Economic Council has estimated that when this investment boom is over, it will have produced more than 250,000 new jobs in Canada. On the American side, business is also booming. Buffalo, New York has reaped some benefits from the agreement, being viewed by those in Toronto as "the cheap side of the border." Shoppers from Toronto head south to purchase computers, clothes, televisions, gasoline, and liquor. Two-way trade between the United States and Canada increased more than 10 percent in the first year of the agreement.

Not everyone is happy with the agreement. Polls in Canada indicate that a majority of the population has turned against it. The Liberal Party has promised to repeal the deal if returned to power. This is understandable because there are winners and losers in free trade. The losers are more visible. Firms that aren't competitive don't survive. The strong Canadian labor unions were opposed to the agreement and still oppose it. Bruce Campbell, an economist with the Canadian Labor Congress, claims that "free trade is a bad deal for Canadians." He would be more correct to say that free trade is a bad deal for Canadian labor union members.

Free trade of sorts is also booming on the southern border of the United States. *Maquiladoras*, or border plants, are booming along the U.S.–Mexican border. Nearly half a million Mexicans are employed in almost 2,000 plants. These plants receive shipments of parts from U.S. manufacturers and assemble the parts into complete products. Any tariffs are due only on the value added. General Motors assembles auto parts in more than thirty *maquiladoras*. In 1986, this trade amounted to $29.7 billion. It grew to more than $65 billion in 1990.

Mexican President Carlos Salinas de Gortari wants free trade between Mexico and the United States to expand. Mexican and U.S. officials have been exploring a free trade agreement like the one negotiated with Canada. Administration officials look favorably on such proposals, but face tough opposition in Congress. Organized labor in the United States, like that in Canada, is strongly opposed to such an agreement. Labor leaders argue that Mexican firms enjoy an unfair advantage because they do not have to meet the environmental and safety standards that U.S. firms do. Owen F. Bieber, president of the United Auto Workers, argues that a free trade pact with Mexico would mean "there'll be a hell of a lot more empty factories in the United States of America." Perhaps Bieber and Campbell have the same speech writer!

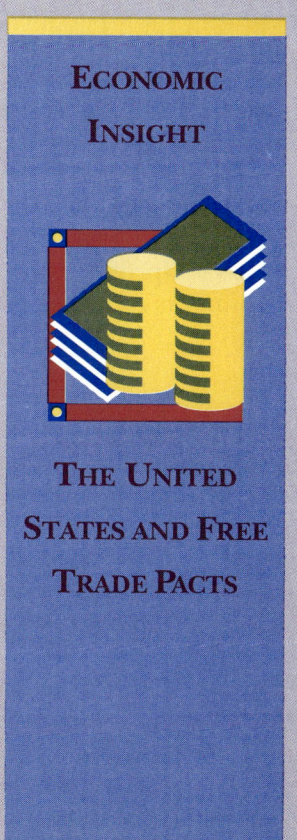

Sources: Stephen Baker, "Along the Border, Free Trade Is Becoming a Fact of Life," *Business Week* (18 June 1990): 41–42; Alan Freeman, "Free-Trade Pact Creates Winners, Losers," *Wall Street Journal* (7 February 1989): A20; Peter Dworkin, "Unhappy Birthday for a Free-Trade Pact," *U.S. News & World Report* (5 February 1989): 54–59.

An alternative solution was suggested by Senator Phil Gramm of Texas (trained as an economist) and former Representative Jack Kemp of New York. Gramm and Kemp are basically in favor of free trade, but are also responsive to political pressures for protection based on fair trade arguments. They propose trading with each country on the basis that it trades with the United States. They believe that this policy would result in freer trade because the U.S. market is so important to other countries that they will lower their barriers rather than see barriers raised in the United States. The appeal of this policy is that it responds to arguments for fair trade and maintenance of the market with economic incentives to promote free trade and specialization based on comparative advantage. This solution demands reciprocity, waving a stick of protectionism in order to get other governments to move toward freer trade.

MOVEMENT OF RESOURCES

If trading countries benefit from the flow of goods and services, what about benefits from the flow of inputs? Labor, capital, and raw materials also move between countries. When they do, objections are sometimes raised by those who are threatened by foreign competition. Foreign competition is unpopular with the owners of factors of production, whether the competition is in product markets or in factor markets. Thus, these owners seek restrictions on the movement of factors as well as on the movement of goods.

Organized labor, for example, opposes immigration of workers and construction of plants abroad. Newly arrived workers compete for jobs and depress wages. An offshore plant of a U.S. firm means more jobs for foreign workers and fewer jobs for American workers. Domestic firms oppose letting their foreign competitors locate inside the country with no tariff wall for protection. Canada is cautious about letting U.S. firms build new plants in that country, and countries such as Kuwait and Japan have even tighter restrictions. Emotional and political arguments are sometimes stronger than economic concerns. Many U.S. citizens are unhappy about the purchase of U.S. banks, farmland, and resort islands by foreign firms and individuals, even when there are no obvious adverse consequences.

The United States puts fewer restrictions than most countries on the inflow or outflow of capital. Except for strategic raw materials (those needed for national defense), there are no restrictions on the flow of natural resources. Exports of natural resources such as oil and copper are often restricted by countries with some market power as suppliers. Some of these countries use controls on exports of these resources to generate revenue for their governments or to attract industries that use the resources as raw materials in manufacturing. Cartels are sometimes formed to take advantage of such market power when that power is shared among a small number of countries.

Immigration policy has been a source of much debate in the United States. After several previous attempts, Congress finally passed a new immigration bill in 1986. The most controversial provisions of that bill centered on illegal aliens, who have come to the United States in large numbers in the last twenty years. The bill made it possible for illegal aliens who resided in the United States prior to 1982 to become citizens but also imposed stiff penalties on employers who hire illegal aliens. The large number of illegal aliens who were residing in the United States when the law was passed was due to past restrictive immigration quotas. Organized labor has generally opposed raising or eliminating immigration quotas because it wants to protect jobs for U.S. citizens.

In general, the movement of inputs between countries can substitute for free movement of goods. If a country is poor in raw materials, capital, or skilled labor, it has two possible remedies. It can import goods that incorporate large quantities of those inputs, or it can import those inputs and produce its own final products. Both kinds of trade should bring benefits. In the absence of artificial barriers, market considerations determine which choice is more efficient—to move the final product or to move the input.

MULTINATIONAL CORPORATIONS

Another important influence on patterns of trade and factor movements is the multinational firm. A **multinational corporation** is a firm with headquarters in one country and plants in one or more other countries. Many large and well-known multinationals are headquartered in the United States, including Ford, General Motors, IBM, and AT&T. (So are many smaller and less-known ones.) Other large multinationals are headquartered in other countries, especially Japan (Honda and Mitsubishi) and European countries (Shell Oil, Nestlé, Michelin, and BASF). Multinationals have been around for a long time, but most of their growth has occurred since World War II.

multinational corporation A firm with headquarters in one country and plants in one or more other countries.

Why Firms Go Abroad

Why do firms build plants in foreign countries? Why not just export or invest in a local firm that can produce the product? Exporting may not be feasible because of trade barriers, perishability, or a need to produce a product tailored to the local market. Investing in a local firm by purchasing stock or making a loan is sometimes feasible. Often, however, the investing firm wants more control over management, product quality, or patented processes. Sometimes the only way to get access to local resources, especially raw materials, is to build a plant.

U.S. labor unions oppose building plants abroad, arguing that firms are in search of cheap foreign labor. Unions would rather see plants built in the United States and goods exported. However, trade barriers or the unique needs of foreign markets are much more common reasons for building foreign plants than the attraction of cheap labor. Furthermore, U.S. workers have found jobs in the many plants in the United States owned by foreign multinationals, especially Japanese-owned firms. The lower wages and different management style of Japanese companies have meant adjustments not only for their American employees but also for their American competitors.

EFFECTS OF MULTINATIONALS

Multinationals are accused by their critics of stifling competition in the countries in which they locate, creating balance of payments problems, and leading to unhealthy concentration of economic and political power. Advocates argue that multinationals often increase competition, speed up the transfer of capital and technology, and help counteract artificial barriers to trade.

COMPETITION. In some cases, the multinational "shakes up" domestic competitors, forcing them to try harder when they can no longer hide behind a protective tariff wall. On the other hand, multinationals often simply buy out local competitors or keep local competition from developing. Sometimes multinationals increase competition, and sometimes they reduce it. Japanese multinationals and others have generally been regarded as beneficial in the United States. They compete for resources and markets with established American firms that must adjust or decline.

TRANSFER OF TECHNOLOGY. Multinationals expedite the flow of technology between countries. They make available to their foreign subsidiaries processes and methods that they would be reluctant to share with competitors. Less developed countries sometimes argue, however, that this transfer doesn't spill over to other industries for maximum benefit. They also argue that multinationals, which are generally from developed industrial countries, don't try very hard to adapt technology to the local mix of available resources.

LARGE MULTINATIONALS AND SMALL COUNTRIES. Probably the most serious concern about multinationals is that small countries are at a disadvantage in dealing with these large firms. Such a firm may have an annual revenue much larger than the host country's GNP. The multinational may be the largest employer, landowner, and taxpayer in a small country. A multinational represents a threat to the sovereignty of a host country when the firm is larger and more powerful than the government.

Despite these problems, there are real benefits to having multinationals. They provide a way for resources and technology to flow around trade and cultural barriers, which has been very beneficial to the world economy. In most cases, they promote the free-trade goals of more output with less effort that were the concern of classical economists two centuries ago when they formulated the theory of comparative advantage.

Chapter 18 International Trade

SUMMARY

1. Trade takes place because both parties benefit. Trade is based on the principle of comparative advantage, which means that each country produces that product for which its opportunity cost is lower in terms of other production.
2. Specialization increases total output, and trade allows that increase to be shared. Trade also increases competition and allows countries to take advantage of economies of scale for some products.
3. Tariffs, quotas, and nontariff barriers interfere with free trade. A tariff or quota will raise the price, reduce imports, reduce consumption, and increase domestic production.
4. The United States has had high tariffs for most of its history but has reduced tariffs and other trade barriers since 1934.
5. Arguments for protection include protecting infant industries, national defense, balance of payments, employment, and cheap foreign labor. The first two have some validity but must be applied with caution. Most arguments for protection are really thinly disguised requests for income redistribution. The optimal tariff and the theory of the second best are two sophisticated arguments for tariffs.
6. Fair trade arguments call for consideration of the costs imposed on firms by U.S. laws.
7. Movements of resources can substitute for trade in goods and services.
8. Multinational corporations may increase competition in some cases and decrease it in others. They increase the transfer of technology between countries but may have too much power in small, less developed countries.

NEW TERMS

gains from trade
absolute advantage
comparative advantage
terms of trade
consumption
  possibilities curve
product cycle
tariff
quota
tariff quota
nontariff barrier
commercial policy
optimal tariff
theory of the second best
fair trade
multinational
  corporation

QUESTIONS FOR DISCUSSION

1. Consider the following situation for Upland and Downland. Each country devotes half of its resources to producing bananas and half to producing apples, and the figures given are what they produce in the absence of trade.

COUNTRY	APPLES (TONS)	BANANAS (TONS)
Upland	40	80
Downland	60	60

Do these figures indicate an absolute advantage, a comparative advantage, or both? What is each country's opportunity cost of producing apples? By how much will total output rise when they specialize? Can you find a better consumption combination for each country through trade?

2. Represent the information in Question 1 on a graph as a pair of production possibilities curves.

3. Who gains and who loses from a tariff? How do the effects of tariffs differ from the effects of quotas?

4. If you were running a small country, why might you have mixed feelings about the building of a plant there by a big multinational?

5. Among the U.S. industries that have received tariff protection in recent years are textiles and autos. Use one or more of the arguments in this chapter to present a case for protection of one of these industries.

6. Write a criticism of the case you made in Question 5, citing the benefits of free trade.

7. A tariff is proposed on imported pineapple. Economists calculate that 1 million pineapple buyers will incur additional costs of $2 each. Five thousand pineapple workers will earn an additional $100 a year. One hundred unemployed workers will find jobs at an average salary of $10,000. One hundred owners of pineapple packing firms will experience an average income increase of $5,000. What are the total gains to the gainers and the total losses to the losers? Are there other losses not counted in these figures? Do you think the tariff is likely to be enacted?

8. Why do multinational firms go abroad?

9. Why do economists generally prefer tariffs to quotas?

10. Why is an economy's consumption possibilities curve different from the production possibilities curve? How does a consumption possibilities curve help explain the benefits of trade as similar to the benefits of economic growth?

11. Can the government completely eliminate imports of some goods even if there is general agreement that such restrictions are appropriate? How does the experience with illegal immigration and illegal drugs support your argument?

12. Assume that the United States can produce 3 mainframe computers or 3,000 pairs of shoes with one unit of resource, and Italy can produce 1 mainframe computer or 2,000 pairs of shoes with one unit of resource. Could specialization and trade increase world output and consumption?

13. Given the data in Question 12, how will firms in the United States and Italy know what to produce? Who or what will tell them what to produce and what to import?

14. Why might competing domestic producers and importing firms prefer quotas to tariffs?

15. U.S. companies are often criticized as being too focused on the domestic market and not concerned enough with exporting. Business schools in the United States have been blamed for this domestic emphasis and have responded by "internationalizing" the business curriculum. Can you suggest economic reasons why U.S. firms have historically concentrated on the domestic market?

Suggestions for Further Reading

Business Week: Special 1990 Bonus Issue (June 15, 1990). An entire special issue devoted to international trade.

Dertouzos, Michael L., Richard K. Lester, Robert M. Solow, and the MIT Commission on Industrial Productivity. *Made in America: Regaining the Productive Edge.* Cambridge: MIT Press, 1989. A report by an MIT commission on U.S. industrial importance that addresses issues of American competitiveness in world markets. Chapter 2 discusses the U.S. economy in the changing world environment.

Helpman, Elhanan, and Paul R. Krugman. *Trade Policy and Market Structure.* Cambridge: MIT Press, 1989. A highly theoretical treatment of trade policy that demonstrates that when markets are not competitive, government intervention can improve welfare. This argument calls into question the argument for a unilateral free trade policy.

King, Philip. *International Economics and International Economic Policy: A Reader.* New York: McGraw-Hill, 1990. A collection of readings on current issues in trade policy. Includes material on Japan's trade policy, strategic trade, Europe 1992, and multinational companies.

Root, Franklyn R. *International Trade and Investment.* Cincinnati, OH: South-Western, 1990. An intermediate-level textbook covering both international trade and international finance.

Vargish, George. *What's Made in the U.S.A.* Saddle River, NJ: Vargish International, 1988. A book written by a businessman that attacks free trade as a "national catastrophe" and repeats many of the arguments for protectionism discussed in this chapter.

Yeager, Leland B., and David G. Tuerck. *Foreign Trade and U.S. Policy.* New York: Praeger, 1976. This book presents the case for free trade and a criticism of protectionism in theory and practice, with many examples and illustrations from Congressional hearings.

AFTER STUDYING THIS CHAPTER, YOU SHOULD BE ABLE TO:

1. Describe how the market for currencies is different from other kinds of markets.
2. Diagram and explain the operation of the foreign exchange market.
3. Explain what causes shifts in supply and demand for foreign exchange and how countries can deal with persistent disequilibrium in the foreign exchange market.
4. Explain the relationship between the foreign exchange market and the balance of payments.
5. Discuss how the forward market works.
6. Identify the components of the balance of payments accounts and measure the deficit or surplus.
7. Describe how the gold standard and the Bretton Woods system worked, and explain why neither is used today.
8. Discuss the advantages and disadvantages of floating rates.
9. Explain what exchange control is and why countries use it.

CHAPTER 19

INTERNATIONAL FINANCE

INTRODUCTION

International finance seems very unlike other topics in economics. It involves foreign exchange markets, hedgers and speculators, floating rates and gold hoarders, balance of payments deficits and surpluses, the ups and downs of the U.S. dollar, and dealing under the table by international banks to affect currency prices. In fact, the foreign exchange market is really very similar to other markets.

The preceding chapter described international trade in goods and services, but not exchange of currencies or financial assets. One important difference that distinguishes trade *within* nations from trade *between* nations is that people in different countries use different currencies. To pay for goods purchased abroad, a buyer must acquire foreign currency. It is relatively easy for U.S. citizens to purchase foreign currency, but obtaining foreign exchange is more difficult in many other countries.

This chapter looks at the market for currencies and what determines the price of one currency in terms of another (the exchange rate). It also describes the accounting statement for the foreign sector—the balance of payments—and its links to the domestic economy. Finally, we will examine different kinds of international monetary systems to see how they work and how they affect trade between countries.

THE MARKET FOR FOREIGN EXCHANGE

The network of banks and financial institutions through which buyers and sellers exchange national currencies is called the **foreign exchange market**. The foreign exchange market works much like the market for wheat, apples, or skateboards. There is a supply curve, a demand curve, and an equilibrium price and quantity. There are also conditions that are held constant (*ceteris paribus* conditions). When these conditions change, the curves shift and the equilibrium price and quantity change.

foreign exchange market The network of banks and financial institutions through which buyers and sellers exchange national currencies.

SUPPLY AND DEMAND FOR FOREIGN EXCHANGE

Figure 1 represents the foreign exchange market as it appears to U.S. buyers and sellers. In this figure, foreign currencies are represented by the German mark (DM). The price of foreign exchange is measured in dollars.[1] Citizens of other countries supply foreign exchange in order to buy U.S. exports, to travel or invest in the United States, or to purchase U.S. services or assets. U.S. citizens demand foreign exchange in order to import foreign goods and services (including traveling abroad) and to invest in foreign assets.

In Figure 1, the equilibrium price of the mark is 50¢, and the equilibrium quantity is 100 million. At a price of 70¢ per mark (equivalent to 1.4 marks per dollar), there would be a surplus of foreign exchange of 60 million marks. Quantity supplied is 130 million marks, and quantity demanded is only 70 million. At 30¢ per mark (equivalent to 3.3 marks per dollar), there would be a shortage of foreign exchange of 60 million marks (130 million marks demanded less 70 million marks supplied).

SHIFTS IN SUPPLY AND DEMAND

Demand for foreign exchange will increase if something causes U.S. citizens to want to import more foreign goods and services or to invest more abroad. The supply of foreign exchange will increase if foreigners want to buy more U.S. goods and services or invest more in the United States. Recall from Chapter 3 that demand curves shift when the *ceteris paribus* conditions change. Some of those demand shifters, including changes in tastes, population, and income, apply here. Others work a little differently because the foreign exchange market is a macroeconomic market.

The price of a good is affected by changes in the prices of related goods. For example, demand for coffee is affected by the price of tea. In the foreign exchange market, it is aggregate rather than individual prices that matter. Aggregate price changes that can affect foreign exchange are

FIGURE 1
THE FOREIGN EXCHANGE MARKET
The foreign exchange market shows the supply of foreign exchange (German marks) from abroad, the demand for foreign exchange by U.S. citizens, and the equilibrium price (50¢ per mark) and quantity (100 million marks).

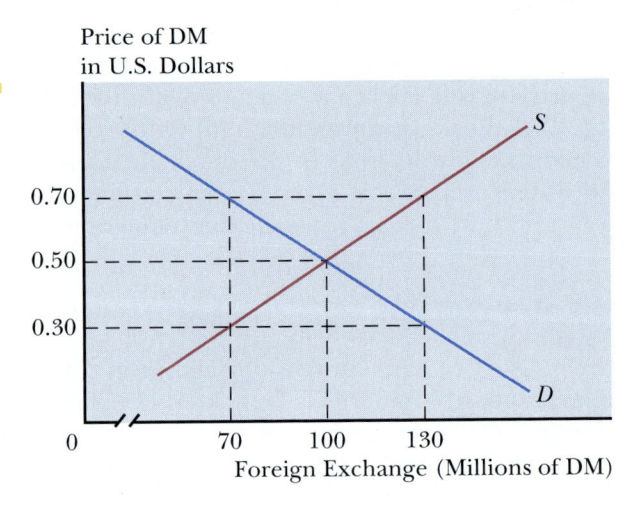

---

1. This market can also be represented as the supply and demand for U.S. dollars, but we will focus on the U.S. market for other countries' currencies.

changes in the price level in the United States relative to the price level abroad or changes in the prices of U.S. exports in general relative to prices of foreign goods. Note that the price on the vertical axis in Figure 1 is the price of foreign exchange. Changes in other prices, including the domestic price level, can shift the supply and demand curves for foreign exchange. If the U.S. price level rises more than foreign price levels, imports become cheaper relative to domestic goods, and Americans will want to buy more imported goods. Rising domestic prices shift the U.S. demand curve for foreign exchange rightward. U.S. citizens demand more foreign exchange to buy more imported goods. At the same time, the U.S. supply curve for foreign exchange shifts to the left because foreigners want to buy fewer American exports at higher prices. In fact, economists who forecast changes in exchange rates find that changes in relative price levels are the most significant determinant.[2]

Changes in relative interest rates also shift demand for foreign exchange. If interest rates are higher abroad, Americans will demand more foreign exchange to buy foreign financial assets, such as bonds or bank deposits. From 1981 to 1985, interest rates in the United States were higher than in most other countries, attracting an inflow of foreign capital. This increased supply of foreign exchange drove the price of foreign currencies down, or the price of the dollar up. As U.S. interest rates fell after 1985, the price of the dollar also fell (that is, the prices of marks, yen, and pounds began to rise).

Another source of shifts in demand for foreign exchange is changes in government restrictions on trade, such as tariffs, quotas, and nontariff barriers. These commercial policy tools are often used intentionally to shift the demand for foreign exchange, either to change the currency price or to "cure" a shortage of foreign exchange (balance of payments

SOURCES OF SHIFTS IN SUPPLY AND DEMAND FOR FOREIGN EXCHANGE

Changes in:
- relative price levels,
- relative incomes,
- relative interest rates,
- tastes and preferences,
- population,
- technology,
- input cost and availability,
- tariffs, quotas, and nontariff barriers,
- export subsidies.

---

2. The theory that changes in exchange rates result primarily from changes in countries' relative price levels is called purchasing power parity. Much attention was given to using price level changes to predict exchange rates in the 1970s and 1980s under floating exchange rates. Most studies indicate that purchasing power parity explains long-run exchange rate changes well but not short-run variations.

deficit). Export subsidies and promotions encourage foreign purchases and shift the supply of foreign exchange to the right. Finally, demand for foreign exchange shifts when there are changes in technology or input costs, which can change demand for foreign inputs or foreign products.

The same kinds of factors that shift one nation's demand for foreign exchange also operate to shift other countries' supply of foreign exchange. Changes in a country's relative price level or income, tastes, population, technology, interest rates, and tariffs and quotas all affect the supply of foreign exchange from other countries.

UNIQUE FEATURES OF THE FOREIGN EXCHANGE MARKET

The foreign exchange market has several unique features. First, the operations of this market have important macroeconomic implications. What happens in the market for foreign exchange affects (and is affected by) interest rates, output, and price levels. Second, governments are often heavily involved in setting the price, often in an attempt to limit its fluctuations. Third, a well-developed forward market exists for foreign exchange, where people make contracts for future deliveries of currency at a fixed price. Finally, the foreign exchange market sometimes suffers from persistent disequilibrium.

MACROECONOMIC IMPLICATIONS. U.S. exports and imports, which are heavily influenced by changes in exchange rates, each constitute about 10–11 percent of GNP. In addition, the foreign exchange market supports some large transactions in financial assets, such as stocks and bonds. Exports, imports, and capital transactions affect the domestic economy in many ways. A rise in exports can increase output, but expanding output puts upward pressure on the price level. Rising imports can reduce domestic output but will also reduce inflationary pressures. An inflow of foreign capital can drive up interest rates, the money supply, and prices. The opposite is true for a capital outflow. Thus, any macroeconomic model of the U.S. economy must incorporate the foreign sector if it is to predict output, employment, prices, and interest rates accurately.

Domestic events also affect exports, imports, and trade in capital assets. Changes in output, prices, and interest rates spill over into the foreign sector. Rising output means rising income, some of which will be spent on more imports. A fall in output and income will reduce imports, as it did in the 1981–1982 recession. Rising U.S. prices (relative to foreign prices) encourage U.S. citizens and foreigners to substitute cheaper goods made in other countries for more expensive American products. When the price level rises faster in the United States than abroad, exports fall and imports rise. Falling prices, or prices rising more slowly than in the rest of the world, stimulate exports and discourage imports. Higher interest rates attract capital from abroad, but lower interest rates encourage U.S. capital owners to try to earn a higher return in other countries. All these changes shift the supply and demand for foreign exchange, and thus change currency prices under the present floating exchange rate system.

GOVERNMENT INTERVENTION. Governments have always been heavily involved in the market for their own currencies. Even with floating rates, governments don't always allow the market to completely determine the prices of their currencies. A government may want to keep the price of its currency from falling because of national pride or because of the effect on the terms of trade.[3] Alternatively, a government may want to keep the price of the currency from rising too high because such an increase would make it more difficult for the country's exporters to compete and easier for imports to undersell domestic goods. In small countries where foreign trade is a large part of total economic activity, monetary authorities may be concerned about the effects of changes in the currency's price on the volume of the country's monetary reserves and the money supply. Finally, a government may want to keep the price of the currency stable in order to encourage trade and foreign investment by minimizing risk and uncertainty.

Governments set and maintain prices in other markets, including minimum wages, farm price supports, and rent controls. In these markets, the government usually sets either a floor price or a ceiling price. In the market for foreign exchange, governments historically have set both a floor and a ceiling.

THE FORWARD MARKET. Another special feature of the foreign exchange market is a well-developed **forward market**, in which contracts are made for future delivery of specific amounts of currency at a specified price. Forward (or futures) markets also exist in other goods and services. Probably the best-known forward market is the commodities market, where contracts for the future delivery of corn, wheat, pork bellies, copper, tin, gold, and other metals and agricultural goods are traded.

Traders who try to reduce their risk by buying or selling contracts for future delivery are called **hedgers**. Those who are willing to assume risk in return for the chance of a profit are called **speculators**. Let's look at a simple illustration of how hedgers and speculators interact in the foreign exchange market. Suppose a Honda dealer in the United States receives a shipment of Hondas from Japan. The dollar cost of the shipment is $100,000, but the contract calls for payment in six months in yen. The yen is trading for 150 yen per U.S. dollar, so the dealer owes 15 million yen. What the dealer needs in six months is not $100,000, but however many dollars it takes at that time to buy 15 million yen. Suppose the dealer thinks the price of a dollar in six months will be only 120 yen. Then the payment will cost the dealer more dollars—$125,000, to be precise. There goes the profit! If the dealer can find someone now who will guarantee a reasonably attractive price, say 145 yen to the dollar, that will eliminate the exchange risk. The dealer can concentrate on the business of selling cars and motorcycles.

What about the opposite situation—that of the speculator? Chances are the speculator is a large commercial bank, with many forward transactions in many directions. There is probably some Japanese firm in need of dollars that can be matched with the U.S. car dealer's need for yen.

forward market
The market in which contracts are made for future delivery of specific amounts of currency at a specified price.

hedgers
People who try to reduce their risk by buying or selling contracts in the forward market for currency.

speculators
People who assume risk in the forward market for currency in return for the chance of a profit.

---

3. If the price of U.S. currency falls, then Americans have to pay more U.S. dollars (and therefore more U.S. goods) for foreign goods. Giving up more U.S. goods per unit of foreign good makes U.S. consumers worse off. The ratio of U.S. goods exchanged to foreign goods received is called the gross barter terms of trade.

Some speculators are gambling on changes in currency prices. Perhaps the speculator who offered the car dealer 145 yen per dollar expects the price of yen to go to 160 yen per dollar. If the dealer can buy dollars at 145 yen per dollar and sell them at 160, there will be a profit of 15 yen on each dollar bought and sold.

The forward market in foreign exchange has been around for a long time. Since 1973, when most countries adopted floating exchange rates, the forward market has played an important role in encouraging foreign exchange by reducing risk.

PERSISTENT DISEQUILIBRIUM. If the price of currency is set by the government, it may not be a market-clearing price. If it isn't, there will be a persistent disequilibrium, that is, constant surpluses or shortages of foreign exchange. This situation is shown for the United States in Figure 2. The market shows a shortage of foreign exchange because the price of 40¢ per mark is too low for equilibrium. The quantity of marks demanded exceeds the quantity supplied by 50 million marks.

One way to deal with this problem is to change the price of the currency. Another way is to try to shift supply or demand for foreign exchange in order to make the curves intersect at the official price. A third possibility is for the government to ration foreign exchange. Finally, if the government has some foreign exchange reserves, it may draw on those reserves to meet the shortage, hoping that the shortage will eventually disappear of its own accord.

A shortage of foreign exchange is equivalent to a balance of payments deficit. A **balance of payments deficit** is an excess of a country's foreign spending over its foreign earnings for a given year. In Figure 2, that difference amounts to 50 million marks. (At 2 marks per dollar, 50 million marks translates into $25 million.) A nation can instead have a balance of payments surplus (foreign earnings exceed foreign spending) or an equilibrium in foreign exchange (inflows and outflows are equal). Before exploring the various ways of dealing with disequilibrium, it would be helpful to know a little more about how such surpluses and deficits are measured. The source of that information is the balance of payments.

balance of payments deficit
An excess of a country's foreign spending over its foreign earnings for a given year.

FIGURE 2
DISEQUILIBRIUM IN THE FOREIGN EXCHANGE MARKET
At 40¢ per mark, the quantity of foreign exchange demanded exceeds the quantity of foreign exchange supplied by 50 million marks. This gap between supply and demand corresponds to a balance of payments deficit.

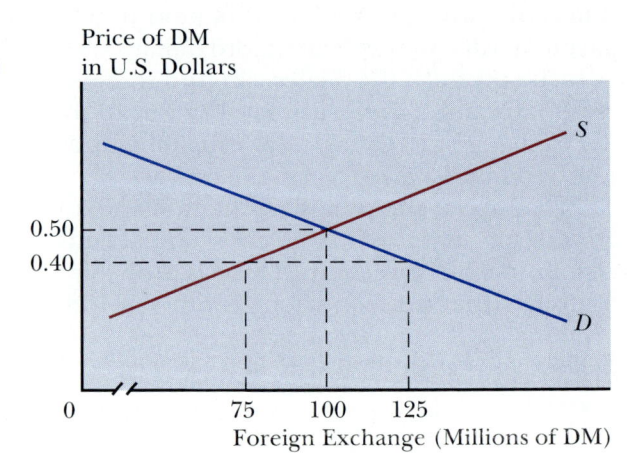

THE BALANCE OF PAYMENTS

The yearly summary of the transactions between residents of one country and residents of the rest of the world is that country's balance of payments. The **balance of payments** is an income statement—a summary of the flows of goods, services, and assets in and out of a country in a given year.

balance of payments An annual summary of the transactions between residents of one country and residents of the rest of the world.

The balance of payments was a matter of great concern to the United States from 1945 to 1973. During that period, there was a fixed rate of exchange for the dollar, or a currency price set and maintained by the U.S. government. Every time the U.S. balance of payments was in deficit (which was most of the time), U.S. reserves fell, putting greater downward pressure on the price of the dollar. Since 1973, the balance of payments has been less important. However, it still provides several kinds of useful information. Table 1 presents a simplified summary of the U.S. balance of payments for 1990.

The pluses and minuses in the table have important meanings. A transaction that gives rise to a payment to the United States or a claim to future payment is entered with a plus sign. A transaction resulting in a payment by the United States or a claim for future payment is entered with a minus sign.

TABLE 1
U.S. BALANCE OF PAYMENTS, 1990
(MILLIONS OF DOLLARS)

CURRENT ACCOUNT		
Merchandise exports	+389,286	
Service exports	+130,623	
Merchandise imports		−497,966
Service imports		−107,699
Investment income (net)	+7,533	
Unilateral transfers		−21,073
Balance on current account		−99,296
CAPITAL ACCOUNT		
Changes in foreign private assets in the United States	+56,767	
Changes in U.S. private assets abroad		−62,063
Changes in government assets other than reserves (net)		−33,749
Balance on capital account		+28,453
STATISTICAL DISCREPANCY		+73,002
Overall balance		−2,159
SETTLEMENT ACCOUNT		
Changes in U.S. reserve assets	+9,151	
Changes in foreign official holdings of dollars	+47,516	
Balance in settlement account		+56,667

Source: Adapted from U.S. Department of Commerce, *Survey of Current Business* (Washington, DC: U.S. Government Printing Office, March 1991).

COMPONENT ACCOUNTS

The balance of payments provides a lot of useful information. The sum of merchandise and service exports and imports (the balance of trade) indicates how competitive U.S. exports are compared to earlier years. The deficit in the balance of trade in the last decade has been a matter of great concern to policy makers. The buzzword "competitiveness" reflects concern for the big gap between U.S. exports and imports.

The current account, which adds investment income and a few other items to the balance of trade, is roughly equivalent to the part of the national income accounts called net foreign investment. The **current account** is the part of the balance of payments that summarizes transactions in currently produced goods and services, including merchandise, services, investment income, and several smaller items. Note that in 1990 the United States had a large deficit for this account, reflecting an excess of imports over exports. From 1960 to 1971, the United States regularly had a surplus on this account. Prior to the 1980s, the largest deficits in the current account were $14 billion in 1977 and $15 billion in 1978. After some small surpluses in 1980 and 1981, the deficit in the current account reappeared and grew rapidly from $9 billion in 1982 to $46 billion in 1983, $117 billion in 1985, and $161 billion in 1987. These figures set off a wave of alarm about loss of U.S. competitiveness with foreign products. Part of the reason for the current account deficit, however, was the high price of the dollar. The price of the dollar was bid up in foreign exchange markets by a demand for dollars to invest in the United States. The value of the dollar began to fall, and, after a lag, there was some decline in the current account deficit beginning in 1988. The current account is linked to the capital account through changes in the market for the U.S. dollar. In 1990, the deficit fell to $99 billion, a decline of 38.5 percent from the 1987 high.

The **capital account** is the part of the balance of payments that summarizes purchases and sales of financial assets, such as bonds, short-term debts, bank deposits, stocks, and foreign plants. This category showed a surplus in 1990, although the surplus was even larger a few years earlier when high U.S. interest rates attracted foreign capital. The figure of $57 billion in foreign private investment in the United States is enormous compared to past experience. The outflow of private U.S. investment of $62 billion is small compared to levels of investment abroad in previous years. This pattern of a large net inflow of foreign private capital has existed only in the last few years.

The category of statistical discrepancy is often rather large. The **statistical discrepancy** is the part of the balance of payments that reflects unrecorded transactions (such as workers' remittances, smuggling, and other illegal activities) and inaccurate estimates of spending by U.S. tourists abroad or by foreign tourists in the United States. There is a good reason for this entry. Balance of payments accountants do not have perfect information. When the discrepancy is large, as it was in the 1980s, it is believed to consist mainly of unrecorded bank deposits. Thus, a negative statistical discrepancy suggests additional (unrecorded) capital inflows.

SURPLUSES, DEFICITS, AND SETTLEMENT ACCOUNT

The sum of the current account, the capital account, and the statistical discrepancy is the surplus or deficit in the balance of payments. In 1990,

---

current account
The part of the balance of payments that summarizes transactions in currently produced goods and services.

capital account
The part of the balance of payments that summarizes purchases and sales of financial assets.

statistical discrepancy
The part of the balance of payments that reflects unrecorded transactions and inaccurate estimates of spending by tourists.

there was a deficit of about $2 billion. At 1990 exchange rates, the demand for foreign exchange in the United States exceeded the supply of foreign exchange by about $2 billion. That figure is not large relative to some of the other sums in the accounts. A moderate balance in the settlement account and a corresponding moderate surplus or deficit in the other three accounts is normal even under a floating exchange rate. When the price of currency is allowed to adjust to clear the foreign exchange market, the small surplus or deficit at the end of the year reflects the fact that the market is moving toward equilibrium but hasn't arrived there. Under a fixed exchange rate, surpluses or deficits would be larger, reflecting the fact that when price is not allowed to adjust, a disequilibrium (surplus or deficit) can be large and persistent.

The **settlement account** is the part of the balance of payments that explains how a deficit or surplus was financed. In 1990, the deficit was settled by selling foreign exchange in the amount of about $2 billion. The Federal Reserve watches changes in foreign exchange reserves closely because they are a component of the monetary base and can affect the size of the U.S. money supply.

Under the present system of floating exchange rates, persistent surpluses or deficits suggest that the price of a country's currency is likely to rise or fall. Under floating rates, a market-determined rise in the price is called **appreciation**, and a market-determined fall is called **depreciation**.

Although the United States and most major industrial countries allow their currency prices to float, many other countries maintain a fixed price for their currencies. However, a floating rate can be either clean or, more commonly, dirty. A clean float means that there is no government intervention to influence the currency's price. A dirty float implies some government involvement in the market to limit fluctuations. This activity has been common in recent years.

settlement account
The part of the balance of payments that explains how a deficit or surplus was financed.

appreciation
A rise in the market price of a currency due to market forces.

depreciation
A fall in the market price of a currency due to market forces.

INTERNATIONAL MONETARY SYSTEMS

Although most industrial countries have floating rates, four different international monetary systems have been tried in the past. Two of them, exchange control and floating rates, continue to be used by most countries. Some economists and policy makers advocate a return to one of the other two systems, the gold standard or the Bretton Woods system. No discussion of international finance would be complete without considering these four alternatives.

Consider what goals an international monetary system might be designed to achieve. Many traders and bankers prefer fixed or at least stable exchange rates. Stable rates reduce much of the uncertainty and the need for hedging in international transactions, making foreign trade more like domestic trade. Another goal that has widespread support is freedom of trade and capital movement, so nations can enjoy the benefits of specialization and trade. Still another goal that many countries want is freedom in domestic monetary and fiscal policy. If the government feels a need to fight recession or contain inflation, it should be free to do so without having to worry about the effects of its policies on the balance of payments or international transactions. Finally, a satisfactory system ensures equi-

International Perspective

Tourism and the Balance of Payments

In Dyersville, Iowa, a baseball field was built for the set of the 1989 movie *Field of Dreams*. The baseball field was carved out of a cornfield owned by farmer Don Lansing. It is beautifully groomed and maintained. *Field of Dreams* was a box office smash in baseball-crazy Japan. As a result of the movie's success, a Japanese tour operator began to include Dyersville, Iowa in one of its tours. Lansing hasn't (yet) started charging tourists to see the ball park, but he took donations from the more than 8,500 Japanese who visited in the first twelve months after the tour began to include his farm. Lansing hasn't made so much that he has give up farming, but his experience is an indication that foreign tourism is becoming big business in the United States.

Until very recently, American spending on foreign tourism was greater than foreign spending on tourism in the United States. The balance of tourism trade was positive in 1989, for the first time since the U.S. Department of Commerce started keeping records on tourism. In other words, the United States became a net exporter of tourism for the first time in 1989, when 39 million foreign tourists spent $44 billion in the United States. This total was $1.2 billion more than U.S. tourists spent in foreign countries in that year. As recently as 1985, the United States had a $9 billion deficit in the tourism account. Foreign tourism continues to grow. The number of foreign tourists visiting the United States in 1995 is projected to be four times the number who came in 1985.

Most foreign tourists in the United States (65 percent in 1989), come from Mexico and Canada. However, Japanese tourists account for much of the spending surplus. Although Japanese tourists represent only 8 percent of the foreign tourists visiting the United States, they are big spenders, accounting for 19 percent of tourists' spending. It appears that Americans are buying Japanese autos and selling Japanese tourists greens fees on golf courses and shopping sprees in fancy boutiques in exchange.

Most foreign tourists in the United States follow the same pattern that Americans do when they go abroad for the first time. They go to major cities. As a result, New York, San Francisco, Los Angeles, and Miami are big draws for foreign tourists. Orlando, home of Disney World, is a close fifth. After foreign tourists have seen the cities, they tend to concentrate on the West. Perhaps all those Western movies are now paying off in tourist dollars!

Source: Evan McGlinn, "Good News for the Balance of Payments," *Forbes* (25 June 1990): 36–38.

librium in the balance of payments. The system should have some way of correcting deficits and surpluses. The various international monetary systems attain these goals in different degrees.

THE GOLD STANDARD

From the late nineteenth century until the 1930s, most industrial countries were on the gold standard. The **gold standard** was an international monetary system in which currencies were defined in terms of gold, money supplies were tied to gold, and balance of payment deficits were settled in gold. Gold served as money in most of the world for centuries. Thus, gold was a logical choice for settling accounts between countries with different national currencies. A country on the gold standard was supposed to observe three rules:

1. To define the value of its currency in terms of gold content. Under the gold standard, the dollar price of an ounce of gold was $20.67 from 1837 to 1934, and the price of gold in British pounds was £4.25. The price of each currency in gold automatically determined the exchange rates between the two countries. The British pound was worth $4.86 ($20.67 divided by £4.25).
2. To have its money supply consist of gold or be tied to the gold stock in some fixed ratio. For example, the ratio of gold to currency in the United States was 1:4 in the nineteenth century. The nation's supply of currency could not exceed four times its gold stock. The money supply could be less than the maximum, however.
3. To require its central bank or monetary authority to buy gold from anyone or to sell gold to anyone at the official price.

CORRECTING DEFICITS AND SURPLUSES. These rules, if followed, automatically corrected deficits and surpluses in the balance of payments. When there was a deficit (surplus of U.S. dollars offered for foreign exchange), the price of foreign exchange would tend to rise. As the dollar price of foreign exchange started to rise, U.S. citizens would find that they could get more pounds or francs per dollar by exchanging their dollars for gold at the Fed, shipping the gold abroad, and exchanging it there for pounds or francs. As gold flowed out of the country, the U.S. money supply would shrink, and prices and output would fall.

When prices fall in the United States, exports rise and imports fall. There is a shift in demand and supply for foreign exchange. Foreigners supply more of their currencies to buy more of relatively cheaper U.S. exports. At the same time, U.S. citizens demand less foreign exchange because they want to buy less of other countries' relatively more expensive products. Also, as U.S. output and national income fall, Americans buy less of everything, including imports.

Figure 3 shows these effects. Again, German marks (DM) represent all foreign currencies. The official price of the mark is 40¢, and the cost of shipping 1 mark's worth of gold is 5¢. In a free market, the equilibrium price of the mark would be 50¢. Because the United States is on the gold standard, the price of foreign exchange cannot rise above the official price plus the cost of shipping the gold to Germany. Thus, at the maxi-

gold standard
An international monetary system in which currencies were defined in terms of gold, money supplies were tied to gold, and balance of payment deficits were settled in gold.

FIGURE 3
AUTOMATIC ADJUSTMENT UNDER THE GOLD STANDARD
At 45¢ per mark, gold flows out of the country to cover the deficit $B - A$. The gold outflow shrinks the money supply, reducing income and prices. Lower income and prices reduce demand for imports (from D_1 to D_2) and increase the supply of foreign currency to buy U.S. exports (from S_1 to S_2). The deficit shrinks from $B - A$ to $E - C$.

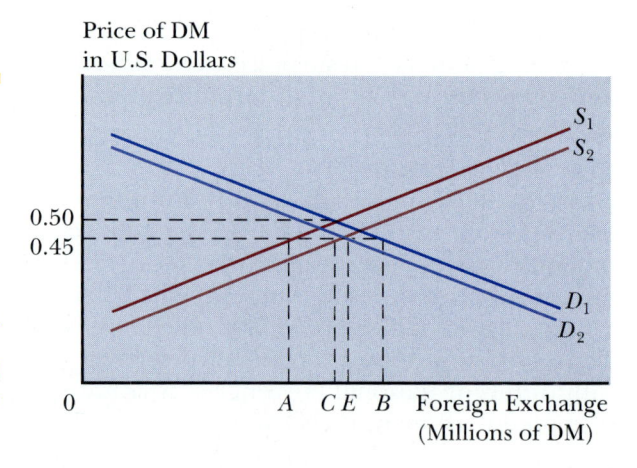

mum price of 45¢, amount $B - A$ of gold flows out of the United States. That outflow shrinks the U.S. money supply, lowering national income and the price level and shifting supply and demand for foreign exchange to S_2 and D_2. The deficit falls to $E - C$. This process of gold flows and shifts in supply and demand continues until the official price is restored and the deficit is eliminated.

The effects of the gold flow are reinforced by events in the other country into which gold is flowing. The other country's money supply expands, raising income and prices and further shifting supply and demand in the correct direction. This automatic correction of deficits and surpluses, recognized in the early eighteenth century by David Hume, is called the **specie flow mechanism**. (Specie refers to coined money with a commodity value, such as gold or silver.)

specie flow mechanism
The automatic correction of deficits and surpluses in the balance of payments through the effects of gold flows on money supplies.

HISTORICAL EXPERIENCE. The gold standard worked fairly well in the late nineteenth and early twentieth centuries. Numerous discoveries of gold in California, Colorado, Alaska, Canada, and South Africa provided an adequate supply of gold for stock. The gold standard meant that governments could not control their money supplies, but nineteenth-century governments didn't pursue an active monetary policy anyway. There were few major disturbances, such as wars and revolutions, that might have caused shifts in supply and demand so great that they would have been difficult and painful to correct.

World War I marked the end of the gold standard, although some countries (including the United States) remained on it until the 1930s. The gold standard's main attractions were fixed exchange rates and automatic correction. The slow growth in the supply of gold in the twentieth century and the gold standard's restrictions on monetary policy were serious problems that could not be resolved.

The gold standard achieved three of the four goals of an international

The idea of returning to the gold standard has never died. It just went underground, surfacing as regularly as the groundhog every February. Although the Reagan administration never officially endorsed returning to the gold standard, some of Reagan's financial advisers were inclined in that direction. Jude Wanniski, in a popular book on supply side economics, *The Way the World Works*, argued very strongly for a return to the gold standard.[a]

Why does this idea keep returning? In part, it is because gold seems to offer a degree of certainty that paper money does not. When governments have gone down in revolutionary flames, new governments have usually restored faith in the currency by tying it to gold. When refugees leave countries in turmoil, the safest way to transport their wealth is in the form of gold. Fifty years after the gold standard was abandoned, some people still think of gold as the only universal money.

Gold buffs, however, are not sentimental. Most of them are hard-headed profit seekers. Many invested in gold as its price made its dramatic rise from $35 an ounce in 1967 (the official price, maintained by central banks) to over $1,000 an ounce in the mid-1970s in a free market. (Some also had the foresight to get out of gold before its price dropped sharply to under $400 an ounce in the early 1980s.) They didn't invest because of the demand for gold to use for jewelry and dental work. They invested because gold was, is, and probably always will be considered money by a substantial part of the world. The gold buffs would like gold to be *the* money of the world again in the same way it was in earlier centuries.

Economic Insight

The Gold Buffs

Gold buffs usually want to return to the gold standard because they do not trust the government to control the money supply. They would rather have the money supply determined by the impersonal forces of the marketplace and the supply of monetary gold. Give governments the freedom to print money, they argue, and political pressures will sooner or later run up the money supply and the price level.

One argument offered against returning to the gold standard is that the chief advantage of gold is also its chief disadvantage. No one can control the supply of gold. Big discoveries can cause inflation and have done so in the past. Very slow growth of the gold supply relative to growth of output and population can lead to deflation, which can be very painful. Gold buffs argue that at $400 an ounce, the supply is much greater than it was fifty years ago, because an ounce now represents much more money and because there is more incentive to mine gold at the higher price. They admit, however, that it would be necessary to fix the price of gold. Over time, that fixed rate would fail to encourage more gold mining as the cost of finding and retrieving gold increases.

The main reason why gold buffs are unlikely to get their way is that governments don't like to tie their own hands. Returning to the gold standard would mean giving up any sort of stabilization policy. No elected government is going to be willing to give up that option. The argument will go on, but as nations adapt to floating rates, the likelihood of going back on the gold standard gets smaller and smaller each year.

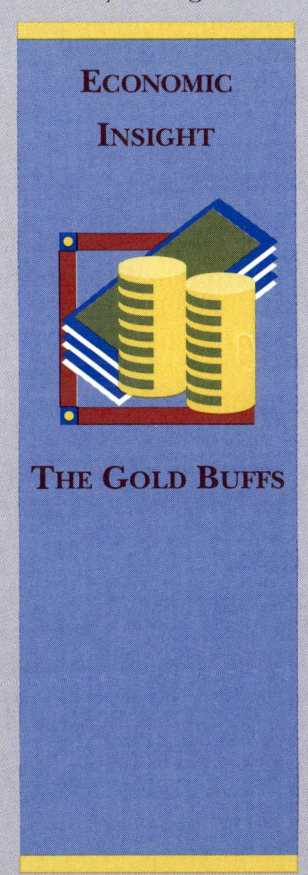

a. Jude Wanniski, *The Way the World Works* (New York: Basic Books, 1981).

monetary system: stable exchange rates, freedom of trade and capital movement, and balance of payments equilibrium. It sacrificed independent monetary and fiscal policy. If the money supply is controlled by gold flows, little discretion is left to the monetary authority to use the money supply to change the levels of output, employment, and prices. This drawback, combined with the problem of ensuring an adequate gold supply, makes a return to the gold standard very unlikely.

Bretton Woods System

From 1945 to 1973, international monetary arrangements were governed by the **Bretton Woods system**, named for the small New Hampshire town where delegates from major countries met to create a new international monetary system. The Bretton Woods system had some of the characteristics of the gold standard and some of the advantages of floating rates.

Bretton Woods system
The international monetary system in effect from 1945 to 1973, based on infrequent changes in currency prices, ample reserves, and the dollar as key currency.

OPERATING RULES. Under the Bretton Woods system, a country defined a par value for its currency in terms of gold. The government was then obliged to keep its currency price within 1 percent of that par value.[4] Central banks bought and sold their countries' currencies in exchange for gold, dollars, or other foreign currencies in order to maintain the currency's price at par value.

The Bretton Woods system differed from the gold standard in that there was no connection between gold, deficits, and the money supply. Countries could pursue independent monetary policies instead of linking their money supply to their holdings of gold. Since there was no automatic correction for deficits and surpluses, a balance of payments disequilibrium might last indefinitely. Because of this problem, the designers of the Bretton Woods system created a pool of **international monetary reserves**, or funds that countries could borrow to settle deficits and repay when they ran surpluses. Reserves consisted of gold, dollars, and other currencies. These reserves were kept at a newly created institution, the International Monetary Fund (IMF). The **International Monetary Fund (IMF)** was the agency that supervised the operation of the Bretton Woods system by recording par values, consulting on devaluations and revaluations, and maintaining a pool of reserves.

international monetary reserves
The pool of gold and major currencies created under the Bretton Woods system, from which countries could borrow to settle deficits and replenish from surpluses.

International Monetary Fund (IMF)
The agency that supervised the operation of the Bretton Woods system by recording par values, consulting on devaluations and revaluations, and maintaining a pool of reserves.

What happened if a country kept running deficits and borrowing from the IMF? The pool of reserves was not intended to sustain deficits forever—just long enough for the situation to get back to normal. If a disequilibrium continued, the Bretton Woods system had a second method for coping with deficits (or surpluses). A country with a persistent deficit could change the currency's price, or the exchange rate. Thus, the Bretton Woods system did not mandate unchangeable currency prices, a central feature of the gold standard. In this respect, the Bretton Woods system was more like floating rates, except that currency prices changed infrequently by large amounts instead of frequently by small amounts.

---

4. The Bretton Woods system, like the gold standard, had both a floor and a ceiling price for each currency. Under the gold standard, the floor and ceiling prices were determined by the cost of shipping gold. Under the Bretton Woods system, the floor and ceiling prices were arbitrarily set at 1 percent above and below the official price.

WHY THE BRETTON WOODS SYSTEM FAILED. The key to the failure of Bretton Woods system lay in the difficulty of finding enough reserves. Since there was not enough gold, the next choice was the U.S. dollar, for two reasons. First, at the end of World War II, the United States had two-thirds of the world's monetary gold stock and was the only nation willing to redeem its currency in gold. Second, the United States dominated world trade as the biggest supplier and the biggest customer. Because dollars were so popular and so useful, they were even used to make payments when no U.S. citizens or firms were involved. A currency that serves as a major reserve asset and is used in transactions between third-party nations is called a **key currency**. The dollar, as the most popular key currency, joined gold as the second major form of international reserves.

Unfortunately, since the Bretton Woods system provided for no built-in corrections, deficits became large and persistent for many countries. Demand for reserves grew rapidly. The United States obliged by creating reserves. To create reserves, the United States ran deficits. The bigger and more frequent these deficits were, the more reserves were created. But the more dollars that were outstanding, the less likely it became that the United States would be able to redeem them from its dwindling gold stock. It became more likely that a devaluation of the dollar would be necessary to correct the deficits. No one wanted to be holding dollars when they were devalued, because of the financial loss. The pending crisis came to a head in 1971, when foreigners started turning in dollars for gold. The United States was forced to suspend the redemption of dollars for gold in August 1971—an event known as the "closing of the gold window." In December 1971, the dollar was devalued by about 8 percent, raising the dollar price of gold from $35 to $38. In February 1973, the dollar was devalued again, raising the dollar price of gold to $42. After the second devaluation, the United States and its major trading partners all switched to floating rates.

The Bretton Woods system was an attempt to have the best of all possible worlds. Nations wanted stable exchange rates, independent monetary policy, and free trade. The Bretton Woods system sacrificed balance of payments equilibrium. The failure of Bretton Woods reminded policy makers that there must be some mechanism to deal with deficits. Once the nations of the world recognized that problem, Bretton Woods could not survive.

FLOATING EXCHANGE RATES

A system of floating exchange rates represents a pure market approach to foreign exchange, in which any shift in supply or demand will change the price of a currency. This system had been tried by some countries, such as Canada, but was not widely adopted until 1973. In February 1973, the United States totally abandoned its commitment to fixed exchange rates. Japan quickly followed suit and allowed the yen to float against the dollar. Within a month, the finance ministers of the European Economic Community announced that they would allow their currencies to float. Most major industrial countries have had floating exchange rates since 1973. Figure 4 shows that the price of the U.S. dollar has fluctuated a great deal under floating rates.

key currency
A currency that serves as a major reserve asset and is used in transactions between third-party nations.

FIGURE 4
THE RISE AND FALL OF THE U.S. DOLLAR
The dollar was devalued in 1971 and again in early 1973. Beginning in 1973, the dollar has floated. Its value has fluctuated in both nominal terms (solid line) and real terms (dashed line—corrected for price level changes) against currencies of the major trading partners of the United States.

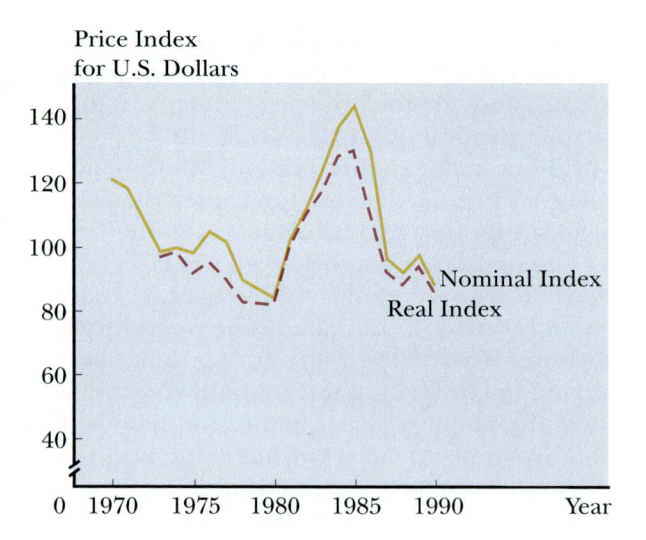

Floating exchange rates work on the basic principles of supply and demand. Floating rates support all of the suggested goals for an international monetary system except stable exchange rates. If exchange rate adjustments clear the market, then the balance of payments should always be at or near equilibrium. Thus, there will be no need to shift the curves to intersect at a fixed price or to use restrictions in order to make international payments balance.

When countries first began to use floating exchange rates, there was widespread fear that the volume of trade would shrink because exchange rates would be very unstable. Although exchange rates have been unstable, well-developed forward markets have ensured that this instability does not discourage international trade. One serious problem has been that when a currency's exchange rate falls, it often falls below its ultimate equilibrium before rising back to that equilibrium. In the interim, the exchange rate is still incorrect but it is too low instead of too high. During this time, price signals to importers, exporters, consumers, and producers are distorted. Decisions are made that would not be profit-maximizing at the correct exchange rate.

Floating rates have not resulted in balance of payments equilibrium. Why? Part of the problem is measurement, but another part reflects a basic truth about market equilibrium. Equilibrium is never where the market is, but rather the direction in which it is headed. If supply and demand shift often, the market may always be in the process of moving from one equilibrium to another. However, deficits and surpluses generally have been much smaller under floating rates than they were under fixed rates.[5] In fact, the floating rate system has worked fairly well during severe shocks (major supply and demand shifts), such as the OPEC oil price hike that created large deficits and surpluses and the 1981–1982 recession.

The floating rate system established in 1973 is not a completely free

---

5. The United States has had large deficits in its balance of trade in recent years, but those have been largely offset by inflows of foreign capital.

market in practice. Governments continue to intervene in the market, buying and selling their own currency to limit swings in the price. Countries have not allowed the market alone to determine exchange rates, but they are closer to doing so than ever in the past. Although there is still some unhappiness with floating rates, there is little pressure to return to a fixed rate system. Many government officials are reluctant to go back on the gold standard or to return to the Bretton Woods system because both would limit their flexibility of action.

Exchange Control

The last international monetary system, exchange control, is used by most less developed countries and sometimes by major industrial nations. **Exchange control** means that a country's government requires all earnings of foreign exchange to be turned over to it and then sells the foreign currencies to those who want to import, travel abroad, or invest in other countries.

Usually, a country adopts exchange control because the currency price is too high and the country doesn't want to change it. Without exchange control, the balance of payments would be in deficit. Typically, the country that uses exchange control has limited reserves and little international credit. By insisting that everyone turn in their foreign currency to the government, which then sells it, the country can make its balance of payments accounts balance.

Exchange control accomplishes three of the goals cited earlier: stable exchange rates, independent monetary and fiscal policy, and no apparent deficit in the balance of payments. However, free trade is sacrificed. In addition, black markets almost always exist. People make side deals in foreign exchange in order to bypass the government. Bribery, smuggling, and falsified reporting of earnings from exports and the cost of imports are regular events in countries with exchange control.

However, exchange control can accomplish other objectives. Often there are multiple exchange rates—different rates for buying, selling, and different uses. Suppose the government wants to encourage factory construction and discourage luxuries. It can charge a low price for foreign exchange to people who want to import machinery and a high price to those who want to buy air conditioners and yachts. Thus, the government can promote specific consumption and production goals. Also, the government can gain revenue for public purposes by buying foreign currencies at a low price and selling them at a higher price.

In some countries, such as China, exchange control involves two kinds of currency. One is used solely by foreigners, such as tourists and approved traders, and the other is used by ordinary citizens. Some stores and service institutions, such as hotels, accept only the first kind. In this way, the government can closely control the use of foreign exchange, deciding who buys imports and who gets the currency that foreigners spend in the country. With this type of exchange control, black markets are less likely, because the country's citizens are not allowed to hold exchangeable currency.

Some degree of exchange control is practiced by all but a few industrialized countries. Total or partial exchange control can coexist with ei-

exchange control
A system in which the government purchases all incoming foreign exchange and is the only source from which foreign exchange can be legally purchased.

International Perspective

Watching Currencies under Floating Rates

One problem of a floating rate system is the difficulty of measuring changes in the price of one currency when others are moving around at the same time. If the price of the dollar is measured in French francs instead of Japanese yen, the picture of what is happening to the dollar may look very different.

One way to obtain a consistent measure of a currency's price is to use special drawing rights (SDRs). These drawing rights are issued by the International Monetary Fund and are only exchanged among central banks. One SDR equaled one U.S. dollar before the 1971 devaluation. This international "currency" provides a constant measuring rod. In the table titled "Currency Units per U.S. Dollar," for example, are the prices of the dollar in March 1977 and February 1991, measured in francs, yen, and SDRs. The SDR price is the most accurate reflection of changes in the price of the dollar because it is the only constant measuring rod. The dollar rose relative to the franc and fell sharply with respect to the yen. The dollar also fell when measured in SDRs. (Note from Figure 4, however, that there were some sharp ups and downs in the interim.)

Measured in SDRs, the dollar and most other currencies have had a lively market since 1973. After the first devaluation (in December 1971), the dollar was worth 0.92105 SDRs. After the second devaluation (in February 1973), the dollar dropped to 0.82895 SDRs. During the ups and downs that followed, the dollar hit a low of 0.74141 SDRs—more than 25 percent below its 1971 price. It rebounded sharply to a high of 1.035 SDRs in 1985 before dropping back to 0.7039 SDRs in February 1991.

Other currencies have seen equally dramatic shifts in prices. The table titled "Currency Units per SDR" gives the high and low values since 1975 for five major currencies. Daily rates (including forward prices) are published in most major newspapers. Long-term trends can be followed in *International Financial Statistics*, a monthly publication of the International Monetary Fund (and the source of these exchange rate figures). Importers, exporters, foreign exchange dealers, lenders, and multinational corporations all follow these figures carefully to make decisions about what to trade, when to trade, and at what price.

Currency Units per U.S. Dollar

	March 1977	February 1991	Percent Change
French franc	4.9780	5.1770	+3.9
Japanese yen	282.7000	132.0000	−53.3
SDRs	0.8639	0.7039	−18.5

Currency Units per SDR

Currency	1971 Value	Low Value (Date)	High Value (Date)
U.K. pound sterling	0.4250	0.8476 (1984)	0.4250 (1975)
French franc	5.6718	9.4022 (1984)	5.2510 (1985)
Canadian dollar	1.0809	1.6703 (1990)	1.1725 (1975)
German mark	3.5481	3.0857 (1984)	2.1378 (1991)
Japanese yen	341.7800	368.4700 (1974)	175.2000 (1987)

ther a fixed rate or a managed float, although fixed rates are more common. The major industrial countries have adopted floating rates, but the majority of nations do not have floating currencies. Most countries still maintain a fixed exchange rate or "peg" their currency to a major currency. For example, many former French colonies in Africa keep a fixed relationship between the price of their currency and the French franc. Since France is still their major trading partner, this link creates a fixed exchange rate for most of their transactions. If the price of the franc falls 10 percent relative to the dollar, the price of a currency pegged to the franc will also fall by 10 percent relative to the dollar. The pegged currency will still have the same relationship to the franc.

A combination of floating rates, managed floats, exchange control, fixed rates, and pegged rates make up the hodgepodge international monetary system of the 1990s. It will be interesting to see how the Soviet Union and the countries of Eastern Europe manage their currency prices as they move from planned economies to market systems.

Summary

1. Unique features of the foreign exchange market are the forward market, government price setting, and effects on important macroeconomic variables.

2. U.S. demand for foreign exchange reflects demand for foreign goods, services, and financial assets. The supply of foreign exchange reflects foreigners' desire to buy U.S. exports of goods and services and/or U.S. financial assets.

3. Surpluses and shortages in the market for foreign exchange are equivalent to surpluses and deficits in the balance of payments.

4. Shifts in supply and demand for foreign exchange result from changes in relative prices, incomes, interest rates, tastes, population, technology, and input cost and availability.

5. The forward market reduces the risk connected with changing currency prices.

6. Disequilibrium often persists in the foreign exchange market. Ways in which government can deal with this disequilibrium include changing the currency's price, shifting the supply and demand curves, rationing, and drawing on reserves.

7. The balance of payments is a summary of transactions between U.S. residents and foreigners. It is divided into four accounts: the current account, the capital account, the statistical discrepancy, and the settlement account. The sum of the first three is the deficit or surplus. The settlement account explains how the deficit or surplus was financed.

8. The gold standard relied on movements of gold to settle deficits. Gold flows changed money supplies, affecting prices and income and shifting supply and demand for currency.

9. The Bretton Woods system was established in 1945 to provide some stability in exchange rates. It relied on reserves to settle deficits. It broke down because it was too dependent on a single currency—the dollar—which could not be devalued.

10. Floating exchange rates, determined in the market, have been widely used since 1973.

11. Under exchange control, all sales and purchases of foreign exchange pass through the government. Many less developed countries use exchange control. Usually, black markets in currency develop under this system.

New Terms

foreign exchange market
forward market
hedgers
speculators
balance of payments deficit
balance of payments
current account
capital account
statistical discrepancy
settlement account
appreciation
depreciation
gold standard
specie flow mechanism
Bretton Woods system
international monetary reserves
International Monetary Fund (IMF)
key currency
exchange control

QUESTIONS FOR DISCUSSION

1. Look up the balance of payments for the United States for the last year in the *Federal Reserve Bulletin*. See if you can put it into the simplified format of Table 1 and calculate the surplus or deficit. How has it changed in the last few years?

2. What might shift a country from equilibrium into a deficit in its balance of payments? How would the deficit be dealt with under each of the four international monetary systems—the gold standard, the Bretton Woods system, floating exchange rates, and exchange control?

3. Why is the forward market especially important with floating exchange rates?

4. How do changes in prices and incomes in one country affect the supply and demand for its currency? What about changes in prices and incomes in other countries?

5. Why do some people want to return to the gold standard? What drawbacks does the gold standard have?

6. If interest rates rise in the United States, what happens to the supply, demand, and price of the dollar? Why? How might this affect U.S. exports and imports of goods and services?

7. In what part of the U.S. balance of payments (Table 1) would each of the following transactions be incorporated?
    a. Sale of tractors to Poland
    b. Gift of tractors to Mexico
    c. U.S. citizen's purchase of a restaurant meal in Canada
    d. British resident's purchase of U.S. government bonds

8. How does a recession in one country affect economic conditions in another country?

9. The ways of dealing with a disequilibrium in the foreign exchange market are to change the currency's price, ration, shift the supply and demand curves into equilibrium at that price, or draw on or accumulate reserves. Identify the international monetary system that uses each of these as its primary way to deal with disequilibrium.

10. Why is there a statistical discrepancy in the balance of payments?

11. Do floating exchange rates do away with a country's need to maintain reserves?

12. How would you describe the current international monetary system? How did it evolve?

13. Stories in the press often draw attention to the fact that the balance of trade between the U.S. and Japan is in deficit. In itself, is this bilateral deficit a meaningful number?

14. How would each of the following be likely to affect supply or demand for the U.S. dollar? What should happen to its price?
    a. A recession in Japan, Canada, and Western Europe, the major trading partners of the United States
    b. A fall in the U.S. interest rate relative to that in the rest of the world
    c. More rapid inflation in the United States than in the rest of the world
    d. An export boom in U.S. movies and television shows

15. Graph the foreign exchange market for the zloty, the currency of Poland, to indicate an equilibrium price of 20¢ and an equilibrium quantity of 50 million. Is there a surplus or a shortage at prices of 40¢ and 10¢?

SUGGESTIONS FOR FURTHER READING

Melamed, Leo (ed.). *The Merits of Flexible Exchange Rates: An Anthology*. Fairfax, VA: George Mason University Press, 1988. A collection of articles by eminent economists in support of flexible exchange rates.

Pool, John Charles, and Steve Stamos. *The ABCs of International Finance*. Lexington, MA: Lexington Books, 1987. A simple, nontechnical discussion of current international finance issues, emphasizing the evolution of the international monetary system and the problems of debtor nations, including the United States.

Root, Franklin R. *International Trade and Investment*, 6th ed. Cincinnati: South-Western, 1990. An intermediate textbook on international trade and international finance.

Yeager, Leland B. *International Monetary Relations: Theory, History, and Policy*. New York: Harper & Row, 1976. A classic reference on international finance with a solid treatment of history and policy.

AFTER STUDYING THIS CHAPTER, YOU SHOULD BE ABLE TO:

1. Define:
   a. capitalism,
   b. socialism,
   c. communism,
   d. fascism.
2. Contrast socialism and capitalism.
3. Describe the major features of and the differences in the economic systems of:
   a. the Soviet Union,
   b. the People's Republic of China,
   c. Cuba,
   d. Yugoslavia,
   e. Great Britain.
4. Define:
   a. input coefficients,
   b. shadow prices,
   c. the socialist controversy,
   d. the competitive solution.
5. Discuss prospects for economic reform in China, Eastern Europe, and the Soviet Republics.
6. Identify the unique characteristics of the Japanese economy.

CHAPTER 20

COMPARATIVE ECONOMIC SYSTEMS IN THEORY AND PRACTICE

INTRODUCTION

The past few years have seen staggering and revolutionary changes in the world. Political and economic reform has been the order of the day in much of the Communist world. Indeed, many writers now use the words "formerly Communist" when referring to some of the countries of Eastern Europe and the Soviet Union. Few would have thought that on November 17, 1989, Berliners from both sides would be dancing on the Berlin Wall as it came tumbling down, while the East German guards watched. A week earlier, getting close to the east side of the wall would have probably meant death.

This chapter will examine the events of the recent past and speculate on what might occur as these economic and political changes mature. There is much uncertainty surrounding these reforms. The introduction of markets and market mechanisms means choice and uncertainty in countries where security and sameness ruled. To some individuals, this choice and uncertainty will be very unsettling.

To begin, it is important to define some basic differences in economic systems. People often discuss other economic systems without really knowing how to define such terms as capitalism, socialism, and communism. What are the key differences among these systems, and to what degree do these differences affect economic outcomes? Chapter 2 stated that all economic systems are mixed systems and that economic theory can be used to analyze any economic system. That statement was valid because the concepts of opportunity cost, the law of demand, the principle of diminishing returns, specialization, exchange, efficiency, and self-interest do not differ from country to country. Competing ideologies may respond to these concepts differently, but no ideology can eliminate their impact on economic life.

You might ask, if the economics you have learned is good for all systems, why include a chapter on comparative systems? The answer is that politics, cultures, and ideology mix with economics to create widely differing economic-political systems. These different mixes will be important as the various countries of Eastern Europe pursue reform. It is therefore necessary to examine the way economics works in different political and historical settings.

To introduce the subject of comparative economics, we will begin with an attempt to define ideological systems. We will then examine some of the different forms of communism as well as recent changes in a number of countries. Next, we will present a decision-making approach to the analysis of differing systems and discuss advantages and disadvantages of economic planning. Finally, we will examine reform movements in China and the Soviet Union and outline the unique features of the Japanese form of capitalism.

IDEOLOGIES

Chapter 2 divided economic systems into three major groups, labeled traditional, planned, and market. The field of comparative economics subdivides the last two categories, which include all modern industrial economies, in order to classify economies more precisely. A very common approach, and perhaps the oldest, is to classify economic systems according to two criteria: the underlying political philosophy, and the ownership of the factors of production. This might be called the *isms* approach because it concentrates on four major political philosophies: capitalism, socialism, communism, and fascism.

Even this approach oversimplifies the diversity that exists in economic systems. There are numerous economic systems in the world. The term *capitalism* is often applied to the economic systems found in Western democracies, but there are significant differences among economic institutions in the United States, Great Britain, France, and Sweden. Similarly, the economic systems in Eastern Europe and the Soviet Union were labeled communist before the reforms began, but there were important differences in the institutions of the Soviet Union, Yugoslavia, and Romania. This complexity makes it difficult to separate the critical elements of the four basic economic systems. Economists must identify the differences in institutions and then determine if these differences are the reasons for differing economic behavior. The most important factor distinguishing the four *isms* is in the ownership of the factors of production.

CAPITALISM

Capitalism is an economic system characterized by private ownership of the factors of production by individuals or groups of individuals. In pure capitalism, these individuals would be free to use their property as they see fit. Any limitations on the use of the property diminish its value to the owner. Private property holders are at the center of the decision-making process in capitalism.

A system based on private ownership is one in which individuals max-

capitalism
An economic system characterized by private ownership of the factors of production by individuals or groups of individuals.

imize their own well-being, in terms of either profit or utility. The term *capitalism* is interpreted very broadly to allow for a great deal of government intervention, as long as the primacy of private ownership is retained. It is therefore possible for systems as divergent as the U.S. economy and the British economy to be labeled capitalist.

Socialism

Under a system of **socialism**, the nonhuman means of production are owned by society or the state. Socialism has its theoretical roots in the work of Marx and its real-world roots in various twentieth-century revolutions and their leaders. Socialism shifts the decision-making authority from individual entrepreneurs to a central authority. This central authority makes the major economic decisions. Utopian socialists see this central authority as promoting the "common good," usually greater equality and/or economic development. Critics of socialism point out that this authority may develop into a centralist, personal dictatorship, such as that of Stalin in the Soviet Union or Nicolae Ceausescu in Romania. Fidel Castro of Cuba is a living example of this tendency.

Like capitalism, socialism comes in many forms. There is utopian socialism, such as the Fourier movement in the United States in the early to mid-nineteenth century. Utopian socialists established communes with shared possessions and cooperative labor. Other variations, such as the Social Democratic parties in Western Europe, have become forceful political movements. For instance, François Mitterand, a socialist, was elected president of France in 1981 and 1988. Because the term *socialism* is used to describe a great variety of people and ideas, it is almost meaningless to label someone a socialist or a set of institutions socialistic.

socialism
An economic system in which the nonhuman means of production are owned by society or the state.

Communism

To Karl Marx, **communism** was the final stage of the progression from capitalism, with socialism representing the middle stage. Under communism, Marx foresaw the end of scarcity, the end of conflict among the classes, and the creation of a new social order. An ideal member of this new order would no longer be the self-interested individual on which most economic analysis is based. The true communist would put the interest of the larger community above personal self-interest. In the final stage, individuals would receive goods and services according to their needs, and the state would wither away until all it did was administer the economy. The organizational structure that Marx foresaw under communism is not at all clear. Presumably everyone would contribute labor in exchange for goods and services needed. One major problem is how those needs would be defined and determined. A second problem is the motivation that would drive the system and create incentives. In the absence of self-interest, the motivation would have to lie in the development of this new economic order.

communism
The final stage in the theory of Karl Marx, in which the state has withered away and economic goods are equally distributed.

Fascism

In the countries that have practiced **fascism** (which include Spain, Portugal, Germany, and Italy), monopoly capitalism and private property were combined with a strong authoritarian central government headed

fascism
An economic system that combines monopoly, capitalism, private property, and a strong authoritarian central government.

International Perspective

China, Hong Kong, and Taiwan

Political-legal developments in China, Hong Kong, and Taiwan and economic comparisons among them demonstrate much about capitalism and socialism. The varying levels of economic development invite comparison because the areas are similar in many ways, including culture. The essential differences are political and economic.

In 1997, the 100-year lease that the British have for Hong Kong expires, and the territory reverts to Chinese rule. This change is expected to have a profound effect on Hong Kong. There are virtually no government impediments to doing business in Hong Kong. A corporation can be started for a fee of only $250, and there are no reporting requirements. Hong Kong has no currency exchange controls, no tariffs, and no quotas. The entrepreneurs in this prosperous capitalist state are casting a wary eye on 1997 and the arrival of the Communist Chinese. In 1997, the country will go from almost pure *laissez-faire* capitalism to communist rule. Many of Hong Kong's successful entrepreneurs are looking for a haven in Taiwan, Singapore, or other parts of Southeast Asia. Some have moved as far away as Jamaica.

Taiwan provides another interesting contrast to mainland China. Chinese nationalists who fled mainland China during the Communist revolution in 1949 went to Taiwan. There they dominated the native Taiwanese majority and established a market-directed economy. The People's Republic of China insists that Taiwan is a province of China and that reunification is inevitable. The Taiwanese insist that they must remain independent. A comparison of China and Taiwan seems to indicate that economic development is faster under capitalism than under socialism. In 1950, the socialistic People's Republic and capitalistic Taiwan had basically the same level of development. Today, the average income in Taiwan is about $3,000 per year, more than ten times the per capita income in China. Perhaps this fact is understood in China, where elements of market capitalism are being introduced in the disguise of economic reform.

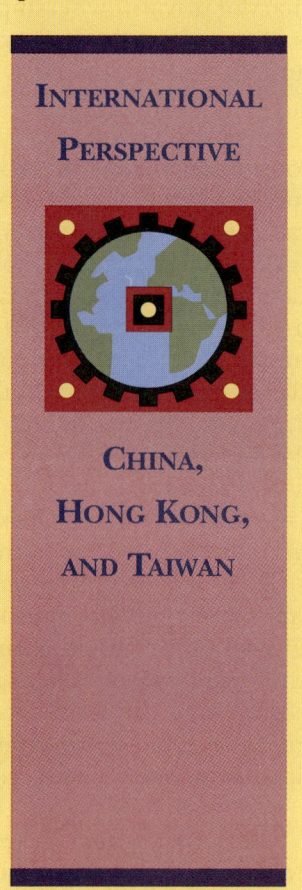

by a charismatic dictator. This combination promoted monopoly and then imposed "national interests" on that monopoly structure. Fascism lacks both the large degree of personal freedom that is a characteristic of free-enterprise capitalism and the egalitarian ideals of socialism and communism.

USE OF THE *ISMS* APPROACH

The drawback of using the *isms* approach to compare economic systems is that it is too simplistic and does not include many of the keys to determining control over resources. The *isms* approach tends to equate ownership with control and control with decision-making power over the factors of production. This connection is becoming less clear over time. For example, in the Soviet Union, before the reform movement, the leaders of the government did not own much of anything, yet they clearly controlled the system. In the United States, many people own land, but they cannot use it as they please because of zoning or environmental regulations.

All economies are mixed in varying degrees. That is, they contain elements of socialism (or planning) and elements of capitalism (or markets). Therefore, the *isms* approach, though often used in political-economic classification schemes (and political rhetoric), has serious limitations. In fact, applying this classification scheme would be likely to produce just two sets of systems, capitalism and socialism. Yet no serious analyst would consider a scheme that places the United States, France, and Great Britain in one category to be very meaningful. However, capitalism and socialism, like pure competition and monopoly, offer theoretical models to aid in understanding real-world mixed systems.

The *isms* approach remains popular because it is the one almost always used by politicians and journalists. A statement made in 1990 by a member of the Leningrad Communist Party is typical. Pyotr S. Filipov is quoted as saying: "We must hurry away from Marxism-Leninism, through Socialism, to Reaganism."[1] What does this mean and how do the Soviets expect to accomplish such a reform? In this chapter we will try to address these issues so you can give an informed answer to such a question.

CONTRASTING CAPITALISM AND SOCIALISM

Recognizing that there is no such thing as a pure system, we can construct a continuum and attempt to place countries on it. Figure 1 presents such a continuum. On one end is pure, market-directed capitalism, and on the other end is pure, centrally planned socialism. (The Soviet Union and the countries of Eastern Europe have been omitted from Figure 1 because it is unclear what the outcome will be in these reforming nations.) Capitalism and socialism are the two polar extremes of economic systems. Contrasting the distinguishing features of these two types of economic systems will help in evaluating real-world systems.

Private property rights are an important feature of capitalism because they create incentives and make exchange possible. In capitalism, the property rights to resources and factors of production, including labor, are vested with the individual. Workers are free to move about, but they

---

1. *National Review* (29 August 1990): 11.

```
                    U.S., Canada,
                    Western Europe              Cuba
PURE                                                                    PURE
MARKET-DIRECTED                                                         CENTRALLY PLANNED
CAPITALISM                                                              SOCIALISM

          Hong    Mexico, Latin        Yugoslavia,        Albania
          Kong    America, Japan       France,
                                       Sweden, Israel
```

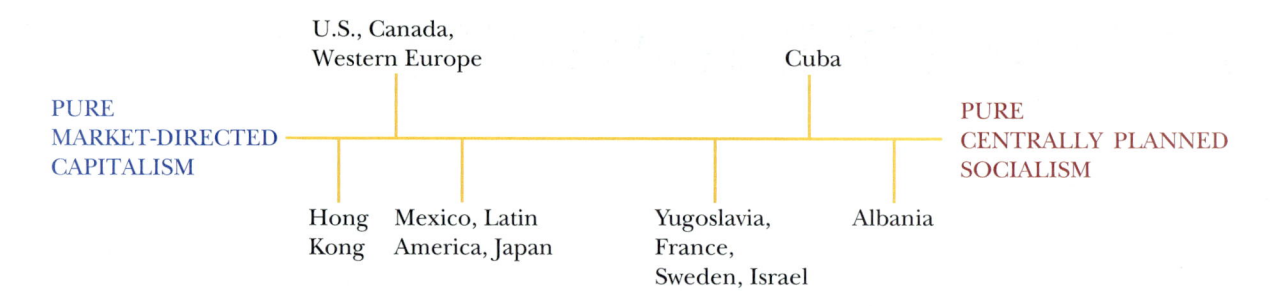

FIGURE 1
A CONTINUUM OF ECONOMIC SYSTEMS
No country has an economic system that represents a pure type. All countries mix market and planning to some degree. It is possible to place countries along a continuum, as shown here, on the basis of their relative reliance on the market or on a plan.

are not guaranteed jobs. In socialism, the state is vested with property rights, including property rights to the individual's labor. As economic reforms proceed in the Soviet Union and Eastern Europe, property rights and who owns what are important issues in these reforms. Government officials in these countries are arguing over the ownership of resources, including a new division between public and private ownership.

Under socialism, especially in China, people are often assigned jobs in certain geographic locations and do not have the freedom to switch occupations or geographic location. The method of job assignment in the U.S. military is similar to that in most socialist states. Workers have greater job security but less freedom to choose jobs than in a market system. Investment decisions follow a similar pattern. Under capitalism, individuals seeking profits make these decisions. Under socialism, a central plan determines the level and composition of investment. Production decisions and decisions that affect the distribution of income are also made by the central planning authority under socialism. These decisions are the *what* and *for whom* questions of Chapter 2.

MARX, MARXISTS, AND MARXISM

Perhaps no other economist has had more effect on the political shaping of the world than Karl Marx, who with Friedrich Engels, published the *Communist Manifesto* in 1848. This book, along with Marx's *Das Kapital*, published in three volumes in 1867, 1885, and 1894, is the philosophical basis for a widely divergent group of economic-political systems. In recent years, almost all communist governments have claimed to be Marxist. Therefore, it is necessary to distinguish between Marx and Marxism (or Marxists).

The central ideas of Marx's economic theory are easy to outline. He believed that every society would evolve through the historical stages of tribal communism, slavery, feudalism, capitalism, socialism, and, finally, communism. The most important transition would come when capitalism decayed because of internal conflict and was succeeded by socialism. The regular cyclical ups and downs of a capitalist economy (the business cycle) would become more and more severe until capitalism finally collapsed. Marx saw the empire building of European countries in the nineteenth century as an attempt to postpone the inevitable failure of capitalism. He believed that when socialism was replaced by communism, scarcity would disappear, and workers would produce without material incentives.

Essential Differences between Capitalism and Socialism

	Capitalism	Socialism
• Property rights	Resources are owned by individuals or groups of individuals.	Resources are owned by the state.
• Labor	Workers have a property right to their own labor. They are self-employed or work for private firms.	Workers are employed by the government and are usually not allowed to change jobs.
• Investment	Investment is determined and undertaken by entrepreneurs.	Investment is determined and undertaken by government.
• Production mix	What is produced is determined by market forces.	What is produced is determined by central plan.
• Distribution of income	Distribution of income is determined by market forces, productivity, and ownership patterns.	Distribution of income is determined by central plan.
• Incentives	Labor, management, and entrepreneurs respond to wages, prices, and profits.	Often many nonmaterial incentives are used.

The countries to which communism has spread have been those in which the level of industrialization was very low. This pattern is inconsistent with what Marx predicted. What, then, is the significance of Marx's writings?

The significance of Marx's writings lies not in the accuracy of his predictions but rather in the theoretical, philosophical, and political movements spawned by his work. Communist parties in many countries consider themselves Marxists and appeal to the writings of Marx to justify their views on various issues. In some respects, they are similar. They all condemn the "exploitation" of workers under capitalism and forbid the use of the term *profit*. Countries in which Communists are in power all claim to have full-employment economies and to have overcome the unemployment problem of capitalistic systems. There are also wide differences among Communist countries, however. Countries as diverse as China, Yugoslavia, the Soviet Union, Albania, Romania, and Cuba have all at one time or another claimed to be the true Marxists. Many of the economic reform movements in these countries still use Marxist terminology in their political statements. The significance of Marx is that he was the father of a political, as well as an economic, movement.

LEADERISMS

Socialism was Marx's intermediate stage between capitalism and communism. Under socialism, the decision-making authority shifts from individual entrepreneurs to a central authority, which Marx called the "dictatorship of the proletariat." In practice, the central authority has almost always been personified by a dominant individual. It is thus possible to view many of the offshoots of Marxism as the products of the interaction of Marxist ideas with the personalities of strong-willed leaders. Thus, for example, the Soviet economic and political reforms may have a curious result if they succeed. Gorbachev had to be a strong leader to initiate the reforms, but any success in these reforms will reduce his power. This effect became evident early in his term of office as competition for the right to lead the Soviet Union quickly developed.

LENINISM

Vladimir Lenin (1870–1924) was active in developing the Communist Party in Russia and led that country's successful Bolshevik Revolution in 1917–1918. He claimed to be a follower of Marx but developed new directions for the achievement of communism. Lenin refused to wait for the maturation of capitalism and instead developed a different model for revolution based on four essential ingredients: (1) a small, revolutionary elite, (2) economic underdevelopment (the opposite of Marx's industrialization), (3) a discontented peasantry, and (4) war against an outside force. Lenin's formula worked in Russia and in Yugoslavia, China, Vietnam, and Cuba. In fact, Lenin's formula applies to almost all cases where communism has taken root. The exceptions are those countries of Eastern Europe in which the Soviet Union imposed communism after World War II.

Lenin was the first Communist to be faced with the task of setting up an economic system after the political system was secure. **War Communism** was the economic system that Lenin imposed on Russia immediately after the Bolshevik Revolution. This system instituted rigid administrative control of the economy in an attempt to marshal the resources needed to engage in a civil war with the non-Communist White Russians. Widespread nationalization of industry took place, and all private trading was outlawed. All labor mobility was rigidly controlled, and money as an exchange mechanism almost disappeared. This period is difficult to evaluate. Some economic historians claim that Lenin instituted War Communism only because of the demands of fighting a civil war.[2]

By 1921, the economy had seriously deteriorated. Lenin responded by abandoning War Communism and instituting a program referred to as the **New Economic Policy (NEP)**. This policy was an attempt at market socialism, with planning for only the key industries in the economy. The remainder of the economy was left to respond to basic market forces. There was very rapid economic growth during this period, and the Soviet economy quickly recovered from the protracted civil war. Lenin died in 1924. In 1926, the NEP came to an end for a variety of reasons. One reason was that the move toward a market economy during NEP greatly reduced the power of the Communist Party to channel and direct the course of economic development. Many parts of the current reform in the Soviet Union resemble the NEP.

War Communism
An economic system of rigid administrative control imposed by Lenin in Russia during the civil war following the Bolshevik Revolution.

New Economic Policy (NEP)
A program that replaced War Communism in 1921 in the Soviet Union and was an attempt at market socialism.

2. Others claim Lenin instituted War Communism out of a desire to see such a system evolve as the economic application of communism. For this view, see Paul Craig Roberts, *Alienation and the Soviet Economy* (Albuquerque: University of New Mexico Press, 1971).

STALINISM

After Lenin's death, there was open dispute in the Soviet Communist Party over the direction of development. The **Great Industrialization Debate** was an open debate that took place in the Soviet Union from 1924 to 1928 concerning the correct way to industrialize the economy.[3] The left wing of the party, led by economist E. A. Preobrazhensky, argued that the country should make a concerted effort toward rapid industrialization of key sectors of the economy. This policy would be carried out by the central allocation of investment expenditures. N. I. Bukharin, who was the spokesperson for the right wing, disagreed with this position and stressed balanced growth of the economy. Bukharin argued that all sectors of the economy must grow together because they all support and feed one another.

Joseph Stalin (1879–1953) was both an observer and a participant in the debate. Stalin played one side against the other while forming a power base. At the time of Lenin's death, Stalin allied himself with the right wing of the party in order to counteract the power of Leon Trotsky and the left wing. This alliance allowed Stalin to discredit and weaken the left wing, a task he accomplished by 1927. He then turned on the right wing and, by 1928, had its leaders denounced by the party. Stalin was then in complete control, since he had purged all dissidents.[4]

The planning system that Stalin adopted was centrally directed and was set up in five-year increments. Five years was chosen since it is possible to complete most investment projects in that period. Stalin's first five-year plan was an extreme version of the left-wing industrialization proposal. Its achievement required very centralized planning, investment in heavy industry, and forced collectivization in the agricultural sector, which was expected to supply food and raw materials. Industrialization was very rapid, but the costs of this policy in human terms were great. Millions of people were purged. Many others starved to death because the peasants resisted forced centralization by destroying crops and livestock.

The Soviet Union's rigid system of central planning up to 1989 was the legacy of Stalin. Today, the term *Stalinism* is associated with a ruthless dictatorship as well as with a highly centralized planning structure. However, Stalinism is not openly practiced in any Communist country today.

Great Industrialization Debate
An open debate that took place in the Soviet Union from 1924 to 1928 concerning the correct way to industrialize the economy.

MAOISM

In China, the Communist Party came to full power in October 1949, after decades of struggle. Mao Zedong was the revolutionary leader who took command, just as Lenin's formula for communist revolutionaries had predicted. In the early years of Chinese Communism, the goal was industrialization, much as it had been in the Soviet Union. However, this policy was formulated without the help of Moscow. The Chinese Communist Party, from the very beginning, was fiercely independent of the Soviet Union.

In 1958, the Great Leap Forward was announced. The **Great Leap Forward** was a modernization plan to increase per capita income in China by 25 percent in five years. Many of the programs were ill-conceived, such

Great Leap Forward
A modernization plan that was launched in 1958 to increase per capita income in China by 25 percent in five years.

---
3. See Alexander Erlich, *Soviet Industrialization Debate, 1924–1928* (Cambridge, MA: Harvard University Press, 1960).
4. For an excellent economic history of the Soviet Union, including this period, see Alec Nove, *An Economic History of the USSR* (London: Penguin, 1975).

as the production of steel on a small scale in backyard furnaces. The result was a product of poor quality that was not useful as input to further manufacturing processes. The Great Leap Forward included the collectivization of Chinese agriculture. Mao sought to mobilize the huge underemployed population of China in collectivized agriculture. The result was disastrous. In two years, agricultural production fell by 20 percent and widespread starvation occurred. Mao was ousted from control, and a pragmatic leadership took over. With the aid of revolutionary youth, Mao was able to return to power in 1966 through a political coup.

The period from 1966 through 1969, called the **Cultural Revolution**, represented the high point of Mao's power. The Cultural Revolution embraced revolutionary values. Mao envisioned a completely classless society, organized as a collective operation rather than as a state enterprise, as in the Soviet Union. The motivation for the society was to be completely altruistic, embracing the concept of the "new man" who responds to social rather than to material incentives. The Cultural Revolution almost destroyed the educational system. Professors were sent to work in communes and factories. Education came to a standstill during this period. The Cultural Revolution was also an economic disaster. As a result, in 1969, Mao turned more authority over to Chou En-Lai, who tempered some of the more drastic policies.

Cultural Revolution
The high point of Mao's power in China, characterized by a radical restructuring of the economy from 1966 through 1969.

The Chinese economy has changed often and in different directions. Not enough information is available to evaluate the success of Maoism in promoting economic development. Several economists who have traveled to China give strikingly different reports. For example, John Gurley argues that China made great strides and has eradicated poverty, but James Tobin claims that there was not much economic progress under Mao.[5] He argues that almost any system that brought peace to the country would have achieved some economic success, since China was torn by revolution and war for several decades before 1949.

After Mao's death in 1976, the new leaders pursued a development strategy that was often openly hostile to Mao's ideas. They attacked the "Gang of Four," Mao's widow and three other radicals. In attacking the Gang of Four, the leaders attacked the ideas of the Cultural Revolution and, in fact, Mao himself, although they were careful not to name Mao. *Newsweek* reported that Chinese officials argued that "Chairman Mao was deceived by the Gang of Four."[6] The Gang of Four were tried and convicted in 1981.

Castroism

Fidel Castro, who overthrew the Batista government in Cuba in 1958, learned the lesson of Lenin's formula for revolution very well. He led a small group of committed revolutionaries in an country with a large, discontented peasant class and an underdeveloped economy. The United States served as an outside enemy that he used to unify the diverse elements within Cuba. In many ways, the Cuban system resembles early Chi-

---

5. John Gurley, "Maoist Economic Development," and James Tobin, "The Economy of China: A Tourist's View," in Edwin Mansfield, *Economics: Readings, Issues, and Cases* (New York: W. W. Norton, 1977).
6. *Newsweek* (30 October 1978): 50.

nese communism. For example, Castro has placed heavy emphasis on creating a "new man."[7] The goal was to remove all social inequities and motivate workers with moral incentives rather than with material ones. Castro's vision is very close to Marx's view of the final stage of communism. His policy was in large part the work of Che Guevara. The Soviets, who were financially underwriting the Cuban economy, were skeptical of the plan.

Rather than attempt to industrialize the Cuban economy rapidly, Castro concentrated on agriculture and sought to exploit the export potential of the sugar cane industry. This policy required the transfer of labor from cities to rural areas, the exact opposite of what occurred under European Communist regimes. The Cuban economy remains heavily reliant on agriculture. Planning in Cuba is carried out by the System of Budgetary Finance, a centralized planning system that views the economy as a single firm to be rigidly controlled by the central authority.

Castro faces severe problems. The Cuban economy had been receiving more than $5 billion annually in subsidies from the Soviet Union. With reform in the Soviet Union, these subsidies were phased out beginning in 1991. When the Soviet aid declined, the Cuban GNP fell 30 percent. Castro responded by sending 100,000 "volunteers" into the countryside to plant and harvest crops. He called on Cubans to tighten their belts and create a new agricultural class. This move created unrest among the youth, but they appear too apathetic or frightened to protest. Many experts predict that Castro will be the next Communist leader to be deposed. In fact, a group of Cuban-Americans in Miami has drafted a constitution and is planning economic programs for a post-Castro Cuba. The group, called The Cuban American National Foundation, is headed by Jorge Mas Canosa, a successful Florida businessman.[8]

RETREAT FROM SOCIALISM: THATCHERISM

Just as strong leaders have had a significant influence on socialism, some leaders have left a mark on capitalism. Margaret Thatcher led a retreat from socialism through significant reprivatization of the British economy. She served the longest continuous term as British Prime Minister in the twentieth century. In December 1990, Thatcher stepped down as Prime Minister when she was challenged for the leadership of the Conservative Party. Thatcher was often linked with former President Reagan as a proponent of supply side economics and privatization. However, her program aimed at decreasing the size of government was far more successful than Reagan's. Thatcher reduced income taxes in order to reverse the "talent drain" of entertainers and other highly paid individuals from Britain. She convinced Parliament to pass legislation that greatly reduced the power

---

7. For a good review of Castro's Cuba, see Carmelo Mesa-Lago (ed.), *Revolutionary Change in Cuba* (Pittsburgh: University of Pittsburgh Press, 1971).
8. See "Gorbachev Will Soon Make Castro More of an Island," *Business Week*, (16 July 1990): 47; Anthony Daniels, "The Last Days of Fidel Castro," *National Review* (5 March 1990): 29–32; "Soon to Come: Capitalist Cuba", *National Review* (17 September 1990): 19–20. The Council for Inter-American Security sponsored a contest, a pool to predict when Castro will fall from power, and received 300 predictions. Former U.N. Ambassador Jeane Kirkpatrick predicted "by the end of 1991," and Texas oilman Nelson Bunker Hunt predicted October 5, 1993. See "Betting on Fidel's Fall," *Forbes* (1 October 1990): 17.

of labor unions by requiring that they poll their members before calling a strike.

Perhaps the most important element of Thatcherism was the privatization of the British economy. When she became Prime Minister in 1979, the economy was best described as one in which large governmental enterprises were deadlocked with large labor unions. (This situation was referred to as the "British Disease.") During her tenure, she reversed the trend by selling off more than $31 billion in state-owned industries to private investors. These sales included the government's share in British Gas, Rolls-Royce, British Airways, and British Petroleum. Her action and the effect it had on productivity (productivity increases have averaged over 3 percent) inspired similar privatization policies in Italy and France.

ORGANIZATION AND DECISION-MAKING APPROACH TO COMPARING ECONOMIC SYSTEMS

We have been comparing economic systems in terms of how the underlying ideology affects their organization. In many cases, a dominant personality's interpretation of that ideology shaped an entire system. Some of you may have found this an exciting and useful way to categorize the world. Others may have found it frustrating to examine individual systems, rather than developing general principles as to how different systems are organized and how they affect behavior. The first approach has been the way most economists have historically examined alternative economic systems. A second approach is to formulate organizational principles using economic theory as a coherent analytical framework.[9]

The Decision Process: Decision Makers, Incentives, and Information

To understand an economic system, it is necessary to examine the organizational setting for the production of goods and services *and* the institutional setting for the distribution of those goods and services. The important questions concern the structure of decision making in production and distribution. One such question is which individuals, and at which levels, make the major decisions concerning production and distribution. In the United States, production decisions are made at the entrepreneurial level. In the Soviet Union, these decisions until recently were made at the planning level.

Once the assignment of decision-making responsibility has been made, the next question concerns the motivation for the decision makers. Do the decision makers bear the costs of wrong decisions or reap the rewards of correct decisions? It is also necessary to determine how one person's participation in the decision-making process influences another's. Also, it is possible to change an individual's internal values. In other words, do institutions affect individuals' value systems?

Once these two aspects of the decision-making structure are determined, the informational structure of the economic system can be ana-

---

9. For a comprehensive development of this approach, see Egon Neuberger and William J. Duffy, *Comparative Economic Systems: A Decision-Making Approach* (Boston: Allyn and Bacon, 1976).

lyzed. The informational structure is the way in which individuals learn about their options so they can act on them. In the U.S. economy, prices are an important source of information. In the Soviet economy, the plan plays this role. As decision making becomes centralized, more and better information is critical because the costs of wrong decisions are so much higher. System questions are largely microeconomic in nature.

THE ENVIRONMENT

A country's environment is its social structure, physical conditions, and international situation. Some of the more critical aspects of the environment in terms of possible impact on the economic system are the level of economic development, the size of the country in area and population, the availability of natural resources within the country and from safe allies, the values of the people (religious, cultural, and so on), the political system, the size of the country relative to its near neighbors, the level of development relative to the rest of the world and relative to near neighbors, and the sphere of influence in which the country lies (American, Soviet, or Chinese, for example). These are only a few of the influences on an economic system, but they are representative of the concept of environmental influence.

ECONOMIC PERFORMANCE

The way in which an economy performs is an important evaluation measure. Economists usually focus on the performance of the gross national product (GNP) and examine growth in per capita production, stability of production (business cycles can be socially destabilizing), and equity in income distribution. These measures of performance are mostly macroeconomic in nature.

POLICY CHANGES

Some policy changes can be made within a system without changing the underlying fabric of the system. These changes consist of marginal changes in the system and its environment in order to affect performance. Policy changes can influence the system in a positive or negative way. A "good" system might develop "bad" policies that produce "bad" performance and in turn result in a negative change in the "good" system. For example, a central planning policy decision to consolidate farms into larger units or to shift from corn to wheat can increase (or reduce) productivity and efficiency. Recent policy changes in the Soviet Union and some countries in Eastern Europe affect the entire system.

INTERACTION OF SYSTEMS, ENVIRONMENT, PERFORMANCE, AND POLICY

Of course, all these organizational elements interact in a complex fashion. Using this terminology, however, can help in understanding how economic systems differ and in what ways they are similar. For example, consider a small country with the Soviet Union or the United States as a close neighbor. How would this affect the development of its economic system? Having the Soviet Union nearby had a profound effect on the countries of Eastern Europe, but the Soviet Union has pulled back, even allowing the reunification of the two Germanys in 1990. Similarly, being close to the United States has affected the trade pattern, the output mix, and the level of development in Canada, Mexico, and the Caribbean. What environmental factors caused the Industrial Revolution to spread from England to the United States but not to Russia?

How might performance influence an economic system? Performance is part of Lenin's formula: If things get bad enough, there might be a revolution. On the other hand, if economic conditions stagnate in a Communist country after a revolution, there might be a move toward capitalism or market socialism. There are many complex questions, and the organization and decision-making approach may give you a start in organizing your thoughts. This approach gives some insight into the many and varied forms of capitalism and socialism.

PLANNING

Throughout this chapter, whether we were using the *isms* approach to systems or a more structured organizational approach, we continually encountered the issue of planning. Who directs production, who makes decisions, and who bears the costs for wrong decisions or receives the rewards for correct decisions? Planning is the essence of the problem of understanding systems. The question is not whether planning should take place but rather who should do the planning. General Motors plans, homebuilders plan, wheat farmers plan—and so do you. The key question is the degree of centralization of planning and control. At the market extreme, the answer would be that only individual consumers and entrepreneurs should plan. At the command extreme, the position would be that only the central authority should plan.

THE SOCIALIST CONTROVERSY

Marx had little to say about the actual workings of the economic system under socialism. Instead, Marx criticized capitalism and left the development of the economics of socialism to his followers. In 1922, a professor at the University of Vienna, Ludwig von Mises, wrote a famous article, "Economic Calculation in the Socialist Commonwealth."[10] This article claimed that rational economic calculations were impossible under socialism. Von Mises based his argument on a number of factors, but the essence was quite simple. If the state owned the factors of production (other than labor), it would have to allocate them among competing uses. Without a market to determine prices, this task would be impossible. A simulated market with shadow prices could not supply correct information because of the absence of the profit motive. **Shadow prices** are simulated market prices used by economic planners.

The **socialist controversy** was a debate between von Mises and Oskar Lange concerning the feasibility of planning without markets.[11] Von Mises argued that "the most serious menace to socialist economic organization"

shadow prices
Simulated market prices used by economic planners.

socialist controversy
A debate between Ludwig von Mises and Oskar Lange concerning the feasibility of planning without markets.

---
10. Ludwig von Mises, "Economic Calculation in the Socialist Commonwealth," in F. A. Hayek (ed.), *Collectivist Economic Planning* (Clifton, NJ: Augustus M. Kelley, 1967), 103.
11. For a thorough discussion of the socialist controversy, see Paul R. Gregory and Robert C. Stuart, *Soviet Economic Structure and Performance* (New York: Harper & Row, 1974).

Chapter 20 Comparative Economic Systems in Theory and Practice

was the lack of rewards for correct managerial decisions and penalties for incorrect managerial decisions. Lange, a famous Polish economist who at the time was on the faculty at the University of Chicago, responded to von Mises by developing a model sometimes referred to as the **competitive solution**. In this model, Lange tried to prove that a socialist economy with a combination of central *and* local decision making can arrive at the same efficiency as attained with perfect competition. Prices are set by the central authority. Local managers are told to maximize profits, although they cannot keep these profits. They are solely accounting profits. If shortages or surpluses develop, the price is changed, and in this way an equilibrium price is finally reached. One of the most telling criticisms of Lange's solution, however, is that in a market system, profits are not merely a measure of success but the *incentive* to succeed.[12]

competitive solution The model developed by Oskar Lange in an attempt to show that a planned economy could theoretically reach the efficiency of an economy with competition.

The debate over the feasibility of centralized planning has never been resolved. Is it possible for a central authority to make the calculations necessary to produce efficiently? In a later article that might be considered an extension of this debate, Nobel laureate F. A. Hayek said no.[13] Hayek argues that information is the friction in the system that causes economic models to diverge from the ideal system of either von Mises or Lange. Information is costly to develop and spread, using up scarce resources that must be taken away from other uses. Hayek argued that market systems are superior because they need less information than do centrally planned systems.

Recall from Chapter 2 what happens in a planned economy and a market economy when an earthquake destroys a copper mine. What happens in each economy? In the market economy, the price of copper will rise, reflecting the decrease in supply. Profit-minded entrepreneurs will substitute cheaper metals to minimize costs. In a planned economy, the planners must first be informed of the disaster. The planners must then make some estimate of the severity of the scarcity. They then inform each user of copper that in the future less copper will be available and that other metals should be substituted. The planners must also contact producers of other metals and tell them to ship to the enterprises that had been using copper. In addition, the planners will have to set priorities for use of the available copper. In the market system, this priority setting was done by the increase in price.

Hayek's position is quite simple: Central planning can never be as efficient as a market system because it requires the use of so many resources in transmitting information. The market system, on the other hand, minimizes the amount of information needed. In 1989, there were severe earthquakes in San Francisco (during the World Series) and in Soviet Armenia. The speed of adjustment in the earthquake zones was much faster in San Francisco, reflecting the positive role that the market can play in speeding the process of economic recovery. Recent developments in planned economies also lead to the conclusion that Hayek was right. The inefficiencies of central planning became too expensive, and market reforms were required to stimulate economic growth.

---

12. Paul Craig Roberts, "Oskar Lange's Theory of Socialist Planning," *Journal of Political Economy* (May-June 1971): 562–568.
13. F. A. Hayek, "The Use of Knowledge in Society," *American Economic Review* (September 1945): 519–528.

How to Plan

The fact that central planning may be inefficient does not change the fact that it is undertaken. Most socialist countries still rely heavily on central planning to move production in the desired direction. Therefore, we need to look at how planning takes place in a command economy.

First, priorities must be established. Someone has to decide what to produce. In the early years of Soviet planning, such decisions were made at the aggregate level. The first plan was, in fact, called the "State Plan for the Electrification of Russia." Until recently, planning was still done by the state planning commission, commonly called the **Gosplan**. Whether to produce consumer or investment goods was the first aggregate planning decision in the Soviet Union. Since the goal of the early leaders was rapid economic growth, they decided to produce investment goods at the expense of consumer goods. As a result, very few consumer goods were available, forcing consumers to save. This pattern of production permitted heavy investment and very rapid rates of economic growth. There were, and still are, shortages of consumer goods in the Soviet Union.

Once planners decided what to produce, they turned their attention to how much to produce. This is a difficult planning problem because the amount produced depends on the productive capacity of the existing industries and on the resources that will be available during the period. Production uses up resources. Therefore, the planners have to make sure that the resources to be used for the final output will be available. At this stage, the various industries are brought into the picture, and the ministries, one for each major industry, make their plans ahead of the overall plan. Once all plans are finalized, they are communicated to productive enterprises so they can take the necessary action to put the plans into operation. Planning is an ongoing process. Even though the planning period is usually expressed in five-year increments, there is continuous revision and implementation.

The planning process itself used up a great deal of time and productive resources. The individuals who engaged in the planning were highly trained engineers and economists, people taken out of other productive activities in order to plan. It is not, therefore, difficult to understand the burden that planning places on an economy. Ironically, many of the poorest countries, where most Communist revolutions have taken place, are the very ones that can least afford the luxury of planning, because of the high opportunity cost of the resources used in the planning process.

Gosplan
The state planning commission in the Soviet Union.

Input-Output Analysis

The complexity of planning led to the development of methods to make it more effective. Input-output analysis, developed by Nobel prize–winning economist Wassily Leontief, shows that everything depends on everything else. These interrelationships are what make planning so difficult, because specific plans must be made as to how much of each good is to be produced, by whom, and for whom. **Input-output analysis** is an attempt to quantify the flows between different sectors of the economy.

Table 1 is an input-output table for a small economy in which there are only a few industries to control. There are only three industries: electric-

input-output analysis
An attempt to quantify the flows between different sectors of the economy for purposes of economic planning.

		Electricity	Trucks	Steel	Consumption	Total Output
				OUTPUTS		
INPUTS	Electricity	1,000	1,500	5,000	1,500	9,000 kilowatts
	Trucks	1,000	1,500	2,000	1,000	5,500 trucks
	Steel	4,000	3,000	8,500	3,500	19,000 tons
	Labor	2,000	500	3,000	0	5,500 worker-days

TABLE 1
INPUT-OUTPUT TABLE FOR A SIMPLE THREE-INDUSTRY ECONOMY

ity, trucks, and steel. There is also a labor sector and a category of consumption. The input to labor is consumption. Reading across the rows of Table 1 gives the output of each industry and of labor and shows how that output is distributed. One of the reasons that input-output tables are especially useful in command economies is that physical units are used, and prices of outputs and inputs are not needed for the analysis. The fact that no prices are needed is important in a system where market prices are not available and the prices that exist do not necessarily reflect relative scarcity.

To interpret this input-output table, read across the rows. For example, the steel industry has a total output of 19,000 tons, which is sold or allocated by the central authority to the following sectors: 4,000 tons to the electricity industry, 3,000 tons to the truck industry, 8,500 tons to the steel industry, and 3,500 tons to the consumer goods sector. Reading down a column shows the inputs that are needed to produce the output. For example, in order to produce the 19,000 tons of steel, the steel industry uses the following inputs: 5,000 kilowatts of electricity, 2,000 trucks, 8,500 tons of steel, and 3,000 worker-days of labor. The simple arithmetic of input-output tables can be used to plan future output.

The key assumption in input-output analysis is that production takes place in all industries at *constant* costs. There are no economies or diseconomies of scale. If planners want to double the production of the steel industry, all they need to do is double the inputs. Regardless of the level of output planned, the amount of inputs required per unit of output remains the same. However, for large increases in output, this assumption is very unrealistic.

The numbers in Table 2 can be used to calculate the input needed to produce additional units of output. These numbers are referred to as input coefficients. An **input coefficient** shows the ratio of the amount of an input to the total output of an industry. Each input coefficient in Table 2 can be calculated by dividing each value in a column of Table 1 by the to-

input coefficient
In input-output analysis, the ratio of the amount of an input to the total output of an industry.

			OUTPUTS	
		Electricity	Trucks	Steel
INPUTS	Electricity	0.11	0.27	0.26
	Trucks	0.11	0.27	0.11
	Steel	0.44	0.55	0.47
	Labor	0.22	0.09	0.16

TABLE 2
INPUT COEFFICIENTS FOR THE ECONOMY OF TABLE 1

tal output of that industry. For example, the input coefficient of electricity in the truck industry is 0.27 kilowatts/truck (1,500/5,500). Input coefficients can be used to plan increases in output. Examine the column for trucks. The input coefficient tells what increase is needed from each supplying industry in order to get a given increase in output of trucks.

The input-output information in Tables 1 and 2 can be used to plan for the three-industry economy. Suppose planners want to expand the output of the electricity industry by 2,000 kilowatts. That expansion in output would require 220 kilowatts of electricity, 220 trucks, 880 tons of steel, and 440 worker-days. These inputs are found by multiplying the applicable input coefficients by the desired increase in output. Planners would, therefore, be able to direct these industries to deliver the required inputs to produce the planned output.

You should note that there are feedback effects in this process. In order to produce more electricity, some electricity must be consumed in producing the additional steel and trucks used to produce electricity. Feedback occurs throughout this interdependent system. The example assumes that there is no limit to the capacity of any sector of the economy. In fact, however, this may not be the case. In order to produce more electricity, it may be necessary to build new power generators. Generators require time to produce, causing a delay in fulfilling the plan.

The problems of using input-output analysis for planning stem from the fact that the coefficients are constant and are calculated on the basis of historical experience. In other words, the required inputs are calculated on the assumption that the same input mix as that used in the time period for which the table of input coefficients was compiled will continue to be used.

Problems of Central Planning

The technique of planning seems simple in theory. The calculations for a realistic economy are usually overwhelming, however. Think about the size of an input-output table for an economy with 100 industries, 1,000 industries, or 5,000 industries. The interdependencies between the industries become mind-boggling, or even computer-boggling.

The significant problems of planning begin after the plan has been created. There are the problems of implementing the plan, as well as the problems of creating and maintaining incentives that induce workers and managers to support the plan. Managers have incentives to overstate their "needs" for inputs and to hoard materials, since they do not have to pay for them. It is not surprising that plans are often announced with a great deal of publicity and fanfare, but the poor results are often played down.

REFORMS: ECONOMIC FREEDOM AND POLITICAL FREEDOM

Socialist countries have found through experience that the application of planning has not necessarily improved economic performance. This failure was evident during the Great Leap Forward and the Cultural Revolution in China and is also suggested by the declining rate of economic growth in the Soviet Union. Because of poor economic performance, both the People's Republic of China and the Soviet Union have entered into a series of reforms aimed at introducing market forces into the economy. The difficulty with such reforms is that the economic freedom of markets always produces pressure for other types of freedom, which would reduce the power of the central authorities. The trade-off is easy to see. In order to stimulate economic growth, incentives are needed. Markets are allowed to develop in order to create these incentives. The markets diminish the control of the party and its large and powerful bureaucracy. The problem becomes acute when the economic reforms produce the inevitable demands for other freedoms. Bureaucrats can use the demands for political freedom as an excuse for reversing the economic reforms and, by so doing, restore their diminished power. Each socialist country has to cope with the conflicting goals of economic growth and tight administrative control. It is helpful to examine the reform movements in China and the Soviet Union in greater detail.

THE PEOPLE'S REPUBLIC OF CHINA

After Mao's death in 1976, there was rapid reform in China, affecting almost every aspect of the economy. Much of this reform was due to the efforts of Deng Xiaoping, Party General Secretary since December 1978.

POLITICAL, SOCIAL, AND INTELLECTUAL REFORMS. Many of the holdovers of Maoism disappeared from China in the 1980s. Before then, class labels from before the 1949 revolution were still used. These labels (peasant, landlord, intellectual, and so on) affected such things as how people were treated by the courts and whether they were allowed into schools. In the 1980s, the labels were eliminated. Intellectuals benefited from these changes, a great contrast to the days of the Cultural Revolution. They were encouraged to debate and exchange ideas with Western scholars. The results were sweeping demands for political freedom that culminated in large demonstrations.

A system of laws also evolved in the 1980s. Mao had removed all laws because they interfered with the "dictatorship of the proletariat." The new system of laws replaced the arbitrary power of party secretaries and brought some stability to the country.

ECONOMIC REFORM. The first stage of the economic reforms championed by Deng required the "readjustment" of some priorities. The first shift occurred in the output mix. To establish economic incentives, it is necessary to increase wages *and*, equally important, to produce consumer goods for people to buy with those higher wages. This change was accomplished by setting lower targets for heavy industries and increasing investment in light, consumer-oriented industries.

Most noticeable was the change away from the Maoist principle of self-reliance, that is, independence from other countries. Trade with the rest of the world was greatly expanded. Between 1975 and 1985, China's international trade increased from 3.5 percent of GDP to 16 percent of GDP.

The basic reforms of the economic system had profound effects. In agriculture, the "household responsibility system" assigned land that had been held in communes to individual families. In exchange, these farmers assumed contractual obligations to provide a certain amount of food to the state. Farmers were allowed to sell production in excess of the contracted amounts. The result was dramatic. Production increased sharply, and peasant farmers became some of the wealthiest people in China.

The industrial sector was also radically reformed. Once production goals were met, industrial enterprises could sell any surplus on the open market, or they could barter it for other goods. Profits and losses were used to reward or penalize managers. In some instances, factories that had been making losses were turned over to workers, just as communal farms were divided among households. In addition, the state started to charge industrial enterprises for the investment capital it supplied. In some cases, these "loans" were made with assigned payment schedules and interest charges, just as in capitalist countries.

The changes brought about by Deng Xiaoping were fundamental. They injected a great deal of market influence into the Chinese economy. With the market influence and the rise in foreign trade, there came other observable changes. Western dress, music, and ideas about democracy crept in. These Western influences created a danger. Deng was responsible for the reforms, which were not popular with all party leaders. The frustration of many leaders was understandable, since the freeing of the economy greatly reduced their power and influence. As a result, a political movement to reverse the reforms surfaced. In 1985, some party leaders began to complain about the "excesses" of the reforms and the "spiritual pollution" that had been created. In January 1987, the conservatives in the party finally acted when students demonstrated for democratic reforms, including freedom of expression. The student demonstrations united the police and military elements in the party leadership. The result was that Hu Yaobang, party leader, reform advocate, and likely heir to Deng's power, made a "self-criticism" and was forced to step down. He was replaced by Zhao Ziyang, whose first act was to fire the top security official for being too lenient with the student demonstrators. Zhao was described in the press as a cautious reformer.

The Chinese reform movement was at a crossroads in 1989. The economic reform produced economic gains, which in turn led to political demands. These demands led to the firing of Hu and a campaign against "bourgeois liberalization." Party leaders started stressing central planning, thrift, and reduced consumption. Factory managers remained quiet while party leaders were reasserting their political control. In June 1989, students gathered in Tiananmen Square demanding democracy. The demonstration, which included the construction of a statue copied from the Statue of Liberty, was covered in great detail by the Western news media. On June 4, 1989, the military opened fire on the students to put down what is officially known in China as "the turmoil." Thousands of students died. The commander of the 38th Army who did not obey orders to attack the students received a ten-year prison sentence. The official line is that the student movement was a counter-revolutionary rebellion. During the turmoil, Jian Zemin emerged as General Secretary of the Chinese Communist Party. He told *U.S. News & World Report*, "We do not regret or criticize ourselves for the way we handled the Tiananmen event because if we had not sent in the troops then, I would not be able to sit here today."[14]

The political backlash has restricted further economic reforms. Some Western firms that had been investing in China fear that the crackdown will reverse the economic gains. Others contend that the economic reforms have gone so far that it would be impossible to reverse them.

THE SOVIET UNION

Recent changes in the Soviet Union have been staggering. Before 1989, planning was the major feature of the Soviet economy. Gosplan supervised the planning and the implementation of the plan through approximately fifty ministries. Each ministry represented a segment of the Soviet economy. The changes were spawned by the Soviet Union's lackluster economic performance. In Stalin's time, growth rates were high. But a succession of general secretaries, including Brezhnev, Andropov, Chernenko, and now Mikhail Gorbachev, have acknowledged the poor economic performance in their speeches.

Concern focused on several areas. First and foremost, economic growth has been slow. Coupled with this slow growth were "imbalances" (shortages) in consumer areas. Wages increased, but the production of consumer goods was too low. As a result, workers had few production incentives. In addition, both shortages and surpluses were common because the plan did not adjust to changes in supply and demand. As Soviet consumers became relatively better off, they resisted purchasing shoddy merchandise, creating surpluses of some products.

The reasons for the poor performance are not hard to pinpoint. The centralization of economic decision making, based on detailed, explicit plans, led to mistakes. There was no good mechanism for channeling feedback from consumers into the plans. Ultimately, the managers of enterprises were only concerned with satisfying the central planners in the relevant ministry. This concentrated central planning, coupled with enterprise security (the firms faced no competition) and employment security (workers faced no job-loss threat), created few incentives to increase productivity or to be more responsive to consumer preferences.

REFORMS. In March 1985, Mikhail Gorbachev was made general secretary of the Soviet Communist Party following the death of Konstantin Chernenko. Gorbachev, in his fifties, represented a change from rule by elderly men from the Stalin era. His first steps in the direction of economic reform were taken in early 1987. The economic reforms are referred to as *perestroika*. Political reforms are known as *glasnost*, or openness.

Perestroika represents the first steps in economic reform. Reform was not easy to accomplish because every step toward markets and efficiency was a step away from central planning. *Glasnost* and *perestroika* are dramatic changes from earlier periods when the Soviet Union intervened first in

perestroika
Restructuring, economic reforms in the Soviet Union.

glasnost
Openness, political reforms in the Soviet Union.

---

14. Emily MacFarquhar, "Back to the Future in China," *U.S. News & World Report* (12 March 1990): 41. This issue of *U.S. News & World Report* contains three very good articles on China.

International Perspective

Reform in East Germany, Poland, Hungary, and Czechoslovakia

While the Soviets struggle with the political aftermath of the failed coup, some of the Eastern European countries are moving much faster in the area of economic reform. It must be kept in mind that these countries differ greatly from the Soviet Republics. For most of these countries, the main obstacle to reform was the Soviet Union. When they realized that the Soviet Union would not intervene militarily as it had in Hungary (1956) and Czechoslovakia (1968), the reform movements gained momentum.

The success of reforms in Eastern Europe is based on many factors. To begin, most of these countries have escaped the ethnic unrest that has been so devastating in the Soviet Republics. In addition, their economies were in better shape than the Soviet economy when the reforms began.

East Germany was the most developed of the Soviet bloc countries. Its reform movement has been greatly helped by its reunification with West Germany. The financial aid from the West German economy is so important that East Germany is a special case by itself. Even there, however, there have been problems. Unemployment has been high, and buyers for state enterprises have been hard to find.

Poland moved toward capitalism in a bold step. Poland's Finance Minister Leszek Balcerowicz is a former economics professor with an MBA degree from St. John's University in New York. He is an admirer of Milton Friedman. With the help of Professor Jeffry Sachs of Harvard University, Balcerowicz drafted a plan for Poland's economic reform. In 1990, inflation dropped to an annual rate of around 30 percent, compared to 3,000 percent in 1989. The stores are well stocked with agricultural products from local farms and high-tech consumer goods from West Germany and Hong Kong. All restrictions on new enterprises were lifted in the fall of 1989, and 80,000 new companies sprang up in the first year. It was expected that 45 percent of all goods and services would be produced by firms in the private sector by the end of 1991.

Problems remain. Unemployment is high and consumers spend most of their income on food and shelter. The main obstacle to continued success in Poland is political. Lech Walesa and Prime Minister Tadeusz Mazowiecki fought for control of the ruling Solidarity movement in November and December of 1990. Walesa won the election and became Prime Minister in December 1990. Critics worry that his political ties to labor will undermine the reforms. Since his election, Walesa has been uncharacteristically silent about his plans.

Hungary is pursuing a very sophisticated reform package, loosely based on a Thatcher-like gradual selling of government-owned enterprises. The ability to attract foreign capital will determine its success. By the end of 1991, 45 percent of the Hungarian GNP was produced by privately owned firms.

The Czech reform is proceeding more slowly. Czech reformers do not want to sell government assets directly to foreigners or to Czech citizens. They favor a gradual approach. The Czech plan calls for vouchers to be given to citizens, who could use them to buy equity in state-owned enterprises. About 10 percent of the Czech economy had been privatized by the end of 1991.

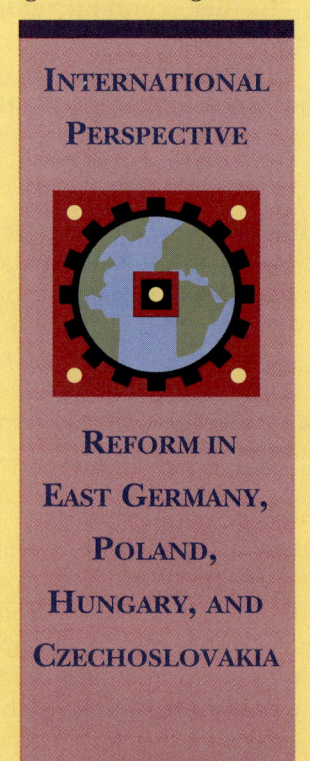

Hungary, then in Czechoslovakia, and finally in Poland to make sure that economic reform did not mean a slide toward capitalism. In 1989, the Soviet Union did not intervene when radical change swept Eastern Europe. The most dramatic event occurred in East Germany where the Berlin Wall came down, but change also occurred in Romania, Hungary, Czechoslovakia, and Poland.

The reforms in the Soviet Union have not gone smoothly. The once powerful Red Army is in disarray. In the first half of 1990, when only 26 percent of the drafted young men showed up, the government chose not to crack down on the draft-dodgers. To complicate the military situation, several independent armies emerged in ethnic republics, including Georgia, Armenia, and Azerbaijan.[15] In August 1991, Gorbachev was the victim of a coup, but he was rescued when Boris Yeltsin's political support defeated the coup.

The reforms face at least eight problems:

1. There is no experience with markets, property rights, and exchange. There is widespread distrust of market processes.
2. Pollution is rampant in the Soviet Union (and the countries of Eastern Europe). An emerging environmental movement is demanding that more attention be paid to the environment. This will be expensive at a time when other matters are more pressing.
3. There is growing ethnic unrest. Independence movements have succeeded in the Baltics, the Ukraine, Moldavia, and Georgia. Fighting has erupted between Armenia and Azerbaijan.
4. There is growing labor unrest. Miners are the most organized and violent. They threaten to strike unless their demands are met.
5. The military is in turmoil. Senior military leaders are unhappy about their loss of status in the political apparatus.
6. Agriculture is in disarray. Although bumper harvests, the best in fifteen years occurred in 1990, food rotted in the fields because the distribution network is not adequate.
7. The economic reformers demand faster and more radical economic changes. At the same time, there is strong resistance from bureaucrats and consumers who fear higher prices.
8. Finally, the economy is in chaos. The widespread shortages are aggravated by panic buying from consumers afraid of higher rates of inflation. An illegal black market thrives. Economic conditions are likely to deteriorate before they get better.

To address these growing problems, Gorbachev teamed with his rival Yeltsin in August 1990 to announce a new 500-day program to replace the failed reform of the previous year. Under the 500-day program, the government's huge subsidies to industry were to end. The twenty remaining industrial ministries would be substantially cut back, further freeing the economy to market forces. Workers, the public, and even foreign investors would be permitted to buy state assets. The republics were to be given more control over their own resources. Most have already declared such

---

15. See "The Enemy Within?" *National Review* (17 September 1990): 7.

control.[16] The future is difficult to predict. The failed coup in August 1991 ended communist rule. The Communist Party and the KGB were shut down in Russia by Yeltsin. Other republics quickly followed suit. It is unclear what the political structure of the former Soviet Union will be.

CAN REFORMS SUCCEED IN THE SOVIET UNION? The next few years will determine whether reforms succeed in the Soviet Republics or are halted by a conservative backlash. The twin forces of *perestroika* and *glasnost* can cause opposing changes. In China, the democracy movement created a setback for the economic reform movement. In some Soviet Republics, the same result could occur.

A major problem that market reform faces is the attitude of consumers. Consumers want the standard of living that capitalism produces, but they like the safety of governmental regulation. If such attitudes prevail, it will be very difficult to institute market reforms in a democratic setting. The breakup of the Soviet Union into a loose federation of republics could be the cause for optimism. The various republics will go their separate ways, and markets may have a better chance with decentralization and the shock destruction of the centralized political power.

JAPAN

In Japan, great strides have been made in a modified capitalistic structure in the last forty years. The Japanese "miracle" is of great interest to developing countries and industrial managers in the United States. The interest stems in part from wanting to borrow those elements of the Japanese success that can be transplanted into other economies.

In 1950, Japan was starting to recover from the devastation of World War II. The U.S. Commerce Department reports that Japanese per capita income in 1950 was only about an eighth of that in the United States. Thirty-five years later, in 1990, the per capita level of income was four-fifths of that of the United States. In the 1950s, the phrase "Made in Japan" implied cheap, shoddy copies of U.S. products. In the 1990s, "Made in Japan" implies the finest of automotive and high-tech products. This rapid economic growth occurred in a country smaller than the state of California with few natural resources (Japan imports almost all of its oil) and a population half as large as that of the United States.

TAXES
Compared to Western Europe and the United States, Japan has very low taxes. Japan's taxes are around 25 percent of national income, compared to 30 percent in the United States, 35 percent in the United Kingdom, and almost 40 percent in West Germany.

16. See "This Time, Gorbachev May Really Turn the Economy Upside Down," *Business Week* (27 August 1990): 8; "Out of Stock," *The Wall Street Journal* (23 July 1990): 1; "Moscow's Bumper Crop of Troubles," *U.S. News & World Report* (3 September 1990): 27–28; "Who's in Charge Here?" *Forbes* (3 September 1990): 32–33; Anthony DeCurtis, "Anarchy in the Soviet Union," *Rolling Stone* (26 July 1990): 29–34; "Yeltsin's Shadow Just Keeps Getting Longer," *Business Week*, (17 September 1990): 28; and "500 Days," *Business Week* (1 October 1990): 29–30.

Supply siders in the United States argue that low taxes are an important reason for growth. They note that the tax structure in Japan is not used to redistribute income. Until very recently, there was no social insurance system, and even now it is very limited. The pre-tax distribution of income is about the same as the post-tax distribution. As a result, there are powerful incentives to engage in risky, entrepreneurial activity.

INVESTMENT AND SAVING

The Japanese people save about 20 percent of their annual incomes. These savings find their way into capital investment, which creates future income. The high rate of Japanese saving is the result of two powerful influences. The first has already been mentioned. Since only a very limited social insurance system exists in Japan, workers must save for their retirement. Second, the tax system is structured in such a way that tax credits are given for saving. In contrast, in the United States, dividends and interest—the returns to saving—are taxed, and Social Security reduces the incentive to save for retirement.

LABOR-MANAGEMENT RELATIONS

Perhaps the aspect of the Japanese economy that has generated the most interest in the U.S. business community is the labor-management relationship. Great loyalty to the firm exists in Japan. Many workers in the manufacturing sector enjoy lifetime employment to age fifty-five, when mandatory retirement occurs. These workers belong to company unions that cooperate with management in setting goals, work schedules, and plans for the company.

Certain aspects of this labor-management relationship are being tried by U.S. businesses. **Theory Z** is the idea that employees are not motivated by negative incentives, such as threats, or by monetary incentives, such as raises and promotions, but are motivated by being included as active participants in the management process. The use of quality circles is one of the tools of a Theory Z style of management. In **quality circles**, workers organize themselves into units to try to improve quality by discussing production problems and suggesting solutions. A quality circle is a kind of activist, organized, suggestion box.

Theory Z
A management theory that workers are motivated to perform if they are made part of the management process.

quality circles
Groups of workers organized to improve quality by discussing production problems and suggesting solutions.

HAS JAPAN PEAKED?

Many observers feel that the Japanese economy may have peaked in the mid-1980s.[17] They point to the fact that Japanese exports have dropped and industrial production has fallen. Other observers have predicted that younger workers in Japan will grow restless because of long working hours and high consumer prices. They will demand higher standards of living, rather than increased investment and production through higher levels of saving.

The Japanese Ministry of International Trade predicts that Japan will lose 560,000 manufacturing jobs by 2000. Some of this loss is due to the increasing tendency for Japanese firms to produce in foreign countries rather than producing in Japan and exporting. Approximately 20 percent

---

17. See "To Have and Have Not in Japan," *U.S. News & World Report* (13 February 1989): 41–42.

of Japanese manufacturing is expected to be "offshore" in 2000, compared to 5 percent in 1987.

The Japanese response to the changing economic position will be important. If Japan opens its market to foreign trade, it will be able to live off its investments rather than its production. This openness will be a challenge because changing the pattern of economic development has been disturbing to Japanese leaders. These leaders have tended to support protectionist policies in the past. In the face of rising production costs at home, a rise in protectionist policies may follow. These trends could represent a cloud on the Japanese horizon.

Still another cloud on the Japanese horizon is growing discontent among Americans about the trade relationship between the United States and Japan. Forty-four percent of Americans say they do not trust the Japanese, and sixty-one percent believe Japanese imports into the United States should be restricted. These negative attitudes are unlike the attitudes of U.S. voters to trade relations with other foreign countries.[18]

SUMMARY

1. The study of comparative systems allows economists to analyze different environments and institutions to determine how they can affect economic outcomes.

2. The most common approach to comparative economics is to classify systems according to dominant ideology. This approach is not very useful. Almost all systems can be labeled as either capitalist or socialist but differ widely within these general categories.

3. Marx's writings provide the basic political framework on which all socialist systems are based. The economic systems of these countries are, however, widely divergent. The variation in the systems has been, in many cases, the result of dominant political leaders. Thus, it is possible to distinguish among Leninism, Stalinism, Castroism, and Maoism as separate forms of socialism.

4. Another way to analyze different economic systems is to examine their organizational and decision-making differences. This approach looks at the level at which decisions are made, the informational requirements and the motivations of the decision-making units, and the interaction of system, environment, performance, and policy.

5. Planning is carried out in all economies. The key difference between systems is the level at which planning is carried out. The higher the level of planning, the greater the informational requirements of the system.

6. Central planning requires the determination of what to produce. In the Soviet Union, such planning resulted in rapid growth because the central authority decided not to produce many consumer goods. This decision generated high rates of investment.

7. Central planning relies on input-output analysis. Input-output analysis starts with historical data on the amounts of inputs necessary to produce a given output. Those data are used to determine what inputs are necessary to produce a desired output. Input-output analysis assumes that the historical production record will continue to hold.

8. After all the technical problems of planning are worked out, it is necessary to put the plan into operation. Implementation requires transmitting the plan to the production units and creating the proper incentives.

9. China and the Soviet Republics face reform movements. Economic growth in each case will depend on whether these reforms are continued or reversed.

10. The Japanese "miracle" is based on low tax rates, high saving rates, and labor-management harmony.

---

18. Lee Smith, "Fear and Loathing of Japan," *Fortune* (26 February 1990): 16.

Chapter 20 Comparative Economic Systems in Theory and Practice

NEW TERMS

capitalism
socialism
communism
fascism
War Communism
New Economic Policy (NEP)
Great Industrialization Debate
Great Leap Forward
Cultural Revolution
shadow prices
socialist controversy
competitive solution
Gosplan
input-output analysis
input coefficient
perestroika
glasnost
Theory Z
quality circles

QUESTIONS FOR DISCUSSION

1. How did the trade union Solidarity threaten the Communist Party in Poland? Why was the Soviet Union so interested in developments in Poland?
2. How did Lenin change the theories of Marx? Which of the two appears to be more important as the inspiration of communist revolutions?
3. Is planning an important function in all economies? Is it more important in market or command economies?
4. How would allowing the input coefficient to vary complicate input-output analysis? Is the assumption of fixed input coefficients a damaging one?
5. List as many problems of maintaining proper incentives under a central planning system as you can. Do these problems exist only in centrally planned economies?
6. How do you evaluate the performance of the Japanese economy? Are there lessons for the U.S. economy?
7. What are the weaknesses of fascism?
8. What was the period of the New Economic Policy in the Soviet Union?
9. Evaluate the two sides of the socialist controversy.
10. What is the connection between economic freedom and political freedom?
11. How can political freedom undermine economic reform in Eastern Europe, China, and the Soviet Union?
12. What are the primary obstacles facing the reform movement in the Soviet Republics?
13. Which reform movement in Eastern Europe has been the most successful? Why? Are there any lessons in this for the rest of the world?
14. Cuba is the last of the Communist countries to continue rigid planning. What are prospects for reform in Cuba?
15. Do the events of the past five years signal the death of communism and the victory of capitalism?

SUGGESTIONS FOR FURTHER READING

Doder, Dusko, and Louise Branson. *Gorbachev: Heretic in the Kremlin*. New York: Viking, 1990. A book billed as the story of how "Gorby got to the top." The authors final prediction: "It is entirely possible that Gorbachev ultimately will be rejected by the nation in a free election."

Galbraith, John Kenneth. *Economics in Perspective*. Boston: Houghton Mifflin, l987. A fast-paced economic history that extends from Adam and Eve to the present.

Gray, Francine du Plessix. *Soviet Women*. New York: Doubleday, 1990. Looks at the reform movement through the eyes of Soviet women and describes the problems they face.

Kahn, Joseph F. "Better Fed Than Red," *Esquire* (September 1990): 186–197; and "Inside Quin Cheng Prison," *Harper's* (August 1990): 17–19. Two accounts of what happened to different groups of students after the Tiananmen Square protest in China. The first chronicles the life of student leader Wu'erkaixi after his escape to Paris. The second describes life in prison for some of the arrested students.

Kotkin, Stephen. *Steeltown USSR: Soviet Society in the Gorbachev Era*. Berkeley: University of California Press, 1991. Shows how difficult Soviet reforms will be, based on interviews in a steel-producing city.

Winiecki, Jan. *The Distorted World of Soviet-type Economies*. Pittsburgh: Pittsburgh University Press, 1988. A book by a respected Polish economist that outlines the problems that faced Soviet-type economies on the eve of the reform movement.

Yoshino, M. T., and Thomas B. Lifson. *The Invisible Link: Japan's Sogo Shosha*. Cambridge, MA: MIT Press, 1986. Examines how the Japanese general trading houses coordinate trade and production.

GLOSSARY

absolute advantage The ability to produce something using fewer resources than other producers use.

accommodating monetary policy Monetary expansion that is undertaken to help the Treasury finance deficits without driving up interest rates very much.

Accord, The The 1951 agreement between the Fed and the Treasury that the Fed was no longer obliged to hold interest rates low to assist with the Treasury's debt financing.

adaptive expectations Expectations about the future that are formed by economic actors on the basis of current and past experience and that adjust slowly to changing conditions.

Agency for International Development (AID) An agency that is part of the U.S. State Department and is in charge of U.S. aid to foreign countries.

aggregate demand curve A graph showing the amounts of total real output that all buyers in an economy wish to purchase at various price levels.

aggregate expenditure (*AE*) Total planned spending by all sectors for an economy's total output.

aggregate production function A graph showing the relationship between total real output and the number of workers employed.

aggregate supply curve A graph showing the amounts of total real output that the producing sector will offer for sale at various price levels.

aggregates Quantities whose values are determined by adding across many markets.

allocation Any activities by government or its agents that affect the distribution of resources and the combination of goods and services produced.

allocative efficiency The use of resources to produce the goods most desired by society. Free markets allow allocative efficiency.

annually balanced budget The view that government revenues should be equal to expenditures on an annual basis.

appreciation A rise in the market price of a currency due to market forces.

appropriate technology Methods of production that have been adapted to take advantage of the mix of resources available in less developed countries.

asset demand for money Demand for money to hold in order to protect the value of one's assets against changes in interest rates. The asset demand for money is negatively related to interest rates.

association-causation fallacy The false notion that association implies causality.

auction markets Markets characterized by good information, many buyers and sellers, and rapid adjustments of price to changing conditions.

automatic stabilizers Changes in tax collections and transfer payments that are automatically triggered by changes in national income and tend to reduce changes in output and employment.

balance of payments An annual summary of the transactions between residents of one country and residents of the rest of the world.

balance of payments deficit An excess of a country's foreign spending over its foreign earnings for a given year.

balance on goods and services The difference between the value of exports and the value of imports for a country in a given year.

balance sheet A statement of assets owned, liabilities owed, and the difference between them at a point in time.

bank deregulation A policy enabling banks to compete more aggressively with nonbank financial institutions by reducing the regulations affecting them.

bank panics Sudden waves of fear that banks will not be able to pay off their depositors.

bar chart A graphic representation that expresses data using columns of different heights.

barter Direct exchange of one good or service for another without the use of money.

big push strategy The development strategy calling for a major thrust on all fronts in the economy by government or by private enterprise with government inducement.

bimetallism The use of both gold and silver as parts of the money stock.

Board of Governors Central governing body of the Federal Reserve System.

bond An interest-earning certificate that is issued by a government or corporation in exchange for borrowed funds and has a fixed face value, annual interest payment, and maturity date.

bond market A market in which the debt instruments of governments and corporations are traded.

Bretton Woods system The international monetary system in effect from 1945 to 1973, based on infrequent changes in currency prices, ample reserves, and the dollar as key currency.

business cycle An observed and repeated pattern of ups and downs in real output, employment, and prices.

business cycle theorists A group of economists in the

G-1

nineteenth and early twentieth centuries who tried to develop explanations for cyclical patterns in economic activity.

business inventories Stocks of goods held by firms from which they can make sales to meet demand.

capital The durable inputs into the production process created by people. Machines, tools, and buildings are examples of capital.

capital account The part of the balance of payments that summarizes purchases and sales of financial assets.

capital consumption allowance The national income accountants' estimate of the amount of the nation's capital stock used up in production during a year.

capital gain An increase in the market price of an asset.

capitalism An economic system characterized by private ownership of the factors of production by individuals or groups of individuals.

certificate of deposit (CD) A deposit made with a financial institution at a specified interest rate for a given (fixed) period of time.

ceterus paribus **assumption** The assumption that everything else will remain constant, used for most economic models. (*Ceterus paribus* is Latin for "all else being equal.")

ceterus paribus **fallacy** The false notion that arises because an observer fails to recognize that variables other than the one in question have changed.

checkable deposit Balances in accounts at depository institutions on which checks can be drawn.

circular flow model A visual representation of the relationships between the factor market (in which income is obtained) and the product market (in which income is used to purchase goods and services).

classical school A group of economists in the eighteenth and nineteenth centuries who believed that the economy automatically tended toward the full-employment level of output.

command economy An economy in which the three basic questions are answered through central planning and control (also called a planned economy).

commercial paper Short-term loans by financial institutions to business firms.

commercial policy The set of actions that a country undertakes to deliberately influence trade in goods and services.

communism The final stage in the theory of Karl Marx, in which the state has withered away and economic goods are equally distributed.

comparative advantage The ability to produce something at a lower opportunity cost than other producers face.

comparative statics A technique of comparing two equilibrium positions to determine the changing relationships between variables.

competitive solution The model developed by Oskar Lange in an attempt to show that a planned economy could theoretically reach the efficiency of an economy with competition.

complementary goods Goods that are jointly consumed. The consumption of one enhances the consumption of the other.

consumer durables Goods that last, on average, a substantial length of time.

consumer nondurables Goods that last, on average, only a short period of time.

Consumer Price Index (CPI) A well-known measure of inflation based on the cost of a selected market basket of consumer goods (also known as the cost-of-living index).

consumer services That part of household consumption composed of nontangible activities.

consumption expenditures Sales to the household sector.

consumption function Any equation, table, or graph that shows the relationship between income of consumers (disposable income) and the amount they plan to spend on currently produced final output.

consumption possibilities curve A line showing the consumption combinations attainable through trade.

contract markets Markets characterized by few buyers and sellers, imperfect information, long-term contracts, and sluggish price adjustments.

contractionary fiscal policy Raising taxes, lowering transfer payments, or reducing government purchases in an attempt to reduce the equilibrium level of output to one that is attainable with available resources.

convergence hypothesis The prediction that income differences among countries will shrink over time because of the transfer of technology and innovation.

coordinates The values of x and y that define the location of a point in a coordinate system.

cost-push inflation Inflation that starts as a result of a decrease in aggregate supply due to wage or price increases.

countercyclical policy Government actions designed to offset the cyclical ups and downs of the macro economy.

credit crunch The 1966 shortage of loanable funds caused by the sudden slowing of monetary growth rates by the Fed.

credit market The aggregate market consisting of financial institutions that channel household savings to business firms that want to invest.

crowding out The negative effect on borrowing for private investment due to competition from the federal government in the credit market.

crude birth rate Number of births per thousand of population.

crude death rate Number of deaths per thousand of population.

Cultural Revolution The high point of Mao's power in China, characterized by a radical restructuring of the economy from 1966 through 1969.

currency Paper money with a specified value, issued by the government or central bank.

currency drain An increase in cash held by the public that causes a dollar-for-dollar decline in bank reserves.

current account The part of the balance of payments that summarizes transactions in currently produced goods and services.

cyclical deficit The part of a deficit that is due to a downturn in economic activity.

cyclical unemployment Unemployment caused by a decline in the level of total output.
cyclically balanced budget The idea that surpluses during expansionary periods should offset deficits during recessionary periods so that the budget balances over the course of the business cycle.

debasement of money The practice of reminting coins of gold or silver with base metals added, thus increasing the number of coins, driving up the prices of goods, and reducing the value of each coin.
decrease in demand A shift in the demand curve indicating that at every price, consumers demand a smaller amount than before.
decrease in supply A shift in the supply curve indicating that at every price, a smaller quantity will be offered for sale than before.
deficit The difference between the federal government's revenues and expenditures in a given year (the fiscal year), when the government spends more than it collects in taxes.
demand The desire and ability to consume certain quantities of a good at various prices over a certain period of time.
demand curve A graph representing a demand schedule and showing the quantity demanded at various prices in a certain time period.
demand deposits Bank deposits on which checks can be written (also known as checking accounts).
demand for money The amount of money households and businesses wish to hold for making transactions and as a financial asset.
demand-pull inflation Inflation that starts as a result of a rise in aggregate demand, usually due to expansionary monetary or fiscal policy.
demand schedule A table that shows quantities demanded at various prices during a specific time period.
demographic transition The bridging of the developmental gap from falling death rates to falling birth rates, resulting in slower population growth.
dependency ratio The percentage of the population not of working age (under fifteen or over sixty-five).
dependent variable The variable, usually plotted on the vertical axis, that is affected or influenced by the other variable.
deposit multiplier Ratio between the maximum increase in the money supply and a given increase in excess reserves. It equals the reciprocal of the reserve ratio.
depreciation (1) The decline in the value of an asset, such as a machine or factory, over time. (2) A fall in the market price of a currency due to market forces.
depression A very severe recession.
discount rate The interest rate the Fed charges on loans to banks.
discretionary fiscal policy Deliberate changes in tax rates, transfer programs, or government purchases designed to change the equilibrium level of national income.
disequilibrium An unstable situation in which variables are moving toward equilibrium but are not yet at equilibrium.

disposable income Income received by households and available to spend or save; equals PI less personal taxes.
dissaving Consuming by drawing on accumulated stocks (inventories) or financial assets.
double coincidence of wants The necessary requirement for barter that each trader has what the other wants and wants what the other has.
dualism The coexistence of a modern, urban, market-oriented society and a rural, agriculture-based, traditional peasant society, characteristic of most less developed countries.

economic growth An increase in the level of real output per capita.
Economic Report of the President An annual report to Congress describing the state of the economy and recommending policy.
economics The study of how people and institutions make decisions about production and consumption and how they face the problem of scarcity.
Employment Act of 1946 A law requiring the federal government to actively promote full employment, steady growth, and stable prices through the use of fiscal and monetary policy.
endogenous variables Variables that are explained or determined within a model.
enterprise The input to the production process that involves organizing, innovation, and risk taking.
equation of exchange An identity based on the quantity theory of money that says that the money supply times the velocity of money equals the price level times real output.
excess reserves Reserves above the level required by law.
exchange control A system in which the government purchases all incoming foreign exchange and is the only source from which foreign exchange can be legally purchased.
exogenous variables Variables that are determined outside of a model and affect endogenous variables.
expansion A period of economic growth extending from a trough to the next peak in a business cycle.
expansionary fiscal policy Cutting taxes, raising transfer payments, or increasing government purchases to try to increase the level of income and employment.
expectations Feelings that individuals have about future conditions.
expected yield The rate of return on an asset that includes expected interest or dividends and the expected increase or decrease in its price.
expenditure multiplier Measures the impact of a given initial change in aggregate expenditures on equilibrium income and output. The multiplier is equal to $1/(1-MPC)$.
exports Goods and services sold to foreign buyers.

factor market Set of markets in which owners of the factors of production sell these to producers.
factors of production The inputs of land, labor, capital, and enterprise that a firm uses to produce outputs.
fair trade The idea that the United States should im-

pose trade barriers equivalent to those that its trading partners place on U.S. exports.

fallacy of composition The false notion that what holds for the parts holds for the whole.

fascism An economic system that combines monopoly, capitalism, private property, and a strong authoritarian central government.

federal funds market The market in which banks borrow reserves from each other.

federal funds rate The interest rate charged in the federal funds market.

Federal Open Market Committee (FOMC) Committee that supervises the conduct of the Fed's monetary policy.

Federal Reserve System (Fed) The central bank of the United States.

fiat money Money that is not a commodity and is not redeemable in any commodity.

final goods Goods that will not be further processed or resold.

fiscal policy The use of government spending and taxes to try to influence the levels of output, employment, and prices.

fixed investment The part of business investment that does not add to inventories; consists of new plants and equipment and residential construction.

flow variable A variable that is defined over a period of time.

foreign exchange market The network of banks and financial institutions through which buyers and sellers exchange national currencies.

45° line A line in the first quadrant, passing through the origin, with a slope of +1, which divides the quadrant in half. If the scales on the axes are the same, the value of the x-variable is equal to the value of the y-variable along the 45° line.

forward market The market in which contracts are made for future delivery of specific amounts of currency at a specified price.

fractional reserve banking The practice of holding a fraction of money deposited as reserves and lending the rest.

free reserves A bank's excess reserves less its loans from the Fed.

free riders People or business firms who consume collective goods without contributing to the cost of their production.

frictional unemployment Unemployment due to workers being temporarily between jobs or new entrants to the work force.

full-bodied money Money that has a value in other uses equal to its monetary value. Coins made of precious metals are the best examples.

full employment The level of employment at which approximately 94 to 95 percent of those who want to work are employed.

full-employment level of output The level of real output associated with full use of all of the factors of production, especially labor.

functional finance The idea that a balanced budget is less important than a stable economy.

gains from trade The increase in economic well-being resulting from specialization and exchange.

GNP deflator A current-weights index used to correct the GNP for price changes.

GNP targeting A monetary policy that calls for the Fed to aim at some level of nominal GNP by influencing a number of variables that affect GNP.

gold standard An international monetary system in which currencies were defined in terms of gold, money supplies were tied to gold, and balance of payment deficits were settled in gold.

Gosplan The state planning commission in the Soviet Union.

Great Industrialization Debate An open debate that took place in the Soviet Union from 1924 to 1928 concerning the correct way to industrialize the economy.

Great Leap Forward A modernization plan that was launched in 1958 to increase per capita income in China by 25 percent in five years.

Green Revolution An agricultural innovation consisting of the development of dwarf, high-yield varieties of wheat and rice that have enabled some less developed countries to improve food production.

greenbacks Paper money issued by the U.S. government during the Civil War that was not redeemable in gold.

gross national product (GNP) The total market value of all final goods and services produced by a nation's domestically owned factors of production during a given time period, usually a year.

gross private domestic investment Purchases by the business sector of final output.

hedgers People who try to reduce their risk by buying or selling contracts in the forward market for currency.

high-employment balanced budget The view that tax rates and transfer payments should be set so as to balance the budget at the full-employment level of output Y^*. (The actual budget need not be balanced.)

human capital The investment made to improve the quality of people's labor skills through education, training, health care, and so on.

impact lag The time that elapses between implementation of a fiscal policy and its full effect on economic activity.

implementation lag The time it takes after a problem is recognized to choose and enact a fiscal policy in response.

imports Goods and services purchased from foreign sellers.

income statement Measure of the total flow of revenue to a household, individual, or firm over a period of time.

increase in demand A shift in the demand curve indicating that at every price, consumers demand a larger amount than before.

increase in supply A shift in the supply curve indicating that at every price, a larger quantity will be offered for sale than before.

increasing opportunity cost The principle that as production of one good rises, larger and larger sacrifices of another are required.

independent variable The variable, usually plotted on the horizontal axis, that affects or influences the other variable.

industrial policy A growth strategy consisting of government programs to identify and encourage promising industries and to ease the decline of old industries.

inferior good A good for which demand decreases as income increases.

inflation A sustained rise in the general, or average, level of prices.

infrastructure The basic facilities and equipment, usually publicly owned, that provide community services.

injections Spending added to the circular flow that is not paid for out of factor income. Business investment, government expenditures, and sales of exports are injections.

innovation The translation of inventions into products and processes that are commercially feasible and cost-effective.

input coefficient In input-output analysis, the ratio of the amount of an input to the total output of an industry.

input-output analysis An attempt to quantify the flows between different sectors of the economy for purposes of economic planning.

insatiable wants The needs and desires of human beings, which can never be completely satisfied.

insider-outsider model An explanation of labor market behavior that assumes that insiders (employed union members) will negotiate for higher real wages for themselves at the expense of jobs for outsiders, thus worsening the inflation-unemployment tradeoff.

institutional investors Large investors, including insurance companies, pension funds, and mutual funds, whose purchases and sales have an impact on the prices of investment assets.

interest The return to capital, one of the factors of production.

intermediate goods Goods that will be further processed before final sale.

International Monetary Fund (IMF) The agency that supervised the operation of the Bretton Woods system by recording par values, consulting on devaluations and revaluations, and maintaining a pool of reserves.

international monetary reserves The pool of gold and major currencies created under the Bretton Woods system, from which countries could borrow to settle deficits and replenish from surpluses.

inventories The stocks of goods that have been produced by business firms but have not yet been sold.

investment Purchases of real, tangible assets, such as machines, factories, or inventories, that are used to produce goods and services.

investment demand schedule A graph that ranks possible investment projects for a firm in order of decreasing expected rate of return.

Investment Tax Credit (ITC) Provision offering tax savings over and above depreciation for business firms investing in new plants or equipment. A percentage of the investment made can be subtracted from tax liability.

invisible hand The idea advanced by Adam Smith that individuals pursuing their own self-interest direct the market system toward socially desirable outcomes.

junk bonds High-yield, high-risk securities that are usually issued to finance a takeover of one corporation by another.

key currency A currency that serves as a major reserve asset and is used in transactions between third-party nations.

Keynesian economists Twentieth-century economists who adopted and extended John Maynard Keynes's idea that there could be persistent unemployment without government intervention.

Keynesian revolution The change in macroeconomic theory and policy that occurred when Keynes's ideas displaced the classical theory of how output and employment are determined.

labor The physical and mental exertion that human beings put into production activities.

labor force Those who are working or actively seeking work.

labor force participation rate The percentage of the adult population that is employed or actively seeking work.

land Natural resources that can be used as inputs to production.

law of demand The quantity demanded of a good or service is negatively related to its price, *ceteris paribus*.

leading sectors strategy The development strategy calling for concentration on a few successful sectors, which will then pull along other sectors in the development process.

leakages Flows out of the circular pattern that occur when factor income is received but not spent directly on purchases from domestic firms. Savings, taxes, and purchases of imports are leakages.

legal tender Money that, by law, must be accepted by private parties and governments in payment of debts and obligations.

lender of last resort A source of funds for rescuing sound banks by lending them as much as they need to meet temporary high demand from depositors.

liquidity The measure of how quickly a financial asset can be converted into the medium of exchange.

M1 money stock The total of all financial assets in the United States that function as a medium of exchange: currency, traveler's checks, demand deposits, and other checkable deposits.

M2 money stock The total of M1 and small-denomination time and savings deposits at all financial institutions, money market accounts, and a few other items.

M3 money stock The total of M2 and large-denomination time deposits, repurchase agreements, and a few other items.

macroeconomic equilibrium The level of output at which there is no tendency to change. The amount that buyers wish to buy is exactly equal to what is being produced.

macroeconomics The study of the economy as a whole or of economic aggregates, such as the level of employment and the growth of total output.

marginal analysis A technique for analyzing problems by examining the results of small changes.

marginal efficiency of investment (*MEI*) curve A graph that sums the investment demand schedules for all firms in an economy. It ranks all investment possibilities for all firms according to their expected rates of return.

marginal propensity to consume (*MPC*) The fraction of any change in income that is consumed. The *MPC* is greater than 0 and less than 1.

marginal propensity to save (*MPS*) The fraction of any change in income that is saved. The *MPS* is greater than 0 and less than 1.

market A place where buyers and sellers meet to exchange goods, services, and productive resources.

market-clearing price The equilibrium price, which clears the market because there are no frustrated consumers or suppliers.

market demand curve The sum of all of the individual demand curves. A market demand curve shows what quantities will be demanded by all consumers in a specific time frame in a certain market at various prices.

market economy An economy in which the three basic questions are answered through the market, by relying on self-interested behavior and incentives.

market equilibrium A point at which quantity demanded by consumers is equal to quantity supplied by producers. The price at which this occurs is the equilibrium price, or market-clearing price.

market for loanable funds The market in which transactions between borrowers and lenders determine the interest rate and equate quantities of loanable funds offered to quantity demanded.

market supply curve The sum of all of the individual supply curves. A market supply curve shows what quantities will be supplied by all firms at various prices during a specific time period.

maximum The point on a graph at which the y-variable, or dependent variable, reaches its highest value.

Measure of Economic Welfare (MEW) An alternative to GNP that tries to provide a better indicator of economic well-being by adding leisure and nonmarket production and subtracting public bads.

medium of exchange A function of money in simplifying transactions by allowing people to exchange the goods and services they produce for money and then exchange money for other goods and services they want.

microeconomics The study of individual market interactions, focusing on production and consumption by the individual consumer, firm, or industry.

minimum The point on the graph at which the y-variable, or dependent variable, reaches its lowest value.

mixed economy An economy in which the three basic questions are answered partly by market forces and partly through government.

model A set of assumptions and hypotheses that is a simplified description of reality.

monetarists Twentieth-century economists who criticize Keynesian economics and stress the role of the money supply.

monetary base The currency in the hands of the public plus reserves held by banks.

monetary policy The use of changes in the money supply to try to influence the levels of output, employment, and prices.

monetary rule A proposed regulation requiring the Fed to make the money supply grow at some predetermined, steady rate.

money Any financial asset that serves as a medium of exchange, a unit of account, a standard of deferred payment, and a store of value.

money multiplier The ratio of the actual money supply to the monetary base.

moral suasion Attempts by the Fed to convince depository institutions to do what the Fed favors.

multinational corporation A firm with headquarters in one country and plants in one or more other countries.

municipal bond Any bond issued by a state or local government to finance a capital project.

mutual fund A financial institution that pools money from many individuals in order to invest in a diversified portfolio of assets.

National Banking System Agency that chartered and regulated national banks during the latter half of the nineteenth century, before the Federal Reserve System.

national banks Banks chartered by the federal government and subject to its rules and regulations.

national debt The total of all past budget deficits minus all past surpluses, or the net amount owed to lenders by the federal government.

national income (NI) Income earned by the four factors of production; consists of wages, rent, interest, profit, and proprietors' net income.

natural rate of unemployment The rate of unemployment that is determined by frictional and structural factors and toward which the economy tends to return.

near money Assets that are very similar to the kinds of assets included in the money stock. Near money is usually highly liquid.

negative externalities Harmful spillovers to third parties that result from production or consumption of certain goods.

negative relationship A relationship between two variables in which an increase in the value of one is associated with a decrease in the value of the other.

net national product (NNP) Equal to GNP minus the capital consumption allowance (depreciation).

net private domestic investment Gross private domestic investment minus the capital consumption allowance (depreciation).

net worth The difference between assets and liabilities for a person or firm at a point in time.

new classical economists Late twentieth-century economists who regard monetary and fiscal policies as ineffective because individuals will anticipate and offset government actions.

New Economic Policy (NEP) A program that replaced War Communism in 1921 in the Soviet Union and was an attempt at market socialism.

New International Economic Order (NIEO) A proposal by the Group of 77 calling for changes in international economic institutions to redistribute income from richer nations to poorer nations through trade preferences, increased aid, and other measures.

nominal rate of interest The rate of interest actually charged, without correction for inflation (also known as the market rate of interest).

nontariff barriers Trade restrictions other than tariffs and quotas.

normal good A good for which demand increases as income increases.

normative statements A set of propositions about what ought to be (also called value judgments).

(not quite) law of supply The quantity supplied of a good or service is usually a positive function of price, *ceteris paribus*.

open market operations Purchases and sales of government bonds on the open market by the Fed in order to affect bank reserves.

opportunity cost The value of the other alternatives given up in order to enjoy a particular good or service.

optimal tariff A tariff that maximizes a nation's net gain from altering its terms of trade.

origin The intersection of the vertical and horizontal axes of a coordinate system, at which the values of both the *x*-variable and the *y*-variable are zero.

paradox of thrift The fact that attempts by consumers to increase saving cause income and output to decline. Therefore actual saving may not increase at all.

peak A high point in a business cycle, where output turns downward.

perestroika Restructuring, economic reforms in the Soviet Union.

permanent income hypothesis The view that consumption does not depend on current income alone but on past income and expected future income as well.

personal income (PI) The income received by households; computed from NI by subtracting corporate profits taxes and undistributed corporate profits and adding net transfer payments.

Phillips curve A graph showing the relationship between the rates of inflation and unemployment for a country over a specified period of years.

pie chart A graphic representation in the shape of a pie that expresses actual economic data as parts of a whole. The sizes of the slices of the pie correspond to the percentage shares of the components.

political business cycle A business cycle that results from the use of fiscal (or monetary) policy to influence the outcome of elections.

positive externalities Spillover benefits to third parties (free riders) that result from production or consumption of certain goods.

positive relationship A relationship between two variables in which an increase in one is associated with an increase in the other and a decrease in one is associated with a decrease in the other.

positive statements A set of propositions about what is, rather than what ought to be.

Post-Keynesians A group of late twentieth century economists who have refined and extended the work of Keynes. They stress market imperfections such as imperfect information, monopoly power, and inflexible wages and prices.

potential output The output an economy could produce if all of its resources were fully employed.

price index A measure of the price level in a given year relative to some base year.

primary effect The dominant or immediate effect of a change in an economic variable.

principle of comparative advantage The idea that output will be maximized if people specialize in producing those goods or services for which their opportunity costs are lowest and engage in exchange to obtain other things they want.

Producer Price Index A group of three indices (for raw materials, semifinished goods, and finished goods) that shows what is happening to prices paid by producers and wholesalers.

product cycle A series of stages, from development to standardization, through which a new product passes.

product market Set of markets in which goods and services produced by firms are sold.

production possibilities curve A graph that depicts the various combinations of two goods that can be produced in an economy with the available resources.

productivity A measure of economic performance that shows changes in output per worker hour from one year to the next.

profit The return to enterprise, one of the factors of production. Profit is whatever remains after all other factors have been paid.

progressive tax A tax that takes a larger share (percentage) of income as income rises.

property rights The legal rights to a specific piece of property, including the rights to own, buy, sell, or use in specific ways. Markets can exist and exchanges can occur only if individuals have property rights to goods, services, and productive resources.

proportional tax A tax that takes the same share (percentage) of income from all taxpayers.

public bads Negative external effects of production or consumption that impact a large number of individuals—for example, acid rain.

public choice economics A branch of economic theory that attempts to integrate economics and politics by examining the motives and rewards facing individuals in the public sector.

public goods Goods that are nonrival in consumption and not subject to exclusion.

quality circles Groups of workers organized to improve quality by discussing production problems and suggesting solutions.

quantity theory of money The theory that changes in the price level will be proportional to changes in the money supply.

quota A limit on the amount of a good or service that can be imported during a given time period.

real business cycle A cyclical pattern of economic activity resulting from changes in aggregate supply (rather than aggregate demand).

real deficit A measure of the federal budget deficit as the change in the real (inflation-adjusted) value of the national debt from one year to the next.

real rate of interest The nominal rate of interest minus the expected rate of inflation.

recession A state of an economy marked by a decline in real output for two or more successive quarters.

recessionary gap The difference between aggregate expenditure and the full-employment level of output.

recognition lag The length of time it takes to determine that an economic problem exists.

redistribution Actions by government that transfer income from one group to another.

regressive tax A tax that takes a smaller share (percentage) of income as income rises.

rent The return to land, one of the factors of production.

representative money Money that is redeemable in a commodity (or commodities), such as gold.

reserve ratio Fraction of deposits that banks are required to hold in reserves.

reserves Bank assets that can be used to pay depositors when checks are presented for payment, consisting of currency on hand and reserve deposits at the central bank.

risk A measure of how much the actual yield on an asset may vary from the expected yield.

risk premium The difference between interest rates charged to the safest borrowers and those charged to less safe borrowers for the same length of time.

saving The part of households' income flow not spent on purchases of goods and services.

savings rate The ratio of combined business, household, and government saving to GNP.

Say's law The idea that supply creates its own demand, a cornerstone of classical economics.

scarcity The central economic problem that there are not enough resources to produce everything that individuals want.

scatter diagram A graph that plots actual pairs of values of two variables to determine whether there appears to be any consistent relationship between them.

secondary effects Effects indirectly related to the immediate effect, often smaller and felt after some time.

self-interested behavior A basic assumption of economic theory that individual decision makers do what is best for themselves.

self-regulating markets Markets that quickly resolve problems of shortage or surplus through price changes, quantity adjustments, or a combination of the two.

settlement account The part of the balance of payments that explains how a deficit or surplus was financed.

shadow prices Simulated market prices used by economic planners.

slope The ratio of the change in the dependent variable (y) to the change in the independent variable (x).

social science An academic field that studies the behavior of human beings, individually and in groups, and examines their interactions.

socialism An economic system in which the nonhuman means of production are owned by society or the state.

socialist controversy A debate between Ludwig von Mises and Oskar Lange concerning the feasibility of planning without markets.

Soil Conservation Service A federal program under which grants were given to encourage farmers to contract production by fallowing fields, contour plowing, and other conservation techniques.

specialization Limiting production activities to one or a few goods and services that one produces best in order to exchange for other goods.

specie flow mechanism The automatic correction of deficits and surpluses in the balance of payments through the effects of gold flows on money supplies.

speculators People who assume risk in the forward market for currency in return for the chance of a profit.

spread The difference between the average interest rate earned on loans and the average interest rate paid on deposits.

stabilization Actions by government to reduce changes in output, employment, and prices.

stabilization policy Government actions designed to smooth out sharp changes in output, employment, and the price level.

stagflation An economic condition of slow growth, high unemployment, and inflation.

standard of deferred payment A function of money in providing borrowers and lenders a medium for the repayment of debt in the future.

state banks Banks chartered and regulated by individual states, as opposed to the federal government.

statistical discrepancy The part of the balance of payments that reflects unrecorded transactions and inaccurate estimates of spending by tourists.

stock A certificate of ownership in a corporation.

stock market A financial market in which ownership claims on corporations are bought and sold.

stock variable A variable that is defined at a point in time.

store of value A function of money in providing purchasing power in a general form that can be held in order to buy goods and services in the future.

structural deficit The part of a deficit that would persist even if the economy were at the full-employment level of output.

structural unemployment Unemployment due to a mismatch between the skills or locations of unemployed workers and those of available jobs.

substitute goods Goods that can be interchanged. The consumption of one replaces the consumption of the other.

supply The quantity of a good offered for sale at various prices during a certain time period.

supply curve A graph representing a supply schedule and showing the quantities supplied at various prices in a certain time period.

supply schedule A table that shows quantities offered for sale at various prices over a particular time period.

supply siders Late twentieth century economists and policy makers who want to fight inflation and unemployment by trying to shift the aggregate supply curve to the right.

surplus (1) The amount by which the quantity suppliers wish to supply at some price exceeds the quantity consumers wish to purchase at that price. A surplus can occur on a lasting basis only when a price floor is in effect. (2) A situation in which the government collects more in taxes than it spends.

surplus value The difference between the value of the goods produced by labor and the subsistence wages the workers received.

T-accounts Partial balance sheets showing changes in assets and/or liabilities resulting from a transaction or group of transactions.

tangent line A straight line just touching a curve (nonlinear graphic relationship) at a single point. The slope of the tangent line is equal to the slope of the curve at that point.

tariff A tax on imported goods or services.

tariff quota A combination of a quota and a tariff that allows a certain amount of a good or service to be imported without paying a tariff and imposes the tariff on further imports.

tax-based inflation policy (TIP) A sophisticated approach to wage and price controls that ties allowable increases in prices and wages to tax breaks and penalties and uses market incentives to attempt to control price increases.

tax wedge The gap between prices paid by consumers and the prices (incomes) received by sellers (factor owners).

terms of trade The ratio at which one product is exchanged for another.

testable hypothesis An inference from a theory that can be subjected to real-world testing.

theory A set of principles that can be used to make inferences about the world.

theory of the second best A theory that a second-best policy of tariffs may be useful to introduce new distortions that eliminate existing distortions.

Theory Z A management theory that workers are motivated to perform if they are made part of the management process.

token money Money whose monetary value is greater than its commodity value. Modern coins, for example, are worth more as money than the metal they contain.

traditional economy An economy in which the three basic questions are answered by custom, or how things have been done in the past.

transactions costs Costs associated with gathering information about markets (prices and quantities supplied) for consuming or producing.

transactions demand for money Demand for money in order to make purchases and carry out other day-to-day market transactions. The transactions demand for money is positively related to income.

transfer payments Income payments to individuals who provide no goods or services in exchange.

transmission mechanism The process of translating money supply changes into changes in demand, output, and the price level.

trough A low point in a business cycle, where output turns upward.

unemployment rate The percentage of the labor force that wants to work but does not currently have a job.

unit of account A function of money in providing a measuring unit in terms of which goods can be valued and thus readily compared with each other.

unplanned inventory changes Changes that occur when the inventory level rises above or falls below that desired by a firm because the production level is too high or too low relative to current sales.

vicious circle of poverty A trap in which many low-income countries are caught—there is little investment because of a low level of income, and a low level of income because of little investment.

wage and price controls Government-imposed restrictions on increases in prices or wages in order to contain inflation.

wages The return to labor, one of the factors of production.

War Communism An economic system of rigid administrative control imposed by Lenin in Russia during the civil war following the Bolshevik Revolution.

x-axis The horizontal line in a coordinate system that shows the values of the independent variable; the horizontal axis.

y-axis The upright line in a coordinate system that shows the values of the dependent variable; the vertical axis.

yield The return on funds invested in an asset measured as a percentage of the price paid for the asset.

Index

absolute advantage, 483–484, 485. *See also* comparative advantage
accommodating monetary policy, 394
accounting, basic concepts of, 125–129
adaptive expectations, 432
Agency for International Development (AID), 472–474
aggregate demand, 153–156. *See also* aggregate demand curve
   equation of exchange and, 159
   expenditure approach to measurement of, 154–156
   fiscal policy and, 266–267
   foreign trade and, 156
   monetary approach to measurement of, 158
   monetary policy and, 369–378
   relationship of to aggregate expenditure, 233–235
   role of in Keynesian economics, 205
   shifts in, 164–165
aggregate demand curve, 154, 159
aggregate expenditure (*AE*), 212–213
   changes in, 228–233
   relationship of to aggregate demand, 233–235
aggregate expenditure (*AE*) function, 212
aggregate production function, 166
aggregate supply, 160–163. *See also* aggregate supply curve
   composite view of, 162
   policies to promote shifts in, 444–450
   shifts in, 164, 165–166
aggregate supply and demand model, 153, 163–168
   competing macroeconomic theories and, 168–179
aggregate supply curve, 420–421
   economic growth and, 435–442
   long run, 429–431
   market imperfections and, 431
   short run, 429–431
   slope of, 160–162
aggregates, 2–3
agriculture, in LDCs, 463, 465

allocative efficiency, 90
annually balanced budget, 278
appreciation, 513
appropriate technology, 475
Argentina, development in, 464
Asian Tigers, 478
asset demand for money, 204, 369. *See also* money
assets, 128
association-causation fallacy, 20–21
auction markets, 433–434
automatic stabilizers, 251–252, 253, 255

balance of payments, 505, 511–513
   protection and, 496
   tourism and, 514
balance of payments deficit, 510
balance of trade, 275
balance on goods and services, 102
balance sheet, 128
   of banks, 316–320, 348–350
   of the Fed, 330–331
Balcerowicz, Leszek, 546
Baldinelli, Elvio, 464
bank notes, 300
bank panics, 323
banking. *See also* banks; Federal Reserve System
   crisis of the 1980s in, 323–324, 328, 329–330, 346–350
   development of, 300, 316, 322–325
   fractional reserve, 316
   interstate, 345
   legislation regarding, 345–346
   recent changes in, 302, 303, 344–345
bankruptcy, 274
banks. *See also* banking; Federal Reserve System
   balance sheets of, 316–317
   creation of money by, 300–304
   currency drain and, 321
   deregulation of, 345–346
   free reserves of, 387
   national, 325
   operations of, 316–322
   reserve ratios of, 320
   reserves of, 317
   safety of, 328

   spread of, 348
   state, 325
bar chart, 37, 38
Barro, Robert, 286, 394
barter, 294
Baumol, William, 460
Bieber, Owen F., 499
big push strategy, 469
bimetallism, 116–118
birth rate, crude, 460–461
Blinder, Alan, 444
blood, supply of, 92
Board of Governors, 326, 328
bond market, 359–361
bonds, 359
   issuers of, 359–360
   junk, 360
   municipal, 360
   versus stocks, 360–361
Bretton Woods system, 518–519, 521. *See also* international monetary systems
Britain
   fiscal policy in, 262
   privatization in, 54, 536
   taxation in, 537
Brunner, Karl, 175
Bryan, William Jennings, 118
Buchanan, James, 263
budget. *See also* deficit; national debt
   debate on balancing of, 278–283
   deficits in, and fiscal policy, 274
Bukharin, N. I., 533
Burtless, Gary, 447
Bush, George, 266
business cycle, 114, 419
   political, 265–266
   real, 442–443
   theories of, 115–116
   in the United States, 116–118
business cycle theorists, 168, 171–173, 199–200
business inventories, 131

Canada, trade with, 499
capital, 41, 42. *See also* human capital
capital account, 512
capital consumption allowance, 135
capital gain, 360
capitalism, 526–527, 528

I-1

Index

contrasted to socialism, 529–530, 531
Castro, Fidel, 534–535
central bank. *See also* Federal Reserve System
   in Europe, 327
certificate of deposit (CD), 302
ceteris paribus, 15
   fallacy of, 21–23
change, responding to, 47
checkable deposits, 300
checking accounts, 302
children, reduction of investment in, 284
China, 528, 533–534
   reforms in, 543–545
Chou En-Lai, 534
cigarettes, as money, 299
circular flow model, 48–52
   adjustments to, 50–52
   components of, 103
   with credit market, 34, 35, 74
   foreign sector and, 51–52, 224–225
   government and, 50–52, 224
   leakages and injections in, 50–52, 100, 222–223, 226–228
   macroeconomics and, 98–103
   national income accounts and, 138–139
   taxes in, 224
   two-sector, 49–50
classical economists, 162, 168, 169, 170–171, 174, 198–199, 418, 421. *See also* Say's law
   ideas of, 185–192
   on money, 370–371
   on population growth, 190
climate, and development, 465
Club of Rome, 441
commercial paper, 362
commercial policy, 493
communism, 527
comparative advantage, principle of, 62–64, 484–488. *See also* absolute advantage
comparative economics, 525–526
   ideologies as basis of, 526, 529
   organizational principles as basis of, 536–538
comparative statics, 84
competitive solution, 539
consumer durables, 131
consumer nondurables, 131
Consumer Price Index, 105–107. *See also* price index
   construction of, 140–141, 143
   problems with, 143
   uses of, 141–143
consumer services, 131–132

consumption, changes in, 232–233
consumption expenditures, 131
consumption function, 212, 213–219
   permanent income hypothesis and, 260, 261
consumption possibilities curve, 487
contract markets, 433–434
contractionary fiscal policy, 258, 267
convergence hypothesis, 460
Cooper, Michael, 92
coordinates, 30
cost-push inflation, 414–415
Council of Economic Advisers, 256, 257
countercyclical policy, 121
credit crunch, 388
credit market. *See also* banking; banks; Federal Reserve System
   in circular flow model, 344, 357
   classical economic view of, 189–192
crowding out, 283, 360, 394
   foreign lending and, 391
   government borrowing and, 389–395
   Keynesians and, 390
   monetarists and, 390–392
Cuba, 534–535
Cultural Revolution, 534
Culver, Anthony, 92
currency, 299–300
currency drain, 321
current account, 512
cyclical deficit, 279
cyclical unemployment, 111

death rate, crude, 460–461
debasement of money, 299
debt, of LDCs, 477–478
defense spending, 440, 472
deficit, 101, 271–274. *See also* budget; national debt
   cyclical, 279–280
   economists' views on importance of, 283
   exchange rate and, 392
   projected vs. actual, 280–281
   real, 287
   structural, 279–280
   "third," 284
   "twin," 275
demand, 69–76. *See also* aggregate demand; supply; supply and demand
   changes in, 85–86
   foreign, 81
   for foreign exchange, 506–508
   law of, 70, 85

   market, 70–71, 73
   for money, 196
   nonprice determinants of, 72–76
   shifts in, 71–76, 85–86
demand curve, 70
demand deposits, 302
demand management policies, 431
   differing views of, 400
   wage and price controls and, 417
demand-pull inflation, 413–414
demographic transition, 476
Deng Xiaoping, 543, 544. *See also* China
Denison, Edward, 443
dependency ratio, 460
dependent variable, 31
deposit multiplier, 320, 333, 336–337
Depository Institutions Deregulation and Monetary Control Act, 345
depreciation, 126
depression, 116
deregulation, 448–449. *See also* regulation
   of banking, 343–350
development assistance, 472–474
Dick, G. William, 470–471
discount rate, 337, 338
discounting, 337. *See also* discount rate; Federal Reserve System
discretionary fiscal policy, 255–259
disequilibrium, 80. *See also* equilibrium
disintermediation, 346
disposable income, 138
dissaving, 218
dividends, 356
dollar, price of, 142, 301, 392
double coincidence of wants, 294
dualism, 465–466
Dumas, Lloyd, 440
dumping, 491–493

Eastern Europe
   markets in, 89
   reforms in, 546
   stagflation in, 406
econometrics, 424–425
economic development
   big push strategy of, 469
   classical economic model of, 466–467
   government role in, 470–475
   leading sectors strategy of, 469–470
   Marx's theories of, 467–468
   military spending and, 472
   obstacles to, 475–478
   private property and, 471

role of assistance in, 472–474
Rostow's stage theory of, 468–469
economic fallacies, 20–23
economic models, 14–15
economic performance, international comparisons of, 147
economic policy makers, 254
Economic Report of the President, 256
economics. *See also* comparative economics; Keynesian economics; supply side economics
  basic elements of, 17–20
  basic questions of, 43–44
  definition of, 2, 3
  international, 22
  policy analysis and, 23–24
  public choice, 261–263
  schools of thought in, 418–420, 421
economies of scale, international trade and, 488
economy. *See also* capitalism; communism; socialism
  changes in, 47
  command, 45
  defense spending and, 440
  market, 43–44, 45–46, 47
  mixed, 47–48
  one-product, 229
  traditional, 44–45
  types of, 43–48
  underground, 306
education, investment in, 439, 462
Eisner, Robert, 286
employment
  balanced budget and, 278–279
  effect of immigration on, 190
  full, 12, 110
  Keynesian view of, 204–207
  protection and, 496
Employment Act of 1946, 255–256
endogenous variables, 84
enterprise, 41, 42–43
environment, economic, 537
equation of exchange, 158, 196, 197
  aggregate demand and, 159
  money supply and, 303–304
equilibrium. *See also* disequilibrium
  aggregate, 163–168
  disequilibrium and, 80–84
  in a four-sector model, 225–226
  macroeconomic, 186–187
  market, 80, 520
  in the money market, 310–311
  in a two-sector model, 220–222
European Community (EC), industrial policy in, 451
excess reserves, 319–320, 373
exchange control, 521, 523

exchange rate, 505. *See also* international monetary systems
  budget deficit and, 392
  floating, 519–521, 522
  imports and exports and, 508
exogenous variables, 84
expansion, 115
expansionary fiscal policy, 245–246, 266
expectations
  adaptive, 432
  aggregate supply and, 431–434
  demand and, 75–76
  Phillips curve and, 408–410, 411
  supply and, 79
expected yield, 356
expenditure multiplier, 230, 232, 378–379
  changes in consumption and, 232–233
  changes in investment and, 230–232
exports, 51, 102
  exchange rate and, 508
externalities
  negative, 56, 57
  positive, 56, 57

factors of production, 41–43. *See also* capital; enterprise; labor; land
faculty offices, allocation of, 92–93
fair trade, 498–500
fallacy of composition, 21
fascism, 527–529
Fed. *See* Federal Reserve System
Federal Deposit Insurance Corporation (FDIC), 328
federal funds market, 338
federal funds rate, 338
Federal National Mortgage Association, 359
Federal Open Market Committee (FOMC), 328
Federal Reserve Act, 325
Federal Reserve System, 316
  balance sheet of, 330–331
  Board of Governors of, 326–328
  discounting by, 337–339
  GNP targeting and, 383–384
  Great Depression and, 386–387
  interest rates and, 383
  monetary policy and, 379–380, 386–389
  money supply and, 331–340
  origins of, 322–325
  political pressures on, 385
  structure and functions of, 325–331
  tools of, for controlling money supply, 331–340
Federal Savings and Loan Insurance Corporation (FSLIC), 328, 345
fei, 297
fiat money, 298–299
final goods, 130
Financial Institutions Reform, Recovery and Enforcement Act, 350
fiscal policy, 174, 241. *See also* banking; banks; Federal Reserve System; money
  aggregate demand and, 266–267
  in Britain, 262
  budget deficits and, 274
  business tax cuts as, 259
  contractionary, 258, 267
  discretionary, 255–259
  expansionary, 245–246, 266, 267
  of four U.S. presidents, 256–259
  government spending as tool of, 246, 250–251
  international effects of, 247
  Keynesian, 241–243, 272
  lags in, 263–265
  multiplier and, 248–249
  operation of, 243–249
  price level and, 266–267
  pros and cons of, 260–266
  taxes as tool of, 246–247
  tools of, 250–251
  types of, 251–255
  varying views of economists on, 241
Fisher, Irving, 184, 203 (note)
fixed investment, 132
floating exchange rates, 520–522
flow variable, 125–126
Forbes index, 140
Ford, Gerald, fiscal policy of, 258
forecasting, 425
foreign exchange. *See also* exchange rate, floating; international monetary systems
  supply and demand for, 506–508
foreign exchange market, 505, 508–510
foreign sector, 59–61, 81
  benefits of trade with, 61–62
  in circular flow model, 51–52, 101–102
  investment by, 437
  and monetary policy, 376, 385, 391, 392
  privatization in, 54
  size of, 60, 61
45° line, 36

forward market, 509–510
fractional reserve banking, 316
free reserves, 387
free riding, 55–56
free trade, 499. *See also* protectionism
freedom, in economic markets, 90
frictional unemployment, 110
Friedman, Milton, 17, 18, 90, 260, 386, 395, 408
   natural rate hypothesis of, 410–412, 430
full-bodied money, 299
full employment, 12, 110
full employment level of output, 161
functional finance, 278

gains from trade, 483
Gall, Norman, 464
Garn-St. Germain Act, 345, 346
General Theory of Employment, Interest, and Money, The, 121, 174, 184, 199. *See also* Keynes, John Maynard
Germany, guest workers in, 190
Ghana, 229
GNP. *See* gross national product
GNP implicit price deflator, 143–144
GNP targeting, 383–384
gold standard, 387, 515–518. *See also* international monetary systems
Goldfeld, Stephen, 375
goldsmiths, as bankers, 300, 316
goods
   complementary, 74–75
   durable, 131
   final, 130
   inferior, 74
   intermediate, 130
   nondurable, 131
   normal, 74
   public, 55–56, 57
   substitute, 74–75
Gorbachev, Mikhail, 532, 545–548
Gosplan, 540
government
   allocation and, 55–57
   borrowing by, crowding out and, 389–395
   in circular flow model, 50–52, 101–102
   economic role of, 46, 52–59
   exchange control by, 521–523
   federal system of, 57
   intervention in markets by, 91–93
   levels of, and budgets, 288
   market for currency and, 508–509
   purchases by, 133–134
   regulation by, supply side view of, 448–449
   role of, in economic development, 470–475
   role of, in income redistribution, 57–58
   spending by, 246, 250–251, 261–263, 393–394
   stabilization and, 58–59, 114
Gramm, Phil, 500
Gramm-Rudman-Hollings Act, 277, 280
graphs, 29–39
   abstract ideas and, 36–37
   descriptive, 37–39
Great Depression, 117, 118–121, 173, 200
   Fed and, 386–387
   Keynes on, 207–209
Great Industrial Debate, 533
Great Leap Forward, 533–534
Green Revolution, 465
greenbacks, 300
Greenspan, Alan, 109, 328, 388
Gresham's law, 296
gross domestic product (GDP), 457–458
gross national product (GNP), 129
   adjustments to, 135–138
   by buying sector, 131–134
   foreign sector in, 134
   problems with, 144–146
   by producing sector, 129–131
   as target of monetary policy, 383–384
gross private domestic investment, 132
growth, 103–105
   in investment and saving, 435–438
   in the labor force, 438
   in natural resources, 441–442
Gurley, John, 534

Hamilton, Alexander, 323
Haveman, Robert, 447
Hayek, F. A., 539, 540
hedgers, 509
Hibbs, Donald, 265–266
high-employment balanced budget, 278–279
Hirschman, Albert O., 469
Hoffman, Dennis, 375
Hong Kong, 478, 528
Hoover, Herbert, 272
housing, 126–127
How to Lie with Statistics (Huff and Geis), 39
Hu Yaobang, 544
Hufbauer, Gary, 492

human capital, 42, 439
   investment in, 438–439
   in less developed countries, 462
Hume, David, 158, 169, 193, 195, 516
hypotheses, 14

immigration, 500–501
   unemployment and, 190
impact lag, 264
implementation lag, 264
implicit price deflator, 143–144
imports, 51, 102
   exchange rate and, 508
income
   consumption, saving, and, 214–218
   disposable, 138
   equilibrium level of, 220–222
   national, 134–137
   personal, 137
   types of, and circular flow, 138–139
income statement, 127
increasing opportunity cost, 11
independent variable, 31
industrial policy, 450–452
inflation, 105, 107–110, 195
   cost-push, 414–415
   demand-pull, 413–414
   effect of, on market for loanable funds, 354–355
   gainers and losers from, 107–109
   unemployment and, 401–403
   war and, 195–196
   zero rate of, 109–110
information, in economic systems, 539
infrastructure, 104
   reduction of investment in, 284
injection, 100. *See also* circular flow model
innovation, 441
input coefficient, 541–542
input-output analysis, 540–541
insatiable wants, 4–5
insider-outsider model, 408
institutional investors, 351
interest, 42
interest rate
   budget deficits and, 276–277, 280, 283
   components of, 353
   crowding out and, 283
   foreign lenders and, 286
   investment demand and, 364–365, 391–393
   nominal, 352

nonbank financial institutions and, 356–357
range of, 351–352
real, 352–353, 354
risk and, 352
role of in Keynesian economics, 206, 369–370
supply of loanable funds and, 391
as target of monetary policy, 383
intermediate goods, 130
international finance, 482
International Monetary Fund, 335, 518
international monetary systems. *See also* balance of payments; Bretton Woods system; gold standard
exchange control in, 521–523
floating exchange rates as, 519–521, 522
goals of, 513–515
international trade, 482. *See also* multinational corporations; protectionism
benefits of, 61–62, 483, 488
factors of production and, 500–501
fair trade arguments and, 498–500
nontariff barriers to, 491–493
reasons for, 483
terms of, 486–487
International Trade Commission (ITC), 492, 493
inventories, 131
effects of changes in, 222
investment, 42, 50, 100
demand for, 219–220, 364–365, 391–393
fixed, 132
gross private domestic, 132–133
growth in, 435–438
Keynesian view of, 201, 205–206
net private domestic, 135
taxes and saving and, 447–448
investment demand schedule, 363-364
Investment Tax Credit (ITC), 259
"invisible hand," 63, 90. *See also* Smith, Adam
Italy, industrial policy in, 451

Jacobs, Barry, 92
Japan
capitalist economy of, 548–550
financial markets in, 347
industrial policy in, 451
investment in United States by, 437
Jevons, William Stanley, 115

Jian Zemin, 544–545
Johnson, Lyndon
federal budget and, 281
fiscal policy of, 257–258
junk bonds, 360

Kemp, Jack, 500
Kennedy, John, fiscal policy of, 256–257
key currency, 519
Keynes, John Maynard, 4, 121, 162, 163, 173–175, 184, 200–204. *See also* Keynesian economics
on the Great Depression, 207–209
on monetary policy, 371–373
on the quantity theory of money, 203–204
on Say's law, 200–201
on self-regulating markets, 201–203
theory of aggregate supply of, 161–162
Keynesian economics, 168, 173, 178, 266, 377, 420, 421. *See also* Keynes, John Maynard
algebra of, 238–240
crowding out and, 390
fiscal policy and, 241–243, 272
interest rates and, 206, 369–370
macroeconomic theory in, 204–207
monetarists and, 395–396
population growth and, 190
role of investment in, 201, 205–206
Keynesian economists, 173. *See also* Keynesian economics
Keynesian revolution, 200–204
kidneys, market for, 92
Kondratieff, Nikolai, 116
Krutilla, John V., 441
Kuznets, Simon, 469

labor, 41–42
labor force, 148
growth in, 438
labor force participation rate, 148–149
labor market, classical economic view of, 188
lags, 264, 384
laissez-faire, 170, 173, 174, 175
land, 41, 42
Lange, Oskar, 538, 539
Lansing, Don, 514
leading sectors strategy, 469–470
leakage, 100. *See also* circular flow model
legal tender, 298–299
lender of last resort, 323

Lenin, Vladimir, 532, 538. *See also* Soviet Union
Leontief, Wassily, 540
less developed countries
agriculture in, 463–465
climate in, 465
death rates in, 461–462
dualism of, 465–466
human capital in, 462
multinationals and, 474–475
negative development in, 464
New International Economic Order and, 474
per capita income in, 457–460
population and birth rate in, 460–461
liabilities, 128
Lindahl, Erik, 120
liquidity, 128, 295
loanable funds
effect of inflation on market for, 354–355
interest rate and supply of, 391
market for, 350, 351
supply of and demand for, 365

M1 money stock, 303–304
M2 money stock, 303–304
M3 money stock, 303–304
macroeconomic equilibrium, 186–187
macroeconomics. *See also names of particular economists and economic schools*
definition of, 2
focus of, 98, 103
goals of, 428
issues in, 12
theories of, 168–179
Malthus, Thomas Robert, 171, 199, 466–467
management, Japanese style of, 549–550
Mao Zedong, 533–534, 543. *See also* China
marginal analysis, 84
marginal efficiency of investment (*MEI*) curve, 364–365
marginal propensity to consume (*MPC*), 215–218, 231, 378
marginal propensity to save (*MPS*), 215–218
market system, drawbacks of, 90–91
markets
auction, 433, 434
bond, 359–361
contract, 433–434
credit, 100
equilibrium, 80
expectations and, 434

Index

factor, 48, 49, 50
freedom in, 90
for loanable funds, 350, 351
product, 48, 49, 50
stock, 357–359
Marshall, Alfred, 196, 197, 202, 203, 204
Marx, Karl, 171, 173, 527, 530–531, 539. *See also* socialism
  theories of economic development of, 467–468
maximum, 34–35
Mazowiecki, Tadeusz, 546
Measure of Economic Welfare (MEW), 146
medium of exchange, 294
mercantilism, 483
Mexico, trade with, 499
microeconomics
  definition of, 2
  focus of, 98
Mincer, Jacob, 439
minimum, 35
Mitchell, Wesley Clair, 199, 442
Mitterrand, François, 527
model, 14
monetarists, 162, 168, 175–176, 178, 377
  crowding out and, 390–391
  Keynesians and, 395–396
monetary base, 380
monetary policy, 175
  accommodating, 394
  aggregate demand and, 369–378
  debate about targets of, 379
  Fed and, 379–380, 386–389
  GNP as target of, 383–384
  interest rates as target of, 383
  international effects of, 376
  Keynesian view of, 371–373
  lags in, 384
  money supply as target of, 379, 380–383
  in the 1960s and 1970s, 387–388
  since the 1970s, 388–389
  sectoral effects of, 384–385
monetary rule, 385
money. *See also* banking; banks; Federal Reserve System; fiscal policy; quantity theory of money
  aggregate demand and, 312
  asset demand for, 307, 308
  banks and, 300–304
  classical economists on, 370–371
  costs of holding, 307
  creation of, 317–319
  definitions of, 292, 293, 295, 303
  foreign, 301
  forms of, 297, 299–300, 300–302, 303

functions of, 294–295
inflation and, 296
inflow of in seventeenth century, 193–195
paper, 293
properties of, 295–299
transactions demand for, 305, 306, 308
velocity of, 309, 310, 378–379
money demand, changes in, 305–312
money market mutual funds, 344–345
money multiplier, 380–383
money supply. *See also* banking; banks; Federal Reserve System; fiscal policy
  contraction of, 322
  effect of increases in, 311–312
  equation of exchange and, 303–304
  expansion of, 319–322
  measurement of, 302–303, 304
  as target of monetary policy, 380–383
moral suasion, 339
multinational corporations (MNCs), 474–475, 501–503
multiplier. *See also* expenditure multiplier
  balanced budget, 249
  deposit, 320, 333, 336, 380
  fiscal policy and, 248–249
  money, 380, 381
multiplier effect, 246
municipal bonds, 360
Murray, Charles, 447
mutual fund, 362
Myrdal, Gunnar, 120

Napoleonic Wars, 195
National Banking Act, 300
National Banking System, 324
national banks, 325
national debt, 271. *See also* budget; deficit
  growth of, 274–277
national defense argument, 495
national income (NI), 134–137
  investment spending and, 365
natural rate hypothesis (of unemployment), 410, 430
  aggregate supply and demand and, 412–413
natural resources, growth in, 441
near money, 303
negative externalities, 56, 57
negative relationship, 33
net national product (NNP), 135
net private domestic investment, 135

net worth, 128
new classical economists, 168, 177, 178, 394
  on market participants, 431–433
New Economic Policy (NEP), 532–533
New International Economic Order (NIEO), 474
Nixon, Richard, 417
Nobel Prize for Economics, winners of, 7
nominal rate of interest, 352, 354
nonbank financial institutions
  interest rates and, 356–357
  types of, 361–363
nontariff barriers, 491
Nordhaus, William, 146
normative statements, 17
(not quite) law of supply, 76–77, 85

Okun, Arthur, 257, 410
open market operations, 331
opportunity cost, 5, 9, 63
  choice and, 6, 8
  comparative advantage and, 484, 486
  increasing, 11
optimal tariff, 496–497
organ donations, 91–92
origin, 30
output
  full employment level of, 161
  potential, 279–280

paradox of thrift, 233, 399
peak, 114
permanent income hypothesis, 260–261, 394
personal income (PI), 137
Phelps, Edmund, 401
Phillips, A. W., 401, 404
Phillips curve
  criticisms of, 408–413
  development of, 404–408
  insider-outsider model and, 407–408
  shifts in, 405–407
  stagflation and, 400–408
Physiocrats, 48, 172
pie chart, 37, 38
Pigou, A. C., 169
planning
  in command economies, 540, 542
  in economic systems, 538–542
  input-output analysis in, 540–542
  socialist controversy in, 538–539
policy makers, 254
political business cycle, 265–266

population
  in less developed countries, 460–461
  as obstacle to economic development, 475–477
positive externalities, 56, 57
positive relationship, 33
positive statements, 17
Post-Keynesians (economists), 168, 177–178, 415–418
potential output, 279
poverty, and population, 477
Preobrazhensky, E. A., 533
price index, 105, 106, 139, 140–141, 143–144. *See also* Consumer Price Index
  construction of, 143
  for the dollar, 142
prices
  functions of, 88–90
  theory of formation of, 85–88
primary effect, 85
privatization, in Britain, 54, 536
Producer Price Index, 144
product cycle, 487
product market, classical economic view of, 188
production, factors of, 41–43
production function, aggregate, 166–168
production possibilities curve, 8–11, 13
  comparative advantage and, 486
  shifts in, 12–13
productivity, 112–113
  growth of, 443–444
profit, 43
progressive tax, 252–253
property rights, 46, 53–55, 529–530
proportional tax, 252
protectionism
  common arguments for, 494–496
  optimal tariff argument for, 496–497
  political pressures for, 493–494
  theory of the second best and, 497–498
  tools of, 488–491
public bads, 56, 57
public choice theory, 261, 263
public goods, 55–56, 57

quality circles, 549
quantity theory of money, 158–159, 169, 184, 192–195, 196–199, 305, 370. *See also* money
  Keynes on, 203–204
Quesnay, François, 48, 50
quota, 488, 489–491

Rasche, Robert, 375
rational expectations school of economic thought. *See* new classical economists
Reagan, Ronald
  deregulation and, 448–449
  fiscal policy of, 258–259, 262, 266, 276
  gold standard and, 517
real business cycle, 442–443
real deficit, 287
real rate of interest, 352–354
recession, 114–115
  budget deficits and, 276
recessionary gap, 245
recognition lag, 263–264
redistribution, 57–58
regressive tax, 252
regulation, supply siders on, 448–449. *See also* deregulation
Reich, Robert, 452
rent, 42
representative money, 298
research and development, public policy toward, 449
reserve ratio, 320
  effects of changes in, 334–338
reserves
  bank, 317
  excess, 319, 320
Resolution Trust Corporation, 350
Ricardian equivalence, 286
Ricardo, David, 195, 196, 466, 483
risk, 356
  interest rates and, 352
risk premium, 352
Robinson, Joan, 415
Roosevelt, Franklin D., administration of, 119–120
Rostow, W. W., 468–469

Sachs, Jeffry, 546
Salinas de Gortari, Carlos, 499
Samuelson, Paul, 17, 18
savings, 50, 100
  factors influencing, 215–216
  growth in, 436–437
  in Japan, 549
  motivation for, according to Keynes, 201
  savings rate and, 436
  taxes and investment and, 447–448
savings and loans, bailout of, and deficit, 277, 280, 281
savings rate, 436–437
Say, Jean-Baptiste, 172. *See also* Say's law
Say's law, 169, 173, 184, 186, 187, 197, 205. *See also* classical economists; Say, Jean-Baptiste
  Keynes on, 200–201
scarcity, 4
scatter diagram, 31–33
Schelling, Thomas, 399
Schick, James, 140–141
Schumpeter, Joseph, 199, 200, 442
Schwartz, Anna, 386
Scully, Gerald, 471
secondary effect, 85
self-interest, 15–17, 63
  Keynes on, 222 (note)
self-regulating markets, 187–188
  Keynes on, 201–203
services, 131–132
settlement account, 513
shadow prices, 538
Simon, Julian, 461
Simons, Henry, 184, 203 (note)
simulation, 425
Singapore, 478
slope, 33–34
Smith, Adam, 62, 63, 90, 170, 193, 466, 483
Smith, V. Kerry, 441
social science, 3
Social Security System, 51, 58, 133, 137, 250, 251, 253, 255, 265, 280. *See also* transfer payments
  relationship of to federal deficit, 281–283
social welfare programs, 119–120. *See also* transfer payments
socialism, 527, 528, 531–532. *See also* Lenin; Mao Zedong; Marx; Soviet Union; Stalin
  competitive solution and, 539
  contrasted to capitalism, 529–530
socialist controversy, 538–539
Solow, Robert, 404
South Korea, 478
Soviet Union, 532–533, 540, 543
  reforms in, 545–548
Spain, money inflow to, 193–195
special drawing rights (SDR), 522
specialization, 61–62
specie flow mechanism, 516
speculators, 509
spread, 348
stabilization, 58–59, 114
stagflation, 118
  in Eastern Europe, 406
  Phillips curve and, 400–408
  Post-Keynesians and, 416–418
Stalin, Joseph, 533
standard of deferred payment, 295
state banks, 325
states, budgets of, 288
statistical discrepancy, 512

Stigler, George, 90
stock, 357
  versus bonds, 360–361
stock market, 357–359
  crashes in, 358
stock variable, 125
Stockholm School of economic thought, 120–121
store of value, 295
Strategic Information Research Corporation, 473
structural deficit, 279
sunspots, and business cycles, 115–116
supply, 69, 76–80. *See also* demand; supply and demand
  changes in, 77–80, 86
  foreign, 81
  of foreign exchange, 506–508
  market, 77
  (not quite) law of, 76–77
supply and demand, 3. *See also* demand; supply
  model of, 69, 82, 85
supply curve, 77
supply side economics, 168, 172, 176–177, 178, 444–446, 450
  government regulation and, 448–449
  in the 1980s, 449–450
  taxes and, 446–448
  transfer payments and, 447
supply siders, 176. *See also* supply side economics
surplus, 101
surplus value, 467
symbols, glossary of, 182

T-account, 318
tangent line, 34
tariff quota, 489
tariffs, 488, 489, 490–491
  optimal, 496–497
tax-based inflation policy (TIP), 418
tax wedge, 446

taxes, 50, 58, 100
  balanced budget and, 278
  as fiscal policy tool, 246–247
  in Japan, 548–549
  policies in foreign countries on, 445
  progressive, 252
  proportional, 252
  regressive, 252
  saving and investment and, 447–448
  supply side economics and, 446–447
taxi industry, 91
terms of trade, 486
testable hypothesis, 14
Thatcher, Margaret, 535–536
theory, 14
theory of the second best, 497–498
Theory Z, 549
Third World. *See* less developed countries
Thomas, Brinley, 190
Thurow, Lester, 415–416
Tobin, James, 146, 263
token money, 299
tourism, 514
trade. *See* international trade
transaction costs, 87–88
transactions demand for money, 204, 369. *See also* money
transfer payments, 51, 58, 133, 137–138, 250–251, 253–255, 280. *See also* Social Security System
  balanced budget and, 278
  supply side view of, 447
transmission mechanism, 371, 372
  problems with, 373–375
Truman, Harry, 116
Tuerck, David, 495

underground economy, 306
unemployment, 11, 12
  costs of, 111–112
  cyclical, 111

frictional, 110, 111
immigration and, 190
and inflation, 401–403
measurement of, 146–149
natural rate hypothesis of, 410, 412–413, 430
rate of, 146, 148
structural, 110–111
unemployment rate, 146, 148
unit of account, 294–295

variables, 29–30, 31
  endogenous, 84–85
  exogenous, 84–85
  flow, 125–126
  stock, 125
velocity of money, 308–309, 378–379
Vernon, Raymond, 487
vicious circle of poverty, 462
Vietnam war, 12, 15
Volcker, Paul, 388
von Mises, Ludwig, 538, 539

wage and price controls, 416–418
wages, 42
Wagner, Richard, 263
Walesa, Lech, 546
Wanniski, Jude, 517
wants, 4–5
War Communism, 532
Wealth of Nations, The, 62, 63, 466. *See also* Smith, Adam
World Bank, 335, 477
World Resources Institute, 135–136
World War II, 12, 208, 272, 285

x-axis, 30

y-axis, 30
Yap, money of, 297
Yeager, Leland, 495
Yeltsin, Boris, 547
yield, expected, 356

Zhao, Ziyang, 544

Year	Population (thousands)	Labor Force (including military)	Labor Force Participation Rate (%)	Unemployed Workers (thousands)	Unemployment Rate (%)	Average Hourly Earnings* (current dollars)	Average Hourly Earnings* (1982 dollars)
1950	152,271	63,377	41.6	3,288	5.2	1.34	5.34
1951	154,878	64,160	41.4	2,055	3.2	1.45	5.39
1952	157,553	64,524	41.0	1,883	2.9	1.52	5.51
1953	160,184	64,246	40.1	1,834	2.8	1.61	5.79
1954	163,026	65,785	40.4	3,582	5.4	1.65	5.91
1955	165,931	67,087	40.4	2,852	4.3	1.71	6.15
1956	168,903	68,517	40.6	2,750	4.0	1.80	6.38
1957	171,984	68,877	40.0	2,859	4.2	1.89	6.47
1958	174,882	69,486	39.7	4,602	6.6	1.95	6.50
1959	177,830	70,157	39.5	3,740	5.3	2.02	6.69
1960	180,671	71,489	39.6	3,852	5.4	2.09	6.79
1961	183,691	72,359	39.4	4,714	6.5	2.14	6.88
1962	186,538	72,675	39.0	3,911	5.4	2.22	7.07
1963	189,242	73,839	39.0	4,070	5.5	2.28	7.17
1964	191,889	75,109	39.1	3,786	5.0	2.36	7.33
1965	194,303	76,401	39.3	3,366	4.4	2.46	7.52
1966	196,560	77,892	39.6	2,875	3.7	2.56	7.62
1967	198,712	79,565	40.0	2,975	3.7	2.68	7.72
1968	200,706	80,990	40.4	2,817	3.5	2.85	7.89
1969	232,677	82,972	35.7	2,832	3.4	3.04	7.98
1970	205,052	84,889	41.4	4,093	4.8	3.23	8.03
1971	207,661	86,355	41.6	5,016	5.8	3.45	8.21
1972	209,896	88,847	42.3	4,882	5.5	3.70	8.53
1973	211,909	91,203	43.0	4,365	4.8	3.94	8.55
1974	213,854	93,670	43.8	5,156	5.5	4.24	8.28
1975	215,973	95,453	44.2	7,929	8.3	4.53	8.12
1976	218,035	97,826	44.9	7,406	7.6	4.86	8.24
1977	220,239	100,665	45.7	6,991	6.9	5.25	8.36
1978	222,585	103,882	46.7	6,202	6.0	5.69	8.40
1979	225,055	106,559	47.3	6,137	5.8	6.16	8.17
1980	227,757	108,544	47.7	7,637	7.0	6.66	7.78
1981	230,138	110,315	47.9	8,273	7.5	7.25	7.69
1982	232,520	111,872	48.1	10,678	9.5	7.68	7.68
1983	234,799	113,226	48.2	10,717	9.5	8.02	7.79
1984	237,001	115,241	48.6	8,539	7.4	8.32	7.80
1985	239,279	117,167	49.0	8,312	7.1	8.57	7.77
1986	241,625	119,540	49.5	8,237	6.9	8.76	7.81
1987	243,942	121,602	49.8	7,425	6.1	8.98	7.73
1988	246,307	123,378	50.1	6,701	5.4	9.28	7.69
1989	248,762	125,557	50.5	6,528	5.2	9.66	7.64
1990	251,394	126,424	50.3	6,874	5.4	10.03	7.54

*Private nonagricultural workers in nonsupervisory positions.

Year	Personal Income (billions of dollars)	Per Capita Personal Income ($)	Consumer Price Index (1982–84 =100)	Per Capita Income (1982 dollars)	Median Family Income (1986 dollars)	Poverty Rate (%)
1950	228.1	1,498	24.1	6,216		
1951	256.5	1,656	26.0	6,370		
1952	273.8	1,738	26.5	6,558		
1953	290.5	1,814	26.7	6,792		
1954	293.0	1,797	26.9	6,681		
1955	314.2	1,894	26.8	7,066		
1956	337.2	1,996	27.2	7,340		
1957	356.3	2,072	28.1	7,373		
1958	367.1	2,099	28.9	7,263		
1959	390.7	2,197	29.1	7,550		
1960	409.4	2,266	29.6	7,655		
1961	426.0	2,319	29.9	7,756		
1962	453.2	2,430	30.2	8,045		
1963	476.3	2,517	30.6	8,225	22,379	15.9
1964	510.2	2,659	31.0	8,577	23,221	15.0
1965	552.0	2,841	31.5	9,019	24,177	13.9
1966	600.8	3,057	32.4	9,434	25,448	11.8
1967	644.5	3,243	33.4	9,711	26,052	11.4
1968	707.2	3,524	34.8	10,125	27,205	10.0
1969	772.9	3,813	36.7	10,391	28,213	9.7
1970	831.8	4,057	38.8	10,455	27,862	10.1
1971	894.0	4,305	40.5	10,630	27,845	10.0
1972	981.6	4,677	41.8	11,188	29,134	9.3
1973	1,101.7	5,199	44.4	11,709	29,734	8.8
1974	1,210.1	5,659	49.3	11,478	28,687	8.8
1975	1,313.4	6,081	53.8	11,304	27,949	9.7
1976	1,451.4	6,657	56.9	11,699	28,811	9.4
1977	1,607.5	7,299	60.6	12,044	28,966	9.3
1978	1,812.4	8,143	65.2	12,489	29,647	9.1
1979	2,034.0	9,038	72.6	12,449	29,588	9.2
1980	2,258.5	9,916	82.4	12,034	27,974	10.3
1981	2,520.9	10,954	90.9	12,050	26,991	11.2
1982	2,670.8	11,486	96.5	11,903	26,619	12.2
1983	2,838.6	12,089	99.6	12,138	27,155	12.3
1984	3,108.7	13,117	103.9	12,624	27,903	11.6
1985	3,325.3	13,897	107.6	12,916	33,595	11.4
1986	3,526.2	14,594	109.6	13,315	34,857	10.9
1987	3,766.4	15,440	113.6	13,591	35,350	10.7
1988	4,070.8	16,527	118.3	13,971	35,549	10.4
1989	4,384.3	17,624	124.0	14,213	35,975	10.3
1990	4,645.6	18,479	130.7	14,139	NA	NA